THE W.D. GANN
STOCK MARKET FORECASTING COURSE

Unlocking Predictive Strategies and Forecasting

W. D. Gann

All rights reserved. No part of this publication may be reproduced, stored in a retrieval system, or transmitted in any form or by any means, electronic, mechanical, photocopying or otherwise, without the prior permission of the copyright owner.

● Copyright 1955 by W.D. Gann

www.snowballpublishing.com
info@snowballpublishing.com

ALL RIGHTS RESERVED

For information regarding special discounts for bulk purchases,
please contact sales@snowballpublishing.com

TABLE OF CONTENTS

Page

A Note About This Master Course iii

General Lessons
- Chapter 1: Speculation A Profitable Profession: A Course Of Instructions On Stocks 1
- Chapter 2: Method For Forecasting The Stock Market (including The Human Body) 45
- Chapter 3: Method For Trading With The Overnight Chart - Mechanical Stock Trading Method 68
- Chapter 4: The Basis Of My Forecasting Method - Geometric Angles 117
- Chapter 5: Seasonal Changes On Stocks 157
- Chapter 6: Natural Resistance Levels And Time Cycle Points 181
- Chapter 7: Master Time Factor And Forecasting By Mathematical Rules (including How To Trade) 214
- Chapter 8: Form Reading And Rules For Determining Trend Of Stocks 237
- Chapter 9: Resistance Levels 259
- Chapter 10A: Forecasting By Time Cycles (including How To Trade) 278
- Chapter 10B: How To Forecast 292
- Chapter 11A: Review Of Bull And Bear Markets: Showing Formations And Buying And Selling Points (1909-1939) - Dow-Jones 30 Industrial Averages 308
- Chapter 11B: Dow-Jones 30 Industrial Averages 350
- Chapter 12: Volume Of Sales 356

Master Calculators
- Chapter 13: The Master Mathematical Price Time And Trend Calculator 371
- Chapter 14: Master Calculator For Weekly Time Periods To Determine The Trend Of Stocks And Commodities 381

Master Charts
- Chapter 15A: Master Charts 388
- Chapter 15B: The Hexagon Chart 418

Other Lessons
- Chapter 16: Auburn Motors 424
- Chapter 17: Time Periods - Seasonal & Yearly 430
- Chapter 18: Time And Price Resistance Levels 435

Options Lessons
- Chapter 19A: How To Make Profits Trading In Puts And Calls 440
- Chapter 19B: How To Sell Puts And Calls 457

A NOTE ABOUT THIS MASTER COURSE

This Master Stock Market Course is a transcribed collection of most, if not all, of W.D. Gann's publicly available stock market lessons. It represents hundreds of hours of lesson sourcing, typing, meticulous proofing and compiling by a relatively small number of dedicated individuals. An overriding objective in developing this resource was to create an electronic searchable reference document to assist students of Gann.

In order to preserve the authenticity of Gann's original work, every effort has been made to precisely transcribe the lessons contained within this Master Course. The lessons have been formatted and paginated to match the source documents as closely as practicable – even to the point of replicating letterheads.

The general approach for dealing with spelling and grammar mistakes was to replicate the original text. However, there were some exceptions:

Corrections were made when the source document appeared to be a previous transcript and the spelling mistakes were blatant. Note that these corrections were minor in nature and great care was taken to ensure that they did not alter the underlying message of the text.

In other instances, suggested corrections were inserted beside apparently erroneous original text. This was only done when the suggested correction could be corroborated by the surrounding context and where it was felt that it would provide greater clarity. All suggestions were contained within square brackets [like this], as is conventional when making editorial comment. Whilst all suggestions were made in good faith, the reader must ultimately decide whether to accept them.

Chapter 1

Speculation a Profitable Profession: A Course of Instructions on Stocks

SPECULATION A PROFITABLE PROFESSION

A Course of Instructions With Rules of Trading in Stocks

FOREWORD

Be ready for opportunities. Knowledge more important than capital. To succeed in any business you must be prepared, and in preparing for a speculative or investment business you must look up the greatest advance or the greatest decline a stock has ever had and the greatest time period from the high or low. Most profits are made in active fast moving markets. Examples: Stocks 1924-1929 – September 29th to November 15th, 1929; November 13, 1929 to April 17, 1930.

FAST ADVANCES

You will find these from June 1949 to June 1950: June 13, 1950 to July 14, 1950 this was a fast decline.

1952 and 1953 – September 1953 to April 1954, fast advance.

SLOW TRADING MARKET

You should keep out of slow trading markets or watch until you get a definite indication of a change in trend. There was a slow trading market from November 1946 to November 1949, that is the range in most stock was narrow because the market was going through a period of consolidation or accumulation and getting ready for the big bull market which followed later.

CROSS CURRENTS

You must learn to know that some stocks sometimes are declining while others are advancing, and that there are cross currents, and you must know about these. Example: 1952 to 1954 Studebaker, Chrysler, Celanese declined while Vanadium, Steel, Dupont and Aircraft stocks advanced. Only by a study of the individual stock and the different groups can you determine what stock is supposed to decline at the time when another stock is going to advance.

HOW TO SELECT THE GROUP OF STOCKS WHICH WILL LEAD AN ADVANCE OR A DECLINE

During 1953 – 1954 the Aircrafts were big leaders. You can see from the chart and the group of the averages on Aircrafts where they broke into new high levels. Example: Douglass Aircraft, Boeing Aircraft, United, Glenn Martin and Lockheed all indicated that they were in a position to advance when the average price or average value of the group of stocks indicated a strong position. Without a knowledge of these things you could not make a success.

2.

LOW PRICE STOCKS DISAPPOINTING

A study of past history proves that buying low price stocks often ties up capital for a long period of time. You wait, and if you do not lose money you lose your patience and when your patience is exhausted in advance of the start you get out. Many low price stocks have held in narrow trading for 5, 10 years or more before they started to advance or to decline and some, after remaining in a narrow trading range for a long period of time, declined to new low levels. The best way to make money is to take higher price stocks and buy them after they have broken into <u>new high ground</u> and show activity as outlined under the rules below.

NEW INDUSTRIES AND GROWTH STOCKS

Select stocks to buy in new industries but make careful study of their prospects and make up charts on stocks that you intend to trade in, and if they are part of a group that you can get a record of, study this group and then pick the individual stock to buy that shows indication of leading the group.

STOCKS OF THE FUTURE

When considering what stocks to buy in the future, you must make up charts and study the companies which are producing Uranium and are developing Atomic Energy machinery for commercial purposes. Among this group of stocks are Babcock & Wilcox Co., Bendix Aviation Corp., Dow Chemical Co., DuPont, General Dynamics Corp., General Electric (which is of the largest in the business and has orders from the U.S. Government as well as a few commercial concerns), Newport News Shipbuilding, Phillips Petroleum, Sylvania Electric Products, Inc., Union Carbide and Carbon Corp., Vanadium Corp. of America and Westinghouse Electric. Corp.

Among the very best of these stocks for the future we consider Vanadium, Molybedeum, General Dynamics Corp., which has now consolidated with Consolidated Vultee.

Among the low priced stocks with future possibilities of enhancement in value due to Uranium deposits is New Park Mining listed on the American Exchange. Fairchilds Engine and Aircraft Corp. also has possibilities of becoming a future leader.

You must, of course, buy any of these stocks at the time the total value of all stocks on the N.Y. Stock Exchange show up-trend and buy the best of the

3.

individual stocks when the individual groups show up-trend, selecting the one you buy that is in the strongest position.

You would not buy any of these higher priced stocks at the present time because the total value of all stocks on the N.Y. Stock Exchange is at the highest levels in history and because the trend of stocks has been up in a general way since 1932 and the last extreme low was April 1942 and the present swing in the bull market started in June, 1949. Therefore it is natural to expect a decline in stocks during the last half of 1954 and you must be cautious on the buying side.

HOW TO MAKE SPECULATION A PROFITABLE PROFESSION

Speculation or investment is the best business in the world if you make a business of it. But in order to make a success of it you must study and be prepared and not guess, follow inside information or depend on hope or fear. If you do you will fail. Your success depends on <u>knowing</u> the <u>right kind of rules</u> and <u>following</u> them.

FUNDAMENTAL RULES

Keep this well in mind. For stocks to show up-trend and continue to advance they must make higher bottoms and higher tops. When the trend is down they must make lower tops and lower bottoms and continue on down to lower levels. But remember, prices can move in a narrow trading range for weeks or months or even years and not make a new high or a new low. But after a long period of time when the stocks break into new lows they indicate lower prices and after a long period of time when they advance above old highs or old tops they are in a stronger position and indicate higher prices. This is the reason why you must have a chart a long way back in order to see just what position the stock is in and at what stage it is between extreme high and extreme low.

THE KIND OF CHARTS TO KEEP

Remember the old Chinese proverb, "One good picture is worth 10,000 words". You should make up charts and study the picture of a stock before you make a trade. You should have a weekly high and low chart, a monthly high and low chart, and a yearly high and low chart. A yearly high and low chart should run back 5, 10, or 20 years, if you can get records that far. Monthly high and low chart should run back for at least 10 years and the weekly high and low chart should run back for 2 or 3 years. When stocks are very active you should have a daily high and low chart. This need not go back more than a few months, especially start the daily chart after the stock breaks into great activity.

FOLLOW THE MAIN TREND

You will always make money by following the main trend of stocks up or down. Remember that stocks are never too high or buy as long as the trend is up and they are never too low to sell as long as the trend is down. Never sell short just because the stock is high or because you think it is too high. Never sell out and take profits just because the price is high. Buy and sell according to definite rules and not on hope, fear or guesswork. Never buy a stock just because the stock is low. There is usually a good reason why it is low and it can go lower.

RULES FOR BUYING AND SELLING

The first thing to remember before you start to apply any rules is that you must always use a STOP LOSS order to protect your capital. When making a trade remember that you can be wrong or that the market may change its trend and the STOP LOSS order will protect you and limit your loss. A small Loss or several small losses can easily be made back with one large profit but when you let large losses run against you it is hard to make them back.

PROVE ALL THINGS AND HOLD FAST TO THAT WHICH IS GOOD

The Bible tells us this and it is well worth remembering. Many people believe that it is wrong to buy at new high levels or sell at new low levels but it is most profitable and you must prove this to yourself because when you do buy at new high levels or sell at new low levels you are going with the trend of the market and your chances for making profits are much better than any guesswork or buying or selling on hope or fear.

PROLONGED ADVANCES

After stocks have had a prolonged advance and wind up with a fast, active, runaway market in most cases they come down very quickly and much faster or in a shorter period of time than when they go up. That is why you must keep up some daily charts at the end of the fast move and keep up the weekly charts to determine the first change in trend and be able to go with it.

SHARP DECLINE IN SHORT PERIOD OF TIME

This usually follows a rapid advance and the first sharp declines which may last from one month to as much as seven weeks usually corrects an overbought position and leaves the market in position for a secondary advance.

When you are able to catch extremes at the end of any great time cycle you can make a large amount of money in one year's time trading in fast active markets. It makes no difference whether you catch the extreme low or the extreme high; the opportunities are great for making money providing you select the stocks that will lead.

LARGE PROFIT ON SMALL RISKS
You can make large profits on small risks provided you use a STOP LOSS order and apply all the rules, then wait for a definite indication of a change in trend up or down before you make a trade.

FIXED IDEAS AND FIXED PRICES
Never get a fixed idea of just how high any price is going to go or just how low they are going. Never buy or sell on a price that you fix because you may be trading on hope or fear and not following the trend of the market and applying rules which will determine when the trend is changing.

HOW TO PROTECT PROFITS
After you have accumulated profits it is just as important to protect them with STOP LOSS orders as it is to protect your original capital because once you have made profits it is your capital and STOP LOSS orders must be used to protect it. The most dangerous thing that you can do is to let a trade start going against you. You lose back your profits. A STOP LOSS order will protect the profits and you can always get in again when you are out with capital. Remember when you are out of the market, the only thing you can lose or miss is an opportunity.

My 52 years' experience has taught me that thousands of people have gone broke trying to hold until the trend turned. Avoid getting out of the market too soon after move starts when you have a small profit. This can be a great mistake. Get out of the market quickly as soon as you see that you have made a mistake. If you place a STOP LOSS order this will put you out of the market automatically.

TOO LATE OR TOO SOON
You can lose money or miss opportunity by getting into the market too soon or getting out too late. That is, not waiting until a definite change in trend is indicated or failing to act in time when you see a definite change in trend. Wait until you have a well defined indication that the trend has changed, then buy or

sell. Follow all the rules in my book "45 YEARS IN WALL STREET". There are many rules in my book "45 YEARS IN WALL STREET" which are not in this course of instruction and by using all the rules you will make a greater success.

HOPE AND FEAR

I repeat this because I have seen so many people go broke trading on hope or fear. You will never succeed buying or selling when you hope the market is going up or down. You will never succeed by making a trade because you fear the market is going up or down. Hope will ruin you because it is nothing more than wishful thinking and provides no basis for action. Fear will often save you if you at quickly when you see that you are wrong. "The fear of the market is the beginning of wisdom". Knowledge which you can only obtain by deep study will help you to make a success. The more you study past records the surer you are to be able to detect the trend of the future.

MAKE THE MARKET MOVE YOUR WAY

You must learn to realize that you cannot make the market go your way, you must go the market's way and must follow the trend. Many successful business men who are accustomed to giving orders to others and have them carried out will often, when they get into the market, especially for the first time, expect the market to follow their orders or move their way. They must learn that they cannot make the market trend go their way. They must follow the market trend as is indicated by fixed rules and protect their capital and profits by the use of STOP LOSS orders. There is no harm in making a few mistakes and a few small losses because small losses are the expense of a successful speculator.

NEVER AVERAGE A LOSS

This is the surest way to lose all or a great part of your capital. If you have bought a stock and it shows you a loss, the trend is moving against you, and it is very foolish to buy more, which will only increase your losses. The time to increase buying is when the market is moving in your favor, and you have a profit. If you intend to make <u>speculation a profitable profession</u>, you must learn all the rules and apply all of them to determine the trend. Professional men, such as lawyers, doctors, accountants and engineers spend years in training and a large amount of money to learn how to succeed in their chosen profession. You must spend time and money to learn the profession and become a successful speculator or investor.

RULES FOR TRADING IN STOCKS

RULE 1. Buy at new high prices or old top levels.

RULE 2. Buy when prices advance above old low price levels.

RULE 3. Sell when prices decline below old top levels or high prices.

RULE 4. Sell at new low price levels. As a general rule it is safer to wait until prices advance at least 1 to 2 points above high levels and still more important to wait until they close above these levels before buying and at the same time it is safer to wait until prices decline 1 to 2 points below old levels and still safer to wait until they close below these old levels before making a trade.

RULE 5. Closing Prices. Wait to buy or sell until prices close above old highs or below old lows on the daily or weekly charts when markets are very active and moving fast; it is important to use the daily high and low chart and the closing price above highs or below lows. Prices may advance rapidly during the day but when it comes to closing time they may run off several points and close lower than the previous day, and at the same time when there is a sharp decline, prices may go below the low of the previous day but when they close they close near the high levels; therefore, it is the closing price that is always important to keep up on the daily, weekly or monthly high or low charts. The longer the time period in days, weeks or months or years when prices exceed old highs or break old lows the greater the importance of the change in trend and the move up or down. Remember the general rule, when prices advance to new high levels they generally react back to the old tops which is a safe place to buy and when they decline below old lows, as a rule they rally back to the old lows which is a safe place to sell. Always, of course, protect with STOP LOSS orders.

RULE 6. **STOP LOSS ORDERS.** Your capital and your profits must be protected at all times with STOP LOSS orders which must be placed when you make the trade and not later.

RULE 7. Amount of capital required. It is very important to know exactly how much of you capital you can risk on any one trade and never lose all of your capital. When you make a trade you should never risk more than 10% of the capital you have to trade with, and if you have one or two losses, reduce you units of trading.

THE BEST BUYING POINT. This point is when prices decline to 50% of the highest price at which a stock has ever sold; the next strongest and best buying price is 50% between the extreme low and the extreme high (See example on Chrysler Motors.)

8.

SELLING LEVEL: When prices advance after they have been considerably below the 50% point and advance for the FIRST TIME, it is a selling level and a price to sell short, protected with STOP LOSS orders 3 points above the 50% level. The first time a stock reaches these levels, if the indications on the daily chart and the weekly chart show it is making tops, you should sell out long stocks and sell short.

The next important selling level is 50% between the extreme low and the extreme high.

CHRYSLER MOTORS: (*Example of 50% Price*)

1946, February high 141½, divide by two and get 50% of the highest selling price. This gives 70-3/4. After Chrysler was split up and sold ex-stock dividend in 1947, it declined to 44 in June 1949; from this level, which was a buying point, the trend started up.

1953, January high 98½; we always expect selling just under 100 and Chrysler made top at this level. We figure the range being 44 and 98½ which gives a 50% price at 71¼.

1953, June Chrysler low 70, just below the 50% price. It rallied to 73 in August which was a very feeble rally and closed at 71 indicating lower and was a short sale.

1932, Chrysler extreme low $5 per share; 1953 high 141½. 50% of these extremes is 73¼ when Chrysler can advance and close above 73¼ it will indicate higher prices.

1954, February Chrysler declined to 57 and has shown very little rallying power. At the time of this writing the main trend is down and when it closes below 57 it will indicate lower. The next price to watch is the old low of 44 made in June 1949.

Look up the extreme highs and low and figure all other stocks in the same way to get buying and selling points and resistance levels.

When you start trading be sure that you know all of the rules and that you follow them, and be sure that you place a STOP LOSS order.

WHERE TO PLACE STOP LOSS ORDERS: You must place STOP LOSS orders below the lows of swings and not just below the lows on the daily chart. STOPS must be above old tops or below old bottoms on a weekly or monthly chart.

9.

STOP LOSS orders should e place below <u>closing prices</u> on the daily, weekly or monthly chart. They are much safer under closing prices and less likely to be caught, because you are trading with the trend. STOP LOSS orders placed above closing prices on the daily or weekly chart are caught a smaller number of times than if you place them below the daily bottoms or daily tops.

The swings or reversals in the market are the prices to place STOP LOSS orders below the price of the swing or above the price of the swing. It is of great importance to know where to place STOP LOSS orders properly.

For stocks selling around $10 a STOP LOSS order is usually safe if you place it 1-point below closing price.

For stocks selling between 20 and 30, STOPS should be placed 2 points below bottoms or below closing prices.

Stocks selling between 90 and 150; in this range of prices STOPS should be 3 points under the lows or closing prices, and 3 points above the high or low closing prices.

When stocks are very active and selling at these extreme high prices, you must depend upon the daily high and low chart to give you the first indication of a change in trend which will later be confirmed on the weekly high and low charts.

When stocks are selling at extreme high levels, follow all the rules in my book, "45 YEARS IN WALL STREET", and if you have taken my Master Forecasting Course apply the rules on <u>Great Time Cycles</u> as well as the minor time periods.

Remember you can never have too much <u>knowledge</u>. Continue to study and learn more for the knowledge can always be turned into profits later.

WHAT TO DO BEFORE YOU MAKE A TRADE. Check all records of prices, daily, weekly, monthl and yearly and note all time periods. Note when the prices are near some old high levels or near some old low levels of recent weeks or years. Then calculate just what you risk will be before you make the trade and after you make it, place the STOP LOSS order for your <u>protection</u> in case <u>you are wrong</u>.

WEEKLY HIGH AND LOW CHART: The weekly high and low chart is a very important trend indicator. When prices get above a series of weekly highs or lows, or decline below a series of weekly lows, it is of greater importance and indicates a greater change in trend which may last for many weeks.

MONTHLY HIGHS AND LOWS: When prices advance above or decline below prices which have occurred for many months past, it means a greater change in trend which can last for several months.

YEARLY HIGHS AND LOWS: When prices advance above or decline below the prices made several years in the past, it is nearly always a sure sign of big moves which will last for a long period of time or at least have a greater advance or decline in a short period of time, and when these old highs are crossed, or lows broken, always watch for a reaction to come back to around the old highs or slightly lower and after they are broken, expect the rally to advance back to around the old highs or slightly below.

Study the yearly highs and lows and you will see the proof. Remember the greater the time period when it is exceeded, the greater the move up or down.

RULES FOR STOCKS

A. How Much Decline To Expect In A Bull Market And How Much Rally To Expect In A Bear Market.

After a bull market gets under way and stocks are moving up fast, the reactions are likely to be quick and sharp but they will never last more than 3 to 4 weeks as a general rule and then the upward trend will be resumed, so you can always figure that stocks are a buy on a reaction of about 1 month in a bull market. In a bear market after the main trend has been established downward, the rallies will run three weeks to four weeks and seldom ever more than one month, but in some cases after sharp, severe declines in a short period of time rallies will last as much as 2 months – just the same there is a possibility of a reaction in a bull market running 2 months after extremes. By keeping these rules in mind you will have a guide as to when the main trend is changing up or down.

B. How To Make The Most Money In The Shortest Period of Time.

People want to get rich quick, that is why they lose their money because they try to get rich quick with out first preparing themselves for getting ready or having the knowledge to know how and when to make the most money in the shortest period of time. I am going to prove to you, by examples, and you can also prove to yourself, when you can make the most money in the shortest period of time. Do not try to lead the market or make the market. Follow the big men with big money and you will make big money. Buy when the big market makers are ready for prices to move up fast and you will make the most money in a short period of time. Sell when the big market money makers have distributed stocks and are ready for them to go down and there is indication of definite trend downward. Then sell short and you will make the most money in the shortest period of time.

11.

It requires time for a market to get ready, time for stocks to be absorbed or accumulated but once we have passed from weak into strong hands, then they move up fast because the offerings are smaller and the big people just have to let the market roll and do a little buying and it goes up easy.

It also requires a long period of time to sell out stocks or distribute them once they have reached the high levels and let the stocks pass from strong hands into weak hands. When this period is over and the market is ready, then it declines fast and if you trade this way and wait until there is a definite indication that the trend has changed, you really can make the <u>most money</u> in the <u>shortest period</u> of <u>time</u>.

Below I am giving you some examples to prove that these rules work and that the market goes up the fastest after a long period of time and down fastest in the last stages after a long period of declining market.

BOEING AIRCRAFT 1949, June low 17¼ 1950 May high 31½ UP 14 points in 11 months.

1950, September. Buy at 37 in new highs; 1951, February high 56, up 19 points in 5 months. This is making the most profits in the <u>quickest</u> and <u>shortest</u> period of time.

1954, February. Buy at 57 at new highs. 1954, April Sell at 83, Up 26 points in 2 months. It takes nerve to buy at new highs but that is what big people do and you are only following them when you buy at new high levels and then you make the most <u>money</u> in the <u>shortest period</u> of <u>time</u>.

DOUGLASS AIRCRAFT: 1951, June low 43½ ; October 1951 high 66½ , UP 23 points in 4 months.

GLENN L. MARTIN: 1949, June low 7; 1951 high 22; 1952, July low 9. Therefore, the low of 9 in July 1952 was a higher bottom, a support and buying level. The trend was up until February 1953, high 18½ . Note last previous high 19½ in September 1951; from this lower top the trend started down.

1953, June to September low 12 at the old tops of April to September 1952, remaining for four months in a range of 2 points and indicated good support and a buying level and you should buy.

1954, February crossed 18½ , the high of February 1953. Here you would follow the rules and <u>buy</u> at <u>new high levels</u>.

1954, high is 25½ on a volume of 384 thousand share for the week ending April 3, 1954. The large volume indicated public buying at high levels and short covering and a reaction was due.

Note April 1948 high 22½ and January 1951 high 22; the price of 25½ was 3½ points above these old high levels indicating a possibility of higher prices.

Later. The reaction during the week ending May 8 brought prices down to 21¾ which was at the old high levels of 1948-1951 and a rally started up from 21¾.

UNITED AIRCRAFT: 1951, May high 41½ ; 1951, July low 26; 1951, October high 33; 1951, December low 28½ ; 1952, February high 33½ , same high as October 1951 and a selling level.

1952, May low 27½ , about the same low as December 1951 and higher than June 1951 low.

1952, September crossed 33, the old high. Buy at new highs.

1953, April high 40½ , just below 41½ the high of May 1951, making this a selling level.

1953, April and May low 32 to 31½ , just below the old tops of 33, a buying level, then the advance was resumed.

1953, October prices crossed 41½, the high of May 1951. Follow the rule and buy at new high levels as the trend was up and continued up with very small reactions.

1954, April high 59½, the highest price since September 1930 when the last high was 65 and the two previous highs were 64; therefore, 64-65 is the next resistance level to watch for tops. The price is now up more than 100% from May 1952 and a natural reaction often comes when stocks have advanced 100%.

Analyze any other Aircraft stock in the same way in which we have analyzed these stocks and in fact any other stock of any other group. First you should keep a chart of the total value of the group as published by the New York Stock Exchange Statistical Bureau and then keep up weekly, monthly and yearly highs and lows on the different individual stocks so that you will have a record far enough back that you will know where the important tops and bottoms are and know when change in trend comes by prices advancing above old highs or breaking below old lows. You cannot have too much information or too many records when you are going to risk your capital. You must be fully prepared and ready, then you can take advantage of opportunities when they come based on scientific mathematical deductions and not hope, fear or guesswork.

13.

DOUGLASS AIRCRAFT: 1953, October buy at new high 74. 1954, April sell at 133. Up 59 points in 6 months. This was making the most money in a short period of time after you bought it at very high levels. Why? Because the big people had absorbed all the stock offered below and offerings were very small, so when buyers come in the market advanced rapidly and profits to the buyers who bought at high levels made profits fast in a short period of time.

LOCKHEED AIRCRAFT: 1943, November low 12½; 1944, August high 24, 11½ points profit in 21 months.

1945, August low 25; 1946, May high 45½, up 21½ points in 5 months. Here you were making nearly as much in 5 months as you made in 21 months previously.

1951, July low 17½; 1953, March 26½, UP 9 points in 20 months. A small profit in a long period of time.

1953, October. Buy at 24 above old highs; 1954, March high 37 profit, 13 points in 5 months. This is making a quick profit and a large profit based on the capital in a short period of time.

GLEN L. MARTIN: 1943, December low 14½ ; 1944, December high 24½, up 10 points in 12 months.

1945, August Buy at 22; 1945, December sell at 46½, UP 24½ points in 4 months. This is again making the most profits in the shortest period of time.

1952, June low 9; 1953, March 18½ , UP 9½ points in 8 months.

1953, June to September low 12. This is a buying level; 1953, October, Buy at 15 after it crossed 5 months tops. 1954, April, sell at 26. Profit 9 points in 6 months.

SOUTHERN RAILWAY: 1951, July low 46½ . September high 56½ , UP 10 points in 2 months.

1952, February low 48; 1952, March buy at 53 after it crossed old tops. 1953, May sell at 99, UP 46 points in 12 months. This is making the most profits in the short period of time.

UNITED AIRCRAFT: 1951, July low 26; 1953, March high 40, UP 14 points in 20 months. 1953, October buy at 40 at new high. 1952, April sell at 59. Profit 19 points in 6 months.

VANADIUM STEEL: 1950, December low 28½; 1952 August high 45½, up 17 points in 20 months.

14.

1953, September. Buy at 32 against a series of old bottoms. 1952, April sell at 59, making 27 points profit in 7 months.

1954, March. Buy at 47 at a new high; 1954, April high 59¾. UP 12¾ points in 1 month. Here you would make the most profits in the shortest period of time after buying at a new high level. Why was this move so fast? Because after a long period of time the insiders or people who were in the know had bought all the Vanadium that was offered and when it all was absorbed and bidding started to come into the market, it advanced very rapidly. In this way, when you buy you are going with the trend and following people who make the market. Therefore, you make the <u>most money</u> in the <u>shortest period</u> of <u>time</u>.

These examples of seven stocks are not exceptions. You can go over the list of stocks and pick out hundreds of them that make moves of a similar nature and you should always have the average of the different groups, and when the average of the groups show up or down, then pick out the stocks in strong or weak position and watch them and buy when they make new highs, or sell them at new lows; in the first and last stage of the market you make the most money in the shortest period of time.

You cannot make money without getting ready to make it and in doing this you have to spend some money for charts, records, books and course of instruction. In this way you are ready to follow the big men who make the market and make big money.

STOCKS NOT MANIPULATED: Before the Stock Exchange started regulating brokers and the control of markets, there was manipulation and pools often were organized that could advance low priced stocks that had very little merit to extreme high levels. This does not happen under present conditions; therefore, most of the buying is by investors and long term speculators and there is practically no manipulation; for this reason it is more necessary to study the market carefully and study individual stocks and get definite indications that they are going to move up, because they will not be put up just by manipulation, as they were years in the past. Under present conditions more traders and investors buy stocks on the prospects of dividends and an increase in their investment. This you can do by a careful study of all the rules.

NEW INDUSTRIES AND GROWTH OF STOCKS: In the future, stocks connected with the atomic energy will naturally be leader because like all new discoveries and inventions, it will prove to be very valuable and a lot of companies will make a lot of money. These companies with prospects on the atomic stocks will be covered later. In selecting stocks to buy under new industries, you should make a careful study of their prospects and make up charts on the individual stocks that you intend to trade in, and if they are part of the group, you can get a record of the group average, study this group average and then pick the individual stock to buy that shows an indication of leading the group.

15.

URANIUM STOCKS: Uranium is now one of the most valuable of all precious metals. It is much more valuable than gold and the stocks that have made discoveries and have Uranium deposits, such stocks as Vanadium have better prospects to be leaders in the future. We will cover other stocks later under the Uranium Stocks.

VALUE OF ALL STOCKS LISTED ON THE NEW YORK STOCK EXCHANGE

The Department of Research and Statistics of the New York Stock Exchange has done a most valuable work for investors and they deserve great credit for it. At the end of each month they publish a total value of all stocks listed on the N.Y. Stock Exchange, the average value of all stocks, the total number of stocks listed and the total number of shares and the total value, that is, the market value of each group of stocks and the average of 39 or more different groups. This is of great value to any investor and trader who will study these records and use them, as I will show how to do later with the charts covering these averages and total value of stocks. The number of stocks list on the N.Y. Stock Exchange is 1536. The total number of shares listed is 2 billion 936 million, nearly 3 billion shares. The market value of all stocks listed on the N.Y. Stock Exchange at the end of March 1934 was nearly 125 billion dollars and the average price of all stocks was 42.53, this is the highest price in recent years.

1932, June – the total value of all stocks was a little less than 16 billion dollars.

1928, November – the flat average price was 97.80 and in March 1929 the average price was 96.67. August 31, 1929 the total value of all stocks on the N.Y. Stock Exchange was 69 billion, 668 hundred million dollars.

1932, July 1 – the total number of companies on the N.Y. Stock Exchange was 831; the total number of issues was 1233, and the number of shares was 1 billion, 315,334,428 and at the present time the total number of shares listed is nearly 3 billion. From this you can see that while the value of stocks increases, the number of shares is increasing all of the time.

1941, June was the last extreme low in stocks. At that time the average price was 40.74 and the total value of all stocks was $63,921,054,342.

1950, May. The value of all stocks $85,624,559,669. The average price 38.48. When prices crossed the high of may 1946, they indicated much higher prices but of course, you have to learn to pick the stocks in the strong groups to buy.

16.

THE AVERAGE VALUE OF ALL STOCKS ON THE NEW YORK STOCK EXCHANGE AND HOW THEY INDICATE TREND OF PRICES

THE DOLLAR TREND: Please refer to Chart; it which shows the total market value of all stocks at the end of each month. Refer to chart on which shows the total market value in dollars of Aircraft stocks. Refer to chart on which shows the total market value of 39 steel and iron stocks ant the end of each month.

HOW TO USE VALUE CHART – AS A GUIDE TO TREND INDICATOR
(The scale on this chart shows 16.24 and up to 135, this means billions of dollars).

EXAMPLE: 1932, June 30 lows show just the low of 16. This means at the extreme low in 1932 the total value of all stocks was 15 billion, 633 million, 633 thousand dollars. We will refer to 26, 36, and 40, etc., which is on the scale and means billions of dollars.

1932, February high just below 28; June low 16; August high 28, 1933, February low 20 billion dollars – this was a secondary decline and made a higher bottom than June 1932. 1933, in April the value line crossed the high of February 1932 and August 1932 this indicated that the main trend was up. 1933, June and August high just above 36 billion dollars. October low just above 30 billion dollars.

1934, January high 37 billion dollars. February, March and April the value held just above 36 billion and when prices broke 36 it indicated lower.

1934, July low just below 31 and above the low of October 1933.

1935, March – low slightly below 31 billion. This made three lows of supports near the same level making it a buying level.

1935, June – the value crossed 37 the high of January 1934. Here is where we use the rule and <u>buy at new high levels</u>.

The advance continued. February and March 1936 high just under 52 billion. April 1936 a one month's decline to 48, less than 4 billions decline.

The upward trend was resumed and on July 1936 the averages crossed 52, the high of March 1936, indicating higher. Again we follow the rule and <u>buy</u> at <u>new high levels</u>.

1937, February and March high, 62½ million dollars. For 3 months the value was in a range of one billion dollars which indicates resistance and good selling as the total volume of sales was very large.

1936, December low 58. 1937, April this low was broken indicating lower prices. Here we follow the rule and sell at lower levels.

1937, June low 55; a rally followed to July high 59, a lower top then broke below 55; the low in June showing down trend. You would remain short and sell more and should be out of all long stocks. The main trend continued down.

1937, December low 39; 1938, February high 41½ , a small rally; 1938, March low, just below 32 billion and above the lows of October 1933. July 1934 and March 1938 the decline was 50% of the high of February and March 1937. Therefore, March 1938 was a buying level.

1938, June the dollar trend crossed 41½ , the high of February 1938 indicating to buy more.

1938, October and December high 47 to 47½ . Under the low of April 1936 where prices broke below 45 indicated lower. 1939, March and April low just above 40. June and August higher bottoms indicating support and good buying.

1939, September Hitler started the war and the value advanced to just below 41-48, a double top against December 1938, a selling level or place to watch indicating a change in trend. 1940, May the price was just above 36, a rally followed to October high 42. 1941, July 41, higher than October 1940. November prices broke the bottom of April 1941 and later went below May 1940 indicating lower prices.

WHEN TO WATCH FOR SUPPORT AND BUYING LEVEL

1948, March low just under 32. 1942, April low 31½ . The average value was 32½ in March and May 1944. Then started to move up showing strong uptrend.

1943 crossed the high of October 1940 and July 1941. Follow the rule, buy more at new highs. 1943, June high just below 49 and above December 1938 and September 1938, indicating higher prices.

1943, September high 49, same high as May and June 1943 indicating good selling.

1943, November low 45½, a decline of less than 5 billion dollars in value and a recovery started. 1944, May prices crossed the highs of June and September 1932. Here we again follow the rule and buy when prices moved up to new highs. August 1945, when the Japanese war ended, prices crossed 62½, the high of February 1937, a sure indication of higher prices. You would buy the stocks in strong groups.

1946, January high 78½ ; February declined to 74, about the same decline as November 1943, not enough to show a change in the main trend.

1946, May high 85 billion dollars up 55 billion from April 1942 low and 22 billions above the highs of February 1937. This was the time to watch for a change in trend.

The high in May 1946 was about 5 billion below the high of August 31, 1929. which is just under 90 billion dollars.

1946, April high was 80 billion dollars; June 80 billion dollars, July low 79 indicating lower. The trend continued down to November 1946 low 65 billion. 1947 January high 68¼, a small rally. May low 63½ billion. July high 69¼ same high as January 1947. The trend continued down.

1948, February low 63 billion 158 million dollars. Slightly lower than May 1947 but still above the highs of February 1937 making this a buying level.

1948, May and June high 74½ under the low of February 1946. 1948 July low indicated lower prices. September 65½ , October high 72¼ , the decline was resumed. 1949, June low just below 64 billion. Same low as May 1947 and February 1948, a buying level at old lows. 1949, August prices crossed the highs of January and March 1949, indicating higher. Buy more. 1949, December the value was 76 billion above the high of May and June 1948. Follow rule and buy at new high levels. A rapid advance followed.

1950, May high 85 billion 624 million dollars, above May 1946 high, an indication of higher prices.

1950, August; the averages crossed the 1946 highs made in May 1950 – follow the rule and buy at new high levels. 1950, December – average value above the high of August 1929. Follow the rule and buy at new high levels.

1951, April high 103 billions. June low 97 billions. An average decline of about the same as June 1950.

July high 104 billions near the high buy at new high levels. 1952, January high 112. February low 108, March new high at 113 billions. April low 108, a decline of 5 billions. A normal decline based on previous reaction. From this level the advance was resumed.

19.

1952 July high 116 billions. September and October low just below 113 billion, a smaller decline than April 1952.

1952, December and January 1953 high 120½ billions. This was 33⅓% more than 1929 high

1953, February low just below 119 billions. This was 3 months with no gain, an indication that a reaction was due, since June 1949 no reaction had been more than 5 billions and a greater reaction was due, possibly 10 billions.

1953, August and September low slightly below 10 billions or 2 times the previous reaction.

1953, October Average 116 billions above July 1953 high, an indication of higher prices.

1954, January the prices crossed 120 billions, the high of December 1952. Again we would follow the rule and buy at new high levels, selecting the stocks in the groups which showed strong up trend. (See charts on U.S. Steel, Vanadium Steel, and the Aircrafts and the average value of these). You can see by the charts on Boeing, Douglass Aircraft, Glen Martin and Vanadium Steel why we would select these stocks to buy and the price of these stocks to move up fast in March and April 1954.

1954, March 31 the average value of all stocks in the New York Stock Exchange was just above 129 billion dollars. We now come to the problem of estimating when the average will meet resistance and good selling. We use 1929 high of 90 billion dollars and add 50% of this which would give 135 billion.

If we add or use approximately 325% on the high of April 1944, we get close to 135 billions as a selling level.

April 30, 1954 is 12 years from the low of April 30, 1942 and from June 30, 1932 low to April 30, 1954 is 262 months. The Dow Jones Industrial Averages made secondary highs at 297½ in April 1930. By going back over past history you find many changes in trend in April and May, therefore the time is near to watch for a change in trend in Stocks and groups like Aircrafts and Steels which have led the 1954 advance.

HOW MUCH DECLINE TO EXPECT: The greatest decline since 1942 lows was from February 1937 to March and April 1938. The decline was 31 billion 168 million dollars. The decline from May 1946 to February 1948 and June 1949 was 21 billion 785 million dollars. This gives you a guide as to how much the first decline may amount to.

20.

The advance from June 1949 to date has already exceeded 100% gain in value of all stocks and this would indicate that the time is near for at least a substantial corrective decline but groups and individual stocks must be studied to indicate their strength and weakness in relation to the average value of all stocks.

WHEN STOCKS ARE IN THE STRONGEST AND WEAKEST POSITION

When a stock has sold at very high levels declines and remains for a very long time at low levels and then finally crosses 50% of the highest prices at which it ever sold, or 50% between the extreme low and the extreme high, it is then in a very strong position and indicates higher prices.

When a stock decline and breaks 50% of the highest prices ever sold, it is in a very weak position and as a general rule when the stocks reach this point they have a moderate rally and sometimes it is a final bottom for a big advance. The next important point is 50% between the extreme high and the extreme low when stocks cannot hold this level and break below it they are in the weakest possible position and indicate much lower prices. In many cases a decline to these points or a rally to these important 50% points remains for weeks or months without advancing above the halfway point of 50% or breaking below it, but when once these points are exceeded, you should reverse the position. If you are short cover shorts and buy. If you are long, sell out longs and sell short. In this way you will make money because you will be going with the trend buying the stocks in the strongest position and selling the stocks in the weakest position. You must remember if it is time to sell out a stock you are doing it because in a weak position the trend is down and it is also equally good then to sell short following, of course, all rules given in this book and all rules given in my book, "45 YEARS IN WALL STREET".

You must give the market time to show a change in trend. Suppose people in the last two years have bought Studebaker too high, Chrysler at high levels or Celanese. When they saw that the main trend had change, if they had a 5 point loss or even a 10 point loss if they sold out, took the loss and went short, they would not only make back the loss they had but make big profits on the short side. This is how money is made by going with the trend. Example: Celanese high 58 in 1951, 50% of this is 29 in April 1953. Celanese broke 29 and never sold 2 points higher before it declined to 16 in 1954. This is the proof of how weak stocks get when once they have lost 50% of their value.

In 1953 Studebaker high 434½. 50% of this high price is 21¾ ; after it broke this level in December 953 it never rallied 2 points before it sold at 15 in April 1954, another proof of why it pays to sell stocks short when they are down 50% from the high level, because when you do this you are going with the trend.

WHY IT IS PROFITABLE TO BUY AT NEW HIGH PRICES AND SELL AT NEW LOW LEVELS

When the stock is in a strong enough position to advance to new highs after several months, weeks or years it has remained below these highs, it is strong as a result of good demand and because powerful interests are buying; therefore, when you buy you are going with the main trend and that's the right way to make profits.

Never buck the trend, go with the trend always and you'll make money.

When stocks decline to new low levels they are in a weak position because the supply is greater than the demand and the selling is better than the buying, and for this good reason you will be right 90% of the time if you sell stocks when they are weak but always protecting with a STOP LOSS order based upon the rules.

MORE PROFIT IN SWINGS: If you will go over any active stock over a period of 5 ,10, or 20 years and note all the moves of 10 points or more, you will see that there is more profit trading for these swings than there is trading for dividends or hold for big increase in capital.

From 1925, where Chrysler has started around 28, it moved up to 141 and after having many swings up and down, running 10 to 50 and 75 points, it finally declined to 5 in 1932. From 1932 up to 1954 Chrysler has made a range from $5 a share to 141, a total of 136 points which would give a profit of $13,600 on 100 shares. During this same time, Chrysler, figuring 10 point moves or more has made a total of 1458 points. Just suppose you could catch 1/2 or 50% of these moves which would give 729 points profit against the range of 136 points. This is proof that it pays to trade for the swings. That is, get out of the market when it shows an indication that prices have reached high and go short and then get in again when there is a definite indication that they have made low trading in and out and not holding and letting the market go up and down over a period of years and receiving nothing but dividends, finally winding up with a small return on you capital counting interest from the time you bought up the time you sold out. Go over any active stocks and you can prove this to yourself.

THE W.D. GANN MASTER STOCK MARKET COURSE

22.

CHANGE WHEN THE TREND CHANGES: Conditions change from time to time and trends change after a period of time, and to make profits you must change with the trend and with the time. Do not hold too long or hold just because you are receiving dividends; trade to increase your capital and don not worry too much about dividends. The value of any rules is, "Will it stand the test of time in actual trading?". I offer proof of all my rules such as buying at new highs and selling at new lows by actual practice and prove to you that it does pay to go with the trend and buy when stocks are reaching new high levels and sell when they break into new low levels. Go over the charts in the Course, Celanese, Douglas Aircraft, Boeing, Lockheed, Glen Martin, Studebaker, United Aircraft and Vanadium Steel and in this way you can prove to yourself how the rules work.

BUYING ONE STOCK AND SELLING ANOTHER SHORT AT THE SAME TIME: To prove this rule, I show the chart on Celanese and Douglas Aircraft and Studebaker and Vanadium Steel.

BUYING AND SELLING A DIFFERENT GROUP OF STOCKS AT THE SAME TIME: 1951, July bought 100 Douglas at 48, August sold 100 Celanese at 52 when both stocks were selling at around the same levels. Suppose you placed a STOP LOSS ORDER ON Douglas at 45 and when you sold Celanese at 52 you placed a STOP at 59, 1 point above the high of 53 in August. Suppose you do not buy More Douglas which you should many times, based on the rules and should have sold short more Celanese based on the rules, and could have made a larger amount of money on a very small risk.

Suppose in April 1954 when Douglas made the final grand rush and was advanced crossing the high of 110, you finally sold the Douglas at 130; you would make 72 points on the Douglas or $7,200 less interest and commission and at the same time you buy in 100 short Celanese at 16 making 34 points at $3,400 profit, less commission, or a total on the two trades of $10,600 on a capital of $5,200, more than 100% in less than 3 years. Refer to the chart on Studebaker and Vanadium Steel where we show why, by buying Vanadium and selling Studebaker short, big profits were made.

1951, March sell 100 Studebaker at 34 short because there were two tops at 36 and the third top was 35, a lower top, place STOP at 37.

1951, August bought 100 Studebaker at 26 because 3 lows around this same level and bought 100 Studebaker for long account.

1951, March bought 100 Vanadium at 32 because it was 6 months around this low level at 31. Place STOP AT 29.

1953, March sell 100 Vanadium at 44½ because the highs previously were 45 and 45½ in August 1952 and March 1952, making this a double top.

1953, March sell 100 Vanadium short at 44½, place STOP at 47.

1953, February Studebaker high at 43½ near the same level as Vanadium.

1953, March sold 100 Studebaker short at 38½ and sold 100 Studebaker that we had for long account at 38½. When it broke under the low of February and the low of 39½ made in May 1952. Place a STOP LOSS order on Studebaker, sold short at 45½.

1953, June Studebaker broke 34; the low of October-November 1952 and you should sell more at 31.

1953, June make STOP on 200 short at 34. Studebaker continues to go down and in September 1953 broke below 21¾, a decline of 50% from 43½, rallied to only 26 and then broke 21¾ which indicated much lower.

1954, January and February high 21¾, a very weak rally, remain short of the 200 shares with STOP 22¾.

1954, April 30 Studebaker low 15 main trend down. Profits, if you close all the Studebaker, are 60 points or $6,000.

1951 March bought Vanadium at 32; 1953 sold 100 at 44½ and sold short 100 at 44½.

1953, bought 100 to cover shorts of 31 because it was at the low of April and May 1951 and at the same time we bought 100 Vanadium for long account at 31 and place a STOP LOSS order at 29.

1954, February bought 100 Vanadium at 41 because it was at the new high above 2 tops of 39½ in July and August 1953, and above 2 tops of 39½ in December 1953 and January 1954.

1954, March bought 100 Vanadium at 47 because it was at new high levels above the high of August and December 1952 & March 1953 showing main trend up and at the highest level since 1931, indicating a very strong position.

1954, April Vanadium reached a high of 59¾. Note September 1953 low of 30½, add 50% gives 61 and a possible high. The volume of sales was the largest for years indicating that it might be reaching a possible top for reactions anyway. So we sell 300 shares that were long at 59½ but would not go short because the main trend is still up. These shares which we sold were bought at 31, 41, and 47. This give a total of 57 points profit or $5,700 less interest and commission. Add this to $6,000 profit on Studebaker give $11,500. in 3 years

24.

time on a capital of about $3,500. or over 300% on the capital, or 100% profit for each year by following rule and not guessing.

I have not picked these stocks because they were exceptions. There are many more in different groups that would have made a showing equally as good.

1953, Vanadium low 30½ and Studebaker 28, just 4 points apart.

1954, April Vanadium was approximately 45 points higher than Studebaker, a spread of 45 points in 7 months time. This proves that it pays to buy the stocks in strong position and sell the ones in weak position, which indicates main trend down.

WHY LOW PRICED STOCKS DO NOT MOVE UP

Changed conditions are the cause why low price stocks or so called "cats and dogs" have not followed the advance from September 1953 to April 1954. With the Dow Jones Stocks up 66 points in 7 months and the total value of all stocks listed on the N Y Stock Exchange up about 24 billion dollars, there must be some reason why the low priced stocks have not followed this advance.

In the old days when pools operated and manipulation and watched sales were permitted, the low priced socks nearly always advanced in the last stage of a bull market but it is not the case now because no pools are operating. The Investment Trusts, and the people with large amounts of money for investment buy into the strong companies where the earnings are good and the dividend prospects are good. They buy good stocks like General Motors, Standard of New Jersey, American Tel. & Tel., Dupont, General Electric, Westinghouse, Douglas, U.S. Steel, Bethlehem Steel and Vanadium Steel.

The public buys and holds the low priced stocks hoping they will follow the high priced stocks and go up, but hope will not put these low priced stocks up. The big people don't want them and the result will be many low priced stocks will decline faster in the next bear market than the high priced stocks. Of course, the day will come when the great time cycle indicates a great depression, that large and small investors will lose confidence and sell the blue chips when they are at very low levels.

AIR CRAFT STOCKS ON THE NEW YORK STOCK EXCHANGE

The New York Stock Exchange, Department of Research publishes at the end of each month the total value of all aircraft stocks listed on the Exchange, and this chart is very valuable as a guide in selecting the best aircraft stocks to buy or sell. The chart which we have made up on these averages we call the <u>Dollar</u> Trend because it is not the average price of stocks but the value in dollars of the entire group, and this is a more important trend indicator than the average price. However, the Research Department does publish the average value of all aircraft stocks at the end of each month as well as all other groups.

1951, September total value 1 billion, 135 million dollars. November low 955 million dollars.

1952, January 1 billion 10 million dollars. April low 892 million dollars. This was the extreme low. At this time you would look up the monthly high and low, and weekly high and low chart on the individual aircraft stocks to decide which is the best buy.

BELL AIRCRAFT

April 1952, in a slow trading range, had been split up and was not one of the best to buy at that time.

1953, September – it was making higher bottoms and was better to buy.

BOEING AIRCRAFT

April 1952. Made low in June after the stock was split up and was good to buy, but was better to buy in September 1953 because the average value of all Aircraft Stocks had made a new low, and were higher in September indicating that the trend was turning up.

1954, February was the time to buy Boeing for <u>quick profits</u> in a <u>short period</u> of <u>time</u> because it had crossed old high levels.

DOUGLASS AIRCRAFT

April 152 was the very best buy among the Aircrafts because it had declined from 66½ to 52, and 50% of the range from 43½ to 66½ was 55 and it closed in April 1952 at 57, making it a good buy with STOP at 51.

1953, September Douglas made low of 62. It had been making higher bottoms since April 1952 and it was one of the very best stocks to buy, protected with STOP at 60. In December 1953 it crossed 74, the old high level, and was one of the best stocks to buy for a fast move up and large profits in a short period of time.

LOCKHEED AIRCRAFT

In April 1952 it made higher bottoms but was slow because it had been split up. It was a much better stock to buy in October 1953 when it crossed old tops.

GLEN L. MARTIN

April 1952 was good to buy because it had held for four months making higher bottoms than 1949 low. It was a still better buy in September 1953 when it was crossing old tops.

UNITED AIRCRAFT

April 1953 was a good stock to buy because it was making higher bottoms but the big profits in a short period of time could have been made by buying in September 1953.

ALL AIRCRAFT STOCK AVERAGES

1953, February the average was 1 billion 180 million dollars.

1954, January the averages made a new high and in February 1954 they were higher, and if you bought Douglass or almost any other Aircraft Stock at that time you could have made large profits in a short period of time.

1954, March 31 the average of all Aircraft Stocks was 1 billion 504 million dollars, the highest for many years, and at the end of April 1954 they had probably advanced 100% from the extreme low of April 1952. (At this writing we do not have the figures for the end of April 1954).

39 STEEL AND IRON STOCKS AVERAGE VALUE

These figures are for the average price on the last day of each month. Study the chart in back of the book of instructions and it will help you to determine the trend of one entire group of steel stocks and when you want to select the best stock to buy or sell, study the chart of the individual steel stocks.

1951, September high 3 billion 805 million dollars. From this level the trend turned down and made lower tops and lower bottoms each month with no gain of more than 100 million dollars in one month until April 1952 when the low was 3 billion 350 million dollars. The trend turned up from this low level and July high 3 billion 635 million dollars.

1952, September and October low 3 billion 384 million dollars, a higher bottom and a buying level. At this time you would look up the individual steel stocks in order to select the best stocks to buy.

BETHLEHEM STEEL

September 1952 low 47, higher than May 1952 and good to buy with a STOP at 45, but it was a much better buy in September 1953 when the average of all steel stocks was 3 billion 105 million dollars. At this time Bethlehem Steel was selling at 44½, not 3 points below the old bottoms and good to buy with STOP at 43.

VANADIUM STEEL

April 1952 low 35½, good to buy because it was making higher bottoms and you would have made fair profits buying it at this time.

1952, September low 30½, higher than the lows of 1950 and 1951, a good buy with a STOP at 29, especially because it had such good prospects for increased profits through its Uranium mines.

1954, February Vanadium was a safe and best buy at 41 because it crossed the old high and you could buy more in March 1954 when it crossed 47, the old highs, and the average value of all steel stocks was up at that time. Vanadium advanced to 59¾ in April 1954, and the volume of sales was very large. If you were keeping up the daily and weekly high and low chart, you would sell out at this time. It reacted to 54 and then advanced to 59 again. It will have to decline below 54 to indicate lower prices and when it crosses 60 and closes above this level, the next resistance level is 67 - 68; after this price is crossed, the next price to watch is 76½, the old high in March 1931.

It will pay you to keep up the average value of each group of stocks monthly and the average price of the group, as well as the total value of all stocks listed on the N Y Stock Exchange each month. These averages of value give you the dollar trend which is much more accurate and valuable than the Dow-Jones 30 Industrial Average which cover only a small percentage of the total stocks listed.

28.

Remember that the harder you work, the more knowledge you will get, and the more profits you will make. King Solomon, the wisest man who ever lived, shows wisdom and understanding above everything else. You will do well to follow his example. "Happy is the man who findeth Wisdom, and the man who getteth understanding". (Proverbs).

The rules which I have laid down in the course are practical. I have followed them and made money, and you can follow them and make money. My greatest pleasure in life comes from helping others.

> "If I can throw a single ray of light,
> Across the darkened pathway of another;
> If I can aid some soul to clearer sight,
> Of life and duty, and thus bless my brother;
> If I can wipe from any human cheek a tear,
> I shall not then have lived in vain while here."

I am nearing my 76th birthday and I have realized happiness and success. I feel that I have not lived in vain, because thousands of people have benefited through my books and my course of instructions and I feel confident they will benefit through the rules in this course, SPECULATION - A PROFITABLE PROFESSION.

W. D. GANN

May 18, 1954

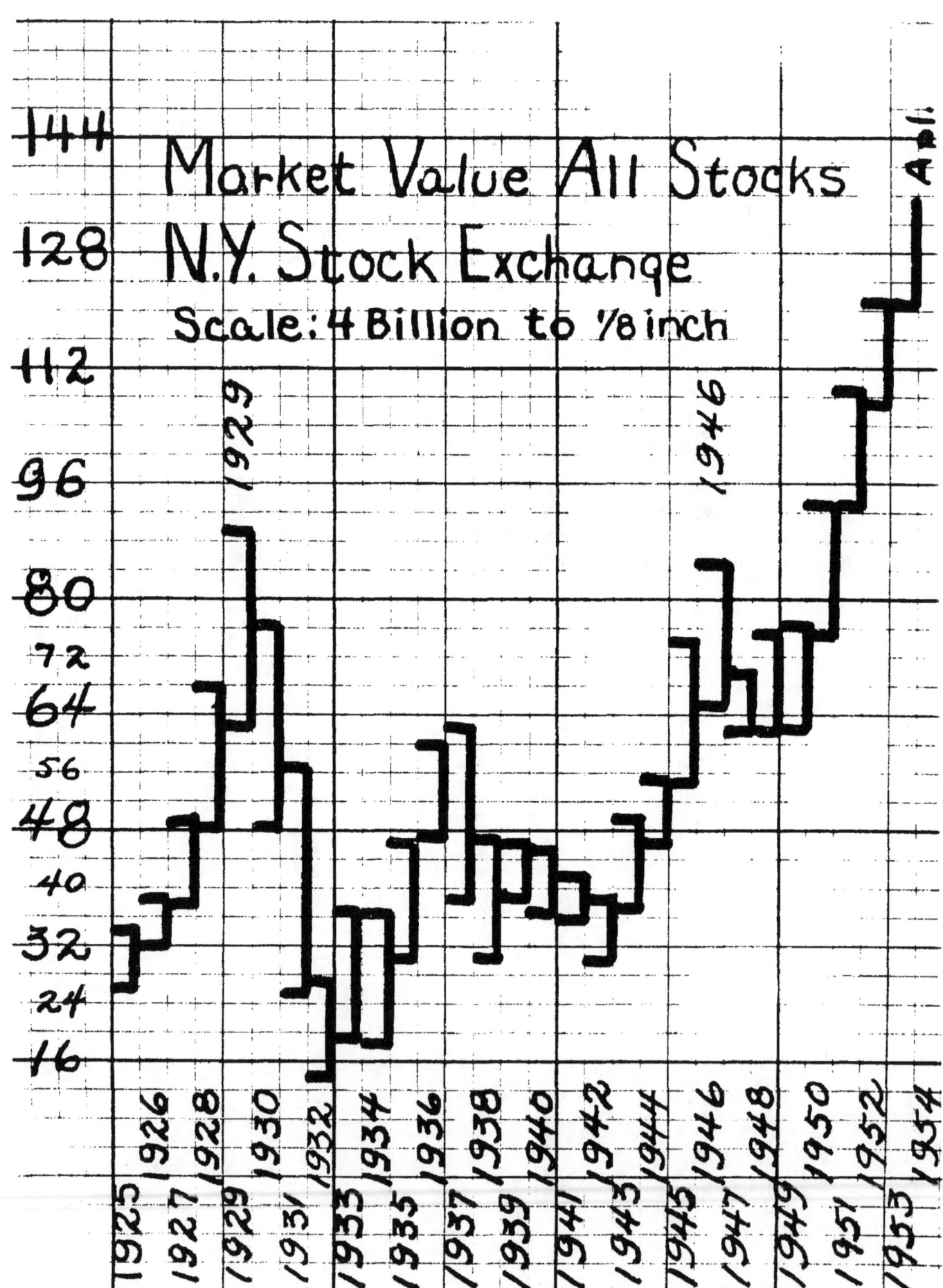

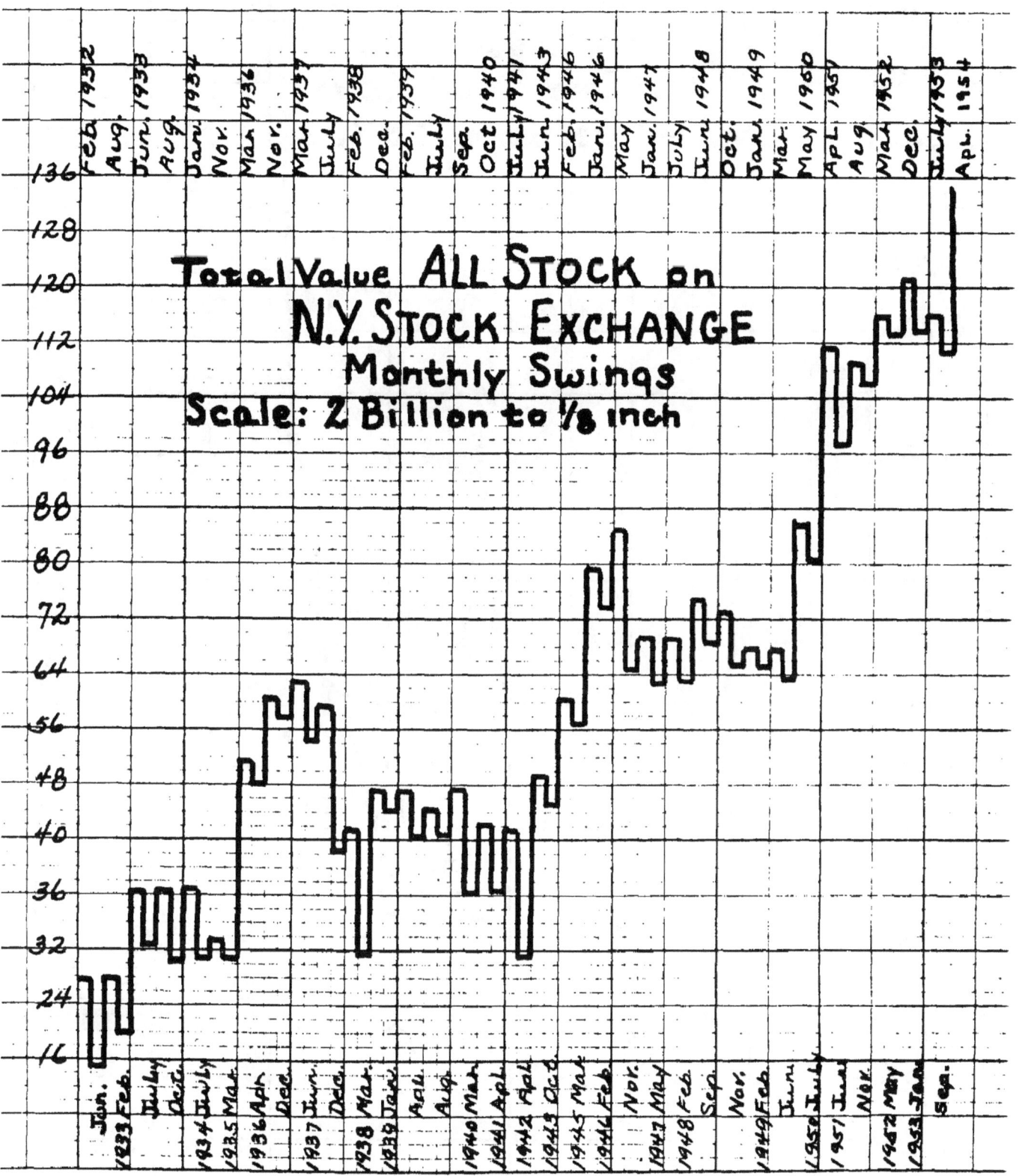

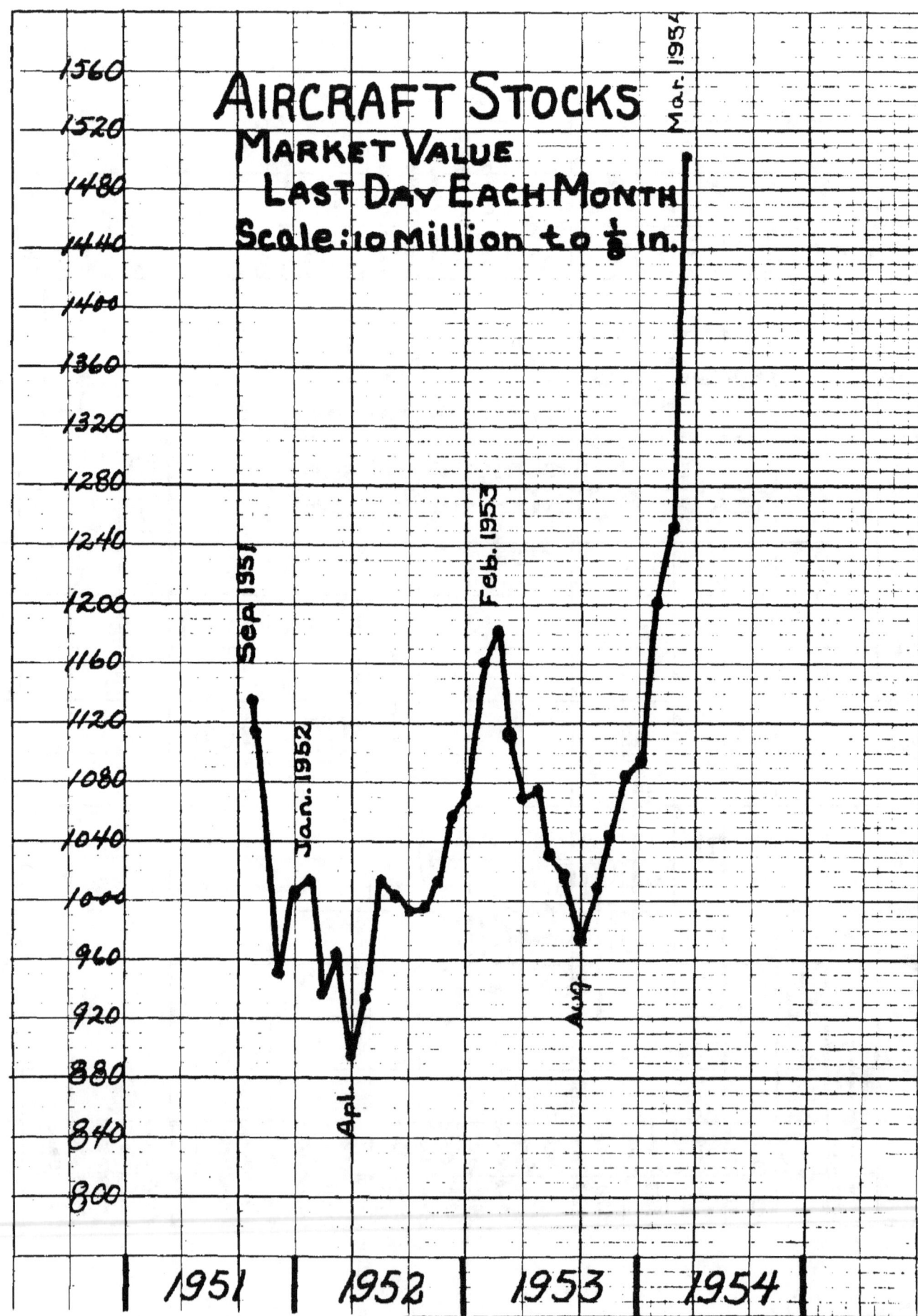

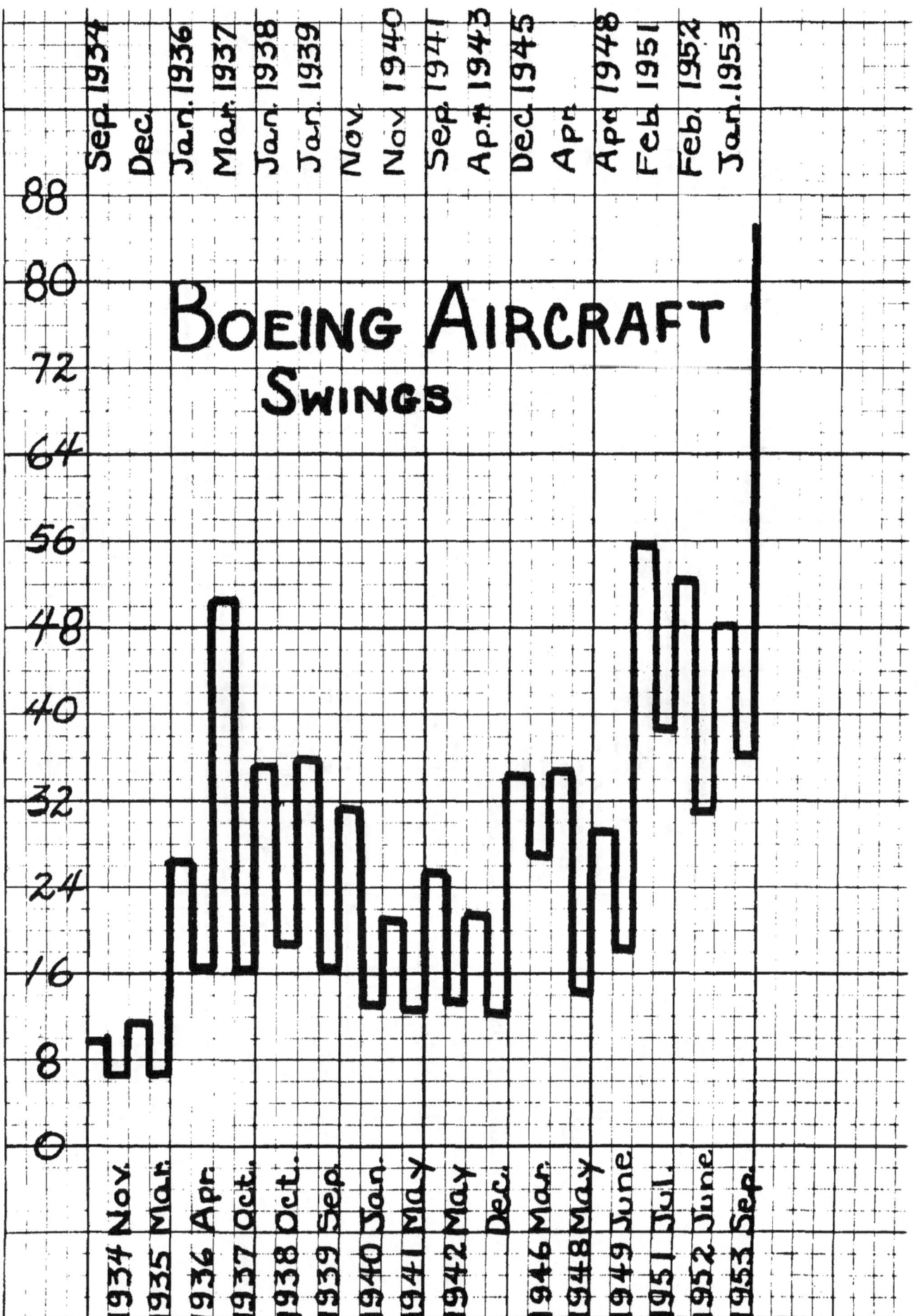

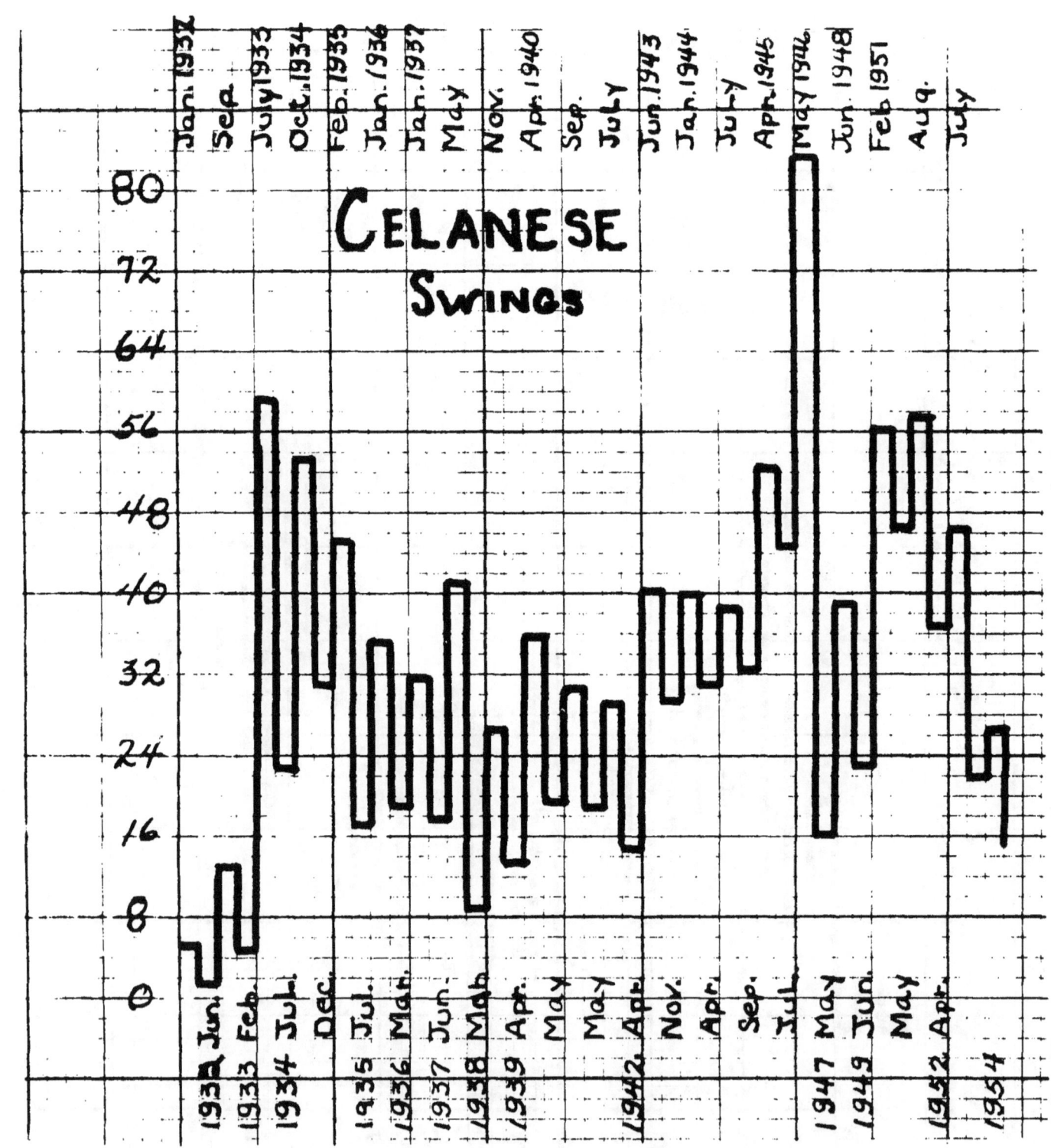

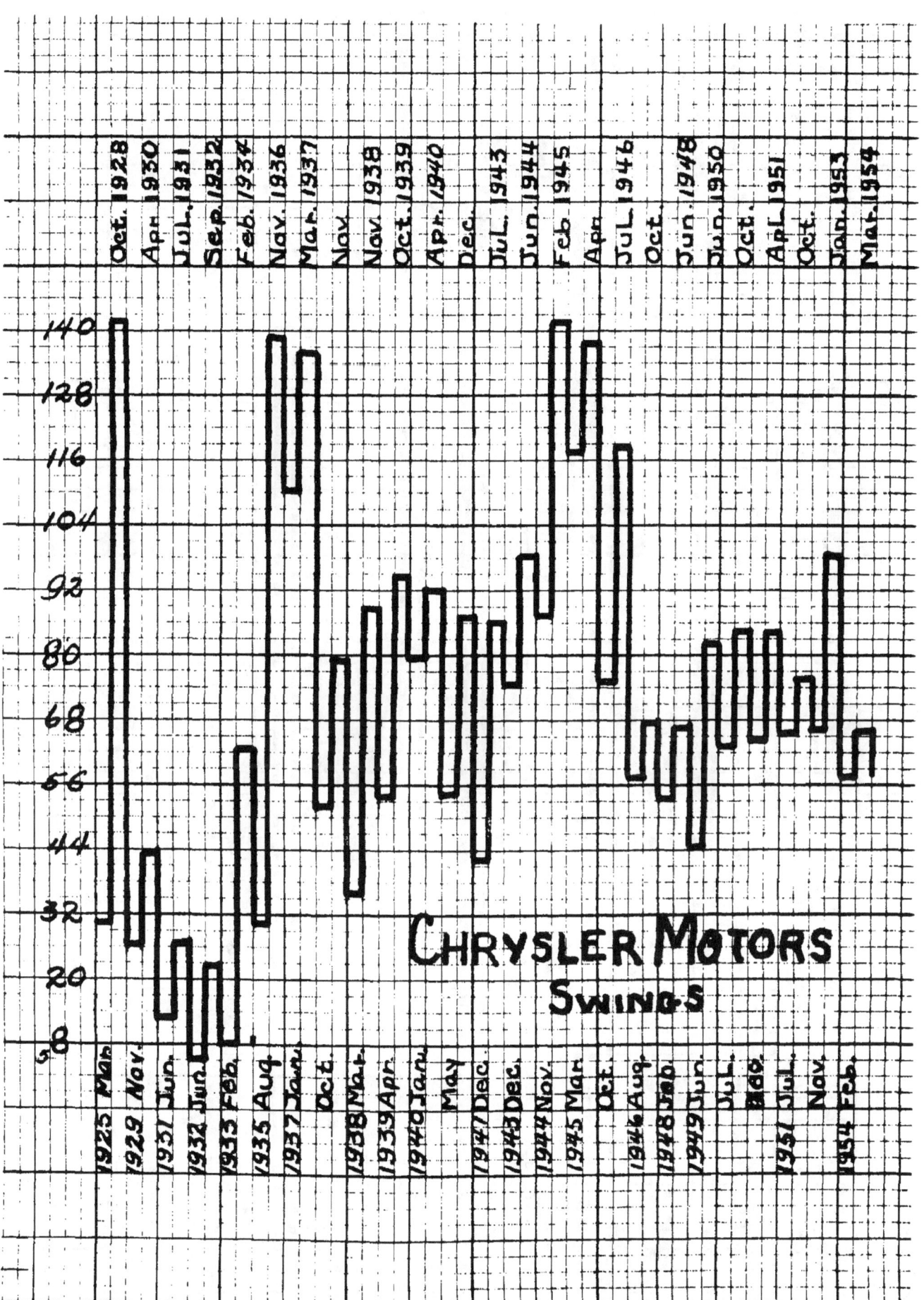

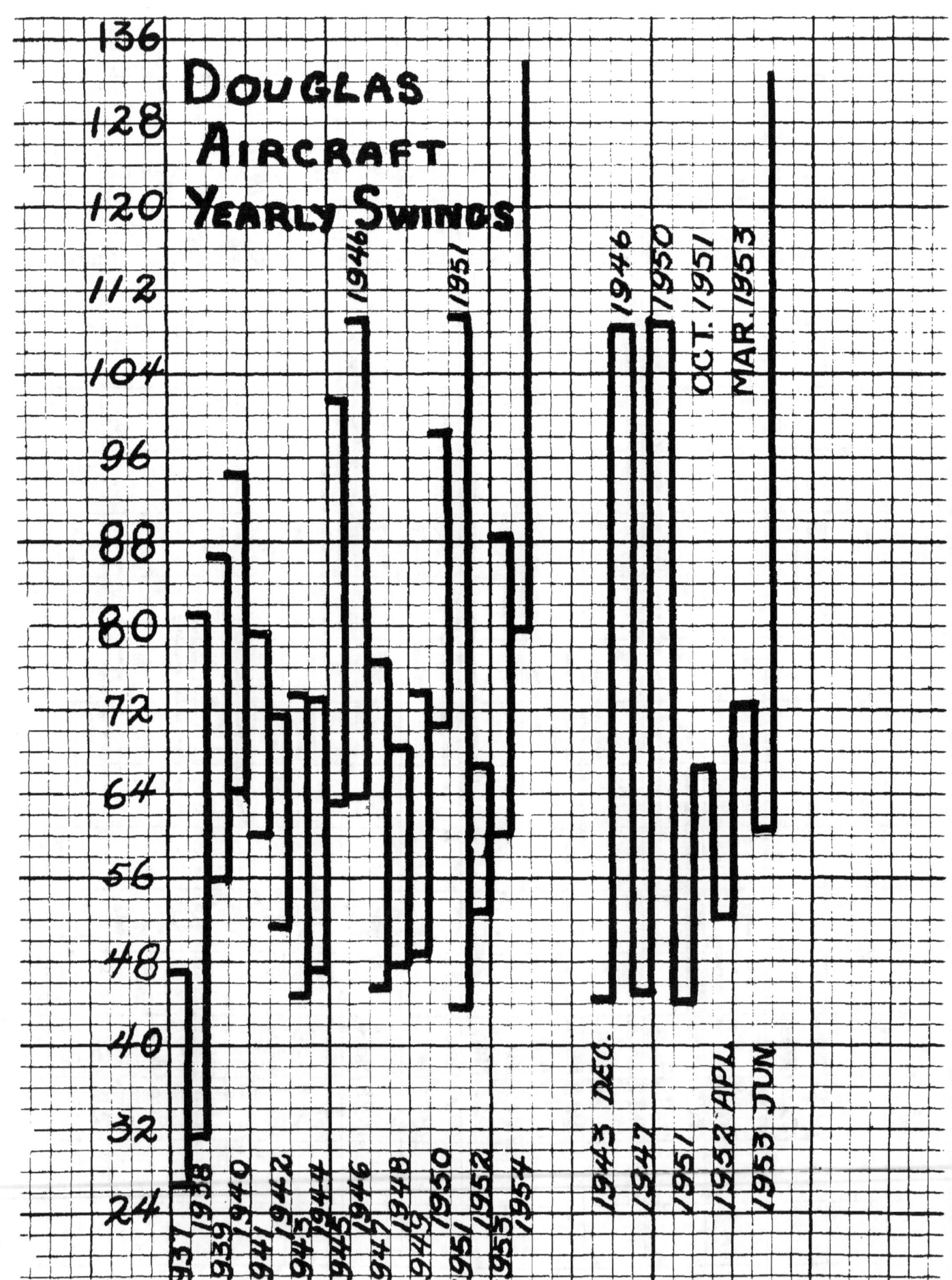

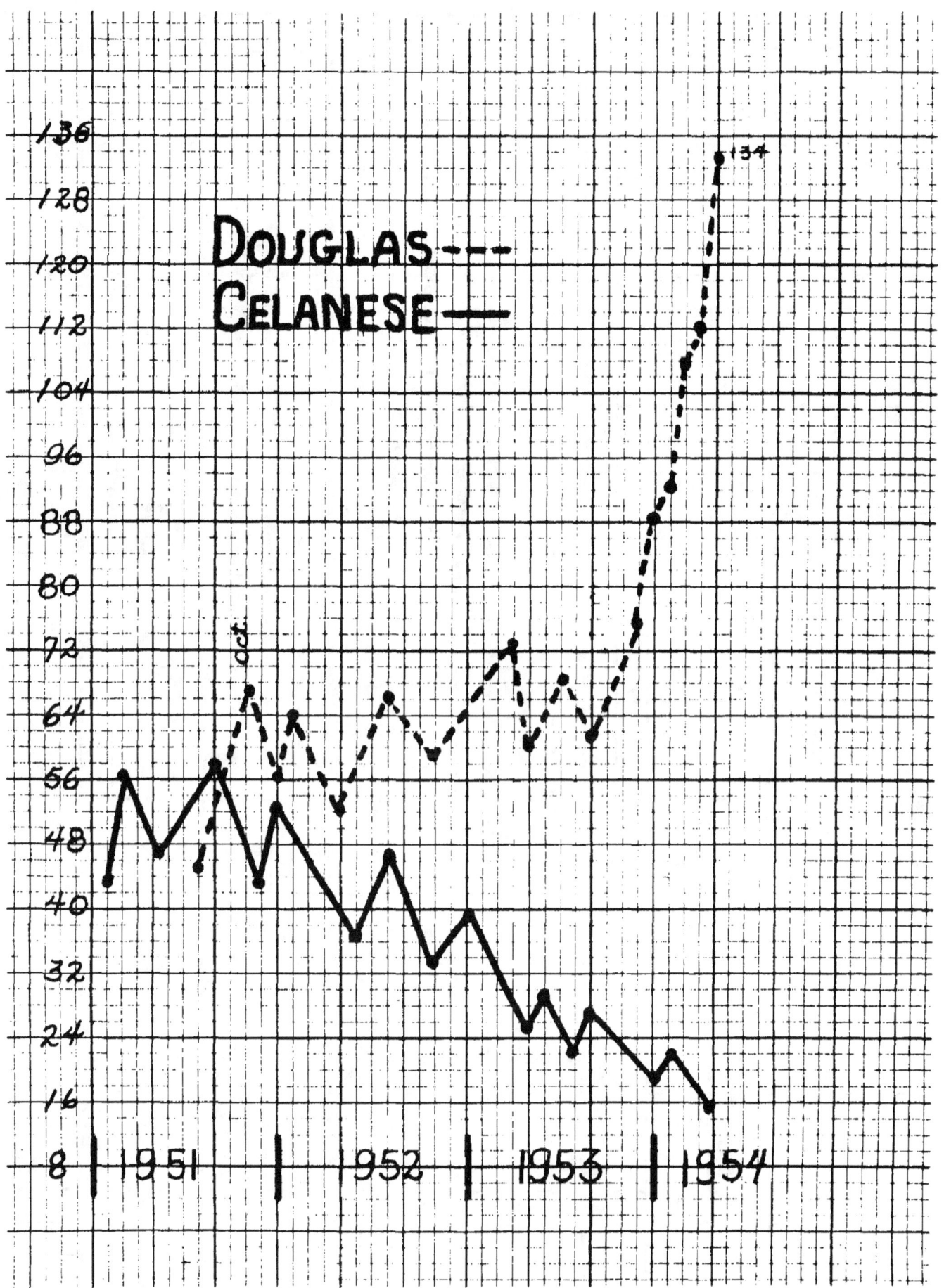

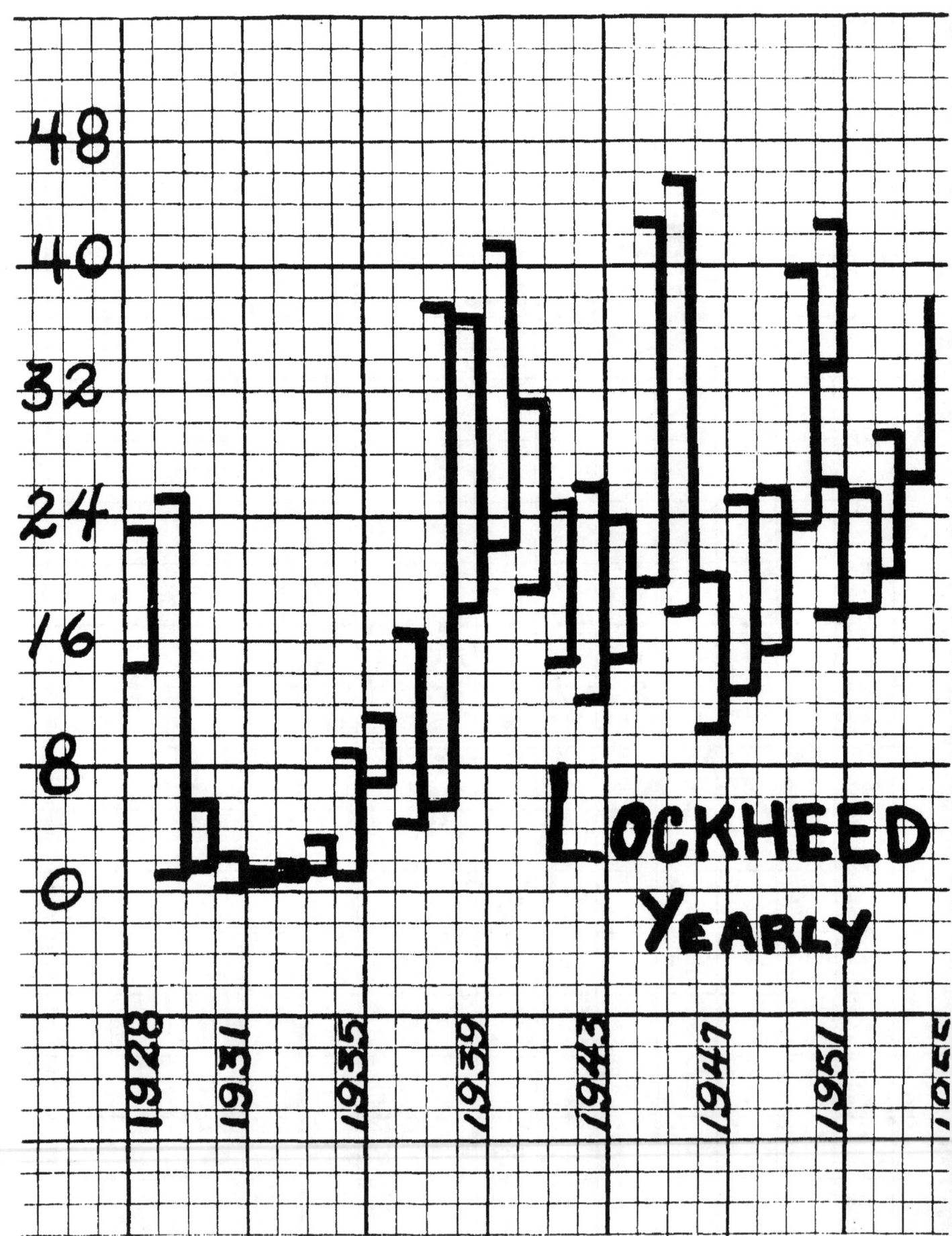

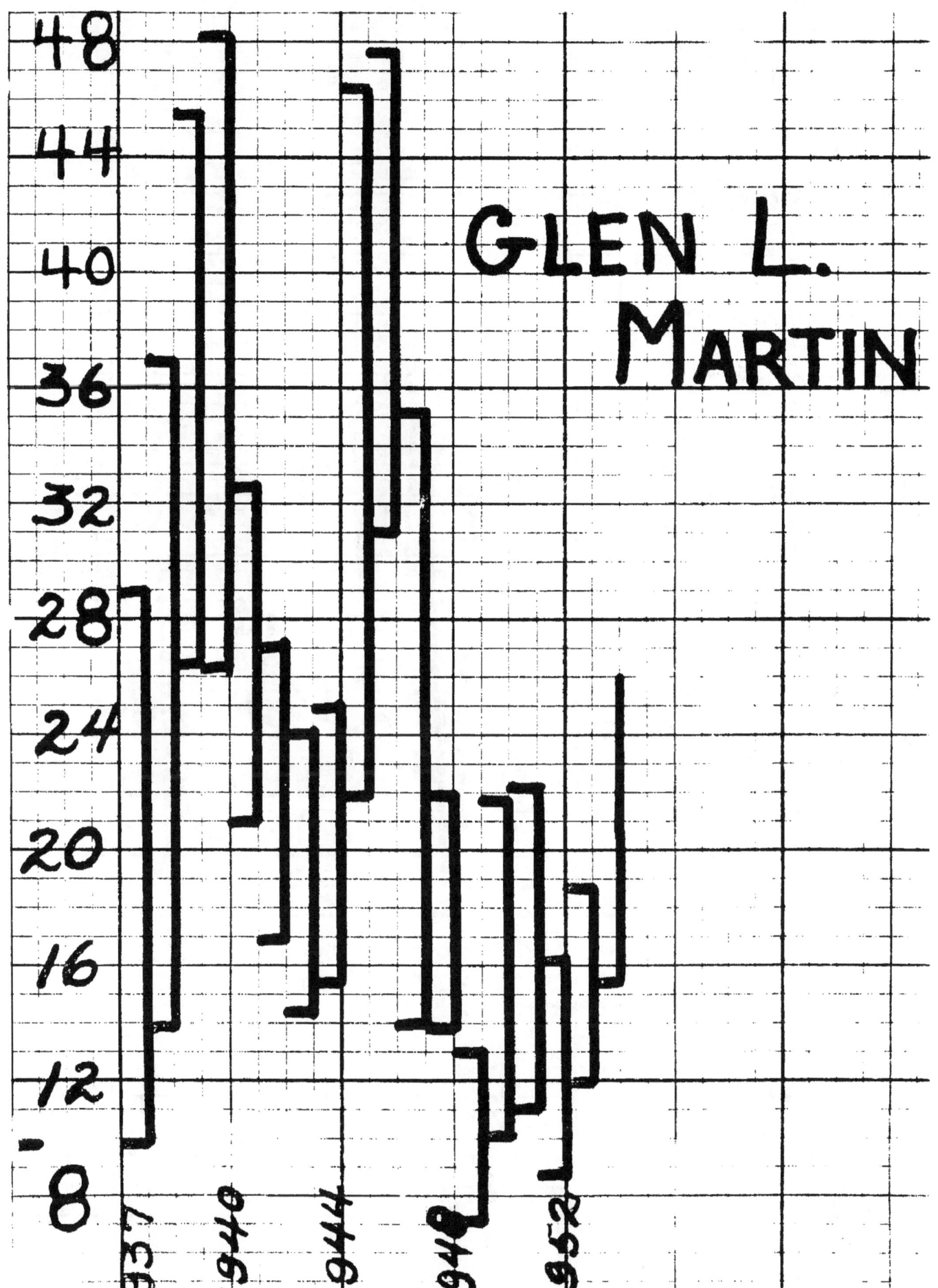

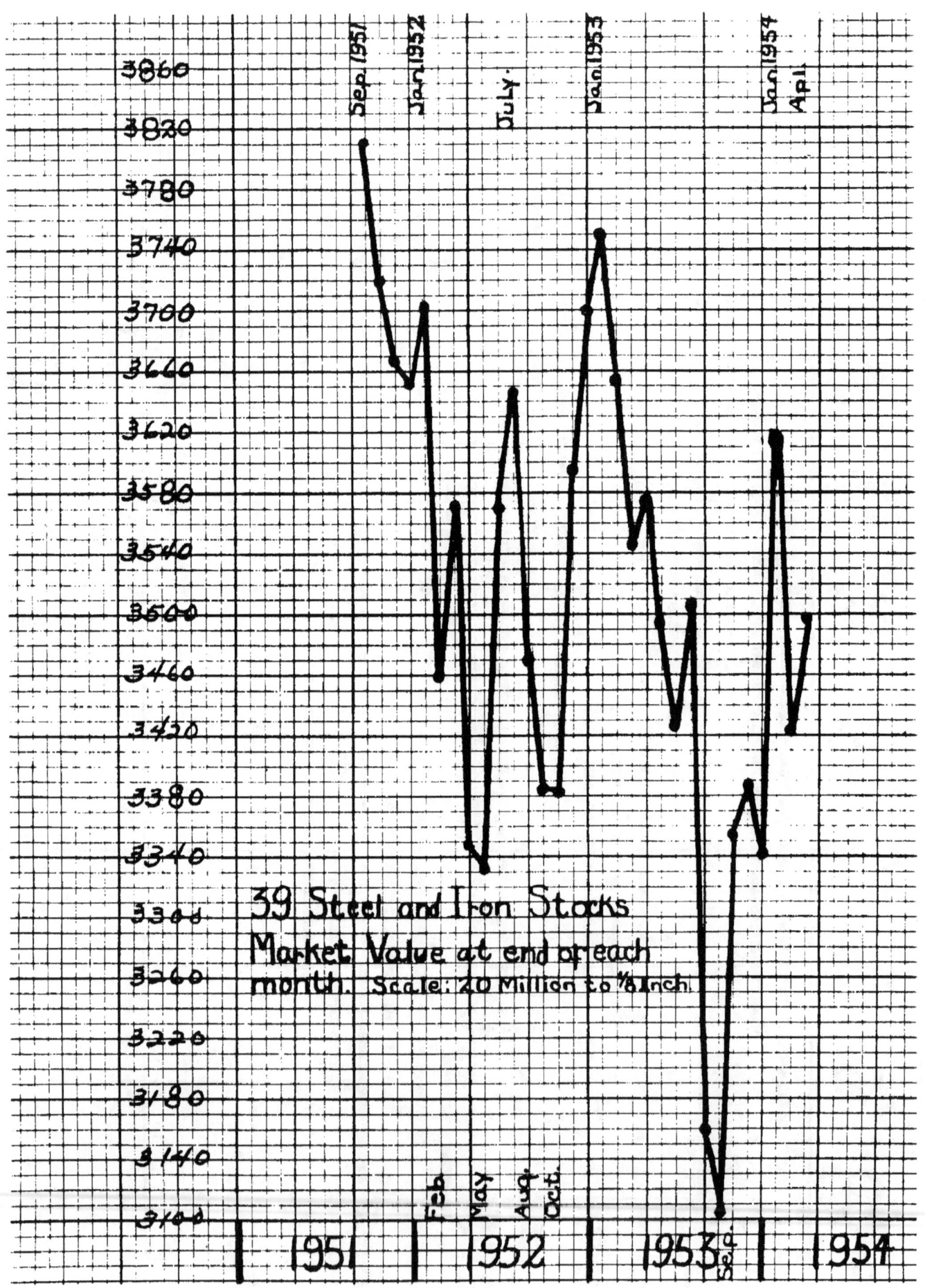

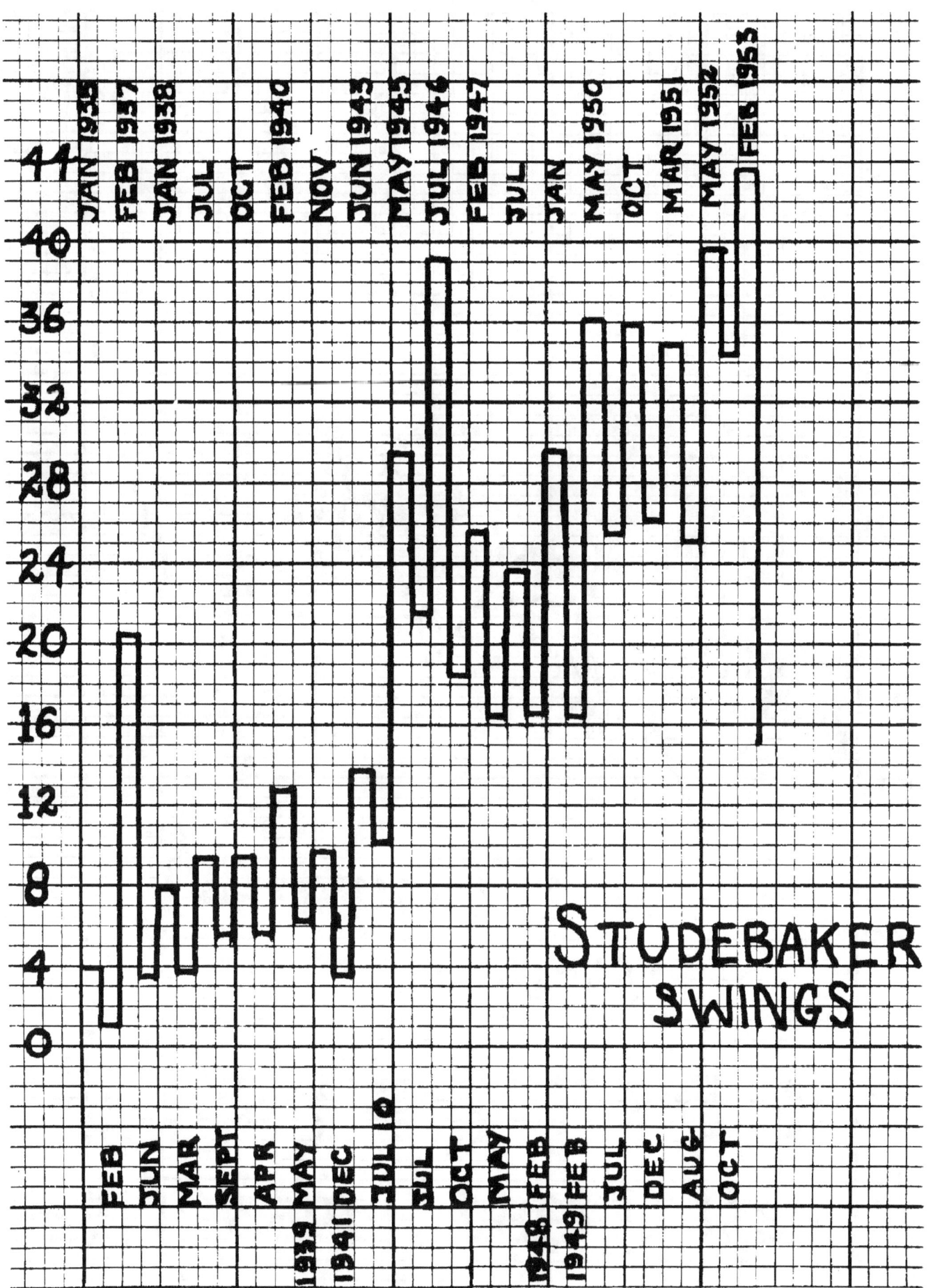

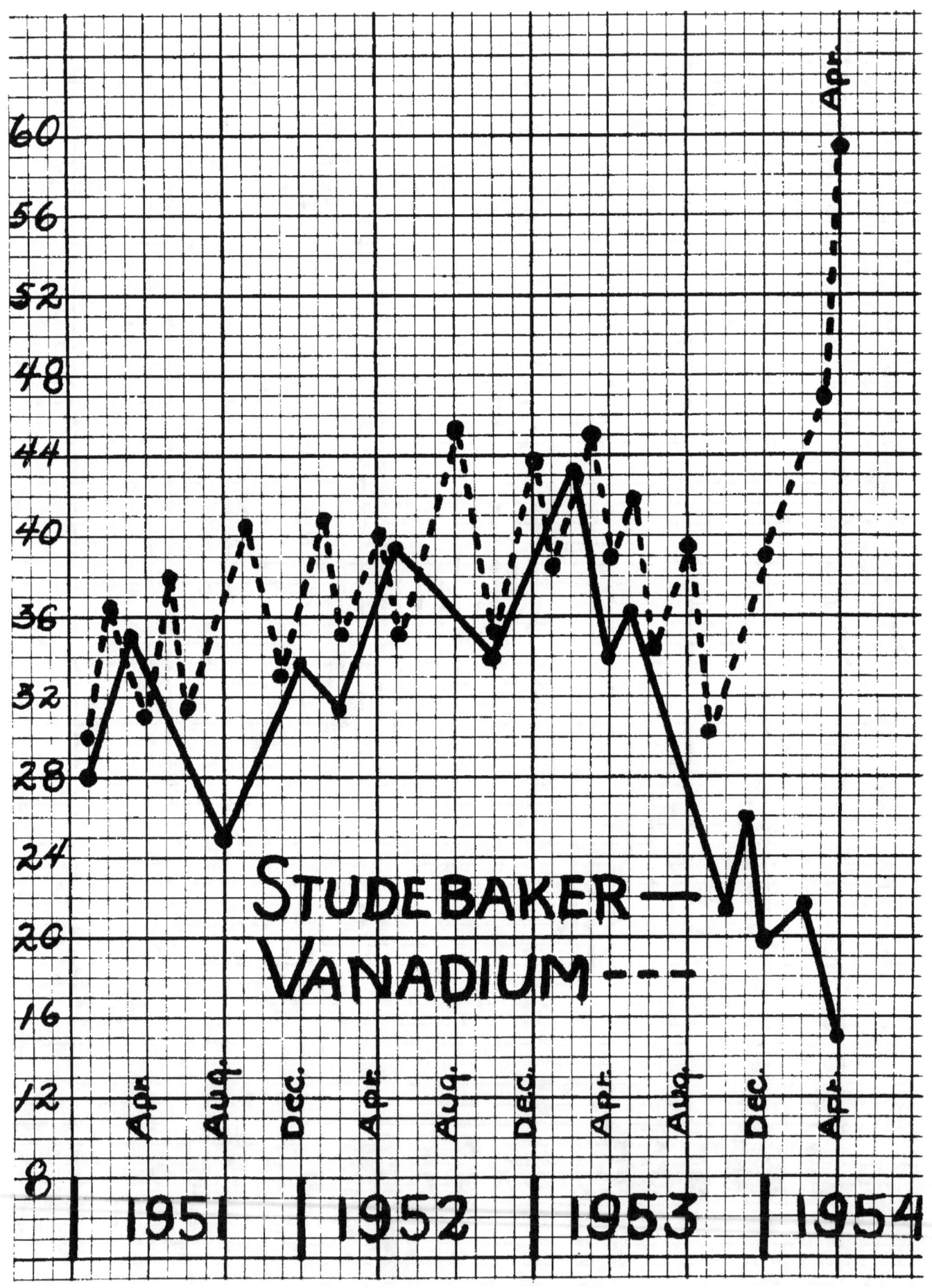

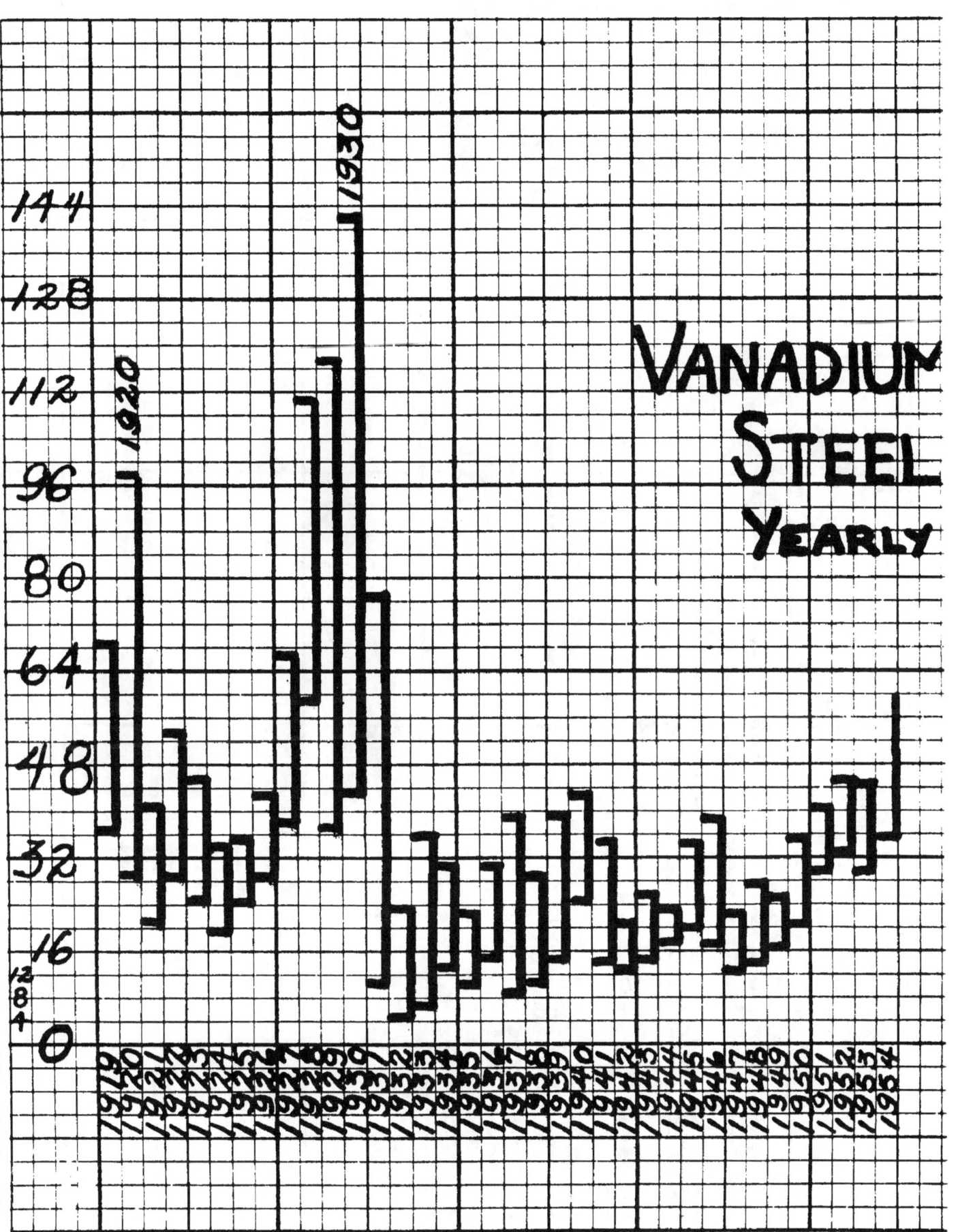

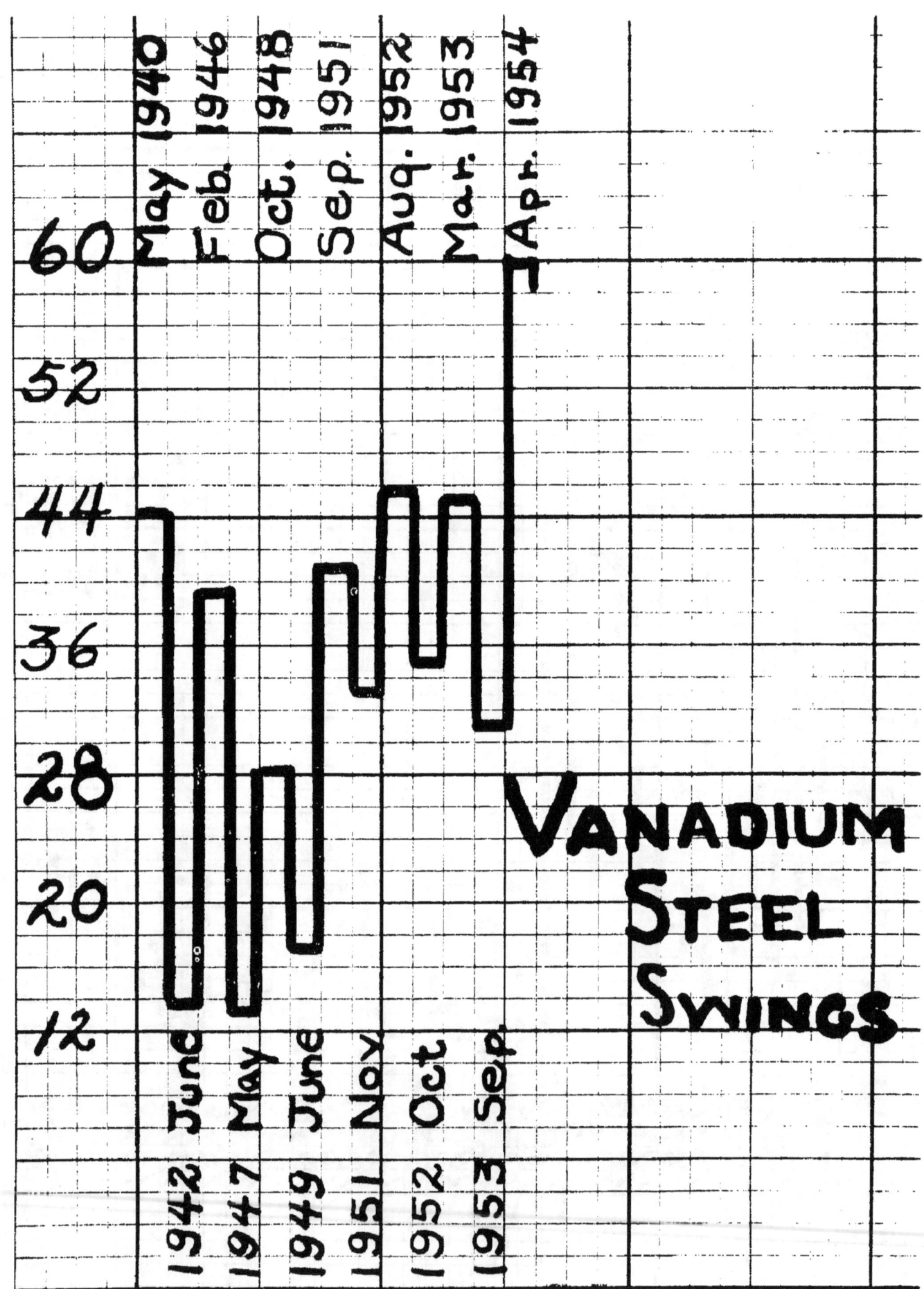

Chapter 2

Method for Forecasting the Stock Market

The Human Body

<table>
<tr><td>Scientific Advice
and Analytical Reports
on Stocks and Commodities
Author of "Truth of the Stock Tape"
and "The Tunnel Thru the Air"</td><td>**W. D. GANN**
78 WALL STREET
NEW YORK</td><td>Member
American Economic Ass'n
Royal Economic Society
Cable Address
"Ganwade New York"</td></tr>
</table>

METHOD FOR FORECASTING THE STOCK MARKET

KIND OF CHARTS

You should keep a yearly, monthly, weekly and overnight chart. You will find on the weekly chart that stocks will often reverse the minor trend and run up two or three weeks, but the third week it will not make a higher top or a higher bottom; yet at other times it will hold for several weeks without advancing above the level made in the first two weeks' rally. In cases of this kind, it is always safe to buy or sell with a stop 3 points above or below the two weeks' reverse move. If the market is going higher, it should continue up the third week, or down, as the case may be. The rules apply in a bear market as in a bull market.

The Overnight Chart, in order to show a reversal in trend, must go 3 points above the last top or bottom. The Overnight Chart is based on Bottoms. As long as higher bottoms are made, it continues upward. As long as lower bottoms are made, it continues downward. The basis of all movements are calculated from bottoms. For a market to advance, bottoms must be progressive or increasing, and if a market declines, bottoms must decrease.

HOW TO FORECAST

Every movement in the market is the result of a natural law and of a Cause which exists long before the Effect takes place and can be determined years in advance. The future is but a repetition of the past, as the Bible plainly states: "The thing that hath been, it is that which shall be; and that which is done is that which shall be done, and there is no new thing under the sun" – Eccl. 1:9.

Everything has a major and a minor, and in order to be accurate in forecasting the future, you must know the major cycle, as the most money is made when extreme fluctuations occur.

The major cycle of stocks occurs every 49 to 50 years. A period of "jubilee" years of extreme high or low prices, lasting from 5 to 7 years occur at the end of the 50-year cycle.

"7" is a fatal number referred to many times in the Bible and it is ruled by the planet Saturn, which brings about contractions, depressions, and panics. Seven times "7" equals 49, which is shown as the fatal evil year, causing extreme fluctuations.

Page #2

The most important Time cycle is the 20-year cycle, or 240 months and most stocks and averages work closer to this cycle than any other. Five years is onequarter of twenty and ten years is one-half of twenty and very important because it is 120 months. Fifteen years is three-quarters of twenty years and important because it is 180 months, just the same as 7-1/2 years is 90 months, because 84-5/8 is 15/16 of 90.

The next important major cycle is 30 years, which is caused by the planet Saturn. This planet makes one revolution around the sun every 30 years. Saturn rules the products of the earth and causes extreme high or low prices in products of the earth at the end of each 30-year cycle, and this makes Stocks high or low. The most important cycle of all is the 20-year cycle.

The next important major cycle is the 10-year cycle, which produces fluctuations of the same nature and extreme high or low every 10 years. Stocks come out remarkably close on each even 10-year cycle. The minor cycles are 3 years and 6 years. The smallest cycle is 1 year, which will often show a change in the 10th or 11th month.

In rapid markets a move will run 6 to 7 weeks and have some kind of a minor reversal in trend, but often markets will continue for several months, only reacting two weeks, then resting possibly two or three weeks and resuming the main trend. Often they move right on up or down in the third week. This same rule applies to daily movements. Fast markets will only move two days in the opposite direction to the main trend and on the third day they will resume their upward or downward course in harmony with the main trend.

In all movements use the angles and also calculate the 1/3, 2/3, 1/4, and 3/4 points of the major or minor move. One-half is the most important as it equals the 45° angle, which is the strongest and most fatal. The next in importance is 2/3, which would equal a triangle, or 120°

All rules based on Natural Law are applied the same to Time, Space and Volume charts.

It never pays to guess. Always consider the main time swing of a market; then watch your weekly and Overnight charts until they show a reversal or time has expired. All markets move in three to four sections. The third or fourth movement up or down marks the culmination. A reverse signal is always given before time expires and then the market may make two or three swings up or down into the same territory, going a little higher or a little lower than the tops or bottoms from which the warning signal was given. When this is taking place the market is either being accumulated or distributed.

Page #3.

TIME RULES FOR FORECASTING STOCKS

The stock market moves in 10-year cycles, which is worked out in 5-year cycles – a 5-year cycle up and a 5-year cycle down.

RULE 1: Bull or bear campaigns do not run more than 3 to 3½ years up or down without a move of 3 to 6 months or one year in the opposite direction. Many campaigns culminate in the 23rd month, not running out the full two years. Watch the weekly and monthly charts to determine whether the culmination will occur in the 23rd or 24th month of the move, or in the 34 to 35, 41 to 42, 49 to 60, 67 to 72, or 84 to 90th months.

RULE 2: A Bull campaign runs five years; – 2 years up, 1 year down, and 2 years up, completing a 5-year cycle. The end of a 5-year campaign comes in the 59th or 60th months. Always watch for the change in the 59th month.

RULE 3: A Bear cycle runs five years down. First move 2 years down, then 1 year up and 2 years down – completing the 5-year down swing.

RULE 4: Add ten years to any top and it will give you another top of a 10-year cycle with about the same average fluctuations.

RULE 5: Add ten years to any bottom and it will give you the next bottom of the 10-year cycle and of the same kind of a year and about the same average fluctuations.

RULE 6: Bear campaigns run out in 7-year cycles, or 3 years and 4 years from any complete bottom. From any complete bottom of a cycle first add 3 years to get the next bottom; then add 4 years to get bottom of 7-year cycle.

RULE 7: From any complete top add three years to get the next top; then add three years to the first top, which will give the second top. Add four years to the second top to get the third and final top of a 10-year cycle.

RULE 8: Add five years to any top, will give the next bottom of a five-year cycle with about the same average fluctuations. In order to get tops of a 5-year cycle, add five years to any bottom and it will give the next top with the same average fluctuations. 1917 bottom of a big bear campaign – add five years – gives 1922 top of a minor bull campaign. Why do I say "Top of a Minor Bull Campaign"? 1919 was top – add five years to 1919, gives 1924 as bottom of a 5-year Bear cycle. Refer to Rule 2 and 3, which will tell you that a Bull or Bear campaign never runs more than two years in the same direction.

Page #4.

The Bear campaign from 1919 was down two years – 1920 and 1921: therefore, we can only get a 1-year rally in 1922; then two years down – 1923 and 1924, which completes the 5-year Bear cycle. Now, look back to 1913 and 1914 and you will see that 1923 and 1924 must be Bear years to complete the 10-year cycle from the bottoms of 1913 and 1914. Then note 1917 bottom of a Bear year add seven years and it gives 1924 also as bottom of a Bear cycle.

RULE 9: How to make up Annual Forecasts for any year. Take ten years back and the future year will run very close to the last 10-year cycle. For instance – 1932 will run like 1902, 1912, and 1922.

There is a major cycle of 30 years, which runs out three ten-year cycles. The 10-year cycle back from the present and the 20-year cycle have the most effect on the future. But in completing the 30-year cycle, it is best to have 30 years past records to check up to make up a future forecast. For instance: In order to make up my 1922 Forecast, I check 1892, 1902, and 1912, and watch for minor variations in monthly moves. But I know that 1922 will run closest to 1912. However, some stocks will run close to the fluctuations of 1892 and 1902. Remember each stock works from its own base or from its own tops and bottoms, and not always according to average tops and bottoms. Therefore, judge each stock individually and keep up weekly and monthly charts on them.

RULE 10: Extreme Great Cycles. There must always be a major and a minor, a lesser and a greater, a positive and a negative; that is why stocks have three important moves in a 10-year cycle, two tops three years apart and the next one four years. This works again the five years moves, 2 years up and 1 year down, then 2 years up – two major and one minor move. The smallest complete cycle or workout in a market is five years, and 10 is a complete cycle. Five times ten equals 50, which is the greatest cycle. At the end of a great Cycle of 50 years, extreme high and low prices occur. Go back over past records arid you can verify this.

The number "7" is the basis of time, and a panic occurs and depression in the stock market every seven years, which is extreme and greater than the three-year decline. Note 1907, 1917, etc. Seven times seven is fatal, which makes 49 years, and causes extreme fluctuations in the 49th to 50th year. Remember that you must begin with bottoms or tops to figure all cycles, whether major or minor. Extreme fluctuations also occur at the end of a 30-year cycle as you can see by going back 30 to 50 years.

RULE 11: Monthly moves can be determined by the same rule as yearly; i.e. add three months to a bottom, then add four, making seven, to get minor bottoms and reaction points. But remember in a Bull market a reaction may only last two or three weeks; then the advance is resumed. In this way, a market may continue up for twelve months without breaking a monthly bottom. In Big up swings a reaction

Page #5.

will not last over two months, the third month swing up, the same rule as in yearly cycle – two down and the third up. This same rule applies in Bear markets – rallies not lasting more than two months. Most moves run out in six to seven weeks. Seven days in a week, and seven times seven making 49 days, a fatal turning point. Always watch your annual trend and consider whether you are in a bear or Bull market. Many times when in a Bull year, with the monthly chart showing up, a stock will react two or three weeks, then rest three or four weeks, going into new territory and advancing six to seven weeks more. Always consider whether or not your big time limit has run out before judging a reverse move, and do not fall to consider your indications on time both from main tops and bottoms.

RULE 12: Daily Charts: The daily swing runs on the same rules as yearly and monthly cycles, but of course it is only a minor part of them. Important daily changes occur every seven and ten days. During a month natural changes in trend occur around the 6th to 7th, 9th to 10th, 14th to 15th, 19th to 20th, 23rd to 24th, 29th to 31st. These minor moves occur in accordance with tops and bottoms of individual stocks. Watch for a change in Trend 30 days from the last top bottom. This is very important. Then watch for changes 60, 90, 120 days from tops or bottoms. 180 days, or six months, is very important and sometimes marks changes for greater moves. Also the 9th and 11th months from tops or bottoms should be watched for important minor and often major changes.

A daily chart gives the first short change, which may run for seven or ten days, the Weekly the next important changes in trend, and the monthly the strongest. Remember weekly moves run three to seven weeks; monthly moves 2 to 3 months or more, according to the yearly cycle, before reversing.

It is important to note whether a stock is making higher or lower bottoms each year. For instance, if a stock has made a higher bottom each year for five years, then makes a lower than previous year, it is a sign of a reversal and may mark a long down cycle. The same rule applies in stocks that are making lower tops for a number of years in a Bear market.

Study all the instructions and rules I have given you. Read them over several times, as each time they will become clearer to you. Study the charts and work out the rules in actual practice, as well as on past performances. In this way you will make progress and will realize and appreciate the value of my method of forecasting.

INSTRUCTIONS FOR FORECASTING THE STOCK MARKET

First, remember time is the most important of all factors and not until sufficient time has expired does any big move up or down start. The time factor will overbalance both space and volume. When time is up, space movement will start and big volume will begin either up or down, Time rules. Always consider your annual Forecast.

Page #6.

Second, consider each individual stock and determine its trend from its position according to distance in time from bottom or top. Each stock works out its 5, 10, 20, 30, 50 and 60-year cycles from its own bottoms and tops, regardless of the movements of other stocks, even those in the same group.

Third, monthly reversals or changes in trend often occur after two to three months. The change starts in the third month, according to the main time factor you are working in.

Fourth, weekly time rules. A stock will run down two to three weeks and sometimes four, but as a rule a reversal or change will occur in the third week and will only run three weeks against the main trend. In a Bull market two weeks' decline, or possible three, and in the middle of the third week the trend will turn up and close higher at the end of the third week. In some cases the change in trend will not come until the fourth week. Then the reversal will come and it will close higher at the end of the fourth week. All of these rules are reversed in a bear market.

Fifth, rapid advances or declines on big volume will run about seven weeks. These are culmination moves up or down. Watch for bottom or top around the 49th to 52nd day, although at times the bottom or top will come on the 42nd to 45th day and a change in trend will start.

Remember that at the end of any big movement, either monthly, weekly, or daily move, some time must be consumed for accumulation or distribution. So, you must allow for this. Watch your angles and time periods. After a market has declined seven weeks, it may have two or three short weeks on the side and then turn up, which agrees with the monthly rule for a change in the third month.

In regard to daily time rules, the daily chart gives the first change but remember it may only run from seven to tens days, then follow the main trend. The weekly chart will give the next important change in trend but remember it may not run more than three to four weeks or in extreme cases not more than six to seven weeks, then reverse and follow the main trend.

The monthly chart may reverse and run down three to four months, then reverse and follow the main trend again, or run up three to four months in a bear market, then reverse and follow the main trend, although as a general rule, in a bear market stocks never rally more than two months. They start breaking in the third month and follow the main trend down.

Page #7.

Never decide that the main trend has changes one way or the other without consulting your angles from top or bottom and without considering the position you are in the cycle of each individual stock. When extreme advances or declines occur, the first time the market reverses over one-fourth or one-half of the distance travelled in the last section, you can consider that the trend has turned up or down at least for the present.

It is important to watch space movements because when time is running out one way or the other, space movements will show a reversal by breaking back over 1/4, 1/3, or 1/2 of the distance of the last move, which indicates the main trend has changed.

HOW TO USE ANGLES FROM TOPS AND BOTTOMS

The angles to be used from a bottom of a stock up start from the point marked "0" and those starting down from the top of the chart marked "T" are the way they are put on from the top running down. Remember, the first thing to do when you want to put angles on from bottom to top is to draw the angle of 45°, then draw next the angle of 2 x 1 on each side of the 45° angle. In many cases, you will not have to use any other angles for a long time, then put on the other angles when they are necessary. Of course, if your stock is advancing very rapidly, then keep your 1 x 4 angle on and your 8 x 1. The same applies when it is having a sharp decline – keep your angle of 8 x 1 and 4 x 1 drawn down, using the scale of 1 point to each 1/8 of an inch, as shown on your Pattern Chart.

A stock to keep above the 45° angle must make a gain of one point per month, i.e. it must raise its bottoms one point per month. To keep above the angle of 8 x 1 going up, it must raise its bottoms eight points per month, and to keep above the angle of 4 x 1 it must raise its bottoms four points per month. To keep above the angle of 3 x 1, it must raise its bottoms three points per month, and to keep above the angle of 2 x 3 [3 x 2?] it must raise its bottoms 1½ points per month or make a gain of 18 points per year. On the left [right?] hand side of the angle of 45°, beginning with the angle of 6 x 1, the stock only has to make a gain of 2 points per year. If a stock cannot rise above an angle of this kind, it is in a very weak position and of course on the bear side of the square.

The angle to the left [right?] of the angle of 3 x 1 [4 x 1?] indicates a gain of 3 points per year and the angle of 3 x 1 indicates a gain of 4 points per year. The next angle of 2 x 1 indicates a gain of 6 points per year or 1/2 point per month.

Coming down after having broken the angle of 45° and breaking this angle, a stock is in a very weak position, especially if it is a long ways from the base, and indicates much low prices.

Page #8.

The angle of 3 x 2 on the left [right?] rises at the rate of 8 points in 12 months or a gain of 3/4 [2/3?] of a point per month in order to keep above this angle. It is not necessary to draw angles from a long ways back. You can make the calculation and determine where they cross. For example: Suppose in 1900, in the month of January, a stock made bottom at 15, and I want to calculate where the angle of 45° will cross 20 years later in January 1930. The 45° angle rises at the rate of 1 point per month, then 10 years would be 120 months or 120 points added to 15 at the bottom; the 45° angle would cross at 135 in January, 1930. All of the other angles may be calculated in a long way back in the same way.

I have marked on the Pattern Chart the measured degrees of the angles, which you will see are 3¾°, 7½°, 15°, 18¾°, 26½°, 30°, 33¾°, 37½°, 45°, 52½°, 56¼°, 60°, 63¾°, 71¼°, 75°, 82½°, 86¼°, and 90°. You do not have to bother about measuring these angles. All you have to do to get the angles correct is to count the spaces and draw your lines or angles accordingly.

You will notice on your Pattern Chart how each angle drawn from the top and from the bottom prove themselves by the point at which they cross. For example: The angle of 8 x 1 drawn from "0" and the angle of 8 x 1 drawn from 90 down both cross at 45, 5-5/8 points over from "0" counting to the right. Then take the angle of 4 x 1 from "0" and 4 x 1 down from 90 and you will notice that they cross at 11¼ on 45, equal distance from the other angle and of course twice the measure.

The reason why these angles prove this way is because the 45° angle or 45 points, degrees, or anything else from "0" to 45 is one-half of 90. Therefore parallel angles beginning at "0" going up and at 90 coming down, must cross on a 45° angle or at the gravity center.

RULES FOR ANGLES FROM BOTTOMS

From any bottom, base or beginning point, two 45° angles can be started, one running up from the vertical angle and one running down from the vertical angle. You can also use a 45° angle or any other angle from any top, running the 45° angle down from the top, which indicates a decline of 1 point per month, week, or day, according to your scale of prices; then running the 45° angle up from the top, which would indicate a gain of 1 point or 1 degree per month.

For example: Take the low of U.S. Steel on November 13, 1929, when it sold at 150. Start the 45° angle up and it gains 1 point per month; then start the 45° angle down from 150 and the stock has to decline 1 point per month to rest on the angle of 45°.

November, 1930, was 12 months from November, 1929, and U.S. Steel made low in November, 1930 at 138, which was on a 45° angle from the bottom at 150.

Page #9.

In December, 1930, U.S. Steel made an extreme low of 134-3/8. This was 2 points under the 45° angle from 150, but rested on the angle of 2 x 1 from the low at 111½, made in January, 1927. In December, 1930, U.S. Steel closed above the 45° angle from the bottom of 150. As long as it stays above this angle, it is in a stronger position, but to regain the strongest position, it will have to cross the angles of 45° from 150 on the up side and stay above this angle.

Remember that when any stock breaks under the 45° angle on the daily, weekly or monthly puts it in a very weak position and indicates a decline to the next angle. However, when a stock can regain the 45° angle, it is in a stronger position. The same rule applies to a 45° angle up from any top. When a stock crosses the angle on the daily, weekly or monthly and stays above the 45° angle, it is in a very strong position.

After a stock once drops below or gets above any important angle and then reverses its position by getting back above the angle or dropping back below it, it changes the trend again.

The angles on the Monthly and Weekly charts are, of course, of greater importance than those on the Daily charts, because the daily trend can change quite often, while only the major changes are shown according to the angles on the monthly high and low and weekly high and low charts.

Always consider the distance a stock is from its base or beginning point when it breaks any important angle or crosses any important angle. The farther away from the base, the [more?] important the change in trend, whether this be crossing an angle from the top or breaking under an angle from the bottom.

Each stock works out its own square according to its extreme high and low points or the square of its tops. For example: U.S. Rubber – 143 was the total high to measure the width; then move over 143 spaces or 143 months to the angle of 90° down and divide up the square, as I have done on the monthly high and low chart. You can see how it worked out to the 1/4 of its square, 1/2, 3/4, 1/3, 2/3, etc. It will require 143 months to pass out of the square, or 11 years and 11 months. This period of time will end in December, 1931, which will be an important point to watch for a change in trend on U.S. Rubber.

WHY GEOMETRICAL ANGLES WORK ON STOCKS

Why is the 90° angle the strongest angle of all? Because it is horizontal or straight up and straight down.

What is the next strongest angle to the 90° angle? The 180° angle because it is square to the 90° angle, being 90° from the 90° angle.

Page #10.

What is the next strongest angle to the 180° angle? 270 because it is in opposition to 90, or 180° from the 90° angle, which equals 1/2 or the circle, the strongest point.

What is the next strongest angle after 270? 360 because it ends the circle and gets back to the beginning point and is opposite 180° or half-way point, or the angle which equals 1/2 of the circle

What angles are next strongest to 90, 180, 270 and 360? 120° and 240° because they are 1/3 and 2/3 of the circle. 120 is 90 plus 30, which is 1/3 of 90. 240 is 180 plus 1/3 or 60, which makes these strong angles, especially strong for measurements of time.

What angles are next in strength? 45, because it is 1/2 of 90, and 135 because it is 90 from 45, and 225 because it is 45 from 180, and 315 because it is 45 from 270. The angle of 225° is 180 from 45 and the angle of 315° is 180 from 135.

The angles of 90, 180, 270 and 360 form the first important cross, known as the Cardinal Cross. The angles of 45, 135, 225 and 315 form the next important cross, which is known as the Fixed Cross. These angles are very important for the measurements of time and space and volume.

Why is the angle of 22½° stronger than 11¼°? Because it is twice as much, being the same reason that a 45° angle is stronger than a 22½. Again the angle of 67½ is 1½ times 45 therefore quite strong when anything is moving up toward 90°. 78¾ is stronger than 67½ because it is 7/8 of 90 and therefore one of the strongest points before we reach 90 and important to watch both on time, space and volume. Many stocks have important moves and make tops or bottoms around the 78th to 80th week, month or day.

Why are the angles of 1/8 or a circle most important for time and space measurement? Because we divide $1 into 1/4, 1/2, and 1/8 parts. We use 25¢ or one quarter, 50¢ or 1/2 dollar, and long years ago we had 12½¢ pieces. But the most important figures of our basis of money are the four quarters, but we do use the 1/8 part or 12¢ in all calculations. Stock fluctuations are based on 1/8, 1/4, 3/8, 1/2, 5/8, 3/4, 7/8 and the whole figure. Therefore, any space measurement, as well as time, will work out closer to these figures when changed into angles of time than 1/3 or 2/3 points for the simple reason that the fluctuations moving in 1/8 proportion must come out closer to these figures. Figuring $100, or par, as a basis for stock prices and changing these prices to degrees, 12½ would equal 45°, 25 would equal 90°, 37½ would equal 135°, 50 would equal 180°, 62½ would equal 225°, 75 would equal 270°, 82½ would equal 315°, and 100 would equal 360°.

For example: When a stock sells at 50 on the 180th day, week or month, it is on the degree of its time angle. On February 1, 1915, U.S. Steel made a low at 38, which is closest to a price of 37½, which is 3/8 of 100 and equals a 135° angle. Steel was

Page #11.

14 years old or 168 months old on February 25 1915 and hit the angle of 135° which showed that Steel was behind time, but that it was in a strong position holding at 38 above the angle of 135°, or the price of 37½. Then when Steel crossed 200, it equalled 2 circles of 360°. When it advanced to 261¾, it was closest to 62½ in the third 100 or nearest the 225° angle. It was the strongest angle after it crossed the half-way point or 180° angle. Steel's half-way point on the third hundred was 250; 262½ would be the next point, or 5/8 point, which equals 225°.

Under the instructions for the Master Timing Angles, you will find how far each timing angle had moved from the time Steel was incorporated up to the time it made extreme top. Study these timing angles and you will see what happens when each of the timing angles reach 24, 36, 48, 60, 72, 84, 90, 120, 135, 157½, 180, 210, 225, 240, 270, 300, 315, 330, 345, and 360 months, the equivalent of 360°. Under the Master Timing Angles we also show you what happens when timing angles #5, 6, 7, 8, and 9 cross the other timing angles, or the place where they were at the time Steel was incorporated. Of course these same rules can be applied to any other stock. You can see what happens when each of these Master Timing Angles returns to the same place it was at the time Steel was incorporated, or to the same place when any extreme high or low price is reached. You will learn when these Master Timing Angles return to the same place or to the same angle or degree from which they started. Therefore you will know the exact measurements of cycles according to moving energy. The instructions on the Master Timing Angles give you the cause of all market movements and they can be worked out ahead as far as the year 2000. The figures which we will use are figures made by the United States Government astronomers and are therefore absolutely accurate. A careful study of all these figures and a comparison of the movements of the various stocks will convince you of their value.

HOW TO USE GEOMETRICAL ANGLES

My Method of operating in the Stock Market is all based on mathematical points or geometrical angles. The Resistance Level[s] are all geometrical angles because they are 1/8, 1/4, 1/2, 3/4, 1/3, 2/3, etc., which are proportional parts of a circle whether large or small and, therefore, represent geometrical angles.

There are three important factors to consider, price, time and space movements. For example, when the price reaches 45, it meets resistance because it is equal to a 45° angle. Then when the price breaks a 45° angle, regardless of whether the price is at 45, 67, 90, 135, 180 or anywhere else, it weakens the position and equals a resistance angle, but is more important when a long ways from the base. The distance the stock breaks the angle of 45° on any other angle from the base is the most important. For example, many times a stock will rest on the angle of 45° in its early stages when advancing, then later in reaction rests on it again, then have a prolonged advance, react and rest on the 45° angle again, and then hit a higher level, break the 45° angle the fourth time, which places it in an extremely weak

Page #12.

position because it is so far away from the base and so much time has elapsed since the stock made low level. Reverse this rule in a bear market or decline and don't forget to consider that the Monthly and Weekly high and low charts are the most important when angles are broken. Daily charts can break angles and recover them and it is possible for a daily high and low chart to maintain an angle of 45° for a very long period of time except when the final grand rush comes at the end of big bull campaigns.

Suppose at the time a stock breaks a 45° angle that it is at 135, and on the 135th month. This would he at a strong Resistance Level, breaking a strong angle, and striking and breaking a strong angle according to time. This would be time and space balancing at Resistance Levels, or geometrical angles, and would indicate a big decline to follow. Reverse the same rule at the end of a bear campaign.

After considering the three important factors, Resistance Levels, time and geometrical angles, the fourth and next very important factor is the volume of sales at tops or bottoms. Sales increase near the top and decrease near the bottom, that is, when a bear campaign has run for a long time and liquidation has about run its course, the volume of sales decrease, which is an indication that the Market is getting ready to make a change in trend.

VANADIUM STEEL, WEEKLY HIGH AND LOW CHART, VOLUME OF SALES

This chart begins September 29, 1928. For each space 1/8 wide, I have used to represent 25,000 shares. For example, during the week ending September 29, 1928, sales were 26,600 shares and the high was 85 and the low 76 which is represented by 1/8. The same with the following week, when sales were 25,000 shares or less and the stock remained in a narrow trading range but gradually worked up until the week ending October 27th, when the volume of sales was 111,400 shares and the stock advanced to 88¼. I made the space 4 wide to represent 100,000 shares. Then note November 10th, or the week ending November 10th, when the stock advanced from 84¼ to 108, sales were 238,900 shares. The following week, sales were, 116,400 shares and the price only went 3 points higher. Then the stock broke the angle of 45° and declined to 85. During the week ending December 8th, and the following week, the price was around this same level, holding above the angle of 4 x 1 from the bottom, and failing to get back to the low reached during the week ending December 10th. The volume of sales on this decline was small. For the week ending December 22nd, sales were only 25,000 shares. Then the stock started up again.

During the week ending January 19, 1929, sales were 138,800. The following week sales were 61,200 and the next week with the stock getting only ½ point lower, sales were only 25,000 shares. Then followed a quick rally ending in the week of February 9th; with sales of 175,000 shares. This was top. A quick

Page #13.

reaction followed with sales of 74,200 shares. In the following week, the bottom was around the same level with sales of 153,000 shares. During the week ending March 2nd, sales were 51,500 shares. Then followed two weeks of small volume, 33,500 shares and 32,200 shares. Here the stock again broke under the angle of 22¼, or 2 x 1 from the level of September 29, 1928 and a decline followed. Bottom was reached at 68 on the week ending June 1st, when sales were only 33,700 shares. The following week sales were only 27,000 shares which indicated that liquidation was not heavy and had run its course. The stock rallied to 97 during the week ending July 20th. The volume of sales was only 48,700 shares, not enough volume to indicate that the buying was strong enough to force the stock higher at that time. A decline followed and the volume of sales was small. Bottom was reached during the week ending August 10th at 77½. During these weeks the sales run 25,000 or less, getting down to 8,800 during the week ending August 31st which indicated that there was not much stock for sale at this price and that some one was just taking what was offered.

During the week ending September 14th, the stock was pushed up to 100 on sales of 138,400. Note that it failed to cross the top of April 6th, and that both of these tops were under the heavy volume of February 16th and 23rd, which indicated the big distribution that took place between 104 and 115 was by people who did not intend to buy the stock back for a long time and that when the stock approached the level of 100, they sold heavily again.

During the week ending September 28th, a decline followed on small volume, but the angle of 45° was broken and the stock continued to work lower. The volume increased during the week ending October 26th to 56,600 shares. The following week it was 50,600 shares, indicating heavy liquidation at this time. Then during the week ending November 9th and 16th, sales dropped to 17,200 shares and 29,000 shares. Final bottom was reached on November 13th at 37½. Then a rally followed up to the week ending December 14th, but the volume of sales was small only getting up to 31,000 shares and on the top week 21,000 shares. A reaction followed but the volume of sales was still smaller, 12,300, 11,300, and 13,800 shares. The bottom was reached during the week ending December 21st, when sales were 19,000 shares, then two narrow weeks on the side with the total volume not exceeding 25,000 shares. This indicated that the stock was thoroughly liquidated and was getting ready to go higher, but the week ending February 1, 1930, when the stock crossed the high of December 14th, volume of sales increased to 92,000 shares. Then during the week of February 8, there was a small reaction, but the volume of sales was only 23,000 shares. The advance was resumed the following week and sales reached 62,400 shares. The next week the sales were 48,300 shares. Then during the week ending March 1, there was a small reaction but the volume of sales were only 36,500 shares which indicated that the buying was better than the selling, and that there was no heavy selling pressure yet.

Page #14.

The advance was resumed and the volume of sales increased every week until the week ending March 29, when the stock sold at 124½ with a volume of sales of 206,000 shares. This was the largest volume of sales of any time since November 1928, a reaction of 20 points followed, but during the week ending April 5th, sales were only 83,600 shares. In the following week the stock made a higher bottom showing that the market had not yet reached top.

During the week ending April 19th, sales were 184,600 share and during the week ending April 26th, sales were 258,100 shares. With the stop [stock?] up 105 points from the extreme low, and the volume of sales almost equalling the total amount of stock outstanding, was a plain indication that top was being reached for a big reaction. During the week ending May 3rd a big decline followed, sales reached 304,000 shares, an angle of 45° from the low at 103½ was first broken, then the angle of 45° from 37½ was broken and the stock declined to 87 during the week ending May 10th on sales of 310,400 shares, breaking all records up to that time. It got down near the angle of 22½°, or the angle of 2 x 1 from the low of 37½. It was a big reaction for two weeks period of time and came down 57 points. Figuring your low of 37½ to the high of 143¼, gives a half-way point of 90-3/8. The stock declined 3-3/8 points beyond this. This was due to the large volume of sales and the momentum. However, often a stock will go 3-3/4 points beyond the half-way point and then recover, especially if it has had a big decline. The greater the decline in number of points, the more allowance can be made for fluctuations around the main center or half-way point and, of course, Vanadium with a very small volume of floating supply of stock makes faster moves and wider range than a stock of large volume.

During the week ending May 10th, the volume of sales of 242,400 shares and the price crossed the top of the following week and advanced to 118½. The following week it advanced to 120¼ on sales of 248,600 shares, showing that the volume of trading was increasing on the way up but the price was not increasing in proportion.

During the week ending May 31st, the stock reached 124 on volume of sales of 135,700 shares, an indication that the selling was better than the buying and that the price level approached where distribution started, it showed that there was again the very best of selling.

During the week ending June 7th, the price advanced to 125. Figuring the top of 143½ to the low of 87, the 2/3 points was at 126¾. Then figuring the total value of the stock 143¼, we find the 7/8 point at 125-3/8. This made 125 a very strong Resistance Level because it was at the 7/8 point, of total value, and close to the 2/3 point on the fluctuating moves. Another reason why 125 was a strong Resistance Level is because 25 is 1/4 of 100.

Page #15

During the week ending June 7th, Vanadium broke the angle of 45° from the low of 87 on heavy volume, the total sales for the week being 237,100. The price got down to 100 and rested on the angle of 22½°, or the angle of 2 x 1 from 37½. On June 9th, Vanadium broke 100 and, of course, was under the angle of 2 x 1 and declined to 89½, this time getting support around the gravity center, or half-way point, from 37½ to 143½. However, Vanadium is in a weak position on angles according to the volume chart, and in a weak position on angles according to the weekly chart, without volume and the Monthly high and low chart and nother [nothing?] but a rally is indicated at this time. However, if it can hold for a while and not break the low of 87 on May 10th, it will indicate a better rally, probably 1/3 to 1/2 of the recent decline.

From the low on November 13, to the high in April, the total volume of sales was 1,672,600 shares figuring 25,000 to each 1/8 space to move over each week would bring this over to the 67th space, which I have marked, and you will see from the volume chart that this runs over which is due to the fact that some weeks volume did not equal 25,000,000 [25,000?] shares. We have to register the top and bottom and this throws us out a little on balance. In the weeks of May 3rd and 10th, the total volume was 614,000 shares, bringing the grand total up to that time to 2,282,000 which brings it to space 91, on the week ending May 10th and puts our volume chart 6 spaces too far over. Note that the volume of these two weeks was about 1/3 of the total volume from 37½ to 143-3/4 and, of course, wiped out half of the advance. Therefore, it is only natural that a rally should follow because the decline was too fast according to time. Bringing the total number of sales up to the week ending June 7, we have 3,170,800 shares. This would bring us to space 126, marked in red ink, and the way we have the volume chart, it is 8 spaces too far over. Therefore, the volume for the week ending June 7th, with the space movement rested exactly on the angle of 2 x 1 from 37½, and 101 to 100¾ would strike up against this angle on the week beginning June 9th. The price on June 9th was 101¾, and the stock declined to 89½. After a stock gets away from a narrow series of fluctuations with small volume and keep your volume chart exact, so as your angles will work out better.

MONTHLY VOLUME CHARTS ON DOW-JONES THIRTY INDUSTRIALS FROM JUNE 1921 TO MAY 1930

A study of this volume chart will prove very interesting and valuable. You can see that in June, July and August, 1921, the volume of sales was down to around, 10,000,000 to 15,000,000 shares per month. In March 1928, sales reached 80,000,000 per month for the first time in history. From this time on the volume of sales was very large, with this group of stocks working higher right along from the reaction in June 1928 when the price was 194 to the top in September 1929 when the price reached 381, there was never more than one month's reaction and at no time did the averages break 10 points under a previous month's bottom. The volume of sales increased enormously in October, 1928, and continued large in

Page #16.

November, December, and in fact, right on up until August, 1929, when sales were again over 100,000,000 shares, and the month of September sales were over 100,000,000 shares; see how the picture looks with this enormous volume at the top and then in October, the first time since May, 1929, the price broke under the level of the previous month, showing that the trend had turned down. All records for volume of sales was broken in the month of October, when sales reached 141,000,000. In the final reaction in November, or the last wave of liquidation, sales dropped down to around 80,000,000. Then the price worked up every month, making higher bottoms and higher tops with a fairly large volume, until March, 1930, when the volume of sales reached 90,000,000. In April, the total volume of sales reached 111,000,000 shares, a very small gain in price. In the early part of May the price broke under the bottom of the month of April, which was the first time since the low was reached in November, and a sharp declined followed. The volume of sales for the month of May was heavy, reaching 80,000,000; then continued in June on fairly heavy volume, with the price getting down to 250 on June 9th. This movement on volume from November, 1929 to April, 1930, shows a rally in a bear market.

Note the bottom from January, 1929 to May, 1929, and that the rally in April just brought prices up under this heavy volume of sales where distribution took place in 1929. Note that the scale on this chart is 2 points to each 1/8 of an inch instead of 1, for in considering the angles from the low in August, 1921 and the low in November, 1923, the angles are doubled in value, that is, the angle of 2 x 1 equals the angle of 45° and the angle of 4 x 1 equals the angle of 2 x 1 or 22½°. For example, the angle of 2 x 1 from the low In June, 1928 equals the angle of 45°. Note that the price rested on this angle in May 1929, and that it was broken for the first time in October, 1929 and the big decline followed. Note that the angle of 4 x 1 from August, 1921, which is the equal of the angle of 22½°, or 2 x 1, fairly in April, 1930, come right up under this angle. Then consider the next angle of 4 x 1 from November, 1923, which is also equal to the angle of 22½°, notice prices in March and April got slightly above this angle, but that when the price opened in May, 1930, it dropped under this angle and then broke the angle of 45° from November, 1929 and the angle of 45° is really the angle of 2 x 1, or 22½°, counting the basis of the chart being at the rate of 2 spaces for one. Then the angle of 2 x 1, from November 1929 is equal to the angle of 45°. This angle crosses at 248 in June 1930, the same place where the angle of 2 x 1, from the corner of the top of October, 1919, angle of 2 x 1, or 45 as it is drawn across there, crosses, making 248 a very important point. Also note that the low in January, 1930, was 246. If this angle is broken and this low of 246, of January, is broken, it will indicate very much lower prices for these averages.

FAST ADVANCES AND FAST DECLINES

Why do stocks that have fast advances, reverse quickly and have sharp, quick declines before breaking the angle of 67½°, or the 45° angle on the monthly and weekly charts?

Page #17.

It is because the large volume of sales moves the prices over until the 45° angle is really broken at a very high level, which can be seen by making the combination time, space and volume chart. The volume chart shows that the angle is broken while the time chart, which only shows one space for each month or week, does not show the angle broken.

For example, make up a volume chart on U.S. Steel weekly from May 31, 1929 to date, and you will see that it broke so sharply after the high in September, 1929, because the volume broke the angle before the angles were broken by the weekly or monthly chart.

We are sending you Vanadium weekly from 1929 to date with volume. This will show you how the stock works when volume of sales is charted with time and space.

Why do stocks take such a long time to recover after a long decline and remain so long at low levels?

Because the volume gets so small near the bottom that it requires a long time to overcome the square of distance. When a stock declines 100 points or more in two or three months, for example, we will say exactly 100 points, then to overcome the square of distance at a low level, it requires 100 months. A stock has to square itself on the weekly, monthly and daily high and low chart. The lower the price crosses the 45° angle, the stronger the position of the stock and the higher the stock is and the greatest distance from the base, or beginning point when the 45° angle is broken or, in fact, any other angle, the weaker the stock is.

Why do stocks often cross the 45° angle on the daily, weekly or monthly high and low chart, then have an advance for a short period of time, decline and rest on the 45° angle?

It is because when they cross the 45° angle the first time, they have crossed it before they have run out or overcome the square of distance. Therefore, on the secondary reaction, when they rest on the 45° angle, it is at a time when they have reached the square of distance, and after that time a greater advance follows. Reverse this rule at the top of a bull market. This accounts for the stocks having a sharp, quick decline from the top and then advancing and making a slightly higher top or a series of slightly lower tops, working over until it overcomes the square of distance at a comparatively high level and breaks the 45° angle, then a fast decline follows.

What rule should be followed when stocks make higher bottoms and lower tops?

Page #18.

As stocks advance and make higher bottoms on the monthly, weekly or daily chart, you should always draw angles from higher bottoms. Then when you reach the last section of a bull market, and these important angles are broken from the last bottom, you know that the trend has turned down. Apply this same rule as a market declines. Draw your angles from each lower top and watch your angles, until the stock again crosses the 45° angle from a second, third, or fourth lower top. The second lower top, or second higher bottom is always very important to draw angles from, and to measure time from, as well.

When a stock is in a very weak, or a very strong position, it will always show it by its position on angles, and a volume chart, made up according to the proper spacing with volume, that is, considering the total number of shares, will show when the stock is in a strong or weak position and show whether buying or selling predominates, enabling you to determine whether supply is increasing, or whether demand is decreasing.

WHAT RULES TO USE WHEN IN DOUBT

When you are in doubt about the position of a stock and do not know what its trend is, you should, of course, not trade in it. Wait until it shows by breaking resistance level, or crossing a resistance level, or until it crosses an important angle, or breaks an important angle before deciding which way it is going to move, especially after it has been in a long deadlock, or in a sideways movement, as referred to in "Wall Street Stock Selector." As a general rule, when a change in trend takes place of importance, the volume of sales will show it. The volume of sales usually increases when a stock starts to advance from low levels or from dullness, and the same after a long period of dullness at a high level when activity starts on the down side, the volume of sales increases. When a stock starts up and is in a strong position, it will show it on angles by keeping above strong angles from the bottom. The same when it starts to decline. If it is in a very weak position and, going very fast, it will show it by the position of angles, that is, dropping below and keeping below strong angles. With the daily, weekly and monthly high and low chart, the important angles cannot be crossed at extremely low levels, until proper time has elapsed, neither can important angles be broken at high levels until sufficient time has elapsed. Therefore, the angles are very important because when broken they usually mean that the time has run out, whether you know it or not, and a change in trend will take place.

MASTER "12" CHART

The MASTER CHART is the Square of "12" or 12 x 12, making the first square end at 144. The Second Square of "12" ends at 288, the Third square of "12" at 432, and the Fourth Square at 576, which will cover most anything that you want, but you can make up as many more squares as you want.

Page #19.

This chart may be used and applies to anything – TIME, SPACE OR VOLUME, the number of points up or down; days, weeks, months and years.

On Square No. 1, which runs from 1 to 144, I have drawn the finer angles to show the grand-center or strongest Resistance Point in each minor square. The minor centers, which are the strongest for minor tops and bottoms are 14, 17, 20, 23, 50, 53, 56, 59, 86, 89, 92, 95, 122, 125, 128, 131.

The major center is where the strongest resistance is met. These numbers are 66, 67, 78, and 79. Stocks going up or coming down to these prices will meet with stubborn resistance. The next strong angle is the 45°, and the numbers of greatest resistance are 14, 27, 40, 63, 66, 79, 92, 105, 118, 131, and 144. The other diagonal 45° angle from 12 is equally strong. The numbers are 12, 23, 34, 45, 67, 78, 89, 100, 111, 122 and 133.

The numbers which are cut by the 45° angles thru the center of each of the 1/4 squares are next in strength. These numbers are 7, 20, 43, 46, 59, 72, 61, 56, 39, 28, 17 and 6, and on the other side of the Square, after you pass the half-way point, these numbers are 75, 86, 99, 112, 125, 138, 139, 128, 117, 106, 95 and 84.

The numbers at the tops and bottoms of the squares are important prices for important tops and bottoms to be made because they are opposition numbers and are equal to the half-way point. These numbers for Square No. 1 are 1, 13, 25, 37, 49, 61, 73, 85, 97, 109, 121, 135. The top numbers are 12, 24, 36, 48, 60, 72, 84, 96, 108, 120, 132 and 144.

The opposition angle, which runs thru the center of the Square, from east to west, equally dividing it, is one of the very strong angles because it equals one-half. Any stock moving up or down and reaching these prices will meet with resistance and make tops or bottoms. These numbers are 6, 7, 18, 19, 30, 31, 42, 43, 54, 55, 66, 67, 78, 79, 90, 91, 102, 103, 114, 115, 126, 127, 138, 139.

Remember, when anything has moved three sections over from the beginning, it reaches the square of its own place, which is the first strong resistance. When it has moved six sections over, it reaches the opposition, or what equals the half-way point of its own place and meets still stronger resistance. Moving over nine places or sections from its own place, it reaches the 3/4 point another square. The 8th and 9th sections are the strongest and hardest points to pass because this is the "death" zone. The next and still stronger is the 12th section or column which ends at 144. Anything getting into this section meets the strongest resistance but once it moves out of this Square and gets as much as 3 points into Square #2, that is, making 147, will indicate much higher, but after reaching this, it should not drop back 3 points or to 141 in Square #1.

Page #20.

When a stock gets into the Second Square of "12", it has faster moves, and when the time or number of months from any bottom or top moves into the Second Square, it is an indication of faster moves, both up and down.

Apply the same rule to the 3rd, 4th, 5th and 6th squares, In the 3rd and 4th squares of the Master "12", you will find that most of the big bull and bear campaigns culminate, when measured by months, which determines the division according to time. All of the other rules given you to apply to Space movements, angles and time, can be used with the Master "12" tables.

SQUARE OF NINE

You have already had the MASTER SQUARE OF TWELVE explained, which represents days, weeks, months and years, and the measurements of TIME in the Square of Twelve or the Square of the Circle.

The SQUARE OF NINE is very important because nine digits are used in measuring everything, and we cannot go beyond 9 without starting to repeat and using the 0. If we divide 360° by 9, we get 40, which measures 40°, 40 months, 40 days, or 40 weeks, and shows why bottoms and tops often come out on these angles measured by one-ninth of the total circle.

If we divide our 20-year period, or 240 months, by 9, we get 26-2/3 months, making an important angle of 26-2/3°, months, days or weeks. Nine times [9?] equals 81, which completes the First square of Nine. Note the angles and how they run from the main center. The Second Square of Nine is completed at 162. Note how this is in opposition to the main center. The Third Square of Nine is completed at 243, which would equal 243 months or 3 months over our 20-year period and accounts for the time which often elapses before the change in the Cycle, sometimes running over 3 months or more. The Fourth square of Nine ends at 324. Note the angles of 45° cross at 325, indicating a change in cycles here. To complete the 360° requires Four Squares of Nine and 36 over. Note that 361 equals a Square of 19 times 19, thus proving the great value of the Square of Nine in working out the important angles and proving up discrepancies.

Beginning with "1" at the center, note how 7, 21, 43, 75, 111, 157, 211, 273 and 343 all fall on a 45° angle, Going the other way, note that 3, 13, 31, 57, 91, 133, 183, 241 and 307 fall on an angle of 45°. Remember there are always four ways you can travel from a center following an angle of 45° or an angle of 180° or an angle of 90°, which all equal about the same when measured on a flat surface. Note that 8, 23, 46, 77, 116 163, 218, 281 and 353 are all on an angle from the main center; also note that 4, 15, 34, 61, 96, 139, 190, 249 and 316 are on an angle from the main center, all of these being great resistance points and measuring out important time factors and angles.

Study the SQUARE OF NINE very carefully in connection with the MASTER TWELVE and 360° CIRCLE CHART.

Page #21.

SIX SQUARES OF NINE

We are sending you six Permanent Charts, each containing 81 numbers. The First Square of Nine runs from 1 to 81. Everything must have a bottom, top, and four sides to be a square or cube. The First Square running up to 81 is the bottom, base, floor or beginning point. Squares #2, 3, 4 and 5 are the four sides, which are equal and contain 81 numbers. The sixth square of Nine is the top and means that it is times times and referred to in the Bible, or a thing reproducting [reproducing?] itself by being multiplied by itself. Nine times nine equals 81 and six times 91 equals 486. We can also use 9 times 81, which would equal 729.

The number 5 is the most important number of the digits because it is the balance or main center. There are four numbers on each side of it. Note how it is shown as the balancing or center number in the Square of Nine.

We square the Circle by beginning at 1 in the center and going around until we reach 360. Note that the Square of Nine comes out at 361. The reason for this is it is 19 times, and the 1 to begin with and one over 360 represent the beginning and ending points. 361 is a transition point and begins at the next circle. Should we leave the first space blank or make it "0", then we would come out at 360. Everything in mathematics must prove. You can begin at the center and work out, or begin at the outer rim and work in to the center. Begin at the left and work right to the center or to the outer rim or square.

Note the Square of Nine or the Square of the Circle where we begin with 1 and run up the side of the column to 19, then continue to go across until we have made 19 columns, again the square of 19 by 19. Note how this proves up the circle. One-half of the circle is 180°. Note that in the grand-center, where all angles from the four corners and from the East, West, North and South reach gravity center, number 191 appears, showing that this point we are crossing the Equator or Gravity center and are starting on the other half of the circle.

We have astronomical and astrological proof of the whys and wherefores and the cause of the workings of geometrical angles. When you have made progress, proved yourself worthy, I will give you the Master Number and also the Master Work.

Study the human body in every way and you will find that it is the work of a Master Mind, and when once you know yourself and know your body, you will know the Law and will understand all there is to know. Remember there is a source of all supply, and that you have within you the power to know all there is to know, but you must work hard, seek and you shall find.

Page #22.

THE HUMAN BODY

There are seven openings in the head – two eyes, two ears and two nostrils, equally divided, three on each side. From this we get our Law of Three and know the reason why the change comes after two and in the third period. The seventh opening in the head is the mouth and everything goes down. Study your seven-year periods and see how your markets go down and make tops and bottoms.

Woman is more perfect than man because she can create. Her body contains 12 openings. Man's body only contains 11. The 12 represents the 12 signs of the Zodiac. The fact that man's body only contains 11 openings proves why a man betrayed Christ and not a woman. Note the angle of 11¼°. Note the number 11 on all of your different charts. Study the position of 7 times 7 or 49 on all of your permanent charts. Then you will understand why the children of Israel marched 7 times around the walls of Jericho, blew the ram's horn 7 times and the walls fell down on the 7th day. This Law is also backed with astrological proof, but anything that can be proved in any way or by any science is not correct unless it can be proved by numbers and by geometry.

The Time Cycles and every measurement of angles are represented by the human body. You have 5 fingers on each hand. They are above the waistline or solar plexus and represent the 10-year cycle or the two 5-year cycles, which are 1/4 and 1/2 of the 20-year cycles. You have 10 toes, but note that there are 5 on one side and 5 on the other. This indicates that one 10-year cycle which is below the base line, must run opposite to the 10 above the base line, but that the 10 and 20-year tops and bottoms will come out according to the proper measurements from the base or beginning point. Study the different divisions of your limbs. Note the 3 divisions of your fingers, and that the third joint or ends of your fingers are shorter than the other two, and that the thumb really contains only two spaces or joints, where your fingers contain 3. Learn the secret of this and you will learn why the thumb is so important. Study all of these Master charts, apply them to Space, Time and you will find the cause of tops and bottoms and will know how to determine Resistance Levels. Go back over any of the old charts you have and study the places where they have had the greatest resistance. Note the price, then determine the time by weeks, months or days, and you will be able to learn how to understand future movements. Look up the position of your Master Twelve Chart and your Square of Nine, then consider your geometrical angles from West to East, according to time, then consider your angles from the different bases or beginning points and you will be able to determine the position of a stock.

The SQUARE OF NINE, the MASTER TWELVE SQUARE, and the GEOMETRICAL ANGLES are all mathematical points and do not contradict each other but harmonize and prove up the different mathematical points.

[W.D. Gann's signature]

January 17, 1931.

Chapter 3

Method for Trading with the Overnight Chart - Mechanical Stock Trading Method

W. D. GANN
91 WALL STREET
NEW YORK

SCIENTIFIC ADVICE
AND ANALYTICAL REPORTS
ON STOCKS AND COMMODITIES
AUTHOR OF "TRUTH OF THE STOCK TAPE"
AND "THE TUNNEL THRU THE AIR"

MEMBER
AMERICAN ECONOMIC ASS'N
ROYAL ECONOMIC SOCIETY
CABLE ADDRESS
"GANWADE NEW YORK"

[MECHANICAL STOCK TRADING METHOD]
METHOD FOR TRADING WITH THE OVERNIGHT CHART

The Overnight Chart and the method for operating it is purely mechanical. You use no judgement but simply follow rules and reverse your position when the Overnight Chart indicates it. If you buy and sell and use stop loss orders according to rules, this Method will make a large amount of profits over a long period of time.

The Overnight Chart is taken from the daily high and low chart and the rule for keeping it is as follows:

As long as a stock makes higher bottoms each day, you move the Overnight Chart up, but the first day it makes ¼ point or more under a previous day's bottom you move the Overnight Chart down to this level, but always recording the highest top reached before the Overnight Chart turns. Then as long as the Overnight Chart makes lower bottoms, you continue to move it down. Should it make a higher bottom and a lower top the same day, you would move it up to the top of that day because the Overnight Chart is based on bottoms. When there is a wide swing and the market runs up early in the day and makes a higher top than the previous day and then runs down later in the day and makes a lower bottom, you first move your chart up to the top, or highest point reached during the day, and then bring it down to the lowest level. Then suppose next day it makes a higher bottom, you move it up to the top of that day.

You can use the Resistance Levels in connection with the Overnight Chart, but the only rule that I use in connection with the trading record on U.S. Steel, which will follow, is the half-way point, or taking extreme low and extreme high of the last move and dividing it by two to get the gravity center or half-way point. Then buy or sell when this point is reached and protect it with a 1 point stop loss order. The other trading indications are according to the Overnight Chart.

When a stock reaches a new high where you have no Resistance Levels between a previous high and a previous low, you simply follow the Overnight Chart and reverse position when the rule indicates it.

You should watch the daily highs and lows, on your daily chart around Permanent Resistance Levels as they will help you to determine a change in the major or minor trend on the Overnight Chart.

RULE 1: Buy or sell on double or triple tops or bottoms with a stop-loss order 1 point above the top or 1 point under the bottom. This is the rule that I use. However, many times you will make more money if you use a 3 point stop loss order but by using a 1-point stop loss order most of the time, the stop will not be caught very often and when it is, it will be time to reverse. The greatest advances and declines usually start from triple tops or bottoms, but remember that these triple tops or bottoms must be several weeks or several months apart to be of great importance. Triple tops or bottoms which are only a limited number of days apart do not mean such big moves as those that occur weeks or months apart.

RULE 2: When a stock reaches the same top or bottom the 4th time, especially if it is several weeks or months apart, it nearly always goes through. Therefore, when you buy or sell the 4th time at a bottom or top, you must always use a 1-point stop loss order over the top or under the bottom.

RULE 3: When the overnight Chart makes top or bottoms on Resistance Levels like the 1/2, 2/3 and 3/4 points, you should buy or sell with a stop loss order 1 or 2 points under these exact Resistance Levels. As a general rule, the stop should be 1 point.

RULE 4: When your stop loss order is caught, it indicates that the Overnight Chart has reversed, so you should reverse position and double up every time it is caught. You will make a great deal more money trading in this way, as will be shown by the trading operations which follow on U.S. Steel. In my trading, the only place where I do not reverse position, that is, double up when the stop loss order is caught, or the trend changes, is where there is no second top or bottom close enough for me to place a stop loss order if I reverse position. As a general rule, I place the stop loss order 1 point above a previous top or 1 point under a previous bottom.

RULE 5: The rule for pyramiding is to sell or buy half as much as your trading unit every 3 to 5 points apart, determining the distance according to the activity of the stock and according to previous Resistance Levels which are broken. Your 3rd trade in a pyramid should be one-half the amount of your 2nd trade, your 4th one-half of the 3rd, and so on. In this way, you take your greatest risk first, then when you make the 2nd, 3rd and 4th trades, you are reducing your trading units, therefore when a stop loss order is caught, your loss will be small on the last trade in the pyramid and large on the ones that you bought or sold the most of first. Suppose you are pyramiding a stock when it has declined or advanced 20 or 30 points and has a fast move up or down without making any change on the Overnight Chart. In nearly every case before the trend changes, the Overnight Chart will make a reverse move and allow you to place your stop loss order at least 3 to 5 points away from the bottom or top, but when you have a very large profit and the market has a sharp move one way or the other, and you have a pyramid, you do not want to lose any more of your profits than you can help. In this case, I usually pull my stop loss order down 5 points from the low level each day or, if on the up side, place it up 5 points under the high level, then when the market makes the first reverse move of 5 points, I am out on stops on all of the pyramiding trades.

RULE 6: For very active, fast moving stocks, especially when they are at high levels, you should wait for a change in trend on the Overnight Chart before reversing position.

By a change in the Overnight Chart, I mean wait until it breaks a previous low level, or crosses a previous high level, in case you are operating on the down side.

RULE 7: After any big advance or decline, reverse position when Overnight Chart shows a change in trend, that is double up on changes and go with the trend. The big money is made by going with the trend. That is why every time the trend changes or a stop loss order is caught, we reverse position. If the trend has changed and it is time to sell out longs, it is also time to go short, and vice versa.

For example: In fast moving markets, like the panic of October and November, 1929, when you pyramid on active stocks and make a large amount of money, if you have very large profits, you should follow down with a stop loss order about 10 points away from the market. Then, after a severe decline reduce stop loss order, placing it about 5 points above the low level, because when a market is moving so fast as this, you should not wait for the Overnight Chart to show a change in trend by crossing a previous top before changing position. In fast moving markets you would also watch for the market to stop around important half-way points. For example: U.S. Steel at 150 had reached the half-way point from 38 to 261¾. You would not wait until the Overnight Chart showed a change but when Steel got around 150, you would cover shorts and buy with a stop at 149, or if you use the 3-point rule, place stop at 147. Suppose Steel had broken this 150 level. When your stop loss order was caught at 149 or 147, whichever was used, you would have gone short.

RULE 8: Watch the daily, weekly, and monthly closing price. When a stock is active and closes for 3 days, 3 weeks or 3 months around the same price, then the trend changes, it will usually go a considerable distance in the direction in which it starts. However, it is not necessary to depend on this rule at all in connection with the Overnight Chart. I am only giving it to help those who study the daily, weekly and monthly charts.

RULE 9: In very weak or very strong markets watch for the first advance of 3 full points from any low level. By 3 full points I mean, for example, from 100 low, a rally to 103 would be 3 full points. Suppose the low was 99½. We would not count 3 full points until the stock rallied to 103. Reverse this rule for a stock when it is advancing. Suppose it advances to 150-7/8 and has not had a 3 full point reaction for some time. Then it if declined to 147, I would consider it a 3 full point reaction and an indication that the minor trend was reversing. In this case, suppose the stock only declined to 147½ or even to 147¼. We would not count it a full 3 point reaction, because full points are based on even figures.

No matter at what point or at what price you begin trading according to this Method, you must follow the rules and not risk more than 3 points on any one trade, then after that use the Overnight Chart and make your stop loss orders 1 point away from the top or bottom which I always do in my trading example which follows on U.S. Steel. Then when the stop loss order

4.

is caught, buy or sell double the amount, reversing your position. When you cover shorts on a stop loss order, you buy and go with the trend. In the same way when you sell out longs on a stop loss order, you reverse position and go short the same amount which keeps you with the trend.

In my trading, I do not use or take advantage of other rules which I know which might help me at points. I make many trades when I know there is going to be a loss just to demonstrate that the Method will work over a long period of years and make money by reversing position every time and using stop loss orders and, at the same time, following the capital rule and not overtrading, always allowing $3000 capital for each 100 shares traded in. If you start with $300 capital, then trade in 10-share lots and never risk more than 3 points, or $30, on each of your initial trades. Do not increase your trading unit on initial trades until your capital has increased so that the loss will be only 10% of your capital, if the loss comes.

In pyramiding, it is different. When you make the 2nd or 3rd trade, you have a profit already and are risking part of your profits, but always keep these risks protected with stop loss orders according to the Overnight Chart, so that if your stop loss orders on a pyramid are caught, your total loss will not exceed 10% of your capital. A man who will follow this rule over a long period of years will not only keep his capital, but will make a fortune. This can be demonstrated on any active stock. Use as little human judgment as possible and you will make better success in trading. The Mechanical Method beats human guesswork, because it reverses at the time the trend reverses and doubles up and goes with the trend, while the man who is guessing or using human judgment will wait. You must have machine-like action in order to succeed, and must buy or sell according to the rules, regardless of what you think or hope. This is exactly what I always do in the trading operations which follow on U.S. Steel.

THE W.D. GANN MASTER STOCK MARKET COURSE

5.

U.S. STEEL TRADES ACCORDING TO OVERNIGHT CHART

1915 - 1930

This trading plan requires $3,000 to start with, to trade in 100-share lots. My rule is never to risk more than 3 points or $300 on any one trade. I protect all trades with stop loss orders.

Follow the rules for Resistance Levels and the rules for using the Overnight Chart. When I pyramid, or buy or sell a second lot, I limit my risk so that I will not lose more than 10% of my original capital. In other words, when I buy or sell a second lot, I place stop so that my loss will not exceed $300.

The following operations are based on trading according to the Overnight Chart and the use of Resistance Levels to determine buying and selling points:

1915

February 1, low 38, February 3, high 41½ - a 3-point rally indicated a buying point. Either buy at market or on a reaction. We buy 100 shares at 41. On February 5 it declined to 38¾, then crossed 41½, the top of February 3, and turned Overnight trend up. Stop would now be at 36½ or 3 points under 39½. Trend continued up to 45 on February 13, then decline to 40¼ on February 24, making a higher bottom than February 5. Raise stop to 38½ or 2 points under 2 bottoms close together.

March 8th high 46, then made 3 bottoms around 43½ to 44¼ on March 5, 13 and 18. Here raise stop to 42½ or one point under three bottoms. Then we buy more at 47 when it goes one point above top at 46. Trend continues up to 49¾ on March 29; again made three bottoms around 47¾ to 48¼; raise stop to 46¾. Then we buy more at 51 and raise stop on three lots to 48. The advance continued to 58 on April 10, reacted to 55¼ on April 13. We raise stop to 52¼ or three points under.

April 19 made top 60¾, reacted to 56¾ on April 24. Raise stop to 55¼, last bottom. April 26 high 59¼, April 27 low 57, a third higher bottom. Raise stop to 56 on all three lots. April 29 high 60-5/8, just 1/8 under top of April 19, April 30 low 58½. Raise stop to 57½.

6.

May 3rd advanced to 60¾, the third top around same level, where we should either sell out and go short with stop at 63¾ or leave stop at 57½. We sold on stop at 57½

1st	purchase	100	at	41	sold at	57½ -	profit	16½ points
2nd	purchase	100	at	47	sold at	57½ -	profit	10½ points
3rd	purchase	100	at	51	sold at	57½ -	profit	6½ points

or a total of .... 33½ points on
100 shares,

gives $3,350
Deduct $100 for commission, Tax and Interest 100

Net Gain $3,250

Then we increase trading to 200 shares but less must be limited to $600, or 3 points on each 100 shares. This would give us 200 short at 57½ with stop at 60½.

Decline followed, broke three bottoms made April 24, 27 and 30. We sell 200 shares more at 54¼. Decline continued to 48¼ where there were three bottoms March 26, 31 and April 1st. Rule says, buy the fourth time with one point stop. We covered 300 shares short at 48½ and bought 200 at 48½ with stop at 46¾, which was one point under bottom of March 26th and April 1st. The profits are as follows:

Sold	200	at	57½	closed at	48½ - profits		$1,800.00
Sold	200	at	54¼	closed at	48½ - profits		1,150.00
					Total		$2,950.00

Commission and Taxes 116.00

Net Profit   2,834.00

Previous Capital & Profits 6,250.00

Gives a Capital of $9,084.00

which will allow 300 shares as a trading unit with risk limited to $900 on each trade. We bought 200 at 48½ when we covered shorts, then we would have 100 more to buy later.

The stock advanced to 55¼ on May 12th. If we were watching the resistance level of 54½ or 1/2 from 60¾ to 48¼, we would expect top and a reaction and could have sold out longs and gone short at 54½ with stop at 57½, but we waited for a change on the Overnight Chart.

May 14th, low 49¾. Here we buy 100 more at 50½, then make stop on 300 at 48. The advance was resumed on May 17th made 53½, then reacted to 51¾, then turned trend up again. We would now raise stop to 49¾, the last bottom.

May 24th high 56¼ and crossing 54½, the 1/2 point, the second time indicated higher.

May 26th and June 1st reacted to 53¼ and made double bottom. Raise stop to 50¾ or one point under previous low level and when it crossed 56¼, last top, buy 200 more at 56½ and raise stop on all trade to 52¼, one point under last double bottom. June 4th the stock advanced to 64-1/8. June 9th declined to 56¾. Holding above 56¼, the 1/2 point from last low of 48¼ to high of 64-1/8, was a sign of strong support and showed that the main trend was up be cause the stock had gone three points above the triple tops made April 19, 29 and May 3rd.

From June 9th a rally followed to June 12th, when the high was 61¼. We now raise stop to 55¾ or one point under low of June 9th.

June 14th declined to 59, then raise stop on all trades to 58. This stop was never caught. The stock advanced to 61¾ on June 22, then after a series of lower tops and bottoms, declined to 58¼ on July 7th, then rallied to 59¼ on July 9th and declined same day to 58¼, making a double bottom from which advance was resumed and on July 17th reached 65-1/8, reacted to 62-1/2 on July 20th, rallied to 62-1/8 on the 26th and declined same day to 62¾, making a double bottom again, then went to new high and crossed 66-3/8, the 1/2 point from 94-7/8 to 38. We bought more at 67 and raised stop on all trades to 61¾ or one point under last low of July 26th. Buy 200 more at 72.

August 10th high 76¾; 11th declined to 73-5/8;
12th advanced to 75½; 14th declined to 73-3/8;
18th advanced to 77-5/8.

We now raise stop on all trades to 72-3/8 or one point under the last bottom at 73-3/8. The stop was caught and we sold short 400 shares at 72-3/8.

The account now stands as follows:

Bought	200	at	48½	closed at	72-3/8	profit $6,725.00
Bought	100	at	50½	closed at	72-3/8	profit 2,162.50
Bought	200	at	56½	closed at	72-3/8	profit 3,125.00
Bought	200	at	67	closed at	72-3/8	profit 1,075.00
						$13,087.50

Bought 200 at 72 closed at 72-3/8
   Less loss of 3/8 on 200   75.00
   Commissions   225.00   300.00
   Net Gain   12,787.50
   Previous Capital and Profits   9,084.00

   Gives an Operating Capital of $21,871.50

8.

This would give a limit of 700 shares as a trading unit.

$$
\begin{array}{llll}
\text{We sold} & 400 & \text{short at} & 72\text{-}3/8 \\
\text{Sold} & 300 & \text{short at} & 69\text{-}3/8 \\
\end{array}
$$

Always calculate the 1/2 point of a previous move.

Last low 58-1/8 July 9th to 77-5/8 high August 18th, making 1/2 point at 67-7/8. August 23rd, decline to 67-3/4. Here we cover shorts and buy 700 longs at 68½, stop 64-7/8. However, a stop at 66-7/8, just one pint under 1/2 point, would have held, as low of 67-3/4 was not reached again.

Here our account stands as follows:

Sold	400	at	72-3/8	closed at	68½	profit	$1,750.00
Sold	300	at	69-3/8	closed at	68½	profit	252.50
							2,002.50
	Less Taxes and Commissions						175.00
							1,827.50
	Previous Capital						21,871.50
	Operating Capital						$23,698.00

We continue with 700 shares as trading unit. We are now long of 700 shares bought at 68½ with stop 64-7/8. Buy 300 at 72.

August 27th, advanced to 77; Sept. 1st, declined to 73-3/4;

Sept. 2nd, rallied to 76-3/4.

Here we raise stop to 72-3/4, just one point under September 1st low

Sept. 10th advanced to 76¼; Sept. 11th declined to 73¾;

Sept. 14th rallied to 76; Sept. 17th declined to 74¼;

making five bottoms around 74¼ to 73-3/4, a sure indication that stop should be at 72-3/4.

September 27th, advanced to 79-3/4, getting above all tops since August 17th. We bought 300 at 78½, stop 75½.

October 1st high 81-3/4; 6th low 76-3/4, advance resumed 19th high 87¼; 20th low 85½; 21st high 87-5/8, stop 84½; 26th low 85¼; 26th high 87¼, the third top around same level.

We could have sold out but we assume stop was caught at 84½, and we went short 700 at 84½.

9.

Our account now reads as follows:

Bought	700 at 68½,	sold at	84½	profit	$11,200.00
Bought	300 at 72	sold at	84½	profit	3,750.00
Bought	300 at 73½,	sold at	84½	profit	1,800.00
	Profit				16,750.00
	Less Tax and Coms.				325.00
					16,425.00
	Previous Capital				23,698.00
	Operating Capital				$40,123.00

We can now raise trading unit to 1000 shares. We are short 700 at 84½. The last low, October 6th, was 76-3/4, high October 21st, 87-5/8. Makes 1/2 point 82-1/8. October 29th, the stock declines to 82¼. Note October 16th low 82¼. Here we would cover shorts and buy with stop at 81¼. Our account now stands:

Sold	700 at 84½	closed	82½	profit	$1,400.00
	Less Commission				175.00
					$1,225.00
	Previous Capital				40,123.00
	Operating Capital				$41,308.00

We now have 1000 shares bought at 82½.

November 1st, advances to 88-3/8; 3rd, low 86; 4th, high 88.

Raise stop to 85, one point under November 3rd low. The stop was caught, and we sold short 1000 at 85. Our account now stands:

Bought 1000 at 82½,	sold at	85	profit	$2,500
Less Tax and Commissions				250
				2,250
Previous capital				41,308
Operating Capital				$43,558

Short 1000 at 85, stop 88-3/8. The stock declines to 83-5/8 on November 9th; then rallies on November 12th to 88-3/8; declines on November 16th and 20th to 86¼; November 26th high 88¼, December 2nd low 84½. December 7th high 88¼, making the same level five times. Our stop should be 89¼. December 13th, 17th, 21st made lows 85¼ to 84-7/8, higher than previous bottoms, and our stop should have been reduced to 87¼, one point above December 20th high. This stop was caught, and we would reverse position and buy 1000 at 87¼. Account now stands:

Sold	1000 at 85	closed at	87¼	loss	$2,250.00
	Commissions				250.00
	Net loss				2,500.00
	Capital of				43,558.00
					2,500.00
	Net Operating Capital				$41,058.00

10.

We have 1000 at 87¼. December 27th advanced to 89½; December 29th, low 86-3/4; December 31st high 89½ a double top- raise stop to 85-3/4. This double top near 90, a strong resistance level, would be the place to sell out and go short, but we stay to see if overnight trend turns down. Stop is caught at 85-3/4, and we sell 1000 short at 85-3/4. Account now stands as follows:

    Bought   1000 at 87¼   sold at   85-3/4   loss $1,500.00
           Commissions   250.00
                                                                     $1,750.00

from capital of $41,058.00 leaves a balance of $39,308.00, and 1000 short at 85-3/4.

1916

January 24th, declined to 82¼, same low as October 16th and 29th, 1915. We cover shorts at 82½ and buy 1000 82½.

Account now stands:
    Sold   1000 at 85-3/4, closed at 82½   profit $3,250.00
          Less commissions   250.00
          Net loss   3,000.00
          Capital   39,308.00
          Operating balance $42,308.00

    Bought   1000 at 82½   stop   81½.

January 26th high 86; 27th low 82-3/4; 28th high 84¼,

Raise stop to 81-3/4, one point under January 27th low. This stop was caught and we go short 1000 at 81-3/4. Account now stands:

    Bought   1000 at 81½   sold at   81-3/4 <u>even</u> counting commissions.
    Capital $42,308.000
    Short 1000 at 81-3/4, stop 86¼.

January 31st low 79 7/8; February 4th high 84-3/4; 5th low 82¼; 10th high 85-5/8

Stop caught and we buy 1000 at 85-5/8. Account now stands:

    Sold   1000 at 81-3/4 closed at 85-5/8   loss $3,787.50

From $42,308.00 leaves $38,520.50, with 1000 bought at 85-5/8, stop 81¼.

11.

February 17th and 24th, made lows at 82½ and 82-3/8. Raised stop to 81½. Stop caught and we go short 1000 at 81½. Account stands:

        Bought   1000 at 85-5/8 sold at 81½   loss $4,125
                Less commissions   250
                                                                     $4,375

        from capital $58,530.00, leaves $34,145, with 1000 short at 81½.

March 1st declines to 79-3/4, same low as January 31st. We cover shorts and buy 1000 at 80¼. Account now stands:

        Sold   1000 at 81½   closed at 80¼   profit $1,250.00
             Less commissions   250.00
             Net   1,000.00

             Added to Capital gives $39,520.00,

with 1000 bought at 80¼, stop 79¼. March 17th high 87¼, March 22nd low 84. We raise stop to 83. April 4th high 86. April 8th and March 31st lows 83-3/4. April 10th high 85¼. Decline follows. Stop is caught at 83 and we go short 1000. Account now stands.

        Bought 1000 at 80¼ sold at 83 profit $2,750.00, less commissions of $250.00, leaves $2,500 net profit. Added to capital gives $42,020.00 with 1000 short at 83.

April 22nd declines to 80 and we cover at 80¼ and buy 1000 because this is same bottom as January 31st and March 1st. We protect with stop 79¼, this being a triple bottom.

April 25th high 84, April 26th low 80-3/8, a higher bottom. May 1st high 84¼, May 5th low 80½, a slightly higher bottom, From high of 89½ on December 31, 1915 to low of 79-3/4 March 1st, 1916, makes 1/2 point 84-5/8, and making 85-5/8 would indicate higher.

May 25th high 86-5/8 and last low on 17th was 84. Therefore we raise stop to 83. The stock declines to 83-5/8 on June 2nd. June 12th advances to 87¼. June 12th low 86. June 14th high 87. We raise stop to 85, which is caught, and we go short 1000 at 85. Account stands:

        Bought 1000 at 80¼ sold at 85 profit $4,750.00, less $250.00 commission, gives net $4,500.00. Added to capital gives $46,520.00 and 1000 short at 85, stop 88.

June 27th declines to 82-3/4 and as top on June 26th was 84¼ we reduce stop to 85¼, which is caught, and we buy 1000 at 85¼. The account now stands:

        Sold 1000 at 85 closed 85¼, loss of 1/4 point and commission makes $500 from $46,520.00, leaves $46,020.00 and 1000 bought at 85¼, stop 81-3/4.

12.

July 6th high 87¼, July 14th low 83¼, we raise stop to 82¼. June 24th high 87¼, July 25th low 85¼, we raise stop to 84¼, July 27, August 2nd and 5th, makes low 85-3/4 and 86, and we raise stop to 84-3/4. A big advance follows and at 90½ we buy 300 more because the stock has gone one pint into hew high after holding for nine months between 89½ and 79-3/4. August 17th high 92-5/8, August 18th low 91. We raise stop on all trades to 90 and at 94 buy 300 more, August 23rd high 99½, the highest in its history. August 24th low 96-3/4. We raise stop to 95-3/4. August 25th high 99¼. August 28th low 95-3/4. Catches stop and we go short 1000 at 95-3/4. The account now stands:

Bought	1000	at	85¼	sold	95-3/4	profit	$10,500
Bought	300	at	90½	sold	95-3/4	profit	1,575
Bought	300	at	94	sold	95-3/4	profit	525
							12,600
	Less commissions						400
	Net profit						12,200
	Capital						$46,030
							$58,220

with 1000 shares short at 95-3/4. We can now increase trading unit to 1200 shares. August 30th low 95¼. The high on 29th was 97, so we make stop to 97. August 31st stop is caught and we buy 1,200 at 97. Account now stands:

Sold 1000 at 95-3/4, closed at 97, loss $1,500 from capital
leaves $56,720, and 1200 bought at 97.

August 31st advances to 99-3/8 for third time and can't go thru 100, so we sell out at 99 and go short 1200 at 99. Account now stands:

Bought 1200 at 97, sold at 99, net profit $2,100.
Added to capital gives $58,820.00 and 1200 short at 99.

September 1st declines to 95, getting only 1/4 under low of August 30th. We reduce stop to 99, which is caught, but we wait to buy until stock can make new high and go through 100 - a very important Resistance Level. Account now stands:

Sold 1200 at 99, closed at 98, profit $900.00.
Added to capital gives $59,720.

The advance continues and at 100½ we buy 1200 with stop 97½, and at 105½ we buy 600 more, and 110½ - 600 more. The lows on September 19th and 20th were 107, so we raise stop to 106 on all trades. At 115½ we buy 300 more. September 25th high 120, a Resistance Level. September 26th low 113-3/4. We raise stop on all trades to 112-3/4. September 29th high 120½. September 30th low 116¼. We raise stop to 115¼. October 2nd, 4th, 5th, makes tops at 118-5/8 to 118-3/4 and low on October 4th was 117, so we raise stop to 116, which is caught, and we go short 1200.

13.

Account now stands:

Bought	1200	at 100½	sold at	116	profit	$18,600
Bought	600	at 105½	sold at	116	profit	6,300
Bought	600	at 110½	sold at	116	profit	3,300
Bought	300	at 115½	sold at	116	profit	150
						28,350
	Less commissions					675
						27,675
	Previous capital					59,720
	Operating Capital					$87,395

and short 1200 at 116, with stop 119. We can now increase trading to 1500 shares.

Decline follows and we sell 600 more at 111, October 9th low 108; October 10th high 113. Reduce stop to 113, October 14th low 108, same as October 9th, a double bottom. We figure from last low September 1st at 95 to high 120½ September 29th and find 1/2 point is 107-3/4, so we cover shorts at 108½ and buy 1500 with stop 106-3/4. The account now stands:

Sold	1200	at 116	closed at	108½	profit	$9,000
Sold	600	at 111	closed at	108½	profit	1,500
						10,500
	Less Commission					950
	Net profit					9,650
	Capital Added					87,395
	Operating Capital					$97,045

With 1500 bought at 108½. Bought 700 more at 114. October 23rd high 121-3/4. Bought 400 more at 121½, because it was a new high. October 26th low 117¼. Raised stop on all trades to 116¼, November 2nd high 122¼. November 4th low 119-3/4. Raised stop to 118-3/4. November 8th high 126. November 9th low 122½. Raised stop to 121½. Stops were caught, and we go short 1500 at 121½. The account now stands:

Bought	1500	at 108½	sold	121½	profit	$19,500
Bought	700	at 114	sold	121½	profit	5,250
Bought	400	at 121½	sold	121½	profit	0
						24,750
	Less Commissions					650
						24,100
	Previous capital					97,045
	Operating Capital					$121,145

with 1500 short at 121½. We can now be very conservative and increase trading to 2000 shares and should we have ten consecutive losses of 3 points each, we would still have half our capital left to operate with, and ten consecutive losses are highly improbable.

14.

November 14th, declined to 120¼, failing to make low of November 4th, which was 119-3/4. We reduce stop to 123¼, which is caught and we buy 2000 at 123¼ with stop at 120. November 27th, high 129-3/4, November 28th low 125-3/4. We raise stop to 124-3/4. This stop was caught, and we go short 2000 shares. The account now stands:

    1500   sold at 121½   closed at 123¼   loss $3,000
    2000   sold at 123¼   closed at 124-3/4   profit $3,000

Leaves a loss of commissions on 3500 shares, which is $875 from capital $121,145, leaves $120,270.00.

with 2000 short at 124-3/4. December 4th high 120½, and we make stop 127½. Decline follows. We sell 1000 more at 119-3/4. December 13th high 120½ and we reduce stop to 121½ on all trades. We sell 500 more at 115½. December 15th low 109¼. December 16th high 114-5/8. We reduce stops to 115-5/8, which are caught, and we go long 2000 at 115-5/8. The account now stands:

    Sold   2000 at 124-3/4   closed   115-5/8   profit $18,250.00
    Sold   1000 at 119-3/4   closed   115-5/8   profit   4,112.50
    Sold   500 at 115-1/2   closed   115-5/8   profit $22,362.50

    Less loss of 1/8 on 500 and commission   937.50
    Profit   21,425.00
    Capital   120,270.00
    $141,595.00

with 2000 bought 15 115-5/8. December 19th high 116¼. The low on 18th was 112½, so we raise stop to 111½, which is caught and we go short 2000 at 111½. Account stands:

    Bought   2000 at 115-5/8   sold at   112½   loss $6,250
    Commissions   500
    $6,750

from capital of $141,695 leaves $134,945, with 2000 short at 111½. The decline continues, and we sell 1000 more at 106½. December 21st panicky decline. Stock sells at 100, a Resistance Level, where we should cover, but we reduce stop to 105, which is caught, and we buy 2000 at 105. Account now stands:

    Sold   2000 at 111½   closed   105   profit $13,000
    Sold   1000 at 105½   closed   105   profit   1,500
    14,500
    Less Commission   750
    Profit $13,750
    Capital   134,945

    Total Capital $148,695

with 2000 bought at 105, and we buy 1000 more at 110.

1917

January 4th high 115-3/4. We figure high 129-3/4 to 110 low and get 1/2 point 114-7/8, and looking back to December 19th, we see last high was 116¼. Therefore, we sell out longs at 114½ and go short with stop 117½. The account now stands:

Bought	2000 at 105	sold at	114½	profit	$19,000
Bought	1000 at 110	sold at	114½	profit	4,500
					23,500
	Less Commissions				750
	Net Profit				$22,750
	Capital				148,695
					$171,445

with 200 short at 114½. The stock declined to 109¼ on January 5th; then advances to 113-7/8 on January 9th, and on 11th makes 109¼, same low as January 5th. We cover shorts and buy 2000, because 108 is 1/2 point from 100 to 115 7/8. The account now stands:

Sold	2000 at 114½	closed at 110	profit	$9,000
	Less Commissions			500
	Profit			$8,500
	Capital			171,445
	Total capital			$179,945

with 2000 bought at 110, stop 107. January 19th and 26th advances to 115½. We sell out at 114½ and sell short with stop 116½; because it is 1/2 point and strong Resistance Level. The account stands:

Bought	200 at 110	sold 114½	profit	$9,000
	Less Commissions			500
	Profit			$8,500
	Capital			179,945
	Total			$188,445

with 2000 short at 114½. We sell 1000 more at 109½. February 1st, just two years from the low of 38 on February 1, 1915, U.S. Steel declines to 99. We cover shorts and buy 2000 at 100, because 100 was low on December 21, 1916. We protect with stop at 99 and stop is caught, and we go short 2000 at 99. The account now stands:

Sold	2000 at 114½	closed at 100	profit	$29,000
Sold	1000 at 109½	closed at 100	profit	9,500
	Profit			$38,500
	Less one point on 2000 and			
	Commissions on 5000			$3,250
	Net Profit			35,250
	Capital			188,445
				$223,695

with 2000 short at 99. February 2nd high 104-1/8. We place stop 105-1/8. February 3rd low 99¼, a higher bottom than February 1st, and counting December 21st, three bottoms around the same level. We reduce stop to 102¼ and stop is caught. We reverse and buy 2000 at 102¼. The account now stands:

Sold	2000	at	99	closed at 102¼	loss	$6,500
	Commissions					500
						$7,000

Deducted from capital leaves $216,695 and 2000 bought at 102¼. The stock advances, making higher bottoms until February 20th and 25th, when it makes double top at 109½ with bottom at 106¼ on February 23rd. We raise stop to 105¼. This stop was caught and we sell 200 short at 105¼. The account now stands:

Bought	2000	at	102¼	sold at 105¼	profit	$6,000
	Commissions					500
Profit						5,500
Capital						216,695
Total						$222,195

with 2000 short at 105¼. March 1st low 103½, same low as March 9th, Figuring 1/2 point from 99 to 109½ high makes the 1/2 point at 104¼ a buying level. We cover shorts and buy 2000 at 104½. The account now stands:

Sold	2000	at	105¼	closed at 104½	profit	$1,500
	Commissions					500
Net Gain						1,000
Capital						222,195
						$223,195

with 2000 bought at 104½, stop 102½. The stock advanced and we bought 1000 more at 110½, when it crossed the last two tops. March 6th high 111½; March 7th low 109½. We raise stop on all trades to 108½. Then buy 500 more at 114½. March 21st high 118; March 22nd declined to 115¼. We raise stop to 114¼ which was caught and we go short 2000 at 114¼. The account now stands:

Bought	2000	at	104½	sold at 114¼	profit	$19,500
Bought	1000	at	110½	sold at 114¼	profit	3,750
Profit						23,250
Less loss of ¼ on 500 and commissions						1,000
Net Profit						$22,250
Capital						223,195
Total						$245,445

17.

with 2000 short 114¼. March 31st declines to 113-3/4. Last tops on March 28th and 30th were at 116. We make stop 117, which is caught, and we buy 2000 at 117. The account now stands:

Sold	2000 at 114¼	closed at 117	loss	$5,500
	Commissions			500
	Net Loss			$6,000
	from capital leaves balance of			$239,445

with 2000 bought at 117. April 3rd advances to 118-3/4. We raise stop to 116-3/4, which is caught, and we go short 2000 at 116-3/4. The account now stands:

Bought	2000 at 117	sold at 116-3/4	loss	$500
	Commissions			500
	Net Loss			$1,000
	Subtract form capital leaves			$238,445

with 2000 short at 116-3/4. The decline follows and we sell 1000 at 112-3/4, because it is under the last three bottoms. March 10th low 108-3/4. From 99 low to 118-3/4 high makes the 1/2 point 108-7/8. We cover shorts at 109¼ and buy 2000 at 109¼, stop 107-7/8. The account now stands:

Sold	2000 at 116-3/4 closed at 109¼	profit	$15,000
Sold	1000 at 112-3/4 closed at 109¼	profit	3,500
			18,500
	Less Commissions		750
	Net Profit		17,250
	Added to capital gives		$245,695

with 2000 bought at 109¼. April 20th last low 110½. We raise stop to 109½. We buy 1000 more at 113½. April 26th and May 1st high 117-3/4, and May 28th low 115¼. We raise stop on all trades to 114¼. The stop was caught, and we go short 2000 at 114¼. The account now stands:

Bought	2000 at 109¼	sold at 114¼	profit	$10,000
Bought	1000 at 113½	sold at 114¼	profit	750
	Net Profit			10,750
	Less Commissions			750
				10,000
	Capital			245,695
	Total			$255,695

18.

with 2000 short at 114¼, stop 117¼; May 9th low 112½; May 8th last high 116¼; May 11th high 116-3/4; May 11th low 114-3/4. Stop was caught at 117-1/4, and we buy 2000 at 117¼. The account now stands:

    Sold   2000 at 114¼   closed at 117¼   loss $6,000
            Commissions   500
            Net Loss $6,500

Deducted from capital leaves balance of $249,695.00

with 2000 bought at 117¼. The advance gets under way, and we buy 1000 more at 119-3/4, because it is one point above high of April 3rd. We buy 500 at 124-3/4; we buy 300 at 129¾ May 31st high 136-5/8. Last low on May 28th was 131¼. We raise stop on all trades to 130¼. This stop was caught, and we sell 2000 short at 130¼. The account now stands:

Bought	2000	at 117¼	sold at	128-3/4	profit	$23,000
Bought	1000	at 119-3/4	sold at	128-3/4	profit	9,000
Bought	500	at 124-3/4	sold at	128-3/4	profit	2,000
						$34,000
Bought	300	at 129-3/4	sold	128-3/4	loss	300
						$33,700
	Less Commissions					950
	Net					32,750
	Capital					249,695
	Total					$282,445

with 2000 short at 128-3/4. June 1st low 126-3/4. June 2nd high 131¼. We make stop 132¼. Stop was caught, and we bought 2000 at 132¼. Account now stands:

    Sold   2000 at 128-3/4 closed at 132¼   loss $7,000
            Commissions   500
            Net Loss $7,500

Deducted from $282,445.00 leaves $274,945.00.

with 2000 bought at 132¼. May 14th high 134-5/8. May 15th low 130¼. We make stop 129¼, which was caught, and we go short 2000 at 129¼. Account now stands:

    Bought   2000 at 132¼   sold   129¼   loss $6,000
            Commissions   500
            Net Loss $6,500

Deducted from Capital leaves $268,445.00

19.

with 2000 short at 129¼. June 20 low 125½. We reduce stop to 129½, which was caught, and we buy 2000 at 129½. Account now stands:

    Sold   2000 at 129¼   closed at 129½   loss $500
            Commissions   500
            Net $1,000

        Deducted from Capital leaves $267,44500

with 2000 bought at 129½. June 27th high 132-3/4. Last low was 128-3/4 on June 26th. We raise stop to 127-3/4, which was caught, and go short 2000 at 127-3/4. Account now stands:

    Bought   2000 at 129½   sold at   125-3/4   loss $6,750
             Commissions   500
             Net $7,250

        Deducted from capital leaves $260,245.00

with 2,000 short at 127-3/4; sold 1000 more at 123-3/4. July 19th low 118-3/4. Last high was 122¼, on July 18th. We reduced stop to 123¼, which was caught, and we buy 2000 at 123¼. The account now stands:

    Sold   2000 at 125-3/4 closed at 123¼   profit $4,500
    Sold   1000 at 125-3/4 closed at 123¼   profit   500
                                                                      $5,000
        Less Commissions   750
        Net   4,250
        Capital   260,245
                                                                     $264,495

with 2000 bought at 123¼. The advance follows, and we calculate from the high 136-5/8 to the low 118-3/4 and find the 1/2 point is 127-5/8. The stock advances to 127-7/8 on August 7th, and we sell out longs and go short 2000 at 127½. The account now stands:

    Bought   2000 at 123¼   sold at   127½   profit $8,000
            Less Commissions   500
        Net   7,500
        Capital   264,495
                                                                  $271,995

with 2000 sold at 127½. We sell 1000 more at 122, because it has broken three bottoms. We sell 500 more at 117½ after it has broken four other bottoms. September 4th low 104½. September 6th high 109½. We reduce stop on all trades to 110½. September 17th low 103¾,

THE W.D. GANN MASTER STOCK MARKET COURSE

20.

and the last high was 108-3/4 on September 14th. We reduce stops to 109-3/4. The stops were caught, and we bought 2000 at 109-3/4. The account now stands:

Sold	2000 at 127½	closed at 109-3/4	profit	$17,500
Sold	1000 at 122	closed at 109-3/4	profit	12,250
Sold	500 at 117½	closed at 109-3/4	profit	4,575
	Total			$34,325
	Less Commissions			875
	Net			$33,450
	Capital			271,995
	Total			$305,445

with 2000 bought at 109-3/4. September 25th high 113-7/8. The last low was 109-1/2 on September 24th. We raise stop to 108½. The stop was caught, and we sell short 2000 at 108½. The account now stands:

Bought	2000 at 109-3/4	sold at 108¼	loss	$2,500
	Commissions			500
	Net Loss			$3,000

Deducted form capital, leaves $302,445.00

with 2000 short at 108½. Sold 1000 more at 103½. October 15th it declines to 99, and we reduce stop to 104, which was caught, and we buy 2000 at 104. The account now stands:

Sold	2000 at 108½	closed at 104	profit	$9,000
Sold	1000 at 103½	closed at 104	loss	500
				$8,500
	Less Commissions			750
	Net Profit			$7,750
	Capital			302,445
	Total			$310,195

with 2000 bought at 104. October 22nd high 107-3/8. October 26th low 103-7/8. We raise stop to 102-7/8. The stop was caught, and we go short 2000 at 102-7/8. The account now stands.

Bought	2000 at 104	sold at 102-7/8	loss	$2,250
	Commissions			500
				$2,750

Deducted from capital leaves $307,445

with 2000 short at 101-7/8. Sold 1000 more at 98. Sold 500 more at 93. November 8th low 88-3/4. November 12th high 94-3/4. Reduced stop to 95-3/4. November 14th low 89¼. Reduced stop to 94-3/4. The stop was caught, and we buy 2000 at 94-3/4.

21.

The account now stands:

	Sold	2000	at	101-7/8	closed at	94-3/4	profit	$14,250
	Sold	1000	at	98	closed at	94-3/4	profit	3,250
								17,500
	Sold	500	at	93	closed at	94-3/4	loss	875
								16,625
	Less Commissions							875
	Net							$15,750
	Capital							307,445
	Total							$323,195

with 2000 bought at 94-3/4. November high 99¼. Last low on November 22nd at 96. We raise stop to 95, and it was caught. We go short 2000 at 95. The account now stands:

Bought 2000 at 94-3/4, sold at 95 makes it even
allowing 1/4 for commissions. Balance $323,195.00.

with 2000 short at 95. Sold 1000 more at 90. Sold 500 more at 85. December 13th low 79-7/8. December 14th high 84¼. December 17th low 80½. December 18th high 83-3/4. December 20th low 79½. As 79-3/4 was last low March 1, 1916, we cover shorts at 80 and buy 2000 with stop at 79. The account now stands:

	Sold	2000	at	95	closed at	80	profit	$30,000
	Sold	1000	at	90	closed at	80	profit	10,000
	Sold	500	at	90	closed at	80	profit	2,500
								$42,500
	Less Commissions							875
	Net							$ 41,625
	Capital							323,195
	Total							$364,820

with 2000 bought at 80, stop 79. Bought 1000 more at 85 and raised stop to 82. Bought 500 more at 90 and bought 300 more at 95.

1918

January 3, 1918 high 98 and January 5th low 82¼. Raised stop on all trades to 91¼. January 8th high 97¼. January 9th low 93½. Raised stop to 92½. The stop was caught, and we went short 2000 at 92½. Account now stands:

	Bought	2000	at	80	sold	92½	profit	$25,000
	Bought	1000	at	85	sold	92½	profit	7,500
	Bought	500	at	90	sold	92½	profit	1,250
								$33,750

22.

						Brought Forward	$33,750
Bought	300	at	95	sold at	92½	loss	750
							$33,000
	Less Commissions						950
	Net						32,050
	Capital						364,820
	Total						$406,870

with 2000 short at 92½. January 15th low 88½. January 16th high 91¼. Reduced stop to 92¼. We figure last low 79½ on Dec. 20th to high 98 on January 3, 1918, and find 1/2 point – 88-5/8. On January 18th low 88-3/4. We cover shorts at 89 and buy 2000 at 89, with stop 87-5/8. February 1st 19th and 27th highs at 98½ to 98, failing to cross top of January 3rd. We sell out at 98 and go short 2000 at 98, with stop 99.

The decline follows. Sold 1000 more at 93-3/4, because it is one point under February 21st. March low 89½. March 6th high 91-7/8. We reduce stop to 92-7/8. March 25th low 86-1/2. April 1st high 90-5/8. We reduce stop to 91-5/8. The stop was caught and we buy 2000 at 91-5/8. April 2nd and 5th low 89-3/4. We raise stop to 88-3/4. Stop was caught and we sell 2000 short 88-3/4. Last top was 91-5/8 on April 5th. We place stop at 92-5/8. The stop was caught. We buy 2000 at 92-5/8. April 22nd high 96-1/4. April 23rd, 26th, 27th and 30th lows at 93-3/4. We raise stop to 93-3/4. May 5th, we buy 1000 more at 99, because the stock has crossed all tops made early in the year. We raise stop to 96-3/8. We buy 500 more at 104 and raise stop to 101, which was one point under May 9th low.

We buy 200 more at 109. May 16th high 113-3/4. May 14th low 109-3/8. We raise stop to 108-3/8. Stop was caught, and we sell short 2000 at 108-3/8. May 22nd high 110½. We make stop 111½. We sell 1000 more at 105½. June 1st low 96¼. We figure from low of 79½ to high 113-3/4 and find 96-5/8 the 1/2 point. We cover shorts and buy 2000 at 97 with stop 95-5/8. After June 10th, we raise stop to 96½. We buy 1000 more at 104½. June 27th high 110½. Last low June 25th 107¼. so we raise stop to 106¼. The stop was caught, and we sell short 2000 at 106¼. July 15 low 101½. Last top July 12th was 104-3/4. We make stop 105-3/4. Stop was caught, and we buy 2000 at 105-3/4. We buy 1000 more at 110-3/4. August 28th high 116½. Last low 110-3/4 on August 22nd. We make stop 109-3/4. Stop was caught and we sell short 2000 at 109-3/4.

23.

September 13th low 107. September 14th high 109-3/4. We reduce stop to 110-3/4. Stop is caught, and we buy 2000 at 110-3/4 September 27th high 113½. Last low 109-3/4, September 25th. We raise stop to 108-3/4. Stop was caught, and we sell short 2000 at 108-3/4.

We figure from June 1st low 96¼ to August 28th high 116½, which makes 106-3/8 the 1/2 point. We cover shorts at 106½ and buy 2000 at 106½, stop 105-3/8. Stop is caught, and we sell short 2000 at 105-3/8.

October 9th low 104-5/8. Last low, October 8th, 108½. We make stop 109-1/8, which is caught, and we buy 2000 at 109-1/8. October 19th high 114½. We raise stop to 111½. The stop is caught, and we sell 2000 short at 111½, sell 2000 more at 107½, sell 500 more at 102½, and on November 7th, high 104¼ we reduce stop on all trades to 105-1/8. November 29th low 94. High same day 96¼. We reduce stop to 97¼. Stop was caught, and we buy 2000 at 97¼. December 11th high 99-3/4. Last low 95¼ on December 6th. We raise stop to 94¼. Stop is caught, and we sell short 2000 at 94¼.

December 26th low 92½. December 30th high 95¼. We make stop at 96¼. Stop was caught, and we buy 2000 at 96¼. Last low December 31st, 93-3/4. We place stop at 92-3/4. Stop was caught, and we sell short 2,000 at 92-3/4.

1919

January 9, 1919, high 94-3/8. We make stop 95-3/8. January 21st low 88-3/4. January 22nd high 90-5/8. January 25th high 94. January 27th low 90-3/4. We make stop 89-3/4. Stop was caught, and we sell 2000 short at 89-3/4. February 10th low 88¼. February 4th high 91. We make stop 92. Stop was caught, and we buy 2000 at 92.

THE W.D. GANN MASTER STOCK MARKET COURSE

24.

The statement below covers trades from January 10, 1918 to February 10, 1919:

								DEBIT	CREDIT
January 10, 1918									$406,870
Sold	2000	at	92½	closed	at	89			7,000
Bought	2000	"	89	"	"	98			18,000
Sold	2000	"	98	"	"	91-5/8			12,760
Sold	1000	"	93-3/4	"	"	91-5/8			2,120
Bought	2000	"	91-5/8	"	"	88-3/4		$5,760	
Sold	2000	"	88-3/4	"	"	92-5/8		7,760	
Bought	2000	"	92-5/8	"	"	108-3/8			31,500
Bought	1000	"	99	"	"	108-3/8			9,380
Bought	500	"	104	"	"	108-3/8			2,190
Bought	200	"	109	"	"	108-3/8		124	
Sold	2000	"	108-3/8	"	"	97			22,760
Sold	1000	"	105½	"	"	97			8,500
Bought	2000	"	97	"	"	106¼			18,500
Bought	1000	"	104½	"	"	106¼			1,750
Sold	2000	"	106¼	"	"	105-3/4			1,000
Bought	2000	"	105-3/4	"	"	109-3/4			8,000
Bought	1000	"	110-3/4	"	"	109-3/4		1,000	
Sold	2000	"	109-3/4	"	"	110-3/4		2,000	
Bought	2000	"	110-3/4	"	"	108-3/4		4,000	
Sold	2000	"	108-3/4	"	"	106-1/2			4,500
Bought	2000	"	106-1/2	"	"	105-3/8		2,240	
Sold	2000	"	105-3/8	"	"	109-1/8		7,500	
Bought	2000	"	109-1/8	"	"	111-1/2			4,740
Sold	2000	"	111-1/2	"	"	97¼			28,500
Sold	1000	"	107-1/2	"	"	97¼			10,250
Sold	500	"	102-1/2	"	"	97¼			2,625
Bought	2000	"	97¼	"	"	94¼		6,000	
Sold	2000	"	94¼	"	"	96¼		4,000	
Bought	2000	"	96¼	"	"	92¾		7,000	
Sold	2000	"	92-3/4	"	"	91-5/8			2,240
Bought	2000	"	91-5/8	"	"	89-3/4		3,760	
Sold	2000	"	89-3/4	"	"	92		4,500	
								$55,644	$603,185
						Commissions		13,050	68,694
						Net Profit			$534,491

25.

Bought 2000 at 92 - February 10, 1919. February 27th high 95-3/4. Low on February 25th 93½. We raise stop to 92½. Stop was caught. We sell short 2000 at 92½. Math 5th low 91-5/8; same low as March 1st. Last high March 3rd at 94-5/8. We make stop 95-5/8. The stop was caught. We buy 2000 at 95-5/8. March 11th low 95½. We make stop 94½. The stop was caught. We sell short 2000 at 94½. March 19th low 94¼, stop 98. Stop was caught and we buy 2000 at 98.

The market makes a series of narrow moves, and on April 23rd makes high at 103. April 25th low 99¾. We make stop 99¾. Stop was caught, and we sell short 2000 at 98¾. May 1st low 96½. May 3rd high 99¾. We make stop 100¾. Stop was caught, and we buy 2000 at 100¾. Buy 1000 at 104.

June 6th high 111¾. June 11th low 106¾. We raise stop to 105¾. The stop was caught, and we sell short 2000 at 105¾. June 16th low 103¼. We figure last low May 1st 96½ to June 6th at 111¾, making 1/2 point 104-1/8. We cover shorts at 104¼ and buy 2000 at 104¼, stop 103-1/8, and buy 1000 more at 109¼.

July 7th high 115-1/8. July 11th low 111-5/8. We raise stop to 110-5/8. Stop was caught. We go short 2000 at 110-5/8. July 24th high 113-3/8. We make stop 114-3/8. We sell 1000 more at 105, because it is one point under 1/2 point from 96½ to 115½.

August 21st low 98½. August 25th high 101-5/8. We reduce stops to 102-5/8. Stops are caught, and we buy 2000 at 102-5/8 with stop 99½.

September 4th high 107½. September 5th low 103¼. We place stop 102¼. Stop was caught and we sell short 2000 at 103¼. September 20th low 100½. We make stop 103½. Stop was caught. We buy 2000 at 103½.

October 10th high 112½. October 23rd low 108. We make stop 107. Stop was caught. We sell short 2000 at 107 and place stop at 110. Stop was caught. We buy 2000 at 110. November 5th high 112½, same high at October 10th. We sell out at 112 and go short 2000 at 112 with stop at 113½. We sell 1000 more at 107. December 1st low 101. December 3rd high 103¼. We make stop 104¼. Stop was caught. We buy 2000 at 104¼, with stop at 100. December 12th low 100½.

1920

January 5, 1920 high 109. January 8th low 105¾. We make stop 104¾. Stop was caught, and we sell short 2000 at 104¾. January 19th low 104½. January 20th high 106. We make stop 107. Stop was caught. We buy 2000 at 107 with stop 104. Stop was caught. We sell 2000 at 100. Sell 1000 more at 99. February 27th low 92½. We reduced stop to 95½. Stop was caught, and we buy 2000 at 95½.

26.

March 20th low 102¼. We raise stop to 101¼. Stop was caught. We go short 2000 at 101¼. March 25th low 101¼. We make stop 103¼. Stop was caught. We buy 2000 at 103¼. April 7th high 107½. April 12th low 104. Make stop 103. Stop caught. We sell 2000 at 103. Sell 1000 more at 99.

May 24th low 89½. Last high June 22nd at 92½. We make stop 93½. Stop caught. We buy 2000 at 93½. June 14th low 92¾. Raise stop to 91¾. Stop caught. We sell 2000 at 91¾. June 23rd low 91½. June 26th high 93. We make stop 94. Stop caught. We buy 2000 at 94. July 8th high 95½. We make stop 92½. Stop caught. We sell 2000 at 92½ and sell 1000 at 87½.

August 95th low 84. August 75th low 96½. We make stop 87. Stop caught. We buy 2000 at 87. September 8th high 91½. August 23rd low 88-1/8. We make stop 87¼. Stop caught. We sell 2000 at 87¼. The decline follows and we sell 1000 more at 85¼.

December 21st low 76¼. December 24th high 97-7/8. We make stop 80-7/8. The stop caught. We buy 2000 at 80-7/8. February 16th high 85. February 21st low 82-3/4. We make stop 81¾. Stop caught. We sell 2000 at 81¾. March 12th low 77¾. We make stop 80¾. The stop was caught. We buy 2000 at 80¾.

The statement below covers trades from February 10, 1919 to March 15, 1921:

							DEBIT	CREDIT
February 10, 1919								$534,491
Bought	2000	at	92	closed	at	92½		1,000
Sold	2000	"	92½	"	"	95-5/8	$ 250	
Bought	2000	"	95-5/8	"	"	94-1/2	2,250	
Sold	2000	"	94-1/2	"	"	98	7,000	
Bought	2000	"	98	"	"	98¾		1,500
Sold	2000	"	98¾	"	"	100¾	4,000	
Bought	2000	"	100¾	"	"	105¾		10,000
Bought	1000	"	104	"	"	105¾		1,750
Sold	2000	"	105¾	"	"	104¼		3,000
Bought	2000	"	104-1/8	"	"	110-5/8		13,000
Bought	1000	"	109	"	"	110-5/8		1,625
Sold	2000	"	110-5/8	"	"	102-5/8		16,000
Sold	1000	"	105	"	"	102-5/8		2,375
Bought	2000	"	102-5/8	"	"	102-1/4	750	
Sold	2000	"	103¼	"	"	103-1/2	500	
Bought	2000	"	103½	"	"	107		7,000
Sold	2000	"	107	"	"	110	7,000	
Bought	2000	"	110	"	"	112		4,000
Sold	2000	"	112	"	"	104¼		1,550
Sold	1000	"	107	"	"	104¼		2,750
Bought	2000	"	104¼	"	"	104¾		1,000
Sold	2000	"	104¾	"	"	107	4,500	
Bought	2000	"	107	"	"	104	6,000	
Sold	2000	"	104	"	"	95½		17,000

(Continued on next page)

27.

							DEBIT	CREDIT
Sold	1000	at	99	closed	at	95½		3,500
Bought	2000	"	95½	"	"	101½		11,500
Sold	2000	"	101¼	"	"	103¼	4,000	
Bought	2000	"	103¼	"	"	103	500	
Sold	2000	"	103	"	"	95½		15,000
Sold	1000	"	99	"	"	95½		3,500
Bought	2000	"	95½	"	"	91½	7,500	
Sold	2000	"	91¾	"	"	94	4,500	
Bought	2000	"	94	"	"	92½	3,000	
Sold	2000	"	92½	"	"	87		11,000
Sold	1000	"	87¼	"	"	87		500
Bought	2000	"	87	"	"	87¼		500
Sold	2000	"	87¼	"	"	80-7/8		12,750
Sold	1000	"	85½	"	"	80-7/8		5,625
Bought	2000	"	80-7/8	"	"	81-3/4		1,750
Sold	2000	"	81-3/4	"	"	80-3/4		2,000
							$51,750	$685,666
						Commissions	18,000	69,750
						Net Profit		$615,916

March 15, 1921, bought 2000 at 80-3/4. March 22nd low 80¾. We make stop 79¾. April 14th stop caught. We sell short 2000 at 79-3/4, stop 82-3/4. Stop caught. We buy 2000 at 82-3/4. May 6th high 86-1/2. We make stop 83-1/2. Stop caught. We go short 2000 at 83-1/2. Decline continues. We sell 1000 at 78-1/2. June 23rd low 70-1/2. We reduce stop to 73-1/2. Stop was caught and we buy 2000 at 73-1/2. June 30th low 73-5/8. We make stop 72-5/8. Stop caught. We go short 2000 at 72-5/8. July 16th low 71-1/2. July 20th high 73-1/2. We make stop 74-1/2. Stop caught. We buy 2000 at 74-1/2.

September 19th, 26th and 30th high 80½. We sell out at 80 and go short 2000 at 80, stop 81½. October 17th low 77¼, October 20th, high 78-5/8 We make stop 79-5/8. Stop is caught, and we buy 2000 at 79-5/8. December 15th low 83-3/4. We raise stop to 82-3/4. Stop is caught, and we go short 2000 at 82-3/4.

1922

January 6th low 82. January 9th high 83½. We make stop 84½. Stop caught. We buy 2000 at 84½ and buy 1000 at 89½. Buy 500 at 94½. Buy 300 at 99½.

April 20th high 100¼. April 18th last low 97. We raise stop to 96. June 6th high 103½, low 102-5/8 on June 5th. We raise stop to 101-5/8. Stop caught. We sell short 2000 at 101-5/8.

The statement below covers trades from March 15, 1921 to June 1922:

							DEBIT	CREDIT
March 15, 1921								$615,916
Bought	2000	at	80¾	closed	at	79¾	$2,000	
Sold	2000	"	79¾	"	"	82¾	6,000	
Bought	2000	"	82¾	"	"	83¾		1,500
Sold	2000	"	83½	"	"	73½		20,000
Bought	2000	"	73½	"	"	72-5/8	1,750	
Sold	2000	"	72-5/8	"	"	74	3,750	
Bought	2000	"	74-1/2	"	"	80		11,000
Sold	2000	"	80	"	"	79-5/8		750
Bought	2000	"	79-5/8	"	"	82-3/4		6,250
Sold	2000	"	82-3/4	"	"	84-1/2	3,500	
Bought	2000	"	84-1/2	"	"	101-5/8		24,250
Bought	1000	"	89-1/2	"	"	101-5/8		12,125
Bought	500	"	94-1/2	"	"	101-5/8		3,562.50
Bought	300	"	99-1/2	"	"	101-5/8		637.50
							$17,000	$695,991.00
						Commissions	5,950	22,950.00
						Net Profit		$673,041.00

June, 1922 sold short 2000 at 101-5/8. June 12th and 16th low 96¾. We make stop 99¾. Stop caught. We buy 2000 at 99¾. Buy 1000 more at 104. September 11th high 106½. September 14th low 104½. We make stop 103½. Stop caught. We go short 2000 at 103½. September 27th and 29th low 100¾. September high 102½. We make stop 103½. Stop caught. We buy 2000 at 103½. Buy 1000 at 107. October 16th high 111½. We make stop 108½. Stop caught. We go short 2000 at 108½. November 1st low 103¼. Make stop 106¼. Stop caught. We buy 2000 at 106¼.

November 9th high 110¾. Make stop 107¾. Stop caught. We sell 2000 at 107¾. November 28th low 99¾. December 2nd high 103½. We make stop 104½ and buy 2000 at 104½. December 26th low 106¼. Make stop 105¼. Stop caught. We go short 2000 at 105¼.

1923

January 31st low 104. Make stop 107. Stop caught. We buy 2000 at 107. March 21st high 109½. March 17th low 107½. We make stop 106½. Stop caught. We go short 2000 at 106½.

29.

The statement below covers trades from June, 1922 to March, 1923:

							DEBIT	CREDIT
June, 1922								$673,041
Sold	2000	at	101-5/8	closed	at	99-3/4		3,750
Bought	2000	"	99-3/4	"	"	103½		7,500
Bought	1000	"	104	"	"	103½	$500	
Sold	2000	"	103½	"	"	103½	--	--
Bought	2000	"	103½	"	"	108½		10,000
Bought	1000	"	107	"	"	108½		1,500
Sold	2000	"	108½	"	"	106¼		4,500
Bought	2000	"	108¼	"	"	107¾		3,000
Sold	2000	"	107¾	"	"	104½		6,500
Bought	2000	"	104½	"	"	105¼		1,500
Sold	2000	"	105¼	"	"	107	3,500	
Bought	2000	"	107	"	"	106½	1,000	
							$5,000	$711,291
					Commissions		5,500	10,500
					Total Profit			$700,791

Sold	2000	at	106½
Sell	1000	"	103
Sell	500	"	98
Sell	300	"	93

June 30th, July 5th, 11th and 17th made lows at 89½ to 89¼, and on July 14th high 91½. We make stop on all trades at 92½. Stop caught and we buy 2000 at 92½. July 23rd high 92¾. July 21st low 91½. We make stop 90½. Stop caught. We sell short 2000 at 90½. July 31st low 85-3/8. August 2nd high 88½. We make stop 89½. Stop caught. We buy 2000 at 89½. August 30th high 94. August 8th low 92. Make stop 91. Stop caught. We go short 2000 at 91. September 25th low 85-5/8, same low as July 31st. We cover shorts at 86½ and buy 2000 at 86½, with stop 84½. We buy 1000 at 90. November 9th low 94. We make stop 93. Stop caught. We sell 2000 at 93. November 17th low 91-7/8. We make stop 94-7/8 and buy 2000 at 94-7/8. Buy 1000 at 98 and 500 at 103.

1924

February 7th high 109. February 8th low 106½. We make stop 105½. Stop caught. We go short 2000 at 106½. Sell 1000 at 101½. March 29th low 97. We figure low of 85-3/8 to high 109 and find 1/2 point 97. We cover shorts at 97½ and buy 2000 at 97½, stop 96. Stop is caught and we go short 2000 at 96.

THE W.D. GANN MASTER STOCK MARKET COURSE

30.

The statement below covers trades from March, 1923 to April, 1924:

							DEBIT	CREDIT
March, 1923								$700,791
Sold	2000	at	106½	closed	at	92½		28,000
Sold	1000	"	103	"	"	92½		10,500
Sold	500	"	98	"	"	92½		2,750
Sold	300	"	93	"	"	92½		150
Bought	2000	"	92½	"	"	91½	$2,000	
Sold	2000	"	90½	"	"	89½		2,000
Bought	2000	"	89½	"	"	91	3,000	
Sold	2000	"	91	"	"	86½		9,000
Bought	2000	"	86½	"	"	93		13,000
Bought	1000	"	90	"	"	93		3,000
Sold	2000	"	93	"	"	94-7/8	3,750	
Bought	2000	"	94-7/8	"	"	105-1/2		21,250
Bought	1000	"	98	"	"	105-1/2		7,500
Bought	500	"	103	"	"	105-1/2		1,250
Sold	2000	"	106-1/2	"	"	97-1/2		18,000
Sold	1000	"	101-1/2	"	"	97-1/2		4,000
Bought	2000	"	97-1/2	"	"	96	3,000	
							$11,750	$821,191
				Commissions			6,325	18,075
				Net Profit				$803,116

Sold 2000 at 96. April 10th, 15th and 22nd low 95½. We make stop 98½, Stop caught. We buy 2000 at 98½. April 26th high 101. We raise stop to 98. Stop caught. We go short 2000 at 98. June 6th low 94-1/8. We make stop 97-1/8. Stop caught. We buy 2000 at 97-1/8, buy 1000 at 102 and 500 at 107. August 20th high 111¾. We raise stop to 108¾. Stop caught. We go short 2000 at 108¾. September 8th low 105¼. We make stop 108¼. Stop caught. We buy 2000 at 108¼. September 25th low 108¼. We raise stop to 107¼. Stop caught. We go short 2000 at 107¼. October 14th low 104¾. October 18th high 107¼. We make stop 108¼. Stop caught. We buy 2000 at 108-1/8. Buy 1000 at 112. November 26th high 119¼. December 2nd low 116. We raise stop to 115 and buy 500 at 117. Buy 300 at 122.

1925

January 23rd high 129½. January 28th low 125¾. We make stop 124¾. Stop caught and we go short 2000 at 124¾. February 19th low 122. We sell 1000 at 121 and 500 at 116. March 30th low 112¼. April 8th high 115½. We make stop 116¼. Stop caught.

The statement below covers trades from April, 1924 to April, 1925:

								DEBIT	CREDIT
April, 1924									$803,116
Sold	2000	at	96	closed	at	98½		$5,000	
Bought	2000	"	98½	"	"	98		1,000	
Sold	2000	"	98	"	"	98-1/8			1,750
Bought	2000	"	98-1/8	"	"	108¾			23,250
Bought	1000	"	102	"	"	108¾			6,750
Bought	500	"	107	"	"	108¾			875
Sold	2000	"	108¾	"	"	108¼			1,000
Bought	2000	"	108¼	"	"	108¼		2,000	
Sold	2000	"	107¼	"	"	108¼		2,000	
Bought	2000	"	108-1/8	"	"	124¾			33,250
Bought	1000	"	112	"	"	124¾			12,750
Bought	500	"	117	"	"	124¾			3,875
Bought	300	"	122	"	"	124¾			825
Sold	2000	"	124¾	"	"	116¼			17,000
Sold	1000	"	121	"	"	116¼			4,750
Sold	500	"	116	"	"	116¼		125	
								$10,125	$909,191
						Commissions		5,700	15,825
						Net Profit			$893,366

We buy 2000 at 116¼. April 18th high 118¼. Raise stop to 115¼. Stop caught. We go short 2000 at 115¼. April 30th low 112¾. We make stop 115¾. Stop caught. We buy 2000 at 115¾. April 21st high 120¼. Raise stop to 117¼. Stop caught. We go short 2000 at 117¼. June 5th low 113½. June 8th high 114½. We make stop 115½. Stop caught. We buy 2000 at 115½. June 15th high 117¼. June 18th low 115¾. Make stop 114¾. Stop caught. We go short 2000 at 115¾. June 29th low 113¼. Make stop 116¼. Stop caught. We buy 2000 at 116¼ and 1000 at 121. August 26th high 125-7/8. We raise stop to 122-7/8. Stop caught. We go short 2000 at 112-7/8. September 3rd low 118¼. Make stop 121¼. Stop caught. We buy 2000 at 121¼. September 15th high 125-7/8. Make stop 122-5/8. Stop caught. We go short 2000 at 122-5/8. September 28th low 118½. We figure from low 112¼ March 30th to high 125-7/8 August 26th and find 1/2 point 119, so we cover shorts and

Buy	2000	at	119¼	with stop 118
Buy	1000	"	124¼	
Buy	500	"	127	
Buy	300	"	132	
Buy	200	"	137	

32.

November 7th high 139-3/8. We raise stop to 136-3/8. Stop caught. We go short 2000 at 136-3/8. Sold 1000 more at 131-3/8. November 10th low 128. Make stop 131. Stop caught. We buy 2000 at 131. November 14th high 138½. We make stop 135½. Stop caught. We go short 2000 at 135-1/2. November 24th low 126-5/8. We make stop 129-5/8. Stop caught. We buy 2000 at 129-5/8. December 8th high 137¼. Make stop 134¼. Stop caught. We go short 2000 at 134¼. December 22nd low 131¾. Make stop 134¾. Stop caught. We buy 2000 at 134¾.

1926

January 4th high 138½. We make stop 135½. Stop caught. We go short 2000 at 135½. Later sell 1000 at 131 and 500 at 127. March 2nd low 120. Make stop 123. Stop caught.

The statement below covers trades from April, 1925 to March 5, 1926:

							DEBIT	CREDIT
Balance brought forward April, 1925								$893,366
Bought	2000	at	116¼	closed	at	115¼	$2,000	
Sold	2000	"	115¼	"	"	115¾	1,000	
Bought	2000	"	115¾	"	"	117¼		3,000
Sold	2000	"	117¼	"	"	115½		3,500
Bought	2000	"	115½	"	"	114¾	1,500	
Sold	2000	"	115¾	"	"	116¼	1,000	
Bought	2000	"	116¼	"	"	122-7/8		13,250
Sold	2000	"	122-7/8	"	"	121¼		3,250
Bought	2000	"	121¼	"	"	122-5/8		2,750
Sold	2000	"	122-5/8	"	"	119		7,250
Bought	2000	"	119¼	"	"	136-3/8		34,250
Bought	1000	"	124¼	"	"	136-3/8		12,125
Bought	500	"	127	"	"	136-3/8		4,687.50
Bought	300	"	132	"	"	136-3/8		1,311.50
Bought	200	"	137	"	"	136-3/8	125	
Sold	2000	"	136-3/8	"	"	131		10,750
Bought	2000	"	131	"	"	135½		9,000
Sold	2000	"	135½	"	"	129-5/8		11,750
Bought	2000	"	129-5/8	"	"	134¼		9,250
Sold	1000	"	134¼	"	"	134¾	500	
Bought	2000	"	134¾	"	"	135½		1,500
Sold	2000	"	135½	"	"	123		25,000
Sold	1000	"	131	"	"	123		8,000
Sold	500	"	126	"	"	123		2,000.00
							$6,125	$1,055,990.00
				Commissions			9,625	15,750.00
				Net Profit				$1,040,240.00

THE W.D. GANN MASTER STOCK MARKET COURSE

33.

We bought 2000 at 123. March 16th high 128-1/8. We make stop 125-1/8. The stop was caught. We go short 2000 at 125-1/8. March 30th low 117-5/8. Make stop 120-5/8. Stop caught. We buy 2000 at 120-5/8. April 6th high 123½. Make stop 120½. Stop caught. We go short 2000 at 120½. April 15th low 117. Make stop 120. Stop caught. We buy 2000 at 120. April 29th high 124-5/8. We make stop 121-5/8. Stop caught. We go short 2000 at 121-5/8. May 17th low 118-1/8. Make stop 121-1/8. Stop caught. We buy 2000 at 121-1/8. Later we buy 1000 at 126-1/8 and buy 500 at 131 and buy 300 at 136 and 200 at 141. July 11th high 144-7/8. Make stop on all trades 141-7/8. Stop caught and we sell short 2000 at 141-7/8. July 24th low 137¼. July 23 high 140½. Later we buy 1000 at 145½. Stop caught. We buy 2000 at 141½. Later we buy 1000 at 145½, and 500 at 150. August 9th high 155¼. We raise stop to 152¼. Stop caught, and we go short 2000 at 152¼. August 12th low 147½. We make stop 150½. Stop caught, and we buy 2000 at 150½. Later we buy 1000 at 155. August 17th high 159½. We raise stop to 156½. Stop caught. We go short 2000 at 156½. August 20th low 148½. We make stop 151½. Stop caught. We buy 200 at 151½.

August 24th high 153. We make stop 150. Stop caught. We go short 2000 at 150. August 25th low 147-5/8. We make stop 150-5/8. Stop caught. We buy 2000 at 150-5/8. September 8th high 152¾. We make stop 149¾. Stop caught. We go short 2000 at 149¾. September 20th low 142¼. We make stop 145¼. Stop caught and we buy 2000 at 145¼. Later we buy 1000 at 150.

October 2nd high 154¾. Raise stop to 151¾. Stop caught. We go short 2000 at 151¾. We sell 1000 at 147 and sell 500 at 142 and 300 at 140. October 20th low 133¾. We make stop 136¾. Stop caught. We buy 2000 at 136¾, and later buy 1000 at 141¾ and buy 500 at 146¾. November 16th high 153½. We make stop 150½. Stop caught. We go short 2000 at 150½.

November 19th low 143½. We make stop 146½. Stop caught. We buy 2000 at 146½ and later buy 1000 at 151½ and 500 at 156½. December 17th and 27th high 160½. We sell out at 160 and go short 2000 at 160, because 159½ was high on August 17th. We place a stop at 162½.

1927

January 4th and 7th low 154. January 5th high 156½. We make stop 157½. Stop caught. We buy 2000 at 157½. January 13th high 159¼. We arise stop to 156¼. Stop caught. We sell 2000 short at 156¼. January 27th low 153½. We make stop 156½. Stop caught. We buy 2000 at 156½. February 24th high 162½. We make stop 159½. Stop caught. We go short 2000 at 159½. March 5th and 8th low 156½. March 7th high 157¾. We make stop 158¾. Stop caught.

THE W.D. GANN MASTER STOCK MARKET COURSE

34.

The statement below covers trades from March 5, 1926 to March 10, 1927:

							DEBIT	CREDIT
Balance brought forward March 5, 1926								$1,040,240.00
Bought	2000	at	123	closed	at	125-1/8		4,250.00
Sold	2000	"	125-1/8	"	"	120-5/8		11,000.00
Bought	1000	"	120-5/8	"	"	120-1/2	$125	
Sold	2000	"	120½	"	"	120		1,000.00
Bought	2000	"	120	"	"	121-5/8		3,250.00
Sold	2000	"	121-5/8	"	"	121-1/8		1,000.00
Bought	2000	"	121-1/8	"	"	141-7/8		41,500.00
Bought	1000	"	126-1/8	"	"	141-7/8		15,750.00
Bought	500	"	131	"	"	141-7/8		5,437.50
Bought	300	"	136	"	"	141-7/8		1,762.50
Bought	200	"	141	"	"	141-7/8		175.00
Sold	2000	"	141-7/8	"	"	141-1/2		750.00
Bought	2000	"	141-1/2	"	"	152-1/4		21,500.00
Bought	1000	"	145-1/2	"	"	152-1/4		6,750.00
Bought	500	"	150	"	"	152-1/4		1,125.00
Sold	2000	"	152-1/4	"	"	150-1/2		3,500.00
Bought	2000	"	150-1/2	"	"	150	1,000	
Sold	2000	"	150	"	"	150-5/8	1,250	
Bought	2000	"	150-5/8	"	"	149-3/4	1,750	
Sold	2000	"	149-3/4	"	"	145-1/4		9,000.00
Bought	2000	"	145-1/4	"	"	151-3/4		13,000.00
Bought	1000	"	150	"	"	151-3/4		1,750.00
Sold	2000	"	151-3/4	"	"	136-3/4		30,000.00
Sold	1000	"	147	"	"	136-3/4		10,250.00
Sold	500	"	142	"	"	136-3/4		2,625.00
Sold	300	"	140	"	"	136-3/4		975.00
Bought	2000	"	136-3/4	"	"	150-1/2		27,500.00
Bought	1000	"	141-3/4	"	"	150-1/2		8,750.00
Bought	500	"	146-3/4	"	"	150-1/2		3,875.00
Sold	2000	"	150-1/2	"	"	146-1/2		8,000.00
Bought	2000	"	146-1/2	"	"	160		27,000.00
Bought	1000	"	151-1/2	"	"	160		8,500.00
Bought	500	"	156-1/2	"	"	160		2,250.00
Sold	2000	"	160	"	"	157-1/2		5,000.00
Bought	2000	"	157-1/2	"	"	156-1/4	2,500	
Sold	2000	"	156-1/4	"	"	156-1/2	500	
Bought	2000	"	156-1/2	"	"	159-1/2		6,000.00
Sold	2000	"	159-1/2	"	"	158-3/4		1,500.00
							$7,125	$1,324,965.00
						Commissions	14,075	21,200.00
						Net Profits		$1,303,765.00

35.

We buy 2000 at 158-3/4. Later we buy 1000 at 163 and 500 at 168. April 11th and 16th, high 172-3/4. We make stop 169-3/4. Stop caught. We go short 2000 at 169-3/4. May 2nd low 164½. We make stop 167-1/2. Stop caught. We discontinue trading in the old stock.

May 9th, we buy 2000 of new stock at 121½. June 1st high 125¾. June 4th low 123. We make stop 122. The stop was caught. We go short 2000 at 122. June 30th low 118-7/8. June 25th last high 121½. We make stop 122½. The stop was caught and we buy 2000 at 122½. Later we buy 1000 at 127 and 500 at 132. August 2nd high 138-3/8. August 1st low 134-5/8. We raise stop to 133-5/8. Stop was caught, and we sell 2000 short at 133-5/8. August 12th low 129¼. We make stop 132¼. Stop was caught and we buy 2000 at 132¼ and later buy 1000 at 136, 500 at 141, 300 at 145, 2000 at 150 and 100 at 155.

September 16th high 160½. We make stop on all trades 157½. The stop was caught, and we go short 2000 at 157½. Later sell 1000 at 152½ and 500 at 147½. September 29th low 145½. We make stop 148½. Stop caught. We buy 2000 at 148½. October 4th high 154-5/8. We make stop 151-5/8. Stop was caught and we go short 2000 at 151-5/8 and later sell 1000 at 146-5/8, sell 500 at 141-5/8, 300 at 136-5/8 and 200 at 131-5/8. October 29th low 128-5/8. We make stops on all trades 131-5/8. Stops caught.

We buy 2000 at 131-5/8 and later we buy 1000 at 136-5/8 and 500 at 141-5/8. November 29th high 147-5/8. Same day low 144-5/8. We make stop 143-5/8. Stop was caught, and we go short 2000 at 143-5/8. December 9th low 138. We make stop 141. Stop caught. We buy 2000 at 141 and later buy 1000 at 145 and 500 at 150. December 24th high 155. We make stop 152. Stop was caught, and we sell short 2000 at 152 and later sell 500 at 147 and 300 at 142. On March 2, 1928 low 137½, just 1/2 point under low of December 9th. We could have covered shorts at 138 and bought with stop at 137, which would not have been caught, but we reduce stop to 140½, because the last three tops were at 140¼. The stop was caught.

The following statement covers trades from March 10, 1927 to March, 1928:

							DEBIT	CREDIT
Balance brought forward March 10, 1927								$1,313,765
Bought	2000	at	158¾	closed	at	169¾		22,000
Bought	1000	"	163	"	"	169¾		6,750
Bought	500	"	168	"	"	169¾		875
Sold	2000	"	169¾	"	"	167½		4,500
		NEW STOCK						
Bought	2000	at	121½	closed	at	122		1,000
Sold	2000	"	122	"	"	122½	$1,000	
Bought	2000	"	122½	"	"	133-5/8		22,250
Bought	1000	"	127	"	"	133-5/8		6,625
Bought	500	"	132	"	"	133-5/8		812.50
Sold	2000	"	133-5/8	"	"	132½		2,750
Bought	2000	"	132¼	"	"	157½		50,500

Bought	1000	at	136	closed	at	157½		21,500
Bought	500	"	131	"	"	157½		13,250
Bought	300	"	145	"	"	157½		3,750
Bought	200	"	150	"	"	157½		1,500
Bought	100	"	155	"	"	157½		250
Sold	2000	"	157½	"	"	148½		18,000
Sold	1000	"	152½	"	"	148½		4,000
Sold	500	"	147½	"	"	148½	500	
Bought	2000	"	148½	"	"	151-5/8		6,250
Sold	2000	"	151-5/8	"	"	131-5/8		40,000
Sold	1000	"	146-5/8	"	"	131-5/8		15,000
Sold	500	"	141-5/8	"	"	131-5/8		5,000
Sold	300	"	136-5/8	"	"	131-5/8		1,500
Sold	200	"	131-5/8	"	"	131-5/8	--	--
Bought	2000	"	131-5/8	"	"	143-5/8	--	24,000
Bought	1000	"	136-5/8	"	"	143-5/8		7,000
Bought	500	"	141-5/8	"	"	143-5/8		1,000
Sold	2000	"	143-5/8	"	"	141		5,250
Bought	2000	"	141	"	"	152		22,000
Bought	1000	"	145	"	"	152		7,000
Bought	500	"	150	"	"	152		1,000
Sold	2000	"	152	"	"	140½		23,000
Sold	500	"	147	"	"	140½		3,250
Sold	300	"	142	"	"	140½		450.00
							$1,500	$1,645,777.50
					Commissions		10,100	11,600.00
					Net Credit			$1,634,177.50

1928

We buy 2000 at 140½ and later buy 1000 at 144½ and 500 at 149½. March 22nd and 26th high 152. We raise stop to 149. Stop caught, and we sell short 2000 at 149, April 2nd and 11th low 145, same low as March 14th and 20th. We reduce stop to 148, although could have covered against double bottom. Stop caught. We buy 2000 at 148. April 12th high 154. We raise stop to 151, Stop was caught, and we sell short 2000 at 151. April 24th low 143¾. April 27th high 147. We make stop 148. Stop caught. We buy 2000 at 148. May 11th high 150¾. We make stop at 147¾. The stop was caught, and we go short 2000 at 147¾, and later sell 1000 at 142¾ and 500 at 137¾, June 11th low 132-5/8. Last low June 21st at 136¼. We make stop 137¼. Stop was caught, and we buy 2000 at 137¼. July 9th high 142. We make stop 139. Stop caught, and we go short 2000 at 139. July 17th low 134. We make stop 137. The stop was caught.

We buy 2000 at 137 and later buy 1000 at 142, 500 at 147 and 300 at 152. September 17th high 160-3/8. We make stop 157-3/8. Stop was caught, and we sell short 2000 at 157-3/8. September 21st low 155. We make stop 158. The stop was caught, and we buy 2000 at 158. Later buy 1000 at 162. October 15th high 166. We make stop 163. Stop caught. We go short 2000 at 163. October 26th low 159-1/8. We make stop 162-1/8. Stop was caught, and we buy 2000 at 162-1/8 and later buy 1000 at 167. November 16th high 172½ and we make stop 169½. Stop was caught and we go short 2000 at 169½. Later sell 1000 at 164½, 500 at 159½ and 300 at 154½. December 17th low 149¾ and December 8th low was 150¼. Also note August 23rd and 28th lows were 149¼ and 150½. These bottoms give us an indication to cover shorts around 150 and buy; besides from the last low of 132-3/8 on June 25th to the high 172½ on November 16th made 1/2 point at 152½ and 3 point stop was never caught. After low of 149¾ on December 17th, we made stop 152¾. Stop was caught, and we buy 2000 at 152¾. Later buy 1000 at 157¾, 500 at 162¾, 300 at 167¾, 200 at 172¾ and 100 at 177¾.

1929

On January 22, 1929, high 190¼. We make stop 187¼. Stop caught. We go short 2000 at 187¼. January 24th low 183½. We make stop 187½. Stop caught. We buy 2000 at 187½. January 25th high 192¾. We make stop 189¾. Stop was caught, and we sell 2000 at 189¾. January 30th low 179½. We make stop 182½. Stop was caught. We buy 2000 at 182½. February 2nd high 188. Make stop 185. Stop caught. We go short 2000 at 185, and later sell 1000 at 180. February 8th low 171-1/8. Make stop 174-1/8. Stop caught. We buy 2000 at 174-1/8. February 13th high 180. We make stop 177. Stop caught. We sell 2000 at 177 and later sell 1000 at 172. February 16th low 168¼. We make stop 171¼. Stop was caught, and we buy 2000 at 171¼. Later we buy 1000 at 176¼, 500 at 181¼, 300 at 186¼ and 300 at 190¼. March 1st high 193¾. We make stop at 190¾. Stop caught.

We go short 2000 at 190¾ and sell 1000 at 185¾. March 6th low 180½. We make stop 183½. Stop was caught and we buy 2000 at 183½. March 8th high 187¼. We make stop 184¼. Stop was caught, and we go short 2000 at 184¼. March 11th low 180½. same low as March 6th. We make stop 183½. Stop was caught and we buy 2000 at 184¼. March 28th high 183¾. Make stop 180¾. Stop caught.

We go short 2000 at 180¾. April 1st low 176¼. We make stop 179¼. Stop caught. We buy 2,000 at 179¼ and later buy 1000 at 184¼. April 5th high 189. We make stop 186. Stop caught. We go short 2000 at 186. April 9th and 17th low 183¾. Make stop 186¾. Stop caught. We buy 2000 at 186¾. April 30th high 190½. We make stop 187½. Stop caught. We go short 2000 at 187½. Later sell 1000 at 182½, 500 at 177½, 300 at 172½ and 200 at 167½. May 31st low 162½. We make stop 165½. Stop was caught, and we buy 2000 at 165½. Later buy 1000 at 170½, 500 at 175½, 300 at 180½, 200 at 185½, 100 at 190½.

In the early part of July, the stock crosses 194, the highest in history, and not having broken an overnight bottom since the low of 162½ shows strong up trend. As we have 30 points' profit in the first purchase at 165½, we start a new pyramid and buy 2000 more at 195½. Buy 1000 at 200½. July 11th low 197½. We raise stop on all purchases to 196½. The

38.

advance continues, and we buy 1000 more at 105½. July 20th and 24th high 209¾ and 210. July 22nd, 24th and 29th made lows at 204½. We raise stops on all trades to 203½. Stops were not caught. We buy 500 more at 210½, 300 at 215½, 200 at 220½, and 100 at 225½. August 9th, the last low was 213½. We raise stops on all trades to 212½. The advance continues with no change in trend on the Overnight Chart. August 14th high 245. August 15th low 235-5/8. We raise stop on all trades to 234-5/8. August 19th low 237-5/8. We raise all stops to 236-5/8.

The rule to follow when you have big profits on a double pyramid is, do no guessing; wait until the Overnight Chart closes your trades by catching a stop one point under a previous low or follow up with a stop 10 points under each day's high level. This rule is to be applied only in active fast markets. For example, from August 14th high to August 15th low there was decline of 9-3/8 points. Therefore, 10 points from the next extreme high level would indicate that the trend was getting ready to turn down.

August 24th high 260½. August 29th low 251½, just 9 points' decline, and would not catch a 10 point stop. We raise all stops to 250½. September 3rd high 261¾, and a stop 10 points down would be 251¾. We sell out all long stock at 251¾.

The following statement covers all trades from March, 1928 to Sept. 5, 1929:

							DEBIT	CREDIT
March, 1928 balance brought forward								$1,623,177.50
Bought	2000	at	140½	closed	at	149		17,000
Bought	1000	"	144½	"	"	149		4,500
Bought	500	"	149½	"	"	149	250	
Sold	2000	"	149	"	"	148		2,000
Bought	2000	"	148	"	"	141	14,000	
Sold	2000	"	141	"	"	148	14,000	
Bought	2000	"	148	"	"	147¾	500	
Sold	2000	"	147¾	"	"	137 14		21,000
Sold	1000	"	142¾	"	"	137¼		5,500
Sold	500	"	137¾	"	"	137¼		250
Bought	2000	"	137¼	"	"	139		3,500
Sold	2000	"	139	"	"	137		4,000
Bought	2000	"	137	"	"	157-3/8		40,750
Bought	1000	"	142	"	"	157-3/8		15,375
Bought	500	"	147	"	"	157-3/8		5,187.50
Bought	300	"	152	"	"	157-3/8		1,612.50
Sold	2000	"	157-3/8	"	"	158	1,250	
Bought	2000	"	158	"	"	163		10,000
Bought	1000	"	162	"	"	163		1,000
Sold	2000	"	163	"	"	162-1/8		1,750
Bought	2000	"	162-1/8	"	"	169½		14,750
Bought	1000	"	167	"	"	169½		2,500
Sold	2000	"	169½	"	"	152¾		33,500
Sold	1000	at	164½	"	"	152¾		11,750
Bought	500	"	159½	"	"	152¾		3,375
Sold	300	"	154½	"	"	152¾		525
Bought	2000	"	152¾	"	"	187¼		69,000

THE W.D. GANN MASTER STOCK MARKET COURSE

39.

							DEBIT	CREDIT
Bought	1000	"	157¾	closed	at	187¼		29,500
Bought	500	"	162¾	"	"	187¼		12,250
Bought	300	"	167¾	"	"	187¼		5,850
Bought	200	"	172¾	"	"	187¼		2,900
Bought	100	"	177¾	"	"	187¼		950
Sold	2000	"	187¼	"	"	187½	500	
Bought	2000	"	187½	"	"	189¾		4,500
Sold	2000	"	189¾	"	"	182½		24,500
Bought	2000	"	182½	"	"	185		5,000
Sold	2000	"	185	"	"	174¼		21,500
Sold	1000	"	180	"	"	174¼		5,750
Bought	2000	"	174-1/8	"	"	177		5,750
Sold	2000	"	177	"	"	171¼		11,500
Sold	1000	"	172	"	"	171¼		750
Bought	2000	"	171¼	"	"	190¾		39,000
Bought	1000	"	176¼	"	"	190¾		14,500
Bought	500	"	181¼	"	"	190¾		4,750
Bought	300	"	186¼	"	"	190¾		1,350
Bought	300	"	191¼	"	"	190¾	150	
Sold	2000	"	190¾	"	"	183½		14,500
Sold	1000	"	185¾	"	"	183½		2,250
Bought	2000	"	183½	"	"	184¼		1,500
Sold	2000	"	184¼	"	"	183½		1,500
Bought	2000	"	183½	"	"	187¾		8,500
Bought	1000	"	188½	"	"	187¾	750	
Sold	2000	"	187¾	"	"	174½		26,500
Sold	1000	"	182¾	"	"	174½		8,250
Sold	500	"	177¾	"	"	174½		1,750
Sold	300	"	172¾	"	"	174½	525	
Bought	2000	"	174½	"	"	180¾		12,500
Sold	2000	"	180¾	"	"	179¼		2,500
Bought	2000	"	179¼	"	"	186		13,500
Bought	2000	"	184¼	"	"	186		1,750
Sold	2000	"	186	"	"	186¾	1,500	
Bought	2000	"	186¾	"	"	187¾		1,500
Sold	2000	"	187½	"	"	165½		4,400
Sold	1000	"	182½	"	"	165½		17,000
Sold	500	"	177½	"	"	165½		6,000
Sold	300	"	172½	"	"	165½		2,100
Sold	200	"	167½	"	"	165½		400
Bought	2000	"	165½	"	"	251¾		172,500
Bought	1000	"	170½	"	"	251¾		81,500
Bought	500	"	175½	"	"	251¾		38,125
Bought	300	"	180½	"	"	251¾		21,375
Bought	200	"	185½	"	"	251¾		13,250
Bought	100	"	190½	"	"	251¾		6,150
Bought	2000	"	195½	"	"	251¾		113,500
Bought	1000	"	200½	"	"	251¾		51,250
Bought	1000	"	205½	"	"	251¾		46,250
Bought	500	"	210½	"	"	251¾		20,625
Bought	300	"	215½	"	"	251¾		10,875

						DEBIT	CREDIT
Bought	200	at 220½	closed	at	251¾		6,250
Bought	100	at 225½	"	"	251¾		2,625.00
						$33,425	$2,833,577.50
				Commissions		24,700	58,125.00
				Net Credit			$2,775,452.50

Now that we have a total capital of $2,775,452.50, you can be ultra conservative and increase trading unit to 5000 shares. We sell 5000 short at 251¾. September 5th low 245¾. We make stop 248¾. Stop was caught, and we buy 5000 at 248¾. August 7th high 252½. We make stop 249½. Stop was caught and we sell short 5000 at 249½. Later we sell 3000 at 244½ and 2000 at 239½. September 10th low 238. September 11th high 243¼. We make stop on all trades 244¼. September 13th and 15th low 230½. We reduce stop to 233½. Stop caught. We buy 5000 at 233½, with stop 229½ and then buy 3000 a 238½ and 2000 at 243½. September 19th high 247½. We raise all stops to 244½. Stops caught. We go short 5000 at 244½ and 3000 at 239½. September 21st low 232. We make stops at 235. Stops caught.

We buy 5000 at 235 and 3000 at 240. September 24th high 241¾. We make stop at 238¾. Stops caught. We go short 5000 at 238¾ and later sell 3000 at 233¾, 2000 at 228¾, 1000 at 223¾, 500 at 218¾ and 300 at 213¾ and 200 at 208¾. October 4th low 206½. We figure from the low of 149¾ in December, 1928 to the high of 261¾ and get 1/2 point at 205¾, but we are in a panic, so we follow down with stop 3 points above the low or at 209½. Stop is caught, and we buy 5000 at 209½ and later buy 3000 at 214½, 2000 at 219½, 1000 at 224½ and 500 at 229½. October 10th high 234, same high as September 26th. We figure from 261¾ high to 206½ low and get 234-1/8, the 1/2 point. We sell out at 233 and go short 5000 with stop 235-1/8. Then sell 3000 at 230-1/8, 2000 at 225-1/8, 1000 at 220-1/8, 500 at 215-1/8, and 300 at 210-1/8. December 21st low 205, just under the 1/2 point. Also note July 22nd, 24th and 29th lows, 204½, showing a strong resistance point, where we should cover shorts, but we reduce stops to 208. Stop caught. We buy 5000 at 208 and later buy 3000 at 213 and 2000 at 218. October 22nd high 218½. We raise all stops to 215½. Stops caught.

We go short 5000 at 215½. Later sell 3000 at 210½ and 2000 at 204, when 1/2 point and bottoms are broken, and sell 1000 at 199, and 500 at 194. October 24th low 193½. As this is a panic day, we pull stops down 5 points from the low. This covers shorts at 198½, and we buy 5000 at 198½. October 25th high 207. We know the 1/2 point is 205¾, so we sell out at 205 and go short 5000 at 205 with stop at 208. Later we sell 3000 at 200, 2000 at 195, 1000 at 190, 500 at 185, 300 at 180, 200 at 175 and 100 at 170. October 29th, the great panic, Steel declines to 166½. We must cover or follow down with stop 5 points from the low, so stop at 171½ is caught, and we buy 5000 at 171½, 3000 at 176½ and 2000 at 181½. October 31st high 193½. We raise stop to 188½. Stop caught. We go short 5000 at 188½. Then sell 3000 at 183½, 2000 at 178½, 1000 at 173½, and 500 at 168½. November 7th low 161½. We reduce stop to 166½. Stop caught. We buy 5000 at 166½ and we buy 3000 at 171½. November 8th high 175½. We make all stops 170½. Stops caught. We go short 5000 at 170½. Then sell 3000 at 165½, 2000 at 160½ and 1000 at 155½.

Here we figure from low 38, February 1, 1915, to high 261¾, and find 1/2 point 149-7/8. We also know the move started from 149¾ on December 17, 1928. Therefore, 150 is the strongest support level. On November 13th U.S. Steel sells at 150, but we do not wait for the last 1/8th. We cover all shorts at 151 and buy 5000 with stop at 148¾. Later we buy 3000 at 156 and 2000 at 161. November 15th high 167½. We make stop 164½. Stop is caught, and we go short 5000 at 164½. December 18th low 159-5/8. We make stop 162-5/8. Stop caught. We buy 5000 at 162-5/8. Then buy 3000 at 167-/58. November 21st high 171-7/8. We make stop 168-7/8. Stop caught. We go short 5000 at 168-7/8. Then sell 3000 at 163-7/8. December 2nd low 159¼, only-3/8 under low of November 18th. We make stop 162¼. Stop caught. We buy 5000 at 162¼ and later buy 3000 at 167¼. December 5th low 164½. We make all stops 163½. Later we buy 2000 at 172¼, 1000 at 177¼, 500 at 182¼ and 300 at 187¼. December 9th high 189. We make stop 186. Stop caught. We go short 500 at 166. then sell 3000 at 181, 2000 at 176, 1000 at 171, and 500 at 166. December 13th low 164¼, same low as December 5th. We make stop 167¼. Stops caught. We buy 5000 at 167¼. Then buy 3000 at 172¼. December 14th high 174¾. We make stop 171¾. Stops caught.

We sell 5000 at 171¾. Later sell 3000 at 166¾. December 17th low 166¼. We make stop 169¼. Stops caught. We buy 5000 at 169¼. December 18th high 173½. We make stop 170½. Stop caught. We sell short 5000 at 170½. Later sell 3000 at 165½. Sell 2000 at 160½. December 23rd low 156¾. We make stop 159¾. Stop caught. We buy 5000 at 159¾. Later we buy 3000 at 163¾. December 29th low 163-5/8. We make all stops 162-5/8. Later we buy 2000 at 169-3/4.

1930

January 2nd high 173-5/8. Low same day 166. We make all stops 165. The price of 166-1/8 is the 1/2 point from 70½, low of June 23rd, 1921, and the extreme high 261¾. Therefore, a strong support and buying level. January 13th low 168-5/8. We make all stops 167-5/8, because since January 2nd the Overnight chart has made lower tops. January 18th low 167¼. Stops are caught at 167-5/8, and we go short 5000 at 167-5/8, with stop at 170-5/8. Stop caught, and buy 5000 at 170-5/8. We buy 3000 at 175-5/8, 2000 at 180-5/8 and 1000 at 185-5/8. February 14th high 189, same as December 9th high. February 17th low 184½. We make all stops 183½. February 18th high 189½. We raise stop to 186½. Stops caught. We go short 5000 at 186½ with stop 190. Later we sell 3000 at 181½. February 25th low 177. We make all stops 180. Stops caught. We buy 5000 at 180. March 1st and 7th high 184. We make stop 181. Stop caught.

The following statement covers from September, 1929 to March 1930:

								DEBIT	CREDIT
September, 1929									$2,775,452.50
Sold	5000	at	251-3/4	closed	at	248-3/4			15,000
Bought	5000	"	248-3/4	"	"	249½			3,750
Sold	5000	"	249½	"	"	233½			80,000
Sold	3000	"	244½	"	"	233½			33,000
Sold	2000	"	239½	"	"	233½			12,000
Bought	5000	"	233½	"	"	244½			55,000
Bought	3000	"	238½	"	"	244½			18,000
Bought	2000	"	243½	"	"	244½			2,000
Sold	5000	"	244½	"	"	235			47,500
Sold	3000	"	239½	"	"	235			13,500
Bought	5000	"	235	"	"	238-3/4			18,750
Bought	3000	"	240	"	"	238-3/4	$1,250	
Sold	5000	"	238-3/4	"	"	209½			146,250
Sold	3000	"	233-3/4	"	"	209½			72,750
Sold	2000	"	228-3/4	"	"	209½			38,500
Sold	1000	"	223-3/4	"	"	209½			14,250
Sold	500	"	218-3/4	"	"	209½			4,625
Sold	300	"	213-3/4	"	"	209½			1,275
Sold	200	"	208-3/4	"	"	209½	150	
Bought	5000	"	209½	"	"	233			117,500
Bought	3000	"	214½	"	"	233			55,500
Bought	2000	"	219½	"	"	233			27,500
Bought	1000	"	224¼	"	"	233			8,500
Bought	500	"	229½	"	"	233			1,750
Sold	5000	"	233	"	"	208			125,000
Sold	3000	"	230-1/8	"	"	208			66,375
Sold	2000	"	225-1/8	"	"	208			34,250
Sold	1000	"	220-1/8	"	"	208			12,125
Sold	500	"	215-1/8	"	"	208			3,562.50
Sold	300	"	210-1/8	"	"	208			637.50
Bought	5000	"	208	"	"	215½			37,500
Bought	3000	"	213	"	"	215½			7,500
Bought	2000	"	218	"	"	215½	5,000	
Sold	5000	"	215½	"	"	198½			85,000
Sold	3000	"	210½	"	"	198½			36,000
Sold	2000	"	204	"	"	198½			11,000
Sold	1000	"	100	"	"	198½			500
Sold	500	"	194	"	"	198½	2,250	
Bought	5000	"	198½	"	"	205			32,500
Sold	5000	"	205	"	"	171½			167,500
Sold	3000	"	200	"	"	171½			85,500
Sold	2000	"	195	"	"	171½			47,000
Sold	1000	"	190	"	"	171½			18,500
Sold	500	"	185	"	"	171½			6,760
Sold	300	"	180	"	"	171½			2,550
Sold	200	"	175	"	"	171½			700
Sold	100	"	170	"	"	171½	150	

THE W.D. GANN MASTER STOCK MARKET COURSE

43.

							DEBIT	CREDIT
Bought	5000	at	171½	closed	at	188½		$85,000
Bought	3000	"	176½	"	"	188½		36,000
Bought	2000	"	181½	"	"	188½		14,000
Sold	5000	"	188½	"	"	166½		110,000
Sold	3000	"	183½	"	"	166½		51,000
Sold	2000	"	178½	"	"	166½		24,000
Sold	1000	"	173½	"	"	166½		7,000
Sold	500	"	168½	"	"	166½		1,000
Bought	5000	"	166½	"	"	170½		20,000
Bought	3000	"	171½	"	"	170½	$3,000	
Sold	5000	"	170½	"	"	151		97,000
Sold	3000	"	165½	"	"	151		43,500
Sold	2000	"	160½	"	"	151		19,000
Sold	1000	"	155½	"	"	151		4,500
Bought	5000	"	151	"	"	164½		67,500
Bought	3000	"	156	"	"	164½		25,500
Bought	2000	"	161	"	"	164½		7,000
Sold	5000	"	164½	"	"	162-5/8		9,375
Bought	5000	"	162-5/8	"	"	168-7/8		31,250
Bought	3000	"	167-5/8	"	"	168-7/8		3,750
Sold	5000	"	168-7/8	"	"	162¼		33,125
Sold	3000	"	163-7/8	"	"	162¼		4,875
Bought	5000	"	162¼	"	"	186		118,750
Bought	3000	"	167½	"	"	186		56,250
Bought	2000	"	172¼	"	"	186		27,500
Bought	1000	"	177¼	"	"	186		8,750
Bought	500	"	182-14	"	"	186		1,875
Bought	300	"	187¼	"	"	186	375	
Sold	5000	"	186	"	"	167¼		93,750
Sold	3000	"	181	"	"	167¼		41,250
Sold	2000	"	176	"	"	167¼		17,500
Sold	1000	"	171	"	"	167¼		3,750
Sold	500	"	166	"	"	167¼	625	
Bought	5000	"	167¼	"	"	171-3/4		22,500
Bought	3000	"	172¼	"	"	171-3/4	1,500	
Sold	5000	"	171-3/4	"	"	169¼		12,500
Sold	3000	"	166-3/4	"	"	169¼	7,500	
Bought	5000	"	169¼	"	"	170½		6,250
Sold	5000	"	170½	"	"	159-3/4		52,500
Sold	3000	"	165½	"	"	158-3/4		17,250
Sold	2000	"	160½	"	"	159-3/4		1,500
Bought	5000	"	159-3/4	"	"	167-5/8		39,375
Bought	3000	"	164-3/4	"	"	167-5/8		8,625
Bought	2000	"	169-3/4	"	"	167-5/8	4,250	
Sold	5000	"	167-5/8	"	"	170-5/8	15,000	
Bought	5000	"	170-5/8	"	"	186½		79,375
Bought	3000	"	175-5/8	"	"	186½		32,625
Bought	2000	"	180-5/8	"	"	186½		11,750
Bought	1000	"	185-5/8	"	"	186½		875
Sold	5000	"	186½	"	"	180		32,500
Sold	3000	"	181½	"	"	180		4,500

44.

			DEBIT	CREDIT
Bought 5000 at 180	closed at 181			5,000
			$41,050	$5,733,677
We go short)	Commissions		71,175	112,225
5000 at 181)	Net Profit			$5,621,452

We go short 5000 at 181. March 13th low 177¾. March 11th and 14th high 182½. We make stop 183½. Stop caught. We buy 5000 at 183½. Later buy 3000 at 188½ and 2000 at 193½. April 1st, 7th 10th and 16th, highs 198¾ to 197, but extreme high 198¾. The last low on April 3rd was 192¾. We make stops at 191¾. Stops caught. We go short 5000 at 191¾. Later we sell 3000 at 186¾, 2000 at 181¾, 1000 at 176¾ and 500 at 171¾.

May 5th low 166¼. We cover shorts and buy 5000 at 167, because 166-1/8 is the 1/2 point from 1921 low to 1929 high and because low on January 2nd, 1930 was 166. We protect purchases with stop at 165. Later we buy 3000 at 172. May 6th high 175. We figure 174-3/8 the 1/2 point from 150 to 198¾. Therefore, we sell out longs at 174 and go short 5000 at 174 with stop at 176. Then sell 3000 at 169. May 8th low 165¾. We cover shorts at 166½ and buy 5000 at 166½, with stop at 165. Later we buy 3000 at 171½. May 14th high 175-3/8. We again sell out longs at 174 and go short 5000 at 174 with stop at 176. Later we sell 3000 at 169. May 20th low 166¼. We again cover shorts and buy 5000 at 166½, with stop at 165. Later buy 3000 at 171½. May 28th high 175. We sell out longs at 174 and sell 5000 short at 174 with stop at 176. Later we sell 3000 at 169.

June 7th, U.S. Steel sells at 166. We cover shorts at 166½ and buy 5000 at 166½ with stop at 165. Stop was caught same day and we go short 5000 at 165. Steel declines to 164 on June 7th. We can now make stop 167 or wait until the Overnight makes a turn, then place a stop 1 point above the top from which the Overnight Chart turns down again or follow down with a stop loss order 3 points above the low of each day.

THE W.D. GANN MASTER STOCK MARKET COURSE

45.

The following statement covers trades from March, 1930 to June 7th, 1930, inclusive:

							DEBIT	CREDIT
Balance Forward								$5,621,452
Sold	5000	at	181	closed	at	183½	$12,500	
Bought	5000	"	183½	"	"	191-3/4		41,250
Bought	3000	"	188½	"	"	191-3/4		9,750
Bought	2000	"	193½	"	"	191-3/4	3,500	
Sold	5000	"	191-3/4	"	"	167		123,750
Sold	3000	"	186-3/4	"	"	167		59,250
Sold	2000	"	181-3/4	"	"	167		29,500
Sold	1000	"	176-3/4	"	"	167		9,750
Sold	500	"	171-34	"	"	167		2,375
Bought	5000	"	167	"	"	174		35,000
Bought	3000	"	172	"	"	174		6,000
Sold	5000	"	174	"	"	166½		37,500
Sold	3000	"	169	"	"	166½		7,500
Bought	5000	"	166¼	"	"	174		37,500
Bought	3000	"	171½	"	"	174		7,500
Sold	5000	"	174	"	"	166½		37,500
Sold	3000	"	169	"	"	166½		7,500
Bought	5000	"	166½	"	"	174		37,500
Bought	3000	"	171½	"	"	174		7,500
Sold	5000	"	174	"	"	166½		37,500
Sold	3000	"	169	"	"	166½		7,500
Bought	5000	"	166½	"	"	165	7,500	
							$23,500	$6,163,077
					Commissions		19,875	43,375
					Net Credit			$6,119,702

ERROR:
March 10, 1927 to June 7, 1930
509,600 shares at $25 per 100 should be
$50 per 100 round turn $127,403

Tax at $4.00 per 100 shares not figured
on 869,700 shares 34,788   162,191

TOTAL NET PROFITS..$5,957,511

June 7th, 1930
    with 5000 shares short at 165.

June 11 low 160½; June 13 high 166. We make stop on shorts at 167. June 16 we sell 3000 at 161. June 18 low 155. We make stop on all trades at 158. Stop caught. We buy 5000 at 158. June 20 high 162¼. We make stop 159¼. Stop caught. We go short 5000 at 159¼. June 25 low 151-5/8. We reduce stop at 154-5/8. Stop caught. We buy 5000 at 154-5/8. We could have bought at 152 with stop at 149 because 150 is 1/2 point from 1914 to 1929.

June 27 low 153½. We make stop 153. June 30 Steel crossed 157½, the tops of June 24 and 26 and for the first time since June 28 makes a higher top on the Overnight Chart. For this reason we buy 3000 more at 157½ and make stop on all trades at 154.

On June 30, 1930 the account stands:

					Profit
Sold	5000	at 165	closed at	158	$35,000
Sold	3000	at 161	closed at	158	9,000
Bought	5000	at 158	closed at	159¼	6,250
Sold	5000	at 159¼	closed at	154-5/8	23,125
					$73,375
	Less Commissions				9,720
	Net Profit				$65,655
	June 7 Capital				5,957,511
	Total				$6,021,166

with 5000 bought at 154-5/8 and stop on all trades at 154 and 3000 bought at 157½.

July 1st high 161-3/8. We raise stop to 158-3/8 because last high on June 20 was 167¼ and failing to cross this level indicated lower. The stop was caught and we went short 5000 at 158-3/8.

July 8th low 153¼. Note low June 27th was 153½, from which the Overnight turned up for the first time since May 28, when the stock sold at 175. We cover shorts and buy 5000 at 153½ with stop at 152½ because this was a double bottom same as June 27th.

July 9 high 158¼; July 10th low 155¾. We raise stop to 154¾.

On July 10, when Steel rallies, to 158½, we buy 3000 more at 158½ and make stop on all trades 155½.

July 14 high 163¾. We raise stops to 160¾ or 3 points from the high. We can either follow up with stop 1 point under each day's lowest or wait until the Overnight Chart makes a turn, then place stop 1 point under the Overnight bottom.

July 19 high 168¾. We sell out longs and go short 5000 at 168, because 169 is 3/8 point from 198¾ to 151-5/8. We make stop 170. July 21 low 162-5/8. In view of the fact that the Overnight Chart still shows up, we note last low at 164¼ on July 16. We calculate the 1/2 point from July 10th bottom, 155¾, to high at 168¾ and get 162¼ as the 1/2 point, so we cover shorts and buy 5000 at 163 with stop at 161.

July 23 high 168½. We sell out longs at 168 and go short July 25 low 164¼. We cover shorts and buy with stop at 162 or one point under the low of July 21. July 28 high 170. We sell out longs and go short. July 31 low 163. We cover shorts and buy at 163½ with stop at 162, because 163 is Resistance Level.

August 5 high 170¼, a double top against July 28. We sell out longs at 170 and go short with stop at 171. Sell more at 165; then sell more at 160 because it has broken bottoms of July 21 and July 31.

The last Resistance Level on July 10 was 155¾. The stock declined to 155½ on August 13. We cover shorts and buy at 156 with stop at 154¾. Then buy more at 161 where the Overnight Chart turned trend up. Steel advanced to 166¾ on August 16. August 18 reacted to 162¾ and resumed advance. We raise stop to 161¾. August 20 high 168½. August 21 low 165¾. Make stop 164¾. August 27 and September 2nd high 172¼. September 4 low 167¼, still above main 1/2 point, 166¼ We make stop 165. September 8 high 173½. Note three tops, May 6, 14, and 28 at 175. The 1/2 point is 174-3/8. September 8 we sell out longs and go short at 173 with stop at 176. If it had crossed the 3 tops made in May, we would buy for long account.

September 16 declines and breaks low of September 4 and we sell more at 167; then sell more at 164, because it has again broken the main 1/2 point, 166¼. September 27 sell more at 159. September 30 breaks 155, under bottoms of July 10 and August 13; then rallies and makes two tops on October 1 and October 3 at 160½. We make stop 161½. Then sell more at 155; then at 149 sell more, because it has broken the low of November 13, 1929, the big 1/2 point.

October 10 and 14 low 144½. We cover all shorts and buy with stop at 142. October 11 and 15 highs 151½ and 152½. We sell out and go short on 2nd top. October 18 we cover shorts and buy at 145 with stop at 143. Then buy more at 150. October 28 high 154, over last 2 tops. We make stop 151. Stop was caught and we go short. Later sell more at 146. Then when it breaks 4 bottoms, sell more at 143.

November 8, 10 and 12 made bottom. We cover shorts on stop at 143 and buy. Then buy more at 147. The next point to watch is 150, the 1/2 point, where 4 tops were made November 15, 20, 21 and 25. Would sell out there and go short with stop at 151. Sell more at 145; then sell more at 140. Cover all shorts and buy for long account at 135, because this is the 1/2 point between 8-3/8 and 261¾, being half of the life fluctuation and the strongest point since 150.

48.

It made double top December 18 and 20. We sell out longs and go short at 140. On December 29th it declines to 135¾. We cover shorts and buy because 135 is the 1/2 point. We buy a second lot at 141 and when it reacts on January 2nd we raise stop to 137. On January 7 and 9 it makes double top and we raise stop to 142, where again sell out and go short. On January 16 and 19 it makes double bottom at 138½. This is also the 1/2 point between 134-3/8 and 145, therefore we cover shorts and buy at 139 and protect with stop at 137. On January 24 and 27 double tops and lower than January 9. We sell out longs at 143 and go short again. On February 5th we cover shorts and buy at 138 because it is the same bottom as was made on January 2 and 19th. We buy more at 143. On February 16 we sell out longs at 148 and go short because it is a double top and under the 1/2 point and also just under the tops made on November 15 to 25.

On February 17 it makes a double bottom just above the 1/2 point of the last move. We cover shorts and buy at 145. On February 26 the stock advances to 152¼, failing to get 3 points above the 1/2 point. We raise stop to 149. Stop is caught and we sell out longs and go short.

On March 4th the stock declines to 143½, the 1/2 point between 134-3/8 and 152¼. We cover shorts at 144 and go long with stop 142. If the stocks crosses 152 and especially if it makes 153 it will be in a very strong position, and indicate much higher.

[undated, but likely *circa* March 1931]   [unsigned]

Chapter 4

The Basis of My Forecasting Method - Geometric Angles

THE BASIS OF MY FORECASTING METHOD

Mathematics is the only exact science. All power under heaven and on earth is given unto the man who masters the simple science of mathematics. Emerson said: "God does indeed geometrize." Another wise man said: "There is nothing in the universe but mathematical points." Pythagoras, one of the greatest mathematicians that ever lived, after experimenting with numbers and finding the proofs of all natural laws, said: "Before God was numbers." He believed that the vibration of numbers created God and the Deity. It has been said, "Figures don't lie." Men have been convinced that numbers tell the truth and that all problems can be solved by them. The chemist, engineer, astronomer would be lost without the science of mathematics.

It is so simple and easy to solve problems and get correct answers and results with figures that it seems strange so few people rely on them to forecast the future of business, stocks and commodity markets. The basic principles are easy to learn and understand. No matter whether you use geometry, trigonometry, or calculus, you use the simple rules of arithmetic. You do only two things: You increase or decrease.

There are two kinds of numbers, odd and even. We add numbers together, which is increasing. We multiply, which is a shorter way to increase. We subtract, which decreases, and we divide, which also decreases. With the use of higher mathematics, we find a quicker and easier way to divide, subtract, add and multiply, yet very simple when you understand it.

Everything in nature is male and female, white and black, harmony or inharmony, right and left. The market moves only two ways, up and down. There are three dimensions which we know how to prove – width, length and height. We use three figures in geometry – the circle, the square, and the triangle. We get the square and triangle points of a circle to determine points of time, price and space resistance. We use the circle of 360 degrees to measure Time and Price.

There are three kinds of angles – the vertical, the horizontal, and the diagonal, which we use for measuring time and price movements. We use the square of odd and even numbers to get not only the proof of market movements, but the cause.

HOW TO MAKE CHARTS

Charts are records of past market movements. The future is but a repetition of the past. There is nothing new. As the Bible says – "The thing that hath been, it is that which shall be." History repeats and with charts and rules we determine when and how it is going to repeat. Therefore, the first and most important point to learn is how to make charts correctly because if you make an error in the chart, you will make an error in applying the rules to your trading.

YEARLY CHART: You should keep a yearly high and low chart, that is, recording the extreme low and the extreme high price made during the calendar year on one line. The spacing for the price can be used one point to each 1/8 inch or two points or more, according to the activity and range of the stock.

MONTHLY CHART: You must always keep up a monthly high and low chart, which is the most important chart of all in determining the main trend. This chart records the extreme high and extreme low price for the calendar month on one line, and each space or 1/8 inch on the cross-section chart paper should represent one point or $1 per share.

WEEKLY CHART: The next and one of the very important charts to keep is a weekly high and low chart. Where stocks are selling below 50, it usually pays to make this chart up using 1/8 inch to represent one-half point, or two spaces to represent one full point, or four points for each one-inch space. When stocks become very active, especially when they are selling above $100 per share, then you can make up the weekly chart using each space or 1/8 inch on the chart paper to represent one point or $1 per share.

SEMI-WEEKLY OR 3-DAY CHART: The next chart of importance to the Weekly Chart is a 3-day chart, that is taking the extreme high and extreme low price made from the opening of the market on Monday morning until the close on Wednesday night, closing the chart on Wednesday night – then from the opening on Thursday to the close on Saturday, taking the extreme high and low and closing the chart on Saturday. This gives you a time period showing one-half of the week. This chart is very important as will be explained later on in the instructions. The spacing for this chart can be the same as for the weekly high and low chart.

WEEKLY MOVING-AVERAGE OR MEAN POINT: To get a Weekly Moving-Average, we take the extreme low for the week and the extreme high for the week and divide by 2, getting the half-way or mean point for the week. This can be recorded on the weekly high and low chart or on a separate chart, recording the Weekly Moving-Average with a dot and using one line on the chart for each week. Importance of this Weekly Mean Point will be explained later.

DAILY CHART: When you are trading in a stock that is active, you should always keep up a daily high and low chart, but for study purposes it is enough to keep up the Weekly and Monthly Charts, which give you the main trend. The Daily Chart show the minor trend and shows a change in trend much oftener than any of the other charts, but the indication does not last as long or run so far. This chart should be kept up the same as the others, except when stocks are selling below 50 or when they are in an inactive trading range – then the spacing should be 1/2-point to each 1/8-inch on the chart paper, allowing two spaces to represent one full point or $1 per share. When stocks are active and advancing very fast, making a wide range each day, then you can make the Daily Chart the same as the Weekly or Monthly, that is using one point for each 1/8 inch on the chart paper. This spacing cuts the chart down and keeps it in a range where it is easy to see and read when fluctuations are wide.

No spaces are skipped on the Daily chart for Holidays or Sundays, therefore the time period is for actual market days and not calendar days. However, you should carry the calendar days along at least every two weeks, as later, under rules for Time Periods for change in trend, you will find that it is necessary to check up and know when the stock is 30,60,80,120,135, etc.

days from a top or a bottom, which means calendar days, the exact measurement of Time for the daily chart. Often the Daily Chart on actual daily movements comes out on an exact mathematical angle of time measurement at the same time the calendar days come out on exact time measurement, making it a doubly important point for change in trend.

GEOMETRICAL ANGLES

After long years of practical experience, I have discovered that Geometrical Angles measure accurately Space, Time, Volume and Price.

Mathematics is the only exact science, as I have said before. Every nation on the face of the earth agrees that 2 and 2 make 4, no matter what language it speaks. Yet all other sciences are not in accord as mathematical science. We find different men in different professions along scientific lines disagreeing on problems, but there can be no disagreement in mathematical calculation.

There are 360 degrees in a circle, no matter how large or how small the circle may be. Certain numbers of these degrees and angles are of vast importance and indicate when important tops and bottoms occur on stocks, as well as denote important Resistance Levels. When once you have thoroughly mastered the Geometrical Angles, you will be able to solve any problem and determine the trend of any stock.

After 35 years of research, tests and practical applications, I have perfected and proved the most important angles to be used in determining the trend of the stock market. Therefore, concentrate on those angles until you thoroughly understand them. Study and experiment with each rule I give you, and you will make a success.

We use geometrical angles to measure Space and Time periods because it is a shorter and quicker method than addition or multiplication, provided you follow the rules and draw the angles or lines accurately from tops and bottoms or extreme highs and lows. You may make a mistake in addition or multiplication, but the geometrical angles accurately drawn will correct this mistake. For example: If you should count across the bottom of your chart 120 spaces, which represents 120 days, weeks or months, then you begin at "0" and number vertically on your chart up to 120 – then from this top point at 120 draw a 45-degree angle moving down, this will come out at "0" on 120 points over from the beginning. If you have made a mistake in numbering, this will correct it.

Angles drawn on a chart always keep before you the position of the stock and its trend whereas if you had a resistance point on time written down, you might mislay it or forget it but these angles are always on the chart in front of you.

These angles or moving-average trend lines correctly drawn will keep you from making mistakes or misjudging the trend. If you wait and follow your rules, these angles will show you when the trend changes.

The moving-average as commonly used is obtained by taking the extreme low price and the extreme high price of the calendar day, week or month, and dividing it by two to get the mean or average price for the day, week or month, and continuing this at the end of each time period. This is an irregular movement in spaces or points per week because at one time it may move up 2 points per week and at another 5 points per week, while the time period is a regular unit. Therefore geometrical angles, which are really moving-averages, move up or down at a uniform rate from any bottom or top on a daily, weekly or monthly chart.

HOW TO DRAW GEOMETRICAL ANGLES

There are three important points that we can prove with mathematics or geometry: the Circle, the Square, and the Triangle. After I have made the Square, I can draw a Circle in it using the same diameter, and thereby produce the Triangle, the Square and the Circle.

The Angles or moving-trend-line averages measure and divide Time and Price into proportionate parts. Refer to Form "1", where I have drawn the square of 28. You will note that this is 28 high and 28 wide – in other words, 28 up and 28 across. It is the same as a square room which has a bottom or floor, a top or ceiling , and side walls. Everything has width, length, and height.

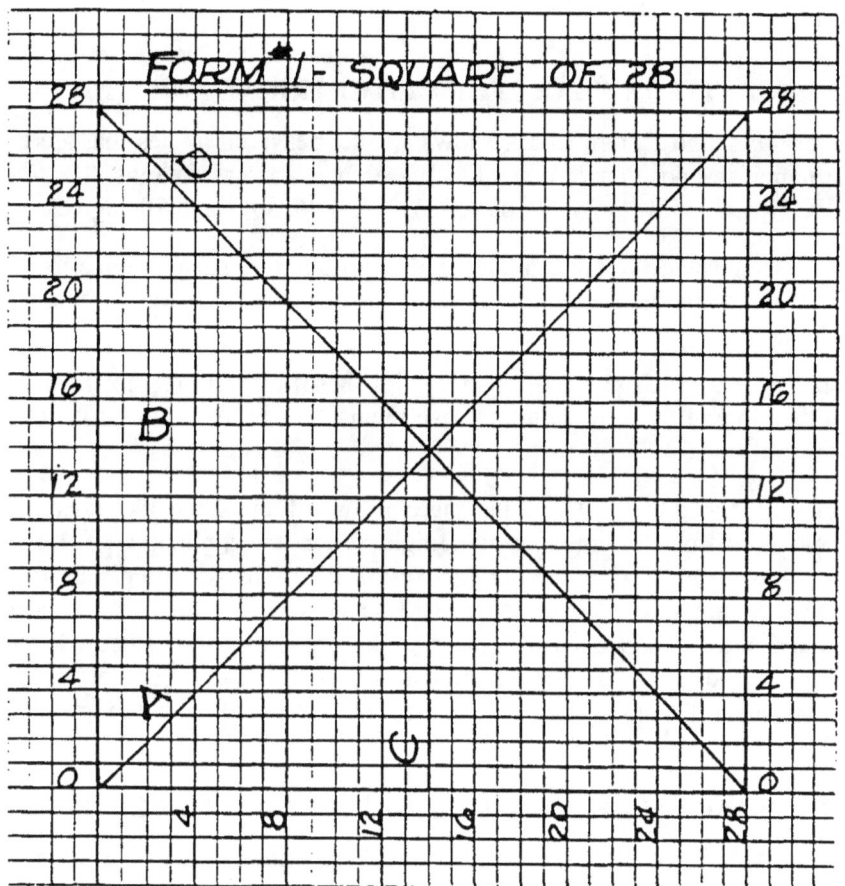

To get the strongest and most important points in this Square, I divide it into tow equal parts by drawing a horizontal and a vertical line. Note angle marked "A", which divides each of the smaller squares into two equal parts and runs from "0" to "28" diagonally. This is a diagonal line moving on a 45° angle and divides the large Square into two equal parts. Then note angle "B" at "14" running horizontally across. This divides the Square into tow equal parts. Note angle "C", which is a vertical line, running up from "14", which is one-half of "28". This crosses at the center of half-way point at 14, where the other angles cross, dividing the Square into two equal parts. Then note angle "D", which forms another 45° angle moving from the N.W. corner to the S.E. corner, crossing "14" at the exact half-way point. You see by this that if we draw the first line thru the center of the square, we divide it into tow equal parts – then when we draw lines from the other directions, we divide it into four equal parts – then by drawing the two lines from each corner, we divide the square into 8 equal parts and produce 8 triangles.

As you look at this Square, it should be easy for you to tell with your eye where the strongest support point is or resistance point is. It is at the center where all the angles cross. Four angles cross at this point, so naturally this would be a stronger support point than a place where only one angle crosses. I could divide each one of these smaller squares into four or eight equal parts by drawing angles in the same way. Later, when I give you the rules and examples, I will explain how to square the Range of a stock, that is, the difference between the extreme low and the extreme high prices, or the difference between any low point and any high point, and also how to square the bottom price. For example: If the tops of a stock is 28, this square of 28 x 28 would represent squaring the Price by Time, because if we have 28 points up in Price, and we move over 28 spaces in Time, we square the Price with Time. Therefore, when the stock has moved over 28 days, 28 weeks, or 28 months, it will be squaring its price range of 28.

PATTERN CHART FOR GEOMETRICAL ANGLES

The Square of 90, or the Pattern Chart, shows all the measured angles that are important to use in determining the position of a stock. These angles are as follows: 3¾, 7½, 15, 18¾, 26¼, 30, 33¾, 37½, 45, 52½, 56¼, 60, 63¾, 71¼, 75, 82½, 86¼, and 90 degrees.

It is not necessary to measure these angles with a protractor. All you have to do to get the angles correct is to count the spaces on the chart paper, using 8 x 8 to the inch, and draw the lines or angles accordingly.

On the square of 90, which you will receive with these instructions, not how equal angles drawn from the top and from the bottom prove themselves by the point at which they cross. For example:

The angle of 8 x 1 drawn from "0" and the angle of 8 x 1 drawn from "90" down both cross at 45, 5-5/8 points over from "0" counting to the right. Then, the angle of 4 x 1 from "0" and the angle of 4 x 1 down from "90", you will notice, cross at 11¼ on 45, equidistant from the other angle and twice the measure. The reason why these angles prove this way is because the 45° angle is one-half of 90. The reason why these angles prove this way is because the 45° angle or 45 points or degrees from "0" to 45 is one-half of 90. Therefore, parallel angles beginning at "0" going up and at 90 coming down, must cross on a 45° angle or at the gravity center.

HOW TO DRAW ANGLES FROM A LOW POINT RECORDED BY A STOCK

An example marked "Form 2" shows you the most important angles to use when a stock is working higher and advancing. (See page 6)

FIRST IMPORTANT GEOMETRICAL ANGLE: The first and always most important
    45° or 1 x 1 angle to draw is a 45-degree angle or moving-average that moves up one point per day, one point per week or one point per month. This is a 45° angle because it divides the Space and Time Periods into two equal parts. As long as the market or a stock stays above the 45° angle, it is in a strong position and indicates higher prices. You can buy every time a stock rests on the 45° angle with a stop loss order one, two or three points under the 45° angle, but remember the rule – never use a stop loss order more than 3 points away.

Unless stocks are near the low levels or just starting in a bull market or selling at very low prices, I always use a stop loss order on point under the 45° angle. If this angle is broken by one point, you will usually find that the trend has changed at least temporarily and the stock will go lower.

An easy way to calculate accurately how to put on this 45° is:
For example: If the time is 28 days, 28 weeks, or 28 months from the point where the stock was bottom, then the angle of 45° must be 28 points up from the bottom and would cross at 28. This is one of the easiest angles to put on and one of the simplest to learn. You can beat the market by trading against the 45° angle alone if you stick to the rule – wait to buy a stock on the 45° angle or wait to sell it against the 45° angle.

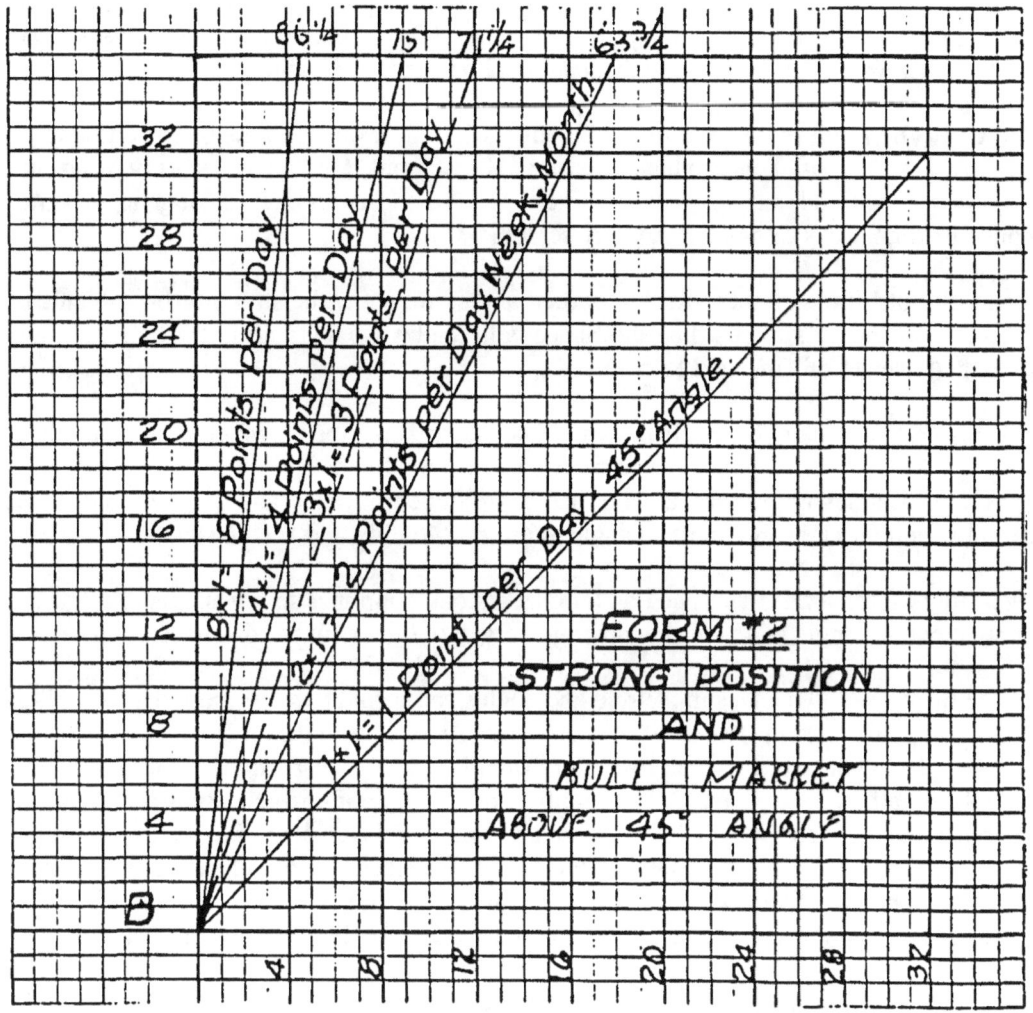

NEXT IMPORTANT ANGLE is the angle of 2 x 1, or the moving-average which moves
       2 x 1   up at the rate of 2 points per day, week or month. It divides the space between the 45-degree angle and the vertical angle into two equal parts and measures 63¾°. That is why it is the next strongest and most important angle. As long as a stock holds above this angle, it is in a stronger position than when it is resting on a 45° angle because it is a more acute angle. When a stock breaks under this angle of 2 x 1, or two points for each time period, then it indicates that it will go lower and reach the 45° angle. Remember the rule of all angles: No matter what angle the stock breaks under, it indicates a decline to the next angle below it.

THIRD IMPORTANT ANGLE which is still stronger as long as a stock hold about it, is
        4 x 1 the angle which moves up 4 points per day, week, or month. This angle is 4 x 1, or 4 points of Space equal one period of Time. It measures 75° and divides the space between the angle of 2 x 1 and the 90° angle into two equal parts. Any stock that continues to advance 4 points per day, 4 points per week, or 4 points per month, and remains above this angle is in a very strong position as long as it stays above it, but when it breaks under, it indicates the next angle or next support point according to the position of the stock on Time.

FOURTH IMPORTANT ANGLE is the angle of 8 x 1 or the one that moves up 8 points
        8 x 1 per day, week or month. This angle measures 82½°, As long as a stock can hold above this angle on daily, weekly or monthly chart, it is in the strongest possible position, but when it reverses trend and declines below this angle, then it indicates a decline to the next angle.

NEXT ANGLE: It is possible to use an angle of 16 x 1, or 16 points of Price to one period
    16 x 1 of Time, which measures 86¼°, but this angle is only used in fast advancing markets, like 1929, when stocks are moving up or down 16 points per day, week or month, and very seldom.

You will note that with these four important angles we show the strong or bullish side of the market. All the time by dividing the Space with angles we are getting the half-way point or the gravity center of Time and Price.

3 x 1 ANGLE: Note the angle drawn in Green, marked "3 x 1", which moves up at the rate of 3 points per day, week or month, measuring 71¼°. This angle is important at times after markets have had a prolonged advance and are a long distance up from the bottom. It is an important angle to use on Monthly and Weekly charts.

These are all the angles you need as long as a stock continues to advance and work up and stays above the angle of 45° or the moving-average of one point per day, week or month.

While there are 360 degrees in a circle and angles can form at any of these degrees, all of the important angles form between "0" to "90" because 90 is straight up and down and the most acute angle on which a stock can rise. For example: The 45° angle divides the space from "0" to "90" in half. The angle of 135° is simply another angle of 45° because it is one-half of the next quadrant between 90 and 180. 225 and 315 in a circle are also 45 ° angles. Therefore all of the angles valuable in determining the trend of a stock are found between "0" and "90" degrees. When we divide 90° by 8 we get the most important angles to use – then divide it by 3 we get 30° and 60° angles, which are important to use for Time and Resistance Points.

WHAT KIND OF BOTTOMS TO DRAW ANGLES
OR MOVING-AVERAGE LINES FROM

DAILY CHART: If a stock has been declining for some time – then starts to rally (by rallying from a bottom it must make higher bottoms every day and higher tops) – then after a 3-day rally on the daily high and low chart, you can put on the 45° angle and the angle of 2 x 1 from the bottom or low point. As a rule, it will only be necessary to put on these two angles at first. If this bottom holds and is not broken, then you can put on the other angles from the bottom.

WEEKLY CHART: If a stock is declining and reacts for more than one week and continues down, we will say, for three weeks or more, then starts to rally and advances two weeks or more, you would start to put the angles on from the low point of the decline, only using the angles above the 45° angle until the stock again breaks under the 45° angle – after that you would use the other angles on the lower or bearish side of the Square.

WHAT TO DO AFTER THE 45° ANGLE FROM BOTTOM IS BROKEN

After a stock makes top, either temporary or otherwise, and breaks under the 45° angle and starts moving down, then the first thing you do is to draw angles below the 45° angle, starting from the bottom or low point. Note example marked "Form #3":

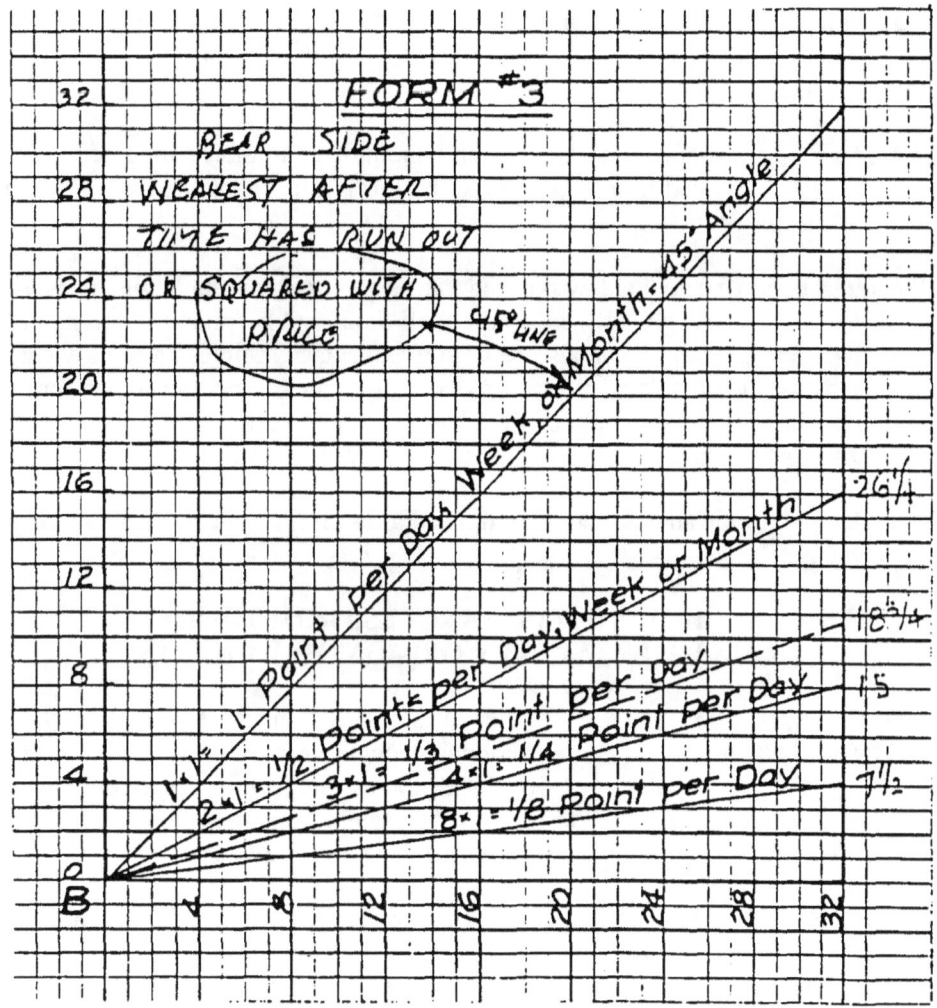

FIRST ANGLE ON BEAR SIDE OF THE SQUARE: The first angle that you draw on the bear side of the Square is the angle of 2 x 1 or 2 points over and one point up, which moves at the rate of one-half point per day, week or month and measures 26¼°. This is the first support angle which the stock should reach after it breaks under the 45° angle. As a general rule, when the stock reaches this angle, it will receive support and rally. Sometimes it will rest on it for a long period of time, holding on this angle and making higher bottoms. But when this angle of 2 x 1, or moving-average of one-half point per day, week or month is broken, then you must draw the next angle of 4 x 1.

NEXT IMPORTANT ANGLE: The next important angle on the bear side of the Square,
4 x 1 which moves up at the rate of 1/4 -point per day is the angle of 4 x 1, measuring 15°. It will be the next strong support angle which the stock should get support on and rally from.

NEXT ANGLE 8 x 1: Then after the 4 x 1 angle is broken, the next important angle that you will put on your chart is the angle of 8 x 1, which moves at the rate of 1/8-point per day, week or month and measure 7½°. This is often a very strong support angle. After a stock has had a big decline, it will often rest on this angle several times or may make final bottom and start up from this angle, crossing other angles and getting back into a strong position again. Therefore this angle is important to use on a monthly or weekly chart after a prolonged decline.

ANGLE 16 x 1: This angle can be used on a monthly chart after a long period of time has elapsed from an important bottom. It moves at the rate of 1/16 point per month and measures 3¾°.

ANGLE OF 3 x 1: This angle, drawn in red ink, is a very important angle, measuring 18¾°. I strongly advise using it at all times and keeping it up on monthly charts from any important bottom. It can also be used to advantage at times on weekly charts, but is seldom of much value on a daily chart. It moves at the rate of one-third point per day, week, or month. By drawing this on the monthly chart for a long period of years, you will soon be convinced of its value and also by testing it on a weekly chart, will find it valuable.

This completes all of the angles that you will need to use from any bottom at any time.

HOW TO DRAW ANGLES FROM TOPS
ON DAILY, WEEKLY OR MONTHLY CHARTS

POSITION UNDER 45° ANGLE After a stock has made top and declined for a
DRAWN FROM TOP: reasonable length of time, say, three days, three weeks or three months, breaking previous bottoms, then you start to draw angles down from the top. Note example marked "Form #4", which is the pattern for drawing angles from the top under the 45° angle. (See page 10)

45° ANGLE FROM TOP: The first angle you draw is the angle of 45° or a moving-average which indicates a decline of one point per day, week or month. As long as the stock is below this angle, it is in the weakest position and in a bear market.

OTHER ANGLES: In many cases a stock will start declining an average of 8 points per day, week or month, or 4 points per day, week or month, or 2 points per day, week or month, therefore you should put on all of these angles from the top, which move down faster than the angle of 45°.

WEAKEST POSITION: The stock is in the weakest possible position when it declines and keeps under the angle of 8 x 1. It is in the next weakest position when it is dropping down at the rate of 4 points per day, week or month, or under the angle of 4 x 1. It is in its next weakest position when it is dropping down under the angle of 2 x 1.

STRONGEST POSITION: The stock is in a stronger position and indicates a better rally when it crosses the angle of 2 x 1, but this depends on how far it is down from the top and how far the angles are apart, as will be explained later under the rules.

CHANGING TREND: As long as a stock is declining one point per day, week or month, or falling below or under the 45° angle, it is still in a bear market and in a very weak position. When a stock rallies and crosses the angle of 45° after a prolonged decline, then you are ready to put on the angles on the other side of the 45° angle, which show that the stock is in a stronger position in a bear market and may be getting ready to change into a bull market.

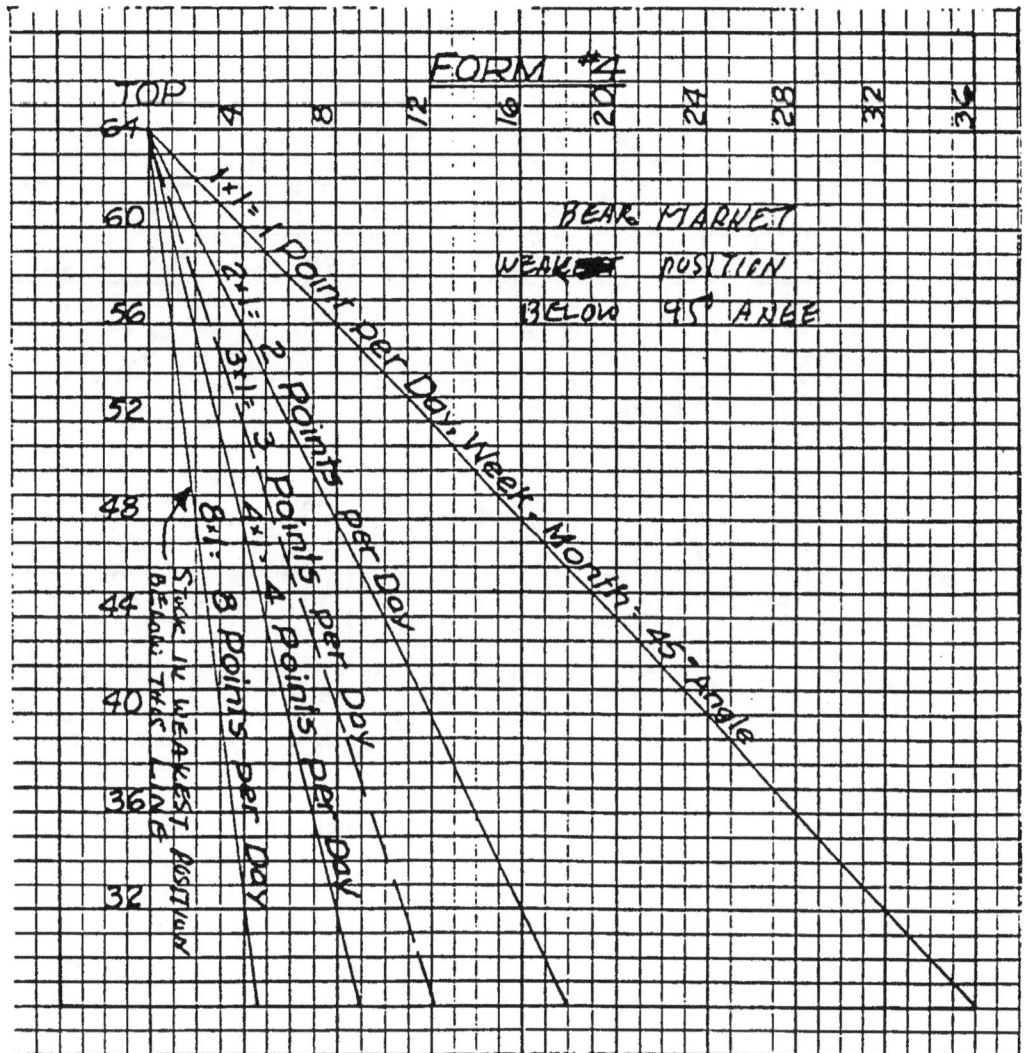

POSITION ABOVE 45° ANGLE DRAWN FROM TOP

Refer to Form #5, which is the pattern for drawing angles above the 45° angle from the top. (See page 11)

2 x 1 ANGLE FROM TOP: The first angle or moving-average you draw after the 45° angle from the top is crossed and after the stock indicates that it has made a temporary bottom is the angle of 2 x 1 moving over 2 points and down one point, or

1/2-point per unit of Time. This is moving down at the rate of 1/2-point per month, week or day.

4 x 1 ANGLE: The next is the angle of 4 x 1 which moves down at the rate of 1/4-point per day, week. or month.

8 x 1 ANGLE: The next angle is the angle of 8 x 1, which moves down at the rate of one point every 8 days, 8 weeks or 8 months, or 1/8-point per time period.

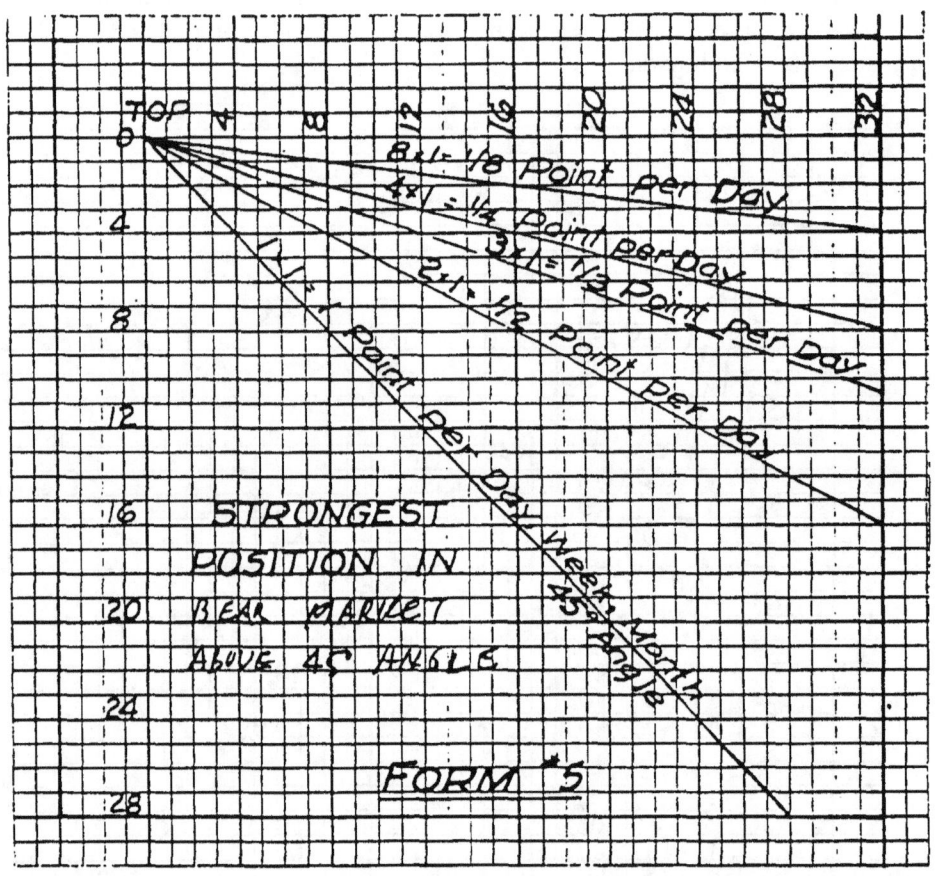

STRONG POSITION: After the stock has crossed the angle of 45° and rallied up to the angle of 2 x 1, it will meet selling and react to some angle coming up from the bottom of the last move, but it is in a stronger position when it holds above this angle of 2 x 1 and is in the next strongest position when it crosses the angle of 4 x 1. Crossing the angle of 8 x 1, which is of least importance, it indicates that it is in a very strong position again from the top. You must always consider a movement coming up from bottom and its position on angles from the bottom to determine its strength. It is important to consider the number of points it has move up from the bottom and how many points it is down from the top.

3 x 1 ANGLE: The angle of 3 x 1 drawn in red on Form #5 moves down at the rate of one point every three days, three weeks or three months, or one third point per day, week or month. This angle is important to use after prolonged declines.

This completes the forms of all the angles that you will need to use at any time from tops or bottoms. Practice putting these angles on tops and bottoms until you thoroughly understand how to do them and know that you are getting them absolutely accurate. Then you can begin to study the rules for determining the trend according to the position of the stock on angles.

DOUBLE AND TRIPLE TOPS OR BOTTOMS

ANGLES CROSSING EACH OTHER: When there is a double bottom several days, weeks or months apart, you draw angles from these bottoms, which are near the same price levels. For example: From the first bottom draw a 45° angle and from the second bottom draw an angle of 2 x 1 – then when these angles cross each other, it will be an important point for a change in trend.

Note on chart marked Form #6 that I have drawn the 45° angle from the first bottom "1B" and the angle of 2 x 1 on the right hand side of the 45° angle. Then, from the second bottom "2B" I have drawn a 45° angle and the angle of 2 x 1, which gains 2 points per day, week or month, on the left hand or bull side of the 45° angle. You will note that the angle of 2 x 1 from the second bottom crosses the angle of 2 x 1 on the bear side from the first bottom at 48, and that when the stock breaks under these angles, a change in trend takes place and it goes lower.

Note that the angle of 2 x 1 from the third bottom "3B" crosses the angle of 2 x 1 on the bear side from the first bottom at 53½ and crosses the 45° angle from the second bottom at 58. This would be a point to watch for change in trend. I have placed a circle where these angles from the different bottoms come together.

Apply this rule to double tops and triple tops in the same way. It is not necessary for the tops or bottom to be exactly at the same price level, but near the same level. Remember, always draw 45° angles from all important tops and bottoms.

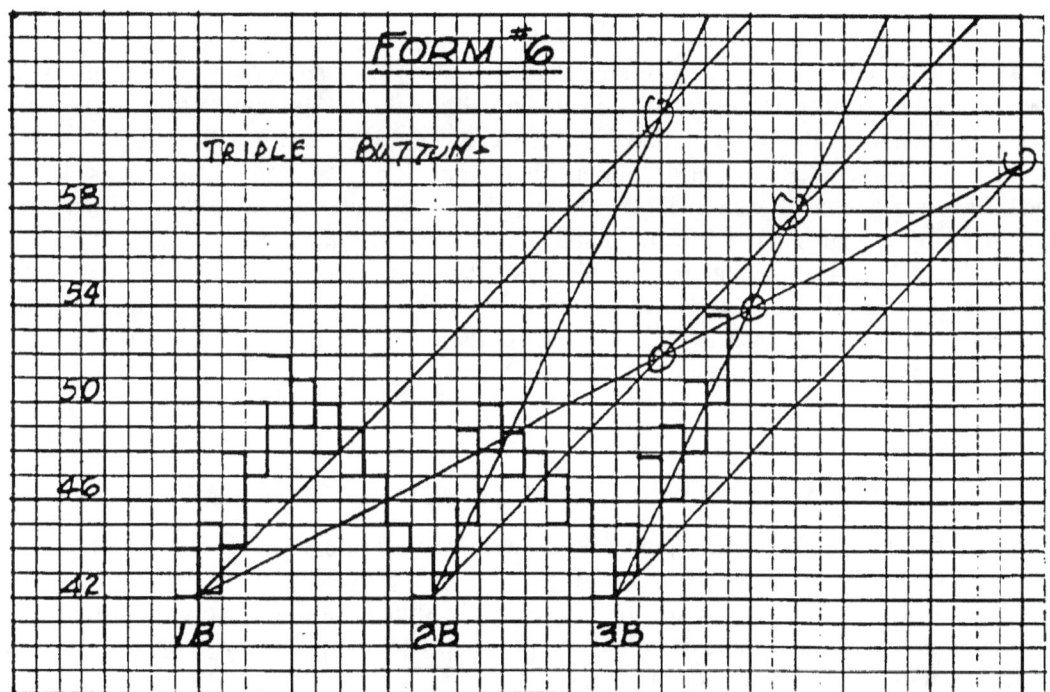

PARALLEL ANGLES

Parallel angles or lines run from important tops and bottoms. As previously explained, the 45° angle is the most important and should be drawn from all important tops and bottoms. If a stock starts advancing, we draw a 45° angle from the bottom – then if the stock makes top, declines and makes a higher bottom – then advances and makes a higher top, we draw a 45° angle from the first top, running the line up. This will give the oscillation or width of fluctuation in a parallel between the 45° angle from the bottom and the 45° angle running up from the top. Often a stock will advance to the 45° angle from the first top, fail to cross it, then decline and rest on the 45° angle from the first bottom – then advance again, working up for a prolonged bull campaign between these parallel angles.

When the angles are very far apart, you can draw another 45° angle equidistant between them, which is often a strong support angle from which a stock will rally, but when it breaks under, it declines to the bottom parallel.

Parallels can form between the angles of 2 x 1 or 4 x 1 just the same as between 45° angles, which often occurs in slow-moving stocks.

GEOMETRICAL ANGLES OR MOVING-AVERAGE LINES DRAWN FROM "0"

When a stock reaches bottom and starts up, you have been instructed to draw angles from this exact low point, which shows the support in time periods, but there are other angles that later on will be just as important and sometimes more important than the angles drawn from the bottom of a stock. These are the angles that begin at "0" or zero and move up at the same rate that they move up from the bottom. The starting pint must be on the same line that the bottom is made on as the time period begins from this bottom, but the angles move up from "0". These angles should be started every time a stock makes a bottom, especially on weekly and monthly charts, and should also be carried up on important movements on the daily chart. Example: See chart marked Form #7 on page 14.

If a stock makes low at 20, as shown on the chart, starting the 45° angle from "0", when will this angle reach 20? Answer: It will reach 20 in 20 days, 20 weeks, or 20 months from the bottom or its starting point. In other words, in 20 days, 20 weeks, or 20 months, it will be up 20 from "0" and at the price where the stock made bottom. Then the angle will continue on up at the same rate, and later, when the stock breaks under the 45° angle from the actual bottom made at 20 and breaks the other support angles drawn from the actual bottom at 20, the next important point for support will be the angle of 45° moving up from "0". When this angle is broken, it is in the weakest possible position and indicates much lower prices, but this depends on how high the stock is selling and how much it has declined at the time it breaks the 45° angle from "0". These angles drawn from "0", especially the 45° angle, proves when Price and Time are balancing or when the stock is squaring out from its bottom.

"0" ANGLES STARTING AT THE TIME TOP IS MADE

When a stock reaches extreme top on a daily, weekly or monthly chart and the trend turns down, you should start an angle of 45° from "0" moving up from the exact space and date that the top is made. This will prove the square of the time period. It is very important when this angle is reached and indicates a change in trend. It is the last strong support and when broken, it will indicate much lower prices.

I have instructed you in each case to first draw the 45° angle from bottom, top and from "0" at bottom and top, but this does not mean that you must not use the other angles. All of the other angles can be used from "0", but the 45° angle is the first and most important. After this angle is broken, then you can use the other angles. It is not necessary to carry all of them along until you need them, but on the monthly chart, after a long series of years, these other angles should be carried along when the stock begins to approach the levels where they would be broken or where the stock would rest on them and receive support.

45° ANGLE FROM "0" TO TOP AND BOTTOM: When a 45° angle moving up from "0" reaches the line or price of the bottom, it is very important – then again when it reaches the point of the extreme high price, it is very important for a change in trend.

You should carry 45° angles and other angles up from "0" from all important first, second, and third higher bottoms, especially those where very much time has elapsed between these bottoms. You should also start the angle of 45° up from "0" from the first, second, and third lower tops, especially those which show much time period elapsed. These angles are the most important to be carried on the weekly and monthly charts.

Never overlook keeping up the angles from "0" because they will tell you when Time is squaring out with Price from tops and bottoms and will locate support angles or moving-average lines at a point on the bear side after the first 45° angle from a bottom is broken. You could not locate this support point in any other way except by the angles from "0".

You should go back over past records and bring up these angles and square out different tops and bottoms so that you can prove to yourself the great value of using these angles.

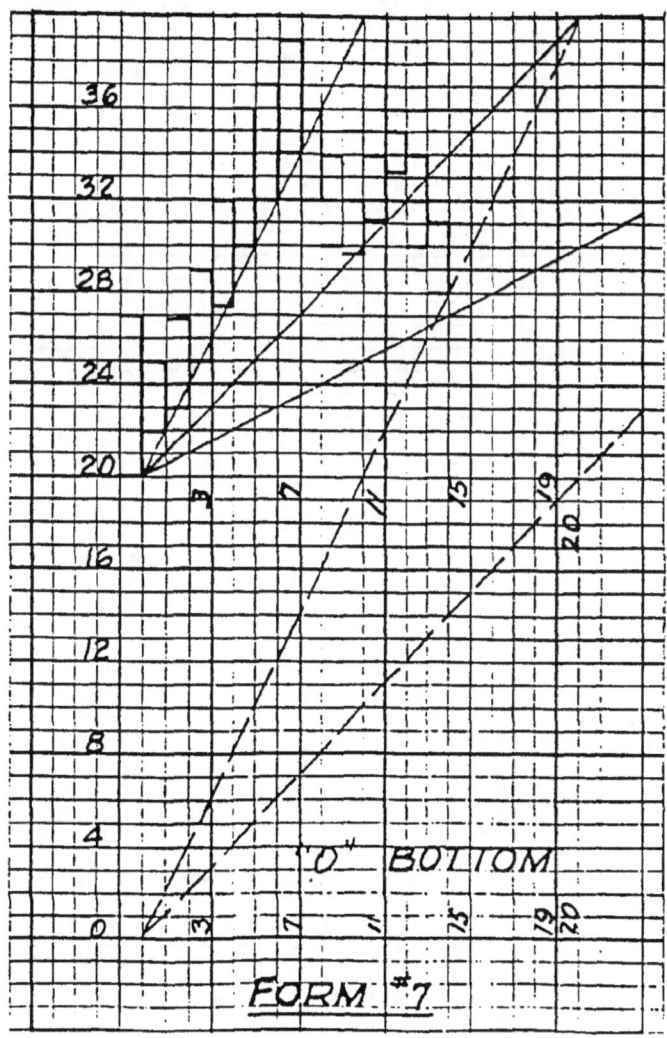

ANGLES FROM TOPS DOWN TO "0" AND UP AGAIN

A 45° angle starting down from any important top on a monthly or weekly chart should be continued down until it reaches "0" and then started up again at the same rate. After a long number of years between important tops and bottoms, this angle coming down and going up again is important. A 45° angle can also be continued down from any important bottom to "0" and then started up again. This will show the squaring of Price and Time from either top or bottom.

Angles can be started from "0" at the time any important time cycle runs out. For example: U.S. Steel made extreme low in 1904. May, 1924 would be the end of a 20-year cycle or 120 months. In May, 1924 Steel made top at 109 against a 45° angle beginning at "0" at the time bottom was made at 38 in February 1915. On account of the importance of this top and a 20-year cycle running out here, we would start a 45° angle and other angles, if we need them, from "0" in May, 1924.

May, 1931 would end a 7-year cycle of 84 months from 1924. The 45° angle running up from "0" in May, 1924 crossed at 84 in May, 1931. Note that Steel made low at 83⅛ in June, 1931. In June, 1924 Steel made the last low at 94¼, showing the importance of the end of the 20-year cycle. The 45° angle moving up from "0" in June, 1924 crossed at 84 in June, 1931, and Steel declined and rested on this angle.

TWO 45° ANGLES FROM THE SAME BOTTOM

As we have previously explained, the 45° angle moves up at the rate of one point per month and moves down at the rate of one point per month.

Refer to example on Chart #8

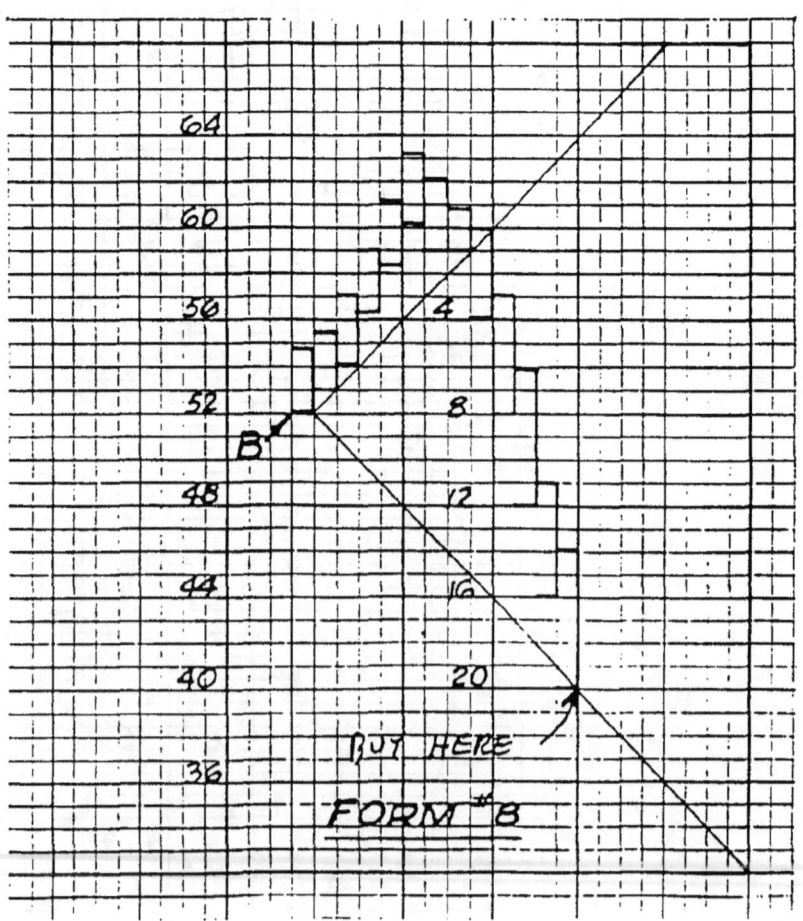

You will note that the low on this chart is shown as 52 and the stock moves up to a high of 63. A 45° angle is drawn up from the bottom, and after the stock reaches top and starts to work down, it breaks the 45° angle, getting under it at a price of 59. You will note that I have drawn another 45° angle down from the bottom at 52. At the point where the stock breaks under the 45° angle moving up from 52 to the 45° angle moving down from 52, the distance in points is 16, therefore the angles have widened until the stock could decline 16 points, if it went straight down, before it reached the 45° angle moving down from the bottom.

Note that I have show on the chart that the stock continues down until it reaches 40, where it rests on the 45° angle from the bottom at 52. This would indicate the strongest support point and at least a temporary rally, especially as the stock is down 23 points from the top. Later you will find under "Resistance Levels" that 22½ to 24 points is a strong support point.

U.S. STEEL: Take the extreme low point of U.S. Steel at 111¼ in January, 1927. Start a 45° angle on the monthly chart moving up at the rate of one point per month – then start a 45° angle moving down at the same rate. This shows the spreading of the angles and what can happen when Steel breaks under the 45° angle coming up from that bottom and the point where it can decline in extreme panicky markets, like 1931 and 1932.

The 45° angle coming up from the low of January, 1927 crossed at 156 in October, 1930. When U.S. Steel broke this angle it went right on down to 134⅜ in December, 1930, where it rested on the angle of 2 x 1 from this bottom of January, 1927 – then rallied to February, 1931, and at the time it broke under the angle of 45° from 111¼, it was on the 45th month, another indication of a sharp, severe decline. Here we look at the 45° angle moving down from 111¼ and find it is 90 points down from the 45° angle moving up from 111¼ . These angle separate at the rate of two points per month and being 45 months from the bottom, the stock would have to decline 90 points to strike the 45° angle moving down from the bottom. The angles being so wide apart indicated that the stock could have a wide open break. This happened in December, 1931, when Steel broke under the 45° angle moving down from 111¼, putting it into a very weak position – in fact, in the weakest position that a stock can get in until it can recover this angle. In June, 1932, when U.S. Steel declined to 21¼, it had dropped under the 45° angle moving down from the last low of 113⅜ made in March, 1925, and closed two months below this angle before it started to recover angles.

This shows that when a stock gets into a very weak position by dropping under important angles moving down from bottoms, after having broken strong angles moving up from bottom, it can decline to very low levels. These extreme fluctuations and declines have happened in the past and will happen again in the future. This proves the squaring out of Time on the down side or the balancing up of Price and Time.

Here is another illustration of the balancing of Price with Time: The angle of 45° moving up from "0" from the bottom at 21⅞ from October, 1907 crossed at 262 in September, 1929 and Steel advance to 261¾, which show that in 262 months from the bottom in 1907 Steel had advanced an equivalent of one point per month. By striking the 45° angle and failing to cross it, it indicated that the Time was up and that the stock was turning downtrend for a prolonged bear market.

ANGLES OR MOVING-AVERAGE LINES FROM ONE TOP TO THE NEXT TOP

Refer to example on Chart #9 on page 17.

THE W.D. GANN MASTER STOCK MARKET COURSE

GA-17

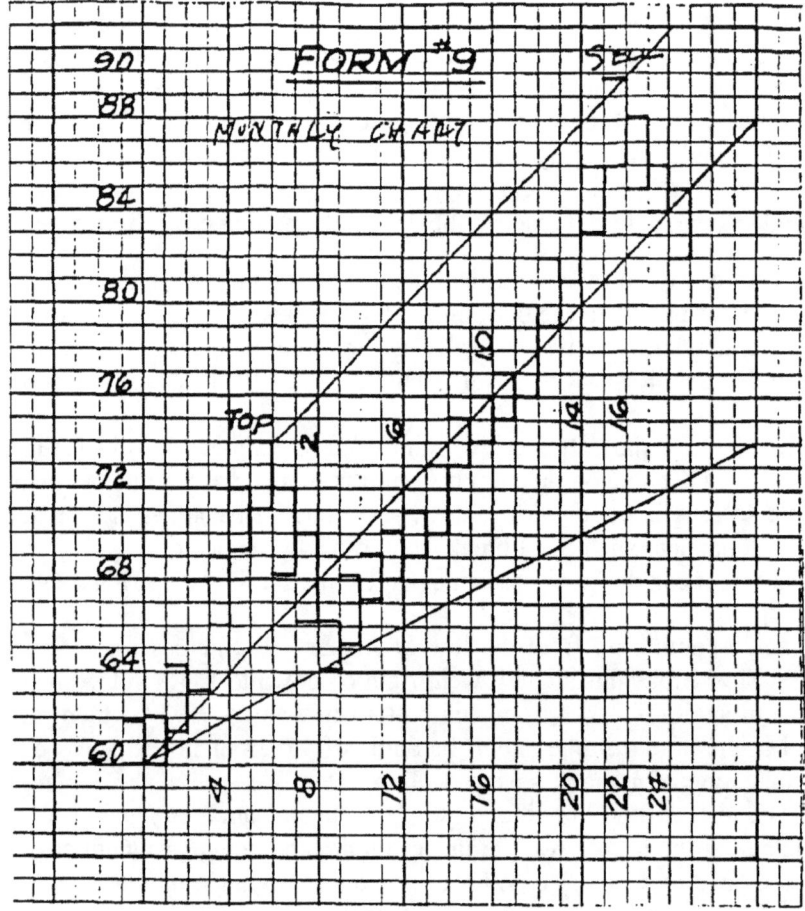

You will see that we have started the bottom at 60. The stock advances six months to 74, to a point marked "T" and makes top – reacts for three months to 64, breaking the 45° angle but resting on the angle of 2 x 1 from the bottom – then starts advancing and finally crosses again the 45° angle from 60, getting into a stronger position, having regained this angle. In order to determine where it might meet resistance, as it is in new high territory, we draw a 45° angle from the top at 74. The stock advances to 90 on the 22nd month from the bottom, striking the 45° angle from the first top at 74, on the 16th month from the first top. Being 16 points up above the first top, the Time equals the advance in the Price above the first top. The 45° angle shows one to three points above the 45° angle. A decline starts and in the third month the stock again breaks under the 45° angle from the bottom (at 60) at a very high level. In other words, it is 24 points up from the bottom and is now in a much weaker position, because it is so far from the base of support, and indicates a decline again to the angle of 2 x 1 (marked in green).

Don't overlook this rule: After a stock has advanced to a new high level, then declines to the old top at 74, this may be a support point unless it breaks 3 points under it. If it does and also breaks the angle of 2 x 1, it will be in a weaker position and the next point to watch for support and a rally would be the next bottom at 64.

ANGLES FROM BOTTOM OF FIRST SHARP DECLINE

When a stock that has been advancing for some time, makes top and holds for several days, several weeks or several months, then turns the trend down and has a sharp, severe decline, there is always a rally after this first decline. It usually makes a lower top on this secondary rally and then starts to work lower again. The bottom of the first decline is a very important point to draw angles from, especially the 45° angle moving down, as I have done on the chart marked Form #10.

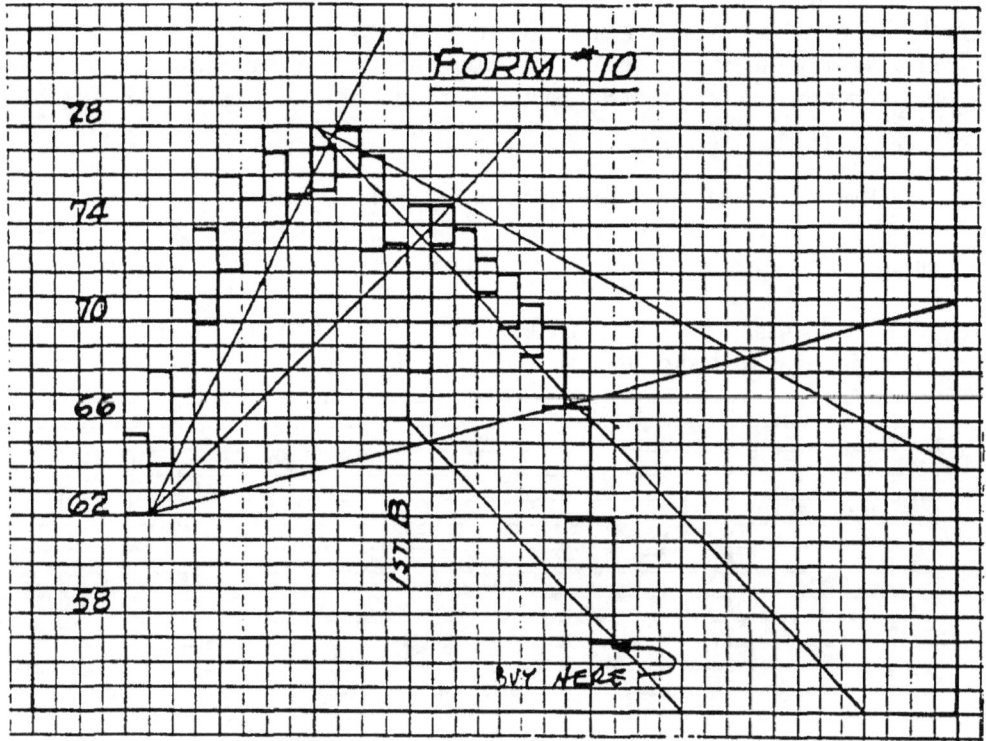

This chart shows the stock rallying up to around 75, where the 45° angle coming up from the last bottom crosses the angle of 2 x 1 coming down from the top. Then the decline started and at 66 the stock broke back under the angle of 45° from the top, which put it in a very weak position. It declined to the angle of 45° coming down from the bottom of the first sharp decline. This would be the squaring out of time from the bottom and would be a place to buy for a rally. A stock will often decline and drop a little below this angle from the bottom – then if it holds for several days or weeks under this angle or on it, it is a place to buy for a rally.

On a Monthly Chart always carry this angle down from the bottom of the first sharp decline, as it often becomes very important later on in a campaign.

After a stock has been advancing for some time and then has a sharp break lasting 2 to 3 days, 2 to 3 weeks, or 2 to 3 months – then rallies and afterward breaks under the lows of this first sharp break, it indicates that the main trend has turned down and that it is going lower.

Apply the same rule when a stock has been declining for a long time and then makes a sharp, quick recovery for 2 to 3 days, 2 to 3 weeks, or 2 to 3 months, then reacts and then crosses this first rally point that it made, an indication of higher prices.

LAST SWING IN A BULL OR BEAR MARKET

It is important to draw angles from the point where the market starts up and makes its last run in a bull market. Refer to Chart #11 on page 19.

In this example note point marked "last bottom". In the last stage of the bull market a fast advance follows to a price of 84. We have drawn the angle of 2 x 1 (a gain of 2 points per day, week or month) and the 45° angle from this bottom. When the angle of 2 x 1 was broken, it indicated that he trend had turned down. The stock declined and rested on the 45° angle – then rallied and made a second lower top – then broke the 45° angle – declined sharply and rested on the 45° angle drawn from the top at 84, which indicated that Time and Price had squared out or were equal. This would be a point to buy, with a stop loss order 2 to 3 points under this angle, for a rally back to the angle of 2 x 1 from the top, as shown on the chart.

In very active fast-moving markets a stock may stay above the angle of 4 x 1 or the angle of 8 x 1 from the "last bottom", but on the daily or weekly chart after this first acute angle is broken, it indicates that the trend has turned down.

Always remember that after a prolonged advance, when the main trend turns down, it is safer to wait for rallies and sell short than to buy against the trend.

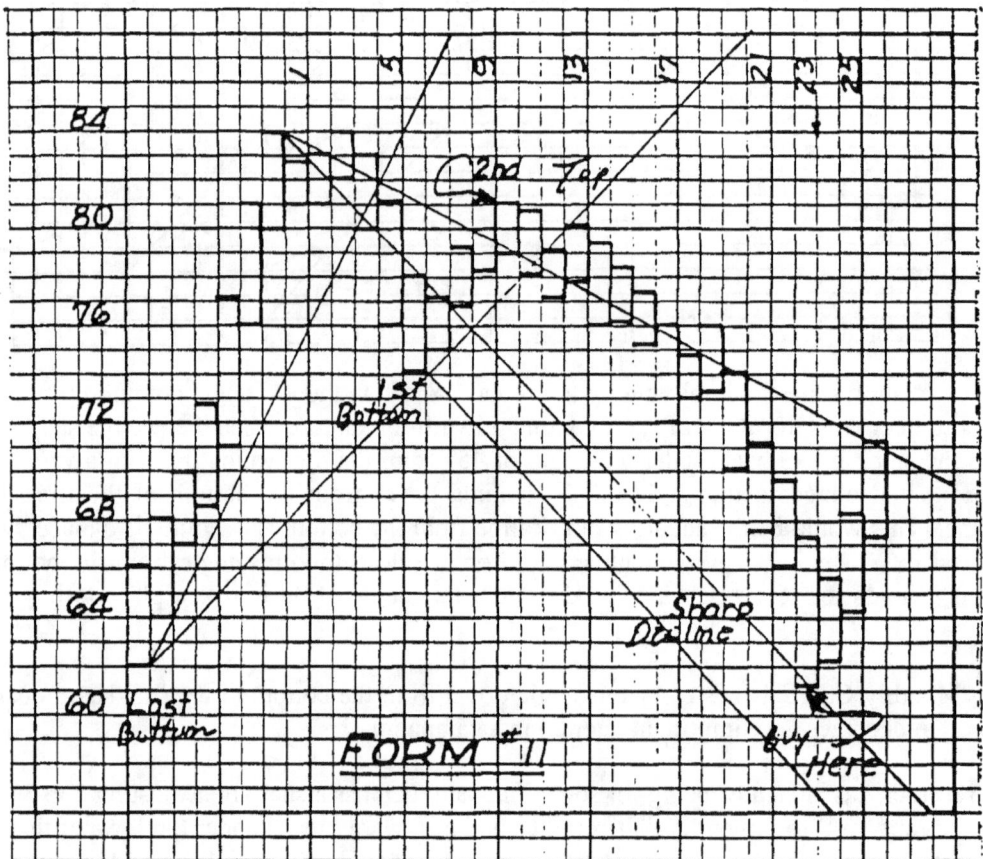

All of these rules are reversed at the end of a bear market or sharp decline. It is important to note when the market starts down from the last top or rally and makes its last run to bottom. Draw angles from this last top and watch when the market reaches these important angles and crossed them. For example:

On March 9, 1932 the Dow-Jones 30 Industrial Averages made last top at 90, from which a decline followed, with very small rallies, reaching bottom at 41 on July 8, 1932. Note on the weekly chart that the angle of 2 x 1 from the top at 90 crossed at 50 in the week ending July 30, 1932 and after they crossed this level they never declined to 50 again, and advanced to 81 in September, 1932. The crossing of this angle was the first definite indication that the main trend had turned up.

It is also important to review the major swing from November 9, 1931, when the Averages reached a high of 119½, to the low at 40½ in July, 1932. This was the last big swing of the bear market, a decline of 79 points. The half-way point of this was at 80. In September, 1932 the Averages rallied to 81 – then after they reacted to 50 and advanced, getting above the half-way point, and crossed 81, they indicated an advance to 119 anyway. After they crossed the half-way point the second time and advanced above 81, they never sold down to it again until they advanced to 149½ in November, 1935.

After a stock has been advancing for a long time, in the last run when there is a lot of momentum, it may cross angles from previous tops or bottoms, then fall back under them, which is an indication of weakness. When a stock has a sharp decline and is making bottom, it will drop under important angles and then recover quickly, getting above them, which show that it is getting into a strong position and changing trend.

ANGLES FROM HIGHER BOTTOMS AND LOWER TOPS

What rule should be followed when stocks make higher bottoms and lower tops?

As stocks advance and make higher bottoms on the monthly, weekly or daily chart, you should always draw angles from higher bottoms. Then, in the last section of a bull market, if these important angles are broken from the last bottom, you know that the trend has turned down.

Apply this same rule as a market declines. Draw the angles from each lower top and watch the angles until the stocks again cross the 45° angle from a second, third, or fourth lower top. The second lower top or second higher bottom is always very important to draw angles from and to measure Time from as well.

Example: Dow-Jones Industrial Averages –
September 3, 1929 – Extreme high-
November 13, 1929 – Bottom of first sharp decline-
April 17, 1930 – Big rally in bear market, second lower top-
July 8, 1932 – Extreme low, final bottom-
September 8, 1932 – Top of first sharp advance after bear market ended-
February and March, 1933 - Second higher bottom from which bull market was resumed.

These are the most important tops and bottoms to draw angles from.

SECTIONS OF MARKET CAMPAIGNS:

All market campaigns, up or down, move in 3 to 4 week sections. When an advance starts, the market runs for several weeks or several months and then halts for several weeks or months, moving up and down over a range of 5 to 20 points, according to the price of the stock – then the advance is resumed and the stock crosses the high level of the first section, moves higher, halts again, and reacts for a period of time – then crosses the top of the second section and moves up again for another period of time and halts for the third time, which is a very important point to watch as markets often culminate at the end of the third section and a bigger decline follows,

Most market run out in three important sections or campaigns. However, after resting and reacting, if a stock crossed the third top, it will then move up to the top of the fourth section. This fourth advance may be a shorter period of time than the previous sections, or in some cases may consume a greater period of time, especially if the stock is very active and high-priced. This fourth top is very important and generally marks a culmination and a reversal for a bigger decline.

For example: On March 12, 1935 CHRYSLER MOTORS declined and made low at 31--

FIRST SECTION: of the advance carried the stock up to 49¾ on May 16, then the stock declined to 41¼.

SECOND SECTION: On June 27, the advance started and the stock advanced to new high levels, reaching 62¾ on August 10, which was top of the second section – then there was a reaction to 57½ and a resting period.

THIRD SECTION: Then there was another advance which started August 28. The stock crossed the top of the second section and reached high at 74 on September 11, top of the third section. Then followed a reaction to 68 on September 21.

FOURTH SECTION: In October the top of the third section was crossed and on November 18 Chrysler reached 90, top of the fourth section, where it held for 5 weeks in a 6-point range while distribution was taking place. This was a most important point to watch for a final top and a change in trend. Then the trend turned down.

Reverse this rule in a bear market. Watch the action of the market when it makes the third and fourth decline. But, remember, in a bear market when rallies come, they may make only one section or one move or in extreme cases only make the second section – then reverse and follow the main trend down.

You will find it very helpful to study and watch these various sections of a campaign and by applying the angles from tops and bottoms you can detect the first minor and major changes in trend.

STRENGTH OR WEAKNESS DENOTED BY POSITION ON ANGLES

The angles on the Monthly and Weekly Charts are of greater importance than those on the Daily Chart because the daily trend can change quite often, while only the major changes are shown according to the angles on the Monthly and Weekly Charts.

Always consider the distance a stock is from its beginning point when it breaks any important angle or crosses any important angle. The further away from the beginning point, the more important the change in trend, whether this is crossing an angle from the top or breaking under an angle from the bottom.

WHEN A STOCK IS IN THE WEAKEST POSITION:

A stock is in the weakest position when it has completed distribution and broken under a 45° angle from an important bottom on the weekly or monthly chart. It is also in the weakest position when it has broken under the half-way point between any important top or bottom. The longer the time period has run and the higher the price, the weaker the position. For example:

If a stock has advance to 150 and has only moved down 25 points when the 45° angle from an extreme low on a weekly or monthly chart is broken, then it is in a very weak position because it is so far above the half-way point on its price movement, already having squared out the time period with price.

Weakness in a stock develops when it breaks the 3/4-point, the 2/3-point, the 1/2-point, etc., but the position on the timing angles from the bottom tells you still more about the weak position. A stock shows its first weakness when it breaks the first important angle coming up from the last bottom in the final run in a bull market.

WHEN A STOCK IS IN THE STRONGEST POSITION:
A stock is always in the strongest position coming up from a bottom when it is holding above the very acute angles on the daily, weekly or monthly charts, especially on monthly and weekly charts.

As long as a stock hold above the angle of 2 x 1 (a gain of 2 points per day) on the daily chart, it is in a very strong position as far as the bottom is concerned. In fact, it is always in a strong position on the daily as long as it holds above the 45° angle. The same applies to weekly and monthly charts, which are the most important trend indicators.

I have found that the stocks which have the biggest advances are those that always hold above the angle of 2 x 1 on the monthly chart or gain 2 points per month for a long period of time. I have seen stocks rest 10 or 15 times on the angle of 2 x 1 and never break it until they have advanced 100 points or more. In this way a stock stays ahead of time and stays within the square of time by being far above the angle of 45°, and therefore is in a very strong position. But the time must come when the cycle has run out and the main trend begins to change from a bull market to a bear market – then the breaking of the angle from the last bottom shows a change in trend.

Another indication that a stock is in a strong position is when it advances and moves up above the half-way point of the previous price movement and then holds the half-way point, that is, advances above it and then reacts and fails to break under it. This is just the same as resting on a 45° angle and indicates a very strong position.

STRONGEST BUYING AND SELLING POINTS:
The cinch buying point is when a stock rests on a 45° angle, placing a stop loss order below it.

Another point to buy is on the half-way point of the price movement, placing a stop loss order under the half-way point.

When the main trend is up, it is also safe to buy when a stock reacts to the angle of 2 x 1 (a gain of 2 points per time period) on the weekly or monthly chart.

REGAINING ANGLES OR CROSSING LINES:
remember, when any stock breaks under the 45° angle from the extreme low point of a move on the daily, weekly or monthly chart, it is then in a very weak position and indicates a decline to the next angle. However, when a stock can regain the 45° angle, it is in a stronger position.

The same rule applies to a 45° angle drawn up from any top. When a stock crosses the angle on the daily, weekly or monthly and stays above the 45° angle or any other angle to the left of the 45° angle, it is in a very strong position.

After a stock once drops below or gets above any important angle and then reverses its position by getting back above the angle or dropping back below it, it changes the trend again.

WHEN A STOCK IS IN A STRONG POSITION FROM BOTTOM AND IN WEAK POSITION FROM TOP:

A stock is in a strong position from the bottom when it is keeping above the angle of 45° or the angle of 2 x 1, but at the same time it can be in a weak position when it rallies up and strikes against a 45° angle or the angle of 2 x 1 coming down from the top – then it is a short sale until it can cross these angles or cross previous tops. When it breaks the angles from the bottom, it is in a weak position and indicates lower.

A stock can be in a strong position from the top and in a weak position from the bottom, that is, it may cross some important angles from the top after a long period of time, but at the same time may break under the 2 x 1 angle or 45° angle from the bottom, which would indicate that it is in a weak position and getting ready to go lower.

WHEN ANGLES FROM EXTREME TOP ARE CROSSED:

The 45° angle drawn from the extreme high point of a stock is most important and when it is crossed, a major move may be expected. For example:

> On the weekly chart of the Dow-Jones Industrial Averages, note the 45° angle moving down from 386, the high of September 3, 1929. January 12, 1935 was 279 weeks from the 1929 top. Taking 279 from 386, we get 107, the price at which the angle of 45° would cross. These Averages advanced to 106½ in the week ending January 12, 1935 – then reacted to 100 in the week ending February 9. This was the first time that they had held within one-half point of this angle and the first time that they had ever reached it since the top was made. During the week ending February 16, 1935, the Averages crossed the 45° angle at 103 for the first time, and during the week ending February 23, 1935 advanced to 108, where they hit the angle of 45° moving up from the low of 85½ in September, 1934, and also hit the angle of 2 x 1 coming up from the low of July 8, 1932. This was a strong resistance point and the Averages reacted to 96 in the week ending March 18, 1935, where they rested on the 45° angle from the 1929 top and also where the 3 x 1 angle (a gain of 1/3 point per week) from September, 1929 coming up from "0" crossed the angle of 45° coming down from the 1929 top. This was a strong support point for a change in trend. The advance started and the Averages moved up to new high levels. This proves the importance of angles, especially the 45° angle drawn from any extreme top, and the point at which any other angle crosses the 45° angle.

Watch the 45° angle from 1929 top when it reaches "0" or when it is 386 weeks down from the top. This will be in the latter part of January, 1937. Note what happens at that time.

ANGLES FOR SEMI-WEEKLY CHART

The semi-weekly chart is a great help at the end of extreme advances or extreme declines. By applying all of the rules and using the geometrical angles from tops and bottoms on the semi-weekly chart, you will often get an indication of a change in trend two to three days before a change in trend is shown on the weekly chart.

A change in trend on the semi-weekly chart is of greater importance than a change in trend on the daily chart. It is much better to rely upon this chart than on the daily chart when markets are in a narrow trading range.

ANGLES FOR NEW LISTED STOCKS

Years of experience and research, which has cost me a large amount of money have enabled me to develop a method that will account for all market movements and give rules to determine the trend from any top or bottom.

It is important to know how to determine the trend when a stock is first listed on any exchange. When a stock has never fluctuated before, we have no top or bottom to draw angle from. Therefore, in order to determine the trend, we use the square of 90, which is 90 up and 90 across, and put all the natural angles on, like the Pattern Chart. As we have said before, the square of 90 is very important because it is one-quarter of a circle of 360°, and as 90° or the vertical angle is the greatest angle that can be used, all of the other angles are found between "0" and "90".

If a new stock opens at 18 or any point below 22½, then you could make out a square of 22½ to determine the position of the stock on angles. If the stock opened at 36 or any point between 22½ and 45, you could make up a square of 45. If it opened at 50 or between 45 and 67, you could make up a square of 67½. However, you could place any stock opening at any price below 90 in the square of 90 and get its proper position and strength or weakness on angles. If the stock opened at 100 or above 90 and under 135, you could make up a square of 135, or could make another square of 90 numbering from 90 to 180.

You could start a monthly chart on a square of 90 at the price where the stock opens or trading begins, as shown on U.S. Steel. (Refer to Special Analysis of U.S. Steel.). After the stock breaks any of these natural angles drawn from "0", it is just the same as breaking under an angle drawn from a bottom. When it crosses any of the angles drawn down from "90", it is just the same as crossing an angle from a top, as you can see by experimenting with U.S. Steel or any other stock, but always consider price resistance levels and how much the stock is up or down from the bottom or top. You can determine the first change in trend by the 3-day or semi-weekly Chart, daily chart, and weekly chart by bringing up the important Geometrical Angles from any higher or lower bottom as the market movements develop.

QUICK CALCULATION OF ANGLES

It is not necessary to draw these angles from a point a long way back. You can make the calculation and determine where they cross. For example: Suppose in 1900, in the month of January, a stock made bottom at 15, and we wish to calculate where the 45° angle will cross 10 years later in January 1910. The 45° angle rises at the rate of one point per month – then 10 years would be 120 points or months – add this to 15 at the bottom – then the 45° would cross at 135 in January 1910. All of the other angles may be calculated a long period back in the same way.

THE W.D. GANN MASTER STOCK MARKET COURSE

ANGLE SELDOM USED

3 x 2 ANGLE: This angle of 3 x 2 on the left side of the 45° angle rises at the rate of 8 points in 12 months. A stock must show a gain of 3/4-point per month in order to keep above this angle. This angle can be used when other important angles from the bottom have spread far apart, as it will show the position and resistance or support point between the other angles.

LATITUDE AND LONGITUDE

On all charts – daily, weekly or monthly – the price must move up or down on the vertical angles. Therefore, the price movement is the same as latitude. You should begin with zero or "0" on any chart – daily, weekly or monthly – and draw the important angles and resistance levels across, which measure latitude.

Next, number the time points in days, weeks or months across, and draw the horizontal angle at each important natural angle, such as 11¼, 22½, 33¾, 45, 56¼, 67½, 78¾, 90, 101¼, 112½, 120, etc. Then you will know when price reaches these important angles and meets resistance.

Longitude measures the time running across the chart, as it moves over each day, week or month. Therefore, you must keep your chart numbered from each important top and bottom in order to get the time measurements according to angles. These important angles, such as 11¼, 22½, 33¾, 45, 56¼, 60, 67½, 78¾, 90, etc from each bottom and top will show you where the strongest resistance in price and time takes place. These angles prove the parallel or crossing point. Study past records and see what has happened when prices on monthly charts reached these important angles or time periods.

For example: 90 points up in price from "0" we draw an angle horizontally across the chart. Then 90 days, weeks or months, going to the right across the chart, we draw a vertical angle up, which will cross the horizontal angle at 90 and prove the square. By keeping all these angles up and understanding them on your charts, you will know when important time cycles are running out.

If the price of a stock at 60 comes out on the 60th day, week or month, it will meet strong resistance because it has reached the square of price with Time. It is at the same latitude or price and the same longitude or time period. You can always put the square of 90 on a chart – either daily, weekly or monthly – and use the natural angles, but I advise only using this on the weekly and monthly. You can begin this square of 90 from any bottom or top, that is, going up 90 points, or from the natural points, which are 90, 135, 180, but you must not fail to square the extreme low and high price as well as the second and third lower tops and higher bottoms with Time.

RULE FOR KEEPING TIME PERIODS ON CHARTS

It is very important that you keep the time periods on all of your charts, carrying them across from the bottom and top of each important move in order to check up and know that you have your angles or moving-averages at the correct point and to see where major and minor cycles indicate changes in trend.

TIME PERIODS FROM BOTTOMS: When a stock makes bottom one month and then the following month makes a higher bottom and a higher top, or anyway, after it makes a higher bottom and rallies for one month or more, you can start numbering from that bottom. The month that it makes the low belongs to the old or downward movement and is the last move down. You count the first month up as one and then number across on the 1/2-inch squares, running them across, adding four each time.

For example: If a stock has made bottom and advanced 50 points, you look down at the bottom of the chart and find that you are on the 25th month – then the angle of 2 x 1, moving up 2 points per month, would cross at 50, while the 45° angle, moving up one point per month, would be at 25, and if the stock broke back under 50 the following month, it would be falling under the angle of 2 x 1 and indicate a further decline. Now, if you had an error on the chart in the timing or numbering across from the bottom, then the moving-average line or angle would not come out correctly.

TIME PERIODS FROM TOPS :

After a stock has advanced and made an extreme high and reacted for a few days, a few weeks, or a few months, and you start putting on the angles from the top down, you must then begin to number the time periods across from the top. Apply the same rule for the top: The month, week or day that a stock makes extreme high finishes the upward movement and is not to be counted. You can count the number of days, weeks or months moving across after that, allowing the top month to be "0", the next month, week or day over to be "1", adding 4 across on the squares to get the correct position. If this Time Period is carried across on all the charts correctly, then you can always check up and find out if you have made any mistake in bringing down the angles or moving-average lines.

For example: After a stock has declined 75 points, either on a weekly or monthly chart, the angles move down the same, except where the spacing is different. Assuming that the spacing is one point per one-eighth inch, after it has moved down 75 points and all the angles are drawn down from the top, there may be an error in the angle of 2 x 1 because your ruler may have slipped and you may not have place it correctly after it is down a distance from the top. Now, in order to prove exactly where the angle of 2 x 1 comes out, you determine the number of time periods there are, If 40 days, weeks or months have been required to decline the 75 points the angle of 2 x 1 moving down 2 points pre unit of time, would be down 80 from the top. If you find that this angle does not cross at 80, then you know that you made an error and should correct it.

This is a simple way to always know when the angles or moving-lines are correct because you simply add the movement to the bottom and subtract it from the top. Suppose the price referred to above, when the stock has declined 75 points, was 150, then subtracting 80 from the top at 150, the angle would cross at 70, and the price of the stock down 75 points would be at 75, therefore it would be above the angle of 2 x 1 from the top and in position for a rally if the time cycle indicated it.

POINTS FROM WHICH TO NUMBER TIME PERIODS

The most important point on the monthly high and low chart to carry the time period from is from the extreme low of the life of a stock and also from the date of incorporation or from the date trading began on the New York Stock Exchange. From the extreme low point the time period should always be carried across on the chart just the same as the important angles should be continued right along for years.

The next important point to number from is a second or third higher bottom, but you should not consider a bottom established until the market has held up or advanced three to four months, then commence numbering from that bottom if it appears to be important. For example:

U.S. STEEL: was incorporated February 25, 1901. Numbering the months across you will not that February, 1931 was 360 months, or 30 years, from the date of incorporation. Then start a new cycle and begin numbering across from "0". This will be working out the second cycle or circle of 360°.

The next important point is the extreme low of 8⅜ made May 14, 1904. On the monthly chart carry the numbers across from this bottom, because it is the lowest bottom and therefore the most important. Note this 30-year cycle or 360 months ended May, 1934.

The next important point to number from and draw the angles from, is the low of 21⅞ in October, 1907, the first higher bottom. Then, the next important is the third higher bottom made in February 1915. Always draw the angles and number the months across from any other important bottoms where campaigns start.

Use this same rule at tops. After top is reached and the trend turns down, then carry the time numbers across from the top, but after any top is crossed or bottom is broken that you are numbering from, then do not count that top or bottom of importance to number from; except to determine a time period on another cycle 3, 5, 7, 10 or 20 years ahead. Tops that stay for a long time without being crossed are always the most important to carry the Time Periods from. The extreme high reached by a stock is always most important until that thigh is crossed – then the next high point made on a secondary rally, which is always a lower top, is the next most important top to number from. For example:

On U.S. Steel you would carry the monthly measurement across first from the high in April 1901 – then from the extreme high in October, 1909, and next from the high in May, 1917 – then from the final high in September, 1929 being the most important to measure from, and also number from the April, 1930 top.

INDUSTRIAL AVERAGES: The Dow-Jones 30 Industrial Averages reached extreme high on September 3, 1929 – then declined sharply in the panic, reaching low in November 1929 – from this low there was a rally to April, 1930, which was the last high and very important to number from because it was a secondary top, the last rally in a bull market. After final low of the bear market was reached on July 8, 1932, a sharp rally followed to September, 1932, when top was reached – then a slow decline followed, reaching bottom in late February and early 1933, making this a secondary higher bottom, from which stocks advance to new high levels. The bottom in 1932 is the most important to number from and the next bottom of March, 1933 is next in importance.

Apply this same rule to weekly and daily bottoms and tops. Discontinue the time periods when any minor top or bottom is exceeded and carry only the main figures on time periods from important tops and bottoms as long as they remain unbroken.

The rule for discontinuing the use of tops and bottoms for Time Periods is: When a bottom or top is exceeded by three points, then discontinue the time period from that bottom or top.

Always note the number of months between extreme high and between extreme low points and note what angle the tops and bottoms come out on.

SQUARING THE PRICE RANGE WITH TIME

This is one of the most important and valuable discoveries that I have ever made, and if you stick strictly to the rule, and always watch a stock when Price is squared by Time, or when Time and Price come together, you will be able to forecast the important change in trend with greater accuracy.

The squaring of Price with Time means an equal number of points up or down balancing an equal number of time periods – either days, weeks or months. For example: If a stock has advanced 24 points in 24 days, then moving the 45° angle or moving-average-line up at the rate of one point per day, the timing line or time period and the price of the stock are at the same level and the stock is resting on a 45° angle and you should watch for an important change in trend at this point. If a stock is to continue uptrend and remain in a strong position, it must continue to advance and keep above the angle of 45°. If it breaks back under this angle, then it is out of its square on the bear side of the 45° angle and in a weaker position. When you are squaring out Time on a daily chart, look at the weekly high and low chart and monthly high and low chart and see if the stock is in a strong position and has yet to run out the time periods, because on a daily chart it has to react and then recover a position, squaring its price many times, as long as the weekly and monthly point up. Market correction or reactions are simply the squaring out of minor time periods and later the big declines or big advances are the squaring out of major time periods.

SQUARING THE RANGE: Refer to Form #12, where a range of 12 points is shown from 48 low to 60 high. Now, suppose a stock remains for several weeks or several months, moving up or down, in this range, never getting more than 12 points up from the bottom and not breaking the bottom: We start the 45° angle from the bottom of 48 and move it up to the top of the range to 60, then when we see the stock is holding this range and not going higher, we move the 45° angle back to the bottom; then back to the top of the range again, moving it up or down over this range until the stock breaks out into new low levels or new high levels. You will find that every time the 45° angle reaches the top of this range or the bottom of this range, there is some important change in trend of the stock.

You can also use the angles 2 x 1 to the right of the 45° angle and the 2 x 1 to the left as they again divide the Time Period into two equal parts and are of some value.

If a stock finally moves out this range on the up side, then the angles would begin at the new and higher bottom and move up, but from the point where the stock went into new high, or from any important bottom made while it was in the range, especially the last bottom that it made, which would be most important, you should then begin an angle at that bottom and continue on up again; watch when this angle is broken or when Time is squared out again with Price, which would be important for another change in trend, either major or minor.

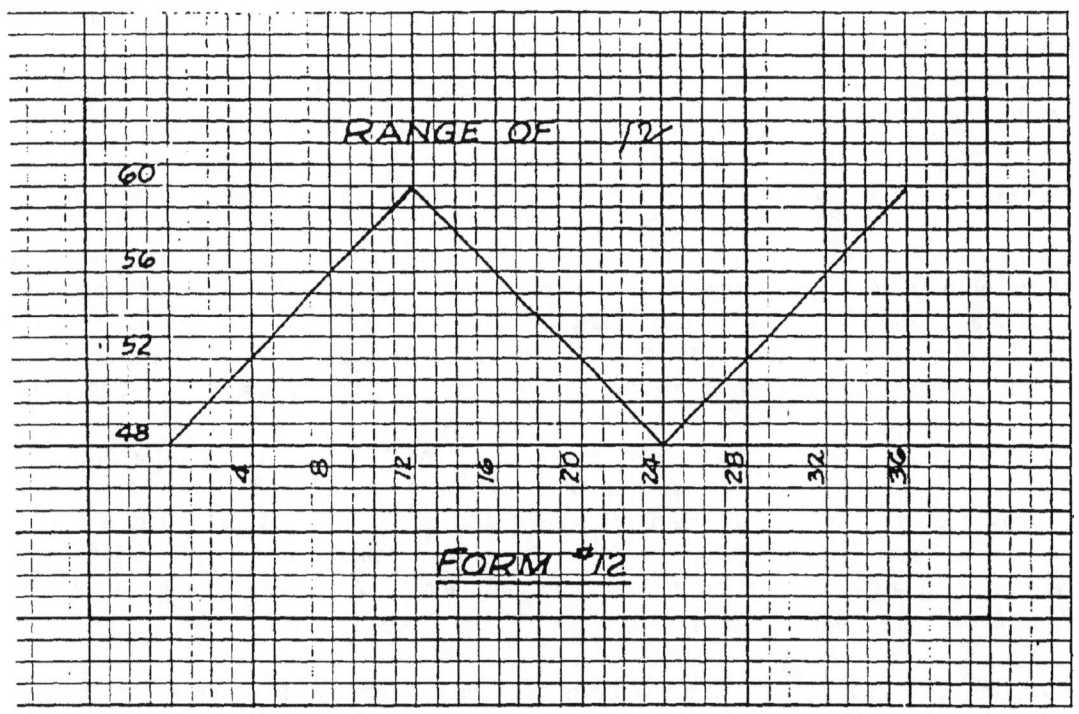

THREE WAYS TO SQUARE TIME AND PRICE:

We can square the Range, that is, the number of points from extreme low to extreme high, with Time – then square the extreme low point with Time – and square the extreme high point with Time. When the market passes out of these squares and breaks important angles, the trend changes up or down.

1. The <u>range</u> that a stock makes between extreme high and extreme low can be squared so long as it remains in the same price range. If the range is 25 points, it squares with 25 periods of Time – days, weeks or months. Continue to use this time period as long as it stays in the same range.

2. SQUARING TIME WITH BOTTOM OR EXTREME LOW PRICE:

    The next important Price to square with Time is the lowest price or bottom of any important decline. For example: If the bottom of a stock is 25, then at the end or 25 days, 25 weeks or 25 months, Time and Price are equal. Then watch for a change in trend as based on its bottom or lowest selling price. As long as a stock continues to hold one bottom and advances, you can always use this time period running across and continuing the time period, noting every time it passes out of the squares. Watch especially when the stock reaches the third square, the fourth square, and again the seventh and ninth squares of its time period. These squares only occur frequently on the daily or weekly charts, as the monthly, in most cases, would move out of a range, up or down, before it squared a bottom as many as 7 or 9 times. However this does sometimes happen when a stock is in a narrow range for many years.

3. SQUARING TIME WITH TOP OR EXTREME HIGH PRICE:

    The other important point to square Time with is the extreme high price of a stock. The Time period must be carried across from the high of the daily, weekly or monthly, and the square of the top price in Time must be noted and watched for a change in trend. If the top of a stock is 50, then when it has moved over 50 days, 50 weeks or months, it has reached its square in Time and an important change is indicated. This can be determined by the position of the angles from top and bottom. For example:

    Dow-Jones Industrial Averages – The high of 386 on September 3, 1929 would require 386 calendar days to equal the Price in Time. This occurred on September 23, 1930. Look at the chart and note how the trend changed and turned around that time. Then, on October 14, 1931, it ran out this period again – and again November 4, 1932, November 25, 1933, December 16, 1934, and January 6, 1936. Look up these dates and you will see that important changes in trend occurred on the Daily Chart when this time period of 386 days balanced the price of 386.

    Both major and minor tops and bottoms on all time periods must be watched as they square out right along. Most important of all is the extreme high point on the monthly high and low chart. This may be very high and work out a long time period before it squares the top, in which case you have to divide the price into 8 equal time periods and watch the most important points, like 1/4, 1/3, 1/2, 3/4, but most important of all is when Time equals Price.

When you are watching the position of a stock after it has squared out from a bottom or a top, always look up the time period and the angles from the opposite direction, If the market is nearing a low point, squaring out a top, see how its relation is to the bottom as it might be in the second or third square period from the bottom, which would be a double indication for a change in trend.

SQUARING WEEKLY TIME PERIODS:

The year contains 52 weeks and the square of this Time and Price is 52 by 52. Therefore you can make up a square of 52 wide and 52 high: put on all of the angles from "0"; then chart the weekly high and low prices of any stock in this square. For example: If the low price of a stock is 50, then the top of this weekly square would be 52 added to 50, which makes 102 as top of the square. As long as the stock stays above 50 and moves up, it will be working in the weekly square of 52. On the other hand, if the stock makes top and works down, you would make up a weekly square 52 points down for the top and 52 over to get the time period.

You can take the past movement of any stock, put on a square of 52 by 52, and study the movement, noting 13 weeks or one-fourth, 26 weeks or one-half, and 39 weeks or three-fourths points on time, and the changes in trend which take place when the stock reaches these important Resistance Points in Time and Price. You would watch for a change in trend around these time periods.

SQUARING MONTHLY TIME PERIODS:

At the time a stock breaks a 45° angle, if it is selling at 135 on the 135th month, it is breaking a doubly strong Resistance Level – a strong angle and a natural Resistance Level. This would be Time and Space balancing at Resistance Levels or geometrical angles and would indicate a big decline to follow. – Reverse this rule at the end of a bear campaign.

On a monthly chart twelve months completes a year, therefore the square of 12 is very important for working out time periods on the monthly chart. The square of 12 is 144 and important changes often occur on even 12 months' periods from a bottom or top of a stock. It will help you if you use the Resistance Levels on prices of the even 12's, noting 24, 36, 48, 60, 72, 84, 96, 108, etc. Watch how the stock acts on angles when it reaches these important Resistance points in Price.

PRICE AHEAD OF TIME

Why do stocks often cross the 45° angle on the daily, weekly or monthly chart, then have an advance for a short period of time, decline and rest on the same 45° angle? Because when the stock crosses the 45° angle the first time, it has not run out or overcome the square of Time with Price. Therefore, on the secondary reaction, when it rests on the 45° angle, it is at a time when the stock has reached the square of distance in Time. After that a greater advance follows.

Reverse this rule at the top of a bull market. When a stock breaks under the 45° angle a long distance from the base or bottom, it is most important. Many times a stock will rest on the 45° angle in the early stages of an advance, then later, on a reaction, rest on it again; then have a prolonged advance, react and rest on the 45° again, and then advance to a higher level; then break the 45° angle next time, which places it in an extremely weak position because it is so far away from the base and so much time has elapsed since the stock made low. Don't forget – It is most important when angles are broken on the monthly and weekly charts.

This accounts for stocks that have a sharp, quick decline from the top and then advance and make a slightly higher top or a series of slightly lower tops, and work over until they overcome the square of the price range at a comparatively high level and break the 45° angle, then a fast decline follows.

STRONGEST ANGLES FOR MEASURING TIME AND PRICE

90° ANGLE: Why is the 90 degree angle the strongest angle of all? Because it is vertical or straight up and straight down.

180° ANGLE: What is the next strongest angle to the 90° angle? The 180° angle because it is square to the 90° angle, being 90° from the 90° angle.

270° ANGLE: What is the next strongest angle to the 180° angle? The 270° angle because it is in opposition to 90, or 180° from the 90° angle, which equals 1/2 of the circle, the strongest point. 270 months equals 22½ years, which is ½ of 45.

360° ANGLE: What is the next strongest angle after 270? It is the 360°, because it ends the circle and gets back to the beginning point and is opposite the 180° or the half-way point, or the angle which equals 1/2 of the circle.

120° AND 240° ANGLES   What angles are the next strongest to 90, 180, 270, and 360°?
Answer: 120° and 240° angles, because they are 1/3 and 2/3 of the circle. 120° is 90 plus 30, which is 1/3 of 90. 240 is 180 plus 1/3 or 60, which makes these strong angles, especially strong for measurements of time.

45° - 135° - 225° - 315°:   What angles are the next in strength?
Answer: 45° angle, because it is 1/2 of 90,
135° angle, because it is 90 plus 45,
225° angle, because it is 45 plus 180, and
315° angle, because it is 45 from 270.
The angle of 225° is 180 from 45 and the angle of 315° is 180 from 135.

CARDINAL & FIXED CROSS: The angles of 90, 180, 270, and 360 from the first important cross, known as the Cardinal Cross. The angles or 45, 135, 225, and 315 for the next important cross, which is known as the Fixed Cross. These angles are very important for the measurements of time and space or price, and volume.

22½° - 67½° - 78¾°:   Why is the angle of 22½° stronger than 11¼°? Because it is twice as much, being the same reason that a 45° angle is stronger than 22½° angle. Again, the angle of 67½° is 1½ times a 45, therefore quite strong when anything is moving up toward 90°. 78¾° is stronger than 67½°, because it is 7/8 of 90, and therefore on of the strongest points before 90 is reached – important to watch both on time, price, and volume. Many stocks have important moves and make tops or bottoms around the 78th to 80th day, week or month, but don't overlook 84 months or 7 years, a strong time cycle.

DIVISION OF $1: 1/8-POINTS   Why are the angles of 1/8 of a circle most important for time and space measurement? Because we divide $1 into 1/2, 1/4, and 1/8 parts. We use 25 cents or one quarter, 50 cents or half dollar, and long years ago we had 12½ cent pieces. While the most important figures of our basis of money are the four quarters, we do use the 1/8, or 12½ cents in all calculations. Stock fluctuations are based on 1/8, 1/4, 3/8, 1/2, 5/8, 3/4, 7/8, and the whole figure. Therefore, any price measurement as well as time will work out closer to these figures when changed into angles of time than 1/3 or 2/3 points for the simple reason that the fluctuations moving in 1/8 proportion must come out closer to these figures.

Figuring $100, or par, as a basis for stock prices and changing those prices to degrees, 12½ equals 45°, 25 equals 90°, 37½ equals 135°, 50 equals 180°, 62½ equals 225°, 75 equals 270°, 82½ equals 315°, and 100 equals 360°. For example:

> When a stock sells at 50 on the 180th day, week or month, it is on the degree of its time angle.
>
> On February 1, 1915, U.S. Steel made a low at 38, which is closest to a price of 37½, which is 3/8 of 100 and equals 135° angle. Steel was 14 years or 168 months old on February 25, 1915, and hit the angle of 135°, which showed that Steel was behind time, but that it was in a strong position, holding at 38 above the 135° angle or the price of 37½.
>
> When Steel reached 200, it equalled 2 circles of 360°. When it advanced to 261¾, it was closest to 62½ in the third 100 or nearest the 225° angle or 5/8 point, which is the strongest angle after it crossed the half-way point at 250 or 180° angle.

[W. D. Gann's signature]

November, 1935

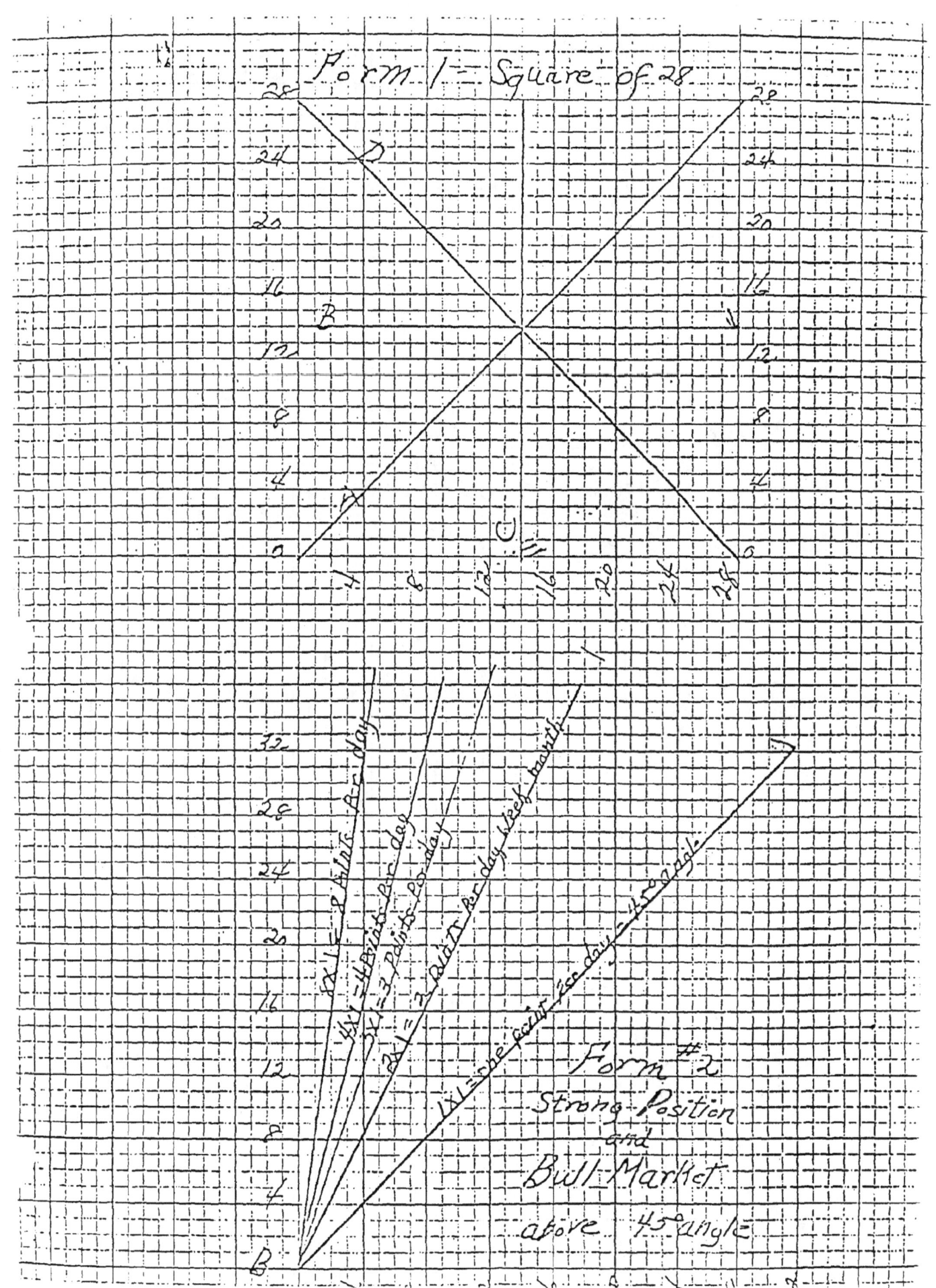

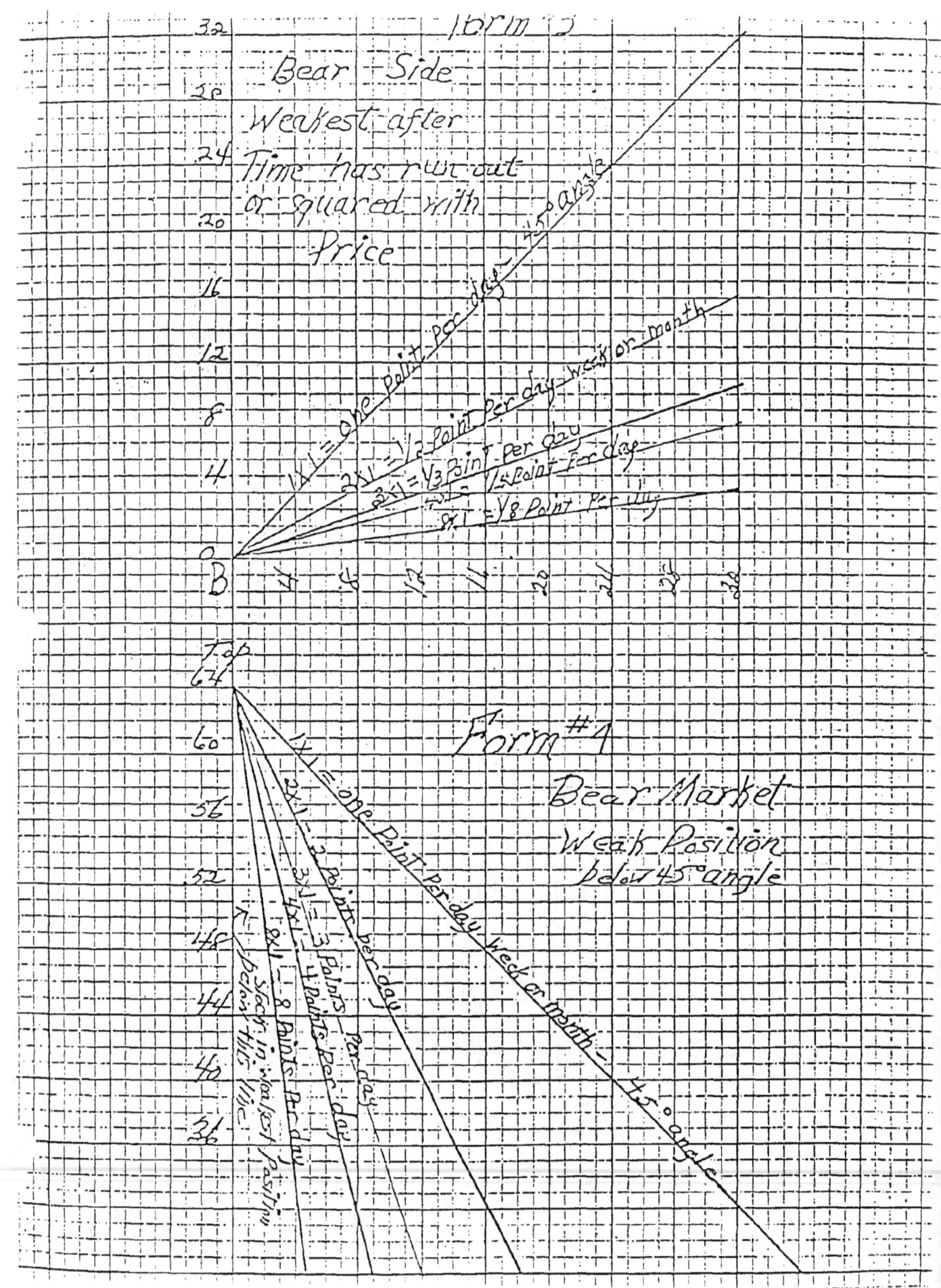

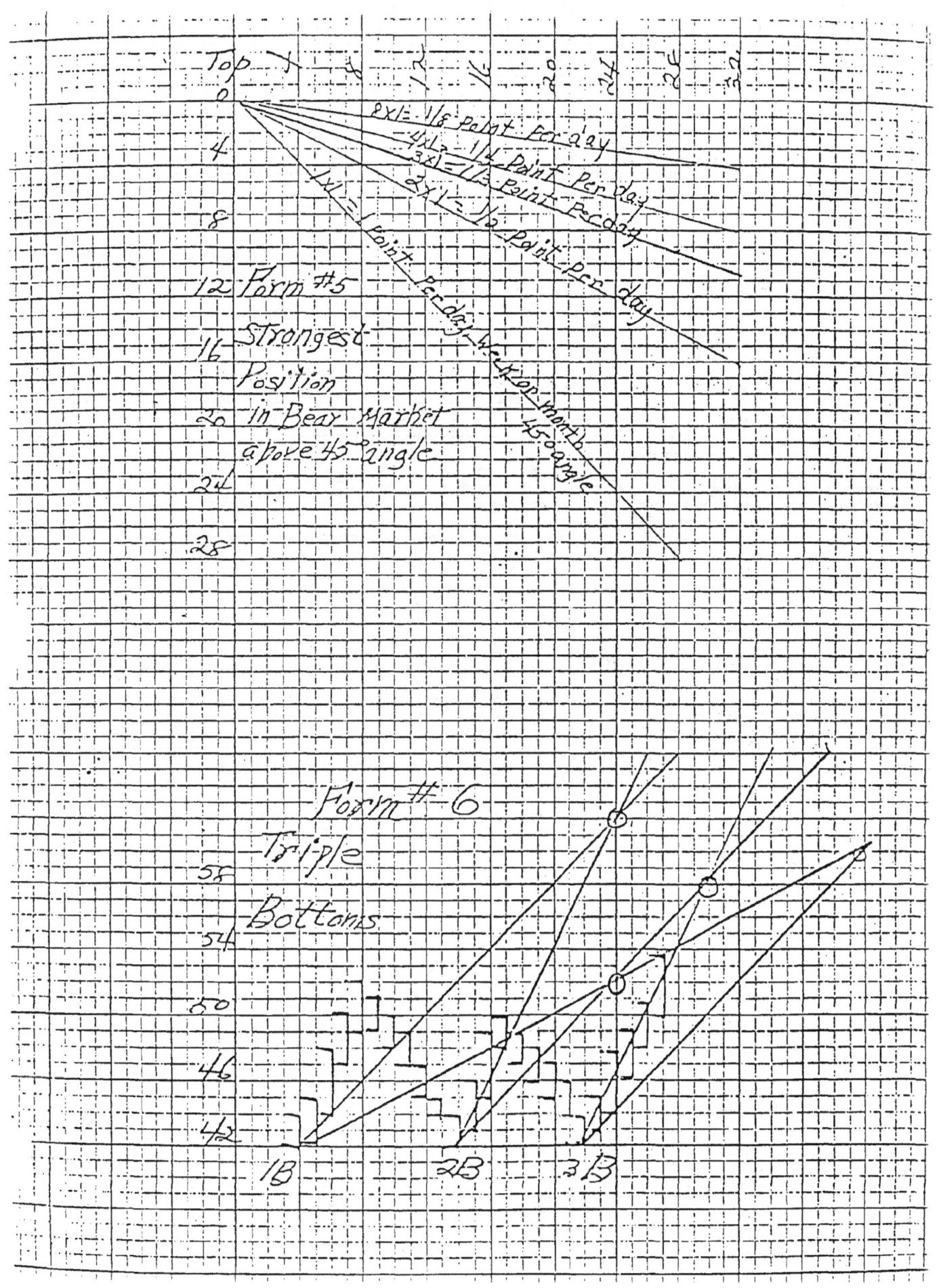

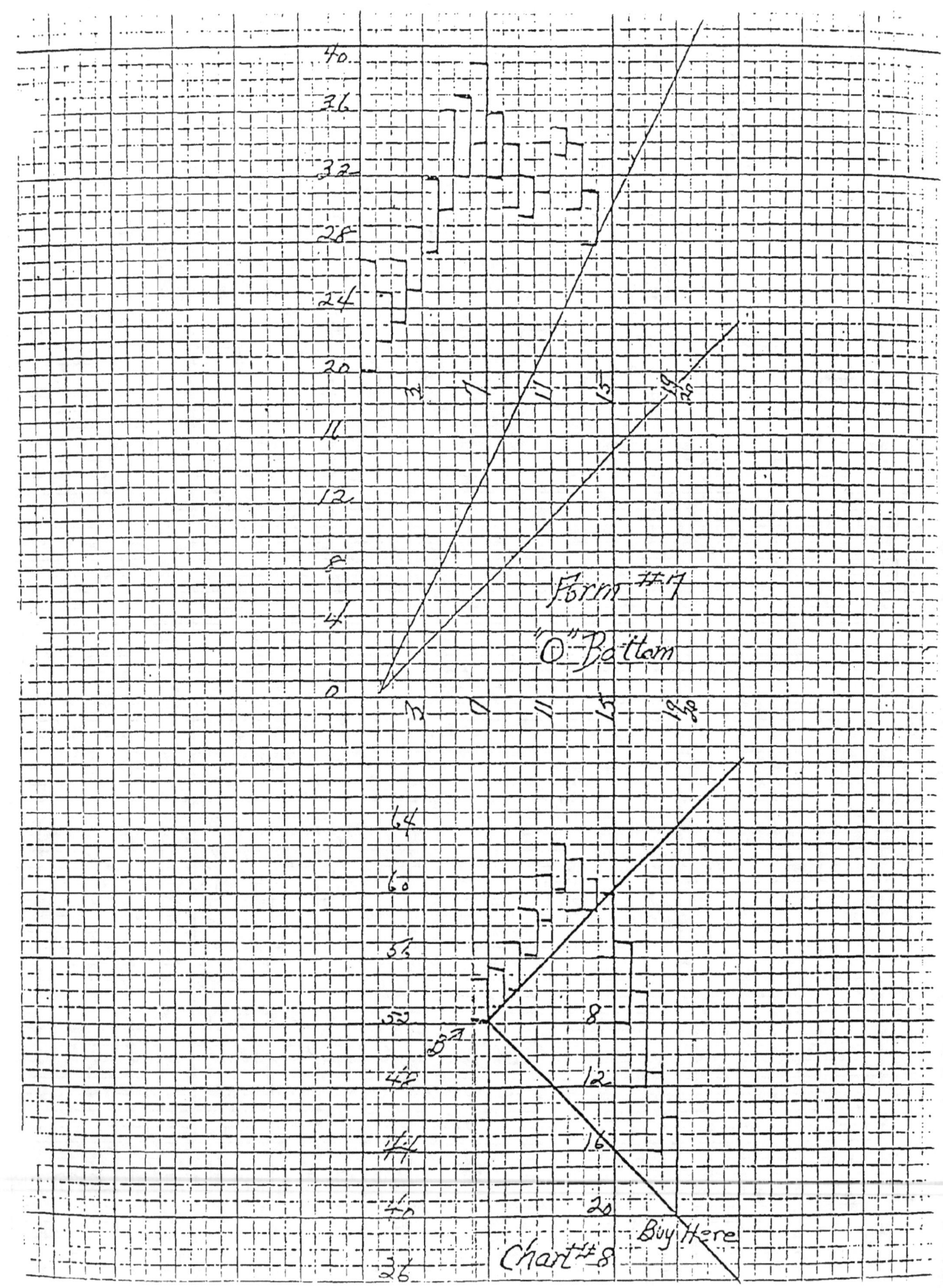

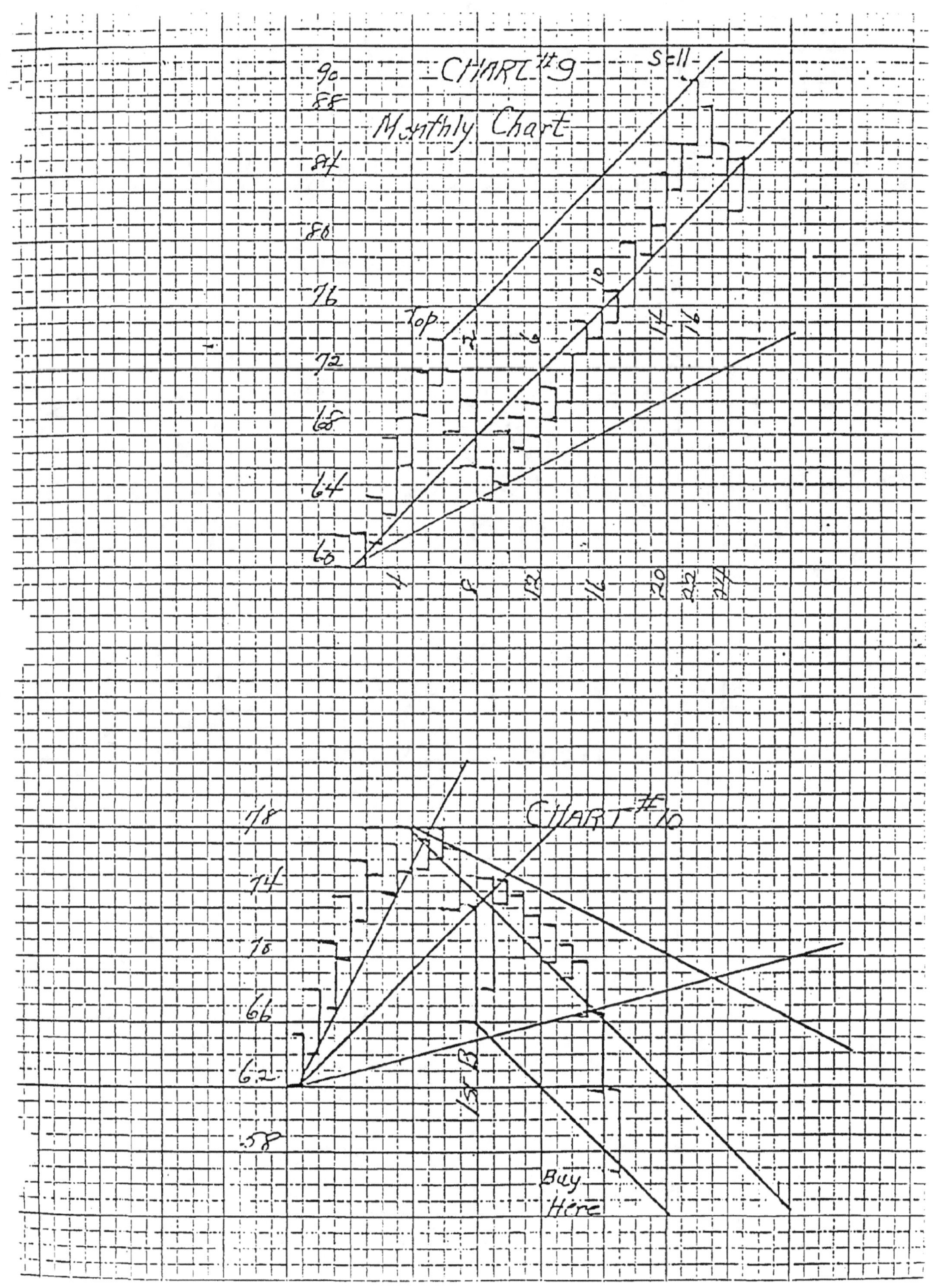

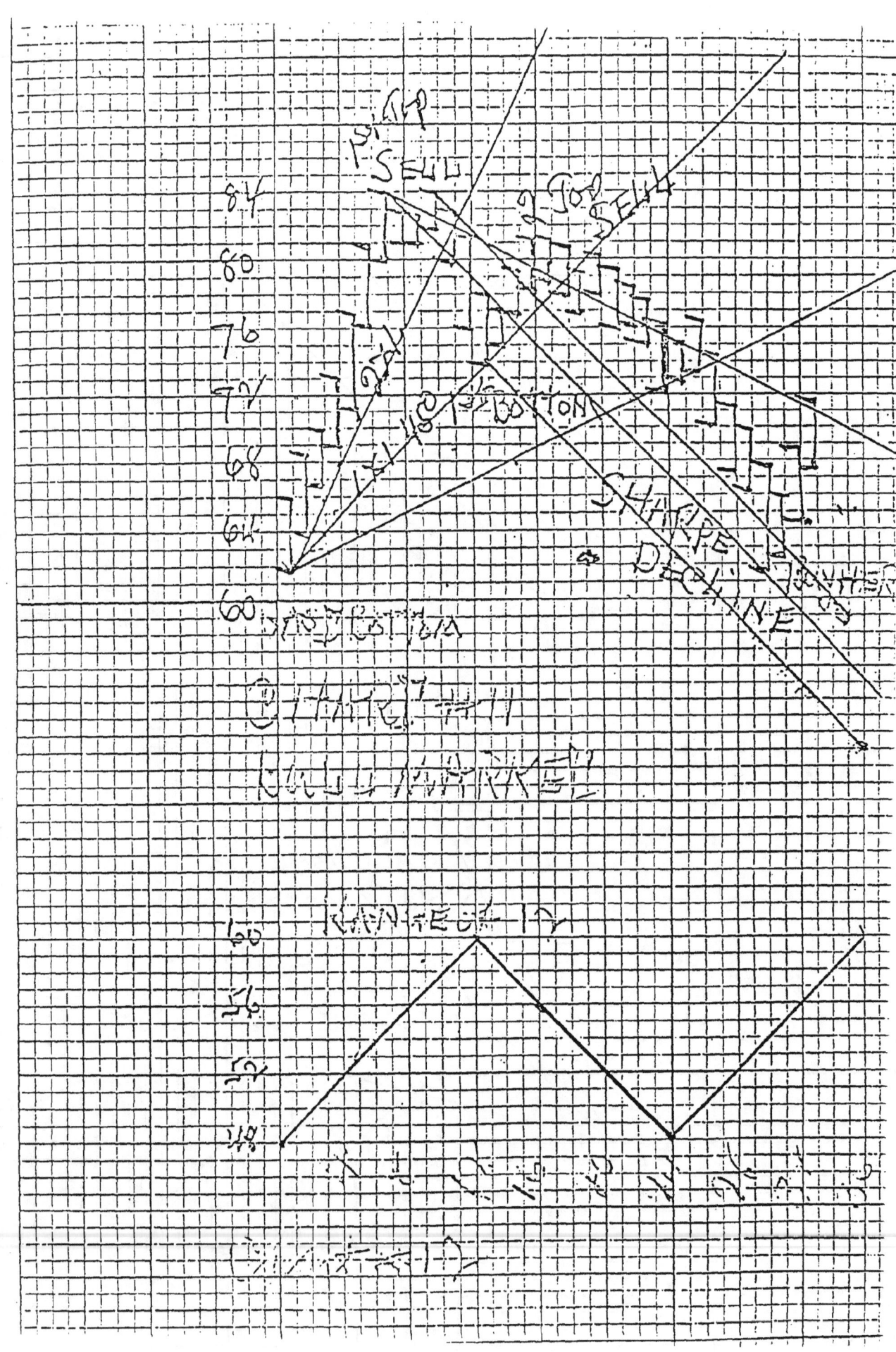

Chapter 5

Seasonal Changes on Stocks

THE W.D. GANN MASTER STOCK MARKET COURSE

W. D. GANN

82-88 WALL STREET

NEW YORK

SCIENTIFIC ADVICE
AND ANALYTICAL REPORTS
ON STOCKS AND COMMODITIES
AUTHOR OF "TRUTH OF THE STOCK TAPE"
"WALL STREET STOCK SELECTOR"
AND "THE TUNNEL THRU THE AIR"

MEMBER
AMERICAN ECONOMIC ASS'N
ROYAL ECONOMIC SOCIETY
CABLE ADDRESS
"GANWADE NEW YORK"

SEASONAL CHANGES ON STOCKS

The average of stocks and many of the individual stocks make important bottoms and tops according to the Seasonal Changes, which are as follows:

The Winter Quarter begins December 22nd, and 15 days from this date is January 5th and 6th, which are always important dates to watch at the beginning of each year, as stocks often make extreme high or extreme low around these dates and a change in trend takes place. When stocks make low in December, just before or just after the 22nd, a January rise usually follows. Dividends are paid on the first of January, and people buy for the dividends, which brings about a rally which often culminates around the 3rd to 7th. However, in some years, the January advance lasts until around the 20th to 21st.

February 5th is 45 days from December 22nd, and minor changes often take place around this date and, sometimes, very important tops and bottoms are reached.

March 21st is 90 days from December 22nd. This is the date when the Sun crosses the equator and Spring begins. The Spring rally in the stock market often starts around this date or culminates if stocks have been advancing previous to this date.

May 6th is 46 days from March 21st or 135 days from December 22nd and equals the 135° angle. Watch for important change in trend around this date.

June 22nd is 93 days from March 21st, which equals 90°, and, of course, it is opposite December 22nd and is important for seasonal change, as Summer begins at this date.

July 7th is 15 days from June 22nd and six months or 180 days from January 7th. July being a dividend month, advances or declines often culminates around this date, and an important change in trend often takes place. It is the next important date to watch after June 22nd.

August 8th is 47 days from June 22nd, but the Sun has only moved 45°, which equals the 45° angle. This is a very important date for change in trend, and you should watch stocks that make tops and bottoms around this date.

September 23rd is 93 days from June 22nd, but the Earth or Sun has only travel 90°. The Sun crosses the equator at this time and is 180° or opposite the point where it crosses the equator on March 21st. Fall begins at this date, and stocks make important changes in trend.

November 8th is 46 days from September 23rd and equals 45°. You will find by checking over the records that many important tops and bottoms and changes in trend occur around this date.

December 22nd is 91 days from September 23rd and 6 months or 180 days from June 22nd. This is where Winter begins, and it is important to watch for important changes in trends.

MONTHLY CHANGES

Stocks make important changes in trend every 30, 60, 120, 150, 210, 240, 300, 330 and 360 days or degrees from any important top or bottom. The seasonal changes or monthly changes based on the beginning of any seasonal changes are important to watch for tops and bottoms.

January 21st is 30 days or 30° from December 22nd, and the Sun changes signs at this date.

February 19th is 60 days or 60° from December 22nd, and the Sun or Earth makes another change in sign.

April 20th is 120 days or 120° from December 22nd.

May 22nd is 150 days or 150° from December 22nd and 60° from March 21st.

July 23rd is 210° from December 22nd and 120° from March 21st.

August 23rd is 240° from December 22nd.

October 23rd is 300° from December 22nd.

November 22nd is 330° from December 22nd.

All of the above dates are important to watch for changes in the major and minor trends.

Next to the 30 day change in trend, the most important are those that occur every 7th, 10th, 14th, 20th and 21st day. You will find some variation in these due to the fact that the Sun changes sign every 30 days, and that the Moon returns to its own place every 28 days and that there is a New Moon around 29 days from the previous New Moon. Sometimes the change will occur on the 28th day from the previous top or bottom, and at other times, on the 33rd or 34th day, due to the changes in the Moon and the time between these changes and the time that the Earth or Sun changes signs.

The dates when companies are incorporated and the dates when stocks are first traded on the New York Stock Exchange or other Exchanges, causes them to make tops and bottoms at slightly different dates than those dates for seasonal changes.

For example: UNITED STATES STEEL was incorporated February 25, 1901 and trading began on the New York Stock Exchange on March 28, 1901. This is why Steel makes so many important changes in trend in the month of February and March. Steel's seasonal changes in trend, based on the date of incorporation, are as follows:

February 25th to April 12th equals 45°.

April 27th equals 60 days or 60° from February 25th.

May 28th equals 90° from Feb. 25th.

June 12th equals 135° from Feb. 25th. June 28th equals 120° from Feb. 25th.

July 30th equals 150° from Feb. 25th.

August 30th equals 180° from Feb. 25th.

October 30th equals 240° from Feb. 25th.

October 14th equals 225° from February 25th.

November 29th equals 270° from Feb. 25th.

December 28th equals 300° from Feb. 25th.

January 11th equals 315° from Feb. 25th.

January 27th equals 330° from Feb. 25th.

February 25th equals 360° or 365 days from February 25th.

By checking over the dates when United States Steel has made minor and major tops and bottoms, you can see how often they have come out very closely to these dates for seasonal changes in trend.

UNITED STATES STEEL QUARTERLY CHART

This chart is made up according to the quarterly seasonal changes and begins and ends each quarter, according to the seasonal changes and not according to United States Steel's individual seasonal changes. The date at the bottom of each quarter is the date when the extreme low is made and the date at the top is the date when the extreme high was made during the Quarter.

The major and minor swings given below are taken from the overnight chart on U.S. Steel from 1901 to date and show most of all the minor swings each month. A study of these tops and bottoms will convince you of the value of the seasonal changes and will show you how tops and bottoms come out 30, 60, 90 days apart, and also will show you that the 7, 10, 14, 15, 20 and 21-day periods work with remarkable regularity.

1901

March 28th – Trading began in U.S. Steel and an advance started.

April 30th – Reached top of rally, the extreme high of quarter, and made second top on May 6th.

May 9th – The day of the Northern Pacific panic. Steel reached extreme low for the quarter.

June 3rd and 5th – Last top at 52-3/8. June 24th – Extreme high for quarter. Never crossed last top. Trend turned down.

July 15th – Extreme low for quarter. July 22nd – Low of reaction.

July 27th – Top of rally.

August 6th – Low of reaction.

September 3rd – Top of rally. Slightly lower than July 27th.

September 13th – Low of reaction. Sept. 26th – Second low of reaction. Narrow market followed from rally to Sept. 28th.

October 28th and November 1st to 5th – Lows of reactions.

November 19th – Top of sharp rally; extreme high for quarter.

November 21st and 27th – Low of reaction.

December 7th – Top of sharp rally.

December 12th – Low of reaction; extreme low of quarter.

December 24th – Last low of reaction and low for quarter. Rally followed.

1902

January 6th – High for-year and high for quarter.

January 21st-26th – Low of reaction.

February 26th – Top of rally.

March 12th and 21st – Lows of reactions in narrow market.

April 4th – Low of reaction since January high.

April 25th – High of rally and high for quarter.

June 19th – Extreme low of reaction and low for quarter.

June 24th – Second low of reaction.

July 2nd – Extreme low for quarter.

August 7th – Low of reaction.

September 5th – Top of rally; extreme high for quarter.

September 24th and 29th – Low of reaction.

October 20th – High of rally and high for quarter.

November 7th – Sharp decline started.

December 12th and 15th – Extreme low of year and of quarter. A bear year, high in January - low in December.

1903

January 5th and 7th – Top of rally. Slow market. High for quarter.

February 5th and 9th – Top of rally; 3/4 point above Jan. 7th top.

March 9th – Extreme low of quarter. March 21st – Top of small rally. Trend turned down. March 22nd – High of quarter. Just starting.

April 24th – Low of reaction.

May 5th – Top of small rally. Decline started.

June 19th – Low of reaction and low of quarter. Small rally to July 1st.

July 1st – High of quarter.

August 6th – Low of reaction. Aug. 18th top of rally.

September 8th – Fast decline started. Sept. 21st low of quarter. Sept. 29th – Low for small rally.

October 13th – Low for rally. Oct. 28th – Top of rally and high of quarter.

November 10th – Low of year.

December 11th and 22nd – Extreme low of quarter. Same lows as Nov. 10th. A bear year, high in January – Low in December.

December 30th – High of quarter.

1904

January 6th – Low of reaction and extreme low of quarter.

January 22nd – Top of small rally.

March 16th – High of small rally. Very dull and narrow.

March 28th – High of quarter.

May 14th – Low 8-3/8 -- of it's history.

June 24th – 9-1/2 last low of reaction and low of quarter. Trend turned up.

August 3rd and 8th – Top of rally in slow, dull market.

August 22nd – Last low of reaction.

September 17th – Top of rally and high for quarter. September 23rd – Last low of reaction 16 before big advance turned trend up.

September 24th – Low of quarter. Just started.

November 1st – Started upward, more active.

November 30th – Extreme high of year and high for quarter.

-6-

December 8th – Low of sharp reaction. Dec. 13th – Low of second reaction.

The year of final low bear market ended.

1905

January 7th – Low of reaction. Jan. 25th – Same low again. Low of quarter.

March 13th – High of rally. Extreme high of quarter.

March 23rd – Low of reaction.

April 6th and 18th – Top of Spring rally and extreme high of quarter.

May 22nd – Extreme low of reaction and low of quarter.

June 2nd and 6th – And about same low as May 22nd.

June 19th – Trend turned up.

June 23rd – Low of quarter.

August 3rd – Low of small reaction.

August 29th – Same high as April 18th.

September 7th and 11th – Low of reaction.

September 18th – High of quarter.

October 3rd and 23rd – Top of rally.

November 10th and 13th – Low of reaction and of quarter.

December 12th – High of rally and of quarter.

December 18th – Low of reaction.

December 26th – Extreme high of year.

1906

January 5th – Low of small reaction.

January 25th – High of rally and of quarter.

January 30th – Same low as January 5th.

February 2nd – High of rally.

February 7th and 9th – Top of small rally, from which big declined followed and broke low of January 5th and 30th.

March 21st – Extreme low of reaction. Low of quarter.

April 16th – Extreme high of rally and of quarter.

April 21st and 25th – Lower top.

May 2nd – Low of sharp decline and low of quarter.

June 5th – Top of rally, only small rally from 22nd to 23rd; then went lower.

July 3rd and 13th – Extreme low of year and quarter. Trend turned up.

August 4th and 9th – Lows of small reactions.

September 6th – Top of rally and high of quarter.

September 28th – Extreme low of reaction and of quarter.

October 12th – Extreme high of year and of quarter.

November 12th – Low of reaction.

December 12th and 15th – High of rally.

December 19th and 24th – Low of reaction.

1907

January 7th – Extreme high of year and of quarter.

January 31st – Low of sharp decline.

February 8th and 15th – High of rally.

March 14th – Low of silent panic and low for quarter.

March 26th – Extreme low of quarter. Low made 1½ points lower than March 14th.

April 10th – Top of rally and high of quarter.

May 3rd – Top of small rally. Decline started.

May 27th – Extreme low of reaction.

June 17th and 22nd – Make lows 3/4 of point above May 27th low.

July 8th – Top of rally and high of quarter.

August 12th and 17th – Lows of reactions.

September 7th – Top of rally. Sept. 16th – Low of quarter.

September 21st – Top of small rally. Trend continued down.

September 23rd – High of quarter just starting.

October 23rd – Low 21-7/8, extreme low of year and of quarter.

November 6th and 12th – Top of rally.

November 19th and 26th – Lows of reactions.

December 6th – Top of rally.

December 16th and 26th – Lows of reactions and low of quarter. A bear year closed, only four points above the low of the year.

1908

January 2nd – Extreme low of year. Jan. 20th – Top of rally.

February 10th – Low of reaction. Advanced started.

March 16th – High of quarter. March 24th – Top of rally.

April 4th – Low of reaction and of quarter.

April 28th – Top for small reaction.

May 3rd – Low of reaction. May 18th – High of rally and of quarter.

May 27th – Low of reaction.

June 2nd – Top of small rally.

June 24th – Low of reaction and of quarter. Slightly above May 27th low.

August 10th – Top of rally and high of quarter.

August 15th – Low of reaction.

September 8th – Same high as August 10th. Sept. 22nd – Low of sharp reaction. Sept. 24th – Low of quarter just started.

November 14th – Extreme high of year, 58-7/8 and high of quarter.

December 21st – Low of reaction. Sharp rally to Dec. 29th.

1909

January 6th – Low of reaction. Rally to 8th.

January 14th – Low of reaction.

January 22nd – High of month and of quarter from which they declined followed.

February 23rd – Extreme low of year from which big bull market followed and low of quarter.

March 1st – Top of rally.

March 20th – Low of decline. March 22nd – Low of quarter just starting.

May 3rd – Low of reaction and low for month of May.

May 8th – Top for reaction to May 14th, from where advance was resumed.

June 14th – Top of rally and high of quarter.

June 22nd – Low of reaction. June 23rd – Low of quarter just starting.

August 12th and 16th – High of rally.

August 24th – Bottom of quick decline.

August 27th – Made bottom. Slightly higher than Aug. 20th.

September 3rd – Top of rally; declined to 9th; then went right on up. Sept. 22nd – High of quarter.

October 4th – High for year 94-7/8 and high of quarter.

October 13th – Low of reaction. Oct. 15th – Top of quick rally.

October 23rd and 27th – Made bottom slightly higher than Oct. 13th.

November 5th – Top of rally and same top as Oct. 15th.

November 30th – Low of reaction and low of quarter. Same low as Oct. 13th.

December 18th – Top of rally. December 27th – Low of reaction. Rally to Dec. 30th; high of quarter.

1910

January 7th – First low and three point rally on 8th; then broke low of 7th. Jan. 19th – Low of reaction.

January 22nd – Top of quick rally. Just ¼ point, under Jan. 8th top.

January 25th – Low of reaction. Jan. 29th – Top of rally.

February 8th – Extreme low of early part of year end of quarter.

March 9th – Top of rally. Never went higher during the year.

March 16th – Low of reaction. March 22nd – Trend turned down.

March 31st – Low of reaction.

April 14th – Top of rally and high of quarter.

May 3rd – Low of reaction. May 21st – Top of rally.

June 6th – Low of reaction and low of quarter.

June 22nd – Top of rally and high of quarter.

July 6th – Low of reaction. July 11th and 15th – Top of small rally.

July 26th – Extreme low of year and of quarter. July 29th – Top of sharp rally.

August 2nd – Low of reaction and low for August. Aug. 17th – High of rally and high for month. Aug. 25th – Low of reaction for rally.

September 14th – Top of rally. Sept. 20th – Extreme low of reaction.

September 24th – Low of quarter just starting.

November 4th – Top for quick reaction to 10th . Nov. 4th – High of quarter. Nov. 19th – Top of rally. Slightly lower than Nov. 4th.

December 8th – Low of reaction. Dec. 10th, 15th and 19th – Tops of rally. Dec. 28th – Low of reaction. Extreme low of quarter, but higher than Dec. 8th bottom; a rally to Dec. 31st.

1911

January 3rd – Low of reaction and low was not broken until late in August.

February 6th and 10th – Top of rally and high of quarter.

March 4th – Low of reaction. March 21st – Top of rally.

April 24th – Low of reaction and of quarter.

May 1st – Top of rally. May 6th – Low of reaction.

May 18th and 22nd – Top of rally and high of quarter.

June 1st – Low of reaction. June 15th – Top of rally.

June 22nd – Low of reaction.

July 22nd – Top of rally and high of quarter from which big declined followed.

August 5th – Low for small rally to August 7th. Aug. 26th – Low for month.

September 6th – Top of rally. Sept. 22nd – First low of decline and low of quarter. Sept. 25th – Extreme low of month.

October 2nd – Top of rally. Oct. 7th – Low for rally to 14th.

October 19th – Low of the same as Oct. 7th low. Oct. 20th and 24th – Last rallies before big break. Oct. 27th – Low 50, extreme low for year and of quarter.

November 6th – Top of rally. Nov. 8th – Low of reaction, but Nov. 3rd was extreme low of month. Nov. 27th – Top of rally.

December 8th – Low of reaction. Dec. 20th – Top of rally and high of quarter. Dec. 29th – Low of reaction.

1912

January 2nd – Top of rally and high of quarter.

February 1st and 13th – Low of reaction and of quarter.

March 25th – Top of rally; declined to 28; then went higher.

April 8th and 30th – Same tops and highest of quarter. From April 30th, a sharp declined followed.

May 7th – Low of declined and end of quarter. May 20th – Top of rally.

June 1st – Low of reaction.

July 2nd – Top of rally. July 11th – Low of reaction and low of quarter.

August 2nd – Top for small reaction. Aug. 7th – Low of reaction.

August 21st and 28th – High for month.

September 12th – Low of reaction. Sept. 23rd – High of quarter.

October 4th – Top of rally and high for year and quarter.

October 30th – Low of reaction.

November 4th – Low of reaction from Oct. 31st. Nov. 7th – Top of quick rally and high for month. Nov. 12th and 16th – Same lows of reaction. Nov. 21st – Last top from which big declined followed.

December 11th and 16th – Low of decline and of quarter.

December 21st and 28th – Top of rally. Dec. 30th – Low of reaction.

1913

January 2nd – High for month, quarter and year. Jan. 17th and 20th – Low for rally. Jan. 31st – Top of rally.

February 4th – Top of rally and high for month.

February 25th – Low of reaction.

March 3rd – Top of rally. Mar. 10th – First low of reaction and of quarter. Mar. 19th – Second low for rally.

April 4th – Top of rally and high of quarter.

April 29th – Low of reaction.

May 5th and 8th – Top of rally. May 12th and 14th – Low of small reaction. May 26th – Top of rally from which big decline started.

June 11th – First low of reaction and of quarter.

June 21st – Second low, slightly higher than June 11th.

July 9th – Low of quarter.

August 13th – Top of rally and high of quarter. Aug. 16th and 22nd – Lows of reaction. Aug. 29th – Top of rally.

September 4th – Low of reaction. Sept. 13th – Top of rally, slightly lower than Aug. 13th. Sept. 22nd – Top of last rally. Big declined followed. Sept. 23rd – High of quarter just starting.

October 17th – Low of decline. Oct. 27th – Top of rally.

November 10th – Same low as Oct. 17th and low of quarter.

December 8th – Top of rally. Dec. 15th – Low of reaction.

December 24th – Low of quarter. Dec. 26th – Top of rally.

1914

January 3rd – Low of reaction. Jan. 31st – High for year and high of quarter.

February 4th and 14th – Tops of small rallies.

March 7th – Low of reaction. March 21 and 24th – Top of rally.

March 25th – Low of quarter.

April 25th – Low of reaction.

May 1st – Low of small reaction. May 28th – Top of rally and high of quarter.

June 25th – Low of reaction.

July 8th – Top of rally and high of quarter. July 16th – Low of reaction. July 22nd – Top of rally. July 30th – Low at 50; extreme low of quarter. Exchange closed until Dec. 15th on account of war.

December 15th – High 55, of quarter. Declined followed. Dec. 22nd – Low of quarter. Dec. 26th – Low 48 for small rally.

1915

January 4th – Low of reaction. Jan. 21st – High of rally 53¼ and high of quarter; big break followed.

February 1st – Steal past dividend. The stock sold at 38, made low for the month and extreme low for the year and quarter.

February 13th – Top of rally. Feb. 24th – Low of reaction.

March 8th – Top of rally. Mar. 18th – Last low of reaction.

March 24th – Low of quarter just starting.

April 19th – Top for reaction. April 24th – Low of reaction.

May 3rd – Top of rally for big, quick decline. May 10th – Low of reaction. May 14th – A higher bottom.

June 4th – Top of rally and high of quarter. June 9th – Low of reaction. June 22nd – Top of rally.

July 7th and 9th – Low of reaction and low of quarter, but higher than June 9th low.

August 10th – Top of sharp advance. Aug. 14th – Low of reaction.

August 18th – Top for month and high for quarter. A quick ten point break followed. August 27th – Top of rally.

September 11th and 17th – Low of reaction. Sept. 24th – Low of quarter.

October 1st – Top of rally. Oct. 6th – Low of reaction; same as Sept. 24th low. Oct. 21st – High of rally and high for month. Oct. 29th – Low of reaction.

November 1st and 4th – High of rally. Nov. 9th – Low of reaction.

November 12th and 26th – High of rally and of quarter.

December 2nd – Low of reaction. Dec. 7th – Top of rally.

December 17th and 21st – Low of reaction. Dec. 27th and 31st – High of rally and of quarter.

1916

January 7th – Low for rally to 8th; then went lower.

January 31st – Low for month and low for quarter.

February 10th – Top of rally.

March 1st – Low of reaction. Mar. 17th – High of rally.

March 27th – Low of reaction.

April 4th – Top of rally. Apr. 22nd – Low of reaction and low of quarter.

May 1st – Top of rally. May 5th – Low of reaction.

June 12th – Top of rally and high of quarter.

June 23rd and 27th – Low of reaction and of quarter.

July 6th – Top of rally. July 14th – Low of reaction.

July 24th and 26th – Top of rally.

August 5th – Low of reaction; trend turned up strong.

August 23rd – Top of rally.

September 1st – Low of reaction. Sept. 22nd – High of quarter just ending. Sept. 25th and 29th – Top of rally.

October 9th and 14th – Same lows from which big advance followed.

November 8th – Top of rally. Nov. 14th – Low of reaction.

November 27th – High of the year and quarter.

December 21st – Low of big break and low of quarter.

1917

January 4th – Top of rally and high of quarter. Jan. 5th and 11th – Low of reaction. Jan. 26th – Top of rally. Did not cross top of Jan. 4th.

February 1st – Low of big break and of quarter.

February 3rd – Made slightly higher bottom.

March 21st – Top of rally. Mar. 27th – Low of reaction.

April 3rd – Top of rally. Apr. 10th – Low of reaction and of quarter. Made higher bottom on 17th and 20th. Apr. 26th – Top of rally.

May 9th – Low of reaction. May 31st – High of month, quarter and year.

June 1st and 4th – Low of reaction. June 14th – Top of rally.

June 20th – Low of reaction. June 27th – Top of rally and high of quarter.

July 19th – Low of reaction.

August 7th – Top of rally.

September 17th – Low of reaction and of quarter.

September 25th – Top of rally and high of quarter.

October 15th – Low of reaction. Oct. 22, and 27th – Top of rally.

November 8th – Low of reaction. Nov. 26th – Top of rally.

December 20th – Extreme low of decline for sharp quick rally. Low of quarter.

1918

January 3rd – Top of rally. Jan. 15th, 18th and 23rd – Lows of reaction.

February 1st – High of rally. Feb. 19th and 27th – high of quarter, slightly lower tops.

March 25th – Low of reaction and of quarter.

April 22nd – Top of rally for small reaction.

April 25th and 27th and 30th – Lows of reaction.

May 16th – High of quarter. Top of rally for sharp decline.

June 1st – Low of reaction. June 27th – Top of rally.

July 15th – Low of reaction and low of quarter.

August 10th – Top for reaction. Aug. 15, 17th and 22nd – Lows of reaction. Aug. 28th and Sept. 3rd – Last tops before big decline and high of quarter.

September 13th – Low of reaction. Sept. 27th – Top of rally.

Oct. 9th – Bottom of reaction. Oct. 19th – Top of rally and high of quarter.

November 2nd – Bottom for small rally. Nov. 7th – Top of rally. Nov. 13th – Low of reaction. Nov. 21st – Top of rally. Nov. 29th – Low of decline and low of quarter.

December 11th – Top of rally. Dec. 26th – Low for month.

1919

January 3rd – Top of rally.

February 10th – Extreme low of decline and low of quarter.

March 12th – Top of rally. Mar. 19th – Low of reaction. Mar. 22nd – Top of rally and high of quarter. Mar. 26th – Low of quarter; low of reaction and higher than Mar. 19th.

April 23rd – Top of rally.

May 1st – Bottom of reaction. May 5th – A higher bottom.

June 6th – Top of rally and high of quarter. June 16th – Low of reaction.

July 7th – Top of rally and high of quarter. July 11th – Low of reaction.

July 14th – Top of rally. Just ¼ point higher than July 7th.

July 22nd – Low of reaction. July 20th – Top of rally.

August 8th – Low for small rally. Aug. 11 and 13th – Top of rally.

August 21st – Low for big rally. Extreme low of quarter.

September 4th – Top for reaction. Sept. 20th – Low of reaction.

October 10th – Top of rally and high of quarter. Oct. 25th – Low of reaction.

November 5th – Same top is Oct. 10th.

December 12th – Low of reaction and of quarter. Dec. 27th – Top for small reaction. Dec. 29th – Low of reaction.

1920

January 5th – Top of rally and high of quarter. Jan. 6th – Low of reaction. Jan. 10th – Top of small rally. Failed to reach top of Jan. 5th. Jan. 19th – Low of reaction. Jan. 27th – Top of rally.

February 13th – Low of reaction. Feb. 18th – Top of rally.

February 27th – Low of decline for big rally; low of quarter.

March 11th – Top of rally. Mar. 17th – Low of reaction. Mar. 22nd – Top of rally. Mar. 25th – Last low of reaction.

April 8th – Extreme top of rally and high of quarter. Apr. 12th – Low of small reaction. Apr. 14th – Top of small rally. Apr. 23rd – Low of sharp decline. Apr. 27th – Top of small rally.

May 3rd – Low of decline. May 8th and 10th – Top of rally.

May 13th – Low of decline. Slightly lower than May 3rd. May 15th – Top of rally. May 19th – Extreme low of decline. May 28th and 29th – Top of rally.

June 1st – Low of small reaction. June 5th – Top of rally.

June 8th – Low of reaction. June 12th – Top of rally. June 20th – Low of quarter. June 23rd – Low of reaction. June 24th – First low of quarter just starting. June 26th – Top of small rally. June 28th – Low of small reaction, higher than 23rd.

July 8th – Top of rally and highest of quarter. July 16th – Low of reaction. July 23rd – Top of rally.

August 9th – Low of reaction and extreme low of quarter. Aug. 27th – Top of rally

September 13th – Low of reaction. Sept. 18th – Top of rally.

October 1st – Low of reaction. Oct. 5th – Top of rally. Oct. 13th – Low of reaction. Oct. 25th – Top of rally and high of quarter. October 28th – Low of reaction.

November 1st – Top of rally. Nov. 19th – Low of reaction. November 23rd – Top of rally.

December 1st – Low of reaction. Slightly lower than Nov. 19. Dec. 2nd and 6th – Top of rally. Big decline followed. Dec. 21st and 22nd – Extreme low of month, quarter and year.

1921

January 4th – High of rally. The Jan. 5th – Small reaction. Jan. 11th – Top of rally. Jan. 14th – Low of reaction. Jan. 19th – Top of rally the low top of 11th. Jan. 22nd – Low of reaction. Same low as Jan. 5th. Jan. 28th – Top of rally.

February 4th – The low of reaction; the same low as Jan. 5th and 22nd. Feb. 17th – High of rally and quarter; ¼ above Jan. 11th high.

March 14th – Low of reaction. Mar. 23rd – Top of rally.

April 14th – Low of reaction. Apr. 26th – Top of rally. Apr. 28th – Low of small decline.

May 6th – Last top before big decline and high of quarter. May 16th – Low of reaction. May 23rd – Top of rally.

June 21st – Low of quarter just ending. June 23rd – Made extreme low of month and year at 70½ and low of quarter.

July 7th – And top of rally. July 16th – Low of decline.

August 2nd – Top of rally. Aug. 24th – Low of reaction.

September 19 high of quarter and 26th – top of rally.

October 17th – Low of reaction and quarter. Oct. 29th – Top of rally.

November 2nd and 7th – Last low before big advance. Nov. 28th – Top of rally. Nov. 30th – Low of reaction.

December 15th – Top of rally and high of quarter. Dec. 23rd – Low of reaction. Dec. 28th and 31st – Tops of rally.

1922

January 6th – Low of month and of quarter. Jan. 20th – Top of rally.

January 31st – Low of reaction.

February 7th – Top of rally. February 9th – Low of small reaction. Feb. 23rd – Top of sharp advance and high of quarter.

March 6th – Low of reaction. Mar. 18th – Top of rally. Mar. 24th – Last low and low of quarter; advanced followed.

April 10th and 20th – Tops for small reaction.

May 11th – Low reaction.

June 6th – Top of rally and high of quarter. June 12th and 16th – Low of reaction. June 20th – Top of rally. June 27th – Last low of reaction and of quarter.

July 20th – Top of rally. July 26th – Low of reaction. In July 31st – Top of rally and high of quarter.

August 10th and 15th – Low of reaction.

September 11th – Top of rally. Sept. 29th – Low of reaction and low of quarter.

October 16th – Top of rally and high of quarter.

November 1st – Low of reaction. Nov. 9th – Top of rally. Nov. 28th – Low of reaction.

December 18th – High of rally. Dec. 21st and 28th – Low of reaction and of quarter.

1923

January 4th – Top of rally and high of quarter. Jan. 17th – Low of reaction. Jan. 26th – Top of rally. Jan. 31st – Low of reaction and quarter.

February 26 and March 3rd – And top of rally.

March 12th – Low of reaction. Mar. 21st – Top of rally and highest of quarter. Mar. 26th – Low of reaction.

April 2nd – Top of rally. Slow and narrow market. Made last top April 18th. Started decline on April 25th.

May 5th – Top of small rally. May 22nd – Low of reaction. May 28th – Top of rally.

June 2nd – Low of reaction. June 7th – High of rally. June 21st – Extreme low of quarter and low for small rally to 23rd. June 30th – Low for month.

July 3rd – Top of rally. July 5th, 11th and 17th – Low's near same level around 89½. July 23rd – Top of small rally. July 31st – Low of reaction and quarter.

August 30th – High of rally and of quarter.

September 4th – Low of small reaction. Sept. 6th and 11th – Top of rally, but not up to Aug. 30th high. Sept. 23rd – Low – Same low as July 31st. Sept. 25th – Low of quarter just starting.

October 4th – Top of small rally. Oct. 17th – Low of reaction.

October 24th – Top of small rally. Oct. 29th – Last low from which big advance started.

November 12th – Top of rally. Nov. 17th – Low of reaction.

November 27th – Top of rally and high of quarter.

December 19th – Low of reaction. December 23rd – Low of quarter.

December 31st – Top of rally.

1924

January 4th – Low of reaction and low for month.

February 7th – Top of rally and high of quarter. Feb. 27th – Low of reaction. Feb. 29th – Top of rally.

March 29th – Low of reaction.

April 5th – Top of rally. Apr. 10th, 15th and 22nd – Lows around same level. April 26th – Top of rally and high of quarter. April 30th – Low of reaction.

May 2nd – Top of small rally. May 20th – Bottom of reaction. May 26th – Top of rally. May 29th – Low of reaction.

June 4th – Top of rally. June 6th – Low of reaction and low of quarter. June 23rd – Low of quarter just starting.

July 10th – Top of rally. July 17th – Low of reaction.

August 4th – Top of rally. Aug. 12th – Low of reaction. Aug. 20th – Top of rally and high of quarter.

September 8th – Low of reaction. Sept. 25th – Top of rally.

October 2nd – Same top the Sept. 25th. Oct. 14th – The last low from which big advance then started and low of quarter.

November 26th – Top for small reaction.

December 11th – Bottom of reaction. Dec. 19th – High of quarter. Dec. 24th – Low of quarter just starting. Dec. 29th – Top of rally. Dec. 31st – Low of small reaction.

1925

January 3rd and 5th – Top of rally. Jan. 6th – Low of small reaction.

January 23rd – Top of rally and high of quarter.

February 3rd – Low of reaction. Feb. 5th – Top of rally. Feb. 17th – Low of reaction.

March 6th and 7th – Top of rally. Mar. 30th – Extreme low for month and quarter.

April 18th – Top of rally. Apr. 30th – Low of reaction. Slightly above Mar. 30th low.

May 21st – High of rally and high for quarter.

June 9th – Low of reaction. June 15th and 19th – Top of rally.

June 29th – Last low of quarter and higher than low of Apr. 30th and Mar. 30th. This was a triple bottom and a big advance followed.

July 29th – High for the month. July 31st – Low of reaction.

August 26th – High of month and of quarter.

September 3rd – Low of reaction. Sept. 15th – Top of rally. Slightly lower top and Aug. 26th. Sept. 28th – Low of reaction and low of quarter. A little higher than Sept. 3rd.

October 1st – Low of month. Oct. 24th and 26th – High of month.

October 29th – And low of small reaction.

November 7th – Top for the year and quarter. Nov. 10th – Low of short decline. Nov. 14th – Top of quick rally, but not as high as Nov. 7th top. Nov. 24th – Low of month.

December 8th – Top of rally. Dec. 22nd – Low of reaction. Dec. 28th – Top of rally. Dec. 31st – Low of reaction.

1926

January 4th – Top of rally and high for quarter. Jan. 6th – Low of small reaction. Jan. 7th – Top of rally. Failed to reach top of Jan. 4th. Jan. 22nd – Low of month. Jan. 25th – Top of rally.

February 1st – Low of small reaction. Feb. 4th – Top of small rally. Feb. 26th – Extreme low of month.

March 1st – Top of small rally. Mar. 2nd – Low of small reaction and low of quarter. Mar. 16th – Top for month. Mar. 30th – Extreme low for month.

April 6th – Top of rally. Apr. 15th – Low of reaction and low of quarter. Apr. 29th – High for month.

May 3rd – Low of reaction. May 6th – Top of small rally. May 17th – Low for month; big advance started.

June 17th – Top of rally and high of quarter. June 18th – Quick decline of five points. June 26th – Low of quarter just started.

July 2nd – Top of rally. July 9th – Low of reaction. July 16th – Top of rally. July 24th – Low of reaction.

August 17th – Extreme high for month, quarter and year. Aug. 25th – Low of reaction.

September 8th – Top of rally. Sept. 20th – Low of reaction.

October 2nd – Top of sharp rally. Oct. 20th – Low of short decline and low of quarter. Oct. 28th – Top of rally.

November 3rd – Low of reaction. Nov. 16th – High of month. Nov. 19th – Low of sharp decline. Nov. 27th – Top of rally.

December 6th – Low of reaction. Dec. 17th – High of quarter - and 27th – high for month and one point above the high of Aug. 17, 1926.

1927

January 4 and 7th – Low of reaction. Jan. 11th – Top of rally.

January 28th – Extreme low for month, quarter and year on the new stock.

February 24th – High for month. Feb. 25th – Low of small reaction.

March 1st – Top of rally. Mar. 8th – Low for month; big advance followed. Mar. 17th – High of quarter. Mar. 22nd – Low of quarter just starting.

April 11 and 16th – Top of rally.

May 2nd – Low of reaction; then up balance of month.

June 1st – Top of rally and high of quarter. June 30th – Low of month and last low before big advance. Low of quarter.

-20-

July 29th – High for month.

August 1st – Low of reaction. Aug. 2nd – Top of rally. Aug. 12th – low of reaction.

September 9th – Top of rally. Sept. 12th – Low of reaction.

September 16th – Top of rally and high of quarter. Slightly higher than Sept. 9. Sept. 29th – Low of month.

October 4th – Top of rally. Oct. 29th – Low of month and quarter and last low before big advance started.

November 29th – High for month.

December 9th – Low of reaction. Dec. 22nd – High of quarter.

December 24th – Top of rally and high of quarter just started.

1928

January 5th – Low of reaction. Jan. 7th – Top of rally; declined and broke low of 5h. Jan. 17th – Low of reaction. Jan. 24th – Top of rally. Jan. 25th – Same low as 16th. Jan. 27th – Top of rally; lower than 24th.

February 4th – Low of reaction. Feb. 9th – Top of rally. Feb. 27th – Low of month.

March 1st – Top of small rally. Mar. 2nd – Low of reaction and low of quarter; one point lower than Feb. 20th. Mar. 22nd – Top of rally. Mar. 23rd – Low of quick reaction. Mar. 26th – Top of rally; slightly lower than Mar. 22 top.

April 2nd – Low of reaction. Apr. 12th – Top of rally and high of quarter; 1¼ points above high of Jan. 7th. Apr. 24th – Low of reaction.

May 7th – Top of rally. May 9th – Low of reaction. May 11th – Top of rally. May 22nd and 29th – Low of month.

June 1st – Top of rally. June 11th – Low of quarter. June 25th – Low for month and quarter and low of year from which big advance followed.

July 9th – Top of rally. July 17th – Low of reaction. July 28th – Top of rally.

August 3rd and 9th – Low of reactions.

September 17th – Top of rally and high of quarter. Sept. 21st – Low of reaction. Sept. 27th – Top of rally and high for month.

October 3rd – Low of reaction and first low of quarter. Oct. 4th – Same top as Sept. 27th. Oct. 9th – Low of reaction. Oct. 24th – High for month. Oct. 26th and 31st – Low of reaction.

November 2nd – Top of small rally. Nov. 3rd and 8th – Low of reaction. Nov. 16th – Top for month and high of quarter. Nov. 21st – Low of reaction. Nov. 23rd and 26th – Tops of rally; big break followed.

-21-

December 17th – Extreme low of quarter; low of 149-3/4, last low before big advance. Dec. 24th – Top of rally. Dec. 27th – Low of reaction and of quarter.

1929

January 3rd – Top of rally. Jan. 8th – Low of reaction, 157¼; advance started and crossed high of Jan. 3rd. Jan. 25th – High of month. Jan. 30th – Low of reaction.

February 2nd – Top of rally. Feb. 16th – Low of month.

March 1st – Top of rally and high of quarter. Mar. 6th and 11th – Low of reaction. March 15th – Top of rally. Mar. 26th – Low of sharp decline.

April 12th – Top of rally and high of quarter. Apr. 17th – Low of reaction. Apr. 30th – Top of rally.

May 2nd – Broke low as of Apr. 9th and 17th; turning trend down. May 3rd – Small rally. May 31st – Low of month, low of quarter and last low before big advance.

June 17th – Top for small reaction. June 20th – Low of reaction.

June 25th – Low of quarter just started.

July 20th – Top of rally. July 22nd – Low of reaction. July 24th – Top for month. July 29th – Low of reaction.

August 2nd – Top for reaction. Aug. 6th – Low of reaction. Crossed high of Aug. 2nd. Aug. 24th – High for month. Aug. 29th – Low of reaction.

September 3rd – High of quarter and final high 261-3/4, up 95 days from last low made May 31st. Sept. 13th – Low of sharp decline. Sept. 19th – Last top of quick rally. Sept. 24th – High of quarter just started.

October 4th – Low of sharp decline. Oct. 10th – Top of quick rally. Oct. 29th – Low of month. Oct. 31st – Top of sharp two-day rally.

November 7th – Low of reaction. Nov. 8th – Top of quick rally. Nov. 13th – Extreme low for month and quarter and 150, down 111-3/4 points in 71 days. Nov. 21st – Top of rally.

December 2nd – Low of reaction. Dec. 9th – Top of sharp rally. Dec. 23rd – Low of month and quarter and last low before advance started.

1930

January 2nd – Top of rally. Declined same day from 173-3/4 to 166 which was low of month. Jan. 10th – Top of rally. Slightly lower than Jan. 2nd top. Jan. 18th – Low of reaction.

February 18th – Top of rally and high for the month and quarter. Feb. 25th – Low of reaction.

March 1st and 7th – Top of rally. Mar. 13th – Low of reaction; made higher bottom on March 17th.

April 7th – Extreme high of rally and high for month and high for quarter. April 8th – Low of reaction. April 10th – Top of rally. April 15th – Low of reaction. April 16th – Quick rally. Big break followed.

May 5th – First low of reaction. May 6th – Top of quick rally. May 8th – Low of reaction and extreme low for the month. May 14th – Top of rally. May 20th – Low of reaction; slightly higher than low on 8th. May 28th – Top of rally; same high as May 6th and one half point lower than May 14th top. Then declined to lower levels, breaking support points.

June 25th – Bottom of decline and low for the quarter.

August 5th – Top of rally. August 13th – Bottom of sharp reaction. Then slowly worked higher.

September 8th – High of quarter and year the highs of May 6th, 14th, and 28th. Trend turned down and prices worked lower. September 24th – Last rally; high for that quarter.

October – Broke support points in declined to new low levels.

December 17th – Reached bottom; low of the quarter. Rally followed.

1931

February 26th – Top of advance and high of quarter.

March 25th – High for that quarter. Then followed a fast decline.

April – Broke bottom of December 17, 1930; showed very weak position and indicated much lower prices.

June 2nd – Bottom of decline and low of quarter. Rally followed.

July 3rd – Top of rally and high of the quarter.

September 21st – Low of the quarter. September 23rd – Top of minor rally; high of quarter. Trend continued down.

December 18th – First low of decline; rally to 19th.

1932

January 4th – Nearly same low as December 18th; low of the quarter. Rally followed.

February 19th – Top of rally; high for quarter. Declined followed.

March 22nd – High of the quarter. April – Declined to new lows.

June 10th – Low of the quarter, the lowest close of any quarter since 1907. June 28th – Extreme low of decline, 21¼, and low of quarter. Note the low of October, 1907, was 21-7/8, a double bottom and support point. Advance followed.

-23-

September 6th – Top of advance; failed to cross top of February 19th, 1932. Also high of quarter. Decline followed. September 20th – Bottom of reaction. September 26th – Last high before decline; high of quarter.

October – Secondary decline continues.

December 22nd – Low of quarter. December 28th – Temporary low.

1933

January 11th – Top of rally; high of quarter.

March 2nd – Low of quarter. Range during the quarter only 8½ points, the shortest range for years on very small volume. Making higher bottom than June 28, 1932, the stock indicated good support. Trend turn up. March 31st – Low of minor reaction.

June 13th – High of quarter. Trend continued up.

July 18th – Top of advance; high for the quarter. Declined followed.

September 22nd – Low of quarter. September 23rd – High of next quarter.

October 21st – Low point of decline and low of quarter. Trend turn up.

1934

December 27, 1933 and January 5, 1934, same low; low of quarter.

February 19th – Top of advance; high of quarter. Trend turn down.

March 26th – High of next quarter.

June 2nd – Low of decline and low of the quarter.

July 11th – High of next quarter.

September 17th – Low of decline and low of quarter.

October 30th – Another low and low of quarter.

December 6th – Top of rally; high of quarter.

1935

January 8th – Top of rally and high of quarter.

March 18th – Last low before the uptrend started; low of the quarter, and a still higher bottom than that of March 31, 1933.

April 3rd – Low of next quarter. Trend turned up.

[undated, but likely *circa* 1935] [unsigned]

Chapter 6

Natural Resistance Levels and Time Cycle Points

W. D. GANN
88 WALL STREET
NEW YORK

SCIENTIFIC ADVICE
AND ANALYTICAL REPORTS
ON STOCKS AND COMMODITIES
AUTHOR OF "TRUTH OF THE STOCK TAPE"
"WALL STREET STOCK SELECTOR"
AND "THE TUNNEL THRU THE AIR"

MEMBER
AMERICAN ECONOMIC ASS'N
ROYAL ECONOMIC SOCIETY
CABLE ADDRESS
"GANWADE NEW YORK"

NATURAL RESISTANCE LEVELS AND TIME CYCLE POINTS

The Resistance Levels given below are based upon natural law and can be applied to the measurement of both Time and Space. Around these points stocks meet resistance going up or down or travelling the same number of points from a top to a bottom. Tops and bottoms of major and minor movements come out on these Resistance Levels.

When man first began to learn to count, he probably used his fingers, counting 5 on one hand and 5 on the other. Then counting 5 toes on one foot and 5 on the other, which made 10, he added 10 and 10 together, which made 20, adding and multiplying by 5 and 10 all the way through. This basis for figuring led to the decimal system, which works out our 5, 10, 20, 30 and other yearly cycles, as well as other resistance points. Man's basis for figuring is 100, or par, on stocks and $1.00 as a basis of money value. Therefore, the 1/4, 1/8, 1/16 points are all important for tops and bottoms and for buying and selling levels.

Taking the basis of 100, the most important points are 25, 50 and 75, which are 1/4, 1/2 and 3/4. The next most important points are 33-1/3 and 66-2/3, which are 1/3 and 2/3 points. The next points in importance are the 1/8 points, which are 12½, 37½, 62½ and 87½. The next in importance are the 1/16 points, which are 6¼, 18¾, 31¼, 43¾, 56¼, 68¾, 81¼ and 93¾.

-2-

Since 9 is the highest digit, it is very important for Resistance Levels in Time and Space. The most important levels according to 9 are: 9, 12, 27, 36, 45, 54, 63, 72, 81, 90, 99, 108, 117, 126, 135 and 144. You will note that many of these points correspond with the other Resistance Levels and correspond with the Master 12 Chart which gives important Resistance Levels, because 12 is simply 9 with 1/3 of 9 added to it.

The second important Resistance Levels formed by the digit of 9 are the 1/2 points, which are as follows: 4½, 22½, 31½, 40½, 49½, 58½, 67½, 76½, 85½, 94½, 103½, etc. You simply add 1/2 of 9, or 4½, to any even figure, or figure coming out on equal numbers of 9.

The next important Resistance Levels are those formed by 12 and its multiples. These are very important on account of the 12 months in the year. The points also come out very close to many of the other important Resistance points measured on the basis of 100 and 9 and also the points in the division of the circle of 360°. The most important points of resistance according to 12 are: 12, 18, 24, 30, 36, 42, 48, 54, 60, 66, 72, 78, 84, 90, 96, 102, 108, 114, 120, 126, 132, 138, 144 and the other points which you can see on the Master 12 Chart or Square of 12 x 12. A separate explanation of the Master 12 Chart gives these other important points. Tops and bottoms of most stocks come out remarkably close to a basis of 12.

The circle of 360°, when divided into its geometrical parts, proves the reason of all Resistance Levels and measures time and volume as well as space very accurately. It is important to divide the circle by 2, 3, 4, 5, 6, 8, 9 and 12, to get the important Resistance Levels.

We first divide the circle by 2 and get 180, which is the strongest resistance level because it is the gravity centre or 1/2 point. It equals 180 months or 15 years, which is 3/4 of the 20-year cycle and 1/2 of the 30-year cycle, which is very important.

We next divide the circle by 4 and get 90, 180, 270 and 360. These are very important points because they equal 7-1/2 years, 15 years, and 22-1/2 years, which is 3/4 of the circle. These points in days, weeks, or months mark the beginning and the ending of important Time Cycles, as well as being important Resistance Levels when the price reaches them, especially when the time is up.

The next important levels we obtain by dividing 360 by 3, getting 120 as 1/3 and 240 as 2/3 point. These equal the 10-year cycle and the 20-year cycle and, of course, the third point, or 360, is the 30-year cycle.

Dividing the circle by 12, we get the following important points, which correspond with other points: 30, 60, 90, 120, 150, 180, 210, 240, 270, 300, 330 and 360. 150 and 210 are very important because 150 is within 30 months of the 180° angle or 1/2 between 120 and 180. 210 is 1/2 point between 180 and 240.

After dividing the circle by 12, it is next important to divide by 24, because there are 24 hours in a day, and the Earth moves 15° every hour or 360° in 24 hours. Therefore, we get the following points: 15, 30, 45, 60, 75, 90, 105, 120, 135, 150, 165, 180, 195, 210, 225, 240, 255, 270, 285, 300, 315, 330, 345, 360. If we divide 15 by 2, we get 7½. Adding this to any of the other points gives an important point which corresponds to many of the other Resistance Levels. For example: Adding 7-1/2 to 15 gives 22-1/2, which is 1/16 of a circle. 150 is an important point and if we add 15 to this, we get 165, which is the 1/2 point between 150 and 180; 180 being one of the strongest angles. Get your other important points in the same way by adding 7-1/2 or 15.

Dividing the circle by 8, we also get very important points, which are: 45, 90, 135, 180, 225, 270 and 315. 135 [225?] is very important because it is 180° from 45. 315 is very important because it is the opposite of 135 and 90° from 45.

The next important points for resistance and measurement of time are obtained by dividing the circle by 16, which gives 22½, 45, 67½, 90, 112½, 135, 157½, 202½, 225, 247½, 292½, 315 and 337½.

The points obtained by dividing the circle by 32 are also important because they measure out cycles closely in accordance with the Master 12 Chart and come out closely with the months. These points are 11¼, 33¾, 56¼, 78¾, 101¾, 123¾, etc., just simply adding 11¼ to any of the other figures to get the next figure.

The lowest division of the circle of any importance is 1/64, which is 5-5/8 of 1/2 of 11¼. These are of minor importance but tops and bottoms often come out on these points, especially when we are nearing the end of a major cycle. These points are as follows: 5-5/8, 16-7/8, 28-1/8, 39-3/8, 50-5/8, 61-7/8, 73-1/8, 84-3/8, 95-5/8, 106-7/8, 118-1/8, 129-3/8. All of these points are the 1/2 points between the other important points. 22-1/2 is 1/2 of 45, 11-1/4 is 1/2 of 22-1/2, and 5-5/8 is 1/2 of 11-1/4.

It is very important to divide the circle by 9 because 9 is the highest digit used. Dividing by 9 we get the following important points: 40, 80, 120, 160, 200, 240, 280, 320, 360, all very important Resistance Levels and corresponding with many of the other Resistance Levels calculated from the different points.

Dividing these points by 2, we get 20, 40, 60, 80, 100, 120, 140, 160, 180, 200, 220, 240, 260 280, 300, 320, 340, 360. Many stocks work to these points of a circle in division of time, making tops and bottoms according to price and according to months. I use these points and the Master 12 points and the other important points obtained through dividing the circle by 2, 4 and 8, as the most important Resistance Levels in measuring the Time cycles.

If you will take the time to go over any stock running back 10 to 30 years, checking all important tops and bottoms, you will see how well these points work out both in Time and Space. In checking the Weekly High and Low Chart, you will find more of them working out than you can see on the Monthly, because there are bottoms and tops made on weekly moves which do not show on the Monthly High and Low Chart. Then checking up on the Daily Chart, you will find minor moves working to these points which do not all show on the Weekly High and Low Chart.

To determine Monthly movements, it is important to divide the year by 4, which gives the seasonal changes or the four quarters, which equal about 90° in time or 90 days and come to the strong Resistance Levels. Watch for changes every 3, 6, 9

-6-

and 12 months. Most stocks make changes of importance at the end of each 12-month period. The next important thing to do is to divide the year by 3, making 4 months, 8 months and 12 months important points to watch. Dividing 52 weeks or one year by 4 gives 13 weeks, 26 weeks, 39 weeks, as important points to watch for changes in trend. Divide 52 weeks by 3 to get the 1/3 points. On this basis the 17th to 18th weeks and the 35th to 36th weeks will be important points to watch for a change in trend.

When any important Time Cycle is running out, watch your Daily and Weekly High and Low Charts for an indication that top or bottom is being reached. Keep up your angles closely, as the angles will determine when the trend is changing. One good rule to use after a very extended campaign, which has run 50 points or more in space, is to take the greatest move on the way up or down and then when it exceeds this on a reaction it indicates that the trend is changing. Another way is to take 1/12 of the total movement. Suppose a stock has advanced 144 points, then 1/12 of 144 points is 12 points. As a rule, when a stock has advanced this much and reacts 12 points, especially if reactions have been smaller up to this time, it indicates that the move is coming to an end. Some stocks will go up and never react more than 1/4 of the total distance travelled, others will react 1/3 of the distance and others will react to the 1/2 point. Always calculate from where the move starts the last time and watch the 1/2, 1/4 and 1/3 points from the last bottom or top, as well as your calculations from the major bottoms and tops.

-7-

The example given below will show you how we work out the campaigns in U.S. Steel according to time and space movements.

UNITED STATES STEEL CORPORATION

This company was incorporated February 25, 1901. Trading in the common stock began on the New York Stock Exchange on March 28, 1901, when it opened at 42-3/4. Now, this being a new stock, which was not listed on the Exchange before, we have no high and low to go by, so the first rule to apply is: If the stock moves down 3 points first, it will indicate still lower; if it advances 3 points, it will indicate that it is going higher. Next, we put on the Square of 90°. You will see that I have drawn the angles up from "0" beginning with March, 1901, and drawn the angles down from "90" beginning March, 1901. These angles will show whether the stock is in a strong or weak position after it fluctuates for a short time.

Using the 3-point rule, the stock advanced to 46 from 43, which is 3 points up and would indicate higher, especially as it had crossed 45. But you will note it is below the 8 x 1 angle drawn from "90" which shows a weak position, while from the bottom it is above the 8 x 1 angle and is strong for some kind of a rally. It goes to 55. Now note your Resistance Levels. 56¼ is the Resistance Level because it is 45 plus 11¼. 54 is the Resistance Level on the Nine Square and on the Master 12 Square. 55 is one of the psychological points where the public buys a stock after it crosses 50 because they think it is going much higher. After the stock has gone up to 55, then take 1/2 from 43 to 55, which is 49. Breaking 49, the halfway point, shows trend down. After breaking this level it broke the low level at 43.

-8-

The next way to calculate is to take 1/2 of 55, which is 27½. During the panic of May 9, 1901, U.S. Steel declined to 24. 24 is an exact point on the Master 12 Chart and 22½ is the support level on the angles. Take the half-way point of the stock, 27½, and the angle of 22½° and get the half-way point between these. It is exactly 25, which indicated around 25 would be a strong support level and a place to buy for a rally.

Next, from the top 55 to the low 24, we get the half-way point which is 39½. If the stock crosses this point, then the next resistance point is the 3/4 point, which is 47. It advances to 48 in July, 1901, and holds for several months without breaking back below 39½. However, it fails to cross the 45° angle from "90" and from 55. In October, 1902, it breaks 39½ and breaks below the 45° angle from the 24 bottom, putting it into a weak position. Notice that in July, 1923, the 45° angles from "0" and from "90" cross at 28 and that 27½ is the halfway point of 55. The stock breaks under the 45° angle from "0" for the first time; then goes straight down to 8-3/8 in May, 1904 and rests on the angle of 4 x 1 from "0", the base or beginning point, reaching bottom on the 39th month from March, 1901, and 36 months from the bottom of May, 1901, coming out on an even cycle. Being down 46 points from the top would indicate a strong support level, because 45 points down is equal to the 45° angle and indicates strong support. 9 is 5/6 of 55, a support level and any stock getting down around 9, the digit, always receives good support. This is a strong number for stocks to make bottom on.

In August, 1904, the stock crosses the angle of 2 x 1 from 90 for the first time and gets active in September, crossing the 45° from 55, which shows uptrend. 20 is 1/4 point from 55 to 8-3/8. It crosses this level, which indicates higher. The next point is the 1/3 point which is 23-5/8, which level is also crossed. The next point is 1/2 which is 32-7/8. In December, 1904, it makes 33, where it hits the angle of 2 x 1 from 55, reacts, then crosses 33 and goes to 38 in April, 1905, which is 5/8 of the distance from 8-3/8 to 55. Note that 39 was the last top in February, 1903. The stock declines to 25 in May, rests on the angle of 2 x 1 from "0" March, 1901, and on 2 x 1 from left of 45° angle from "0" May, 1904, showing strong support, also because 23⅛ was 1/2 from 8-3/8 to 38. The angles held the stock above the halfway point.

Top reached was 46 in February, 1905. At 45 we naturally expect resistance. Besides, 43¼ is 3/4 from 8-3/8 to 55 and it is 60 months, or at the end of a 5-year cycle, and a reaction is due. In July, 1906, it declines to 43. The half-way point from 25 to 46 is 35½, and 33¾ is a strong resistance level. Again, 32-7/8 is 1/2 from 55 to 8-3/8. The stock is still above the angle of 2 x 1 from "0" in March, 1901, and only 2 points below the 45° angle from the low in May, 1904, making this a strong buying level. The next top is at 50 in October, 1906 and again the same top was reached in January, 1907. There was 4 months' distribution in a 5-point range, holding above 45. January, 1907, the last month that top was reached, was 69 months from the top in April, 1901 and 71 months from the date of incorporation, February, 1901, also 32 months from the low in May, 1904. Going into the 7th year indicated lower prices. The 7th year is always a year for a

-10-

panicky decline, and failing to go 3 points above the top made in July, 1901, was a sign of weakness. 50 is a Resistance Level because it is 1/2 of 100; 45 plus 5-5/8 equals 50-5/8.

In January, 1907, Steel broke the angle of 2 x 1 from 33. In March, 1907, it broke the 45° angle from the bottom of May, 1904, and also got below the 45° angle from "0" in 1904, putting it into a very weak position. It declined to 32, the support level of July, 1906, and one-half from 8-3/8 to 55. 29-3/4 is one-half from 8-3/8 to 50. It made bottom for 3 months around 32. In July, 1907, it rallied to 39. Note the angle of 2 x 1 from "0" in March, 1901, and the 45° angle from "0" in May, 1904, crossed at 38, making this a strong Resistance Level and hard to pass. In August, 1907, Steel declined and broke 32. This was the fourth time at this level and my rules say that when a stock reaches the same level the fourth time it nearly always goes through and makes a higher top or a lower bottom.

In November, 1907, Steel declined to 21-7/8. The Resistance Level is at 22-1/2 and 20 is 3/4 point from 8-3/8 to 55; besides 24 is a strong support level, as shown on the Master 12 Chart. It failed to decline to the angle of 4 x 1 from "0" March, 1901, and 2 x 1 from "0" May, 1904, showing strong support. Bottom was made on the 78th month from the top of April, 1901. Note that 78¾ is a strong Resistance Level because it is 3/4 [7/8?] of 90. This was 80 months from March, 1901. Note that the last low in June, 1904, was on the 40th month, and 40 months later makes bottom again when time had balanced. The reason that 40 is strong is because it is 1/9 of 360 and 1/3 of 120, the 10-year cycle.

In January, 1908, Steel crossed the angle of 2 x 1 from January, 1907, and in March crossed the angle of 2 x 1 from May, 1901, and 3 x 2 angle from "0", 1904, putting the stock into a strong position. Later, the stock crossed 36, the half-way point from 50 to 21-7/8, which indicated higher. In August, 1908, which was 90 months from March, 1901, the angle of 2 x 1 from "0" and "90" March, 1901, crossed at 45; also the 2 x 1 from 21-7/8 crossed at 45. The stock advanced to 48 in August and reacted to 42 in September. Being now out of the first square of 90°, having moved over 90 months, put it in a strong position. My rule says that stocks always go higher in the 8th and 9th years of a 10-year cycle.

In November, 1908, Steel crossed 50 and advanced to 58¾ on the 90th month from the top in April, 1901, which would indicate top and a strong resistance, but the fact that the stock got 3 points above 55, the high of 1901, indicated higher prices later, especially as it was out of the square of 90. The stock was up 50 points from 1904 low and 1/3 would bring it back to 42, which was the last low made in September, 1908. In February, 1909, Steel declined to 41⅛. The writer predicted the top for 58¾ in November, 1908, and the bottom for 42 in February, 1909. See the Ticker Magazine of December, 1909.

The April, 1909, Steel crossed 1/2 point from 58¾ to 41⅛, regained the angle of 2 x 1 from "0" March, 1901, and in May crossed 58¾, the top, getting above 45° angle from "0", 1904, putting it in a very strong position. Now, the question arises how to figure how far the stock will go when it has gotten into new territory after

-12-

so many years. If we add 45 to the last important top, which was 50 in 1906 and 1907, we get 95. Steel sold at 94-7/8 in October, 1909. Remember my rule says that tops and bottoms become half-way points. 21-7/8, the bottom, to 58-7/8 equals 37 points. Add this to 58-3/4 and we get 95-3/4. The top at 94-7/8 made 58-1/2 the halfway point from 1907 to 1909. The writer sold Steel short at 94-7/8, stating that it would not go to 95. This is recorded in the Ticker Magazine of December, 1909. When Steel sold at 94-7/8 it got slightly above the 45° angle from the top at 50 in January, 1906. This was exactly 73 points from the 1907 low and 86-1/2 points from May, 1904 low. Any time a stock advances 84 to 90 points from the bottom or base, it is in selling territory. While this price was 4-7/8 points over 90, it was only 86½ points up from its base; therefore, it would have to cross 99 to be out of the square of 90 from its extreme low in May, 1904. This is figuring according to Space movement. The stock was up 53¾ from the low of February, 1909, which was one of the strong Resistance points. It made top on the 102nd month. The Resistance point is 101-1/4. It was 24 months from November, 1907, coming out on an exact cycle and 65 months from May, 1904. It started to break when it reached 67½ or the angle of 67½°. This was 104 months from 1901. The 105th month or 8-3/4 years is an important resistance point.

To determine Resistance Levels, we first calculate the 1/8, 1/4, 3/8, 1/2, 5/8, 3/4, 7/8, 1/3 and 2/3 points of the Space movement. 76-5/8 is one-fourth of the movement from 21-7/8 to 94-7/8. In February, 1910, Steel declined to 75, getting strong support at the 1/4 point. In March, 1910, it advanced to 89, making top 3/4 of the distance from 75 to 94-7/8 and just under the 45° angle from 94-7/8. In July, 1910, Steel declined to 61-1/8 and failed to make 58-1/2, the half-way point from 1907 and 1909, which showed that it was getting strong support. 63-1/4 was one-third of 94-7/8, which indicated a support level. The advance started and it worked up to 82 in February, 1911, just under 2/3 point from 94-7/8 to 61-1/8, hitting the 45° angle from "0" in 1904, and a decline followed.

April, 1911, ended the 10-year cycle from the top in 1901. In August, 1911, Steel broke the 45° angle from 61-1/8 and in September, 1911, broke the 45° angle from November, 1907, and in October, 1911, declined to 50. Note this was on the 89th month from the low in May, 1904, working out the 7½-year cycle and reaching the angle of 90°. The bottom at 50 was down 44-7/8 points from the top, making this a strong support level because it was down 45 points, and equal to the 45° angle. 50-5/8 being a Resistance Level showed that this was the point to buy Steel again; also 51-5/8 was one-half from 8-3/8 to 94-7/8, and 47-3/8 was one-half of 94-7/8, the high point of the stock, all of which shows that this was a very strong support level. The stock was just below the angle of 2 x 1 from May, 1904, which angle the stock soon regained by getting back above it. It was down 2 years or exactly 24 months from the top and was 48 months from November, 1907, bottom, which balanced time and was an indication for another upward move to start. It was the 128th month from March, 1901, which put it out of the hexagon movement. See Hexagon Chart.

In September and October, 1912, Steel made top at 80, which was 3/4 from 94-7/8

-14-

to 50 and failed to cross the high of May, 1911. Now note top 10 years back, September, 1902, from which a decline followed. In October, 1912, a decline started and in December it broke the angle of 2 x 1 from 50, afterwards getting weaker and breaking all support angles from 1901 to 1904 and 1907 to 1909 bottoms. In June, 1913, again declined to 50, the same Resistance Level as October, 1911, and 44 months down from the 1909 top, 52 months from February, 1909 bottom, 68 months from 1907 low and 109 months from 1904 low. This was 7 years or 84 months from the 1906 bottom. You can see from this that the stock was still in a strong position according to the Space movement or Resistance Levels, but in a weak position on angles and was running down to complete the 7-year cycle from 1907.

In February, 1914, Steel rallied to 67, just 2 points above the 1/3 point from 94-7/8 to 50. Note that it made 67 for 2 months, hitting against the angle of 2 x 1 from May, 1904, and failed to reach the angle of 2 x 1 from October, 1909. To run out a 10-year cycle from low in 1904 would indicate bottom in May and June, 1914, and 7 years from low in November, 1907, would be November, 1914. The Stock Exchange closed at the end of July, 1914, on account of War and U.S. Steel sold around 32 on the New Street Curb in the month of November, 1914. So for the purposes of calculating, November, 1914, should be considered, according to time, the month when Steel reached low. However, this level was lower than it sold after the Exchange opened, so we must also calculate the exact date that Steel made the extreme low. This was in February, 1915, when it sold at 38, just 168 months or

-15-

14 years from March, 1901, 64 months, from 1909 top, 72 months from February, 1909, bottom, and on the 88th month from 1907 bottom, all strong time cycles indicating bottom. The stock went below the angle of 4 x 1 from May, 1904, but quickly recovered and stayed above it. This bottom at 38 was just above 2/3 point from 94-7/8 to 8-3/8, and 3/4 point from 21-7/8 to 94-7/8 was 40. February, 1909, bottom was at 41-1/8. 37-1/2 is a natural Resistance Level, being 30 plus 7-1/2 or 22-1/2 plus 15, and 7/8 of 45 is 39-3/8 – all strong resistance points on Space movements.

How to forecast from this point according to TIME: Going back 10 years we see that in 1905, 1906 and in January, 1907, the stock advanced; then in 1915, 1916 and 1917 it should be up trend. We add 7 years to October, 1909 top and get October, 1916. Top was reached in the early part of November, 1916, when the stock sold at 129, and a sharp decline followed to December, 1916, when the stock sold at 101, but final low was not reached until February, 1917, when it sold at 99. This was close enough to the 10-year cycle from March, 1907, when there was a panic, and 7 years from the top of February, 1910. The top at 129 was 21 months from February, 1914, bottom. It broke on the 22nd month, had a small rally in the 23rd month, made bottom 24 months from February, 1915, low. Note strong position on angles at 99, which was 90 or square above the base of 8-3/8 and exactly on the angle of 2 x 1 from 80 bottom in April, 1916.

The 180th month or 15-year cycle ended with February, 1916, with the stock holding above the angle of 2 x 1 from May, 1904, low, still below the price of 90. In August, 1916, it crossed the 1909 top at 94-7/8, which indicated much higher.

-16-

Now we want to know what price to expect Steel to advance to, so we look back and see top at 80 in 1909, 1910, 1911 and 1912. In 1916 there was 3 months' bottoms at 80. This being the last low must become an important centre or halfway point. Take the 1909 top, 94-7/8, and subtract the 1915 low at 38 and get 56-7/8. Add this to 80 and get 136-7/8. The exact high on May 31, 1917, was 136-7/8, the stock being up 98-5/8 points from 1914 low, and 128 points from the 1904 low. It is always important to go back 5, 7, 10, 15, and 20 years to bottoms and tops. Taking 1907 low at 21-7/8 and 1917 top at 136-7/8, we find the halfway point to be 79-1/4, proving that the starting point at 80 was to become the center of gravity or halfway point for a 10-year cycle.

The 1917 top was 91 months from October, 1909, top, and exact square angle of 90°, being only 1 month over it. It was 193 months or 16 years from 1901 top. Note November, 1908 top was 90 months from April, 1901 top. Sixteen years is 4/5 of the 20-year cycle. Stocks make their best advances in the 8th to 9th years of a cycle. May, 1917, was 16 years and 3 months from March, 1901. There is a cycle of 32 years and 6 months. Steel had worked out one-half of this cycle to the top. In view of the fact that top was reached on the 91st month and on the exact Space movement was evidence that the stock was top for a further decline. In 1917 top, coming out on the price indicated and on the 91st month, indicated top and a short sale. Besides, the volume of sales was very large, indicating distribution.

We know that 1907 was a panic year and that stocks made low in October and November, 1907; then 1917 must repeat. 1910 was also a bear year and 1917, or seven years later, indicated a decline. The trend turned down in June, 1917, and in

-17-

the panic of December, 1917, Steel sold at 80, the half-way point from 1907, getting just below the angle of 2 x 1 from 1907 and getting support 1 point below the angle of 2 x 1 from "0" May, 1904. December, 1917, was 90 months from July, 1910, and 30 months from February, 1914, the exact angle being at 33-3/4. This was another indication of bottom for a rally. We know that Steel went up in 1908 and 1909. Therefore in 1918 and 1919, 10 years later, we expect it to work like 1908 and 1909. Steel advanced in 1918 and made last top in October and November, 1919, just 10 years from 1909 top. In 1920 and 1921, Steel followed 1901, 1910 and 1911. In June, 1921, made bottom 7 years from the low in July, 1914, nearly 14 years from the 1907 low, 76 months from the 1915 low, 49 months from 1917 top and 242 months from the top in April 1901, working out the 20-year cycle, the most important cycle.

By taking the top at 136-5/8, we find that one-half of the total value is 68¼. The stock got support above the half-way point of its total value, indicating a good buying price. It was down 66¼ points from top, another Resistance Level. The 1/2 point from 8-3/8 to 136-5/8 was 64. The fact that it held above these halfway points indicated strong support and much higher prices to follow. The next point, 87-1/4, was one-half from 38 to 136-5/8. It made bottom in February, 1918 and February, 1919 at this level. In 1920, after Steel broke 87, it never rallied again to 91 until it declined to 70-1/2 in June, 1921. In 1922, Steel crossed 88, the half-way point; went to 111; then declined to 86. It remained 4 months at this same bottom without getting 2 points below the halfway point from 1915 low to 1917 high. This was proof enough that there was strong buying and good support at this main

-18-

center and that the stock would go much higher later. In May and June, 1924 – just 20 years from May, 1904 when Steel made the low – it sold at 95 and has never sold at that price again, before the high was made at 261¾, making higher tops and higher bottoms each year.

In November, 1928, Steel made top 20 years from November, 1908 top. In January, February and March, 1929, tops were around the same level, 192 to 193. Steel declined and made the last low in May, 1929, at 162½, a little lower than February and March, 1929 lows.

On September 3, 1929 Steel reached the highest in its history, 261¾. Note that tops were reached in July, 1919 and in October, 1909. This was one month sooner than the 1909 top and one month later than the 1919 top. The top was reached on the 343rd month from March, 1901. This is a very important number, which marks culminations and indicates tops or bottoms, because it is 7 times 49, and 49 is composed of 7 time 7. The top was reached 98 months from the 1921 low, or 8 years and 2 months, making top early in the 9th year. Note that the top on the sold stock before it sold ex-stock divided, was reached in May, 1927, 10 years from the top of May, 1917. September, 1929, was 174 months from 1915 low and nearing 180 months indicates a big decline. It was 147 months from the 1917 top, 62 months from 1924 low, 72 months from 1923 low, 56 months from August, 1926 top, 24 months from September, 1927 top, and 147 months from May, 1917. This is important because 135 plus 11¼ equals 146¼, an important Resistance Level on the Master 12 x 12 Chart.

-19-

From September, 1904, when the trend turned up, to September, 1929, was 300 months, an important cycle, which indicated the end. It is important here to figure the Space movement. Figuring from the low of 38 in 1915 to the high of 261¾ in 1929, we get 223¾ points. We know that 225 is one of the very strong Resistance Levels. Then figuring from the low of 21-7/8 in 1907 to the top at 261¾, find the Space movement 240 points, another very strong Resistance Level, because it is 2/3 of the circle of 360°. From the extreme low in May, 1904, Steel was up 253-3/8 points. 255 is the half-way point between 240 and 270, therefore a very strong Resistance Level.

Figuring from the low of 70½ in 1921 to the top in 1929, the Space movement equalled 191¼ points. This is exactly 180 plus 11¼, another strong resistance point. The last run on Steel from 162½ in May, 1929, to the top was nearly 100 points. My rule says, when stocks have sharp advances, getting up 90 to 100 points, it is time to watch for top and a change in trend.

I have found, after years of experience, that over a long period of years a stock cannot maintain a gain of more than one point per month, or that it cannot do better than to hold the 45° angle. When a stock in its early years goes up too fast and gets ahead of time, sharp reactions have to take place while the stock is squaring itself or adjusting itself to the time period. One of my rules is, when Time and Space balance, the stock makes top or bottom. This was the most important indication of all that Steel was top at 261¾.

October, 1907, was the next important low level after Steel reached extreme low in

-20-

May, 1904. From October, 1907, to September, 1929, was 262 points. To be exact, this time was up on August 23, 1929. The top was reached at 261¾ on September 3, 1929, within 1/4 point of the 45° angle from "0" in October, 1907, showing that the stock had made its return to the 45° angle. This indicated that Time and Space had balanced. Suppose the stock had crossed this angle. So long as it stayed above it, it would have indicated higher prices, but just as soon as it got below it, it would be an indication for lower prices. Analyze other stocks according to this same rule. Allowing one point gain per month for the stock to follow the angle of 45°, Steel was behind time in May, 1929. That is why the fast advance of 100 points took place, bringing it up to strike the angle of 45° and make final top when Time and Space balanced.

I have stated before that important tops and important bottoms become half-way points or main centers. Now, it is very important to know why Steel made low at 150 in November, 1929. We go back to December, 1928, and find the last low on Steel was 149¾, having declined from a top at 172½. There were three weeks' bottoms around this level. After advancing from this level to 192 and 193, it declined to 162½; then advanced to 261¾. From the 149¾ level, Steel advanced to a new high level of its history up to that time. Therefore, 149¾ or 150 must become an important center or half-way point. The last important low level was at 38 in 1915. We subtract 38 from 149¾ and get 111¾. We then add 111¾, which gives us exactly 261½. The stock made top at 261¾, which makes the half-way point from 1915 to 1929 at 149-7/8. U.S. Steel declined to 150 in November, 1929, which was a strong buying point, protected with stop at 147.

Figuring the total value of the stock, 261¾, we find the 3/4-point at 196¼, therefore a strong Resistance Level. Then, figuring from the last low, 70½, in June, 1921, to the extreme high of 261¾, we find the 2/3 point at 198. The writer advised selling U.S. Steel short in April, 1930, with stop at 199. On April 7, 1930, Steel sold at 198¾. It was below the angle of 8 x 1 from 261¾, a weak position on angles from the top, but we must always consider the position on angles from the bottom. At this time, Steel was above the 45° angle from 1914 and 1921 lows.

It is important to consider the position of the stock according to the Time Cycle. April, 1930, was 10 years from high in April, 1920, and the high in 1910, 20 years back, was reached in March and April. Going back 7 years, we find the high in April, 1923, and going back 90 months from April, 1930, we find that Steel made top in October, 1922, and a sharp decline followed in November. All of these Time Cycles indicated top for Steel in April and when it reached strong Resistance Levels and the Daily and Weekly Charts showed down, it was a sure sign to go short and pyramid on the way down.

LOOKING AHEAD

Knowing the date of incorporation of U. S. Steel, February 25, 1901, you would look back to see what happened at the end of the 5, 10, 15, 20 and 30 year cycles.

You would find that in 1901, 1902, 1903 and 1904, Steel was in a bear market and worked lower. Therefore, you would expect at the end of the 30-year cycle very much lower prices, especially after Steel had reached extreme high in 1929, being the third high top in the bull campaign. You would also refer back 20 years to 1911 and 10 years to 1921. These cycles indicated that 1931 should be a bear year. Then you would look for geometrical angles to tell when Steel was getting into a bearish position from the bottom, as it already was in a very bearish position on angles coming down from 1929 top.

May, 1930: When Steel broke below the bottoms of the previous three months, getting under 178, it broke under the 45° angle from "0" from the bottom of 1915, and when it was under 174, it broke the 45° angle from the 1921 low, placing it in a very weak position and indicating lower prices.

In December, 1930, Steel declined to 135, on the angle of 2 x 1 from the low of 111¼ from January, 1927. This, being the half-way point of the life fluctuation, was a strong support point.

1931

The stock rallied to 152-3/8 in February, 1931. This was the end of 360 months or the end of the first 30-year cycle from the date of incorporation. A change in trend of Steel nearly always comes in the month of February. The trend turned down at this time when it went into the new cycle. On this last rally to 152-3/8, it failed to reach the 45° angle coming up from 111¼ bottom. Then, declined and broke the 45° angle from "0" from May, 1918.

-22-

In April, 1931, it broke the 135 bottom; broke the angle of 2 x 1 from 111¼ and the angle of 2 x1 from 38 low in 1915; then broke the angle of 2 x 1 from the 1921 low, which put it in a very weak position. Dropping below the angle of 45° coming down from the 150 low of November, 1929, and below the 45° angle from 1950 of December, 1928, it was in such a weak position behind these 45° angles that it indicated very little rally.

In June, 1931, low was 83¼. The price rested on the 45° angle coming up from "0" from the low of May, 1924, where the bottom was made at 95. Note that the 4 x 1 angle from 1904 and 1915 crossed near these levels, and the 4 x 1 angle coming up from "0" in September, 1929, crossed at 84, making this a strong support point for at least a rally.

In July, 1931, Steel rallied to 105½, still weak on angles from the top and from the bottom.

September, 1931, Steel broke 83, under the 2 x 1 angle from "0" in May, 1924, and under the 2 x 1 angle coming down from 111¼, January, 1927 and also behind the 8 x 1 coming down from the 1929 top. As most all of the strong angles from the bottom were broken, it was in a very weak position.

December, 1931, declined to 36 on a 45° angle from "0" in December, 1928, when the low was 150. At 36 it rested on the 45° angle coming down from the last low of 114 in June, 1925. This was 2 points under the 1915 low of 38 and was 242 months from 1911 low and 60 months from January, 1927 low. The stock held here for a temporary rally to February, 1932, when it sold at 52½.

1932

This was 12 months in a new 30-year cycle. Note 1902 top in January was 30 years back, and also 1912 top in January, 20 years back.

The decline continued and in June, 1932, low was reached at 21¼, the same low as October, 1907. This was 34 months from 1929 top. At the time bottom was reached, it was under the 45° angle from the low of March, 1925. Note the 45° angle coming down from May, 1924, reached "0" in June, 1932, an indication for bottom and a change in trend. In view of the fact that Steel made extreme low in May, 1904, we would watch for change in trend in May and June, or when the cycle runs out. June, 1932, was 336 months from May, 1904, low and 26 months from April, 1930, top. Note May and June, 1912, low for a rally.

September, 1932, U.S. Steel had a sharp rally to 52½. This was the same high as the top of February, 1932, which it failed to cross. It was still in a weak position on angles from the top and a decline followed.

1933

February, 1933, Steel declined to 23¼. This was a secondary low and a higher bottom than 1932; indicated good support. It was 42 months from September,

1929, or one-half a 7-year cycle, and 34 months from April, 1930, top and 24 months in the new 30-year cycle. In 1913, February was low for a small rally; in 1903, February was top for a decline. Steel nearly always makes a change in trend in February. Looking back 7 years to 1926, you will find the low in March and April.

Note the 45° angle from "0" in February, 1931, which was the end of the 30-year cycle, crossed at 24 in February, 1933. Therefore, the stock rested on this angle, which was a strong support angle.

July, 1933, high 67½. Note that in 1923 lows were made in July and August; in 1913, high in August; in 1903, new lows were made in July.

October, 1933: Steel declined to 34½. This was 49 months from September, 1929, top and 42 months from April, 1930 top. October, 1923 was low, 120 months or 10-year cycle. 1913 also low in October, 1903, low in November. Looking back 7 years to October, 1926, we find a low, and looking up the 5-year cycle, in October, 1928, we find a low. Fifteen years back, or 180 months, September, 1918, was high. Therefore, there are many indications for a change in trend and bottom in October, 1933.

1934

The stock started up and advanced to February, 1934, when it made a high of 59¾. Again, we find the trend turning down and changing in February. The stock failed to reach the highs of July, 1933, a bearish indication and sign of lower prices. The top at 59¾ was under the 45° angle from the July, 1933, top. Looking ahead, we find that May, 1904, was the extreme low of the stock, therefore we would expect the stock to be down until May, 1934. May, 1934, ended a 30-year cycle from the bottom. Also, look up 1914 and 1924 to tell how Steel should run in 1934.

September, 1934, low 29½. This was 60 months or 5 years from the 1929 top and indicated a change in trend. Note October, 1924, was low, and in 1914 Steel was low in the month of November on the Curb, the New York Stock Exchange being closed. In 1904 Steel started up in September. Look back 7 years to 1927; we find low in October.

1935

January: Steel high at 40½, a weak rally and still under the 45° angle from 1932 and 1933 lows. However, it crossed the angle of 2 x 1 coming down from February, 1934, top, but never closed above this angle, indicating a weak position. The trend turned down again in February, breaking the 2 x 1 angle from the bottoms of 1932 and 1933.

March: Low 27½, still higher than the bottoms of 1932 and 1933 and getting higher support indicated that it was in a position to rally.

-24-

It was under the 4 x 1 angle from 21¼ low, but above the 45° angle from "0" in February, 1933, and on the 2 x 1 angle from July, 1933 high. Note in 1925 the low was made in March; in 1915 the low was made in February; in 1905 April was top. Note that it was 25 months from 1933 low and 33 months from 1932 and 49 months in the second 30-year cycle. Looking back 7 years, we find March, 1928, low. Now, we look at 1905, 1915 and 1925 and find that they were all years of advancing prices for U.S. Steel.

In April, 1935, U.S. Steel started up and crossed the angle of 2 x 1 from February, 1934, top and for the first time held above this angle. In July, 1935, high 44 against the 45° angle from July, 1933 top. In August, Steel crossed the 45° angle from 1933 top and got back above the 45° angle from "0" from June, 1932. This indicated that it was in a stronger position. Note the 2 x 1 angle coming up from "0" at the time of the top in February, 1934. It rested on this angle in May and June, 1935; also on the 45° angle from the low of June, 1932, and on a reaction in October, 1935, rested on the 2 x 1 angle from the low of March, 1935, and where the 45° angle from July 1933 coming down crossed the 2 x 1 angle from March, 1935, low. The low price at this time (October, 1935) was 42. This showed that it was getting strong support on these angles.

In November, 1935, it advanced to 50. Note the 45° angle coming down from the last top of 105½ made in July, 1931, will cross at 53½ in November, 1935. Looking back at the previous cycles, we find 1905 – high of the year in December; 1915 – high of the year in December; 1925 – high in November; 1928 – low in December. Looking at 1930, 5 years back – which was a bear year, however, we find the low in December. In 1935 Steel is following and repeating the bull cycles of 1905, 1915 and 1925.

FUTURE FORECAST: **1936**

In order to forecast Steel for the year 1936, you look back at 1906, 1916, 1926, 1921, 1922 and 1929. Note 1906 and 1916 highs were reached in January and the trend turned down, but in both of these years the trend was strong up from July and August to December. In 1926, high in January; low reached in May; high in August; low in October; and then rallied sharply, making high of the year in the month of December.

Apply these same rules to any other stock in forecasting its future trend. Bring up all of the angles from tops and bottoms; look up the Resistance Levels; study the volume of sales and watch the position on the weekly high and low chart as well as the monthly chart. By applying all the rules and considering all indications, you will be able to get a more accurate forecast.

TIME AND RESISTANCE POINTS ACCORDING TO SQUARES OF NUMBERS

Every price at which a stock stops on the up or down side is some important mathematical point, which can be determined either by a division of the circle of 360° or by the square of 12, the square of 20, or the square or half-way point of some other number.

There is no top and bottom price which cannot be determined by mathematics. Every market movement is the result of a Cause and when once you determine the Cause, it is easy enough to know why the Effect is as it is.

Everything moves to a gravity center or to a point half-way between some bottom and top or some other important resistance point. For example: We divide the circle of 360° by 2 and get 180. We divide by 4 and get 90; then divide 90 by 2 and get 45; divide 45 by 2 and get 22½; divide 22½ by 2 and get 11¼; divide 11¼ by 2 and get 5-5/8; divide 5-5/8 by 2 and get 2-13/16, which is the lowest division of the circle that we can use for time periods. Each of these points is one-half of one of the other important divisions of the circle.

Stocks work out the square of different numbers, triangle points of different numbers, the square of their bottoms, the square of their tops, or to a half-way point of the different squares according to the time period. Therefore, it is important for you to study the Resistance Levels according to these numbers, as outlined below:

SQUARE OF NUMBERS

The squares of each number and the half-way point between the square of one number and the next point are very important. For example:

The square of 2 is 4; the square of 3 is 9. The half-way point between 4 and 9 is 6½.

The square of 4 is 16. The half-way point between the square of 3 and the square of 4 is 12½.

The square of 5 is 25. The half-way point between 16 and 25 is 20½.

The square of 6 is 36. The half-way point between 25 and 36 is 30½.

The square of 7 is 49. The half-way point between 36 and 49 is 42½.

The square of 8 is 64. The half-way point between 49 and 64 is 56½.

The square of 9 is 81. The half-way point between 64 and 81 is 72½.

The square of 10 is 100. The half-way point between 81 and 100 is 90½.

The square of 11 is 121. The half-way point between 100 and 121 is 110½.

The square of 12 is 144. The half-way point between 121 and 144 is 132½.

You can figure out the squares of 13, 14, etc., in the same way.

An important thing to remember is that a stock which makes low on an odd number will work out to the odd squares, that is, a stock that makes a low on 3, 5, 7, 9 or 11 will work out to the odd squares, while a stock which makes a low on 2, 4, 6, 8 or 10 will work out to points in the even squares.

THE W.D. GANN MASTER STOCK MARKET COURSE

-26-

When stocks are selling at low levels, they make bottoms or tops and meet resistance around 2, 4, 6½, 9, 12½, 16, etc. All of these points are also important for time periods, especially on the monthly chart, and should be watched on the weekly chart. When stocks are very active and reach high levels and the time period is a long distance from top or bottom, then these square points should be watched on the daily chart.

IMPORTANT NUMBERS FOR RESISTANCE - 12 to 100

11 to 12: This is an important point for resistance, both on Time and Price, because 12 equals 12 months and 11¼ is 1/32 of a circle of 1/2 of 22½°.

15 and 16: The next important resistance point is 16, the square of 4. 15 is important because it is 1¼ years.

18: An important number for resistance in Time and Price because it is twice 9, 1½ times 12, 1/20th of a circle.

20½: The half-way point between 16 and 25, therefore important at times.

22½ and 24: 22½ is 1/16 of a circle, 1/2 of 45. The reason why stocks often make top or bottom in the 23rd month is because the angle of 22½° comes out at this point.

24 and 25: These are very important because 24 is twice 12 and 25 is the square of 5 and 1/4 of 100.

26: When you consider the square of 4, which is 16, and the even square of 6, which is 36, the half-way point between them is 26, which is sometimes an important resistance point for Time and Price.

27 and 28: Important tops and bottoms often come out around 27 to 28 months, and major or minor campaigns end on this time period. The reason for this is that 4 times 7 is 28 and that 28 is 2-1/3 years. Three times 9 is 27 and anything that comes out on multiples of 3 is very important, because it is the first odd number that we can square, as the square of 1 is 1.

30: Any half-way point or gravity centre is also important. Therefore, 30, which is 2½ years, is an important time period for changes in trend. Because 30½ is the half-way point between 25, the square of 25, and 36, the square of 6, it makes this period important.

34 to 36: 33¾ is 3/4 of 45. You will recall that the bear campaign which ended in July, 1932, was 34 months from the 1929 top. It is always important to watch for changes in trend around the 34th to 36th months. 36 being the square of 6 makes this a strong resistance point. Three times 12 or the end of the 3rd year is another reason for strong resistance at this point.

Page 207

39 and 40: 40 is a number referred to many times in the Bible. The children of Israel wandered 40 years in the wilderness. The food lasted 40 days. 40 equals 3-1/3 years. 7/8 of 45 is 39-3/8. Forty is 1/9 of a circle. All of this makes these numbers important for time periods and resistance levels on price.

42: is the next important number for resistance in Time and Price. It is 3½ years of time or 1/2 of a 7-year cycle. Also, 42½ is the half-way point between the square of 6 and the square of 7.

45: This is the master of all numbers because it contains all the digits from 1 to 9. The 45° angle divides the 90° angle in half, making it an important gravity centre. It is 1/8 of 360 and 5 times 9. Fast moves up or down often occur in the 45th month. On any kind of chart that you make up with squares, you will find that 45 will come out on the 45° angle or a 90° angle or an angle that is the equivalent of these angles. Notice how 45 comes out on the square of 9, the square of 20 and the square of 12, all proving that 45 is a Master Number. Use 45 in every way possible for measuring Price, Time, Space and Volume movements.

48 and 49: are strong and important numbers for changes in trend. 49 is 7 times 7, or the square of 7, and 48 is 4 times 12, or the end of the 4th year. On a decline to 49 to 50, a stock often meets resistance and has a good rally from this point. The same with a stock on an advance to around 49 to 50, meeting resistance around this point and reacting to 45 anyway.

50: is important because it is one-half of 100. If we add 5-5/8 to 45, we get 50-5/8.

52: This number has some importance because there are 52 weeks in a year and 51-7/8 is one-seventh of a circle of 360°. It is 4-1/3 years. 52½ is the half-way point between 45 and 60, which makes this important to watch for resistance.

56 and 57: These are very important because 56¼ is 45 plus 11¼ or the half-way point between 45 and 67½. 56½ is the half-way point between 49 and 64.

60: This is one of the very important numbers to watch for resistance. It is an important time period because it equals 5 years in time or 1/2 of the 10-year cycle or 1/4 of a 20-year cycle. It is one of the most important time periods after 45 to 49. 60 is 1/6 of the circle. Here again we use the rule of 3, multiplying 20 by 3, we get 60. 60 is 1/3 of 180 and the halfway point between 45 and 75. Watch stocks that advance to around 60 or decline to around 60. If they hesitate several days, weeks or months, you will know that they are meeting resistance at this point and a reverse move will occur.

63 to 64:   62½ is 5/8 of 100. 63 is 7 times 9. 64 is the square of 8, and is 5-1/3 years, and the next important point to watch after 60.

66 and 67:   66 is 5½ years or 5½ times 12. 67½ is 45 plus 22½ or 3/16 of a circle.

70 to 72:   The number 70 is referred to many times in the Bible. It is three score years and ten, the allotted span of the life of man. 70 is 7 times 10; 3½ times the 20-year cycle. 72 is 6 years and 72½ is the halfway point between the square of 8 and the square of 9. 72 is 1/5 of 360. It is also the square of 12 and a very important time period.

78 to 80:   These are all important because 78-3/4 is 7/8 of 90; 80 is 4 times 20 and twice 40. 80 equals 1/18 of 360° circle and is 4/5 of 100. The square of 9 is 81. Great resistance occurs around these price levels, and the endings and beginnings of cycles take place around these months as you will find by looking them up on your charts.

84 to 85:   Strong resistance levels, because 84-3/8 is 15/16 of 90 and 84 is 7 times 12 and equals the 7-year cycle. At this point, the greatest resistance is met before a stock reaches the 90th month or a price of 90. After it breaks under 90, it is the first important resistance level below 90.

89 and 90:   90 is one of the strongest points of all because it equals a vertical angle and represents 1/4 of the circle. 90½ is the half-way point between 81 and 100, the square of 9 and the square of 10. In active markets, moves straight up and straight down occur when the 90th month, 90th week or 90th day is reached. The 90th month is the most important, but the 90th week is also quite important.

You should always watch the 89th month for tops and bottoms and important changes in trend. Many important campaigns begin and end in the 89th month; some run to the 91st month. Note U.S. Steel monthly 1915 to 1916 and see what happened around the 89th to 90th months.

On the daily chart the change often comes on the 92nd to 93rd day, but a movement often runs to around the 98th day before an important change. It is important to watch this point on a daily chart.

95 to 96:   This is 8 times 12. 95-5/8 is 90 plus 5-5/8 and quite a strong resistance level for price and time changes. When an important time period comes out on the 96th to 98th month, you will often find an important change in trend because this is 8 times 12 and starts the 9th year. The 9th year is always important and marks the ending of important campaigns with extreme high or low prices.

Stocks often advance to 95 to 97 and fail to make 100; then they often decline to 97 to 95 and meet strong support, rally and cross 100 again.

99 to 100: Important because 100 is the square of 10. 99 is 11 times 9. 100 is a psychological number for the public to buy and sell, or to hope for prices to reach. Stocks often go to 99 and fail to make 100 and often decline to 99 and then start up again.

Study all of these important squares and gravity centers or half-way points and the squares of numbers above 12, as shown on the 360° Circle Chart. All of these mathematical points will help you to determine changes in trend and resistance points.

[W.D. Gann's signature]

November, 1935.

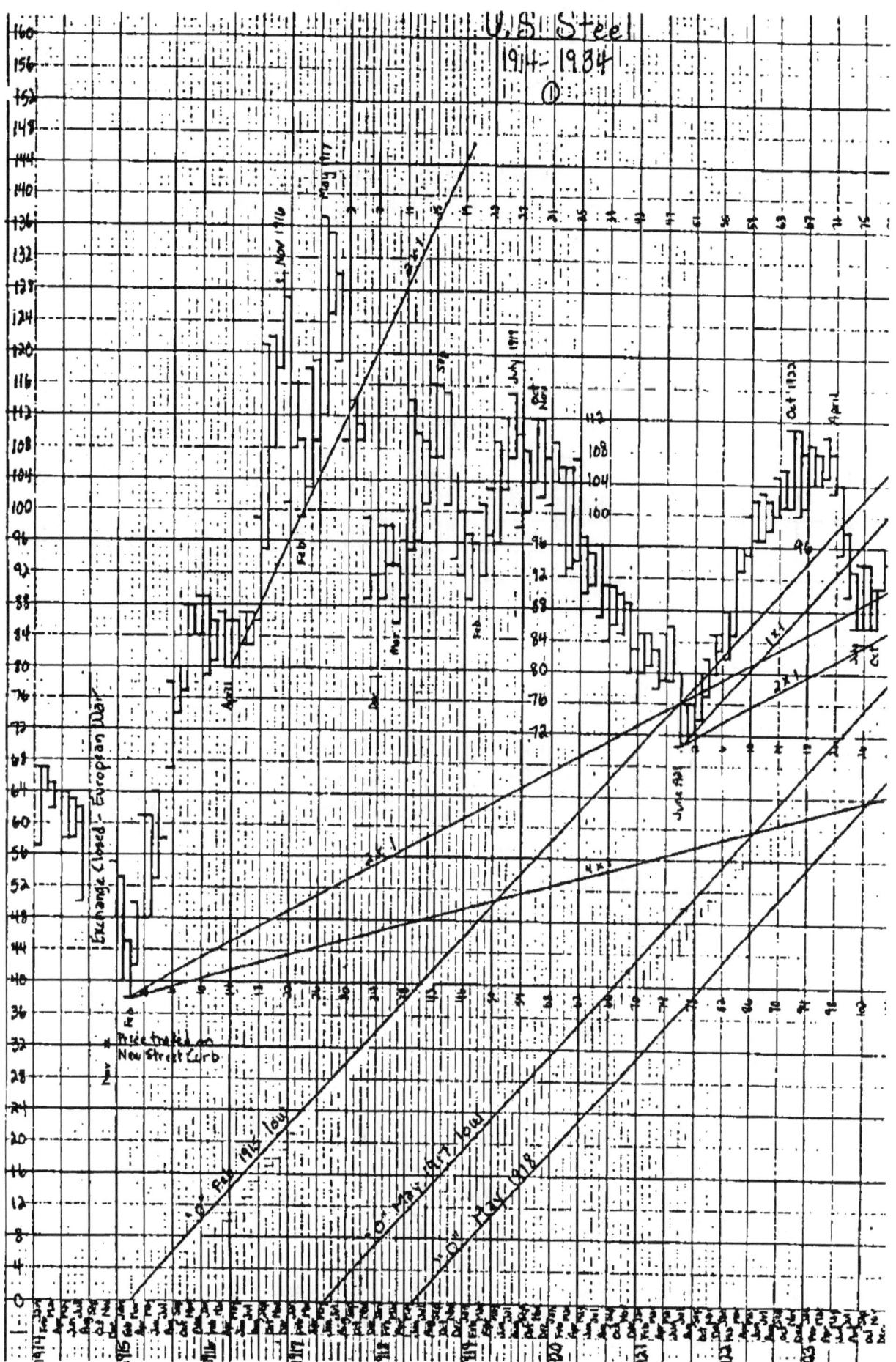

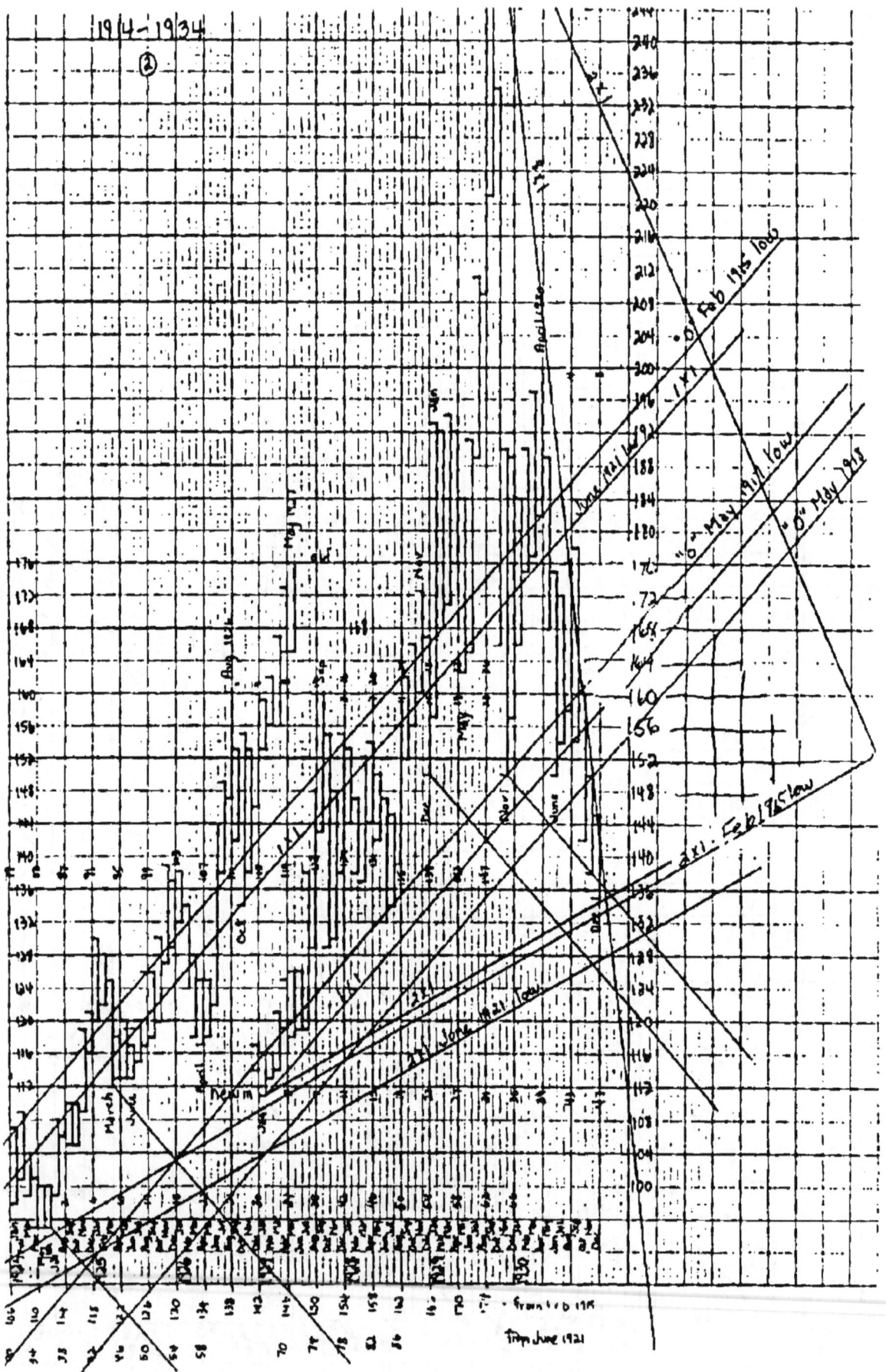

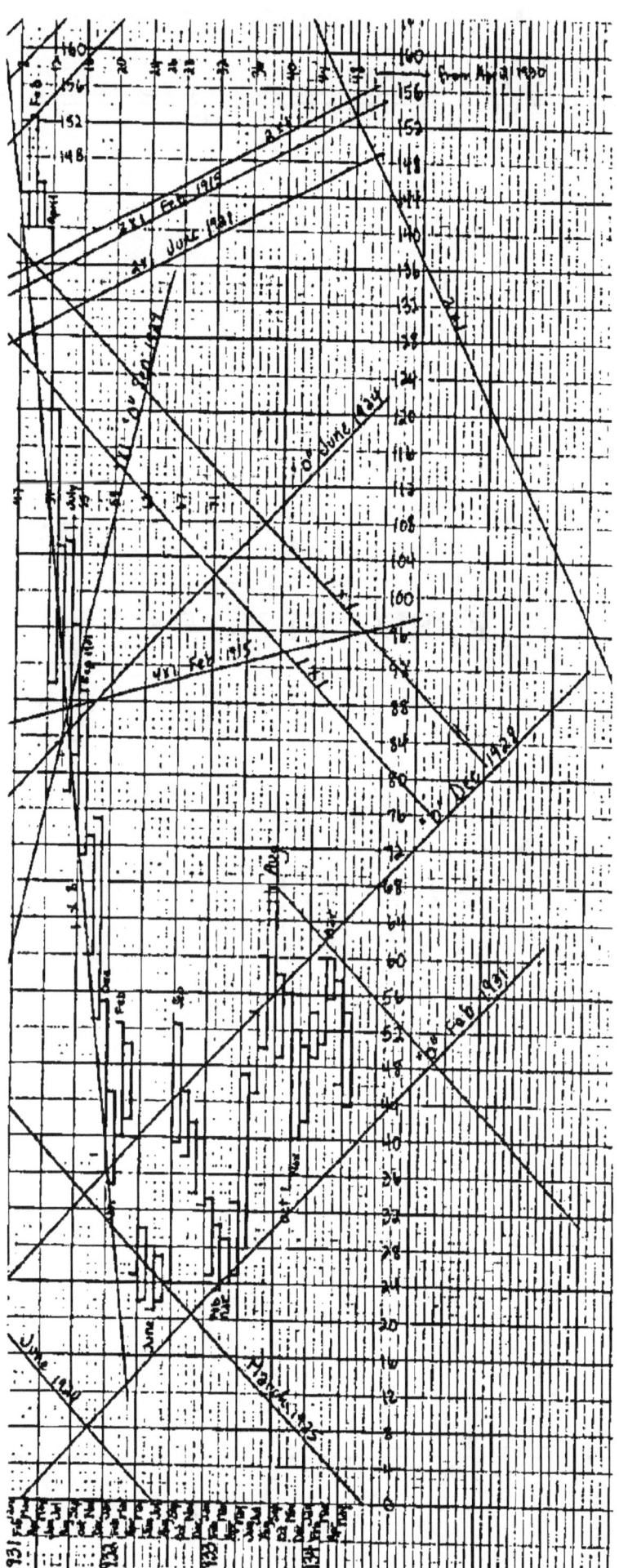

Chapter 7

Master Time Factor and Forecasting by Mathematical Rules

How to Trade

W. D. GANN
88 WALL STREET
NEW YORK

SCIENTIFIC ADVICE
AND ANALYTICAL REPORTS
ON STOCKS AND COMMODITIES
AUTHOR OF "TRUTH OF THE STOCK TAPE"
"WALL STREET STOCK SELECTOR"
AND "THE TUNNEL THRU THE AIR"

MEMBER
AMERICAN ECONOMIC ASS'N
ROYAL ECONOMIC SOCIETY
CABLE ADDRESS
"GANWADE NEW YORK"

[MASTER TIME FACTOR AND FORECASTING BY MATHEMATICAL RULES]

FORECASTING

Every movement in the market is the result of a natural law, and a Cause which exists long before the Effect takes place and can be determined years in advance. The future is but a repetition of the past, as the Bible plainly states:

> "The thing that hath been, it is that which shall be; and that which is done is that which shall be done, and there is no new things under the sun." Eccl. 1:9.

Everything moves in cycles as a result of the natural law of action and reaction. By a study of the past, I have discovered what cycles repeat in the future.

MAJOR TIME CYCLES

There must always be a major and a minor, a greater and a lesser, a positive and a negative. In order to be accurate in forecasting the future, you must know the major cycles. The most money is made when fast moves and extreme fluctuations occur at the end of major cycles.

I have experimented and compared past markets in order to locate the major and minor cycles and determined in what years the cycles repeat in the future. After years of research and practical tests, I have discovered that the following cycles are most reliable to use:

GREAT CYCLE - MASTER TIME PERIOD - 60 YEARS

This is the greatest and most important cycle of all, which repeats every 60 years or at the end of the third 20-year cycle. You will see the importance of this by referring to the war period from 1861 to 1869 and the panic following 1869; also 60 years later – 1921 to 1929 – the greatest bull market in history and the greatest panic in history followed. This proves the accuracy and value of this great time period.

50-YEAR CYCLE

A major cycle occurs every 49 to 50 years. A period of "jubilee" years of extreme high or low prices, lasting from 5 to 7 years, occurs at the end of the 50-year cycle. "7" is a fatal number referred to many times in the Bible. It brings about contraction, depression and panics. Seven times "7" equals 49, which is shown as the fatal evil year, causing extreme fluctuations.

30-YEAR CYCLE

The 30 year cycle is very important because it is one-half of the 60-year cycle or Great Cycle and contains three 10-year cycles. In making up an annual forecast of a stock, you should always make a comparison with the record 30 years back.

20-YEAR CYCLE

One of the most important Time Cycles is the 20-year cycle or 240 months. Most stocks and the averages work closer to this cycle than to any other. Refer to the analysis of "20-year Forecasting Chart" given later.

15-YEAR CYCLE

Fifteen years is three-fourths of a 20-year cycle and most important because it is 180 months or one-half of a circle.

10-YEAR CYCLE

The next important major cycle is the 10-year cycle, which is one-half of the 20-year cycle and one-sixth of the 60-year cycle. It is also very important because it is 120 months or one-third of a circle. Fluctuations of the same nature occur which produce extreme high or low every 10 years. Stocks come out remarkably close on each even 10-year cycle.

7-YEAR CYCLE

This cycle is 84 months. You should watch 7 years from any important top and bottom. 42 months or one-half of this cycle is very important. You will find many combinations around the 42nd month. 21 months or 1/4 of this cycle is also important. The fact that some stocks make top or bottom 10 to 11 months from the previous top or bottom is due to the fact that this period is 1/8 of the 7-year cycle.

There is an 84-year cycle, which is 12 times the 7-year cycle, that is very important to watch. One-half of the cycle is 42 years – 1/4 is 21 years, and 1/8 is 10½ years. This is one of the reasons for the period of nearly 11 years between the bottom of August ,1921 and the bottom of July, 1932. A variation of this kind often occurs at the end of a Great Cycle or 60 years. Bottoms and tops often come out on the angle of 135° or around the 135th month or 11¼-year period from any important top or bottom.

5-YEAR CYCLE

The cycle is very important because it is one-half of the 10-year cycle and 1/4 of the 20-year cycle. The smallest complete cycle or work-out in a market is 5 years.

MINOR CYCLES

The minor cycles are 3 years and 6 [2?] years [N.B. Gann said 2 years in a later course]. The smallest cycle is one year, which often shows a change in the 10th or 11th month.

F-3

RULES FOR FUTURE CYCLES

Stocks move in 10-year cycles, which are worked out in 5-year cycles – a 5-year cycle up and a 5-year cycle down. Begin with extreme tops and extreme bottoms to figure all cycles, either major or minor.

Rule 1 - A bull campaign generally runs 5 years – 2 years up, 1 year down, and 2 years up, completing a 5-year cycle. The end of a 5-year campaign comes in the 59th or 60th months. Always watch for the change in the 59th month.

Rule 2 - A bear cycle often runs 5 years down – the first move 2 years down, then 1 year up, and 2 years down, completing the 5-year downswing.

Rule 3 - Bull or Bear campaigns seldom run more than 3 to 3½ years up or down without a move of 3 to 6 months or one year in the opposite direction, except at the end of Major Cycles, like 1869 and 1929. Many campaigns, culminate in the 23rd month, not running out the full two years. Watch the weekly and monthly charts to determine whether the culmination will occur in the 23rd, 24th, 27th or 30th month of the move, or in extreme campaigns in the 34th to 35th or 41st to 42nd month.

Rule 4 - Adding 10 years to any top, it will give you top of the next 10-year cycle, repeating about the same average fluctuations.

Rule 5 - Adding 10 years to any bottom, it will give you the bottom of the next 10-year cycle, repeating the same kind of a year and about the same average fluctuations.

Rule 6 - Bear campaigns often run out in 7-year cycles, or 3 years and 4 years from any completed bottom. From any complete bottom of a cycle, first add 3 years to get the next bottom; then add 4 years to that bottom to get bottom of 7-year cycle. For example: 1914 bottom – add 3 years, gives 1917, low of panic; then add 4 years to 1917, gives 1921, low of another depression.

Rule 7 - To any final major or minor top, add 3 years to get the next top; then add 3 years to that top, which will give you the third top; add 4 years to the third top to get the final top of the 10-year cycle. Sometimes a change in trend from any top occurs before the end of the regular time period, therefore, you should begin to watch the 27th, 34th, and 42nd month for a reversal.

Rule 8 - Adding 5 years to any top, it will give the next bottom of a 5-year cycle. In order to get top of the next 5-year cycle, add 5 years to any bottom. For example: 1917 was bottom of a big bear campaign; add 5 years gives 1922, top of a minor bull campaign. Why do I say, "Top of a minor bull campaign?" Because the major bull campaign was due to end in 1929.

1919 was top; adding 5 years to 1919 gives 1924 as bottom of a 5-year bear cycle. Refer to Rules 1 and 2, which tell you that a bull or bear campaign seldom runs more than 2 to 3 years in the same direction. The bear campaign from 1919 was 2 years down – 1920 and 1921; therefore, we only expect one-year rally in 1922; then 2 years down – 1923 and 1924, which completes a 5-year bear cycle.

Looking back to 1913 and 1914, you will see that 1923 and 1924 must be bear years to complete the 10-year cycle from the bottoms of 1913-1914.

Then note 1917 bottom of the bear year; adding 7 years gives 1924 also as bottom of a bear cycle. Then, adding 5 years to 1924 gives 1929 top of a cycle.

FORECASTING MONTHLY MOVES

Monthly moves can be determined by the same rules as yearly:

Add three months to important bottom, then add 4, making 7, to get minor bottoms and reaction points.

In big upswings a reaction will often not last over two months, the third month being up, the same rule as in yearly cycle – 2 down and the third up.

In extreme markets, a reaction sometimes only lasts 2 or 3 weeks; then the advance is resumed. In this way a market may continue up for 12 months without breaking a monthly bottom.

In a bull market, the minor trend may reverse and run down 3 to 4 months; then turned up and follow the main trend again.

In a bear market, the minor trend may run up to 3 to 4 months, then reverse and follow the main trend, although, as a general rule, stocks never rally more than 2 months in a bear market; then start to break in the 3rd month and follow the main trend down.

FORECASTING WEEKLY MOVES

The weekly movement gives the next important minor change in trend, which may turn out to be a major change in trend.

In a bull market, a stock will often run down 2 to 3 weeks, and possibly 4, then reverse and follow the main trend again. As a rule, the trend will turn up in the middle of the third week and close higher at the end of the third week, the stock only moving 3 weeks against the main trend. In some cases, the change in trend will not occur until the fourth week; then the reversal will come and the stock close higher at the end of the fourth week. Reverse this rule in a bear market.

In rapid markets with big volume, a move will often run 6 to 7 weeks before a minor reversal in trend, and in some cases, like 1929, these fast moves last 13 to 15 weeks or 1/4 of a year. These are culmination moves up or down.

As there are 7 days in a week and seven times seven equals 49 days or 7 weeks, this often marks an important turning point. Therefore, you should watch for top or bottom around the 49th to 52nd day, although at times a change will start on the 42nd to 45th day, because a period of 45 days is 1/8 of a year. Also watch for culminations at the end of 90 to 98 days.

After a market has declined 7 weeks, it may have 2 or 3 short weeks on the side and then turn up, which agrees with the monthly rule for a change in the third month.

Always watch the annual trend of a stock and consider whether it is in a bull or bear year. In a bull year, with the monthly chart showing up, there are many times that a stock will react 2 or 3 weeks, then rest 3 or 4 weeks, and then go into new territory and advance 6 to 7 weeks more.

After a stock makes top and reacts 2 to 3 weeks, it may then have a rally of 2 to 3 weeks without getting above the first top; then hold in a trading range for several weeks without crossing the highest top or breaking the lowest week of that range. In cases of this kind, you can buy near the low point or sell near the high point of that range and protect with a stop loss order 1 to 3 points away. However, a better plan would be to wait until the stock shows a definite trend before buying or selling; then buy the stock when it crosses the highest point or sell when it breaks the lowest point of that trading range.

FORECASTING DAILY MOVES

The daily movement gives the first minor change and conforms to the same rules as the weekly and monthly cycles, altho it is only a minor part of them.

In fast markets, and there will only be a 2-day move in the opposite direction to the main trend and on the third day the upward or downward course will be resumed in harmony with the main trend.

A daily movement may reverse trend and only run 7 to 10 days; then follow the main trend again.

During a month, natural changes in trend occur around

| 6th to 7th | 14th to 15th | 23rd to 24th |
| 9th to 10th | 19th to 20th | 29th to 31st |

These minor moves occur in accordance with tops and bottoms of individual stocks.

It is very important to watch for a change in trend 30 days from the last top or bottom. Then watch for changes 60, 90, 120 days from tops or bottoms. 180 days or six months – very important and sometimes marks changes for greater moves. Also around the 270th and 330th day from important tops or bottoms, you should watch for important minor and often major changes.

JANUARY 2ND TO 7TH AND 15TH TO 21ST

Watch these periods each year and note the high and low prices made. Until these high prices are crossed or low prices broken, consider the trend up or down.

Many times when stocks make low in the early part of January, this low will not be broken until the following July or August, and sometimes not during the entire year. This same rule applies in bear markets or when the main trend is down. High prices made in the early part of January are often high for the entire year and are not crossed until after July or August. For example:

U. S. Steel on January 2, 1930, made a low at 166, which was the half-way point from 1921 to 1929, and again on January 7, 1930 declined to 167¼. When this level was broken, Steel indicated lower prices.

JULY 3RD TO 7TH AND 20TH TO 27TH

The month of July, like January, is a month when most dividends are paid and investors usually buy stocks around the early part of the month. Watch these periods in July for tops or bottoms and the change in trend. Go back over the charts and see how many times changes have taken place in July, 180 days from January tops or bottoms. For example:

July 8, 1932 was low; July 17, 1933, high; and July 26, 1934 low of the market.

HOW TO DIVIDE THE YEARLY TIME PERIOD

Divide the year by 2 to get 6 months, the opposition point or 180° angle, which equals 26 weeks.

Divide the year by 4 to get the 3 months' period or 90 days or 90° each, which is 1/4 of a year or 13 weeks.

Divide the year by 3 to get the 4 months' period, the 120° angle, which is 1/3 of a year or 17-1/3 weeks.

Divide the year by 8, which gives 1½ months, 45 days and equals the 45° angle. This is also 6½ weeks, which shows why the 7th week is always so important.

Divide the year by 16, which gives 22½ days or approximately 3 weeks. This accounts for market movements that only run 3 weeks up or down and then reverse. As a general rule, when any stock closes higher the 4th consecutive week, it will go higher. The 5th week is also very important for a change in trend, and for fast moves up or down. The 5th is the day, week, month, or year of Ascension and always marks fast moves up or down, according to the major cycle that is running out.

BULL AND BEAR CALENDAR YEARS

By studying the yearly high and low chart and going back over a long period of time, you will see the years in which bull markets culminate and the years in which bear markets begin and end.

Each decade or 10-year cycle, which is 1/10th of 100 years, marks and important campaign. The digits from 1 to 9 are important. All you have to learn is to count the digits on your fingers in order to ascertain what kind of a year the market is in.

No. 1   in a new decade is a year in which a bear market ends and a bull market begins. Look up 1901, 1911, 1921.

No. 2   or the 2nd year, is a year of a minor bull market, or a rally in a bear market will start at some time. See 1902, 1912, 1922, 1932.

No. 3   starts a bear year, but the rally from the 2nd year may run to March or April before culmination, or a decline from the 2nd year may run down and make bottom in February or March, like 1933. Look up 1903, 1913, 1923.

No. 4   or the 4th year, is a bear year, but ends the bear cycle and lays the foundation for a bull market. Compare 1904, 1914.

No. 5 or the 5th year, is the year of Ascension, and a very strong year for a bull market. See 1905, 1915, 1925, 1935.

No. 6 is a bull year, in which a bull campaign which started in the 4th year ends in the Fall of the year and a fast decline starts. See 1869, 1906, 1916, 1926.

No. 7 is a bear number and the 7th year is a bear year, because 84 months or 84° is 7/8 of 90. See 1897, 1907, 1917, but note 1927 was end of a 60-year cycle, so not much decline.

No. 8 is a bull year. Prices start advancing in the 7th year and reach the 90th month in the 8th year. This is very strong and a big advance usually takes place. Review 1898, 1908, 1918, 1928.

No. 9 the highest digit and the 9th year, is the strongest of all for bull markets. Final bull campaigns culminate in this year after extreme advances and prices start to decline. Bear markets usually start in September to November at the end of the 9th year and a sharp decline takes place. See 1869, 1879, 1889, 1899, 1909, 1919, and 1929 – the year of greatest advances, culminating in the fall of the year, followed by a sharp decline.

No. 10 is a bear year. A rally often runs until March and April; then a severe decline runs to November and December, when a new cycle begins and another rally starts. See 1910, 1920, 1930.

In referring to these numbers and years, we mean the calendar years. To understand this, study 1891 to 1900, 1901 to 1910, 1911 to 1920, 1921 to 1930, 1931 to 1939.

The 10-year cycle continues to repeat over and over, but the greatest advances and declines occur at the end of the 20-year and 30-year cycles, and again at the end of the 50-year and 60-year cycles, which are stronger than the others.

IMPORTANT POINTS TO REMEMBER IN FORECASTING

TIME is the most important factor of all, and not until sufficient time has expired does any big move up or down, start. The Time factor will overbalance both Space and Volume. When Time is up, space movement will start and big volume will begin, either up or down. At the end of any big movement – with monthly, weekly, or daily – Time, must be allowed for accumulation or distribution.

Consider each individual stock and determine its trend from its position, according to distance in time from bottom or top. Each stock works out its 1, 2, 3, 5, 7, 10, 15, 20, 30, 50 and 60-year cycles from its own base or bottoms and tops, regardless of the movements of other stocks, even those in the same group. Therefore, judge each stock individually and keep up weekly and monthly charts on them.

Never decide that the main trend has changed one way or the other without consulting the angles from top or bottom and without considering the position of the market and cycle of each individual stock.

Always consider the annual forecast and whether the big time limit has run out or not before judging a reverse move. Do not fail to consider the indications on Time, both from main tops and bottoms, also Volume of Sales and position on Geometrical Angles.

A daily chart gives the first short change, which may run for 7 to 10 days; the Weekly Chart gives the next important change in trend; and the Monthly the strongest. Remember, weekly moves run 3 to 7 weeks, monthly moves 2 to 3 months or more, according to the yearly cycle, before reversing.

Yearly bottoms and tops: it is important to know whether a stock is making higher or lower bottoms each year. For instance, if a stock has made a higher bottom each year for five years, then makes a lower bottom than the previous year, it is a sign of reversal and may mark a long down cycle. The same rule applies when stocks are making lower tops for a number of years in a bear market.

When extreme advances or declines occur, the first time the market reverses over 1/4 to 1/2 of the distance covered in the previous movement, you consider that the trend has changed, at least temporarily.

It is important to watch space movements. When Time is running out one way or the other, space movements will show a reversal by breaking back over 1/4, 1/3 or 1/2 of the distance of the last move from extreme low to extreme high, which indicates that the main trend has changed.

Study all the instructions and rules that I have given you; read them over several times, as each time they will become clearer to you. Study the charts and work out the rules in actual practice as well as on past performance. In this way, you will make progress and will realize and appreciate the value of my Method of Forecasting.

HOW TO MAKE UP ANNUAL FORECASTS

I have stated before that the future is but a repetition of the past; therefore, to make up a forecast of the future, you must refer to the previous cycles.

The previous 10-year cycle and 20-year cycle have the most effect in the future, but in completing a forecast, it is best to have 30-years past record to check out, as important changes occur at the end of 30-year cycles. In making up my 1935 Forecast on the general market, I checked the years 1905, 1915, and 1925. For the 1929 forecast, I compared 1919 – 10 years back, 1909 – 20 years back, 1899 – 30 years back, and 1869 – 60 years back, the Great Cycle.

You should also watch 5, 7, 15, and 50-year periods to see if the market is repeating one of them closely.

MASTER 20-YEAR FORECASTING CHART
1831 – 1935

In order to make up an annual forecast, you must refer to my Master 20-year Forecasting Chart and see how the cycles have worked out and repeated in the past.

And stated before, the 20-year cycle is the most important cycle for forecasting future market movements. It is one-third of the 60 year cycle and when three 20-year cycles run out, important bull and bear campaigns terminate.

In order for you to see and study how the cycles repeat, I have made of a chart of 20-year cycles, beginning with the year 1831. To show all of the cycles from 1831 to date, we have carried through on this chart the monthly high and low on railroad and canal stocks from 1831 to 1855. Beginning with 1856 we have used the W. D. Gann Averages on railroad stocks until the beginning of the Dow-Jones Averages in 1896. After that we have used the Dow-Jones Industrial Stock Averages.

After the end of the 20-year cycle in 1860,

> the next cycle begins at 1861 and runs to 1880,
> the next cycle begins at 1881 and runs to 1900,
> the next cycle begins at 1901 and runs to 1920,
> the next cycle begins at 1921 and runs to 1940.

By placing the monthly high and low prices for each of these 20-year periods above each other, it is easy to see how the cycles repeat. The year of the cycles are marked from "1" to "20". Study the chart and note what happened in the 8th and 9th year of each cycle – that extreme high prices have always been reached. For example:

1929 FORECAST

According to my discovery of the 60-year cycle, I had figured that 1929 would repeat like 1869, 1909, and 1919. Looking back 20 years, we find that top was reached in August, 1909, and 60 years before, top was reached in July, 1869. If you will read my Annual Forecast for 1929, you will see that I had figured the top must come not later than the end of August and stated that a "Black Friday" would come in September. Following strictly the 1869 top, the top would have come in July, 1929, and some stocks did make top at that time. Following the 1909 top, we could expect top in August, and the actual high of the averages and many individual stocks was reached on September 3, 1929. Going back to 1919, we find that the Averages made first top in July and a big decline followed, but extreme high was made in the early part of November.

From all of these tops – 1869, 1909, and 1919 – sharp declines followed in the fall of the year, just as they did in 1929. Therefore, you see how easy it was to follow this great advance and determine when it would culminate. There is no other way, outside of using the 20 and 60-year cycle that we could have forecast this great bull campaign and its culmination so closely in 1929.

1869-73 VS. 1929-33

After the 1869 top, stocks continued to decline and reached low in November, 1873. See how many other bottoms were reached around this time in other cycles. After the big decline from 1929, notice that in October, 1933, the last low was reached on the Dow-Jones averages; then followed an advance to new high levels, crossing the top of July, 1933.

1935 FORECAST

Figuring out the Forecast for 1935, we see on this 20-year Chart that we are running against 1855, 1875, 1895, 1915. Therefore, we look to see what happened in those years. We find that in 1895, the high was reached in September, in 1915, the high of the year was reached in December.

Then, look back at 1865, 1885, 1905, and 1925, the years in the 5th zone or the 10-year cycles. We find that in 1865 the high was reached in October; in 1905 the high was in October: in 1925 the high was in November.

Then, we would have a good guide in making out the Forecast for 1935, and we would know what months to watch for top and a change in trend. My Annual Forecast for 1935, which was made up in October, 1934, indicated top for October 28 and a secondary top for November 15-16, 1935.

There are other ways of using this Chart to advantage. One method of determining the trend is to compare the years of previous cycles in the same zone. For example: after the Dow-Jones 30 Industrial Averages crossed 108 in May, 1935, they were above the average high price of all the previous years in the 15th-year zone. Therefore, the market indicated higher prices and showed that there would be a bull campaign.

1936 FORECAST

If we wish to make up a forecast for the year 1936, we compare the years in the 16th year zone, viz. 1856, 1876, 1896, and 1916. As 60 years back is a very important cycle, we look at 1876 first, then 1896, and 1916.

1876 - We find that the averages run up and reach high in March; then decline to the end of the year.

1896 - Next, we look at 1896, which is 40 years back, or two 20-year cycles, a very important presidential election year, just as 1936 will be. We find that there was a moderate rally into February, a decline to March, then a small rally to May, from which a panicky decline followed, culminating on August 8, 1896, with the averages at the lowest levels in years. From that point, a bull campaign started, with prices working higher to December.

1916 - The next important cycle is 20 years later, or 1916. We find that prices declined in January, rallied moderately in February, then declined sharply to April, rallied to June, then declined and made bottom in July, from which a big bull campaign started, making top in November, 1916, in a war market. A panicky decline followed from the latter part of November into December.

This completes our comparison of the 60, 40, and 20-year cycles back from 1936. Next, we look at the cycles on the other side of the Chart, in the 6th year of the 20-year cycle, or the 6th zone, of the 10-year cycles. These years are 1866, 1886, 1906, and 1926.

1866 - We find that in 1866 there was a sharp decline, reaching bottom in February; then an advance, with top of the year in October.

1886 - We find a sharp decline and bottom in January, a moderate rally into March, then a sharp decline to new lows in May; a sharp advance, reaching high in November, and a sharp decline in December.

1906 - The next important cycle to consider is 1906. In that year, the great McKinley boom, which began in 1896, culminated. The railroad averages reached the highest price in history up to that time. From the high of January, a sharp decline followed to May. Much of this selling was caused by the San Francisco earthquake. Then, there was a rally into June, followed by a sharp decline to low in July, with the bottom just slightly higher than the low of May. From this low there was an advance to September, when another top was made, but lower than the top in January; then followed a decline into December and a panic followed in 1907.

1926 - The next important 10-year cycle to consider is 1926, when the great Coolidge bull campaign was underway. From the low in December, 1925, stocks rallied to February, 1926; then had a sharp decline into March, some stocks breaking as much as 100 points. From this bottom there was a sharp advance to new high levels, reaching top in August; then another sharp decline to bottom in October, from which a rally followed to December, but stocks did not get back to the high reached in August that year.

Now, when I get ready to make up my Forecast for 1936, I will consider all of the cycles. I will go back and also check the 7-year cycles, the 14-year and 15-year cycles, which is half of the 30-year cycle. But, at this writing, with my knowledge and experience of the future cycles, I expect the 1896 cycle to repeat in 1936.

1936 is likely to be a very uncertain election year just as it was in 1896, when the Bryan silver scare caused a panicky decline into August. There is a possibility of a three-cornered fight, with two Democratic presidential candidates and one Republican. There certainly is going to be a time during 1936 when the investors are going to get scared and speculators are going to get scared and sell stocks, causing sharp declines.

My opinion, at this writing, is that the first decline will start in the month of January and wind up with a sharp decline. February – the market may drift along in a narrow, trading range with some rallies, but there will be another decline in the month of March, just as there was in 1926. I am confident that there will be another break in the months of May and June, especially in the latter half of May, as this will be running out four years from the 1932 low and 6 years from April, 1930 high, all of which are indications of important changes in trend.

We know that presidential nominations will take place in July, therefore this is a month to watch for uncertainties and declines, unless sharp declines have come before that time. The ending of the cycle from 1896 in August is quite important and regardless of how high or how low stocks are, there are likely to be some sharp declines before the end of August. Again, in the last half of September, uncertain conditions and possibility of sharp declines are indicated. This may mark the last low and an election rally may start if there are indications of a change in Administration by the election of a Republican president, which, I believe, at this writing, will happen.

September, October, and November are all important because these months are 7 years from the top in September, 1929 and 7 years from the panicky decline in October and November, 1929. I would expect a rally to take place after the election in November, which would last anyway until the early part of December. If conditions show signs of improvement and if the people are satisfied with the man elected, then the advance will probably continue into December, with high prices around the end of the year.

This is merely a general outline that I am giving without completing all of my calculations and making up the Annual Forecast in detail.

INDIVIDUAL STOCKS

I have told you before that you should not depend upon the Averages to forecast the trend of individual stocks. These Averages give you the general trend, and while many stocks will follow this average trend, you should figure out each stock individually and let its position on geometrical angles and time periods determine the different months in the year when the stock is likely to make tops and bottoms.

Take any individual stock and make up the chart like the Master Forecasting Chart, carry it across 10 years or 20 years, and see how it's tops and bottoms come out. I have made up a chart of the 10-year cycles on US Steel and also a chart of the 20-year cycles, and am always glad to furnish these charts to students of my Course on Forecasting, so that they may study the individual stocks and be convinced that the theory will work on an individual stock even better than it will work on the Averages.

No man can study the Master 20-year Forecasting Chart and the cycles without being convinced that time cycles do repeat at regular intervals, and that it is possible to forecast future market movements. By studying Resistance Levels, Geometrical Angles, and Volume of Sales in connection with the Cycles, you can determine when the trend is changing at the end of campaigns.

FAST MOVES AND CULMINATIONS AT IMPORTANT TIME PERIODS

It is important to go over the monthly chart of Industrial or Railroad averages or any individual stock and look up the months when fast advances and fast declines have occurred and figure the number of months from any important top and bottom.

Watch how bottoms and tops come out on the important Geometrical Angles or proportionate parts of the circle of 360°, which are:

11¼	56¼	*90	123¾	168¾	213¾	247½	292½	326¼
22½	*60	101¼	*135	*180	*225	258¾	*300	337½
33¾	67½	112½	146¼	191¼	236¼	*270	303¾	348¾
*45	78¾	*120	157½	202½	*240	281¼	*315	*360

(*very important)

These angles measure the time periods. Always watch what happens around 45, 60, 90, 120, 135, 180, 225, 240, 270, 300, 315 and 360 months from any important top or bottom, as all of these angles are very strong and important, just the same as the 45 degree angle, and indicate strong culmination points.

REVIEW OF DOW-JONES INDUSTRIAL STOCKS FROM 1896

Go back to the extreme low of August, 1896 –

1897 - A secondary low was recorded in April, 1897. We find that there was a fast advance in the 11th to 13th months from August, 1896 low.

1898 - A fast advance occurred in the 16th and 24th months from the bottoms of 1897 and 1896, and a fast declined in the 17th and 25th months.

1899 - A bull year. Fast advance occurred in the 29th to 32nd months from 1896 and in the 21st to 24th months from 1897 bottom. Fast declines occurred in the 32nd and 40th months from these bottoms.

1900 - Fast advance 42nd to 44th months from 1897 and 50th to 52nd months from 1896 bottom.

1901 - A fast decline on the 49th month from 1897 and 57th month from 1896 low. Top reached in June.

1903 - A bear year. 22nd to 28th month from 1901 top, a fast decline – also 72nd to 78th months, from 1897 bottom, and 80th to 86th months from 1896 bottom. Bottom reached in October and November, 1903.

1904 - Fast advance, 12 to 14 months from 1903 bottom.

1905 - Fast move up in the 16th to 18th months; fast decline in the 19th month, and a fast advance in the 25th to 27th months from 1903 bottom.

1906 - Top of campaign reached in January. Fast decline in the 30th month from 1903 bottom.

1907 - Fast decline in the 14th month from 1906 top and in the 19th to 22nd months. Extreme low reached in November, 1907, in the 135th month from 1896 bottom, 127 months from 1897 low, and 22 months from 1906 top.

1909 - Top of campaign reached in October, 45 months from 1906 top and 23 months from 1907 bottom, 158 months from 1896.

1914 - July, a fast decline in the 57th month from 1909 top, 21 months from 1912 top. Extreme low of campaign in December, 107 months from 1906 top, 26 months from 1912 top, 220 months from 1896 low, 84 months or 7 years from 1907 bottom and 134 months from 1903 bottom.

1915 - This was a war year. March and April – Fast advance on the 3rd and 4th months from the 1914 bottom. May – A sharp, severe decline, 90 months from November, 1907 bottom and 225 months from 1896 bottom.

1916 - April – A sharp decline, 16 months from the 1914 bottom, 123 months from 1906 top, and 236 months from 1896 low. September – Fast advance, 21 months from 1914 low, and 240 months from 1896 low, the end of the 20-year cycle, indicating an important change in trend. In November – Top of a fast advance; Dow-Jones Industrial Averages at the highest price in history up to that time. This was 23 months from 1914 bottom and 243 months from 1896 bottom. December – A sharp decline, 24 months from 1914 bottom.

1917 - August to December – A fast decline, 9 to 13 months from November, 1916 top, 32 to 36 months from the 1914 bottom, 117 to 121 months from the 1907 bottom and 252 to 256 months from 1896 low.

1919 - A fast advance started in February and lasted until July. This was 27 to 32 months from the 1916 top, and 50 to 55 months from the 1914 low. February, 1919 was

135 months from the 1907 low and 270 months from the 1896 bottom. The 135th and 270th months, being 3/8 and 3/4 of the circle, were very important for changes in trend and starting of moves. October and early November – Final top, 36 months from 1916 top. November – A panicky decline, 23 months from 1917 low, 59 months from 1914 bottom (end of a 5-year cycle), and 279 months from 1896 bottom.

1920 - November and December – A fast decline, 12 to 13 months from 1919 top, 35 to 36 months from 1917 low, 72 months from 1914 bottom, 157 months from 1907 bottom, and 291 to 292 months from 1896 bottom.

1921 - August – Low of bear campaign, 21 months from 1919 top, 80 months from 1914 bottom, 165 months from 1907 bottom, and 300 months from 1896 bottom.

1924 - May – The last low was made, from which a fast advance started one of the greatest bull campaigns in history, ending in 1929. This was 54 months from the 1919 top, 33 months from 1921 low, 113 months from 1914 low, and 333 months from the 1896 low.

1926 - March – A big decline, with some stocks declining 100 points. This was 23 months from May, 1924 low, 29 months from 1923 low, 55 months from 1921 low, 135 months from 1914 low, and 355 months from 1896 low. August – Stocks reached the highest price up to that time, the Dow-Jones Industrial Averages selling at 166. This was 27 months from May, 1924 low, 34 months from October, 1923 low, 60 months from 1921 bottom, 225 months from 1907 low, and 360 months or 30 years from 1896 low. Then a 20-point decline followed to October, which was 2 months in a new 30-year cycle from the bottom of 1896.

1928 and 1929 were years of some of the fastest moves in history.

1929 - May to September – One of the fastest moves, advancing nearly 100 points on Averages. Final high in September. This was:

> 118 months from 1919 top,
> 240 months from 1909 top,
> 42 months from March, 1926 low,
> 64 months from May 1924 bottom,
> 71 months from October, 1923 low,
> 97 months from August, 1921 low,
> 177 months from 1914 low,
> 262 months from 1907 low,
> 37 months in the second cycle of
>   30 years from 1896 low.

Note the strong time angles on the Monthly Chart running out in October and November, 1929, which are 32, 40, 67½, 75, 120, 180.

1930 - April – Last top before another big decline. This was 49 months from March, 1926 low, 71 months from 1924 low, and 78 months from the 1923 low. May – A sharp severe decline. This was 270 months from 1907 low and 45 months in the second cycle from 1896 low. Then there were fast declines to in 1931.

1931 - September – A decline of 46 points on the Dow-Jones Averages. This was 24 months from the 1929 top, 95 and 86 months from 1923 and 1924 lows, 121 months or the beginning of a new 10-year cycle from 1921 low, 201 months from 1914 low, and 61 months in the new cycle from 1896.

F-15

1932 - July 8 – Extreme low of the bear campaign was reached. This was 71 months in the new cycle from 1896 low, 131 months from 1921 low, 105 and 96 months from 1923 and 1924 lows, 27 months from April, 1930 top, and 34 months from 1929 top. August and September – A sharp, fast advance in stocks. This was 35 and 36 months from the 1929 top; 28 and 29 months from April, 1930 top, 72 and 73 months in the new cycle from 1896 low, and 132 to 133 months from 1921 low.

1933 - April to July – A fast advance. This was 43 to 46 months from 1929 top. Always watch for combinations around the 45th month and multiples of 45. It was also 36 to 39 months from the 1930 top, 9 to 12 months from 1932 low, and 80 to 83 months in the new cycle from 1896, or running out a 7-year cycle in the new 30-year cycle. October, 1933 – Low of reaction, 42 months from April, 1930 top, 49 months from 1929 top, and 15 months from 1932 low.

1934 - February – Top. This was 46 months from the 1930 high, 53 months from 1929 high, 12 months from 1933 low, 19 months from 1932 low, and most important of all, 90 months in the new 30-year cycle from August, 1926. From this top a sharp decline followed. July – This marked the last low before a big bull campaign started. This was 58 months from 1929 top, 51 months from 1930 top, 24 months from 1932 low. Going into the 9th year of this cycle, the market indicated a big bull campaign to follow in 1935, as explained before.

Go over individual stocks and work out their cycles in the same way. Look up the months when extreme highs and lows have been made and note the months when each bottom and top in fast advances and declines have taken place. By keeping up the time periods from important tops and bottoms, you will know when important time periods are running out and when a change in trend is likely to take place. Also watch the seasonal changes in trend around March to April, September to October, and November to December.

All of this will help you to pick the stocks that are going to have the greatest advances and the ones that are going to have the greatest declines. The more you work in study, the more you will learn and the greater profits you will make.

NEW YORK STOCK EXCHANGE PERMANENT CHART

This Master Chart is a square of 20, or 20 up and 20 over, making a total of 400, which can be used to measure days, weeks, months or years, and to determine when tops and bottoms will be made against strong angles as indicated on this Permanent Chart. This chart works out the 20-year cycles remarkably well because it is the square of 20. For example:

The New York Stock Exchange was incorporated on May 17, 1792. Therefore, we began at "0" on May 17, 1792. 1793 and is on "1", when the stock exchange was one year old. 1812 will come out on 20, 1832 on 40, 1852 on 60, 1872 on 80, 1892 on 100, 1912 and 120, and 1932 on 140. Note that 140, or 7 times 20, in 1932 is equal to 90° angle and is at the top of the 7th zone or the 7th space over, which indicated that 1932 was the ending of a bear campaign and great cycle and the starting of a bull market. We would watch for a culmination around May to July, 1932 as the cycle ended May 17, 1792 [1932?].

Page 229

You will notice that the numbers which divide the square into equal parts, run across 10, 30, 50, 70, 90, 110, etc., and that the year 1802 comes out on a 10, the year 1822 on 30, the year 1842 on 50, the year 1862 on 70. Note that the year 1861, when the Civil War broke out, was on the number 69, which is on a 45° angle. Then note that 1882 ended in May on the 90° angle and at the 1/2-point, 180° angle, running horizontally across.

Again in 1902 it was at 110, the 1/2-point, and in 1903 and 1904 hit the 45° angle. Note that the years 1920 and 1921 hit the 45° angle on No. 129, and 1922 – the first year of the bull market – was at 130 at the 1/2-point.

Note that 1929 was on the 137th number, or 137th month, and hit an angle of 45°, and that the year 1930 was at the 1/2-point on the 4th square, a strong Resistance Point, which indicated a sharp, severe decline.

1933 was on 141 or the beginning of the 8th Zone and at the center or half-way point of the 2nd quarter of the Square of 20, indicating activity and fast advances and fast declines.

The years 1934 and 1935, ending in May, were on 142 and 143, and 1935 comes out on the 45° angle at the grand–center in the 8th Zone, and at the half-way point of the second 2nd, going to 1/2 of the total Square, which indicated great activity.

You can also use this chart from October 12, 1492, when Columbus discovered America. 1892 was end of 400 years or Square of 20. 1932 was 40 years in the new Square of 20.

You can use this Square of 20 for time periods on individual stocks and for price resistance levels.

If you will study the weeks, months, as well as the years, and apply them to these important points and angles, you will see how they have determined the important tops and bottoms in the past campaigns.

HOW TO TRADE

After you have thoroughly mastered all of the lessons, be sure you are right before you make a trade. Never guess. Trade on mathematical indications only.

WHAT YOU MUST KNOW BEFORE YOU START TRADING
You must know exactly how to apply all the rules; how to draw the geometrical angles or moving-average lines from tops and bottoms; how to square Time with Price, how to bring up the important 45° angles or lines, which represent a moving average. You must know where to place a stop-loss order and must look up what cycle the year is in, that is, determine from the Master Forecasting Chart whether it is a bull or bear year, whether the main trend should be up or down.

Before you make a trade, either buying or selling, consider the position of each individual stock on the monthly chart; next consider the weekly chart and then the daily chart. If they all confirm an uptrend, it is a cinch to buy, provided you have located the point at which to place a stop-loss order. On the other hand, if the cycle shows that it is a bear year and the monthly, weekly and daily chart show downtrend, then it is time to go short, but again, you must look for the most important point – where to place the stop loss order so that it will not be more than 3 points away and closer if possible.

WHAT TO LOOK UP BEFORE YOU MAKE A TRADE
Following are the most important points that you must consider before buying or selling a stock:

1. Annual Forecast determines year of Time Cycle, whether bull or bear year, and main trend of the general market, up or down.

2. Cycle of individual stock, whether up or down year.

3. Monthly position on angles from tops and bottoms and time periods.

4. Weekly position on time periods from tops and bottoms and on angles from tops and bottoms. See if it is squaring out Time from top or bottom.

5. Daily position on angles from important tops and bottoms and time periods. See whether a stock is near square of recent top or bottom.

6. Resistance levels on price. See whether the stock is near any half-way point or other points of support or resistance.

7. Look to see if stock has held for several days, weeks or months around the same level, and whether it is about ready to cross or break important angles from tops or bottoms.

8. Look up volume of sales. See whether a stock has increased or decreased volume over past few days or weeks.

9. Look up space or price movement, up or down, for past movements. Find out what was the greatest advance or decline for past few weeks or months. For example: if a stock has reacted 5 points several times and at the time you look it up, if you find it is 3

10. points down from the last top and the trend is up on monthly, weekly and daily with the price near support angle, you could buy with a stop loss order 2 to 3 points away; then if the stock broke back over 5 points, the previous reaction limit, it would show a change in trend and you should be out of it.

11. Remember, the most important factor to depend on to determine the position of a stock is Geometrical Angles. Be sure to bring up the angles from "0" from recent tops and bottoms.

12. Never overlook the fact that you must have a definite indication before making a trade.

13. Most important of all – Always locate the point at which to place a stop loss order to limit risk.

PRACTICE TRADING ON PAPER

After you feel sure that you have mastered all the rules and know exactly how to determine the trend of a stock and the place to begin trading, then to make yourself doubly sure and establish confidence, practice trading on paper and until you thoroughly understand how to use the rules and when to use them. If you make mistakes trading on paper, then you would make mistakes at that time in actual trading and you are not ready to begin trading. When you feel that you are competent to start trading, apply all of the rules and <u>trade only on definite indications</u>. If you are not sure of the trend or the buying and selling price and not sure where to place a stop loss order, then wait until you get a definite indication. You can always make money by waiting for opportunities. There is no use getting in partly on guesswork and losing.

WHEN TO CLOSE A TRADE

After you start actual trading, when you make a trade, don't close it or take profits until you have a definite indication, according to the rules that it is time to sell out or buy in or to move up the stop loss order and wait until it is caught. The way to make a success is to follow the trend always and not get out or closer trade until the trend changes.

WHEN TO WAIT AND NOT TRADE

It is just as important to know when not to enter the market as it is to know when to enter it. The time not to make a trade is when you find a stock has been holding in a narrow trading range for some time, say, a 5-point or a 3-point range, but has not broken under bottoms previously made or crossed tops previously made. A stock may stay for weeks or months or even years in a trading range and will not indicate any big move or change in trend until it crosses a previous top or breaks a previous bottom. If a stock is inactive in this position it is no time to start trading in it.

Another time not to make a trade is when a stock has narrowed down between two important angles – has not broken under one or crossed the other. Wait until it gets out in the clear and gives a definite indication before you trade.

After a prolonged decline stocks nearly always narrow down and hold in a trading range for some time. Then you should wait until the angles from the bottom are broken or the angles from the top are crossed and the stock breaks over an old top before you make a trade. In other words, at all times, trade when you have a definite, well-defined trend.

CAPITAL REQUIRED FOR TRADING

Before you do any trading, you must know the amount of capital required to make a success trading and the exact amount that you must risk on any one trade in order to always have capital left to trade with.

You can begin trading in 10 shares, 100 shares, 1000 shares or any other amount, but the main point is to divide your capital properly and to distribute the risks equally to protect your capital.

Whatever amount of capital you use to trade with, follow this rule: Divide your capital into 10 equal parts and never risk more than 10% of your capital on any one trade. Should you lose three consecutive times, then reduce your trading unit and only risk 10% of your remaining capital. If you follow this rule, your success is sure.

As a general rule, I have always considered it advisable to use at least $3000 capital for every 100 shares of stock traded in and to limit risks to 3 points or less on every trade. In this way, you will be able to make 10 trades on your capital and the market would have to beat you 10 consecutive times to wipe out your capital, which it will not do. You should try to make trades a price where it will only be necessary to use one to two-point stop loss orders, which will cut down the risk.

If you want to start trading in small units of stock, use a capital of $300 for each 10 shares and never risk more than 3 points on the initial trade. Try to make the first trade, if possible, where your stop loss order will not be more than one or two points.

ALWAYS FOLLOW RULES: Decide this important point before you start trading. If you do not intend to follow the rules strictly, do not begin trading. Never allow guesswork or the human element to enter into your trading. Stick to the "Capital" rule, and under no condition risk more than one-tenth of your capital on any one trade. Follow the mathematical rules and you will make a success.

PYRAMIDING

You should only pyramid or increase your trading in active markets where volume is above normal. The position on angles and volume of activity will show you when to pyramid. You should never begin pyramiding until a stock has gotten into a strong position on angles or into a weak position on angles, or until it has broken out of a trading range by crossing old tops or breaking old bottoms.

HOW TO PYRAMID

If you are trading at 100 shares, after you have made your first trade with a risk limited to 3 points or 10% of your capital, then do not pyramid, or buy or sell a second lot, until the market has moved at least 5 points in your favor; then when you buy or sell a second lot, use a stop loss order not more than 3 points away on both trades.

Example: We will assume that after buying the second lot, the trend reverses and the stop loss orders on both trades are caught 3 points away from where you bought the last lot. This will give you a loss of 3 points on the last trade and a profit of 2 points on the first trade, or a net loss of only one point. On the other hand, if the market continues to move in your favor, your profits will be twice as much after buying the second lot.

When the market has moved 5 points more in your favor, you buy a third lot, moving up the stop loss orders on the first and second lots and placing a stop on the entire lot of three trades not more than 3 points away and closer, if possible.

Continue to pyramid as long as the market moves 5 points in your favor, always following up with stop loss orders. When a stock selling between 5 and 75 a share, has moved 15 to 25 points in your favor, you should begin to watch for a change in trend and be careful about buying or selling another lot in which you may have to take a loss.

THE RUN OR PYRAMIDING MOVE

The big money in pyramiding is made in the run between accumulation and distribution, that is, after a stock passes out of the zone of accumulation. Pyramids should be started after double or triple tops are crossed and the stock clears the zone of accumulation. Then, when you get into this run, buy every 5 points up, protecting with a stop loss or not more than 3 points away from the last trade.

Reverse this rule in a declining market: After double or triple bottoms are broken and the stock clears the zone of distribution, sell every 5 points down, protecting with stop loss orders not more than 3 points above the last trade.

FAST MARKETS AND WIDE FLUCTUATIONS

When stocks are very active and moving very fast, selling above $100, then you will find it best to make trades 7 to 10 points apart. The angles and price Resistance Points, as well as old tops and bottoms will determine points to place stop loss orders with safety.

In fast-moving markets, like the panic of October and November, 1929, when you pyramid on active stocks and have very large profits, you should follow down, with a stop loss order about 10 points away from the market. Then, after a severe decline reduce stop loss orders, placing them about 5 points above the low level. When a market is moving as fast as this, you should not wait for the stock to get into a strong position on angles. Reverse this rule in an advancing market.

SAFEST PYRAMIDING RULE

One of the safest rules to use for pyramiding when stocks are selling at extremely high levels or extremely low levels is to start with 100 shares and when the market moves 5 points in your favor, buy another 50 shares; then when it moves 5 points more, buy or sell 30 shares; then on the next 5-point move in your favor buy or sell 20 shares, and continue to follow the market up or down with this amount until there is a change in the main trend.

WHEN NOT TO PYRAMID

Safety is the first consideration in starting or continuing a pyramiding campaign in a stock. Mistakes are made by buying or selling a second lot too near the accumulation or the distribution point. After a big move up or down, you must always wait for a definite change in trend before starting a pyramid.

Never buy a second lot for a pyramid when a stock is near a double top or sell a second lot when a stock is near a double bottom.

A stock often holds several days or weeks in a range of 10 to 12 points, moving up and down, not crossing the highest top or breaking the last bottom made. As long as it remains in this range, you should not pyramid. When it gets out of this range, crossing the highest top or breaking the lowest bottom, then it will indicate a bigger move and you should start to pyramid.

Always check and double check, follow all the rules, study the major and minor time cycles for forecasting, the angles from tops and bottoms, the Resistance Points of Price between tops and bottoms. If you ignore one important point, it may get you wrong. Remember, the whole can never exceed all of its parts, and all of the parts make up the whole. If you leave out one of the parts or one of the rules, you do not have a complete trend indicator.

[W. D. Gann's signature]

November, 1935

NYSE PERMANENT CHART

	1	2	3	4	5	6	7	8	9	10	11	12	13	14	15	16	17	18	19	20
	1812	1832	1852	1872	1892	1912	1932	1952	1972	2012	2032	2052	2072	2092	2112	2132	2152	2172	2192
20	40	60	80	100	120	140	160	180	200	220	240	260	280	300	320	340	360	380	400
19	39	59	79	99	119	139	159	179	199	219	239	259	279	299	319	339	359	379	399
18	38	58	78	98	118	138	158	178	198	218	238	258	278	298	318	338	358	378	398
17	37	57	77	97	117	137	157	177	197	217	237	257	277	297	317	337	357	377	397
16	36	56	76	96	116	136	156	176	196	216	236	256	276	296	316	336	356	376	396
15	35	55	75	95	115	135	155	175	195	215	235	255	275	295	315	335	355	375	395
14	34	54	74	94	114	134	154	174	194	214	234	254	274	294	314	334	354	374	394
13	33	53	73	93	113	133	153	173	193	213	233	253	273	293	313	333	353	373	393
12	32	52	72	92	112	132	152	172	192	212	232	252	272	292	312	332	352	372	392
11	31	51	71	91	111	131	151	171	191	211	231	251	271	291	311	331	351	371	391
	1802	1822	1842	1862	1882	1902	1922	1942	1962	1982	2002	2022	2042	2062	2082	2102	2122	2142	2162	2182
10	30	50	70	90	110	130	150	170	190	210	230	250	270	290	310	330	350	370	390
9	29	49	69	89	109	129	149	169	189	209	229	249	269	289	309	329	349	369	389
8	28	48	68	88	108	128	148	168	188	208	228	248	268	288	308	328	348	368	388
7	27	47	67	87	107	127	147	167	187	207	227	247	267	287	307	327	347	367	387
6	26	46	66	86	106	126	146	166	186	206	226	246	266	286	306	326	346	366	386
5	25	45	65	85	105	125	145	165	185	205	225	245	265	285	305	325	345	365	385
4	24	44	64	84	104	124	144	164	184	204	224	244	264	284	304	324	344	364	384
3	23	43	63	83	103	123	143	163	183	203	223	243	263	283	303	323	343	363	383
2	22	42	62	82	102	122	142	162	182	202	222	242	262	282	302	322	342	362	382
1	21	41	61	81	101	121	141	161	181	201	221	241	261	281	301	321	341	361	381

MAY 17 1792

W.D. GANN

Chapter 8

Form Reading and Rules for Determining Trend of Stocks

THE W.D. GANN MASTER STOCK MARKET COURSE

AUTHOR:
"Truth of the Stock Tape"
"Wall Street Stock Selector"
"New Stock Trend Detector"

W. D. GANN

Statistician and Economist
82 WALL STREET
NEW YORK, N.Y.

———

2101 N.W. 18th TERRACE
MIAMI. FLA.

MEMBER
New Orleans Cotton Exchange
Commodity Exchange, Inc. N.Y.
American Economic Ass'n
Royal Economic Society

FORM READING
and
RULES FOR DETERMINING TREND OF STOCKS

REQUIREMENTS FOR SUCCESS IN SPECULATION OR INVESTMENT

KNOWLEDGE

One of the vital and most important factors for making a success in speculation or anything else is KNOWLEDGE. The well-posted man or the man who knows his business is the man who succeeds. Therefore, put it down as a rule that hard work in acquiring knowledge will surely bring success in speculation or business.

PATIENCE

After you have acquired knowledge you will need to learn PATIENCE, if you have not already learned the value of patience. You must learn to wait for a definite indication of a change in trend before buying or selling. You must not guess or gamble on hope or fear. You must have ability to act and to act quickly at the right time, acting after you have acquired knowledge and know it is the time to act.

COURAGE

You must have the COURAGE to act. Courage and boldness will come after you have acquired knowledge because you will have confidence in proven rules and confidence in your ability. Therefore, the acquiring of knowledge will give you the courage for action at the time when the real opportunity comes.

STUDY

A man who will not work hard and STUDY and pay in advance for success will never get it. If you will put in the time, study, and go over the record of the Dow-Jones Industrial averages form 1892 to date, you will be convinced that the rules work and that you can make money by following the main trend of the market.

THE W.D. GANN MASTER STOCK MARKET COURSE

FORM READING

Eight-five per cent of what any of us learn is from what we see. It has been well said, "One picture is worth a thousand words." That is why FORM READING or the reading of various formations at different periods of time is so valuable. The future is but a repetition of the past. The same formation at tops or bottoms or intermediate points at different times indicates the trend of the market. Therefore, when you see the same picture or formation in the market the second and third time, you know what it means and can determine the trend.

You do not have to accept my word that the rules I give you will work in the future as they have in the past but you owe it to yourself to prove by past records that these rules work; then you will have the faith to follow them and make money.

CAPITAL REQUIRED

The first point to consider in operating any method on the stock market is the amount of capital required, with which you can trade and never lose your capital and over a period of 5, 10, or 15 years be able to make profits, because a method that will make profits and never lose your capital is the kind of a method that every man should follow to make a success.

As a general rule, I have always considered it advisable to use at least $3,000 capital for every 100 shares of stock traded in and to limit stop loss orders to not more than 3 points on every 100 shares. In this way you will be able to make 10 trades on your capital and the market would have to beat you 10 consecutive times to wipe out your capital, which it will not do. Whatever amount of capital you use to trade with, follow this rule: Divide you capital into 10 equal parts and never risk more than 10% of your capital on any one trade. Should you lose for 3 consecutive time, then reduce your trading unit and only risk 10% of your remaining capital. If you follow this rule, your success is sure.

On stocks selling around $15 to $30 per share, you can start with a capital of $1,500. The first trade should be made at a time when you can place a stop loss order not more than 2 points away and you should try to start when your risk will only be 1 point. In other words, with a capital of $1,500 you must figure that you would be able to make at least 7 to 10 trades and the market would have to beat you 7 to 10 consecutive times to wipe out your trading capital. With this Method it is impossible for that to happen, provided you follow the rules and trade on definite indications.

This Method will make the most money trading in high-priced stocks, and for trading in stocks selling above $100 per share, you should use a capital of $4,000 and adhere strictly to all the rules.

If you want to start trading in small units of stock, use a capital of $300 for each 10 shares and never risk more than 3 points on the initial trade. Try to make the first trade, if possible, where your stop loss order will not be more than 1 or 2 points. Never risk more than one-tenth of your capital on any one trade.

KIND OF CHARTS TO USE

A busy man or specialist should keep a weekly high and low chart on the Dow-Jones 30 Industrial averages and the 15 Public Utility averages and should keep weekly high and low charts on 5 to 10 of the leading active stocks in the different groups. He could also keep up monthly high and low charts on a few stocks selling below 20 or below 10 and watch these different low-priced stocks when they indicate a change in trend. By crossing old tops and showing activity, it would indicate a good time to buy them.

MAJOR AND MINOR TRENDS

You will always make the most money by following the main trend of the market, altho to say that you must never trade against the trend means that you will miss a lot of intermediate moves which will make big profits, but your rule must be: When you are trading against the trend, wait until one of your rules gives you a definite indication of a buying or selling point at bottom or top, where you can place close stop loss orders.

There are always two trends -- a major trend and a minor trend. The minor trend is a reversal of the main trend, which lasts for a short period of time. When the main trend is down, it is much safer to sell stocks short on rallies at a point where the rules indicate that they are top than it is to buy on a reaction. In a Bull Campaign or advancing market, it is much safer to wait for minor reactions and buy when the rules indicate that it is time to buy than it is to sell short on rallies. You will always make the most money by waiting for a definite indication of the trend before buying and selling.

TREND LINE INDICATIONS

GREEN TREND LINE
This Green Trend Line indicates uptrend, either the minor or the main trend.

We use the GREEN TREND LINE for an advancing market or when a stock or the averages are making higher tops and higher bottoms each week. The first week that a higher bottom and a higher top is made than a previous week, the Green Trend Line is moved up to the top of that week. Then, as long as the stock or the averages make higher bottoms and higher tops, the Green Trend Line continues to be moved up to the high point of each week.

RED TREND LINE
The first week that a stock or the averages make a lower bottom than the previous week, the Trend Line changes to red and is moved down to the low of that week and continues to be moved down as long as the stock or the averages make lower bottoms. This Red Trend Line means that the minor or the main trend has turned down and that you should follow the RED TREND LINE until it reverses. The first week a higher bottom and a higher top are made, the Trend Line changes again to green.

BUY WHEN THE RED TREND LINE CHANGES TO GREEN
SELL WHEN THE GREEN TREND LINE CHANGES TO RED

For study purposes we have used the Dow-Jones 20 Railroad Stock averages ... weekly high and low...from 1896 to July, 1914, because the rails were leader during that period and moved faster, making a wider range, than the Industrial Stocks, therefore, were better trend indicators and more profitable to trade in.

You should follow the Trend Lines and apply the rules given here for buying points:

THREE BUYING POINTS

1 - BUY AT OLD BOTTOMS OR OLD TOPS

When a stock declines to an old bottom or to an old top, it is always a buying point with a stop loss order. In fact, you should never buy unless you can figure where to place a stop loss order 1 to 3 points away and in high-priced stocks never more than 5 points away.

Remember, it is safe to buy when a stock reacts to old tops the first, second, or third time, but when it declines to the same level the fourth time, it is dangerous to buy as it nearly always goes lower.

Buy when a stock declines 1 to 3 points under old tops or old bottoms. However, a stock is always strongest if it holds just around the old tops or old bottoms and does not break 1 to 3 points under. Holding slightly higher than these old levels is a still stronger indication.

Stocks selling above $100 a share -- After they cross old tops they can react 5 points under the old tops but not more, and if the market is really strong, they should not go as much as 5 points under, except in very rare cases when the market is in a wide trading range and very active.

2 - SAFER BUYING POINT

Buy when a stock crosses former tops or crosses a series of tops of previous weeks, showing that the minor or the main trend has turned up as indicated by the Green Trend Line.

3 - SAFEST BUYING POINT

Buy on a secondary reaction after a stock has crossed previous weekly tops and the advance exceeds the greatest rally on the way down from the top.

Buy when the first rally from the extreme bottom exceeds in time the greatest rally in the preceding Bear Campaign.

Buy when the period of time exceeds the last rally before extreme lows were reached. If the last rally was 3 or 4 weeks, when the advance from the bottom is more than 3 or 4 weeks, consider the trend has turned up and stocks are a safer buy on a secondary reaction. Examples later will prove this rule.

THREE SELLING POINTS

When we refer to selling points we mean to either sell out long stocks or sell short.

1 - SELL AT OLD TOPS OR OLD BOTTOMS

An important point to sell out longs and go short is at old tops or when a stock rallies to old bottoms first, second or third time. As a rule it is risky to sell the fourth time that a stock advances to the same level because it nearly always goes higher. When you sell short, place stop loss orders 1,2 or 3 points above old tops or old bottoms.

When prices are at high levels above $100, the averages can go 5 points above old tops or 5 points above old bottoms without changing the main trend. But this seldom happens, as a study of previous tops and bottoms will prove. As a rule, when the market is weak and the main trend down, the rally stops right under old bottoms and should not go more than 2 points above them. If it goes 3 points above, it is an indication that the market is strong and likely to go higher. If it declines under these old levels, this indicates that the market is very weak.

2 - SAFER SELLING POINT

Sell when a stock breaks the low of a previous week or a series of bottoms of previous weeks as indicated by the Trend Line.

3 - SAFEST SELLING POINT

Sell on a secondary rally after the stock has broken the previous bottoms of several weeks or has broken the bottom of the last reaction, turning trend down. This secondary rally nearly always comes after the first sharp decline in the first section of a Bear Campaign.

Sell after the first decline exceeds the greatest reaction in the preceding Bull Campaign or the last reaction before final top.

Sell when the period of time of the first decline exceeds the last reaction before final top of the Bull Campaign. Example: If a stock has advanced for several months or for one year or more and the greatest reaction has been four weeks ... which is an average reaction in a Bull Market ... then after top is reached and the first decline runs more than 4 weeks, it is an indication of a change in the minor trend or main trend. The stock will be a safer short sale on any rally because you will be trading with the trend after it has been definitely defined.

FORMATIONS AT BOTTOMS AND TOPS

Buy studying stock formations of the past you will be able to determine what is going to happen when similar formations occur in the future, just as you know that there is going to be a rainstorm when you see a heavy dark cloud form.

After accumulation or distribution at bottom or top has been completed, there is a BREAKAWAY POINT. When you buy or sell stocks at this point, you make money very quickly.

Study the volume of sales, the space and price movements and the last and most important time period. Similar action of the market occurs around the same month years apart. When we come to the Lesson on "Volume" it will give you more rules and information.

Study the different types of bottom formations -- Sharp, double, triple, flat and ascending bottoms.

SINGLE "V" OR SHARP BOTTOM

This formation can be a sharp, fast decline followed by a fast advance, or even a sow decline followed by a quick rally from the bottom with no secondary reactions until it advances to higher levels.

Example: July 26, 1910, the Dow-Jones 20 Railroad averages had a sharp decline to 105¾; then rallied sharply to 114¾ ... a 9-point advance with no reactions ... and did not later go back to make a double bottom.

"U" BOTTOM OR FLAT BOTTOM

This "U" bottom is a formation where a stock remains for 3 to 10 weeks or more in a narrow trading range, making about the same top and bottom levels several times; then when it crosses the intermediate tops, it has formed a "U" or flat bottom and is a t the breakaway point ... a safe place to buy.

Example: March 12 to April 30, 1898 ... The 20 Railroad averages held between 56 and 60, hitting the bottom level 4 times. This was a flat bottom and when the crossed 60, the averages indicated higher prices.

"W" BOTTOM OR DOUBLE BOTTOM

When a stock declines and makes bottom; then rallies for 2 or 3 weeks or more; declines and makes a bottom around the same level the second time; then advances and crosses the previous top, it has formed a "W" or double bottom. It is safe to buy when it crosses the top or middle of the "W" ... which is a BREAKAWAY POINT.

Example: December 23, 1899, low 72½. June 23, 1900, low 73.

"W V" BOTTOM OR TRIPLE BOTTOM

This is a third higher bottom after a double bottom or three bottoms near the same level. It is safe to buy when a stock has formed a "W" and a "V" on the side and crosses the second top of the "W".

Example: Dec. 23, 1899 - 1st bottom at 72½
Jun. 23, 1900 - 2nd bottom at 73
Sep. 29, 1900 - 3rd bottom at 73¼
This formed a "W V" bottom after the averages advanced above 78 ... the BREAKAWAY POINT ... a runaway advance followed, the market advancing 44 points in 28 weeks.

"W W" BOTTOM OR 4-BOTTOM FORMATION

This formation shows first, second, third and fourth bottoms. The safest point to buy is at the BREAKAWAY POINT or when a stock crossed the middle point of the second "W".

Example: Aug. 8, 1903, low 90¾ .... rallied to 98¾ on Aug. 22, 1903
Oct. 17, 1903, low 89-3/8 .... rallied to 99-5/8 on Jan. 23, 1904
Mar. 19, 1904, low 91¼ .... rallied to 97¾ on Apr. 16, 1904
May 21, 1904, low 93½

When the averages crossed 97¾, the middle of the second "W" they went on thru the top of 99-5/8, top the first "W". This was the BREAKAWAY POINT and the market advanced 27 points with out reacting to 99 again.

TOP FORMATIONS
You should study various types of tops -- Sharp, flat ,double, triple and descending tops.

SINGLE "A" OR SHARP TOPS
After a prolonged advance or at the end of a Bull Campaign, the averages or individual stocks often make a single sharp top ... advancing 17 to 26 weeks or more with only small reactions lasting sometimes 10 days or two weeks .... then follows a sharp, quick decline. It is safe to sell on a subsequent or secondary rally and safer to sell when it breaks the last leg of the "A" or when it breaks the bottom of the first sharp decline.

Example: The 20 Railroad averages advanced from 117½ to 129¼ in 16 weeks from May 24 to September 13, 1902; then had a sharp decline to October 18, and only rallied to 123¼ . When they broke 118¼, it was an indication of weakness and the Bear Market continued.

" ⊓ " TOP OR FLAT TOP
When the market makes several tops near the same level and the bottoms on reactions are near the same level ... holding in a narrow trading range ... it forms a " ⊓ " top or flat top. It is safe to sell short when it breaks under the series of weekly bottoms.

Example: May 13, to July 29, 1911, the Railroad averages held in a range of 2½ points for 8 weeks, forming a flat top, and the market was a safe short sale when the averages broke 121, under the low point of this narrow range.

"M" TOP OR DOUBLE TOP
When a stock or the averages reach top after a substantial advance; then react 3 to 7 weeks or more and rally again to around the same top, an "M" or double top is formed. Then, when it declines and breaks under the low of the last reaction or under the middle of the "M", it is safe to sell short.

Example: 1906, September 15 high 137¾; November 17 low 131½;
December 15 high 137½; then followed a quick decline, Breaking the low of 131 ½, and a Bear Market followed.

"M A" TOP OR TRIPLE TOP
This formation occurs when a stock or the averages make 3 tops near the same level or the 2nd and 3rd tops are slightly lower. When these formations are made at tops after a long advance, they are signals for a major decline. The more time between tops, the stronger the indications for a big decline. It is safe to sell when a stock breaks the last bottom or breaks the end of the "M" and safer when it breaks the bottom of the "A" ... which is the BREAKAWAY POINT.

Example: 1st top – Jan. 19, 1906, high 138-3/8 ... end of Bull Market;
          May   5, 1906, sharp decline to 120¼;
          2nd top – Sep. 22, 1906, high 137¾, slightly lower than Jan. 1906 top.
          Nov. 17, 1906, low of 6-point reaction;
          3rd top – Dec. 15, 1906, high 137½, near same level ... a signal for a big decline. Panic followed in 1907 and the averages declined 57 points in 11 months.

"M M" OR 4-TOP FORMATION

This formation occurs when a stock or the averages make 4 tops at the same level or slightly lower. It is safest to sell short when a stock breaks the second point of the second "M" or the low of the last reaction.

Example: 1st top – July 22, 1911, high 124;
          2nd top – Aug. 17, 1912, high 124;
          Sep. 14, 1912, reacted to 120½;
          3rd top – Oct. 5, 1912, high 124-3/8;
          Nov. 2, 1912, reacted to 119-5/8;
          4th top – Nov. 9, 1912, last rally to 122¾;
          When the averages broke under 119-5/8, low of the last reaction, this was the BREAKAWAY POINT and a big decline followed.

SECTIONS OF MARKET CAMPAIGNS

A Bull or Bear Campaign in stocks or the averages runs out in 3 to 4 sections --

BULL MARKET

1st Section – Advance after final bottom; then a secondary reaction.

2nd Section – Advance to higher levels, above the highs of previous weeks and of the first advance; then a reaction.

3rd Section – Advance to new high for the move. In many cases this means the end of the campaign, but you must watch for a definite indication before deciding that the 3rd run up means a change in the main trend.

4th Section – Often four sections are run out and this 4th move or run-up is the most important to watch for the end of a Bull Campaign and a change in trend.

Minor Bull Campaigns of short duration, running one year or less, often run out in two sections, especially if the first section is from a sharp bottom. Therefore, always watch the action of the market after the second advance to see if it is forming a top and gives indications of a change in trend.

BEAR MARKET

A Bear Campaign runs opposite to a Bull Campaign --

1st Section – There is a sharp, severe decline, which changes the main trend; then a secondary rally on which stocks are safer short sales. That marks the end of the 1st Section.

2nd Section – Then there is a second decline to lower prices, followed by a moderate rally.

3rd Section – A third decline or move to still lower prices, which may be the end of the campaign.

4th Section – There is often a 4th move, when you must watch closely for the bottom. In determining whether it is final bottom, you use all of the other rules ... watching old tops and old bottoms for definite indication that the main trend is ready to change.

Minor Bear Campaigns of short duration, running one year or less, often run out in two sections, especially if the 1st Section is from a sharp top. Therefore, always watch the action of the market after the 2nd decline to see if it is forming a bottom and gives indication of a change in trend.

In extreme cases, like 1929 and the Bear Campaign which followed from 1929 to 1932, there are as many a 7 sections up or down, but his is abnormal and unusual and only occurs many years apart.

Go back over all of the campaigns we have worked out and you will see how these sections or moves run out.

HOW TO DETERMINE CHANGE IN THE MAIN TREND

SPACE MOVEMENT

RULE FOR DETERMINING CHANGE IN TREND ACCORDING TO SPACE MOVEMENTS: When a decline in points exceeds the greatest decline of a previous reaction by one or more points, it is an indication of a change in trend.

When the market has run out 3 or more sections in a Bull Campaign, go back over the record and find out what the greatest reaction has been in any section, whether 10, 15, 20, 30 points or more. Suppose the averages have been advancing for a long time and the greatest reaction in the market has been 10 points and the market has reached the 3rd or 4th Section of the campaign. Then the first time the averages or the price of a stock breaks back more than 10 points, or more than the greatest reaction, it is an indication that the main trend has changed or will change soon. This does not mean that a rally cannot take place after this definite signal of reversal has been given, as usually after the first signal of a change in trend is given, there is a secondary rally in a Bull Market and time has to be allowed at top for distribution to take place. Therefore, just because you get a definite indication that the main trend has changed, do not jump to the conclusion that you can sell short right at that time and that there will be no rally. Always sell on rallies, if possible, although there are times that you can sell at new low levels or when bottoms are broken. Judge this by applying all of your rules.

TIME PERIOD -- Another way to tell when the main trend is changing.

RULE -- When a campaign has only 3 or 4 sections and the TIME period on a reaction exceeds the greatest time of a previous reaction, consider that the main trend has changed.

Go back over the record and find the greatest time period from any minor top or the duration of a reaction in previous sections of the Bull Market. If you find that the greatest reaction has been about 4 weeks, then the first time the market decline consecutively for 5 weeks or more, it is an indication that the main trend has changed and that stocks will be short sales on a secondary rally.

Apply the same rules in a Bear Market. When the SPACE movement or number of points that a stock or the averages have rallied during a Bear Campaign is exceeded, the trend is changing. When the TIME period of the greatest reverse movement is exceeded, then the main trend is changing and a Bull Campaign is starting.

A reversal in SPACE movement after the second run or 2nd Section in a Bull or a Bear Market, would not mean as important a change in trend as if it came after the 3rd or 4th Section had run out, either up or down.

Examples of all these rules will be referred to in the working out of each Bull and Bear Campaign from 1892 to 1939 so that you will know how to apply the rules in future market movements.

MANY WEEKS IN NARROW RANGE

When a stock or the averages hold for 2 to 6 weeks or 10 to 13 weeks in a narrow range, then cross tops or break bottoms of previous weeks, the trend has changed and you should go with it. The longer the period of time in a narrow range, the greater the advance or the decline when they break out of the range, either up or down.

Example: 1897, January 16 to March 20, the Railroad averages held in 2-point range; then broke the low of 52 and went lower. 1897, April 10 to May 22, held in a 2-point range for 6 weeks; then crossed the top at 51 and the Bull Market started.

ACCUMULATION OR DISTRIBUTION ON SIDE

After a market has advanced to the 3rd or 4th Section, then has a sharp decline and rallies, it will often remain for a long period of time in a range while DISTRIBUTION is taking place ON THE SIDE. The top of the range may be several points below the extreme high. In FORM READING it is very important to note the range from high to low in this zone of distribution. The stock is a short sale at the top of this range of distribution on the side and a safer sale when it breaks the low point of this range ... which is the BREAKAWAY POINT.

At the end of a Bear Campaign, after the first sharp advance there is a secondary reaction; then a long period of ACCUMULATION ON THE SIDE, with several moves up to the top of the range and back to the bottom of the range of accumulation. The market is a buy at the bottom of this range and a safer buy when the tops of this range are crossed as that is the BREAKAWAY POINT and a signal for a fast advance.

Examples of these sideways accumulation and sideways distribution will be shown in the different campaigns worked out.

LAST STAGE OF BULL OR BEAR MARKET

In fast, advancing markets in the last stage of the campaign reactions get smaller as stocks work to higher levels, until the final section or run has ended. Then comes a sharp, quick reaction and a reversal in trend.

In the last stage of a Bear Market, after all old bottoms and resistance levels have been broken, rallies get less or smaller as prices work lower. Therefore, people who buy have no chance to sell on rallies until the final bottom has been reached and the first rally takes place.

This is why it never pays to buck the trend in the last stage of a Bull Market or the last stage of a Bear Market.

RANGE OF BOTTOMS

Never consider that a major or a minor trend has reversed or changed until the bottoms of previous weeks have been broken or the tops of previous weeks have been crossed. The number of points that a stock or the averages should decline below a bottom to indicate a change in trend to lower levels, varies according to the price at which the averages or the stock is selling. We consider a range within 1 to 3 points a double or triple bottom or a double or triple top. In a strong market a stock will break only 1 point under a bottom and then rally and, in extreme cases, not more than 2 points. As a rule when bottoms are broken by 3 full points it is an indication for lower prices before any rally of importance.

RANGE OF TOPS

The same at the top. The range for double tops is about 3 points. These tops can be in a range of 1 to 3 points and still be considered double and triple tops. Advancing 1 to 2 points above an old top does not always indicate that the main trend has changed and that stocks are going up immediately but advancing 3 points above old tops is nearly always a definite indication that higher prices will follow before much reaction. At the end of Bull and Bear Markets some false moves are often made and quick reversals follow.

HOW FAR SHOULD STOCKS DECLINE BELOW OLD TOPS AFTER THEY ADVANCE ABOVE THEM?

In order to still show uptrend, after a stock or the averages have advanced above old tops, then reacted, when in strong position they will stop right around the old tops or sometimes go 1 to 2 points below the old tops but seldom more that 3. Regardless of how high a stock is selling, a decline of more than 5 points below the old top would indicate that the trend had reversed and at that immediate time the stock would not go higher but would go lower for awhile. It can decline 5 points under old tops and still be in a Bull Market, all depending on what section the market is in. A signal in the last section is most important.

HOW FAR STOCKS CAN GO ABOVE OLD BOTTOMS IN BEAR MARKETS

Reverse this rule in a Bear Market. When stocks advance to old bottoms, they are short sales because bottoms become tops and tops become bottoms. They should not go more that 1 to 2 points above the old bottoms and on an average should not go more than 3 points. Therefore, even when stocks are at high levels if they advance more than 5 points above an old bottom, it is an indication that they going higher and are not going to work lower immediately with the main trend.

SEVERAL FAST MOVES UP OR DOWN OVER A RANGE OF 5 TO 7 OR 10 TO 12 POINTS

Whether the market is very active or in a slow trading range, all indications are more accurate and more valuable when the market is quite active.

After a stock or the averages have been advancing for some time and have run out 3 or 4 sections, if there are several moves of 10 to 12 points up or down in a range, making several bottoms and several tops in this range, it indicates either accumulation or distribution. When the bottoms in a range of this kind are broken it is an indication of lower prices and when the tops in a range of this kind are crossed, it is an indication of higher prices. Note the range on sideways accumulation and the range on sideways distribution.

An advancing market may have several reactions of 10 to 12 points; then have a reaction of 20 to 24 points; then after an advance if it declines from any top more than 20 points, it will usually run 30 to 40 points. Go over the stocks or averages when they have been selling at very high levels and prove to yourself the value of this rule.

WHEN THE MARKET IS IN STRONGEST OR IN WEAKEST POSITION

A stock or the averages are in the strongest position after there has been a prolonged decline and the market starts making higher bottoms, especially after a sharp, fast decline, when rallies have been small. After the 2nd or 3rd higher bottom has been made and then the top of a previous rally has been crossed, the stock is in the strongest position. Rising bottoms always indicate strength and an advance usually starts from the 3rd or 4th higher bottom, that is, the big advance which runs for a long time with only small reactions. You make money quickest when you get in on a move of this kind.

Reverse this rule in a Bear Market. A market is weakest when it is making lower tops. The 3rd or 4th lower top is the safest place to sell. After the 3rd or 4th lower top, when it breaks the last low or previous bottom, it is in the weakest position and indicates that the main trend is down and declines will be faster.

HOW TO DETERMINE CHANGE IN MINOR TREND

MINOR ADVANCE

When a market is advancing and makes a top around the same level for 2 or more weeks, especially when the range is very narrow near top levels, then prices break under the bottom of 2 weeks or more, the minor trend has turned down and you would follow it until there is another definite indication of a change in trend.

MINOR REACTION

After the averages or a stock has been declining for several weeks or several months and prices make bottom 2 weeks or more around the same level and hold in a narrow trading range for 2 weeks or more and then cross the tops of 2 or 3 weeks on the upside, the minor trend has changed, at least temporarily, and you should go with it.

DULL MARKET

A dull market, in a narrow trading range at any point, indicates that it is getting ready for some kind of a change and you should follow it whichever it breaks out, up or down, after these narrow, dull periods.

DURATION OF MINOR MOVES

RULE FOR TIME OF MINOR REACTION IN BULL MARKETS --

In an advancing market or Bull Campaign when indications are given for a minor reaction, prices will react 3 to 4 weeks but as a rule in the 4th week they will rally and close higher. In some cases there will only be a sharp, quick reaction of 2 weeks and then the main trend will be resumed, but after a decline of 3 to 4 weeks should the market have a minor rally; then break back under the bottom of the 3rd or 4th week, it will be an indication of a greater change in the trend and probably a change in the main trend.

In extreme cases, after a secondary rally in a bull Market, prices will decline as much as 6 to 7 weeks, seldom more, before the main trend is resumed.

RULE FOR TIME OF MINOR RALLIES IN BEAR MARKETS --

These rules are reversed in a Bear Market. Rallies in a Bear Market last 2 to 4 weeks. Should a rally hold into the 5th week, it is likely to run into the 6th or 7th week; then you can watch for an important change in trend.

After a rally of 3 to 4 weeks and a secondary reaction in a Bear Market, should the market advance and cross the level made at the end of the 3 or 4 weeks' rally, then the trend is changing, at least temporarily, and higher prices ... even in a Bear Market ... are indicated.

HOW TO DETERMINE FIRST CHANGE IN TREND BY OPENING AND CLOSING PRICES

<u>The Weekly high and low Chart with the opening and closing prices on it is one of the best charts to use for determining trend of stocks or the averages. That is why we have used the Weekly Chart on the Dow-Jones 30 Industrial averages and given all the indications according to it.</u>

The closing price at the end of the week or at the end of any day is most important because regardless of how high or how low stocks have been during the week or during the day, the closing price show exactly what they have lost or gained at the end of the period.

After a stock or the averages have been advancing for a considerable period of time and have reached an old top or a section of the campaign which indicates that a change in trend could take place, it is very important in very active markets to watch the opening price on Monday morning. Should the averages or a stock not sell more than one point above the opening price on Monday morning and then decline and close at or near the low levels of the week on Saturday, it is the first indication of a change in trend on the Weekly Chart. But don't fail to use your other rules and wait for the proper declines in TIME or SPACE or until previous weekly bottoms have been broken deciding that there is a definite change in trend.

Reverse this rule at the bottom of a decline or after there has been a sharp, fast decline in a very active market. Watch the opening price on Monday morning. Should a stock decline rapidly to around the middle or latter part of the week, then after making bottom, reverse and rally quickly and on Saturday close at or near the opening on Monday morning or above this opening, it is an especially strong indication that the trend is reversing and that prices are going higher temporarily. But use all of your other rules ... the crossing of previous weekly tops ... the reversal of the SPACE movement in points ... also reversal in TIME ... before deciding that a definite change in trend is indicated.

It is also very important at the end of the week if prices close under old bottoms or under bottoms of previous weeks or close above old tops or above tops of previous weeks as it is an indication of weakness or strength.

WHEN STOCKS ADVANCE INTO NEW HIGH GROUND OR DECLINE INTO NEW LOW GROUND

When stocks advance to higher levels than they have been before in their previous history or decline to lower levels than they have ever sold before in their history, they are in new high or new low ground and you must have a rule to follow when stocks reach new high or new low record prices.

First, apply all of your other rules and do not buy or sell until there is a definite indication of a change in the main trend.

When a stock or the averages advance to a new high level that they have never sold at before in their history, it is an indication of an advance of 7,10,15,20 to 24 points or more, especially if it is in the 1st or 2nd section of the Bull Campaign. Should new highs be made in the 3rd or 4th Section, then the advance into new high ground may not be very many points before final high is reached and the trend changes.

You should watch the action of the market when it has advanced 7 points into new high territory, 10 points, again around 15 points, and on an extreme advance watch around 20 to 24 points, where there is likely to be resistance and top made. These are average moves and it depends upon the activity and price of a stock whether it will stop on any of these points. By following the trend indications and rules you will be able to determine when the first move into new high territory has run out and the trend has changed.

Reverse the above rules in a Bear Campaign.

When the averages or stocks selling between 50 and 125 advance in to new high ground, these average movements of 7, 10, 15, 20 and 24 points, work out quite accurately. After stocks advance above 125. Above 200, the movements increases and the range is much wider. The same when stocks or the averages get above 300 ... they have a still greater range and faster moves, all of which depends upon how long the campaign has been running and how many moves or sections the campaign has run out and how high the stocks are from the last bottom or how far down from the last top.

WHEN TO USE DAILY HIGH AND LOW CHART

When markets are very active and fluctuating over a wide range, especially in the last stages of a Bull Market or the last fast decline in a Bear Market, you should keep up a Daily high and low Chart on the averages or individual stocks and put on the Trend Lines, applying the same rules as used for the Weekly Chart, because the Daily Chart will give you the first change in the minor trend, which may later be confirmed by the Weekly Chart into a change of the main trend. Full instructions will follow under "Resistance Levels."

Again I remind you ... Don't try to get ahead of the market. Don't guess if it is making a change in trend and be wrong. Wait until it shows a definite change in trend. You will be right when you form your judgment after definite indication is give according these rules.

July 6, 1939 [unsigned]

DOW-JONES 20 RAILROAD AVERAGES
BOTTOM AND TOP FORMATIONS
1896 - 1914

1896	Aug.	8	Sharp bottom or single "V" - Low 42.
1897	Jan.	16	to 23 and March 20 - Flat double top "M".
	Apr.		Sharp bottom and 4 weeks narrow on side in 1-point range.
	Sep.		Sharp or "A" top at 1/2 point from 42 to 92.
	Nov		Sharp or "V" bottom.
1898	Feb.		Flat top ... 2 weeks in 1-point range.
	Mar.	5	to April 23 - Flat bottom ... triple bottom near same level.
	Aug.		Sharp top.
	Oct.	1	to Nov. 5 - Flat bottom ... 6 weeks in 1-point range.
1899	Apr.	1	to 29 - Flat top ... 5 weeks in 2-point range.
	Jun.	3	Sharp bottom.
	Jul.	29	to Sep. 9 - Flat top ... 7 weeks in 2-point range; 1st lower top after April.
	Nov.		Sharp top ... 4 weeks on side in 2-point range ... 2nd lower top.
	Dec.	23	Sharp bottom.
1900	Apr.	7	Sharp top ... 4th lower top.
	Jun.	23	Sharp bottom ... 1st higher bottom and double bottom against Dec 1899 low.
	Aug.	18	Flat intermediate or middle top.
	Sep.	29	Sharp bottom ... a triple bottom and 3rd higher bottom ... strong and good buying point.
1901	May	4	Sharp top.
	May	9	Sharp bottom ... panic.
	Jun.	15	Sharp top ... 2 narrow weeks on side ... a double top.
	Aug.	10	Sep. 14 and Oct. 12 - Sharp bottoms ... triple bottoms with 2nd and 3rd bottoms higher than the 1st ... strong.
1902	Sep.	13	A sharp top and sharp decline followed.
	Nov.	15	and Dec. 13 - Two sharp bottoms ... double bottoms.
1903	Jan.	10	Sharp top with 5 weeks on side in 2-point range.
	Jul.	11	Sharp top ... 2 weeks rally followed.
	Aug.	22	Sharp top ... 3 weeks on side in 2-point range.
	Sep.	19	to Nov. 14 - Triple bottoms ... 3rd bottom higher.
1904	Jan.	23	Sharp or "A" top.
	Feb.	27	to Mar. 19 - Flat bottom ... 3 weeks in 2-point range.
	Dec.	3	Sharp top ... 3 weeks' reaction.
1905	Mar.	18	and Apr. 15 - A double flat top.
	May	27	Sharp bottom
	Sep.		to Nov. - Flat top but only declined 4 points.
1906	Jan.	19	Final sharp top ... sharp decline followed.
	May	5	Sharp bottom ... sharp rally followed.
	June.	16	Sharp top ... sharp decline followed.
	Jul.	7	Sharp bottom ... sharp rally followed.
	Sep.	18	to Oct. 13 - Flat top ... 7 weeks in 2-point range, just under January top.
	Nov.	17	to Dec. 22 - Flat top ... 4 weeks in 3-point range. A panicky decline followed this 3rd lower top.

BOTTOM AND TOP FORMATIONS 1896 - 1914 (Continued)

1907	Mar.	14	to 25 - A sharp bottom.
	Apr.	6	to May 11 - Sharp double tops.
	Jun.	8	Flat bottom ... 4 weeks in 2-point range.
	Jul.	6	to 27 - Flat top ... 4 weeks in 3-point range.
	Nov.	23	Sharp bottom and sharp rally followed.
1908	Jan.	18	Sharp bottom and sharp decline followed.
	Feb.	15	to Mar. 7 - Flat narrow bottom ... 3 weeks in 1½ point range.
	May	23	Sharp top.
	Jun.	27	Sharp bottom.
	Sep.	12	Sharp top.
	Sep.	22	Sharp bottom ... quick, sharp rally followed.
1909	Jan.	2	Sharp top.
	Feb.	27	Sharp bottom.
	Aug.	14	Sharp top followed by sharp reaction.
	Sep.	11	Sharp bottom.
	Sep.	18	to Oct. 9 - Flat top ... 4 weeks in 2-point range ... 1st lower top.
1910	Jul.	26	Sharp bottom ... end of Bear Market ... quick rally followed.
	Oct.	22	Sharp top.
	Dec.	10	Sharp bottom.
1911	Feb.	4	to 18 - Flat top ... 3 weeks in 2-point range.
	Mar.	11	and Apr. 22 - Double bottoms.
	Jun.	10	to Jul. 29 - Flat narrow top ... 7 weeks in 2-point range.
	Sep.	30	Flat bottom ... 4 weeks in 2-point range.
1912	Aug.	17	to Oct. 3 - Double tops ... narrow range ... 3rd top from July 22, 1911. A prolonged decline followed.
1913	Jun.	14	Sharp bottom.
	Nov.	15	to Dec. 20 - Flat double bottoms.
	Sep.	13	to 27 and
1914	Jan.	24	to Feb. 7 - Double flat tops ... narrow range.
	Apr.	25	A sharp bottom ... slow rally followed.
	May	23	to July 11 - Flat top ... 9 weeks in 2-point range ... a panicky decline followed.

BREAKAWAY POINTS IN BULL & BEAR MARKETS
DOW-JONES 30 INDUSTRIAL AVERAGES
STUDY THESE POINTS ON THE CHART

YEAR							WEEKS	POINTS
1897	June	5	to	Sept.	4		12	16
1897	Oct.	2		Mar.	26	1898	10	14
1898	May	7		Aug.	28		12	15
1898	Dec.	3		Apr.	29	1899	9	20
1899	Dec.	9		Dec.	23		3	15
1900	Oct.	20		Apr.	20	1901	10	18
1901	July	13		Oct.	14		15	14
1903	Mar.	28		Oct.	17		29	25
1904	July	9		Apr.	15	1905	40	33
1905	June	24		Jan.	19	1906	30	28
1906	Feb.	17		May	5		8	14
1906	July	28		Oct.	13		11	8
1907	Feb.	9		Mar.	25		7	16
1907	July	6		Nov.	15		19	25
1908	Feb.	29		Aug.	14		23	25
1909	Apr.	3		Oct.	2		25	16
1910	Jan.	3		Feb.	12		6	13
1910	Apr.	30		July	26		13	16
1910	Oct.	1		Oct.	29		4	6
1911	Aug.	5		Sept.	30		8	12
1911	Nov.	11		Sept.	7	1912	46	15
1912	Dec.	7		Mar.	22	1913	15	12
1913	Apr.	26		June	14		7	9
1913	July	19		Sept.	13		8	8
1913	Oct.	4		Dec.	20		11	6
1913	Dec.	27		Mar.	24	1914	12	5
1914	July	25		Dec.	24		21	27
1915	Mar.	20		May	1		6	13
1915	July	24		Dec.	30		32	28
1916	Jan.	22		Apr.	29		14	10
1916	Aug.	12		Nov.	14		14	13
1916	Dec.	9		Feb.	3	1917	8	12
1917	June	16		Dec.	22		26	30
1918	Jan.	5		Oct.	19		41	14
1919	Feb.	22		July	19		21	30
1919	Aug.	2		Aug.	23		3	10
1919	Aug.	30		Nov.	8		10	18
1919	Nov.	15		Feb.	28	1920	17	23
1920	Mar.	6		Apr.	10		5	10
1920	Apr.	24		May	29		5	14
1920	July	24		Dec.	25		23	23
1921	May	21		Aug.	24		15	13
1921	Sept.	10		Oct.	28	1922	59	13
1923	Mar.	24		Aug.	4		19	16
1923	Nov.	10		Feb.	9	1924	13	10
1924	Mar.	23		May	24		10	9
1924	June	14		Aug	23		18	14
1924	Nov.	8		Mar.	14	1925	18	16

THE W.D. GANN MASTER STOCK MARKET COURSE

#2

BREAKAWAY POINTS IN BULL & BEAR MARKETS
DOW-JONES 30 INDUSTRIAL AVERAGES (Cont.)
STUDY THESE POINTS ON THE CHART

YEAR							WEEKS	POINTS
1925	May	9		Feb.	27	1926	41	36
1926	Mar.	1		Apr.	17		9	19
1926	June	5		Aug.	21		11	18
1926	Sept.	12		Oct.	16		5	12
1927	Apr.	16		Sept.	24		22	31
1927	Sept.	30		Oct.	15		2	14
1928	Mar.	17		May	12		8	14
1928	Aug.	18		Oct.	8		15	68
1928	Oct.	8	to	Oct.	22		2	24
1928	Oct.	22	to	Feb.	9	1929	16	40
1929	Mar.	22		Mar.	30		1	4
1929	Apr.	30		May	11		2	8
1929	May	18		June	8		3	9
1929	July	6		Sept.	3		8	38
1929	Sept.	7		Nov.	13		9	160
1929	Nov.	16		Dec.	14		4	46
1930	Jan.	25		Apr.	17		13	38
1930	Apr.	19		July	5		11	64
1930	Sept.	20		Nov.	15		8	62
1930	Nov.	29		Dec.	20		3	27
1931	Feb.	7		Feb.	24		3	20
1931	Mar.	7		Jun.	2		12	64
1931	Jun.	9		Jul.	27		2	27
1931	Jul.	2		Aug.	8		5	20
1931	Aug.	31		Oct.	3		5	45
1931	Oct.	10		Nov.	9		4	24
1931	Nov.	16		Jan.	9	1932	8	42
1932	Mar.	19		July	8		17	38
1932	July	16		Sept.	8		8	31
1932	Sept.	7		Oct.	30		7	16
1933	Feb.	4		Feb.	27		3	8
1933	Apr.	8		Jul.	17		17	44
1933	July	18		Jul.	21		1	18
1933	Sep.	23		Oct.	21		4	15
1933	Nov.	18		Feb.	5	1934	12	15
1934	May	5		Jul.	26		12	17
1934	Nov.	24		Feb.	23	1935	14	8
1935	Apr.	13		Apr.	6	1936	52	54
1936	Apr.	10		Apr.	30		4	15
1936	May	30		Nov.	21		25	32
1936	Nov.	28		Dec.	26		4	4
1937	Jan.	16		Mar.	8		8	8
1937	Mar.	27		Jun.	17		14	22
1937	Jul.	3		Aug.	14		6	20
1937	Aug.	21		Oct.	19		9	65
1937	Oct.	19		Oct.	29		1	18
1937	Nov.	23		Jan.	15	1938	7	15

BREAKAWAY POINTS IN BULL & BEAR MARKETS
DOW-JONES 30 INDUSTRIAL AVERAGES (Cont.)
STUDY THESE POINTS ON THE CHART

YEAR						WEEKS	POINTS
1938	Mar.	10	Mar.	31		3	28
1938	Jun.	25	Jul.	25		4	24
1938	Sept.	17	Sept.	26		1	10
1938	Sept.	28	Nov.	10		7	25
1939	Jan.	14	Jan.	28		2	14
1939	Mar.	18	Apr.	11		3	25
1939	Apr.	12	Jun.	9		8	15
1939	Jun.	10	Jun.	30		3	7
1939	Jun.	30	Jul.	25		3	12

TIME PERIODS FOR DIFFERENT FORMATIONS

DOW JONES 20 RAILROAD AVERAGES

The RUN OR ADVANCES

AFTER BREAKAWAY

IN A BULL MARKET **EXAMPLES:**

Nov.		1898	to	April	1899, in 21 weeks advanced 38 points after the breakaway.
Mar.		1902	to	Sept.	1902, in 21 weeks advanced 15 points.
July	9,	1904	to	Mar.	1905, in 36 weeks advanced 29 points.
June	24,	1905	to	Jan. 19,	1906, in 27 weeks advanced 19 points.
Mar.	7,	1908	to	Sept. 12,	1908, in 26 weeks advanced 20 points.
Mar.	20,	1909	to	Aug. 14,	1909, in 21 weeks advanced 16½ points.

BREAKAWAY POINTS

IN A BEAR MARKET **EXAMPLES:**

Feb.	21,	1903	to	Oct. 13,	1903, in 33 weeks declined 30 points.
Dec.	22,	1906	to	Mar. 25,	1907, in 15 weeks declined 36 points.
Aug.	10,	1907	to	Nov. 21,	1907, in 15 weeks declined 24 points.
Jan.	15,	1910	to	July 26,	1910, in 27 weeks declined 22 points.
Aug.	5,	1911	to	Sept. 30,	1911, in 8 weeks declined 12 points
Dec.	7,	1912	to	June 14,	1913, in 27 weeks declined 17 points.
July	18,	1914	to	Dec. 23,	1914, in 22 weeks declined 11 points.

CHAPTER 9

RESISTANCE LEVELS

AUTHOR: "Truth of the Stock Tape" "Wall Street Stock Selector" "New Stock Trend Detector"	**W. D. GANN** Statistician and Economist 82 WALL STREET NEW YORK, N.Y. ——— 2101 N.W. 18th TERRACE MIAMI. FLA.	MEMBER New Orleans Cotton Exchange Commodity Exchange, Inc N.Y. American Economic Ass'n Royal Economic Society

RESISTANCE LEVELS

If we wish to avert failure in speculation we must deal with causes. Everything in existence is based on exact proportion and perfect relation. There is no chance in nature, because mathematical principles of the highest order lie at the foundation of all things. Faraday said: "There is nothing in the Universe but mathematical points of force."

Every stock makes a top or bottom on some exact mathematical point in proportion to some previous high or low level.

The movement of a stock between extreme high and extreme low, either in a major or a minor move, is very important and by a proper division of this range of fluctuation, we determine the points where resistance or support will be met on a reverse move, either up or down. By carefully watching these Resistance Levels in connection with your Trend Lines, you can make a greater success and trade with closer stop loss orders. You can tell by the Resistance Points why the averages or a stock should receive support or meet selling at old tops or bottoms.

RANGE OF FLUCTUATIONS

1/8 POINTS

Take the extreme low and extreme high of any important move; subtract the low from the high to get the range; then divide the range of fluctuation by 8 to get the 1/8 points, which are Resistance Levels or buying and selling points. When a stock stops around these levels and makes bottom or top on or near them and shows a turn on the Trend Line, this is the place to buy or sell. Sometimes the averages or a stock will hold for 3 to 7 days, making bottom or top around these important Resistance Levels, and at other times may hold for several weeks around them.

1/3 and 2/3 POINTS

After dividing a stock by 8 to get the 1/8 points, the next important thing to do is to divide the range of fluctuation by 3 to get the 1/3 and 2/3 points. These 1/3 and 2/3 points are very strong, especially if they fall near other Resistance Points of previous moves or when they are divisions of a very wide move.

HIGHEST SELLING PRICE

Next in importance is the division of the highest price at which a stock has ever sold and each lower top.

R-2

Divide the highest selling price by 8 to get the 1/8 points and also divide by 3 to get the 1/3 and 2/3 points.

This is very important as a stock, after breaking the half-way point of the fluctuation range, will often decline to the half-way point of the highest selling price, and will also work on the other Resistance Points in the same way.

When a stock is advancing, it will often cross the half-way point of the highest selling point and then advance to the half-way point of the fluctuation and meet resistance.

MOST IMPORTANT STOCK MOVEMENTS TO CONSIDER

The first and most important point: Consider the Resistance Levels between the extreme high and extreme low of the life of a stock.

Next important point to consider: Resistance Points or divisions of the highest price at which the stock has ever sold.

Then consider the fluctuation of each campaign which runs one year or more. Take the range between extreme high and extreme low and divide into 8 equal parts to get the Resistance Points.

Then take a third or fourth lower top and divide it by 9 to get the Resistance Points.

SECONDARY BOTTOMS AND TOPS

After the market has made final top [bottom?] in a Bear Campaign and the first rally takes place, then follows a secondary reaction, making a higher bottom, the half-way point between the high of the first rally and the low on secondary decline is very important to figure resistance Levels from. The half-way point between the top of the first rally and the bottom of the secondary reaction is a strong support point.

Example: Dow-Jones Industrial averages – 1932 Bear Market
            Jul. 8, 1932 final low 40-1/2;
            Sep. 8, 1932 high of first rally 81-1/2;
            Feb. 27, 1933 bottom of secondary reaction 49-1/2;
            half-way point 61.

After final top in a Bull Campaign has been reached and the first sharp decline takes place and a secondary rally follows, making a lower top, this lower top is an important point to figure Resistance Levels from. The half-way point between the bottom of the first reaction and secondary top is a strong Resistance Level.

Example: 1937, Mch. 8 high 195-1/2;
            Jun. 17 low of first decline 163;
            Aug. 14 high of secondary rally 190-1/2;
            half-way point 179-1/4

Also figure the half-way point between the secondary bottom of 49-1/2 made on February 27, 1933 and the secondary top of 190-1/2 reached on August 14, 1937.

This was 120, a very important Resistance Level. The low of April 11, 1939 was 120, where the trend turned up again. There were many other bottoms and tops formed around this level in the past.

ORDER OF RESISTANCE LEVELS

When a stock is advancing and crosses the 1/4 point, the next most important point to watch is the half-way point (1/2 point) or gravity center, or the average of the move fluctuation.

Then the next point above the half-way point is the 5/8 point.

The next and strongest point after the half-way point is crossed is the 3/4 point.

Then if the range is very wide, it is important to watch the 7/8 point of the move. This will often mark the top of an advance.

But in watching these Resistance Points, always watch your Trend Lines on the Weekly Chart and follow rules given on Formations. If the stock starts making tops or bottoms around these Resistance Points, it is safe to sell or buy.

THE AVERAGE OR HALF-WAY POINT

Always remember that the 50% reaction or half-way point of the range of fluctuation or of the extreme highest point of a stock or any particular move is the most important point for support on the down side or for meeting selling and resistance on the way up. This is the balancing point because it divides the range of fluctuation into two equal parts.

To get this point, add the extreme low of any move to the extreme high of that move and divide by 2.

When a stock advances or declines to this half-way point, you should sell or buy with a stop loss order of 1,2, or 3 points according to whether the stock is selling at very high or very low levels.

The wider the range and the longer the time period, the more important is this half-way point when it is reached.

You can make a fortune by following this one rule alone. A careful study and review of past movements in any stock or the averages will prove to you beyond doubt that this rule works and that you can make profits following it.

Buy or sell at the most important half-way point of the major move and place stop loss orders 1 to 3 points under the half-way point or 1 to 3 points above the half-way point. By major moves we mean the half-way point between the extreme low and extreme high when the range runs 25 to 100 points or more. A minor half-way point would be the 1/2 point between a minor top and a minor bottom. Reactions usually run back half of the last move or to the half-way point.

When the range between the 1/2 point and the 5/8 point is 5 to 10 points or more and the stock crosses the half-way point, it will go to the 5/8 point and meet resistance and then react or

R-4

decline. The 5/8 point is a very important point to watch for top or reaction. A stock will often reaction from the 5/8 point back to the half-way point and be a buy again.

The same rule applies when a stock is declining. If the range is 5 to 10 points or more between the 1/2 point and the 3/8 point, then the stock breaks the half-way point, it will decline to the 3/8 point and make bottom and rally to the 1/2 point or higher.

When a stock is in a narrow trading range, it will often fluctuate between the 5/8 point on the upside and the 3/8 point below the half-way point, making bottom sand tops around the half-way point and at the 5/8 and 3/8 points, moving in 1/4 of the full range of fluctuation. See examples of 1/2, 3/8, 5/8 points on the Dow -Jones 20 Railroad averages 1896 to 1914 and the 30 Industrial averages 1903 to 1939.

When a stock advances to a half-way point and reacts several points from this level, then finally goes thru it, you can expect it to make the next resistance point indicated on your Resistance Level Card or the next old top.

The same applies when a stock declines and receives support several times on a half-way point, then breaks thru it. It will then indicate the next resistance point on your Resistance Level Card or the next important bottom.

The greatest indication of strength is when a stock holds one or more points above the half-way point, which shows that buying or support orders were placed above this important Resistance Level.

A sign of weakness is when a stock advances and fails to reach the half-way point by one or more points; then declines and breaks the Trend Line or other Resistance Points.

NEXT RESISTANCE LEVELS
AFTER THE MAIN HALF-WAY POINT HAS BEEN BROKEN

The next Resistance Level to watch after the main half-way point has been broken is the next half-way point of some previous move. By main half-way point I mean, the half-way point of the extreme fluctuating range of the life of a stock.

Another very important Resistance Level after the main half-way point is crossed is the half-way point of 1/2 of the highest selling price. This is a stronger support level than the half-way point of minor fluctuating moves because it cuts the highest selling price in half, and is a strong buying or selling point until it is crossed by 1, 2, or 3 points, according to the price of a stock, whether it is very high-priced, medium or low-priced.

RESISTANCE POINTS NEAR SAME LEVELS

When two half-way points or any other two Resistance Points, either in the range of fluctuation or the division of the highest selling price, occur near the same level, you should add these two points together and divide by 2, as the half-way point between these two points will often be a support point on a decline or a selling point on a rally.

HOW TO LOOK UP RESISTANCE LEVELS

When you find an important Resistance Level or the strongest one - the half-way point - at a certain level, look to see if any other Resistance Level, whether it be 1/8, 1/4, 3/8, 5/8 or 2/3 point, falls around this same price. You may find 3 or 4 Resistance Levels around the same price. The more you find, the stronger resistance the stock will meet when it reaches this level. Then take the highest Resistance Level around this same price and the lowest, and add them together to get the average point of resistance.

Watch the activity of the stock when it reaches these Resistance Levels. If it is advancing very fast or declining very fast on large volume, do not consider that it is going to stop around these Resistance Levels unless it stops or holds one or two days around these levels; then sell or buy with stop loss orders. Also consider whether the market is in 3rd or 4th section from bottom or in 3rd of 4th section from top down.

AVERAGE AND EXTREME FLUCTUATIONS

In normal markets the rallies and reactions on the Dow-Jones 30 Industrial averages run 10 to 12 points and when they exceed this number of points they run 20 to 24 points and then 30 to 40 points. When there are great extremes between main tops and main bottoms, like August 8, 1896, low 28-1/2 to September 3, 1929, high 386, and from 386 high to a low of 40-1/2 on July 8, 1932, you can divide by 16 and 32 to get closer mathematical points instead of dividing by 8 to get the 1/8 points. These points will correspond to minor top and bottoms of other movements.

Use all the rules and figure that the important tops and bottoms will come out on the strongest points, like the 1/3, 2/3, 1/4, 3/8, 1/2, 5/8 and 3/4 points.

Do not overlook the fact that it requires time for a market to get ready at the bottom before it advances and requires time to distribute at the top. The longer a market has been running, the more time it will require to complete accumulation or distribution.

WHEN STOCKS DECLINE UNDER OLD TOPS

When stocks drop back under old tops of previous campaigns, the Resistance Levels between old bottoms and these old tops will be important points for support and resistance.

Example: After the 1929 high the averages dropped back below 119-5/8, the top of 1919, and declined to 85-1/2 in October, 1931, which was also the low of October 27, 1923. On November 9, 1931, they rallied to 119-5/8, the old top of 1919. After that, as long as the averages stayed below 120, you would watch the old Resistance Levels from 28-12 low, 38-1/2 low, 42 low, 52 low to 119-5/8 high. Then, when the averages advanced above 120, you would watch Resistance Levels to higher tops. The important ones were at 195-1/2 to 197.

SMALL GAINS IN LAST STAGE OF BULL OR BEAR MARKET

When a bull or advancing market is nearing the end of a campaign, the gains or runs will often get smaller, which is a sign that the averages or stocks are meeting with greater selling pressure.

Example: Suppose a stock is moving up and crosses a previous top and advances 20 points, then reacts 10 points; then crosses the last top and advance 15 points and reacts 5 to 7-1/2 points; again advances above the last top but only goes 10 points above it and reacts 5 points or more, this would be a sign of weakness or that the top was near because each move was making a smaller gain. In very active fast markets, when volumes of sales are large, the last run may be a greater number of points. Reverse this rule in a declining market.

If a stock has made several moves down of 10, 15 or 20 points and each one gets shorter or when the stock breaks bottom and the declines get smaller, it is a sign that the selling pressure is decreasing and that a change in trend is near, but in fast panicky markets the last decline may be a large number of points with very small rallies. This is a final wave of liquidation.

In the last stages of Bull or Bear Campaigns use only the half-way point of short or minor moves. It is most important to watch the Resistance Levels of the final move, which may run several weeks or months, particularly the half-way point. When it is exceeded by 3 full points, the trend usually reverses.

LOST MOTION

As there is lost motion in every kind of machinery, so there is lost motion in the stock market due to momentum, which drives a stock slightly above or be-low a Resistance Level. The average lost motion is 1-7/8 points.

When a stock is very active and advances or declines fast on heavy volume, it will often go from 1-7/8 points above a half-way point or other strong Resistance Level and not go 3 points. The same rule applies on a decline. It will often pass an important Resistance Point by 1-7/8 points but not go 3 full points beyond it.

This is the same rule that applies to a gravity center in anything. If we could bore a hole thru the earth and then drop a ball, momentum would carry it beyond the gravity center, but when it slowed down it would finally settle on the exact center. This is the way stocks act around these important centers.

A study of the Resistance Levels between bottoms and tops of individual stocks or the averages will prove how accurate the market works out to these important points.

[unsigned]

July 6, 1939

RESISTANCE LEVELS

DOW JONES 30 INDUSTRIAL AVERAGES
COMPARATIVE BOTTOMS AND TOPS

Resistance points are figured to show you why bottoms and tops were made around these levels. You can use your resistance cards and levels in the same way to determine future bottoms and tops.

1896	Aug. 8	Low	28½	was	3/8 of	78-3/4	the Last High	
1896	Nov. 12	High	45	was	1/2 of	78-3/4	to	28½
1898	Mar. 19	Low	42	was	1/4 of	94½	to	28½
1898	Aug. 7	High	61	was	1/2 of	94½	to	28½
1898	Oct. 22	Low	51-5/8	was	1/2 of	78-3/4	to	28½
1900	Sept. 29	Low	53	was	1/2 of	77-5/8	to	28½

From 42 Low to 78-5/8 the 1/2 point was 60-1/4
From 53 Low to 78-1/4 the 1/2 point was 65-6/8
From 53 Low to 78-1/4 the 5/8 point was 68-3/8

1902 Apr. & Sept.)
1904 Feb.)   Tops 68-1/2 to 67-3/4 was 5/8 of 53 to 78-1/4

1904   Broke 65-6/8   was 1/2 of 53   to 78-1/4
1903 Nov. 9   Low 42-1/8 an old bottom of March 1898 and
                                       was 1/4 of 28½   to 78-3/4
                Later crossed 53-5/8 was 1/2 of 28½   to 78-3/4
                and a big Bull Market followed.

1906 Jan. 19   High 103   A sharp decline followed.
1906 May 5   Low 86½   was 3/4 of 38½   to 103
1906 July 14   Low 85½   was 3/4 of 28½   to 103
1906 Aug. 13   High 96
1907 Jan. 12   High 96-3/4   was 7/8 of 53   to 103
                                       and 3/4 of 76¼   to 103
                Later broke 85
                declined to 78   was 1/2 of 53   to 103
                A Bear Market followed.

1907 Nov. 23   Low 53 (same as 1900) was 1/3 of 28½   to 103
                                       and 1/4 of 38½   to 103
                (Note: 1/2 of 103 is 51½. Holding above this
                1/2 point was a strong support and buying
                point at 53, the old bottom.)

1908 Jan. 18   High 66-3/4   was 5/8 of 103   to 53
1908 Sept. 22   Low 77-1/4   was 1/2 of 103   to 53
1909 Oct. 2   High 100½   was
                (Note: 3 bottom at 96 was 7/8 of 53   to 103
                          and 94½   was 7/8 of 53   to 100½
                Then broke 96 and 96½ and declined fast.)

THE W.D. GANN MASTER STOCK MARKET COURSE

RESISTANCE LEVELS, Cont'd

DOW JONES 30 INDUSTRIAL AVERAGES
COMPARATIVE BOTTOMS AND TOPS

1910 July 26	Low 73-5/8	was 1/2 of 42	to 103		
1911 June 24	High 87	was 1/2 of 73-5/8	to 100½		
1911 Sept. 25	Low 73	was 1/2 of 42	to 103		

and same low as July 26, 1910.
A double bottom and place to buy.

1912 Oct. 10	High 94	was 3/4 of 73-5/8 to 100½	
Made several bottoms around	88	was 3/4 of 53 to 100½	
Later Broke	87	was 1/2 of 73-5/8 to 100½	

1913 June 14	Low 72-1/8	was 3/8 of 53 to 103
		and 1/2 of 42 to 103

A third time at this level -
a buying point.

1913 Sept. &)		
1914 March)	High 83-3/8	was 1/2 of 72-1/8 to 94-1/8
		and 3/8 of 73 to 100½
1914 July declined to	71-1/4 under three old bottoms	
and under		1/2 of 42 to 103
and		3/8 of 53 to 103

A sure sign of lower prices.

1914 Dec. 24   Low 53-1/8. This was third time at this level.
                 1900 -- Low 53
                 1907 -- Low 53
                 1914 -- Low 53-1/8
                 Holding above 51½   the 1/2 of 103
                                         and 1/3 of 28½ to 103
                                         and 1/4 of 38½ to 103
                 Made this a good support and buying point
                 in a panic

                 The War Bull Market Followed.

1915 May	High 71-3/4 just under the 3/8 of 53 to 103	
	and under three old bottoms.	
1915 June	Low 60½ a secondary reaction	
	60½ was 1/3 of 38½ to 103	
	and 62-3/8 was 1/2 of 53-1/8 to 71-3/4	
1919 Jan.	High 99	
1916 Apr.	Low 85 was 5/8 of 53 to 103	
1916 Nov. 21	High 110-1/8 a sharp reaction followed.	
1917 Feb. 2	Low 87 was 5/8 of 53-1/8 to 110-1/8	
1917 June 9	High 99 was 7/8 of 28½ to 110-1/8	
	and 1/2 of 85 to 110	
	Later broke all important 1/2 points	
	including 81½ was 1/2 of 53 to 110-1/8	

Page 267

RESISTANCE LEVELS, Cont'd

**DOW JONES 30 INDUSTRIAL AVERAGES
COMPARATIVE BOTTOMS AND TOPS**

1917	Dec. 19	Low 66	was 1/3 of 42	to 110-1/8
			and 3/8 of 38½	to 110-1/8
1918	Oct. 19	High 89	was 3/4 of 28½	to 110-1/8
			and 5/8 of 53	to 110-1/8
1919	Feb. 8	Low 79-1/8	was 1/2 of 53	to 110-1/8
			and 5/8 of 28½	to 110-1/8

A Big Bull Market followed.

1919	Nov. 3	A New High 119-5/8	A sharp decline followed.
1920	Feb. 25	Low 90	was 3/4 of 28½	to 110-1/8
			and 5/8 of 42	to 119-5/8
			and 2/3 of 28½	to 119-5/8
1920	Apr. 8	High 105	was 5/8 of 79-1/8	to 119-5/8
			and 3/4 of 66	to 119-5/8
			and 1/2 of 90	to 119-5/8

Later declined,
to 99 was 1/2 of 79-1/8 to 119-5/8

1921	Aug. 24	Low 64 Just 2 points under 1917 Lows.
		Low 64	was 1/3 of 38½ to 119-5/8
		62-5/8	was 3/8 of 22½ to 119-5/8

This was a final low and the greatest
Bull Market in history followed.

(Note: When averages crossed 80 they
were above   1/2 of 42   to 119-5/8
and   1/2 of 38½   to 119-5/8

Note: 91-7/8 was 1/2 of 119-5/8 to 64 and
after averages crossed 92 did not reach 91
before they advanced   to 105-5/8

1923	Mar. 20	High 105-5/8	was 3/4 of 64	to 119-5/8
1923	Oct. 27	Low 85-3/4	was 3/8 of 64	to 119-5/8
			5/8 of 28½	to 119-5/8
			1/2 of 53	to 119-5/8

A Strong Support Point.

1924	May 20	Last Low 88-3/8	was 2/3 of 28½	to 119-5/8
1924	Dec.	Crossed old top of 1919 at 119-5/8		

A Big Bull Market followed.

In view of the fact that the averages made - High 103 in 1906 and in 1916 made a new High of 110-1/8 and in 1919 another record High 119-5/8 and in 1921 decline[d] to 64, holding more than 4 points above 1/2 of 119-5/8, was a strong indication of much higher prices because of such a long period of time between these top levels. From January 1906 to December 1924, when averages went above 119-5/8, was nearly 19 years. You could figure they would first double the highest selling price or make 240. After that figure was crossed, you figure three times 119-5/8 of about 360.

RESISTANCE LEVELS, Cont'd

DOW JONES 30 INDUSTRIAL AVERAGES
COMPARATIVE BOTTOMS AND TOPS

1929 Sept. 2	High 386	

If you take the range from extreme Low 28½ to 119-5/8 the range was 91-1/8. Multiply this range by 4 and we get 364½ as a probable top. The proper procedure after the averages were in new high, was to follow the trend and use all rules until there was a change in the main trend.

1926 July	High 162¼	
1926 Apr.	Low 135-1/8 was just under	
	1/2 of 115 to 162¼	
	150-5/8 was 1/2 of 162¼ to 135-1/8	

When averages crossed this level the second time they went right up to new highs.

1927 Oct.	High 199-7/8	
1927 Oct.	Low 179 was 1/2 of 165-3/4, the last low to 199-7/8	
	189-3/8 was 1/2 of 119-7/8 to 179	

When crossed this level never sold below 190½ again.

1928 Dec.	High 299
1928 Dec. 12	Low 254½ was near 250 the 1/2 of 200-7/8 to 299

Holding above the 1/2 of last move indicated higher.

1929 Jan.	High 324½
1928 Mar. 30	Low 281½
	279 was 1/2 of 234 to 374½ the

last low, and holding above 1/2 point was strong.

1929 May	High 331	Last reaction before top
End of May	Low 290	3/4 of 281½ to 331 was 287½

holding above this indicated support.

Then when crossed	306	the 1/2 of 281½ to 331
and crossed	310½	the 1/2 of 331 to 290
	indicated higher.	
1929 Sept. 3	High 386	Final Top.

After the trend turned down, we calculated the Resistance Points from bottoms from 1896 to date, to get points to watch on the way down. The first 1/2 point for the last move from 281½ to 386, making 333-3/4, - this was broken on the first decline to 321, which was 1/2 of 255 to 386.

1929 Oct. Last Rally	358	the 1/2 of 386 to 321 was 253½, did not go 5 points above it -- then broke wide open.
1929 Oct. 29	Low 213	was 1/2 of 38½ to 386
1929 Oct. 31	High 273½	was 2/3 of 42 to 386
		and 2/3 of 53 to 386
	and just under	2/3 of 64 to 386

THE W.D. GANN MASTER STOCK MARKET COURSE

#5.

RESISTANCE LEVELS, Cont'd

**DOW JONES 30 INDUSTRIAL AVERAGES
COMPARATIVE BOTTOMS AND TOPS**

1929   Nov. 13   Low   195½
This was a very important panic bottom and there was a strong mathematical point which indicated they should stop around this level.
When   225   was 1/2 of 64   to 386 was broken
       219½   was 1/2 of 53   to 386
       214   was 1/2 of 42   to 386
       207¼   was 1/2 of 28½   to 386

The extreme high according to our rules is the next important point, or 1/2 of 386 the highest selling point - which is 193 - and the averages held 2½ points above this strong point, indicating bottoms for a big rally.

1930   Apr. 17   High   296-3/8   was 3/4 of 28½   to   386
and just 5 points above
                       291   the 1/2 of 386   to   195-3/8
when the averages dropped back under   290
they never rallied to   291   again.
245-3/4 was 1/2 of 195-3/8 to 296-3/8, they never
broke this 1/2 point, never sold at 250 again.

1930   June to Aug.
       Bottoms at   208 to 214 which   was 1/2 of 28½   to   386
                                          and   42   to   386

1930   Sept. 10   Last High 247   was 1/2 of 195-3/8   to   296-3/8
Then followed a big decline breaking all main 1/2
points and when the average broke 193 the 1/2 of 386
in Oct. 1930 they never sold above 198½ again.

1930   Dec. 17   Low   155½   was 1/3 of 38½   to   386
                                             1/3 of 42   to   386

1931   Jan.   High   175½   was 3/8 of 53   to   386
                                             1/3 of 64   to   386

1931   Jan. 24   Low   160   was 1/4 of 85-3/4 to   386
                              165½   was 1/2 of 155½   to   175½
When it crossed this level it never sold at 163 until it
made next Top.

1931   Feb. 24   High   197¼   was just above
                              193   the 1/2 of 386 and under low of
Nov. 1929 and last Top of Nov. 1930 - making this a
safe point to Sell Short.

The next important point to watch ... 176-7/8   was 1/2 of 155½   to   197¼
1931   Mar. 14   Low   175-3/4   was 1/2 of 155½   to   197¼
1931   Mar. 20   High   189   was 5/8 of 297
                                             1/3 of 85-3/4 to   386
                                             3/8 of 64   to   386

Latter part of Mar. broke   176   the 1/2 of 155½   to   197¼
and a panic decline followed.
Later broke   161   which was 1/4 of 85-3/4   to   386
Then broke   Low   155½ and declined fast.

RESISTANCE LEVELS, Cont'd

**DOW JONES 30 INDUSTRIAL AVERAGES
COMPARATIVE BOTTOMS AND TOPS**

1931 June 2	Low 120	was 1/4 of 85-3/4 to 386
		and 3/4 of 157½
	and a back to 1919 Top. A strong support for a rally.
1931 June 27	High 157½	was 1/3 of 42 to 386
	and just under	1/2 of 197¼ to 120
	and Lows of Dec. 1930 made this a Sure Selling Level.
1931 Oct. 5	Low 85½ Same Low as Oct. 27, 1923
	85	was 1/8 of 386 to 42
1931 Nov. 9	High 119-5/8 was under 1/2 of 157¼ to 85½
		and 1/4 of 28½ to 386
		and 1/8 of 85-3/4 to 386
	A sharp decline followed.
1932 Jan. 7	Low 70	was 1/8 of 28½ to 386
1932 Mar. 8	High 89½	was 3/8 of 119-5/8 to 70
	79-3/4	was 1/2 of 70 to 89½
	When it broke under 79 it declined fast.
1932 July 8	Low 40½
	Final Low – End of Great Bear Market
	Down to Lows of 1898.
1932 Sept. 8	High 81½	was 1/2 of 119-5/8 to 40½
		under 3/8 of 386 to 40½
		1/3 of 157½ to 40½
	61	was 1/2 of 40½ to 81½
1933 Feb. 27	Low 49½	was 3/4 of 40½ to 81½
1933 Mar. 18	High 64½	was 1/2 of 49½ to 81½
1933 Apr. 1	Last Low 54-3/4 not 3 points under
		1/2 of 49½ to 64½
	A rapid advance followed,
	crossed	1/2 of 49½ to 81½
	and	1/2 of 40½ to 81½
1933 July 17	High 110½	was 3/8 of 296-3/4
	just under	5/8 of 146½ to 40½

Why did prices of the Dow Jones 30 Industrial Average make High at 110½ and 111½ in 1933 and 1934?

The highest selling point in 1929 was 386. 1/3 of this is 128-5/8. 1/4 of 386 is 96½. The half-way point between 13/ and 1/4 points is 112½. This is one of the reasons that so many tops were made around this level for such a long period of time before they were crossed.

THE W.D. GANN MASTER STOCK MARKET COURSE

#7.

RESISTANCE LEVELS, Cont'd

DOW JONES 30 INDUSTRIAL AVERAGES
COMPARATIVE BOTTOMS AND TOPS

Why 82½ Low, October, 1933?

In September 1932, the old Top 81. From the low of 49½ to 111½, the half-way point is 80½. From the breakaway point 55½ to 111½ the half-way point is 83½. The fact that the averages held above the extreme half-way point was a sign of strength and good support. From 111½ to 82½, the half-way point was 97.

In March 1935, the averages started up from 95½, not 3 points under this half-way point and on March 31, 1939, the averages declined to 97½ which was also the half-way point of the highest selling point 195½ in 1937.

1933	Oct. 21	Low 82 ½	was above 1/2 of 49½ to 110½
			and 1/8 of 386 to 40½
			and 1/2 of 54-3/4 to 110½

Holding above these important 1/2 points, indicated strong support.

1934	Feb. 5	High 111½
		Low 82½ to 111½ made 97 the 1/2 point.
1934	Mar. 31	Low 97 rallied to 107
1934	July 26	Low 84½ was 3/8 of 157½ to 40½
		From 111½
		To 84½ the 1/2 point was 98

1935	Feb. 18	High 108½
1935	Mar. 18	Low 95½ just under 1/2 of 87½ to 111½
		and 1/2 of 195½
		and 1/4 of 386
		From 108
		To 95½ the 1/2 was 101-3/4

Crossed this minor 1/2 point and crossed Old Tops 110½ to 111½ and Big Bull Market followed.

1936	Apr. 6	High 163¼ was 3/8 of 28½ to 386
		was 3/8 of 386 to 49½
1936	Apr. 30	Low 141½ was 7/8 of 40½ to 157½
		Just 3 points under 1/2 of 176¼ to 163¼

| 1937 | Mar. 10 | High 195½ Same as Low Nov. 13, 1929 and Last High Oct. 1930. |

Just under High of Feb. 1931. This was not 3 points above 193, the 1/2 of 386 and a sure place to go Short.

| 1937 | June 17 | Low 163 was 3/8 of 28½ to 386 |
| | | was 1/2 of 141¼ to 195½ |

RESISTANCE LEVELS, Cont'd

**DOW JONES 30 INDUSTRIAL AVERAGES
COMPARATIVE BOTTOMS AND TOPS**

    1937   Aug. 14   High 190½   just 2½ points under
                                                                   1/2 of 386 and a lower Top-
                                                                   a sign of weakness.
                                 The 1/2 point from 163 to 195 was 179¼ and 163
                                 to 190½ was 176-3/4. When these levels were
                                 broken a panicky decline followed.

    1929 [1937?] Oct. 19   Low 115½   was 1/2 of 195½ to 40½
    1929 [1937?] Oct. 29   High 141½   was 2/3 of 195½ to 40½
                                 and under   3/8 of 386

    1937   Nov. 23   Low 112½   was 3/8 of 196-3/4
    1938   Jan. 15   High 134½   was 3/8 of 40½ to 296-3/4
                                                               and 3/8 of 95½ to 195½

    1938   Mar. 31   Low   97½
    Final Bottom Panic   97½   was 1/2 of 195½
                                                            and 3/8 of 40½ to 195½
                                                            and 1/3 of 296-3/4
                                                            and 1/4 of 386
                               This wasa safe buying point.

    1938   Apr. 18   High 121½   just above 1/2 of 40½ to 195½
                                                        and 2/3 of 157½ to 140½
                                                        and 5/8 of 195½
    1938   May 27   Low 106½   just above 1/4 of 40½ to 296-3/4
                                                     and 1/3 of 195½ to 97½
                                 109¼   was 1/2 from 97½ to 121½
                               When it crossed 110 showed strong up and
                               advanced fast.

    1938   July 25   High 146¼   was 1/2 of 195½ to 97½
    1938   Sept. 26   Low 128   was 1/3 of 386
                                                 and 1/3 of 195½ to 97½
                                             and 1/2 of 106½ to 146¼
                             A Strong Support Level and Buying Point.

    1938   Nov. 10   High 158-3/4
                             When the averages crossed   146½
                                                  1/2 of 97½ to 195½
                           indicated the 5/8 point at   158-3/4.
                                 158-3/4   was 5/8 of 97½ to 195½
                                                    and 1/3 of 40½ to 386
                                                    and 3/4 of 195½ to 40½
                           Making this a sure point to Sell Shirt [N.B. Hopefully W.D.
                           meant, 'Sell Short'?].

THE W.D. GANN MASTER STOCK MARKET COURSE

RESISTANCE LEVELS, Cont'd

DOW JONES 30 INDUSTRIAL AVERAGES
COMPARATIVE BOTTOMS AND TOPS

1939	Nov. 28	Low 145	was 1/2 of 195½	to 97½
			and 3/4 of 195½	
			1/2 of 128	to 158-3/4
			3/8 of 97½	to 158-3/4
			and 5/8 of 40½	to 195½

1939   Mar. 10   High 152½   was 7/8 of 97½   to 158-3/4
                 Last Low 136-1/8
                 to   158-3/4 the 1/2   was   148¼
                                       and 1/3 of 136-1/8 to 152½
                                       was   144¼
                 When broke this 1/2 point declined fast.

1939   Apr. 11   Low 120   was 3/8 of 97½   to 158-3/4
                                     and 3/4 of 158-3/4
                 Note 118   was 1/2 of 40¼   to 195½
                 This was the strongest 1/2 point and the averages
                 held 2 points above, also 118¼ was
                                     1/4 of 28½   to 386

1939   May 10   High 134-5/8   was 3/8 of 158-3/4 to 120
                                     also 3/8 of 195½   to 97½
1939   May 17   Low 128-3/8   was 1/2 of 97½   to 158-3/4
1939   June 9   High 140-3/4   was 1/2 of 120   to 158-3/4
1939   June 30   Low 129   was 1/2 of 97½   to 158-3/4
                                     and 1/3 of 386
                 A strong support point and buying level.
                 The Market rallied and crossed 139-3/8
                 the 1/2 of 120 to 158-3/4
                 and on July 25th advanced to 145-3/4 just
                 under 1/2 of 97½ to 195½
                 and   2/3 of 120 to 158-3/4.

THE W.D. GANN MASTER STOCK MARKET COURSE

RESISTANCE LEVELS, Cont'd

DOW JONES 20 RAILROAD AVERAGES

Aug. 8, 1896		Low	42 WHY?					
			46	was	1/2 of	92, the last high		
			49½	was	1/2 of	99, the extreme high		
Apr.	1897	Low of reaction	48¼	was	1/2 of	54¼	to	42
Sept.	1897	High	67½	was	1/2 of	42	to	92
Nov.	1897	Low	57½	was	1/2 of	48¼	to	67¼
Apr.	1898	Low	58-3/4	was	1/2 of	42	to	67¼
Aug.	1898	High	70¼	was	1/2 of	42	to	99
Oct.	1898	Low	65-3/4	was	1/2 of	42	to	92 close

After averages crossed 70½, the 1/2 of 42 to 99 never sold lower and advanced to 138-3/4 Jan. 19, 1906.

Apr.	1899	High	87	was	7/8 of	99		
				and	2/3 of	42	to	99
June	1899	Low	77¼	was	1/2 of	66	to	87
Dec.	1899	Low	72½					
			just above		1/2	42	to	99
				and	1/2 of	56	to	87

(Note triple bottom near this level)

June		Low	73					
Oct.		Low	73-3/4					
(Note)			79-3/4	was	1/2	87	to	72½
		and	80½	was	1/2 of	62	to	99 and in

Nov. 1899 the breakaway came when averages crossed 80½ after making triple bottoms above the 1/2 of 42 to 99, - later crossed 99, the old top advancing quickly to 117-3/4 May, 1901 and on Sept. 30, 1902 made high at 129¼.

May 9, 1901		Low	103¼	was	1/8 of	42	to	117-3/4
				and	1/4 of	56	to	117-3/4
				and	1/3 of	72½	to	117-3/4
(Note)			106½	was	1/4 of	72½	to	117-3/4

and on secondary reaction after double top, the market made 3 bottoms: 105, 105¼, 106¼, starting up from 106¼ and advancing to new highs.

Sept. 10, 1902		High	129¼					
Dec.	1902	Low	113¼					
			just above		3/4 of	56	to	129¼
Jan.	1903	High	121¼		at 1/2 of	110¼	to	129¼

(Note) 101¼ was 1/2 of 72½ to 129½, broke this level and rallied 2 points above, then broke under and decline further.

Oct.	1903	Low	89-3/8		at 1/2 of	48¼	to	129¼
Jan.	1904	High	99-3/4		at 1/4 of	129¼	to	89-3/8
				and under	1/2 of	72½	to	129¼

Aug. 1904 crossed old top and crossed 1/4 of 129¼ to 89-3/8, then came the breakaway and rapid advance to new highs.

	Later crossed	1/2 point		129¼	to 89-3/8

Page 275

THE W.D. GANN MASTER STOCK MARKET COURSE

RESISTANCE LEVELS, Cont'd

DOW JONES 20 RAILROAD AVERAGES

Mar. & Apr. 1905 made double tops at 127
July 1905 .... Low 114½ at 3/4 of 89-3/8 to 129¼, later crossed
121 above 1/2 of 114½ to 127 advanced to
138-3/8 [on] Jan. 19, 1906.
May 1906 .... Low 120½ (This was first sharp reaction).
....at 3/4 of 89-3/8 to 129¼
Last Low 114½ ....to 138-3/8, the 1/2
point...126½ and 1/2 of 138-3/8 to 120¼ was 129.
The first rally was to....................131
Then secondary reaction..............121-3/4
Then crossed...............................129
And advanced to........................137-3/4, making triple tops.

Showed down when they broke the...........................1/2 of 120¼ to 138-3/8
and was still weaker when they broke.....................1/2 of 98-3/8 to 138-3/8.

Mar. 14, 1907 .... Low 98-3/8 at 3/8 of 138-3/8 to 72½
and 1/2 of 56 to 138-3/8
May 1907 .... High 110-3/8 at 1/4 of 98-3/8 to 138-3/8
and 2/3 of 56 to 138-3/8

(Note) .... 1/2 of 98-3/8 to 110-3/8 was 104.
When they broke this level, they declined to new lows.

Nov. 23, 1907 .... Low 81-3/8 at 3/8 of 48¼ to 138-3/8
Jan. 1908 .... High 95-3/4 at 1/2 of 81-3/8 to 110-3/8 and
later a secondary reaction to............86¼
Just under 1/2 of 81-3/8 to 95-3/4. Later
crossed top at....................... 95-3/4 and 1/4 of 138-3/8 to 81-3/8.

Sept. 1908 .... High 110¼ at 1/2 of 138-3/8 to 81-3/8
Sept. 22, 1908 reacted to 103-3/8 the 1/2 of 98 to 110-3/8
Jan. 1909 .... High 120-3/4 at 2/3 of 138-3/8 to 81-3/8
Mar. 1909 .... Low 113-3/4 above 1/2 of 103-3/8 to 120-3/4
Aug. 14, 1909 .... High 134¼
(Note) ....131 was 1/8 of 138-3/8 to 81-3/8
Last move up 113-3/4 to 134¼
the 1/2 at 124.
When the averages broke this level they never sold above 125-3/4
Until declined to 105-5/8
On July 26, 1910. This Low was just under 1/8 of 81-3/8 to 134¼

Oct. 1910 .... High 118-3/8 the 1/2 of 105-5/8 to 118-3/8 was 112
Dec. 1910 .... Low 111½
good support @ 1/2 point
July 1911 .... High 124 at 2/3 of 105-5/8 to 134¼
.... 3/4 of 81-3/8 to 134-3/8 at 121
and .... 1/2 of 105-5/8 to 134¼ at 120
When this level was broken, sharp decline followed.

THE W.D. GANN MASTER STOCK MARKET COURSE

#12.

RESISTANCE LEVELS, Cont'd

DOW JONES 20 RAILROAD AVERAGES

Sept. 25, 1911 .... Low 109-3/4	at 3/8 of 105-5/8	to 124
(Note) 117	was 1/2 of 124	to 109-3/4.
Averages advanced to 119		
Reacted to 115		
Then crossed the 1/2 at 117	and went higher.	

Oct.   1912 .... High 124-5/8   at 2/3 of 105-5/8   to 134¼
(Note) 117   was 1/2 of 109-3/4 to 124-5/8

When averages broke this level never rallied above 118
June   1913 .... Low 100½   at 3/8 of 81-3/8   to 134¼
Sept.   1913
       and
Jan.   1914 .... High 109¼   at 3/8 of 105-5/8   to 124-5/8
 .... and under .... 1/2 of 124-5/8   to 100½
Later broke under 105   the 1/2 of 100½   to 109¼
And declined wit very small rallies.

July   30, 1914 .... Low   89½

(Note) From 1896 .... Low   42
                to
Jan.   19, 1906 .... High 138-3/8   the 1/2 was 90-1/8
and on July 30, 1914 the averages closed under the 1/2 point from extreme low to the extreme high, closing in a panic under this strongest point indicated lower prices later.

When Exchange opened in December 1914, the 20 RAILROAD AVERAGES declined to 87½.

Chapter 10a

Forecasting by Time Cycles

How to Trade

AUTHOR:		MEMBER
"Truth of the Stock Tape"	**W. D. GANN**	New Orleans Cotton Exchange
"Wall Street Stock Selector"		Commodity Exchange, Inc N.Y.
"New Stock Trend Detector"	Statistician and Economist	American Economic Ass'n
	82 WALL STREET	Royal Economic Society
	NEW YORK, N.Y.	
	2101 N.W. 18th TERRACE	
	MIAMI. FLA.	

FORECASTING BY TIME CYCLES

TIME is the most important factor in determining market movements and by studying the past records of the averages or individual stocks you will be able to prove for yourself that history does repeat and that by knowing the past you can tell the future.

The ancient hunters had a rule that when they were searching to locate an animal in his den, they always followed his tracks backwards, figuring that it was the shortest route to his lair. The quickest way for you to learn how to determine future market movements is to study the past.

> "The thing that hath been, it is that which shall be; and that which is done is that which shall be done, and there is no new things under the sun." Eccl. 1:9.

There is a definite relation between TIME and PRICE. In the previous Lessons, you have learned about FORMATIONS and RESISTANCE LEVELS around old tops and bottoms. Now, by a study of the TIME PERIODS and TIME CYCLES, you will learn why tops and bottoms are formed at certain times and why Resistance Levels are so strong at certain times and bottoms and tops hold around them.

MAJOR TIME CYCLES

Everything moves in cycles as a result of the natural law of action and reaction. By a study of the past, I have discovered what cycles repeat in the future.

There must always be a major and a minor, a greater and a lesser, a positive and a negative. In order to be accurate in forecasting the future, you must know the major cycles. The most money is made when fast moves and extreme fluctuations occur at the end of major cycles.

I have experimented and compared past markets in order to locate the major and minor cycles and determined in what years the cycles repeat in the future. After years of research and practical tests, I have discovered that the following cycles are the most reliable to use:

10-YEAR CYCLE

The important cycle for forecasting is the cycle of around 10-years. Fluctuations of about the same nature occur which produce extreme high or low every 10-years. Stocks work out important tops and bottoms very close to the even 10-year cycle, although at times bottoms or tops come out around 10-1/2 to 11 years in extreme markets.

The 10-year cycle is equal to 120 months. We divide this just the same as we divide the range between bottoms and tops to get Resistance Levels. One-half of the cycle would be five years or 60 months. One fourth would be 2-1/2 years or 30 months. One-eighth would be 15 months and one-sixteenth 7-1/2 months. One-third would be 40 months and two-thirds of the cycle would be 80 months. All of these time periods are important to watch for changes in trend.

7-YEAR CYCLE

The cycle is 84 months. You should watch 7 years from any important top or bottom and 42 months or one-half of the cycle. You will find many combinations around the 42nd to 44th months. 21 months is one-fourth of 84 months, also important. You will find many bottoms and tops 21 to 23 months apart. At times, some stocks and the averages make bottom or top 10 to 11 months from the previous top or bottom. This is due to the fact that this period is 1/8 of the 7-year cycle.

5-YEAR CYCLE

The cycle is very important because it is one-half of the 10-year cycle and the smallest complete cycle that the market works out.

MINOR CYCLES

The minor cycles are 3 years and 2 years. The smallest cycle is one year, which often shows a change in trend in the 10th or 11th month.

RULES FOR FUTURE CYCLES

Stocks move in 10-year cycles, which are worked out in 5-year cycles – a 5-year cycle up and a 5-year cycle down. Begin with extreme tops and extreme bottoms to figure all cycles, either major or minor.

1 - A bull campaign generally runs 5 years – 2 years up, 1 year down, and 2 years up, completing a 5-year cycle. The end of a 5-year campaign comes in the 59th or 60th month. Always watch for the change in the 59th month.

2 - A bear cycle often runs 5 years down – the first move 2 years down, then 1 year up, and 2 years down, completing the 5-year downswing.

3 - Bull or bear campaigns seldom run more than 3 to 3-1/2 years up or down without a move of 3 to 6 months or one year in the opposite direction, except at the end of Major Cycles, like 1869 and 1929. Many campaigns culminate in the 23rd month, not running out the full 2 years. Watch the weekly and monthly charts to determine whether the culmination will occur in the 23rd, 24th, 27th or 30th month of the move, or in extreme campaigns in the 34th to 35th or 41st to 42nd month.

4 - Adding 10-years to any top, it will give you top of the next 10-year cycle, repeating about the same average fluctuations.

5 - Adding 10-years to any bottom, it will give you the bottom of the next 10-year cycle, repeating the same kind of a year and about the same average fluctuations.

6 - Bear campaigns often run out in 7-year cycles, or 3 years and 4 years from any completed bottom. From any complete bottom of a cycle, first add 3 years to get the next bottom; then add 4 years to that bottom to get bottom of 7-year cycle. For example: 1914 bottom – add 3 years, gives 1917, low of panic; then add 4 years to 1917, gives 1921, low of another depression.

7 - To any final major or minor top, add 3 years to get the next top; then add 3 years to that top, which will give you the third top; add 4 years to the third top to get the final top of the 10-year cycle. Sometimes a change in trend from any top occurs before the end of the regular time period, therefore, you should begin to watch the 27th, 34th, and 42nd month for a reversal.

8 - Adding 5 years to any top, it will give the next bottom of a 5-year cycle. In order to get top of the next 5-year cycle, add 5 years to any bottom. For example: 1917 was bottom of a big bear campaign; add 5 years gives 1922, top of a minor bull campaign. Why do I say, "Top of a minor bull campaign?" Because the major bull campaign was due to end in 1929.

1919 was top; adding 5 years to 1919 gives 1924 as bottom of a 5-year bear cycle. Refer to Rules 1 and 2, which tell you that a bull or bear campaigns seldom runs more than 2 to 3 years in the same direction. The bear campaign from 1919 was 2 years down – 1920 and 1921; therefore, we only expect one-year rally in 1922; then 2 years down – 1923 and 1924, which completes a 5-year bear cycle.

Looking back to 1913 and 1914, you will see that 1923 and 1924 must be bear years to complete the 10-year cycle from the bottoms of 1913-1914. Then, note 1917 bottom of the bear year; adding 7 years gives 1924 also as bottom of a bear cycle. Then, adding 5 years to 1924 gives 1929 top of a cycle.

FORECASTING MONTHLY MOVES

Monthly moves can be determined by the same rules as yearly:

Add 3 months to an important bottom, then add 4, making 7, to get minor bottoms and reaction points.

In big upswings a reaction will often not last over 2 months, the third month being up, the same rule as in yearly cycle – 2 down and the third up.

In extreme markets, a reaction sometimes only lasts 2 or 3 weeks; then the advance is resumed. In this way a market may continue up for 12 months without breaking a monthly bottom.

In a bull market, the minor trend may reverse and run down 3 to 4 months; then turn up and follow the main trend again.

In a bear market, the minor trend may run up to 3 to 4 months, then reverse and follow the main trend, altho, as a general rule, stocks never rally more than 2 months in a bear market; then start to break in the 3rd month and follow the main trend down.

FORECASTING WEEKLY MOVES

The weekly movement gives the next important minor change in trend, which may turn out to be a major change in trend.

In a bull market, a stock will often run down 2 to 3 weeks, and possibly 4, then reverse and follow the main trend again. As a rule, the trend will turn up in the middle of the third week and close higher at the end of the third week, the stock only moving 3 weeks against the main trend. In some cases, the change in trend will not occur until the fourth week; then the reversal will come and the stock close higher at the end of the fourth week. Reverse this rule in a bear market.

In a rapid markets with big volume, a move will often run 6 to 7 weeks before a minor reversal in trend, and in some cases, like 1929, these fast moves last 13 to 15 weeks or one quarter of a year. These are culmination moves up or down.

As there are 7 days in a week and 7 times 7 equals 49 days or 7 weeks, this often marks an important turning point. Therefore, you should watch for top or bottom around the 49th to 52nd day, altho at times a change will start on the 42nd to 45th day, because a period of 45 days is 1/8 of a year. Also watch for culminations at the end of 90 to 98 days.

After a market has declined 7 weeks, it may have 2 or 3 short weeks on the side and then turn up, which agrees with the monthly rule for a change in the third month.

Always watch the annual trend of a stock and consider whether it is in a bull or bear year. In a bull year, with the monthly chart showing up, there are many times that a stock will react 2 or 3 weeks, then rest 3 or 4 weeks, and then go into new territory and advance 6 to 7 weeks more.

After a stock makes top and reacts 2 to 3 weeks, it may then have a rally of 2 to 3 weeks without getting above the first top; then hold in a trading range for several weeks without crossing the highest top or breaking the lowest week of that range. In cases of this kind, you can buy near the low point or sell near the high point of that range and protect with a stop loss order 1 to 3 points away. However, a better plan would be to wait until the stock shows a definite trend before buying or selling; then buy the stock when it crosses the highest point or sell when it breaks the lowest point of that trading range.

FORECASTING DAILY MOVES

The daily movement gives the first minor change and conforms to the same rules as the weekly and monthly cycles, altho it is only a minor part of them.

In fast markets there will only be a 2-day move in the opposite direction to the main trend and on the third day the upward or downward course will be resumed in harmony with the main trend.

A daily movement may reverse trend and only run 7 to 10 days then follow the main trend again.

During a month, natural changes in trend occur around 6th to 7th, 9th to 10th, 14th to 15th, 19th to 20th, 23rd to 24th, 29th to 31st. These minor moves occur in accordance with tops and bottoms of individual stocks.

It is very important to watch for a change in trend 30 days from the last top or bottom. Then watch for changes 60, 90, 120 days from tops or bottoms. 180 days or six months – very important and sometimes marks changes for greater moves. Also around the 270th and 330th day from important tops or bottoms, you should watch for important minor and often major changes.

January 2nd to 7th and 15th to 21st:
Watch these periods each year and note the high and low prices made. Until these high prices are crossed or low prices broken, consider the trend up or down.

Many times when stocks make low in the early part of January, this low will not be broken until the following July or August, and sometimes not during the entire year. This same rule applies in bear markets or when the main trend is down. High prices made in the early part of January are often high for the entire year and are not crossed until after July or August. For example:

U. S. Steel on January 2, 1930, made a low at 166, which was the half-way point from 1921 to 1929, and again on January 7, 1930 declined to 167-1/4. When this level was broken, Steel indicated lower prices.

July 3rd to 7th and 20th to 27th:
The month of July, like January, is a month when most dividends are paid and investors usually buy stocks around the early part of the month. Watch these periods in July for tops or bottoms and the change in trend. Go back over the charts and see how many times changes have taken place in July, 180 days from January tops or bottoms. For example:

July 8, 1932 was low; July 17, 1933, high; and July 26, 1934 low of the market.

HOW TO DIVIDE THE YEARLY TIME PERIOD

Divide the year by 2 to get 1/2 or 6 months, which equals 26 weeks.

Divide the year by 4 to get the 3 months' period or 90 days, which is 1/4 of a year or 13 weeks.

Divide the year by 3 to get the 4 months' period, which is 1/3 of a year or 17-1/3 weeks.

Divide the year by 8, which gives 1-1/2 months or 45 days. This is also 6-1/2 weeks, which shows why the 7th week is always so important.

Divide the year by 16, which gives 22-1/2 days or approximately 3 weeks. This accounts for market movements that only run 3 weeks up or down and then reverse. As a general rule, when any stock closes higher the 4th consecutive week, it will go higher. The 5th week is also very important for a change in trend, and for fast moves up or down. The 5th is the day, week, month, or year of Ascension and always marks fast moves up or down, according to the major cycle that is running out.

IMPORTANT POINTS TO REMEMBER IN FORECASTING

TIME is the most important factor of all, and not until sufficient time has expired, does any big move up or down, start. The TIME factor will overbalance both Space and Volume. When TIME is up, space movement will start and big volume will begin, either up or down. At the end of any big movement – monthly, weekly, or daily – TIME, must be allowed for accumulation or distribution.

Never decide that the main trend has changed one way or the other without consulting the RESISTANCE LEVELS from top to bottom, and without considering the position of the market and CYCLE of each individual stock.

Always consider whether the main TIME limit, has run out or not before judging a reverse move. Do not fail to consider the indications on TIME, both from main tops and bottoms.

A DAILY chart gives the first short change, which may run for 7 to 10 days; the Weekly Chart gives the next important change in trend; and the Monthly the strongest. Remember, WEEKLY moves run 3 to 7 weeks, MONTHLY MOVES 2 to 3 months or more, according to the yearly cycle, before reversing.

YEARLY BOTTOMS AND TOPS: It is important to know whether a stock is making higher or lower bottoms each year. For instance, if a stock has made a higher bottom each year for 5 years, then makes a lower bottom than the previous year, it is a sign of reversal and may mark a long down cycle. The same rule applies when stocks are making lower tops for a number of years in a bear market.

When extreme advances or declines occur, the FIRST TIME the MARKET REVERSES over 1/4 to 1/2 of the distance covered in the previous movement, you consider that the trend has changed, at least temporarily.

It is important to watch SPACE movements. When TIME is running out one way or the other, space movements will show a reversal by breaking back over 1/4, 1/3 or 1/2 of the distance of the last move from extreme low to extreme high, which indicates that the main trend has changed.

STUDY all the INSTRUCTIONS AND RULES that I have given you; read them over several times, as each time they will become clearer to you. Study the charts and work out the rules in actual practice as well as on past performance. In this way, you will make progress and will realize and appreciate the value of my Method of Forecasting.

INDIVIDUAL STOCKS

You cannot depend upon the Dow-Jones 30 Industrial averages to forecast the trend of all stocks, altho most active leaders followed the trend of the averages. Individual stocks do not always make tops and bottoms at the same time that the averages make tops and bottoms, but most of them make tops and bottoms very close to the time that the averages reach culminations.

THE W.D. GANN MASTER STOCK MARKET COURSE

T-7

The averages give you the general trend, but some stocks move opposite to this trend. By keeping up a weekly high and low chart on individual stocks and also keeping up a daily high and low chart when the market is very active, you will be able to figure the individual trend and determine whether it is following the trend of the averages.

Consider each INDIVIDUAL STOCK and determine its trend from its position according to distance in TIME from bottom or top. Each stock works out its 1, 2, 3, 5, 7, and 10-year cycles from its own base or bottoms and tops, regardless of the movements of other stocks, even those in the same group. Therefore, it is always important to study each stock individually and apply all of the rules to determine its future course.

COMPARISON OF TIME CYCLES
1896-1939

Review of Dow-Jones 30 industrial averages:

1896 - August 8, extreme low.

1897 - A secondary low was recorded in April, 1897. We find that there was a fast advance in the 11th to 13th months from August, 1896 low.

1898 - A fast advance occurred in the 16th and 24th months from the bottoms of 1897 and 1896, and a fast declined in the 17th and 25th months.

1899 - A bull year. Fast advance occurred in the 29th to 32nd months from 1896 and in the 21st to 24th months from 1897 bottom. Fast declines occurred in the 32nd and 40th months from these bottoms.

1900 - Fast advance 42nd to 44th months from 1897 and 50th to 52nd months from 1896 bottom.

1901 - A fast declined on the 49th month from 1897 and 57th month from 1896 low. Top reached in June.

1903 - A bear year. 22nd to 28th month from 1901 top, a fast decline; also 72nd to 78th months, from 1897 bottom, and 80th to 86th month from 1896 bottom. Bottom reached in October and November, 1903.

1904 - Fast advance, 12 to 14 months from 1903 bottom.

1905 - Fast move up in the 16th to 18th months; fast decline in the 19th month, and a fast advance in the 25th to 27th months from 1903 bottom.

1906 - Top of campaign reached in January. Fast decline in the 30th month from 1903 bottom.

1907 - Fast decline in the 14th months from 1906 top and in the 19th to 22nd months. Extreme low reached in November, 1907, in the 135th month from 1896 bottom, 127 months from 1897 low, and 22 months from 1906 top.

THE W.D. GANN MASTER STOCK MARKET COURSE

T-8

1909 - Top of campaign reached in October, 45 months from 1906 top and 23 months from 1907 bottom, 158 months from 1896.

1914 - July, a fast decline in the 57th month from 1909 top, 21 months from 1912 top. Extreme low of campaign in December, 107 months from 1906 top, 26 months from 1912 top, 220 months from 1896 low, 84 months or 7 years from 1907 bottom, and 134 months from 1903 bottom.

1915 - This was a war year. March and April – Fast advance on the 3rd and 4th months from the 1914 bottom. May – A sharp, severe decline, 90 months from November, 1907 bottom and 225 months from 1896 bottom.

1916 - April – A sharp decline, 16 months from the 1914 bottom, 123 months from 1906 top, and 236 months from 1896 low. September – Fast advance, 21 months from 1914 low, and 240 months from 1896 low, the end of two 10-year cycles, indicating an important change in trend. In November – Top of a fast advance; Dow-Jones Industrial Averages at the highest price in history up to that time. This was 23 months from 1914 bottom and 243 months from 1896 bottom. December – A sharp decline, 24 months from 1914 bottom.

1917 - August to December – a fast decline, 9 to 13 months from November, 1916 top, 32 to 36 months from the 1914 bottom, 117 to 121 months from the 1907 bottom, and 252 to 256 months from 1896 low.

1919 - A fast advance started in February and lasted until July. This was 27 to 32 months from the 1916 top, and 50 to 55 months from the 1914 low. February, 1919 was 135 months from the 1907 low and 270 months from the 1896 bottom. October and early November – Final top, 36 months from 1916 top. November – A panicky decline, 23 months from 1917, low, 59 months from 1914 bottom (end of a 5-year cycle), and 279 months from 1896 bottom.

1920 - November and December – A fast decline, 12 to 13 months from 1919 top, 35 to 36 months from 1917 low, 72 months from 1914 bottom, 157 months from 1907 bottom, and 291 to 292 months from 1896 bottom.

1921 - August – Low of bear campaign, 21 months from 1919 top, 80 months from 1914 bottom, 165 months from 1907 bottom, and 300 months from 1896 bottom.

1924 - May – The last low was made, from which a fast advance started one of the greatest bull campaigns in history, ending in 1929. This was 54 months from the 1919 top, 33 months from 1921 low, 113 months from 1914 low, and 333 months from the 1896 low.

1926 - March – A big decline, with some stocks declining 100 points. This was 23 months from May, 1924 low, 29 months from 1923 low, 55 months from 1921 low, 135 months from 1914 low, and 355 months from 1896 low. August – Stocks reached the highest price up to that time, the Dow-Jones Industrial Averages selling at 166. This was 27 months from May, 1924 low, 34 months from October, 1923 low, 60 months from 1921 bottom, 225 months from 1907 low, and 360 months or 30 years from 1896 low. Then a 20-point decline followed to October.

1928 and 1929 were years of some of the fastest moves in history.

1929 - May to September – One of the fastest moves, advancing nearly 100 points on Averages. Final high in September.

        118 months from 1919 top,   71 months from October, 1923 low,
        240 months from 1909 top,   97 months from August, 1921 low,
        42 months from March, 1926 low,   177 months from 1914 low,
        64 months from May 1924 bottom,   262 months from 1907 low,

1930 - April – Last top before another big decline. This was 49 months from March, 1926 low, 71 months from 1924 low, and 78 months from the 1923 low. May – A sharp severe decline, which was 270 months from 1907. Then there were fast declines to in 1931.

1931 - September – a decline of 46 points on the Dow-Jones Averages. This was 24 months from the 1929 top, 95 and 86 months from 1923 and 1924 lows, 121 months or the beginning of a new 10-year cycle from 1921 low, 201 months from 1914 low.

1932 - July 8th – extreme low of the bear campaign was reached. This was 131 months from 1921 low, 105 and 96 months from 1923 and 1924 lows, 27 months from April, 1930 top, and 34 months from 1929 top. August and September – A sharp, fast advance in stocks. This was 35 and 36 months from the 1929 top; 28 and 29 months from April, 1930 top; and 132 to 133 months from 1921 low.

1933 - April to July – A fast advance. This was 43 to 46 months from 1929 top. Always watch for culminations around the 45th month and multiples of 45. It was also 36 to 39 months from the 1930 top, 9 to 12 months from 1932 low. October, 1933 – Low of reaction, 42 months from April, 1930 top; 49 months from 1929 top, and 15 months from 1932 low.

1934 - February – Top. This was 46 months from the 1930 high, 53 months from 1929 high; 12 months from 1933 low, 19 months from 1932 low, and most important of all, 90 months in the new 10-year cycle from August, 1926. From this top a sharp decline followed. July – This marked the last low before a big bull campaign started. This was 58 months from 1929 top, 51 months from 1930 top, 24 months from 1932 low. Going into the 9th year of this cycle, the market indicated a big bull campaign to follow in 1935, as explained before.

1935 - After the low of March 18, the market advanced during 1935 and 1936, just as it did in 1915 and 1916 and again in 1925 and 1926, working out the 10-year cycle.

1936 - April 6, high 163. In 1926, February 11, high 162-3/8. The averages were at almost the same high 10 years later. 1936, April 30 low 141-1/2; 1926, March 30 low 135-1/4, April 16 low 136-1/2 ... close to the same old prices and dates as 10 year previous.

1937 - March 8, final high 195-1/2, which was 90 months or 7-1/2 years from the high of September, 1929; and 7 years from the high of April 17, 1930; 56 months from July 8, 1932, low. Previous 10-year cycle ... 1917, March 20, high of rally; never went one point higher during the year.

    1937, June 17, low 163; 1927, June 27, low 165-3/4 ... almost at the same level 10 years later.

1937, August 14, high 190-1/4; 1917, August 6, last high before big decline; 1927, August 2, high 185-1/2, top for reaction.

1937, October 19, low 115-1/2; 1917, October 15, low; 1927, October 29, low of the reaction.

1937, November 23, low 112-1/2, low for the year; 1917, November 8, low; 1907, November 15, low of the panic.

Thus, 1937 was working out the 3rd 10-year cycle back to 1907 and the second 10-year cycle back to 1917.

1938 - March 31, low of panic, 97-1/2. Note, February 10, 1908, low; April 11, 1918, low; February 20, 1928, last low; February 27, 1933, low 49-1/2 ... 61 months back; March 21, 1933, last low 55, which was 5 years back; March 18, 1935, low 95-1/2, 3 years back; April 30, 1936, low 141-1/2, two years back. October 3, 1935, low 127, 30 months or 2-1/2 years back. Look back over your records and you'll find all of the years, running on even 10-year cycles, that is 1908, 1918, and 1928, were years of advancing prices and the advance started from a low in February or March.

1938, July 25, high 146-1/4; August 6, high 146-1/2. 1908, August 10, high. 1918, October 18, high; November 9, high. 1928, August 7, high; November 28, high.

1938, September 26-28, low 128. Note 1908, September 22 was last low.

1938, November 10, high 158 3/4.   Comparison:
    1923, October   27, low   15 years back
    1931, October   5, low   7 years back
    1933, October   21, low   5 years back
    1935, November 20, low   3 years back
    1936, November 18, high   2 years back
    1937, November 23, low   1 year back

1939 - January 3-4, high 155-1/2. 1909, January 3-4, high; 1919, January 4, high; 1929, January 2, high for reaction.

1939, April 11, low 120; 1909, February 23, low; 1919, February 8, low; 1929, March 30, last low. In all of these years an advanced or Bull Market followed.

1939, May 10, high 134-5/8; May 17, low 128-3/8, was the last low; June 9, high 140-3/4; June 30, last low 128-7/8; July 25, high 145-3/4.

In order to determine how 1939 will run for the balance of the year, we will make the following comparison:
    1909, October 2 and November 19, high.
    1919, August 14 and November 3, high.
    1929, September 3, extreme high ... 10 years back.
    1932, September 8, high ... 7 years back;
        also November 12, is second high in 1932.
    1934, October 11 and 17 and December 5, high ... 5 years back.
    1936, November 18, high ... 3 years back.
    1937, August 14, last high ... 2 years back.
    1938, July 25, high. August 6, high. November 10, high of
        the year and 158-3/4 ... 1 year back.

The above dates are the ones to watch for important changes in trend and for tops and bottoms during the rest of 1939. 10 years will be up on September 3; also September 8 will be seven years from the top in 1932. Therefore, should the averages start advancing after September 3 or 8, watch for top in October or November, according to past cycles.

At this writing, August 3, 1939, the Dow-Jones 30 Industrial averages have again advanced to around the half-way point from 97-1/2 to 195-1/2, and when they can get above this half-way point and close above it and hold, they will indicate higher prices.

1940 - First 10-year cycle is 1930.   April 17, 1930, high.
        1920, April 8, high.   1910, April 16, last high.
        1935, March 18, low.   1933, February 27, low; July 17, high.
        1937, March 8, high.   1938, March 31, low. 1939, April 11, low.

Therefore, March and April, 1940, will be very important for change in trend, and if the market advances up to that time and makes top, the trend should turn down and work like 1910, 1920, and 1930.

It is always important to consider the Resistance Levels and the position on the weekly high and low chart at the time these important time periods are running out. Then you will be able to detect the first minor change in trend, which may later become a change in the main trend.

Go over individual stocks and work out their cycles in the same way. Look up the months when extreme highs and lows have been made and note the months from each bottom and top in fast advances and declines have taken place. By keeping up the time periods from important tops and bottoms, you will know when important time periods are running out and when a change in trend is likely to take place. Also watch the quarterly changes in trend around March to April, June to July, September to October, and November to December.

All of this will help you to pick the stocks that are going to have the greatest advances and the ones that are going to have the greatest declines. The more you work and study, the more you will learn and the greater profits you will make.

CHANGES IN TREND AROUND HOLIDAYS

If you will go back over your charts for many years, you will find that changes in trend often occur just before or just after holidays. The following dates are important to watch for changes:

> January 2 to 4, January 7 or the first week's range at the beginning of the year.
> February 12 and 22.
> March or April - around Easter.
> May 30
> July 4
> September - Labor Day and Jewish holidays.
> October 12.
> November 2 to 8 - around Election.
> November 26 [to] 30 - around Thanksgiving
> December 21 to 27 - during Christmas holiday week

T-12

HOW TO TRADE

After you have thoroughly mastered all of the lessons, be sure you are right before you make a trade. Never guess. Trade on mathematical indications only.

WHAT YOU MUST KNOW BEFORE YOU START TRADING

You must know exactly how to apply all the rules. You must know where to place a stop loss order and must look up what cycle the year is in, that is, whether it is a bull or bear year, whether the main trend should be up or down.

Before you make a trade, either buying or selling, consider the position of each individual stock on the monthly chart; next consider the weekly chart and then the daily chart. If they all confirm an uptrend, it is a cinch to buy, provided you have located the point at which to place a stop loss order. On the other hand, if the cycle shows that it is a bear year and the monthly, weekly and daily chart show down trend, then it is the time to go short, but again, you must look for the most important point ... where to place the stop loss order so that it will not be more than 3 points away and closer if possible.

WHAT TO LOOK UP BEFORE YOU MAKE TRADE

Following are the most important points that you must consider before buying or selling a stock:

1. TIME CYCLE ... whether Bull or Bear year, and whether main trend of the general market is up or down.

2. CYCLE OF INDIVIDUAL STOCK ... whether up or down year.

3. MONTHLY position on TIME PERIODS from tops and bottoms.

4. WEEKLY position on TIME PERIODS from tops and bottoms.

5. RESISTANCE LEVELS ... see whether the stock is near any half-way point or other points of support or resistance.

6. Study all FORMATIONS. If a stock has held for several days, weeks or months around the same level, determine whether it is about ready to cross tops or break bottoms.

7. Look up VOLUME OF SALES. See whether a stock has increased or decreased Volume over past few days or weeks.

8. Look up SPACE or price movements from previous tops and bottoms and find out the greatest advance or decline for past few weeks or months. Example: If a stock has reacted 5 points several times and at the time you look it up, if you find it is 3 points down from the last top and the trend is up on monthly, weekly and daily with the price near a support point, you could buy with a stop loss order 2 to 3 points away. If the stock should break back over 5 points, the previous reaction limit, it would show a change in trend and you should go short of it.

T-13

9. Never overlook the fact that you must have a definite indication before making a trade.

10. Most important of all ... always locate the point at which to place a stop loss order to limit risk.

PRACTICE TRADING ON PAPER

After you feel sure that you have mastered all the rules and know exactly how to determine the trend of a stock and the place to begin trading, then to make yourself doubly sure and establish confidence, practice trading on paper and till you thoroughly understand how to use the rules and when to use them. If you make mistakes trading on paper, then you would make mistakes at the time in actual trading and you are not ready to begin trading. When you feel that you are competent to start trading, apply all of the rules and TRADE ONLY ON DEFINITE INDICATIONS. If you are not sure of the trend or the buying and selling price and not sure where to place a stop loss order, then wait until you get a definite indication. You can always make money by waiting for opportunities. There is no use getting in partly on guesswork and losing.

WHEN TO CLOSE A TRADE

After you start actual trading, when you make a trade, don't close it or take profits until you have a definite indication, according to the rules that it is time to sell out or buy in or to move up the stop loss order and wait until it is caught. The way to make a success is to always follow the trend and not get out or close a trade until the trend changes.

WHEN TO WAIT AND NOT TRADE

It is just as important to know when not to enter the market as it is to know when to enter it. The time not to make a trade is when you find a stock has been holding in a narrow trading range for some time, say, a 5-point or a 3-point range, but has not broken under bottoms previously made or crossed tops previously made. A stock may stay for weeks or months or even years in a trading range and will not indicate any big move or change in trend until it crosses as a previous top or breaks a previous bottom. After a prolonged decline stocks nearly always narrow down and hold in a trading range for some time. If a stock is inactive in this position, it is no time to start trading in it.

FOLLOW ALL RULES

Remember, follow all rules; check and double check; study the major and minor cycles for forecasting; watch closely the Resistance Levels; study the different Formations and bottoms and tops and between bottoms and tops. If you ignore one important point, it may get you in wrong. The whole can never exceed all its parts and all the parts make up the whole. If you leave out one of the rules, you will not have a complete forecasting method or trend indicator.

Your success with the method depends upon you doing your part, studying and learning how to apply the rules and not mixing any inside or outside information or reasoning against the mathematical indications. No man ever made a success at anything who did not work hard. I have done my part, and it is now up to you to do yours.

[W.D. Gann's signature]

August 3, 1939

Chapter 10B

How to Forecast

F-1

HOW TO FORECAST

By studying the Tables and records given of past cycles and the time from tops to bottoms and from main bottom to main bottom and the time from main top to main top, you will be able to make up the forecast one year or more in advance. Then, by watching your weekly high and low chart and applying all of the other rules, you can tell when the main trend is changing.

After a bottom or top is made or at the beginning of any calendar year, you should go back over 3, 5, 7 and 10-year periods to see if the market is repeating and which one of these periods is running closest to.

12, 20, AND 30 INDUSTRIAL AVERAGES
FROM MAIN TOPS TO MAIN TOPS OF BULL CAMPAIGNS

Year		Low	Time	From
1892 Mar. 4 and				
Apr. 18		94½		
1895 Sep. 4		84½	42 months	Mar. 4, 1892
1899 Apr. 25		77.28	43 months 21 days	Sep. 4, 1895
Sep. 5		77.61	48 months	Sep. 4, 1893
1901 Jun. 17		78.26	21 months 12 days	Sep. 5, 1899
1906 Jan. 19		103.	53 months	Jun. 17, 1901
1907 Jan. 7		96.37	11 months 19 days	Jan. 19, 1906
1909 Oct. 2		100.50		
Nov. 19		100.53	46 months	Jan. 19, 1906
1912 Sep. 30		94.15	36 months	Oct. 2, 1909
1916 Nov. 21		110.15	49 months 22 days	Sep. 30, 1912
1919 Nov. 3		119.62	35 months 14 days	Nov. 21, 1916
1923 Mar. 20		105.38	40 months 17 days	Nov. 3, 1919
1929 Sep. 3		386.10	77 months 14 days	Mar. 20, 1923
1933 Jul. 17		110.50	46 months 14 days	Sep. 3, 1929
1934 Feb. 5		111.50	53 months 2 days	Sep. 3, 1929
1937 Mar. 8		195.50	37 months 3 days	Feb. 5, 1934
			43 months 19 days	Jul. 17, 1933
1938 Nov. 10		158.75	20 months 2 days	

It is important to study the TIME PERIODS between each important top and the next top.

During the period from 1892 to 1898 the time periods between the tops were as follows: There were 2 at 53 months apart; 7 at 42 to 49 months apart; 4 and 35 to 40 months apart; 2 at 20 to 21 months apart; and 1 at 11 months, 19 days.

One of the greatest Bull Markets of all time ... March 20, 1923 to September 3, 1929 ... was 77 months. This was abnormal, unusual, and an extreme, but it is well to know this time period because you may need to use it in the future.

From the above, you can see that most campaigns make tops between 3 and 4 years or between 35 and 49 months, only 2 cases running in extreme of 53 months and 2 running out in 20 to 21 months and 1 in the little less than a year.

THE W.D. GANN MASTER STOCK MARKET COURSE

F-2

FROM MAIN BOTTOMS TO MAIN BOTTOMS OF BEAR CAMPAIGNS

Year	Low	Time	From
1893 Jul. 26	62½		
1896 Aug. 8	28½	34 months 13 days	Jul. 26, 1893
1900 Jun. 23	53	46 months 15 days	Aug. 8, 1896
Sep. 23	53	49 months 15 days	Aug. 8, 1896
1903 Nov. 9	42-1/8	40 months 17 days	Jun. 23, 1900
		37 months 16 days	Sep. 23, 1900
1907 Nov. 15	53	48 months 6 days	Nov. 9, 1903
1910 Jul. 26	73-5/8	32 months 11 days	Nov. 15, 1907
1911 Sep. 25	73-5/8	46 months 10 days	Jul. 26, 1910
1914 Dec. 24	53-1/8	39 months	Jul. 26, 1910
		48 months 28 days	Sep. 25, 1911
1917 Dec. 19	66	36 months	Dec. 24, 1914
1921 Aug. 24	64	44 months 5 days	Dec. 19, 1917
1923 Oct. 27	85¾	26 months 2 days	Aug. 24, 1921
1924 May 20	88-3/8	33 months	Aug. 24, 1921
1932 Jul. 8	40½	104 months 11 days	Oct. 27, 1923
		97 months 18 days	May 20, 1924
1933 Oct. 21	82½	15 months 13 days	Jul. 8, 1932
1934 Jul. 26	85	24 months 18 days	Jul. 8, 1932
1938 Mar. 31	97½	44 months 5 days	Jul. 8, 1932

The market always moves down in a shorter period of time than it moves up. It is important to study the distance between main bottoms in order to tell when the next one should come out.

There was only one period 49 months, 15 days apart; 6 at 44 to 48 months apart; 1 at 40 months; 6 at 32 to 39 months; 1 at 26 months; 1 at 24 months; and 1 at 15 months. Thus you will see that more bottoms came out 3 to 4 years apart than any other time period.

The greatest time period was from the bottom of October 27, 1923 to the bottom of July 8, 1932 ... 104 months, 11 days. The next period was from the last bottom, May 20, 1924, to July 8, 1932 ... 97 months, 18 days. These great extremes occur at very rare intervals, but unless you know the greatest as well as the least movement, you cannot do accurate forecasting.

DOW-JONES 20 RAILROAD AVERAGES
FROM MAIN BOTTOMS TO MAIN BOTTOMS OF BEAR CAMPAIGNS

Year	Low	Time	From
1890 Dec.	76½		
1893 Jul. 26	62	34 months	Dec. 1890
1896 Aug. 8	42	35 months 18 days	Jul. 26, 1893
1900 Jun. 23	73	46 months 15 days	Aug. 8, 1896
1903 Oct. 27	89-3/8	40 months 4 days	Jun. 23, 1900
1907 Nov. 23	81-3/8	48 months 27 days	Oct. 27, 1903
1910 Jul. 26	105-5/8	32 months 3 days	Nov. 23, 1907
1911 Sep. 30	109-5/8	14 months 4 days	Jul. 26, 1910
1914 Dec. 24	87½	38 months 24 days	Sep. 30, 1911
1917 Dec. 19	70¾	36 months	Dec. 24, 1914

The greatest time period between main bottoms was 48 months, 27 days; next 46 months, 15 days; next 40 months, 4 days; next 38 months, 24 days. There were 4 at 32 to 36 months apart and one minor at 14 months apart. Again, you'll see that these important bottoms came at the end of 3 and 4-year periods.

FROM MAIN TOPS TO MAIN TOPS OF BULL CAMPAIGNS

Year	Low	Time	From
1886 Dec.	94 ½		
1890 May	99	41 months	Dec. 1886
1891 Apr.	89	11 months	May 1890
1892 Mar.	94	22 months	May 1890
1895 Sep. 4	92 ½	41 months	Mar. 1892
1899 Apr. 25	87	43 months 21 days	Sep. 4, 1895
1902 Sep. 9	129.36	40 months 15 days	Apr. 25, 1899
1906 Jan. 19	138.29	40 months 10 days	Sep. 9, 1902
1906 Sep. 17	137.4	9 months	Jan. 19, 1906
1906 Dec. 11	137.56	51 months	Sep. 9, 1902
1909 Aug. 14	134.46	42 months 26 days	Jan. 19, 1906
1912 Aug. 14	124.16	36 months	Aug. 14, 1909
1912 Oct. 5	124.35	37 months 21 days	Aug. 14, 1912
1916 Oct. 4	112.28	48 months	Oct. 5, 1912
1918 Nov. 9	92.91	25 months 5 days	Oct. 4, 1916
1919 May 26	91.13	31 months 2 days	Oct. 4, 1916

There was one period between tops 51 months; one at 48 months apart; 6 at 40 to 43 months apart; 2 at 36 to 37 months apart; 1 at 31 months apart; 2 at 22 to 25 months apart; 1 at 11 months and 1 at 9 months apart. This again proves that most of the tops came out around 3 to 3-1/2 years apart, and in extremes around 4 years apart. A few of them came out around 2-year periods and only 2 at less than one year, again confirming the working out of the 10-year cycle.

DOW-JONES 30 INDUSTRIAL AVERAGES
TIME FROM MAJOR AND MINOR TOPS TO MAJOR AND MINOR TOPS

High		Time	From
1895 Sep. 4		40 months 17 days	Apr. 18, 1892
1896 Apr. 22		7 months 17 days	Sep. 4, 1895
1899 Sep. 5		40 months 14 days	Apr. 22, 1896
1901 Jun. 17		21 months 12 days	Sep. 5, 1899
1906 Jan. 19		55 months	Jun. 17, 1901
1907 Jan. 7	Minor top	11 months 19 days	Jan. 19, 1906
1909 Oct. 2		44 months 12 days	Jan. 19, 1906
Nov. 19		46 months	Jan. 19, 1906
Dec. 22		47 months 3 days	Jan. 19, 1906
1912 Sep. 30		36 months	Oct. 2, 1909
1915 Dec. 27		38 months 27 days	Sep. 30, 1912
1916 Nov. 21		84 months 2 days	Nov. 19, 1909
1917 Jun. 9	Last high	6 months 15 days	Nov. 21, 1916
1919 Jul. 14	Minor top	25 months 5 days	Jun. 9, 1917
Nov. 3		35 months 13 days	Nov. 21, 1916
1920 Apr. 8	Second top	5 months 5 days	Nov. 3, 1919
1922 Oct. 14	Minor top	35 months 11 days	Nov. 3, 1919
1923 Mar. 20		40 months 17 days	Nov. 3, 1919
Mar. 20		5 months 6 days	Oct. 14, 1922
1924 Feb. 6	Minor top	10 months 17 days	Mar. 20, 1923
Feb. 6		15 months 23 days	Oct. 14, 1922
1925 Nov. 6		21 months	Feb. 6, 1924
1926 Feb. 11			Feb. 6, 1925
Feb. 11		34 months 22 days	Mar. 20, 1923
Aug. 14		40 months 24 days	Mar. 20, 1923
Aug. 14		81 months 11 days	Nov. 3, 1919
Aug. 14		76 months 6 days	Apr. 8, 1920
1927 Oct. 3	Minor top	13 months 19 days	Aug. 14, 1926
Oct. 3		22 months 27 days	Nov. 6, 1925
1928 May 14		62 months	Mar. 20, 1923
May 14		27 months 3 days	Feb. 11, 1926
Nov. 28	Minor top	27 months 14 days	Aug. 14, 1926
1929 Feb. 5		29 months 22 days	Aug. 14, 1926
Feb. 5		36 months	Feb. 11, 1926
May 4		12 months	May 14, 1928
May 4		39 months	Feb. 11, 1926
Sep. 3	Final top	118 months	Nov. 3, 1919
Sep. 3		82 months 20 days	Oct. 14, 1922
Sep. 3		77 months 14 days	Mar. 20, 1923
Sep. 3		36 months 24 days	Feb. 11, 1926
Sep. 3		9 months 6 days	Nov. 28, 1928
Sep. 3		6 months 29 days	Feb. 5, 1929
Sep. 3		4 months	May 4, 1929
Sep. 3		1 month	Aug. 3, 1929

TIME FROM MAJOR AND MINOR TOPS TO MAJOR AND MINOR TOPS

Date		Note	Duration	From
1930	Apr. 17	Secondary top	7 months 14 days	Sep. 3, 1929
	Sep. 10	Top of rally	4 months 24 days	Apr. 17, 1930
1931	Feb. 24		29 months 21 days	Sep. 3, 1929
	Feb. 24		10 months 7 days	Apr. 17, 1930
	Feb. 24		5 months 14 days	Sep. 10, 1930
1931	Jun. 27		21 months 24 days	Sep. 3, 1929
	Jun. 27		14 months 10 days	Apr. 17, 1930
	Jun. 27		4 months 3 days	Jul. 23, 1931
	Nov. 9	Minor top	26 months 6 days	Sep. 3, 1929
	Nov. 9		18 months 23 days	Apr. 17, 1930
	Nov. 9		8 months 16 days	Feb. 24, 1931
	Nov. 9		4 months 13 days	Jun. 27, 1931
1932	Mar. 8		30 months	Sep. 3, 1929
	Mar. 8		22 months 20 days	Apr. 17, 1930
	Feb. 19		24 months	Feb. 24, 1931
	Mar. 8		4 months	Nov. 9, 1931
	Sep. 8		36 months 5 days	Sep. 3, 1929
	Sep. 8		28 months 22 days	Apr. 17, 1930
	Sep. 8		24 months 2 days	Sep. 10, 1930
	Sep. 8		18 months 15 days	Feb. 24, 1931
	Sep. 8		14 months 12 days	Jun. 27, 1931
	Sep. 8		10 months 1 day	Nov. 9, 1931
	Sep. 8		6 months	Mar. 8, 1932
1933	Jul. 17		10 months 9 days	Sep. 8, 1932
	Sep. 18	Lower top	12 months 10 days	Sep. 8, 1932
	Sep. 18		2 months	Jul. 17, 1933
1934	Feb. 5		17 months	Sep. 8, 1932
	Feb. 5		6 months 19 days	Jul. 17, 1933
	Feb. 15		5 months	Sep. 18, 1933
1935	Feb. 18		19 months 1 day	Jul. 17, 1933
	Feb. 18		12 months 1 day	Feb. 5, 1934
1936	Apr. 6	Minor top	13 months 19 days	Feb. 18, 1935
1937	Mar. 8		90 months 5 days	Sep. 3, 1929
	Mar. 8		82 months 19 days	Apr. 17, 1930
	Mar. 8		78 months	Sep. 10, 1930
	Mar. 8		72 months 12 days	Feb. 24, 1931
	Mar. 8		54 months	Sep. 8, 1932
	Mar. 8		43 months 19 days	Jul. 17, 1933
	Mar. 8		37 months 3 days	Feb. 5, 1934
	Mar. 8		11 months	Apr. 6, 1936
	Aug. 14	Secondary top	49 months	Jul. 17, 1933
	Aug. 14		42 months	Feb. 15, 1934
	Oct. 29		7 months 21 days	Mar. 8, 1937
	Oct. 29		2 months 15 days	Aug. 14, 1937
1938	Jan. 15	Minor top	10 months 7 days	Mar. 8, 1937
	Jan. 15		5 months 1 day	Aug. 14, 1937
	Jul. 25		16 months 17 days	Mar. 8, 1937
	Jul. 25		11 months 11 days	Aug. 14, 1937
	Nov. 10		20 months 2 days	Mar. 8, 1937
	Nov. 10		10 months 5 days	Mar. 8, 1937

DOW-JONES 30 INDUSTRIAL AVERAGES

BULL CAMPAIGNS – MAIN BOTTOMS TO MAIN TOPS
BEAR CAMPAIGNS – MAIN TOPS TO MAIN BOTTOMS

				Time
1893 Jul. 26 low 62½	to	1895 Sep. 4 high 82½	25 months 9 days
1895 Sep. 4 high 82½	to	1896 Aug. 8 low 28½	11 months 4 days
1896 Aug. 8 low 28½	to	1899 Apr. 25 high 77.28	32 months 17 days
1896 Aug. 8 low 28½	to	1899 Sep. 5 high 77.61	36 months 20 days
1899 Apr. 25 high 77.28	to	1900 Jun. 23 low 53.63	14 months
1899 Sep. 5 high 77.61	to	1900 Sep. 24 low 52.96	12 months 19 days
1900 Jun. 23 low 53.63	to	1901 Jun. 17 high 78.26	12 months
1900 Sep. 24 low 52.96	to	9001 Jun. 17 high 78.26	8 months 24 days
1901 Jun. 17 high 78.26	to	1903 Nov. 9 low 42.15	28 months 23 days
1903 Nov. 9 low 42.15	to	1906 Jan. 19 high 103	26 months 10 days
1906 Jan. 19 high 103	to	1907 Nov. 15 low 53	21 months 27 days
1907 Nov. 15 low 53	to	1909 Oct. 2 high 100.50	22 months 17 days
1907 Nov. 15 low 53	to	1909 Nov. 19 high 100.53	24 months 4 days
1909 Nov. 19 high 100.53	to	1910 Jul. 26 low 73-5/8	8 months 7 days
1909 Nov. 19 high 100.53	to	1911 Sep. 25 low 73	22 months 6 days
1909 Oct. 2 high 100.50	to	1911 Sep. 25 low 73	23 months 23 days
1910 Jul. 26 low 73-5/8	to	1912 Sep. 30 high 94-1/8	26 months 4 days
1912 Sep. 30 high 94-1/8	to	1914 Dec. 24 low 53-1/8	26 months 24 days
1914 Dec. 24 low 53-1/8	to	1916 Nov. 21 high 110-1/8	23 months
1916 Nov. 21 high 110-1/8	to	1917 Dec. 19 low 66	13 months
1917 Dec. 19 low 66	to	1919 Nov. 3 high 119-5/8	22 months 14 days
1919 Nov. 3 high 119-5/8	to	1921 Aug. 24 low 64	21 months 21 days
1921 Aug. 24 low 64	to	1923 Mar. 20 high 105-3/8	18 months 24 days
1923 Mar. 20 high 105-3/8	to	1923 Oct. 27 low 85¾	7 months 3 days
1923 Mar. 20 high 105-3/8	to	1924 May 20 low 88-3/8	14 months
1923 Oct. 27 low 85¾	to	1929 Sep. 3 high 386.10	70 months 7 days
1924 May 20 low 88-3/8	to	1929 Sep. 3 high 386.10	63 months 14 days
1929 Sep. 3 high 386.10	to	1932 Jul. 8 low 40½	34 months 5 days
1932 Jul. 8 low 40½	to	1937 Mar. 8 high 195½	56 months
1937 Mar. 7 high 195½	to	1938 Mar. 31 low 97½	12 months 23 days

BULL CAMPAIGNS FROM BOTTOMS TO TOPS 1892-1939

There was one campaign 56 months apart; one at 36 months apart; one at 32 months apart; 4 at 24 to 28 months apart; 3 at 21 to 23 months apart; 1 at 18 months apart, 2 at 8 to 12 months apart. The greatest campaign ran from Oct. 27, 1923 to Sep. 3, 1929 ... 70 months, 7 days. Next from the last bottom, May 20, 1924, to Sep. 3, 1929 ... 63 months, 14 days.

From the above, you'll see that, except for the extreme move up to 1929, there was only one other period that ran above 4 years. The greater number of periods lasted between 2 years and 2 years, 4 months, only two periods running out in less than one year and one running out in 1-1/2 years, again proving the working out of the 1, 2, 3, 4 and 5-year periods in the 10-year cycle.

BEAR CAMPAIGNS FROM TOPS TO BOTTOMS

A Bear Market always runs out the same number of points or more in a much shorter period of time than a Bull Market. Like everything else that is going downhill, gravity helps to pull it down faster and momentum is gained faster on the downside than on the upside.

The greatest Bear Market of all time lasted from Sep. 3, 1929 to Jul. 8, 1932 ... a period of 34 months, 5 days ... a decline of 345-1/2 points, the greatest in history. The next periods were 2 campaigns of 26 and 28 months; 4 at 21 to 23 months; 6 at 11 to 14 months; 3 at 7 to 8 months. Thus, you will see that the greatest Bear Campaign ran out and less than 3 years, and only 2 ran a little over 2 years, and 4 ran slightly under 2 years and 6 ran 11 to 14 months, about one-year periods, and 3 minor ones at 7 to 8 months apart.

This will help you to figure, after a market starts down in a Bear Campaign, how long it should run and by using your other tops and bottoms and time periods, you can tell about when it should run out. Before deciding that a Bear Market has made a final bottom, apply all of the rules and wait for a definite change in trend to the upside before deciding that final bottom has been reached.

DOW-JONES 30 INDUSTRIAL AVERAGES
BULL AND BEAR CAMPAIGNS
FROM TOP TO BOTTOM AND BOTTOM TO TOP

Year	Low or High		Points Up or down	Period of Time	
1892 Mar. 4 and Apr. 18 high 94½					
1893 Jul. 26	low	62½	32	16 months	22 days
1895 Sep. 4	high	82½	20	23 months	9 days
1896 Aug. 8	low	28½	54	11 months	4 days
1897 Sep. 10	high	55-7/8	27-3/8	13 months	2 days
1898 Mar. 23	low	42	17-7/8	6 months	15 days
1899 Sep. 5	high	77-5/8	35-7/8	17 months	11 days
1900 Sep. 24	low	53	24-5/8	12 months	19 days
1901 Jun. 17	high	78¼	25¼	8 months	24 days
1903 Nov. 9	low	42-1/8	36-1/8	28 months	23 days
1906 Jan. 19	high	103	61	26 months	22 days
1907 Nov. 15	low	53	50	21 months	27 days
1909 Nov. 19	high	100½	47½	24 months	4 days
1910 Jul. 26	low	73-5/8	26-7/8	8 months	7 days
1911 Jun. 19	high	87	13-3/8	10 months	24 days
Sep. 25	low	73	14	3 months	6 days
1912 Sep. 30	high	94-1/8	21-1/8	12 months	5 days
1913 Jun. 11	low	72-1/8	22	8 months	12 days
1914 Mar. 30	high	83½	11-3/8	9 months	9 days
Dec. 24	low	53-1/8	30-3/8	9 months	2 days
1912 Sep. 30 to	high	94-1/8			
1914 Dec. 24	low	53-1/8	41	26 months	25 days
1916 Nov. 21	high	110-1/8	67	23 months	
1917 Dec. 19	low	66	44-1/8	12 months	28 days
1919 Nov. 3	high	119-5/8	53-5/8	22 months	14 days
1921 Aug. 24	low	64	55-5/8	21 months	21 days
1923 Mar. 20	high	105-3/8	41-3/8	30 months	24 days
Oct. 27	low	85¾	19-5/8	7 months	3 days
1924 Feb. 6	high	101¼	15½	3 months	10 days
May 20	low	88-3/8	12-7/8	3 months	14 days
1929 Feb. 5	high	322	233-5/8	56 months	15 days
Feb. 16	low	295-7/8	26-1/8		11 days
Mar. 1	high	321-1/8	25¼		13 days
Mar. 26	low	296½	24-1/8		25 days
May 4	high	327	30½		39 days
May 27	low	290	37		23 days
Sep. 3	high	386	96		69 days
Oct. 29	low	230	156		56 days
Oct. 31	high	273½	43½		2 days
Nov. 13	low	195-3/8	78-1/8		13 days

THE W.D. GANN MASTER STOCK MARKET COURSE

F-9

INDUSTRIAL AVERAGES – FROM TOP TO BOTTOM AND BOTTOM TO TOP (Continued)

Year	Low or High	Points Up or down	Period of Time	
1924 May 20 to	low 88-3/8			
1929 Sep. 3	high 386	297-5/8	63 months	13 days
1929 Sep. 3 to	high 386			
Nov. 13	low 195-3/8	190-5/8		71 days
1930 Apr. 17	high 296½	101-3/8	5 months	4 days
Dec. 29	low 158½	138	8 months	12 days
1931 Feb. 24	high 196¾	38¼		57 days
Jun. 2	low 120	76¾		98 days
Jun. 27	high 157½	37½		25 days
Oct. 5	low 85½	72		100 days
Nov. 9	high 119½	34		35 days
1932 Jan. 5	low 70	49½		57 days
Mar. 8	high 89½	19½		63 days
Jul. 8	low 40½	49		122 days
1929 Sep. 3 to	high 386			
Jul. 8	low 40½	345½	34 months	5 days
1932 Sep. 8	high 81½	41		62 days
1933 Feb. 27	low 49½	32	5 months	19 days
Jul. 17	high 110½	61	4 months	20 days
Oct. 21	low 82½	28	3 months	4 days
1934 Feb. 5	high 111½	29	3 months	15 days
Jul. 26	low 85	26½	5 months	21 days
1936 Apr. 6	high 163	77	20 months	11 days
Apr. 30	low 141½	21½		24 days
1937 Mar. 8	high 195½	54	10 months	8 days
1932 Jul. 8 to	low 40½			
1937 Mar. 8	high 195½	155	56 months	
1934 Jul. 26 to	low 85			
1937 Mar. 8	high 195½	110½	31 months	10 days
1937 Jun. 17	low 163	32½		71 days
Aug. 14	high 190½	27½		58 days
1938 Mar. 31	low 97½	98	12 months	23 days
Nov. 10	high 158¾	61¼	7 months	10 days
1939 Apr. 11	low 120.07	38-5/8	5 months	1 day
1937 Aug. 14	high 190½			
1938 May 27	low 106½	84	8 months	13 days
1937 Aug. 14	high 190½			
1939 Apr. 11	low 120.07	70-3/8	20 months	

Page 301

INDUSTRIAL AVERAGES – FROM TOP TO BOTTOM AND BOTTOM TO TOP (Continued)

Year	Low or High	Points Up or down	Period of Time
1939 May 10	low 134.66	14.59	29 days
May 17	low 128.35	6.31	7 days
Jun. 9	high 140.75	12.40	23 days
Jun. 30	low 128.90	11.85	21 days

MINOR TIME PERIODS 1892-1939

The above Table gives the number of points up or down and the time periods for major moves and minor moves of less than a year. There were 7 minor moves covering 8 to 9 months; 6 moves of 4 to 6 months; 2 moves of 7 months; and 5 moves of 3 months. This will show that you can watch for changes in trend around 3 months and then again around 4 to 6 months; a few changes around the 7th month and a greater number around 8 to 9 months. Many fast Bull Markets and Bear Markets have run out in 8 to 9 months once they got away from the Breakaway Point.

MINOR MOVES OF 17 TO 36 days

These periods are runs that last over 2 weeks and culminate at the end of about 5 weeks. From 1896 to 1939, or in a period of 42 years, 10 months, 24 days, there were 204 moves on the averages running from 18 to 36 days. These were moves either up or down. This would mean that on an average every 2-1/2 months there was a reaction or rally lasting 18 to 36 days. Therefore, based on the average, when a market has advanced 3 to 4 months, with only 10 to 15-day reactions, you could expect a reverse move that would run possibly 36 days or more.

For 1929, 1930, 1931 and 1939, when the market was very active, we have shown the minor moves of 7 days or more, and the number of points advanced or declined to help you check how far an active market will move in these shorter time periods.

F-11

DOW-JONES 30 INDUSTRIAL AVERAGES
FROM MAJOR AND MINOR BOTTOMS TO MAJOR AND MINOR BOTTOMS

Low		Time	From
1896 Aug. 8	low 28½		
1898 Mar. 25		19 months 17 days	Aug. 8, 1896
1899 Dec. 18		40 months 10 days	Aug. 8, 1896
Dec. 18		20 months 23 days	Mar. 25, 1898
1900 Jun. 23		46 months 15 days	Aug. 8, 1896
Sep. 24		49 months 16 days	Aug. 8, 1896
Jun. 23		6 months 5 days	Dec. 18, 1899
1901 Dec. 12		24 months	Dec. 18, 1899
Dec. 12		64 months 4 days	Aug. 8, 1896
Dec. 12		44 months 17 days	Mar. 25, 1898
1902 Dec. 15		12 months	Dec. 12, 1901
1903 Nov. 9		87 months 1 day	Aug. 8, 1896
Nov. 9		67 months 14 days	Mar. 25, 1898
Nov. 9		37 months 16 days	Sep. 24, 1900
1904 Mar. 12		4 months 3 days	Nov. 9, 1903
May 18		18 months 9 days	Nov. 9, 1903
1905 May 22		12 months 4 days	May 18, 1904
May 22		18 months 13 days	Nov. 9, 1903
1906 May 3		30 months	Nov. 9, 1903
Jul. 13		32 months 4 days	Nov. 9, 1903
1907 Mar. 14	and 25	40 months 5 days	Nov. 9, 1903
Mar. 14		34 months	May 18, 1904
Nov. 15	final low	48 months 6 days	Nov. 9, 1903
Nov. 15		42 months	May 18, 1904
Nov. 15		135 months 7 days	Aug. 8, 1896
Nov. 15		115 months 21 days	Mar. 25, 1898
1908 Sep. 22	low of reaction	10 months 7 days	Nov. 15, 1907
1909 Feb. 23		15 months 8 days	Nov. 15, 1907
Feb. 23		5 months	Sep. 22, 1908
1910 Feb. 8		11 months 16 days	Feb. 23, 1909
Feb. 8		16 months 7 days	Sep. 22, 1908
Feb. 8		26 months 24 days	Nov. 15, 1907
Jul. 26		5 months 18 days	Feb. 8, 1910
Jul. 26		32 months 11 days	Nov. 15, 1907
1911 Sep. 25		46 months 10 days	Nov. 15, 1907
Sep. 25		36 months 3 days	Sep. 22, 1908
Sep. 25		14 months	Jul. 26, 1910
1913 Jun. 11		20 months 15 days	Sep. 25, 1911
Jun. 11		34 months 15 days	Jul. 26, 1910
1914 Dec. 24		85 months 9 days	Nov. 15, 1907
Dec. 24		53 months	Jul. 26, 1910
Dec. 24		18 months 13 days	Jun. 11, 1913
Dec. 24		133 months 15 days	Nov. 9, 1903
Dec. 24		127 months 6 days	May 18, 1904
1916 Apr. 22		16 months	Dec. 24, 1914
Jul. 13		18 months 19 days	Dec. 24, 1914

FROM MAJOR AND MINOR BOTTOMS TO MAJOR AND MINOR BOTTOMS - 2

Low			Time		From
1917	Feb. 2		25 months	9 days	Dec. 24, 1914
	May 9		28 months	15 days	Dec. 24, 1914
	Dec. 19	low decline	20 months		Apr. 22, 1916
	Dec. 19		36 months		Dec. 24, 1914
	Dec. 19		121 months	4 days	Nov. 15, 1907
	Dec. 19		168 months	10 days	Nov. 9, 1903
1918	Nov. 25		11 months	6 days	Dec. 19, 1917
	Nov. 25		47 months		Dec. 24, 1914
	Dec. 8	same low as 11/25			
1919	Feb. 8		19 months	6 days	Jul. 2, 1917
	Feb. 8		48 months		Feb. 24, 1915
	Aug. 20	Minor bottom	20 months	1 day	Dec. 19, 1917
	Aug. 20		56 months		Dec. 24, 1914
	Aug. 20		59 months	10 days	Jul. 30, 1914
	Nov. 29	and Dec. 22	60 months		Dec. 24, 1914
	Nov. 29		24 months	3 days	Dec. 19, 1917
	Nov. 29		12 months		Nov. 25, 1918
1920	Feb. 11	and 25	61 months	18 days	Dec. 24, 1914
	Feb. 11		26 months		Dec. 19, 1917
	Dec. 21	low of big decline	60 months		Dec. 24, 1914
	Dec. 21		36 months	2 days	Dec. 19, 1917
	Dec. 21		25 months		Nov. 25, 1918
1921	Aug. 24		80 months		Dec. 24, 1914
	Aug. 24		44 months	5 days	Dec. 19, 1917
	Aug. 24		165 months	9 days	Nov. 15, 1907
	Aug. 24		134 months	2 days	Jul. 26, 1910
	Aug. 24		119 months	1 day	Sep. 25, 1911
1922	Nov. 27	Minor reaction	15 months	3 days	Aug. 24, 1921
1923	Oct. 27	Last low	26 months	3 days	Aug. 24, 1921
	Oct. 27		70 months	8 days	Dec. 19, 1917
	Oct. 27		11 months		Nov. 27, 1922
1924	May 20		33 months		Aug. 24, 1921
	May 20		18 months		Nov. 27, 1922
	Oct. 14		25 months	18 days	Aug. 24, 1921
	Oct. 14		11 months	17 days	Oct. 27, 1923
	Oct. 14		118 months		Dec. 24, 1914
	Oct. 14		81 months	20 days	Dec. 19, 1917
1925	Mar. 30		43 months	6 days	Aug. 24, 1921
	Mar. 30		17 months	3 days	Oct. 14, 1923
	Mar. 30		10 months	10 days	May 20, 1924
	Nov. 24		51 months		Aug. 24, 1921
	Nov. 24		25 months		Oct. 27, 1923
1926	Mar. 30		12 months		Mar. 30, 1925
	Mar. 30		22 months	10 days	May 20, 1924
	Mar. 30		29 months	3 days	Oct. 27, 1923
	May 19		24 months	1 day	May 20, 1924
	Oct. 19		36 months		Oct. 27, 1923
	Oct. 19		62 months		Aug. 24, 1921
	Oct. 19		126 months		Apr. 22, 1916

FROM MAJOR AND MINOR BOTTOMS TO MAJOR AND MINOR BOTTOMS - 3

	Low	Time	From
1927	Jan. 25	10 months	Mar. 30, 1926
	Jan. 25	22 months	Mar. 30, 1925
	Jan. 25	39 months	Oct. 27, 1923
	Jan. 25	27 months 11 days	Oct. 14, 1924
	Jan. 25	119 months 28 days	Feb. 2, 1917
	Jan. 25	110 months 6 days	Dec. 19, 1917
	Oct. 22 and 29	12 months 8 days	Oct. 19, 1926
	Oct. 22	44 months 15 days	Oct. 14, 1924
	Oct. 22	48 months	Oct. 27, 1923
1928	Feb. 20	16 months	Oct. 19, 1926
	Feb. 20	51 months 24 days	Oct. 27, 1923
	Jun. 18	55 months 22 days	Oct. 27, 1923
	Dec. 8	61 months 11 days	Oct. 27, 1923
	Feb. 20	78 months	Aug. 24, 1921
	Jun. 18	82 months	Aug. 24, 1921
	Dec. 8	87 months	Aug. 24, 1921
1929	Feb. 16	90 months	Aug. 24, 1921
	Mar. 26	91 months	Aug. 24, 1921
	May 27	93 months	Aug. 24, 1921
	Jul. 29	95 months	Aug. 24, 1921
	Aug. 9	95 months 16 days	Aug. 24, 1921
	Oct. 29	98 months 5 days	Aug. 24, 1921
	Nov. 13	98 months 20 days	Aug. 24, 1921
	Dec. 20	99 months 26 days	Aug. 24, 1921
	Oct. 29	72 months 2 days	Oct. 27, 1923
	Nov. 13	72 months 17 days	Oct. 27, 1923
	Oct. 29	60 months 15 days	Oct. 14, 1924
	Nov. 13	61 months	Oct. 14, 1924
	Oct. 29	36 months 10 days	Oct. 19, 1926
1930	Jun. 24	8 months	Oct. 29, 1929
	Jun. 24	7 months 11 days	Nov. 13, 1929
	Dec. 17	61 months 23 days	Nov. 24, 1925
	Dec. 17	120 months	Dec. 21, 1920
	Dec. 17	132 months 3 days	Dec. 22, 1919
	Dec. 17	156 months 2 days	Dec. 19, 1917
	Dec. 17	192 months 7 days	Dec. 24, 1914
	Dec. 17	13 months 4 days	Nov. 13, 1929
1931	Apr. 29	17 months 16 days	Nov. 13, 1929
	Jun. 2	18 months 20 days	Nov. 13, 1929
	Aug. 6 and 10	20 months 24 days	Nov. 13, 1929
	Oct. 5	22 months 22 days	Nov. 13, 1929
	Aug. 6	119 months 13 days	Aug. 24, 1921
1932	Jul. 8	130 months 14 days	Aug. 24, 1921
	Jul. 8	174 months 19 days	Dec. 19, 1917
	Jul. 8	210 months 23 days	Dec. 24, 1914
	Jul. 8	247 months 23 days	Nov. 15, 1907
	Jul. 8	344 months	Nov. 9, 1903
	Jul. 8	422 months 19 days	Apr. 19, 1897
	Jul. 8	431 months	Aug. 8, 1896

FROM MAJOR AND MINOR BOTTOMS TO MAJOR AND MINOR BOTTOMS - 4

Low		Time	From
1932	Dec. 23	24 months	Dec. 17, 1930
	Dec. 23	36 months	Dec. 20, 1929
	Dec. 23	85 months	Nov. 24, 1925
	Dec. 23	120 months 20 days	Nov. 27, 1922
1933	Feb. 27	7 months 19 days	Jul. 8, 1932
	Feb. 27	26 months 10 days	Dec. 17, 1930
	Feb. 27	39 months 14 days	Nov. 13, 1929
	Feb. 27	112 months	Oct. 27, 1923
	Feb. 27	137 months 3 days	Aug. 24, 1921
	Jul. 21	12 months 3 days	Jul. 8, 1932
	Jul. 21	43 months 24 days	Nov. 13, 1929
	Jul. 21	120 months	Jul. 31, 1923
	Oct. 21	15 months 13 days	Jul. 8, 1932
	Oct. 21	34 months 4 days	Dec. 17, 1930
	Oct. 21	47 months 8 days	Nov. 13, 1929
	Oct. 21	120 months	Oct. 27, 1923
	Jul. 21	4 months 24 days	Feb. 27, 1933
	Oct. 21	7 months 24 days	Feb. 27, 1933
	Oct. 21	3 months	Jul. 21, 1933
1934	Jul. 26	24 months 18 days	Jul. 8, 1932
	Sep. 17	26 months 9 days	Jul. 8, 1932
	Jul. 26	17 months	Feb. 27, 1933
	Jul. 26	12 months 5 days	Jul. 21, 1933
	Jul. 26	9 months 5 days	Oct. 21, 1933
1935	Mar. 18	12 months	Mar. 27, 1934
	Mar. 18	17 months	Oct. 21, 1933
	Mar. 18	24 months	Mar. 21, 1933
	Mar. 18	24 months 19 days	Feb. 27, 1933
	Mar. 18	32 months 10 days	Jul. 8, 1932
	Mar. 18	120 months	Mar. 30, 1925
1936	Apr. 30	13 months 12 days	Mar. 18, 1935
	Apr. 30	25 months	Mar. 27, 1934
	Apr. 30	37 months	Mar. 21, 1933
	Apr. 30	38 months	Feb. 27, 1933
	Dec. 21	12 months	Dec. 19, 1935
	Dec. 21	24 months	Dec. 19, 1934
	Dec. 21	36 months	Dec. 19, 1933
1937	Jun. 17	51 months 21 days	Feb. 27, 1933
	Jun. 17	59 months 9 days	Jul. 8, 1932
	Oct. 19	48 months	Oct. 21, 1933
	Nov. 23	32 months 5 days	Mar. 18, 1935
	Nov. 23	39 months 28 days	Jul. 26, 1934
	Nov. 23	49 months	Oct. 21, 1933
	Nov. 23	56 months 27 days	Feb. 27, 1933
	Nov. 23	239 months 4 days	Dec. 19, 1917
1938	Mar. 31	4 months 8 days	Nov. 23, 1937
	Mar. 31	23 months	Apr. 30, 1936
	Mar. 31	36 months 13 days	Mar. 18, 1935
	Mar. 31	48 months 4 days	Mar. 27, 1934

FROM MAJOR AND MINOR BOTTOMS TO MAJOR AND MINOR BOTTOMS - 5

Low	Time	From
1938 Mar. 31	61 months 4 days	Feb. 27, 1933
Mar. 31	68 months 23 days	Jul. 8, 1932
Mar. 31	117 months 13 days	Jun. 18, 1928
Mar. 31	121 months 11 days	Feb. 20, 1928
Mar. 31	132 months 9 days	Mar. 22, 1927
Mar. 31	199 months 7 days	Aug. 24, 1921
Mar. 31	243 months 12 days	Dec. 19, 1917
1938 May 27	11 months 10 days	Jun. 17, 1937
May 27	24 months 27 days	Apr. 30, 1936
May 27	48 months 13 days	May 14, 1934
May 27	60 months	May 22, 1933
May 27	84 months	Jun. 2, 1931
May 27	108 months	May 27, 1929
May 27	119 months 9 days	Jun. 18, 1928
1938 Sep. 26	5 months 26 days	Mar. 31, 1938
Sep. 26	24 months	Sep. 25, 1936
Sep. 26	48 months 9 days	Sep. 17, 1934
Sep. 26	59 months 25 days	Oct. 21, 1933
Sep. 26	84 months	Oct. 5, 1931
Sep. 26	108 months	Sep. 29, 1929
Sep. 26	120 months	Sep. 27, 1928
1938 Nov. 26	60 days	Sep. 26, 1938
Nov. 26	6 months	May 27, 1938
1938 Nov. 26	7 months 26 days	Mar. 31, 1938
Nov. 26	12 months	Nov. 23, 1937
Nov. 26	108 months 18 days	Nov. 13, 1929
1939 Apr. 11	12 months 11 days	Mar. 31, 1938
Apr. 11	16 months 19 days	Nov. 23, 1937
Apr. 11	35 months 12 days	Apr. 30, 1936
Apr. 11	48 months 24 days	Mar. 18, 1935
Apr. 11	56 months 16 days	Jul. 26, 1934
Apr. 11	65 months 22 days	Oct. 21, 1933
Apr. 11	73 months 15 days	Feb. 27, 1933
Apr. 11	81 months 3 days	Jul. 8, 1932
Apr. 11	120 months 16 days	Mar. 26, 1929

[undated, but *circa* July 1939 onwards]   [unsigned]

Chapter 11a

Review of Bull and Bear Markets Showing Formations and Buying and Selling Points (1909-1939) - Dow-Jones 30 Industrial Averages

AUTHOR: "Truth of the Stock Tape" "Wall Street Stock Selector" "New Stock Trend Detector"	**W. D. GANN** Statistician and Economist 82 WALL STREET NEW YORK, N.Y. 2101 N.W. 18th TERRACE MIAMI. FLA.	MEMBER New Orleans Cotton Exchange Commodity Exchange, Inc N.Y. American Economic Ass'n Royal Economic Society

REVIEW OF BULL AND BEAR MARKETS

Showing Formations and Buying and Selling Points 1903 - 1939
Dow-Jones 30 Industrial averages

2nd BEAR MARKET

The second Bear Market Started on Jun. 23, 1901 and reached final low on Nov. 9, 1903. After that there was a period of accumulation which lasted until Jul. 3, 1904.

1903   END OF 2ND BEAR MARKET

Jul.   The averages broke 53 and 51 and there was no rally or sign of support at these old levels, indicating great weakness and lower prices. After the old bottoms were broken, the next point to watch for support and bottom was 42, the low of Mar. 25, 1893.

Oct. 15   Low 42-1/4. Support came at the old bottom. A 2 weeks' rally followed to 45-1/2; then a 2 weeks' decline to Nov. 9, when the averages reached 42-1/8, a DOUBLE BOTTOM, just above the old bottom at 42 in Mar., 1898. This was TIME TO BUY with close stop-loss orders. A rally followed and prices crossed 45-1/2, over the tops of the past 3 weeks ... the first sign that the minor trend had turned up and the Bear Market ended.

You should now review the second Bear Market from the top at 78-1/4 in Jun., 1901, to the bottom at 42-1/8 on Nov. 9, 1903.

> From 78-1/4 high to 42-1/8 low, the total range was ... 36-1/8 points. The greatest rally in the Bear Market was ... 8 points, from 59-5/8 to 67-7/8. Therefore, when the averages advanced 9 points, or one point more than the greatest rally in the Bear Market, it would be a definite signal for a Bull Market and a safe place to buy.

1904   **3rd BULL MARKET**

ACCUMULATION ON SIDE BEFORE IT STARTS

Jan. 27   High 50-1/2, up 8-3/8 points from the low at 42-1/8, not yet 9 points to confirm Bull Market ready to go ahead.

Feb. 6   In this week prices broke under the lows of the two previous weeks, indicating a reaction. The averages failing to reach old bottoms at 51-1/2 to 53, indicated that the selling was not yet over.

THE W.D. GANN MASTER STOCK MARKET COURSE

1904   **3rd BULL MARKET (Continued)**

SECONDARY REACTION ... SAFE TO BUY

Mar. 12   Low 46-1/2, a decline of 4 points from the top and a loss of one-half the gain from 42-1/8 to 50-1/2. This reaction lasted 6 weeks from the top and held for 8 weeks in 1-1/2 point range; then crossed tops of 3 previous weeks, indicating higher prices.

Apr. 7   High 49-7/8. Fail to reach last top at 50-1/2, a sign that it was not yet ready to go up. A slow decline followed, lasting 6 weeks.

May 18   Low 47-1/2, off only 2-3/8 points and 6 weeks, indicating very little selling; also volume of sales very small. This was dullness at bottom. A slow advance started and it required 7 weeks for prices to cross the top at 50-1/2.

SAFEST PLACE TO BUY

Jul. 16   Prices crossed 51 and advance to 52-1/2, up over 10 points from the bottom and a greater advanced than a rally of 8 points in the previous Bear Market. From Nov. 9, 1903 to July 9, 1904, prices held in a range of 8 points and most of the time in a 4-point range ... a period of 8 months of accumulation on the side, getting ready for a Bull Market.

Study this information of sideways accumulation 4 points above the low levels so that you will know what it means when you see it again. After July, 1904, prices advance to 53, the old bottom; reacted one point in one week; then the advance was resumed. The old tops at 68 were crossed in Nov. There was no reaction and prices moved right on up, indicating a strong Bull Market. The next point to watch would be a round the old tops at 78 to 78-3/4.

1905

Mar. 13   The averages made 78-1/4.

     22   Reacted to 76-1/2.
          Then went through old tops, advancing to 80 before end of March.
          The next old top was 84-1/2 made Sep. 4, 1895.

Apr. 14   High 83-3/4, just under old bottom at 84-1/2. Prices held 3 weeks in 2-1/2 point range at top; then broke under 3 weeks' bottoms, indicating minor trend down, and stock should have been sold out.

May 22   Failing to make bottom at 78, the old top, indicated lower. On May 22 the averages reached 71-3/8. The last old top in Jul. and Aug. was 72-3/4.

Jun. 3   In this week crossed top of previous week, indicating higher.
          After low of 71-3/8. The next 4 weeks each bottom was higher.

Jun. 17   and 24 ... In these weeks, the high was 75-1/4 and the following week crossed tops, indicating higher.

Nov.   The averages advanced to 84-1/8, the old tops. Then reacted to 81. The advance was resumed and prices crossed old tops at 84-1/2. The Next old high was 94-1/2 made in March and April, 1892.

Dec.   The averages advanced to 96; reacted to 94 and held for three weeks, making bottoms and 94 and failing to break 94, an indication of strong uptrend and higher prices. There was no change in trend at this level and no weekly bottoms broken. Refer to Rule, "When Stocks Advance into New High Ground."

THE W.D. GANN MASTER STOCK MARKET COURSE

1906   **3rd BULL MARKET (Continued)**

Jan. 19   High 103. END OF BULL MARKET.
This was 8-1/2 points above old top. When prices of average or stocks reach 100 to 105 there is nearly always heavy selling, but when prices get above 100, you must wait for a signal that top has been made by prices breaking the low of the previous week or weeks.

Jan. 27   In this week there was a narrow range of one point, and slightly lower than 103.

Feb 3   In this week prices broke under the lows of 2 previous weeks. Breaking back (under 100) to 98-1/2 indicated that minor trend had turned down. There was a rally of one week to 100-1/2 or 2 points up. Then the following week prices broke 98, a more definite indication of lower prices and a time to sell short.

Review of Bull Market – Nov. 1903 to Jan. 1906:
The greatest reaction was from April, 1905 to May, 1905 – 83-3/4 to 71-3/8 or 12-3/8 points. The smallest reaction was 4 points. Therefore, you must watch for a decline of more than 12-3/8 points to indicate a definite change in the main trend.

3rd BEAR MARKET

DISTRIBUTION ON SIDE BELOW TOP LEVELS.

Mar. 10   The averages declined to 92-7/8, down 10 points and broke under 4 weeks' bottoms and 94, indicating lower. SELLING SIGNAL.
A rally of one week followed to 96-3/4.
A reaction followed in the next week to 93.
A rally of the following week to 96-3/4, making a double top. In the weeks ending Feb. 17 and 24 there were to tops at 97-1/4. Therefore, these tops at 96-3/4 gave sign of good selling.
A decline followed, breaking bottoms at 93.

May 3   Low 86-1/2, down 16-1/2 points from 103. Breaking more than 12-3/8 points, the greatest reaction in the previous Bull Market, indicated main trend down and a Bear Market would follow. There was an old top at 86-3/4 on April 7, 1893, and a top at 83-3/4, in April, 1905, indicating that a rally could occur from this level. Refer to rule ... After first sharp decline there is a secondary rally, which is safe to sell on. The market advanced 5 weeks.

Jun. 4   High 95-1/4, lower than the last tops at 96-3/4, indicating weakness. Held last week in one-point range and following week broke lows of three previous weeks, indicating minor trend down again. SELLING SIGNAL.

Jul. 13   Low 85-1/4, still above old top at 83-3/4 and one point under low of May 3, 1906, a sign of support for a rally.

Jul. 7   and 14 – During these weeks the highs were 87-7/8 and 87-3/4.

21   Crossed 88, over 2 weeks' tops ... Minor trend up ... BUYING SIGNAL. The next week and a rapid advance followed.

Oct. 9   High 96-3/4, the THIRD TOP at the same level. The week's range was less than one point ... Signal to SELL OUT AND SELL SHORT. SAFE SELLING LEVEL. In the following week prices broke under 3 weeks' lows ... a safe place to sell short.

Nov 17   Low 92-3/8.

Dec 15   A rally followed. High 95-3/4.
A reaction of two weeks to 93 followed.
Then a rally for two weeks.

1907   **3rd BEAR MARKET (Continued)**

Jan. 7   High 96-3/8, the 4th time at this level, but lower than first two ... a SAFE POINT TO GO SHORT with close stops.

      12   In this week to range was 3/4 point, a narrow week same as Oct., 1905.

      19   In this week prices broke under 3 weeks' lows and then broke minor bottom at 93.

Feb 2   Declined to 90-1/2.
Rallied two weeks to 93-1/4, the old bottom. The top of this last rally was in a range of 5/8 point. Dull and narrow at top of small rally was a sign of weakness.

Mar. 9   During this week prices broke low of 86-3/8 and 85-1/4, a very bearish indication. A rapid decline followed.

      14   SILENT PANIC ... Stocks, like Union Pacific and Reading, which were active leaders at that time, broke 20 points in one day.
Our rule says, cover shorts and buy on panic days.

      14   Low 76-1/4, just under old tops at 78.
A rally followed to 82.
SECONDARY REACTION ... SAFEST TO BUY.

      25   Stocks had a secondary reaction after the panicky decline and made a slightly lower bottom at 75-3/8, less than one point under Mar. 14 low, a double bottom and place to by with stop, as main trend was down. But with averages down 28 points from the top at 103 and down 21 points from Jan. 1907, a rally was due.

May 3   High 85, up less than 10 points. Note rally from July, 1906 to Jan., 1907 was 11 points, making 10 to 11 points up a point to watch for a change in trend. There were three weeks' tops at 84-3/4 to 85; then prices broke under 3 weeks' lows, an indication that the trend had turned down and SHORT SALES should be made. The market worked lower and rallies were small, not more than 3 points.

Aug.   Prices broke 75, the low of March, 1907, and in the same month broke 71, under the low of May, 1905, making the position very weak.

Refer to our rule: In the LAST STAGE OF A BEAR MARKET rallies get less as market gets weaker. After May, 1905, low was broken, at what point should we expect resistance, support or bottom?

Review: Oct. 1898, low 51-1/2; Jun. 1900, low 53-1/2; Sep. 1900, low 53; Jul. 1904, last low after main trend turned up was 52-1/4 and last bottom in May, 1904, was 47-3/8, so the first important points would be 53-1/2 to 51-1/2.

Nov 15   PANIC BOTTOM ... low 53 ... time to buy.
Last week of fast decline was 4 points on averages.
Next week after low there was a 2- point range.
In the following week there was a fast advance, crossing top of previous week at 55.
Minor trend turned up ... A SAFE POINT TO BUY.
This was a SHARP SINGLE BOTTOM and indicated that BEAR MARKET HAD ENDED.

Review of 3rd Bear Market: Four Sections or movements down.
Greatest rally in the Bear Market ... 11 points. Therefore, there must be an advance of 12 points or more to show main trend up.

1907   **4th BULL MARKET**

Dec 7   In this week the high was 61-3/4.
Three weeks' rally ... up 8-3/4 points ... not enough to confirm main trend up as the averages must advance 12 points.

     17   Low 56-7/8, a 5-point reaction in 2 weeks. You would buy as this was a SECONDARY REACTION WITH HIGHER BOTTOM.

     26   In this week the market was narrow, within range of previous week.

1908

Jan. 4   In this week the averages crossed 60, above 3 weeks' tops ... a SAFER POINT TO BUY as trend was up.
Later crossed 62, over last rally ... DEFINITE SIGNAL FOR HIGHER.

     18   Advanced to 66-7/8 in this week. Low was 64-1/4, making the range 1-5/8 points, a narrow week at the top. In the following week broke bottom of previous week, indicating further reaction.

Feb 8   Low 58-7/8, down 7 points from 65-7/8 top, and 2 points higher than low of December, 1907, the first higher bottom.

     15   SECOND HIGHER BOTTOM ... SAFER TO BUY. In this week, the range was 3/4 point and the following week, the range was 1-1/2 points; crossed top of previous week ... safer to buy because 2nd higher bottom from sharp panic bottom.

Mar. 7   Crossed 62, top of Dec. 1907, and tops of 3 weeks in Jan & Feb, 1908.

May 21   In this week crossed 65-7/8, old top of Jan. 1908, a DEFINITE SIGNAL FOR HIGHER prices and a bull market to follow ... a safe point to buy or to buy more if you had already bought at lower levels.
Fast moves came after secondary tops are crossed.
The next point to watch for a reaction was around the old bottoms of March, 1907, at 75 to 76. The market advanced right thru these levels with no reaction, showing strong up trend.
The next point to watch was the top at 85 in May, 1907.

Aug. 10   High 85-3/8. The market was advancing very fast and in the same week that top was reached at 85-3/8, it reacted to 80-5/8; then rallied to 84-1/2, holding 2 weeks at a lower top, indicating good selling under old tops.

Sep. 19   In this week broke under 4 weeks' bottoms, indicating MINOR TREND DOWN and lower prices.

Sep. 22   Low 77-1/8, down 8-1/4 points from the top. Last reaction Jan. 1908 to Feb. low was 7 points, making this a BUYING POINT, just above old bottom of March, 1907. This was only 3 weeks from secondary tops at 84-1/2.

Oct. 3   During this week crossed top of previous week... SAFER TO BUY. The advance continued and crossed old tops at 85-1/2, which indicated higher.

Nov 13   High 88-3/8. THREE SECTIONS OR MOVES UP IN BULL MARKET.
Dull at top. Range 1-3/8 points for the week.
The next week broke low of previous week, indicating TOP FOR REACTION.
Held 4 weeks between 86-1/8 and 87-1/2.
Then following week broke under 4 weeks' bottoms, indicating lower.

1908   4th BULL MARKET (Continued)

Dec 26   In this week the low was 83-3/8, just under old tops at 85. A rally followed to 87. Made tops 2 weeks at 87, under old top. Then reacted to 84-1/8.

1909

Feb 20   In this week made top at 86-3/4, the 2nd LOWER TOP.
Declined and broke lows of 7 weeks past.

      23   Last low 80, down 8-3/8 points from the top of 88-3/8 in Nov. 1908 ... same number of points as reaction from August to Sept. 1908, making this up BUYING POINT. This was the 4th reaction in the Bull Market, but made higher bottom than low of Sep. 22, 1908, indicating main trend still up. A rally followed to 83-1/4; reacted to 81-1/2; then crossed 83-1/2, but a SAFER BUYING POINT.

May   Crossed top of 88-3/8 made in August, 1908, and did not reacted at all – A sure sign of much higher prices. Next point to watch was old tops in 1906 and 1907 and 96-3/4 to 97-1/2.

Jul.   Went through all these tops with no reaction.

Aug. 14   In this week the high was 99-1/8; reacted 3 weeks to 96. Holding above old tops showed strength.

Oct. 2   High 100-1/2, under 1906 top and 103. FINAL TOP.

      23   Low of reaction 95-7/8, same as last low in Sep. and at old tops.

Nov 4   High 100-1/2, a DOUBLE TOP
In the following week reacted to 98-1/2.

      19   Then rallied to 100-1/2 on Nov. 19, THE 3rd AND LAST TOP. END OF BULL MARKET.

REVIEW: The advance from the low of 53 on Nov. 15, 1907 to the high of 100-1/2 on Nov. 19, 1909, was ... 47-1/2 points. During that time the greatest reaction was ... 8-1/2 points. The last reaction was ... 4-3/4 points. Therefore, when the average broke back over 5 points, it would be the first indication of a change in trend. And when they broke back over 9 points, it would be a signal that the main trend had turned down.

4th BEAR MARKET

Dec 2   Declined to 96-5/8, just above old bottoms and the 3rd time at these levels. A rally followed.

      11   High 99, a 4th TOP LOWER ... a SIGNAL TO SELL
Held for 3 weeks in less than one point range.
Then broke 4 weeks' bottoms.

1910

Jan. 15   In this week broke 96. This was 4th time at this level and went lower, never rallying more than 4 points and rallies lasting only 10 days to 2 weeks ... a sign of great weakness in a Bear Market.

Jul. 26   Low 73-5/8. There was a sharp decline in the last week, but closed well, up from the bottom and failed to go 5 points under 77, the last low of Sep. 1908, and less than 2 points under the low of 75-3/8 made in Mar. 1907. This was a PANIC BOTTOM and rule will be given in next lesson for proving why this is a SAFE POINT TO BUY.

1910   4th BEAR MARKET (Continued)

END OF 1st SECTION OF BEAR MARKET

Aug. 6   In this week, the range was 76 to 78 and in the following week the average is crossed 78, top of two previous weeks, indicating change in trend and a SAFER POINT TO BUY. Next apply Space Rule. The greatest rally or secondary move-up was 4-3/4 points, and there was a 2nd rally in Jun., 1910 of 4-1/4 points. therefore, to change trend the averages must advance more than five points from 73-5/8 or to above 79.

Aug. 13   During this week they crossed 79 and on Aug. 17 advance to 81-1/2, under old bottoms and to tops of 3 previous weeks' levels.

Sep. 6   A SECONDARY REACTION followed to a low of 78-3/8, only 3-1/8 points' decline, became dull and narrow and made bottoms for 4 weeks near same level ... a sign of support and a SAFE BUYING POINT.

Oct. 1   Crossed tops of 5 previous weeks, and later crossed 82, above old tops, indicating strong uptrend.

Oct. 18   High 86. There were 2 old tops in June at 86-3/8 and 86-1/4.

Oct. 29   In this week broke the low of the previous week.
Rallied one week to 85-3/4.
Then broke lows of 3 previous weeks.
Held for 2 weeks in a narrow range.

Dec 6   Low of sharp decline to 79-5/8, just above secondary bottoms at 78-3/8 to 78-5/8, a higher bottom and support and buying level. This was 5-3/8 points' decline. Rallied to 28 [82?]; reacted to 80-1/2, making higher bottom; then crossed 82, indicating higher.

1911

Feb 4   High 86, same level as top of Oct. 18, 1910 – A. DOUBLE TOP and SELLING LEVEL. Held 3 weeks in narrow range.

Mar. 4   Declined to 81-7/8.
A 2- weeks' rally followed to 84.

Apr. 22   Then declined to 81-1/4, making two bottoms near same level. Holding more than one point to above low of Dec. 1910 indicated support and not yet ready to decline.

Jun. 19   High 87, making 5/8 to 1 point above old tops. Market became very dull and narrow, holding for 6 weeks between 86-5/8 and 85-5/8, in one point range. This was a point to watch and wait for a definitive change in trend as there were 3 tops at same level.

Aug. 5   In this week, the SELLING SIGNAL came when the averages declined to 85, breaking under 9 weeks' bottoms ... a sign that the distribution on the side had been completed and that the downtrend would be resumed. Note DISTRIBUTION ON SIDE after first section of Bear Market. The averages held in a range of 6 to 7 points between 80 and 87 from Dec. 1910 to July 1911.
A sharp, severe declined followed, with volume of sales increasing.

Sep. 25   Low of Bear Market, 73. This was a PANICKY DECLINE and the averages made a DOUBLE BOTTOM against low of 73-1/2 on Jul. 26, 1910. BUYING POINT. A quick rally followed.

5th BULL MARKET

Oct.   Crossed 2 weeks' tops, a second indication that the trend was up.

1911 — 5th BULL MARKET (Continued)

Oct. 14 High 78, under old bottoms of 1910, a selling level for a reaction. There had been only two weeks' rally so they were not yet ready to go further before a reaction.

Oct. 27 Low 74-7/8 after two weeks. SECONDARY REACTION, a higher bottom and SAFER PLACE TWO BUY.

Nov 11 In this week, the average is crossed to 78-1/2, tops of 4 previous weeks, indicating main trend up and safe to buy at this level. Reactions were very small and prices worked higher.

1912

Mar. 22 Prices crossed 87, the old tops. This was the 4th TIME AT SAME LEVEL (Refer to Rule) and there was no reaction from old tops, and indication of a strong uptrend. The advanced continued with only small reaction.

Sep. 30 High 94-1/8, under old bottoms at 96 made in 1909 and failing to reach these old bottoms was a sign of weakness. END OF BULL MARKET.

The averages made 3 weeks' tops at 94, holding in one-point range.

Oct. 19 During this week broke under the lows of 3 previous weeks, indicating MINOR TREND DOWN.

REVIEW: From 73 low in Sep. 1911 to 94-1/8 high in Sep. 1912, the averages had advanced 23-1/8 points. The greatest reaction had been 3-3/4 points. Therefore, they must react over 4 points to indicate a greater decline.

5th BEAR MARKET

Woodrow Wilson, a Democrat, was elected President.

Nov. 16 The averages declined to 89-1/2, down 4-5/8 points, a second indication of lower prices and a better SHORT SALE on any rally.

A weeks rally followed, lasting two weeks. High 91-1/4.

Dec. 7 In this week broke 89 and a faster declined followed.

Dec. 11 Low 85-1/4, just under 4 old tops and a point for a rally.

A slow advanced followed lasting 3 weeks.

1913

Jan. 19 High 88-1/2, up only 3-1/4 points – a weak SECONDARY RALLY.

The following week, the averages broke 85, indicating a Bear Market, and lower prices followed with weak rallies.

Jun. 11 Low 72-1/8, the THIRD BOTTOM at the same level and only one point under the low of Oct., 1911, a BUYING POINT with close stops.

The greatest rally from 94 to 72-1/8 (a decline of 21-7/8 points) was 3-1/4 points. Therefore, a rally from 72-1/8 of 4 points or more would indicate that the trend was turning up.

Jun. 21 Rallied to 75-3/4.

Held for three weeks on the side in a range from 75-3/4 to 74-3/8, a narrow, but no lower bottom.

Jul. 9 In this weak crossed to 76, above 5 weeks' tops and up more than 4 points – a second indication of change in trend.

Sep. 12 High 83-1/2. Note two weeks' tops at 83-3/4 and 83-1/2 in February, 1913, which was the last rally before a big decline started. Prices held two weeks on the side in a narrow range; then broke under 3 weeks' lows – MINOR TREND DOWN.

THE W.D. GANN MASTER STOCK MARKET COURSE

1913   **5th BEAR MARKET (Continued)**

Dec 15   Low 75-1/4, back to last low of July, 1913, and at 5 old weekly tops a support level for a rally.
       The averages made bottoms for six weeks between 76 and 75-1/4 showing support and a PLACE TO BUY.

      27   Crossed to 78, tops of 7 previous weeks – A SAFER POINT TO BUY.

1914

Feb   3   High 83-1/8, the SECOND TOP at this level.
       Prices held 3 weeks in 5/8-point range; then broke under 3 weeks' lows indicating lower.

Mar.   6   Low 81-1/8, a very narrow, dull market.

      20   High 83-1/2, the THIRD TOP at same level.
       Was dull and narrow for 3 weeks in range of 1-1/2 points.
       Then broke under lows of 7 weeks, a definite indication of lower prices.

Apr. 25   Low 77, just above old tops of Nov. and Dec. 1913.
       A slow rally followed.

Jun. 10   High 81-7/8, just under old bottoms.

      25   Low 79-1/4, slow and narrow.

Jul.   8   High 81-3/4, last high and 4TH TOP at lower level – a sure SELLING SIGNAL and a time to go short.

      28   Broke bottom at 78, a definite signal for lower prices.
       The market was declining on heavy volume of sales and WAR NEWS was causing heavy selling from Europe.

      30   The averages broke 75, the low of Dec. 1913, and the same day broke triple bottoms at 73-1/2, 73, and 72-1/8, making the 4th time at this level and closing under 72 was a definite sign for much lower prices.

      31   STOCK EXCHANGE CLOSED ON ACCOUNT OF WAR.

Dec 18   Exchange opened and the averages started at 54-3/8.
       In 1907 the low was 53 and in 1898 and 1900 the lows were made at 53 so these old bottoms should be the next support and buying points.

Dec 24   Low 53-1/8 ... END OF BEAR MARKET.
       REVIEW: From the last high 94-1/8 on Sep. 30, 1912, to the low of 53-1/8 on Dec. 24, 1914 ... a decline of 41 points ... the greatest rally was from 72-1/8 to 83-3/8 or 11-1/4 points. Therefore, when the averages advance above 64-1/2, they will indicate strong uptrend.

1915   **6th BULL MARKET**

Jan. 23   High 58-1/2, only 5-3/8 points rally, not enough to show big move up was ready. Then the SECONDARY REACTION AFTER PANIC ... SAFER TO BUY.

Feb 24   Low 54-1/4, a higher bottom by more than one point and a good buying level.

Mar. 27   This week the averages crossed 56-1/2, top of first rally ... a second signal that main trend was up and a Bull Market under way. SAFEST BUYING POINT.

Apr. 10   The averages crossed 64-1/2 ... the THIRD DEFINITE INDICATION of main trend up and higher prices. This was a POINT TO BUY more stocks.

      30   The market advanced fast and made high at 71-3/4, under 4 old bottoms at 71-1/2 to 73-1/2 ... SELLING LEVEL.

THE W.D. GANN MASTER STOCK MARKET COURSE

1915   6th BULL MARKET (Continued)

May   Prices held one week between 70 and 71-3/4, above tops of two previous weeks. Then broke fast on U-boat scare.

    14   Low 60-3/8, but only two weeks' decline and failed to reach top at 58-1/2 ... a sign of good support. This was a natural reaction in a Bull Market ... 11 point decline and SAFE TO BUY. Then the advance was resumed. There were two weeks' tops at 65-1/2. When these were crossed prices moved up faster.

Jun. 22   High 71-7/8, same top as April and under old bottoms. It was only natural that some selling and resistance would be met. A two weeks' reaction followed to 67-7/8, down only 4 points.

Jul. 24   During this week the averages crossed 72 on big volume and very active.
This was the place to buy more stocks.
The advance continued with reactions of only 3 to 5 points.

Sep. 20   The averages crossed old tops at 81-3/4 to 83-1/2 and did not react, proving STRONG UPTREND. The next old tops were 91 to 94.

Oct. 2   High 92.

    6   Prices reacting to 88-1/4, a small reaction; then went through 94, the top of Sep. 1912. The next tops were 100-1/2, the high of 1909.

Dec 27   High 99-1/8, just under 1909 tops ... a SELLING LEVEL as prices were up 47 points with only one 11-point reaction
The advance slowed down and in 4 weeks there was a gain of only one point ... indicating good selling.

1916

Jan. 8   Prices broke under lows of 3 previous weeks ... a sign that the MINOR TREND head turned DOWN.

    31   Low 90-5/8, not yet down over 11 points, to overbalance the greatest reaction.

Feb 11   Rally to 96-1/8, a lower top and selling level.

Mar. 2   Low 90-1/8, same as Jan. 31 low. The averages would have to break this level to indicate lower. A rally followed.

    16   High 96, slightly lower than Feb. 11 top ... a SELLING LEVEL.

Apr. 22   Low 85, just above old tops ... a BUYING LEVEL as this was a sharp panic, decline lasting only 3 weeks from last top at 94-1/2 in early April.
A quick rally followed.

Jun. 12   High 93-5/8, under old bottoms and at April top ... A SELLING LEVEL.

Jul. 1   This week made low at 87-5/8. A rally of one week followed.

    13   Low 86-1/2, a higher bottom than April and above old tops, A BUYING POINT. A rally to 89-3/4 followed. Then reacted to 88.
Held for 3 weeks with bottoms at 88, showing good support.
Then crossed tops at 90-1/2, indicating higher.

Sep. 21   Averages crossed tops at 96 and went through 1915 top at 99-1/8; 1909 top at 100-1/2; also through 103, the high of 1906 ... STRONG SIGNALS FOR HIGHER PRICES.

Oct. 5   High 104-1/8 ... new high by 1-1/8 points and a signal for higher prices.

    14   Reacted to 99, the old top of Dec. 1915, A BUYING LEVEL as this was only a 5-point reaction and the greatest reactions from 1914 lows were 11 and 15 points. This was a 9-points' reaction and in two weeks prices crossed the top of 104, showing strong uptrend.
You now must follow rules to determine how far averages can go into new high ground. The rules say 7, 10, 15, 20, or 24 points but the safest rule says, wait until minor trend turns by breaking under previous weekly bottom.

Page 318

1916   6th BULL MARKET (Continued)

Nov 21   High 110-1/8. This was 7-1/8 points higher than old top of 1906 and 10 points above 1909 top.
The averages made to weeks' tops at 110-1/8. FINAL TOP.

Dec 2   Then broke under two weeks' lows, turning minor trend down and ending Bull Market.

REVIEW: The ending of this 6th Bull Market was the culmination of the greatest advance in the Industrials up to that time ... up 57 points in 23 months ... with the greatest reaction 14 points and the last reaction 7 points. Therefore, a decline of 7 points or more would be the first signal for lower prices, and breaking 88, the last reaction point, would be a definite signal for a Bear Market to start.

6th BEAR MARKET

During December a wide-open break occurred on heavy scale, the averages breaking 99 and indicating SAFE SHORT SALES.

Dec 21   Low 90-1/8, down 20 points in 4 weeks' time and at old tops ... BUYING LEVEL. A rally was due and a sharp advance followed.

1917

SECONDARY RALLY AFTER TREND TURNED DOWN:

Jan. 3   High 99-1/8, under old bottoms and at old tops ... a SELLING LEVEL on 9-point rally, the first secondary rally ... safe short sales.
DISTRIBUTION ON SIDE after trend turned down ... Prices held for 3 weeks in a narrow range from 97-7/8 to 95.

Feb 2   Prices broke fast on U-BOAT SCARE and fear that the United States would enter the World War. Low 87, down 23 points from 110 top and 12 points from the last top. Note 85, the low of April, 1916, and 86-1/2, the low of Jul., 1916, where last advance started, making 87 to 85 a support or BUYING LEVEL, especially as this was a panicky decline, with prices breaking 10 to 25 points in two days. Remember our rule, always buy in panics for a quick rally. The rally followed with reactions of only 4 to 5 points.

Mar. 20   High 98-1/4, just under old bottoms and tops ... A SELLING LEVEL.

May 9   Low 89-1/8, same level as Dec. 1916 ... a point for a rally.

Jun. 9   High 99, the THIRD TOP at the SAME LEVEL and a SAFE POINT to go short as market became dull on this rally. Held 3 weeks in a narrow range.
Then broke under 3 weeks' bottoms and went lower.

Jul. 19   Low 90-1/2, old bottom. A small rally followed.

Aug. 6   Last rally. High 93-7/8. Held a narrow for 4 weeks.
Then broke under 5 weeks' lows.

Sep. 12   BROKE OLD BOTTOMS at 87 and 85, indicating a very weak market and much lower prices. Rallies were small, only 3 to 5 points. A panicky decline followed.

Nov 8   Low 68-5/8. Note last bottom at 67-7/8 in July, 1915. A rally followed.

     23   High 74-1/4, a 5-5/8 point rally in 2 weeks.
Then a sharp decline of 4 weeks, ending in a weak, panicky market.

THE W.D. GANN MASTER STOCK MARKET COURSE

1917   **6th BEAR MARKET (Continued)**

Dec 19   Low 66, just 2-1/2 points under November low and 1-7/8 points under last low of July, 1915, making 66 a BUYING LEVEL. 6th BEAR MARKET ENDED.

REVIEW: The greatest rally in the 6th Bear Market from the high of 110-1/8 in November, 1916 to the low of 66 in December, 1917 was 12 points. The last rally was 5-5/8 points. Therefore, the first indication of higher prices would be a rally of 6 points or more, and the signal for a change in the main trend would be a rally of over 12 points.

7th BULL MARKET

Dec 29   The advance started, crossing the top of the previous week and giving the FIRST MINOR INDICATION of a change in trend. The advance was rapid, reaching 72-1/2 the first week. There were old bottoms at old tops around 72, but the following week the advance went right through these old resistance levels, showing great strength.

1918

Jan. 2   The averages advance to 76-5/8, up 10 points from the low. At this level they were UNDER THE OLD BOTTOMS of Dec. 1913 and up to the top of the last rally before the final decline started. Then a reaction of two weeks occurred.

1   5   Declined to 73-3/8. This was a secondary reaction and prices held well above the old tops at 72, showing great strength. The fact that after a 3 weeks' sharp rally of more than 10 points, the market only reacted 2 weeks and only lost 3 points, showed good support in strength, making this a SAFE POINT TO BUY on a SECONDARY REACTION.

The advance was resumed and the averages crossed 78, up 12 points from the low level and exceeding the greatest rally in the bear market, a definite indication that the main trend had turned up. Also crossing the previous high, indicated THE MAIN TREND UP.

Feb 19   The averages advance to 82. This was up to old tops and old bottoms, as you can see on the chart, and was a natural point for a reaction. During the week that prices reached top, the range was 82 and 80-1/2, ...1-1/2 point range. The following week, and prices broke back under the low of the previous week, indicating the first change in the minor trend and the signal for a reaction.

Apr. 11   The averages declined to 75-1/2, a reaction of 6-1/2 points, about the average reaction in bull markets. Note that there were 3 weeks' tops at 76. Therefore, this was a logical support and BUYING POINT. The market held around these bottoms for 4 weeks, showing good support.

May 15   Advanced above the tops of 3 previous weeks; crossed the old top at 82 and advanced to 84. This was again under old bottoms and a point where a MINOR REACTION could take place.

The averages reacted to 78, down 6 points. Then held in a narrow trading range for several weeks.

Jun. 1   Advance to 83-7/8, just under the old top. A modern reaction followed.

The averages were down to 80-1/2, holding well above the last low level of Jun. 1.

Sep. 311   The fact that this reaction was not as great as the previous reaction ... which was 7 points, this one being only 6 ... was still an indication that the main trend was up and that stocks were still SAFE TO BUY.

1918   7th BULL MARKET (Continued)

Oct. 18   The advance was resumed and the top at 84 crossed. High was 89. Note old bottoms around 87 to 90. The next week, the market held in a narrow trading range. The second week in broke the bottom of two previous weeks and reacted to 84, off 5 points, the FIRST INDICATION that the minor trend was changing to the down side. Then followed a secondary rally.

Nov 9   The averages reached 88, one .under the previous high. Failing to reached the old top, after the minor trend had turned down, was a SELLING SIGNAL on the SECONDARY RALLY.

     25   The averages broke under the bottom of the first reaction at 84, indicating a further decline, and reached 79-7/8. Then followed a 2 weeks' rally to 84-1/2, a THIRD LOWER TOP, just under the first old bottom, a SELLING LEVEL.

1919

Feb 8   The market gradually worked lower but narrow down into a trading range of about two points and the averages reached a low of 79-1/8. Note OLD TOPS AROUND THIS LEVEL and the last weekly bottom from which the advance started, was around 77-1/2. Therefore, this bottom was higher than the previous bottom and only 3/8 point under the low of November, 1918, ... an indication of support. The market held for 4 weeks between 81-3/4 and 79-1/8.

     22   The averages crossed the tops of four weeks at 82 ... a signal for higher prices and a SAFE POINT TO BUY.

Mar.   Reached old top of 89 and only reacted a little over 2 points, showing great strength.

Apr.   Crossed the last old top at 89 and advance right on up with only minor reactions.

Jul. 14   The averages reached high of 112-1/4. This was 2 points into new high ground, crossing the old top of Nov. 1916, and a SIGNAL FOR HIGHER PRICES later.

     19   The range this week was 110-1/4 to 112-1/4, a very narrow range at the top after a big advance. The following week, the averages broke back under 110 and broke the bottoms of two previous weeks, A SIGNAL that the minor trend was turning down FOR A REACTION. The fact that the market had advance from 79-1/8 to 112-1/4 without ever having a 5-point reaction was an indication that a temporary reaction was in order.

Aug. 20   A sharp, quick decline followed, lasting a little over 4 weeks, making bottom and 98-1/2. This was down to old tops and a natural support level just under 100. The fact that the reaction only ran 4 weeks, then the advance was resumed, was an indication that it was still a bull market and that prices were going higher. A SAFE PLACE TO BUY on this reaction would have been after the high of the last week's decline, 100-3/4, was crossed.

Oct.   Prices advance right on up with nothing more than 3 to 4 point reactions, crossing the old high at 112 and October.

Nov 3   Advance to 119-5/8, FINAL HIGH. This was 9-1/2 points above the old high of 1916 and 7 points above the high of July 14, 1919. Remember, our rules says that prices can advance 7 to 10 points into new territory and then react.

1919   **7th BULL MARKET (Continued)**

COMPARISON: in 1916, after the old high of 103 was crossed, the averages advance to 110 or 7 points into new high ground. In 1919, the averages went 9-1/2 points into new high territory before the Bull Market ended and the trend turned down. During this last run in 1919 the volume was very heavy in the last 60 days. Everybody was bullish and buying stocks and talking about the greatest boom in history, and higher prices than had ever been seen, but the end came and the top was reached. A sharp decline followed, wiping out people who had overtraded on margin, and had bought on hope instead of facing facts and following the trend.

REVIEW: In the 7th Bull Market, which started at 66 low in December, 1917, and culminated at 119-5/8 on November 3, 1919, the greatest reaction was from 89 to 79-1/8, or 9-7/8 points, and the last reaction before the end of the bull campaign was from 112-1/4 to 98-1/2, a decline of 11-3/4 points. Therefore, the signals to watch for a definite indication that a bear market was starting, would be a decline of more than 12 points, or the breaking of the last low at 98-1/2 or the breaking of the low ofND the first sharp decline after final top.

7th BEAR MARKET

Nov   The lows of the last 3 weeks were 114-7/8 to 115-1/2.

Dec 13 A sharp, severe decline followed, with prices breaking under these last 3 weeks bottoms, showing a definite change in the MINOR TREND to the DOWN side.

   22   Low 103-1/2, down 16 points from the high and exceeding the greatest reaction in a bull market, which was 11-3/4 points. This was a definite signal that the trend had turned down and that prices would go lower but the market had not yet had the secondary rally, which always occurs after the first sharp decline. The averages held for five weeks, making bottoms around 104 to 103-1/2. This was above the old top levels at 103 and a natural point for support. The fact that bottoms were made for five weeks at this level showed that there was good support and this was a point to **COVER SHORTS AND BUY** and wait for a secondary rally to sell on again.

1920

Jan. 3 The SECONDARY RALLY and occurred, reaching high of 109-7/8, a rally of a little over 6 points, and up under the old top level of 1916, SELLING LEVEL. There was heavy selling on this rally and prices failed to hold. The second week, the range was 108-3/4 to 106-1/2 and the following week prices broke the lows of the previous week and also broke under five weeks' bottoms around 103-1/2 ... a definite indication that the main trend had turned down because the bottom of the secondary reaction had been broken. The decline continued, the averages reaching 102; then rally to 104-1/2, just under the old bottom, holding dull and narrow for one week.

Feb 7   Heavy selling broke out and a sharp, severe decline followed, the averages breaking 98-1/2, the last bottom made in Aug. 1919, another confirmation that the MAIN TREND was DOWN and that a bear market was under way. The decline was swift and severe with very small rallies; in fact, it was a panicky decline.

1920   7th BEAR MARKET (Continued)

Feb 25   Low 90. This was a support and buying level against old top of Oct. 1918 and February, 1920. There were two weeks' bottoms around this level, one and 90-1/2 during the week ending February 14 and the last bottom and 90, showing that there was support around this level and a point to buy.

Mar. 6   The averages crossed the top of the previous week, the THIRD SIGNAL that the minor trend was turning up. The greatest rally on the way down was 6 points. Therefore, when the averages advance more than 6 points, they indicated a further rally.

13   The averages crossed 98 and failed to halt at the old bottoms around 99.

Apr. 8   Advance to 105-5/8, just 2 points under the series of old bottoms where the main trend turned down, making this a SAFE SELLING LEVEL on an advance of 15 points after the market had declined 30 points. After 2 weeks at the top in a narrow trading range; the market started to break.

24   Broke back under the bottoms of the past five weeks, indicating that the MAIN TREND had again turned DOWN. A sharp decline followed with very small rallies.

May 19   Low 87-3/8, just 2-5/8 points under the low of February and down to a series of old tops and bottoms from which a moderate rally could occur. The market held for two weeks, making two bottoms just under 88; then the rally followed.

Jul. 8   High 94-1/2, a rally of 7 points, which is a fair sized rally in a weak, bear market. During the last week, the range was 94-1/2 to 93 ... 1-1/2 point range. SELLING LEVEL. The following week, the averages broke back under the low of this week and broke the lows of the 3 previous weeks, indicating that the main trend would continue down. All support levels were broken.

Aug. 10   The averages reached 83-1/4. A rally followed to 89-7/8 ... another rally of less than 7 points, practically the same as the last rally and a point at which to again SELL SHORT. The decline continued with only rallies of 2 to 3 points in the averages.

Nov 19   Low 73-1/8.

Dec 4   Top of rally 77-5/8 ... 4-1/2 point rally. Remember, the rule is that the lower prices get in a bear market, the smaller the rallies are because the market is getting weaker all the time, and is a safer short sale.

21   Low 66-3/4. BUYING LEVEL. This was down near the old low of 1917, which was 66, and a point to watch for support and a rally. Remember, the rule is, buy against old bottom and protect the stop-loss order.

The last three weeks of the decline ran from 77-1/2 to 66-3/4. The last week of the decline was 69-5/8 to 66-3/4.

The following week, the averages crossed the top of the previous week, and advanced to 71-7/8, indicating a change in the minor trend, but a rally of 7 points or more, which would exceed the past two rallies, would indicate a further advance. This was confirmed by the averages advancing about 75.

1921

Jan. 5   The averages advanced to 76-1/2, just under old bottoms and a point from which there should be a reaction.

1921   **7th BEAR MARKET (Continued)**

Jan. 11 The averages reacted to 72-3/8. Holding one point above the low of Nov. 1920, was an indication of support and a point at which to BUY FOR A RALLY, protected with stop loss order under the old bottom. The advance was resumed and the previous minor tops were crossed.

Feb 16 Reached 77-1/4, under the old bottom, where a minor reaction was indicated.

Mar. 11 Low 72-1/4. This was down to OLD BOTTOM LEVELS AND OLD TOP, a natural support point. A slow advanced followed.

May 5 High 80 market, very dull and narrow on this advance. Note that 80 was under a series of old bottoms, which occurred between September, 1918 and February, 1919, making this a natural SELLING LEVEL, where you should go short, especially as the market became dull and narrow. The averages were up 13-1/4 points, which was an average rally in a bear market.

14 The averages broke back under the lows of the previous weeks' bottoms, showing that the MINOR TREND was again turning DOWN. From this level the decline continued with very small rallies.

Jun. 20 Low 64-7/8. This was one-point under the low of Dec. 1917; and 2 points under the low of Dec. 1920, a point to watch for support and resistance. A rally followed. This was a slow, feeble advance.

Aug. 2 High 70, a 5-point rally in 5 weeks, not enough to indicate a change in the main trend. The following week, prices broke under the lows of the past 5 weeks.

24 Low 64, 2 points under the low of Dec. 1917 and back to the lows of the weekly bottoms for the advance started in May, 1915, but the fact that the averages failed to break 3 points under the lows of 1917, where the bear market ended at that time, was an indication of support and a BUYING POINT, as the volume of sales ran very low, indicating that liquidation had run its course. But the safest and best indication for buying would-be to wait until the market showed that it could rally by crossing the tops of previous weeks.

REVIEW: From the top at 119-5/8 on November 3, 1919, to the low of 64 on August 24, 1921, the greatest rally in the 7th Bear Market was 15 points and the last rally to May, 1921 was 13 points. Therefore, the first indication of a greater advance and a change in the main trend would be when the averages advanced more than 13 to 15 points.

8th BULL MARKET

Sep. 3 The averages crossed 66, the highs of the two previous weeks, making this a SAFER PLACE TO BUY.

10 Crossed 70, the top of the last rally, a further confirmation of higher prices, making the market a safer purchase on reactions. The averages reached 71-7/8. This was an old bottom and old top level and resistance point for a reaction, but the reaction was very small.

Oct. 17 Low 69-1/2. The averages held for 6 weeks between 71-5/8 and 69-1/2, indicating that there was good buying just above or around the old top at 70, and when the averages made bottom a SECOND TIME, 4 weeks later, at 69-1/2, it was a SAFE POINT TO BUY.

1921   8th BULL MARKET (Continued)

Oct. 29   The safest and best point was when the main trend turned up by crossing 72. This was confirmation of MAIN TREND UP and showed that accumulation had been completed; that liquidation was over.

Dec 15   The averages crossed 80, the last top of May 1921, another definite indication of a Bull Market and higher prices. The advance continued and reactions were very small.

1922

Sep. 11   The averages made 102, the high of Apr., 1920. From this level there was 2 weeks' reaction to 96-1/4. Holding above 3 weeks' bottoms where last advance started, indicated good support and a BUYING LEVEL for higher prices.

Oct. 14   High 103-1/2. Note the last high in April, 1920, was 105-1/2. Therefore, the averages were reaching a level from which a reaction could take place, especially as they had advance from 64 to 103-1/2 without any important reaction. The market held in a narrow range for two weeks, then the third week broke the low of the two previous weeks, indicating temporary top and a reaction to follow. The decline continued and after the averages held for one week with a moderate rally, the lows at 96 were broken.

Nov 27   Low 92, down 11-1/2 points from the top, a natural reaction in a Bull Market. There was a series of old tops and bottoms around 92, a support and BUYING POINT, especially as the reaction had run 7 weeks from the top, which is about the average reaction in a bull market when the decline exceeds 4 weeks. However, the SAFEST POINT TO BUY would have been when the averages crossed 96, three weeks' tops, which they did in the week ending Dec. 9, 1922. The advance continued with very small reaction.

1923

Mar. 20   High 105-3/8, at the old top of April, 1920. SELLING LEVEL. The market gave a definite indication that there was heavy selling at this level because for 3 consecutive weeks the high was around the same level and for 2 weeks, the low was around 103-7/8.

25   Broke under 2 weeks' bottoms ... a signal for a bigger reaction and a point to sell out long stocks and GO SHORT.

REVIEW: From the low of 64 on Aug. 24, 1921, to the high of 105-3/8 on March, 1923, the greatest reaction in the 8th Bull Market had been 11-1/2 points. Therefore, a decline of 12 points or more from the high would indicate main trend down but breaking the last series of four weeks' bottoms around 97 would be the first definite indication that the main trend had turned down and that the Bull Market had ended for the present.

8th BEAR MARKET

May 21   Low 93, holding one above the low of Dec. 1922, from which the last run in the Bull Market occurred.

29   Rallied to 97-5/8, under the old bottom. A SELLING LEVEL. The decline continued and broke 92, the low of Dec. 1922, another definite confirmation that this was a bear market and going lower. The trend continued down.

1923   8th BEAR MARKET (Continued)

Jul. 12   Low 87-5/8, old top and bottom levels, from which a rally could occur.

20   High 91-3/4, just under the two previous bottoms and a SELLING LEVEL.

Market held for two weeks, then declined.

31   Reached 87, holding slightly under the bottom of July 12, which INDICATED A RALLY, especially as the market became very dull and narrow. When it crossed the top of the previous week at 88-1/2, it indicated a moderate further rally.

Aug. 29   High 93-3/4, which was under the old bottom level and just above the last rally. The market held for two weeks in a range of 1-1/2 points. SELLING LEVEL.

Sep. 15   Declined rapidly, breaking back under the four weeks' bottoms and indicating that the minor trend had again turned down.

Oct. 27   Low 85-3/4, just one point under the low of July 30 and down to a line of old bottoms and tops in previous campaigns. The market was very dull and narrow here, but the volume was exceedingly small, indicating that temporarily, at least, liquidation had run its course and the market was making bottom and should be bought for a rally, especially as this was really a DOUBLE BOTTOM.

REVIEW: The greatest rally in the 8th Bear Market from the top at 105-3/8 on March 20, 1923 to the low at 85-3/4 on Oct. 27, 1923 was 6-1/2 points, from 87 to 93. Therefore, when the averages could advance more than 6-1/2 points, it would be an indication that the main trend was up in time for a Bull Market to start.

9th AND GREATEST BULL MARKET

This was really a continuation of the Bull Market that began in August, 1921, as the reaction from the top in 1923 was 20 points, which would only be considered a natural reaction and a resting point or accumulation period for the big Bull Market to follow.

Nov 3   The SAFEST PLACE TO BUY would have been around 88-1/2 during the week ending Nov. 3 after the market had crossed the highs of 3 previous weeks. The advance continued and later crossed the tops at 93 to 93-1/2, indicating that the main trend was up. When prices got above 94, it would have been a still safer place to buy or pyramid, if you had already bought at lower levels.

1924

Feb 6   High 101-3/8. This was under a series of 4 weeks' bottoms, where the market broke away from after the trend turned down from 105-1/2 ... a natural point or SELLING LEVEL for a reaction. The range of the top for the week ending Feb. 9, was very narrow, only about a point. A sharp decline followed, breaking the bottoms of the three previous weeks, indicating that the minor trend had again turned down. In the latter part of February the averages declined to 95-3/8.

1924   9th BULL MARKET (Continued)

March   There was a SECONDARY RALLY to 98-3/4. This was a very feeble rally, requiring 3 weeks to go up a little over 2 points ... A SAFE RALLY TO SELL ON. But a safer time to sell was when the averages broke 96, under 3 weeks' bottoms. The trend continued down with very small rallies.

May 20   Low, 88-3/8. This was 2-1/2 points above the low of Nov. 1923 and 1-1/2 points above the low of July, 1923, making this a TRIPLE BOTTOM and a SAFE PLACE TO BUY, especially as the volume of sales was very small and the market holding for several weeks in a narrow trading range, indicating that liquidation had run its course, and that there was not enough selling to break the previous low levels. But a safe rule to follow would be to wait until the market had definitely proved its strong position by crossing the tops of previous weeks. The market held for three weeks between 88-3/8 and 90-1/2. Then crossed 3 weeks' tops.

Jul. 14   During this week crossed other tops at 92-3/8, indicating a definite change in the trend to the upside and a SAFE POINT TO BUY as accumulation had taken place between 90 and 86.

Aug. 20   High 105-1/2, the same top as March, 1923, and same top as April 1920. The THIRD TIME at this level made it a natural SELLING LEVEL for at least a temporary reaction. During the second week, the averages broke under the previous week and declined to 102-7/8.

Sep. 6   This week a rally followed.

     24   High 104-5/8. Failing to reach the old top by 1 point and only two weeks' rally indicated weakness. SELLING LEVEL – lower top.

Oct. 14   Low 99-1/8, final and last low before the big advance. SELLING LEVEL. This was down to old bottom and top level and a natural resistance point and a 6-point reaction in about 7 weeks, the average time for a reaction and a bull market after it exceeds 3 weeks and the average number of points for stocks at these levels.

Nov 3   The safe point in which to buy would be to wait until after the market confirmed that it had made bottom, which it did promptly, by crossing the tops of the two previous weeks, during the week ending Nov. 3, indicating higher prices. The advance was rapid. The averages crossed the triple top at 105, making the FOURTH TIME AT THIS LEVEL ... a definite indication of a BULL MARKET and higher prices. The next point to watch was the high in history ... the old top of November 1919. The averages went right on thru the old top of 119-5/8 without a reaction, indicating a very strong market.

1925

Jan. 22   High 123-5/8, a new high point, and there had been no reaction of as much as 5 points since the averages started up from just above 88 in May 1924.

Feb 16   The averages reacted to 118, just under the old top, and the advance was resumed.

Mar. 6   High 125-5/8.

Mar. 30   Low 115, a reaction of 10 points and 4-5/8 points under the old top of 119-5/8. Our rule says that a reaction under an old top should never be greater than 5 points, if the main trend is to continue up. This reaction was only 24 days, a little over three weeks, which is a natural reaction in a Bull Market, and this would have been the

1925   9th BULL MARKET (Continued)

point at which TO BUY stocks, or you could have waited until the tops of the previous weeks were crossed, or until the averages advanced above the old top of 120, again, and then bought. They promptly advanced and crossed the high of 125-5/8 reached on Mar. 6, and continued right on up with only small reactions.

Nov 6   High 159. Market was very active and moved rapidly at this level.
     10   The averages reacted to 151.
     13   High 157-3/4. Lower top ... SELL.
     24   Low 148-1/4, less than a 3 weeks' reaction and 11 points on average, a natural reaction in a Bull Market. BUYING LEVEL.

1926

Feb 11   High 162-3/8, another new high. Here the market held for several weeks, moving up and down. The fact that the averages could not go 5 points above the top of November 6, indicated that some distribution was taking place and the market-making top for a reaction. SELLING LEVEL. You should have sold, especially as soon as the weekly bottom of previous week was broken. The market declined fast.

Mar. 30   Just one year from where the advance started at 115, the averages reached low of the reaction at 135-1/4, down 27 points from the top and the greatest reaction. The decline lasted only a little over six weeks, which is a natural reaction in a big Bull Market.

Apr. 6   The market rallied to 142-3/8.
     16   A reaction to 136-1/4, higher bottom, BUYING LEVEL.
     25   A rally to 144-7/8.

May 19   A reaction to 137-1/8, making the THIRD HIGHER BOTTOM between March 30 and May 19, indicating good support at these levels. This third higher bottom was a SAFE PLACE TO BUY. However, a safer place to buy would be to wait until after the top of Apr. 24 was crossed, showing a definite change to the upside. The market advanced rapidly, crossing all tops of previous weeks.

Aug. 9   High 166-1/8.
     11   Low 161-5/8.
     14   High 166-5/8, a DOUBLE TOP against the previous top. SELLING LEVEL.
     25   Low of reaction, 160-1/2.

Sep. 7   High 166, a THIRD TOP slightly lower ... a SELLING INDICATION, especially as the market had made no gain since August 9. A definite change in the minor trend was made when it broke the low of August 26. The market declined fast.

Oct. 19   Low 145-5/8, down a little over 20 points, but not as much reaction as from February 11 to March 30, and holding the previous weekly bottom ... another six weeks' reaction ... an average reaction in a Bull Market. BUYING LEVEL. You should watch for the resumption of the main trend.

Dec 18   High 161. This was up to the old top levels and bottom levels where a reaction could take place. SELLING LEVEL.

1927

Jan. 25   Low 152-3/4, a DOUBLE BOTTOM, the same low as Nov. 19th, and a PLACE TO BUY with stop loss order, especially as weekly tops have been crossed on the upside.

Feb 28   High 161-7/8.
Mar. 7   Low 158-5/8.

1927 9th BULL MARKET (Continued)

Mar. 17 High 161-3/4, three times at the same level. SELLING LEVEL.

    22 Low 158-1/2, a DOUBLE BOTTOM. BUYING LEVEL. Two times at the same level and no weekly bottoms broken. The main trend was still up. A SAFE PLACE TO BUY would be when the averages crossed 162, getting above three tops. The market started moving up fast at the end of March.

Apr. 22 Reached a high of 167-3/8, getting above all previous tops, a signal for higher prices.

    28 Low 163-1/2, down to old top levels and a natural BUYING POINT. The advance was resumed on big volume and a very active market.

May 31 High 172-7/8.

Jun. 3 A reaction to 169-5/8.

    6 High 171-1/8, a slightly LOWER TOP.

    14 Low 167-5/8.

    16 High 170-1/4, making the THIRD SLIGHTLY LOWER TOP, an indication for a reaction. SELLING LEVEL.

    27 Low 165-3/4, down 7 points from the high of May 31st, a 4 weeks' reaction ... just under the top of April 22nd and still above the low of April 30th ... A BUYING INDICATION.

Jul. 9 A safer rule to follow would be to wait until the trend turned up, which it did this week, crossing the top of three previous weeks. Then advanced right on thru, crossing all tops.

Aug. 2 High 185-1/2, low 182-5/8 the same week; close at the low and at practically the same level as the previous week. SELLING LEVEL ... Advancing to a new high and closing on the bottom was an indication of a further reaction. To play safe, you should have sold out long stocks and waited.

    12 Low 177-1/8, an 8-point reaction, only a natural reaction. One week's reaction, not declining to old tops. The following week, the averages crossed the tops of the previous week. BUYING LEVEL. Advanced to the level of August 2 and closed strong, at the top, the highest closing in history up to that time and an indication of higher prices. The following week stocks advanced to new high levels.

Sep. 7 High 197-3/4. Remember this rule: Watch selling at all even levels, that is, 100, 200, 300, etc. SELLING LEVEL.

    12 Reacted to 194.

Oct. 3 Made extreme high at 199-7/8, just under 200 ... SAFER SELLING LEVEL. Looking back, you will find 3 bottoms, in fact, 4 weekly bottoms around 194; therefore, this would be a level to watch. If you had not sold out around 200, where a change in trend was indicated, then you would sell when the market broke back under 3 weeks' bottoms, after an advance from 165 to 200, as this would be an indication for a reaction.

    18 After opening and high levels, the market broke 194 this week and declined to 190, indicating LOWER PRICES. A rapid decline followed.

    29 Low 179-1/2, a decline of 20 points from the top, not as great as the decline from Feb. 11 to Mar. 30, 1926, which was 27 points. This was another 3 weeks' reaction. A natural reaction in a Bull Market, and a BUYING LEVEL, but it would be safer to wait until the averages crossed the top of the previous weeks.

There was a narrow week on the side: High 185-1/4, low 181. The following week the bottom was higher, 181-1/2, and the averages crossed the top at 185-1/2. The advance continued.

THE W.D. GANN MASTER STOCK MARKET COURSE

1927   **9th BULL MARKET (Continued)**

Nov 30 High 198-7/8, just under old tops and still under 200 ... SELLING LEVEL.

Dec 8 Low 193-1/2, a 5-point reaction. Did not break 1 point under the bottom of the previous week. BUYING LEVEL.

1928

Jan. 3 High 203-3/8. Crossing 200 was a SIGNAL FOR MUCH HIGHER PRICES.

    18 Low 194-1/2, a 9-point reaction, only a natural reaction of 15 days and holding above the low of Dec. 8 ... BUYING LEVEL.

    23 Advanced to 201.

Feb 3 Low 196-3/8, the SECOND HIGHER BOTTOM and a level at which to BUY and protect with a stop-loss order.

    9 High 199-3/8.

    20 Last low 191-3/8, breaking 2 points under the low of Dec. 8. With the market at these high levels, this was not enough to indicate lower prices. It should break at least three points under the previous lows to show a definite change in trend. The market remained for 3 weeks in a narrow trading range. In the second week, the extreme low as 191-3/8 and the high 194-1/4, closing at the top, and indication of higher prices. You would buy and protect with stop loss orders under the old bottoms. The advance was resumed and prices went through the 200 level and crossed the old top of Jan. 3 at 203-3/8, a DEFINITE INDICATION OF HIGHER PRICES.

May 14 High 220-7/8. Opened at the top this week and closed near the bottom, closing under the low of previous week ... the FIRST SIGNAL OF TOP for reaction.

May 22 Declined to 211-3/4.

May 25 Advanced to 217-3/4, A LOWER TOP.

May 28 Declined to 214, holding above the bottom of the first reaction.

Jun. 2 High 220-3/4, a DOUBLE TOP. SELLING LEVEL. Closed at the high on Saturday, but opened down about 2 points on Monday morning, and indication that there was good, selling at the top. This was the third top around this level and three consecutive weeks' selling had been met, therefore a reaction was indicated, but a definite change in the minor trend came when the averages broke 214, the low of the previous week.

Jun. 12 Low 202-5/8, down from the old top of Jan. 3, still holding above the 200 level. BUYING LEVEL. This nearly always happens after prices cross high levels at figures like 200; and they stay above that level until the Bull Campaign is completed.

Jun. 23 This was a narrow week: High 204-1/4, low 202, slightly lower than Jun. 12. After a 3 weeks' sharp decline, this narrow range at the bottom indicated that selling was over and TIME TO BUY stocks again, as a natural reaction of about 4 points had run from the top, which is all you could expect in a real Bull Market. The SAFE PLACE TO BUY would be when the averages crossed 205 the following week, getting above the top of the previous week. Advance was resumed.

Jul. 5 High 214-1/2.

Jul. 16 Low 205-1/8, a two weeks' reaction and a higher bottom, still holding well above the 200 level. BUYING LEVEL. The advance was then resumed and prices crossed 215, the previous top.

Aug. Later crossed 221 into new high ground, where you could AGAIN BUY stocks with confidence.

1928   **9th BULL MARKET (Continued)**

Sep. 27   Low 236-7/8, a 5-point reaction, a very small reaction with prices at this level and an indication that prices were going higher.

Oct. 5   High 243.

Oct. 8   Low 236-3/4, a higher bottom. Then, in the latter part of October, prices crossed the top of Sep. 7 and a rapid advance followed with reactions very small, only 3 to 5 points on the averages. SIGNAL FOR HIGHER PRICES.

Nov 28   High 295-5/8, just under the 300 level and a point to watch for reaction before the even figure was crossed. SELLING LEVEL. A sharp quick decline followed.

Dec 8   Low 255-1/8, down 38-1/4 points, the greatest decline since the Bull Market started, but this decline lasted only 10 days. The following week, the high was 272 and the low 264, making higher bottoms ... a DEFINITE INDICATION TO BUY. The following week, prices cross the top of the previous week at 272 and advanced rapidly.

1929

Jan. 2   High 307.

Jan. 8   Low 297, a 10 point reaction.

Jan. 11   Low 301-5/8.

Jan. 15   Low 297-5/8, holding above the bottom of Jan. 8, an indication of strength and in view of the fact that the averages did not get below the top for the week ending Dec. 29th, showed that there was still good buying and indicated higher prices. BUYING LEVEL. The advance followed.

Feb 5   High 324-1/2. SELLING LEVEL. On Monday morning the market opened unchanged from Saturday's close; and advanced from 219-1/2 [319-1/2?] to 322; then broke fast and later broke the low of the previous week at 312.

Feb 16   Low 295, down 27 points from 322, double bottom against Jan. 15 ... BUYING LEVEL.

Mar. 1   High 324, making a DOUBLE TOP ... SELLING LEVEL. Quick rally followed.

Mar. 6   Low 305-1/8.

Mar. 16   High 320, making a third lower top ... SELLING LEVEL for reaction. The decline followed. Broke 3 weeks' bottoms around 303 to 306.

Mar. 30   Low 281-1/2, a decline of 43 points from the high of 324-1/2 made on Feb. 5. Strictly on a space movement, this would be a BUYING LEVEL because the greatest previous decline since the averages started up in August, 1921, was 44 points and 10 days, from Nov. 28, 1928, high of 299 two Dec. 28, low of 255. One of my rules is that reactions or advances can run to around 40 points when prices are at an extreme level. You could have bought on this extreme decline because it was very sharp, panicky break, or you could have waited until the trend turned up by crossing the previous week's top. The market held for two weeks in a range from 294 to 308; then crossed the 308 top, showing that the trend had turned up again and making it a SAFER PURCHASE.

May 11   High 331, or 6-1/2 points above the top of Feb. 5 and March 1. The rally failed to hold and the following week, the high was 324-1/2, the same level as the previous old top ... SELLING LEVEL. Breaking back under the low of the previous week, indicated a further reaction.

THE W.D. GANN MASTER STOCK MARKET COURSE

1929　　　　　　　　　**9th BULL MARKET (Continued)**

May 27　Low 290, down 41 points from 331 high, a smaller reaction than the two previous reactions, which were 43 and 44 points. You will note that there were several old bottoms around 292, making this a logical support point and as it was a decline of only 16 days, less than 3 weeks, it was a natural support or BUYING POINT in a Bull Market. However, you could have waited until the top of the low week was crossed at 306, then bought on a reaction around the price. It reacted to around 302. Then, the advance was resumed and the market moved up fast, crossing the old top at 331 and advancing to a new high level.

Jul.　8　High 350-1/4. The low for the two previous weeks was 332 and 331.

Jul.　11　Low 343.

Jul.　12　High 349-3/4, a slightly LOWER TOP ... SELLING LEVEL.

Jul.　15　Low 340.

Jul.　23　High 349-1/2. Three weeks' tops at this point ... SELLING LEVEL. A reaction followed.

Jul.　29　Low 336-3/8; made low for two weeks at this level, making four weeks' bottoms in a range of less than 3 points, indicating good support and BUYING LEVEL. The advance was resumed.

Aug.　3　New high 358-3/8.

Aug.　7　Low 338-1/2, a 10 point reaction.

Aug.　8　High 352, a lower top.

Aug.　9　Low 336-1/8, a 12 point reaction and not enough to show any change in the main trend. There were 2 weeks' bottoms around this level ... BUYING POINT. Then the advance was resumed.

Sep.　3　High of history 386-1/8, making 50 points' advance on the last run in 25 days, and 90 points from the low of Mar. 30, 1929. From May 27 low of 290, there was an advance of 96 points. SELLING LEVEL.

Sep.　7　The range this week was 386-1/8 high and 367-3/8 low, making a higher top and then breaking back to a lower bottom than the previous week. This is what we call a SIGNAL TOP or final top, making a new high and the same week breaking the low of the previous week and closing lower.

　　　　REVIEW: From the extreme low of 64 on Aug. 24, 1921, to the extreme high of 386-1/8 on September 3, 1929, the greatest reaction in the Bull market was 44 points; the last reaction before final top was 41 points; the last small reaction 10 points. Therefore, breaking back more than 10 points was the FIRST SIGNAL that the trend had changed; breaking back under the 4 weeks' bottoms around 336-1/2, was the SECOND DEFINITE SIGNAL that the main trend had changed, and when this level was reached, the averages had broken back over 44 points, giving the THIRD DEFINITE SIGNAL that the main trend had turned down, and that a real BEAR MARKET was starting.

9th BEAR MARKET

Oct.　4　The averages reached 320-1/2, down 66 points from the top in one month. A sharp, quick SECONDARY RALLY followed, lasting one week.

Oct.　10　High 358-3/4 ... A SELLING LEVEL.

Oct.　19　This week declined to 321, the same bottom as Oct. 4. High was 333 the next week; then the bottom at 320-1/2 was broken and a wide open decline followed.

Oct.　29　Averages at 212-3/8 and over 16 million shares traded in ... the largest day's sales in the history of the New York Stock Exchange. PANIC ... BUYING LEVEL for rally. A quick advance followed.

1929   **9th BEAR MARKET (Continued)**

Oct. 31 High 273 1/2. There was heavy selling on this rally ... SELLING LEVEL after 60 point rally. Decline continued.

Nov 6 Low 232-1/8.

   7 Moderate rally to 239-1/8.

   13 Than followed a sharp decline, reaching final low Nov. 13, 1929, at 195-3/8. The averages were down 190 points and 70 days. Look back on your chart and you will find a period of tops and bottoms between 194 and 200, which was the reason for support and bottom at this level. On this decline, the volume of trading was smaller, indicating that liquidation had run its course and that stocks were meeting support. BUYING LEVEL IN PANIC.

   In fast markets of this kind, by keeping up a daily high and low chart and watching the first-time tops of previous days are crossed, you get the first indication to buy. But I would consider that when the averages rallied above 212 again, the bottom of Oct. 29, it would be an indication that the rally would go further and would consider this a SAFE BUYING LEVEL. Movements were very rapid at this time, up and down.

   21 High 250.

   26 Low 235-1/2. SECONDARY REACTION ... BUY.

Dec 4 High 254-5/8. SIGNAL FOR HIGHER PRICES.

   5 Low 251-1/2. Then advance was resumed.

   7 High 263-1/2, failing to reach the last top at 273 and a 4 weeks' rally, market was high enough for a reaction, which followed quickly. Lower top ... SELLING LEVEL.

   21 Low 227-1/4.

   26 Low 226-3/8. This was the secondary reaction after the first advance from a panic bottom, stocks reacting more than 50% from the first run-up. This would be the PLACE TO BUY with close stop loss orders.

1930

Jan. 4 A safer place to buy would be after the high of the previous week was crossed, which occurred this week when the averages crossed 246 ... SIGNAL FOR HIGHER. After that there were 4 bottoms around 242 to 244 and 3 weekly tops around 252 to 253-1/2. The fact that the market held 4 weeks without breaking the bottom, was another indication of good support and A PLACE TO BUY. But, again, it was still safer to buy when it crossed the 4 weeks' tops at 254. The advance continued and crossed the top at 267-1/2.

Feb 13 High 275, under old bottom and top ... SELLING LEVEL. Note high of last rally on Oct. 31, 1929, was 273-1/2. The averages made top 4 weeks around 274 to 276, indicating a reaction.

Mar. 1 After 2 weeks', reaction, the averages declined to 260 during this week. Holding above the old top level was an indication of support. BUYING LEVEL. Advance was resumed and the averages rallied above the top of 275; reacted to 268-3/4 and made bottom for 3 weeks and failing to break them indicated higher. Advance continued.

1930   9th BEAR MARKET (Continued)

Apr. 17   High 297-1/4 ... SELLING LEVEL ... top of SECONDARY RALLY. Why did the averages stopped at this level? Look back over your chart and you will find a series of bottoms from 292 to 298. The averages were up over 100 points from the extreme low and at a point to watch for a change in trend, to sell out longs and go short. There were 3 weeks' high as around this level, one 296-1/4, one 297-1/4 and one at 295. The averages advanced for 7 weeks without breaking below the previous week's bottoms, therefore, the first signal for a change in the minor trend would be breaking bottoms of the previous weeks.

Apr. 26   During this week, the averages broke the lows of 3 previous weeks, indicating MINOR TREND had turned DOWN and it was SAFE TO SELL out longs and go short. The greatest reaction was 40-5/8 points. The last reaction before the last advance of 37 points was 15 points. Therefore, the first break of 15 points would be a second signal or indication that the trend had turned down.

May 3   This week broke under 282, more than 15 points down, and declined the same week below the last bottom at 260.

10   Declined to 249-1/2 this week. Note 4 weeks' old tops around 252 to 253, indicating SUPPORT around this level FOR A SECONDARY RALLY. Remember, according to the rules, after the first sharp decline in running 3 weeks or more, there is always a secondary rally. This first decline had run three weeks and had declined 47 points, therefore, the rally was sharp and quick.

17   Averages advanced to 277 this week. There was one week's reaction to 261, followed by one weeks rally to 276-3/4, DOUBLE TOP ... SELLING LEVEL. Also note series of old tops around 274-75, making this a selling level and a place to go short. But the safe place to sell would be around 269, when the averages broke back under the low of the previous week, after making 3 weeks' tops. The next definite indication of weakness and lower prices, was when the averages broke the weekly bottom at 261.

Jun. 14   This week the averages broke the 4 weeks' bottoms around 244-43.

24   Low 207. This was at the end of four weeks', sharp decline. While the main trend was definitely down, A RALLY WAS DUE.

Jul. 5   The averages crossed the high for the previous week, advancing to 229 ... SIGNAL FOR RALLY. Then followed one week's reaction.

12   Declining to 215 this week, making a higher bottom than the previous week and holding above the low of Oct. 29, 1929, an indication of temporary support ... BUYING LEVEL.

31   The advance was resumed and the averages crossed the 2 weeks' tops at 229, advancing to 243 on July 31 ... SELLING LEVEL. There were 4 weeks' top around 241 to 243, indicating that the market was meeting resistance. The reason for this, if you will look back, was 4 weeks' bottoms around 243 to 245 in February, 1930, showing that this would be a resistance point. Then there was a quick reaction lasting 2 weeks.

Aug. 16   Averages declined to 214-1/2 this week, making a DOUBLE BOTTOM against low in July. This was the third higher bottom ... BUYING LEVEL, protected with close loss orders, especially as they reaction only lasted 2 weeks. Then followed another advance.

Sep. 10   High 247-1/4. This was the last and final high. SELLING LEVEL. Note that this was under the bottom of 250 made in Feb. 1930 and prices failed to reach the low at 250 made on the decline in May. The chart will show you plainly that with 4 weeks' tops around 241 to 243, and then 2 weeks' tops on the next rally, at 244-1/2 to 247-1/4, the market was meeting with good selling around this level.

THE W.D. GANN MASTER STOCK MARKET COURSE

1930   **9th BEAR MARKET (Continued)**

Sep. 20 But the FIRST DEFINITE INDICATION that the MINOR TREND had turned DOWN and the market was again a safe short sale, came during this week when the averages broke back under the lows of the 3 previous weeks. Volume of sales increased and then the decline was fast.

Oct. 4 This week the averages broke the last bottom at 207.

11 This week broke the low of Nov. 13, 1929, at 195-3/8, SIGNAL FOR BIG DECLINE.

Nov. 15 Low of 168-3/8. Note the series of old tops in July and August, 1926, around 166, making this a logical POINT FOR RALLY after such a sharp, severe decline in 9 weeks' time. BUYING LEVEL.

Nov. 29 A 10-day rally followed the averages made tops two weeks at 191-1/4 ... SELLING LEVEL under old bottoms. Failed to reach or bottom at 195-3/8, made in Nov. 1929, an indication of weakness. If you look back over your chart, you will find 3 weekly bottoms around 191 and 192 made in March, 1928, and also in the week ending Nov. 1930, you will see that the top on the last rally was 199. Therefore, the averages failing to reach this high, indicated lower.

Dec. 3 The first signal came this week when the averages broke back under 3 weeks. The decline was swift and wound up in a panicky decline.

17 Extreme low 154-1/2. Referring to Feb. 1927, you will find 2 bottoms at 154-1/4 and the last low at that time at 152-3/4. There was a series of tops and bottoms in this zone, making this a logical POINT FOR SUPPORT and a rally. A quick rally followed to 170; then reaction to 158-1/2, with bottoms for 2 weeks at this point, making it a SAFER BUYING POINT.

1931

Jan. 9 High 175-1/2 ... SELLING LEVEL. This was a 3 weeks' rally, but failed to hold. Then followed a secondary reaction lasting 2 weeks.

19 Low 160-1/2. This was the SAFE POINT TO BUY, protected with stop loss orders under the 2 bottoms at 158-1/2. A rally followed. There were 3 weekly tops around 172 to 172-3/4. When these tops were crossed, it was a still SAFER POINT TO BUY.

Feb. 14 These tops were crossed during this week and the top at 175-1/2 was Crossed ... BUYING LEVEL. The market advanced sharply.

24 Reached high at 196-7/8, against the old bottom of Nov. 13, 1929, and the last high on Nov. 1, 1930, making this a logical SELLING LEVEL, the old bottom becoming top. From the low of 154-1/2 on Dec. 17, 1930, to this high of 196-7/8, the greatest reaction was 15 points, therefore making back more than 15 points from the top would be a definite signal for lower prices. The first indication that the MINOR TREND had turned DOWN again was the breaking of a weekly bottom at 187-1/4 made in the week ending Feb. 28.

Mar. 7 This week the averages declined below 180.

Mar. 13 Declined to 175-7/8, the old top of Jan. 9, 1931, a logical POINT FOR RALLY. The rally followed, lasting only one week, advancing to 189-1/4 during the week ending March 21 ... SELLING LEVEL. The main trend turned down and the following week, the averages broke under the bottom at 175, indicating definitely that the main trend was again down. The next point to watch was the or bottom at 154-1/2 made in Dec. 1930. The averages did not hesitate or rally at this point because selling was very heavy. They went right on thru this low.

Page 335

1931   **9th BEAR MARKET (Continued)**

Apr. 29   Declined to 141-3/4.

May 9   The averages rallied to 156-1/8, just above the old bottom at 154-1/2 ... SELLING LEVEL. It was one-week rally and the trend continued down.

Jun. 2   Made 120, low of a panicky decline. This was down to the old top of 1919, which was a logical POINT TO BUY for a rally, especially after such a sharp, severe decline. A sharp quick rally followed to 139-1/2; then a reaction to around 128, making 2 weeks' bottoms around this level, showing good support and a point to BUY ON A SECONDARY REACTION.

27   This week the averages crossed 2 weeks' tops at 140 and advanced quickly to 157-7/8, just above the last top at 156-1/8 and against the old bottom of 154-1/2 made in Dec. 1930, a logical SELLING LEVEL, and really only a 3 weeks' rally. The next 2 weeks, the tops were lower.

Jul. 11   This week the averages broke under the low of the previous week, showing that the trend had turned down again. Stocks were again a SHORT SALE.

Aug. 6   The averages declined to 132-1/2, made 3 weeks' bottoms around this level. RALLY DUE.

15   Rallied to 146-1/2, making the third lower bottom. Then held in a range from 148 to 136 the next two weeks.

Sep. 5   A sharp decline started this week and the averages broke back under 132, where there were 4 weeks' bottoms, INDICATING MUCH LOWER PRICES. The decline became worse and the volume of selling was heavy. The averages went right on thru the old bottom at 120 without rallying, an indication of much lower prices.

Oct. 5   Low 85-1/2. You will note that the last low from which this Bull Market started on October 27, 1923, was 85-3/4. Therefore, 85-1/2 or anywhere from 88-3/8 to 85 was a logical BUYING POINT for a rally, especially at the time of a panicky decline. A sharp, quick rally followed with only small reaction.

Oct. 24   Averages advanced to 100-1/2.

29   Then there was a SECONDARY REACTION to 98-1/4, just under 100, a SUPPORT LEVEL, as there were old tops and bottoms around these levels. The advance was resumed and the averages crossed four weeks' tops around 108 to 110.

Nov 9   High 119-1/2, under the low of June 2, 1931, and that the old top of Nov. 1919 ... the logical place to SELL OUT LONGS AND GO SHORT and not to buy until this old bottom and top level could be crossed. The greatest reaction from 85-1/2 low and October to this high was 11 points, therefore breaking back 11 points from the high would be an indication of lower prices, and breaking the previous weekly bottom would indicate trend down again.

21   The market broke back quickly more than 12 points and during this week broke the bottoms of 4 previous weeks, indicating definitely the main trend down.

Dec 12   This week the averages broke the low at 85-1/2, another indication that the main trend was down and the Bear Market would continue and the rallies were very small.

1932   9th BEAR MARKET (Continued)

Jan. 5   Low 70-1/2. The last low on Oct. 17, 1921 was 70 and the other old bottoms 66 and 64. The two weeks previous, the market had rallied from 72. Therefore, this bottom was only 2 points under the previous bottom, indicating that SUPPORT was coming at this time ... BUYING LEVEL. A sharp rally followed.

Jan. 14   High 89-1/2. This was just above the old bottom at 85-1/2. The market met SELLING around this LEVEL.

Feb 10   Declined to 71, only 1 point above the previous bottom and making 3 bottoms around this level ... a POINT TO BUY with stop-loss order. A rally followed.

Mar. 8   High 89-1/2, a DOUBLE TOP against Jan. 14, making the third time that the market had advanced to around these levels and failed to go thru. The market became very dull and narrow, showing there was not much buying power at the top of the rally, indicating stocks were still a SHORT SALE.

     19   The FIRST DEFINITE INDICATION came during this week when the averages broke back under the previous week's bottoms and broke 3 bottoms around 81 to 83-1/2, continuing right on down.

Apr. 7   This week they broke 70, where there were three bottoms, indicating the market was in a very WEAK POSITION and that the main trend was still down. Remember our rule: The lower stocks get, the smaller the rallies until the final clean-out comes and final bottom is reached. The decline continued and the old bottoms at 66 to 64, made back in 1921 and 1917, were all broken. There was no indication of support, showing that the final stage of the panic was on and that stocks would not rally until liquidation had run its course. After breaking 64, the next point to watch was 53, the low of 1914, a support level for several other years in the past.

May 4   The averages declined to 52-1/2, getting support at the old bottom, a quick rally followed.

     7   High 60, only a 3-day rally, which failed to hold. The decline continued and the averages broke the old bottoms at 52 and 51-1/2. The next point to watch for bottoms was the old lows of Mar. 25, 1898 at 42, and the next lower bottom of Apr. 19, 1897 and 38-1/2. The last low Nov. 9, 1903 was 42-1/8. Therefore, there were old triple bottoms around the 42 level a logical place to watch for bottom, anywhere between 42 and 38-1/2. Our rule says that, where there is a series of old bottoms, there should be support.

Jun. 2   Low 43-1/2.

     4   A quick rally to 51-1/2. The first rally of as much as 8 points since the averages started down from 89-1/2. This rally failed to hold.

     9   The averages went back to 44-1/2.

     16   They rallied to 51. Failing to reach the previous top showed that liquidation was still going on and stocks were for sale on rallies. The decline continued and the averages broke the low at 43-1/2.

Jul. 8   Low 40-1/2, receiving support 1-1/2 points under the old support level at 42, thus ENDING THE GREAT BEAR MARKET.

THE W.D. GANN MASTER STOCK MARKET COURSE

1932   **9th BEAR MARKET (Continued)**

In 34 months, the Dow-Jones 30 Industrial averages were down 345-1/2 points, wiping out a gain of more than 30 years. This proves what happens when people lose confidence and everybody gets loaded up and continues to buy on the way down, and finally all have to sell. Prices swung to extreme low levels, the same as they did on the advance, going to extreme and unwarranted high levels. But that is when the man who as knowledge and time makes money, but knowing when to take advantage of extremes, when the public buys on hope and sells on fear.

The FIRST SIGNAL that the market was NEARING BOTTOM came in the week of June 11 when the averages held in a narrow trading range of less than one point and the following week rallied 11 points, making the first high above a previous week since the trend turned down on Mar. 9th at 89-1/2. Then, from 51-1/2, the last high, the averages declined for 3 weeks. Certainly stocks are low enough at these old panic levels for a blind man to know that they were low enough to buy, but having declined so long, people have lost all hope and fear controlled them. Therefore, you could have waited for a definite indication that the trend had turned up and still bought stocks very near the low levels.

REVIEW: Figuring the last decline or last stage of the Bear Market from 119-1/2 high on Nov. 9, 1931, to 40-1/2 low on July 8, 1932, the greatest rally was 19 points, from 70 to 89-1/2, and the next rally around 8 points. Therefore, when the averages advanced more than 8 points, it was the first signal that they were going higher. Advancing more than 19 points indicated a still further advance.

10th BULL MARKET

Jul.   There were 2 weeks' tops at 44-3/4 and 44-1/2.

      16   This week the averages crossed 45, advancing above the 2 weeks' tops, and indication that the minor trend had turned up and that stocks were now SAFE TO BUY.

      30   The averages crossed 53 in this week, getting above 9 weeks' tops, and crossed the tops of previous rallies, being of more than 10 points. This was an indication that the main trend had turned up and with the averages at 52, they were a SAFE PURCHASE for a further advance. The advance was rapid as, naturally, it would be after such a sharp decline and heavy liquidation, cleaning out everybody.

Sep. 8   The averages advanced to 81-1/2, having made higher bottoms and higher tops every week after the low of July 8, advancing for nine weeks. The averages were up under old bottoms and were up 41 points, or an advance of 100%, from low levels and would have to cross 89 to give a definite indication of a real Bull Market and higher prices. There had been no secondary reaction, which always comes after the first sharp advance. Therefore, your FIRST SIGNAL TO SELL out would be the first week that the averages broke the low of the previous week's bottoms, especially after an advance of nine consecutive weeks.

      17   This signal came during this week when the averages broke under the previous bottoms, declining sharply to 64-1/2, down 17 points in 10 days. As they held just above tops of previous weeks and above the old bottom at 64 in 1921, it was a POINT FOR A RALLY. The averages rallied to 76 and made top the next week at 75-1/2. Failing to get above the bottom at 77 reached in the top week, was in indication of GOOD SELLING and lower prices. The decline came and the previous weeks' bottoms were broken.

1932   10th BULL MARKET (Continued)

Oct. 15 This week the averages declined to 57; rallied one week to 66, just above the old bottom level, then had a secondary reaction to 57-1/2, making a DOUBLE BOTTOM at 57 ... BUYING LEVEL. Then there was a rally of one week to 68-3/4, crossing the tops of four previous weeks, but this rally failed to continue the second week, which was in indication that there was GOOD SELLING.

Nov 26 The averages broke the double bottom this week.

Dec 3 Declined during this week to 55-1/4. The market had narrowed down to a slow trading range at this time. A rally of 2 weeks followed.

15 The averages rallied to 62-3/4; then reacted for 1 week to 56, thus forming a series of 5 bottoms between 57-1/2 and 55-1/4, which looked as if it might be good support. A rally followed.

1933

Jan. 14 High 65-1/2. Again the averages had crossed several weeks' tops, but failed to go on, making a LOWER TOP. Then the last high of 68. SELLING LEVEL. Held for 2 weeks in a narrow range; then broke under 2 weeks' bottoms, indicating lower and later broke the bottom at 55-1/4.

Feb 27 The averages declined to 49-1/2, when the banks were failing all over the United States ... BUYING LEVEL – SECONDARY REACTION.

Mar. 4 President Roosevelt took the oath of office as President of the United States and closed all the banks and the Stock Exchange closed. At the time the news was the worst it possibly could be, but stocks made their final lows and another big Bull Market started. Thus you see that in 1929, at the top, the news was bullish and everybody was full of hope. Then, when the banks were failing right and left and it looked as if the world was coming to an end, stocks made bottom and a Bull Market started. Thus, a Bull Market begins in gloom and ends and glory. The averages were holding at 49-1/2, just under the old top levels at 51 and were 8 points above the panic low, after declining from 81-1/2 to 49-1/2, 32 points. A change in trend was due, especially as each weeks' bottoms had been lower for 7 consecutive weeks. After the Stock Exchange opened, the averages opened above the tops of the two previous weeks – opening above 57.

16 They advanced to 64-1/2, about 1 point under the top of Jan. 14 ... SELLING LEVEL.

Apr. 1 Then followed a two weeks' reaction to 54-3/4 during this week. This was a SECONDARY REACTION AFTER THE FIRST SHARP RALLY. From the top of 81-1/2 to 49-1/2, the greatest rally was 11 points, therefore, when the averages advanced to 64-1/2, they were up 15 points, a definite signal that the trend had changed and the market was a buy on a secondary reaction. The first signal came after 54-3/4, when the averages crossed 58, the top of the previous week, and again a SAFE PLACE TO BUY was when they crossed two weeks' tops at 61. Then, crossing 65 and 66, the previous tops, was a safe place to buy. Crossing 69, another safe place to buy because the market did not hesitate at these old tops where a reaction might take place. The accumulation had been so long and the liquidation so thorough that there was very little stock offered and the market advanced rapidly.

THE W.D. GANN MASTER STOCK MARKET COURSE

1933   **10th BULL MARKET (Continued)**

May 6   The averages made the old top of Sep. 8, 1932 this week and only reacted to 76, where there were three previous tops, making this a SAFE POINT TO BUY. Then they crossed 81, indicating a definite Bull Market and higher prices. Reactions were small and the averages went on thru old tops around 89, made in the early part of 1932, advancing rapidly.

Jun. 13   Reached high and 97-1/2.

16   Low 86-1/2, declining 11 points in 3 days. Then advance was resumed.

Jul. 17   High 110-1/2. Note the series of tops in the past. Around 108, and 110-1/2 to 112 SELLING LEVEL. The market was now up 60 points in four and one-half months. The volume on this advance from Mar. to July 1933 was the largest in history for the short period of time. The public had regained confidence and was buying, hoping and believing that there would be another 1929. Everybody was overtrading. It only required some unfavorable news to scare people and bring about a sharp decline. The failure of Dr. E. A. Crawford, who was heavily loaded with all kinds of grain, as well as stocks, started the decline in commodities and stocks followed.

Previous to the high and 110-1/2, the averages had made top for two weeks at 107-1/2 and low at 101-1/2. The fact that they only advanced 3 points above these two tops and started to break back was an indication that they had run into heavy selling, but the first definite indication was when they broke back more than 7 points, exceeding the greatest reaction which occurred when the secondary reaction took place from 64-1/2 to 54-3/4 in March. There was a 10-point reaction in June, which lasted 3 days, therefore, to give the market the benefit of the doubt, when it broke back 10 points to 99, the main trend was down and at that time had broken the lows of the two weeks' bottoms. There were 7 to 10 million share days at this time and stocks were thrown overboard regardless of price and declined rapidly.

21   The averages declined to 84-1/4, down 26-1/4 points in 4 days, a drastic clean-out, but in view of the fact that the averages failed to come back to the old top at 81-1/2 was an INDICATION OF A SUPPORT LEVEL, and rally ... BUYING LEVEL. The market rallied quickly to 97; had a secondary reaction to 87-3/4; then advanced slowly.

Sep. 18   High 107-1/2, a LOWER TOP ... SELLING LEVEL. There had been three weeks previous tops around 105-3/4 and one at 106-1/2, showing that the market was running into heavy selling below the previous tops. The greatest reaction on the way up was 9 points, therefore, a break-back of 9 points, or breaking the bottom of previous weeks would be an indication for lower prices.

23   This week, the averages broke back under previous weeks' bottoms, declining to 95-1/2.

Oct. 7   Declined to 91-1/2 in this week. There was one week's rally and the averages were 100-3/4, under a series of bottoms. 100 is always the SELLING POINT. From this level, there was a sharp decline.

21   Low 82-1/2, down 25 points and a little over 4 weeks, failing to go 2 points under the bottom of July 21 and also failing to reach the OLD LOW of 81-1/2, which was an indication of good support and a POINT TO BUY.

25   The market advanced to 95-3/4. This was a quick, sharp rally.

1933   10th BULL MARKET (Continued)

Oct. 31   A secondary reaction to 86-1/2. This was the SAFEST PLACE TO BUY on the SECONDARY REACTION, protected with stop-loss order under the old bottom. The advance was resumed and the market worked higher with very small reactions.

Dec 11   High 104-1/2, making a THIRD LOWER TOP ... SELLING LEVEL ... and indicating that the market was still meeting resistance. A two weeks' reaction followed.

     20   Low 93-1/2. Note series of tops in Oct. 1933, around this level. The market made four weeks' bottoms at 93-1/2 to 96-1/2, indicating good support at this level, especially after rallying to 101-3/4 and coming back to 96 ... a SAFE POINT TO BUY, protected with stop-loss orders.
The advance was resumed and the market moved on up.

1934

Feb 5   High 111-1/2, getting 1 point above the old high of July 17, 1933 ... SELLING LEVEL. The volume of trading was very heavy and the market too week to cross the top at 112-1/2 and a quick, sharp decline followed.

     10   Low 103, a decline of 8-1/2 points from the top and a definite signal that the market was meeting with heavy selling. The greatest reaction from 82-1/2 low to 111-1/2 was 11 points. The first quick decline of 8-1/2 points was not enough to give a DEFINITE SIGNAL that the market was GOING LOWER. A rally followed.

     15   High 109-1/2, failing by 2 points to reach the old top, an indication of GOOD SELLING.

Mar. 3   The next definite signal that the market was going lower came during this week when the averages broke back under the lows of 3 previous weeks. The decline continued.

     27   Low 97, down 14-1/2 points, indicating a reversal on space movement, but there were 3 bottoms around 96 ... BUYING LEVEL ... and holding above these bottoms indicated a rally. A rally followed.

Apr. 11   High 107 ... SELLING LEVEL. The market may tops 2 weeks at this level and the bottoms for three weeks were around 102-1/2, indicating again that there was good selling.

May 5   This week averages broke under the 3 weeks' bottoms, indicating that the main trend had again turned down. The decline continued.

     14   Low 89. There was a rally to 96 ... SELLING LEVEL ... and a reaction to 90, making 5 weeks' bottoms around these levels ... BUYING LEVEL.

Jun. 19   High 101, failing to reach the bottoms of the previous advance around 100, an OLD SELLING LEVEL. This was only a 3 weeks' rally and there was good selling. A reaction followed to 94-1/2, breaking the bottoms of previous weeks and breaking back under top levels.

Jul. 14   There was another feeble rally during this week to 99-1/2, a lower top. Heavy selling and a sharp, severe decline followed.

Jul. 26   Low 84-1/2. There was a 3-million share day at the bottom, the largest for months, which indicated there was heavy liquidation and that the market was making final bottom. Holding at exactly the SAME LEVEL as July, 1933, and holding above the low of Oct. 21, 1933, indicated good support and again, the fact that the averages never came back to the old top at 81-1/2, made Sep. 8, 1932, indicated that after this top was crossed, it had become a bottom and a BUYING LEVEL. A rally followed quickly.

1934   **10th BULL MARKET (Continued)**

Aug. 25   High 96 ... SELLING LEVEL. Then came a secondary reaction.

Sep. 17   Low 85-3/4, and making a higher bottom. In fact, there were two weeks' bottoms at the same level. This was a SAFE BUYING POINT. After a TRIPLE BOTTOM around the same level and then a higher bottom, it was an indication of good support and stocks should have been brought.

Oct. 17   High 96, back to the same level at Aug. 24 ... SELLING LEVEL. There were four weekly tops around this level.

Nov. 10   This week, a reaction to 92, the last low level. Going back over the charts you can see a series of bottoms and tops around this level. This would make it a logical reaction and a SUPPORT POINT on 1 to 2 weeks' reactions. A rally followed promptly.

Dec. 24   This week the averages crossed 96, where there were 6 weekly tops, an INDICATION of HIGHER PRICES. Dec. 5th, high 104-1/2; Dec. 20th, low of reaction 99, back to the old support level.

1935

Jan. 7   High 107. This was back to the same top reached in Mar. 1934 ... SELLING LEVEL.

     15   Low 99, back to the bottom of Dec. 20 ... BUYING LEVEL.

     21   High 103.

Feb. 6   High 99-1/2, the THIRD TIME and SLIGHTLY HIGHER.

     18   High 108-1/2, 1 point above the old high of March, 1934, and just under the old top ... SELLING LEVEL. Selling developed at this old top level and a decline started.

Mar. 18   Low 95-1/2, back to the same level where it had crossed a series of old tops ... a logical support and BUYING LEVEL. Selling on this decline was light and it was only one month's reaction after the market had given up-signals by crossing a series of tops around 104 to 106, but the safe place to buy was after the market had given a definite up-signal again by crossing the tops of previous weeks.

Apr. 6   This week the averages advanced and crossed the tops of the 3 previous weeks, indicating the MAIN TREND was again turning UP.

     27   The averages advanced and crossed 108 this week and also crossed the old top at 111-1/2 and advanced to 112-1/2. There was a reaction the following week to 107-3/4, just back to the old top. This was a SAFE BUYING POINT after the averages had gone thru to a new high and INDICATED HIGHER PRICES.

May 24   High 117-1/2. The market made 3 weekly tops at this level, just under the old bottom of 119-5/8, and the old top of Nov. 9, 1931 ... SELLING LEVEL. It was natural that the market should meet selling around these old levels. A moderate reaction followed.

Jun. 1   Low 108-1/2, right back on the old top and a SAFE PLACE TO BUY, failing to get back to the low levels reached in the early part of May. This was really one week's reaction and the advance was promptly resumed.

     15   This week crossed the 3 weeks' tops at 117-1/2 and went on through the old bottoms and old tops at 120, only hesitating around 121-1/2 and reacting about 4 points. The market continued to work higher with very small reactions.

Aug. 14   High 129-1/2.

     20   Low 125, this reaction holding well above the old top and bottom levels.

THE W.D. GANN MASTER STOCK MARKET COURSE

1935   **10th BULL MARKET (Continued)**

Sep. 18   High 135-1/2. At this level, there were some old bottoms and tops of the previous campaign and it was natural for a reaction of moderate proportions. SELLING LEVEL.

Oct. 3   Low 127, a two weeks' reaction. The market made 3 weekly bottoms around 128 to 127, holding 2 points above the last low of 125 ... BUYING LEVEL.
The advance was resumed and the averages crossed the top at 135-1/2, indicating still higher prices.

Nov 20   High 149-1/2. There were two old tops around 147 to 148 in the previous campaign, making this a resistance level for at least a reaction ... SELLING LEVEL.

Dec 19   Low 138-1/4 .... BUYING LEVEL; then followed a rally.

1936

Jan. 10   High 148-1/2, making a slightly lower top... SELLING LEVEL.

21   Low 142-1/2, making a higher bottom than the previous bottom ... BUYING LEVEL. From the time that the low was reached July 26, 1934 and 84-1/2, the greatest reaction had been 12 points. There had been reactions of 10 points right along. The reaction of 11-1/4 points from Nov. 20, 1935, to Dec. 19, 1935, was a normal reaction and until the market broke back under some previous bottom or more than 12 points, all indications were that it was still a Bull Market and the main trend up.

Feb   The averages crossed the high of 149-1/2 and continued on up.

Mar. 6   High 159-1/2. Note the old top in June and July, 1931 at 157-1/2, making this a point from which the market should react ... SELLING LEVEL. There was also a bottom at 154-1/2.

13   Low 149, and another 10-1/2 point reaction, the same reaction which had then occurring right along, and lasting only one week ... BUYING LEVEL.
The advance continued and the averages move to a new high for the present move.

Apr. 6   High 163, the low for the week was 159-1/2, making this a narrow week at the top ... SELLING LEVEL. The previous week's high being 161-3/4, show the very little range. In the following week, the averages broke the low of the previous week, and indicating a change in the minor trend. A sharp decline followed.

30   Low 141-1/2, down 21-1/2 points and the greatest reaction which had occurred since the low at 84-1/2. This decline was a little over 3 weeks, a normal reaction in a Bull Market ... BUYING LEVEL. The last low Dec. 19, 1935, was 138-1/4, from which the averages advanced to a new high, therefore, this was an important level that should be broken if a Bear Market was going to start and the averages should continue down more than three weeks if the main trend was going to turn down.
The market did not continue down, but immediately started to advance.

May 23   This week, there were two tops around 152-1/2 and a third higher bottom.

30   The averages advanced to 153-1/2 during this week. Then reacted to 148-1/2, holding above the old top level, indicating strength. This was a GOOD REACTION TO BUY ON. Continued up.

Jun. 27   High 161.

Jul. 11   This week reacted to 154, the old bottom of Jun. 1931. Failing to decline with into the second or third week, indicated strength.

1936   **10th BULL MARKET (Continued)**

        18   The averages advanced to new highs ... SIGNAL FOR HIGHER.

Aug. 10   High 170-1/2 ... SELLING LEVEL.

        21   Low 161, a 9-point reaction in eleven days ... BUYING LEVEL.

Sep. 8   Advanced to a new high 171 ... SELLING LEVEL; then followed a reaction.

        23   Low 165, holding above the last top levels of the previous weeks ... BUYING LEVEL. Reaction was only 9 points, which was an INDICATION of strength and HIGHER prices. The market continued higher.

Oct. 19   High 179.

        26   Low 173, again, only one week's reaction and the averages advanced to new high levels.

Nov 18   High was 187 ... SELLING LEVEL.

Dec 21   Low 175, a 12-point reaction. BUYING LEVEL. The advance was resumed.

1937

Jan. 22   High 187, DOUBLE TOP ... SELLING LEVEL.

        27   Low 182-1/2, a 5-point reaction ... BUYING LEVEL

Feb 11   High 191, a new high ... SIGNAL FOR HIGHER.

        24   Low 185, a 6-point reaction ... HIGHER SUPPORT LEVEL.

Mar. 8   High 195-1/2, END OF BULL MARKET. Why should this be top? Going back to Nov. 13, 1929, you find the low at 195-1/2. Going back to the last high, Feb. 24, 1931, you find the high 197-1/4, and especially in view of the fact that from 1931, the main trend turn down again and continued on down, made this a logical SELLING POINT AGAINST OLD BOTTOMS AND OLD TOPS. But to be sure that this level would not be crossed, you must wait until the bottom of the previous week has been broken and the space movement exceeded.

           REVIEW: From Jul. 26, 1934, low 84-1/2 to Mar. 8, 1937, high 195-1/2, the greatest reaction was 21-1/2 points, from 163 to 141-1/2 in Apr., 1936. Therefore, when the averages broke back more than 21-1/2 points, it would be an indication the Bear Market was starting and main trend had turn down. The last reaction was 12 points when the averages declined to 175 in Dec. 1936. Therefore, breaking back over 12 points would be the first indication that the main trend had turned. There were 3 weeks' bottoms around 185 to 186 in Feb. 1937, and breaking these bottoms would indicate the first change in the main trend.

10th BEAR MARKET

The first decline was sharp and severe.

Mar. 27   This week the averages declined to 183-1/2, breaking under the bottoms of the previous 4 weeks and under the lows of the last reaction of Mar. 6 ... a decline of 12 points. Decline continued. SAFER SHORT SALE, when they broke 185.

Apr. 9   Low 175. Note the last bottom in December, 1936 was 175, making this the logical support point ... BUYING LEVEL for rally. There were 2 weeks' bottoms at 176.

        22   The market rallied to 185, under the old bottom and a SELLING LEVEL. A sharp decline followed, breaking 175, the old bottom and support level.

        28   Low 169.

1937   10th BEAR MARKET (Continued)

May 7   High 176-1/2, rallied back under the old bottoms, a natural SELLING POINT.

     18   Low 166. Note old bottoms around 165 and old tops around 170, making this a point from which the market could rally ... BUYING LEVEL.

     24   High of 176, back to the old bottom and top levels and a SELLING POINT which the averages failed to go thru. Broke back under previous bottoms and declined sharply.

Jun. 17   Low 163. Note there was an old bottom and 164-3/4 and a the top on April 6, 1936, and 163, making this a support and BUYING LEVEL. There was also last low at 161 on Aug. 21, 1930, making this a RALLY POINT. Up to this time there had been no real secondary rally after the trend turned down and you should watch for definite indications of a change in the minor trend to buy for rally. The averages rallied to 172 and reacted to 166. This was the REACTION TO BUY ON, protected with a stop under old bottoms. The advance was resumed and the averages crossed the tops of previous weeks and crossed 176, which was an INDICATION OF HIGHER PRICES. The market advanced slowly this time on very much lower volume than when the top was made in March 1937.

Uug. 14   High 190-1/2, A. LOWER TOP than the main top... SELLING LEVEL. There were two weeks' bottoms at 185-1/2 to 190-1/2; every bottom had been higher on the weekly charge since the advance started.

     21   Therefore, during this week, when the averages broke back under 2 weeks' bottoms, the trend had again turned down and you should SELL SHORT. From 163 to 190-1/2, the greatest reaction was 5 points. Therefore, when they broke back more than 5 points, over balancing the space movement, it was a DEFINITE SIGNAL FOR LOWER PRICES. The decline was rapid and when the averages declined to a series of tops and bottoms at 176, there was no hesitation or any sign of support. The decline continued on down and the old bottom at 163 was reached. There was no rally or no support indicated. Then, finally, broke the low at 160 and continued on down.

Sep. 24   Low 147. This was down into old top levels were there were several weekly bottoms ... BUYING LEVEL.

     30   High 156-1/2, a 9-1/2 point rally. This was up under old bottoms and old top levels of previous campaigns, making this a SELLING LEVEL.

Oct. 19   A panicky decline followed, reaching low at 115-1/2. The volume of sales at this time was the heaviest for many months. Note resistance level and 117 in June, 1935, and the old top and bottom levels at 119-1/2 in 1931, making this a support point for rally, especially on a panicky decline ... and BUYING LEVEL. There was a sharp advance.

     29   High 141-1/2. This was under a series of old bottoms and under the old bottom of Apr. 30, 1936, making it a SELLING LEVEL for a reaction. A sharp quick reaction followed.

Nov. 23   Low 112-1/2, just 3 points under the previous bottom and down to the old 1933 and 1934 tops, a POINT FOR A RALLY.

Dec. 8   High 131 ... SELLING LEVEL.

     13   Low 121-1/2, a SECONDARY REACTION and there were two bottoms around this level ... BUYING POINT.

1937   10th BEAR MARKET (Continued)

21   High 131 ... SELLING LEVEL ... same top as Dec. 8.

29   Low 118, slightly HIGHER BOTTOM and sign of some support ... BUYING LEVEL.

1938

Jan. 15   High 134-1/2 ... SELLING LEVEL ... went over two previous tops, but made top here for two weeks and could not advance. The following week broke back under the low of the previous week, indicating a reaction.

Feb 4   Low 117-1/2, a DOUBLE BOTTOM, same low as Dec. 29, a PLACE TO BUY with a close stop loss order, as the market was holding above the Oct. 19 bottom also.

23   High 133, A. LOWER TOP than January 15, an indication of good selling around this level, where there were old bottoms and tops ... SELLING LEVEL.

Mar. 12   This week, the averages broke back under 2 weeks' of bottoms at 127-1/2, turning the MINOR TREND DOWN again. A sharp decline followed. The double bottoms and 118 were broken, indicating extreme weakness, and no rally occurred from these bottoms. The last low at 112-1/2 was broken and there was no rally or support around the old tops at 110 and 108, indicating that the market was in a very weak position. There was heavy selling and everyone was bearish and had lost hope. Rallies were small, only 4 to 5 points. Remember our rule. In the last stages of a Bear Market, the lower prices get, the smaller the rallies are.

31   Low 97-1/2, END OF PANICKY DECLINE and END OF BEAR MARKET. Why should the averages stop at this point and receive support? Look back on your chart and you will see that on Mar. 18, 1935, the low was 95-1/2, a point from which the real Bull Market got underway; in Nov. 1935, there was a series of tops around 96, making 97-1/2 to 95-1/2 a strong support level and a POINT TO BUY at the end of a panicky decline. But you should follow rules and watch for definite indication that the trend was turning up.

REVIEW: From the high of 195-1/2 on Mar. 8, 1937, to the low of 97-1/2 on Mar. 31, 1938, the greatest advances in the Bear Market was 27-1/2 points, from 163 to 190-1/2, and 22 points, from 112-1/2 to 134-1/2. The last rally was 15 points, from 117-1/2 to 133. The last small rally was 6 points, from low of 121-1/2 on Mar. 12 to high of 127-1/2 on Mar. 16, 1938. Therefore, the first indication of a change in the minor trend would be an advance of more than 6 points. Advancing more than 15 points would indicate uptrend again.

11th MINOR BULL MARKET

Apr. 2   The market started to rally, first indication of higher prices.

9   The averages crossed 108-1/2, the top of the previous week, a SECOND SIGNAL FOR HIGHER PRICES.

18   High 121-1/2, up 23-1/2 points, more than the rally from 112-1/2 to 134-1/2 in the previous Bear Market. This was the THIRD SIGNAL that prices were going higher, but note, the series of bottoms around 121, making this a SELLING LEVEL for a reaction, and at 119 to 120, going back in the past, was a series of bottoms and tops, making it always an important point, and indication that a SECONDARY REACTION was DUE, which always follows the first sharp rally after final bottoms are made.

1938 11th MINOR BULL MARKET (Continued)

May 27 The market worked down slowly. Low 106-1/2, 9 points above the low of March 31. At this level stocks were very dull and narrow, showing that there was no selling pressure, and that this SECONDARY REACTION was a PLACE TO BUY. This was a 3 weeks' reaction from top at 120. You should now watch for the first indication that the minor trend was turning up again. The averages had made a top at 114 and 112-1/2.

Jun. 11 The averages crossed 112-1/2 this week, advancing to 116. Then the following week reacted to 112-1/2 on very small volume, a SURE INDICATION TO BUY.

25 The averages crossed 116, the last top, during this week and went right on through 120-121, the old tops. There was heavy buying and a rapid runaway market. There was no reaction from the old tops at 133 to 134-1/2. Each weekly bottom was higher.

Jul. 25 High 146-1/4. This was under old bottoms. Note 2 weekly bottoms in Oct. 1937. The market made 3 weeks' tops around 146 ... SELLING LEVEL.

28 Reacted to 139.

Aug. 6 Rallied to 146-1/2, making a second or double top ... SELLING LEVEL. Then followed a sharp, quick decline.

12 Low 135-1/2.

24 High 145, a THIRD LOWER TOP, where you should SELL OUT AND GO SHORT as the decline to 135-1/2 had broken under the bottoms of 3 previous weeks. The averages reacted to 136-1/2; rallied to 143-1/2, making a FOURTH LOWER TOP, a sure and SAFE INDICATION TO SELL for lower prices.

Sep. 14 Low 130-1/4 – down against old top levels, but had broken previously weekly bottoms, an indication of lower prices.

21 High 140-1/2, a FIFTH LOWER TOP ... SELLING LEVEL. A sharp, quick decline followed on war news, when Hitler was getting ready to take Czecho-Slovakia and the rumors were that there would be war if Hitler did not have his way, which he did.

26 Low of 127-1/2.

27 A 5-point rally to 132-1/2.

28 Low 127-7/8, a slightly higher bottom than Sep. 26, ... BUYING LEVEL. Stocks showed great resistance and everything indicated that the market was making bottom. The Allies compromised with Hitler and war was averted. You will note at 128. There was a series of old tops and bottoms in past history and a natural support level. More reasons will be given later why this was a SURE BUYING POINT . Then you should watch for the first indication that the trend was turning up. The last rally was 5 points and the greatest rally on the decline 10 points. Therefore, when the averages advanced 6 points, they indicated higher and when they advanced 10 points indicated a still further advance. This they did promptly. You could have bought stocks after the averages were up 5 and 10 points and made plenty of money. The advance continued and the averages moved right on thru the old top at 146, indicated that it was a strong uptrend. You could have bought more stocks after the averages crossed 146 and still made big profits. Reactions were small and there were no weekly bottoms broken.

Nov 10 High 158-3/4 ... SELLING LEVEL. Note top of last rally in September, 1937, at 157-1/2, an indication that stocks would meet selling around this level. But you must follow your rule to determine when the trend is changing.

1938	**11th MINOR BULL MARKET (Continued)**

REVIEW: From the low of 97-1/2 on Mar. 31, 1938, to the high of 158-3/4 on Nov. 10, 1938, there was one reaction of 15 points on the way up and the greatest reaction was 19 points. The smallest reaction was Oct. 14 to 18, 153-1/2 to 148-1/2, 5 points, and the last reaction from 155-1/2 to 150-1/2 was five points. Therefore, when the market broke back 5 points or more, it would indicate lower prices and breaking 150-1/2 would be a signal for lower and breaking back under 148-1/2 would be under a series of weekly bottoms and turned the main trend down.

11th MINOR BEAR MARKET

The decline followed promptly.

Nov 28   The averages reached 145. This was a natural support point for a rally and BUYING LEVEL, because it was down against a series of old tops around 146 to 145. The market had not yet had the secondary rally, which is always indicated after the first sharp break. Therefore, you could have bought around 145 for a rally.

1939

Jan. 4   High 155-1/2 ... LOWER TOP. The market held for several days, in fact, made 2 weekly tops at 155-1/2, just 3 points under the high of Nov. 1938, indicating that it was meeting heavy selling on this secondary rally. This was a point for you to SELL OUT LONG STOCKS AND GO SHORT.

Jan. 14   The FIRST SIGNAL that the minor trend had turned down again and that stocks indicated LOWER PRICES came during this week, when the averages broke back under the bottoms of 3 previous weeks and continued on down.

26   Low 136-1/8. Note 3 weekly bottoms around this level in July, 1938, and tops around this level in Oct. and Dec. 1937, making this a point from which a rally could take place. A quick rally followed and the market worked higher.

Mar. 10   High 152-1/2, a THIRD LOWER TOP and at the breakaway point of the previous moves... SELLING LEVEL. The low for the week was 148-1/2. In the following week when the averages broke back under 148-1/2, it was the first confirmation that the minor trend was turning down again. You should have sold out stocks and gone short. The market moved down fast, breaking all support levels.

31   In this week broke the low at 136, indicating a very weak position, and continued on down. There was no support of any importance or any rally from the old bottoms and 128, made in September 1938, showing that the market was weak and the main trend still down.

Apr. 11   Low 120-1/8 ... BUYING LEVEL. This was a natural support level against old tops and bottoms. Note the last rally before the last decline to 120 during the week ending May 14, making this a logical and natural support point.

REVIEW: From the high at 158-3/4 on Nov. 10, 1938, to the low of 120-1/8 on Apr. 11, 1939, the greatest rally was 16 points and the smallest rally 10-1/2 points. Therefore, when the market advanced 11 points from 120-1/8, it would be an indication that the minor trend was turning up and advancing more than 16 points would turn main trend up again. From the last high point at 152-1/2, made on Mar. 10, 1939, to the low at 120-1/8, the greatest rally was 5 points, therefore, an advance greater than 5 points would be the first indication that bottom had been made and the minor trend, at least, was going to turn up.

12th MINOR BULL MARKET

A quick rally followed.

- Apr. 13 The averages reached 129-1/4, up 9 points. 128 was the old bottom in Sep. 1938 ... SELLING LEVEL. Therefore, it was only natural that from around this level a secondary reaction would take place.

- 14 Low 124-1/2, a higher bottom ... BUYING LEVEL. Then followed a rally.

- 15 High 130-1/2, crossing the previous top by 1-1/4 points ... SELLING LEVEL.

- 19 A secondary reaction to 124-3/4 making a slightly higher bottom ... BUYING LEVEL.

- 22 High 130, same level as Apr. 15 ... SELLING LEVEL.

- 26 Low 126-1/2, a THIRD HIGHER BOTTOM ... BUYING LEVEL.

- 28 High 131-1/2 ... SELLING LEVEL.

- May 1 Low 127-1/2, a FOURTH HIGHER BOTTOM ... BUYING LEVEL.

- 10 High 134-1/2, under old bottoms ... SELLING LEVEL. A reaction followed.

- 17 Low 128-1/2, a FIFTH HIGHER BOTTOM and a support level around the old 128 top and bottom ... BUYING LEVEL. After this last low level the market advanced and tops were crossed. The advance continued.

- Jun. 9 Reached high at 140-3/4, again up to old bottom and old top levels where resistance was met ... SELLING LEVEL. This advance from the extreme low of 120-1/8 in April had carried the averages up over 20 points, an indication of higher prices after a secondary reaction.

- 16 Low 134, back to an old top ... BUYING LEVEL.

- 21 High 138-1/2, a LOWER TOP, an indication of good selling ... SELLING LEVEL. A decline started. The support level at 134 was broken.

- 30 Low 128-7/8, holding above the series of support levels made in April and May, 1939. This was a BUYING POINT on the SECONDARY REACTION. A slow advance started and the averages crossed highs of previous weeks.

- Jul. 13 Crossed 138, the top of June 21, SIGNAL FOR HIGHER PRICES.

- 17 Crossed 140-3/4. The high of June 9.

- 25 High 145-3/4, at the old top levels of July and August, 1938, and at top of last rally of March 21, 1939, a point for at least a reaction ... SELLING LEVEL.

- Aug. 1 Low 142-1/2.

- 3 High 145-3/4, same high as July 25, making a DOUBLE TOP ... SELLING LEVEL.

If you will go over the charts carefully and study all important movements in resistance levels, you will learn how to apply the rules successfully in future market campaigns. The more you study, the greater your success will be.

[unsigned]
_____

August 4, 1939

Chapter 11B

Dow-Jones 30 Industrial Averages

THE W.D. GANN MASTER STOCK MARKET COURSE

#1

DOW JONES 30 INDUSTRIAL AVERAGES

The table below gives the reactions in a Bull Market and the declines in a Bear Market, or the moves that are opposite to the main trend. The number of moves in each campaign is given and the number of weeks of reaction or rally in opposition to the trend. By going over these tables you'll find that only six times in over forty-two years did a move in opposition to a trend last as much as eleven to fourteen weeks. We see that the average moves lasted from two to five weeks and a few from six to eight weeks. This will be a guide for you in future campaigns and enable you to figure about how many weeks a move will run in opposition to the main trend before the market again resumes the main trend.

Year	Moves	Weeks	Year	Moves	Weeks
1st Bull Market Low Aug. 8, 1896			3rd Bull Market		
1896	1	2	1904	1	1
	2	5		2	6
1897	3	13		3	6
	4	7		4	1
1898	5	11		5	1
	6	8	1905	6	6
1899	7	1	End of 3rd Bull Market		
	8	5			
End of 1st Bull Market					
1st Bear Market:			3rd Bear Market:		
1900	1	1	1907	1	2
	2	3		2	5
	3	4		3	9
	4	2		4	4
End of 1st Bear Market			1907	5	2
				6	2
				7	2
2nd Bull Market:				8	2
1900	1	1		9	2
	2	6	End of 3rd Bear Market		
	3	2			
1901	4	3	4th Bull Market:		
	5	1	1907	1	2
End of 2nd Bull Market			1908	2	4
				3	2
2nd Bear Market:				4	5
1901	1	1		5	6
	2	3		6	6
	3	1		7	2
	4	5	1909	8	2
1902	5	8		9	3
	6	3		10	4
	7	2		11	3
	8	4	End of 4th Bull Market		
	9	4			
	10	1	4th Bear Market:		
	11	1	1910	1	3
1903	12	3		2	3
	13	4		3	2
	14	1		4	2
	15	1		5	2
	16	1			
Nov. 9, 1903 End of 2nd Bear Market			July 26 End of 4th Bear Market		

DOW JONES 30 INDUSTRIAL AVERAGES

Year	Moves	Weeks	Year	Moves	Weeks
	5th Bull Market:			7th Bull Market, Cont'd.	
1910	1	4	1918	6	2
	2	7		7	3
	3	4		8	2
1911	4	3	1919	9	5
	5	14	1919	10	2
	6	2		11	5
	7	2		12	1
1912	8	2		End of 7th Bull Market	
	9	2			
	10	2		7th Bear Market:	
	11	2	1919	1	2
	12	2	1920	2	6
	End of 5th Bull Market			3	2
				4	2
	5th Bear Market:			5	5
1912	1	2		6	3
	2	3		7	2
	3	2	1921	8	4
1913	4	1		9	2
	5	2		10	2
	6	13		11	4
1914	7	6		12	6
	8	2		End of 7th Bear Market	
	9	4			
	10	2		8th Bull Market:	
	End of 5th Bear Market		1921	1	2
				2	2
	6th Bull Market:		1922	3	3
1915	1	4		4	2
	2	2		5	2
	3	12		6	2
	4	1		7	7
	5	1	1923	8	2
	6	3		End of 8th Bull Market	
1916	7	5			
	8	3		8th Bear Market:	
	9	6	1923	1	1
	10	4		2	2
	11	1		3	2
	End of 6th Bull Market			4	5
				5	1
	6th Bear Market:			End of 8th Bear Market	
1916	1	2			
1917	2	7		9th Bull Market	
	3	4	1924	1	1
	4	3		2	2
	5	2		3	6
	End of 6th Bear Market			4	2
				5	2
	7th Bull Market:			6	3
1918	1	7		Oct. 18, 1924	
	2	2	1925	7	4
	3	2		8	4
	4	2			
	5	1			

THE W.D. GANN MASTER STOCK MARKET COURSE

DOW JONES 30 INDUSTRIAL AVERAGES

Year	Moves	Weeks
	9th Bull Market, Cont'd.	
1925	9	1
	10	1
	11	2
	12	3
	13	2
	14	7
	15	3
	16	1
	17	6
	18	6
1927	19	1
	20	1
	21	4
	22	1
	23	3
	24	2
1928	25	4
	26	2
	27	3
	28	2
	29	2
	30	2
	31	1
1929	32	2
	33	4
	34	3
	35	2
	End of 1929 Bull Market	
	9th Bear Market	
1929	1	1
	2	2
	End of 9th Bear Market	
	10th Minor Bull Market or Rally in Bear Market	
1929	1	2
1930	2	2
	End of Rally in Bear Market	
	10th Bear Market	
1930	1	2 rally
	2	3
	3	4 rally & 11 wks from low
	4	1
	5	2
	6	3
1931	7	5 rally & 10 wks from low
	8	1
	9	1
	10	3
	11	1

Year	Moves	Weeks
	10th Bear Market, Cont'd.	
1931	12	1
	13	5
	14	2
	15	1
	16	2
	17	1

End of Bear Market July 8, 1932

11th Bull Market, July 8, 1932 to Sept. 1932.

1st Sharp advance lasted 9 weeks no reactions followed by 25 weeks decline which was a reaction in a bull market or accumulation on the side. The greatest rally lasted 6 weeks and the last decline 7 weeks making bottom Feb. 27, 1933.

Bull Market Resumed

1933	1 move	2 weeks
	2 moves	1 week
	3 moves	1 week

July 17 to 21st declined 26 points.

Then followed a trading market or accumulation on the side lasting 91 weeks until March 30, 1935 during this time the averages did not advance 2 points above the high of July 17, 1933 nor decline more than 2 points under the low of July 21, 1933. Holding in a range of 27 points. This long period of time indicated that when the averages crossed 112 the old Tops in March 1935 that they would go very much higher and final top was made March 10, 1937 with averages at 195½.

THE W.D. GANN MASTER STOCK MARKET COURSE

#4

DOW JONES 30 INDUSTRIAL AVERAGES

From July 21, 1933 to March 30, 1935 the moves were as follows:

1 weeks rally

1 weeks reaction

7 weeks advanced to Sept. 1933 making a total of 9 weeks rally.

4 weeks decline to 82½, Oct. 21, 1933. This was the extreme low of the reaction and was 13 weeks from July 21, 1933. The next rally lasted 14 weeks to February 5, 1934, high 111½ then declined to July 26, 1934. The last low 84½ - 24 weeks from February 5, 1934. There was no rally lasting more than 4 weeks and from this low the Bull Market was resumed. February 5, 1934 to July 26, 1934. 11 - a Minor Bear Market or reaction in a Bull Market.

Year	Moves	Weeks		Year	Moves	Weeks	
	11th Bull Market, Con't.				12th Bull Market		
1934	1	4		1938	1	2	
	2	2			2	2	
	3	2			3	1	August reaction
1935	4	3					
	5	4			4	4	weeks reaction or 8 wks from top
	March 18, 1935 last low						
	6	1					
	7	2					
	8	2					
	9	4					
1936	10	1		Nov. 10, 1938 End of 12th Bull Market			
	11	1					
	12	1					
	13	3			12th Minor Bear Market		
	14	1		1938	1	4	
	15	1			2	6	
	16	2					
	17	1					
	18	1					
	19	5					
1937	20	1					
	21	2					
	End of the 11th Bull Market March 10, 1937.						
	11th Bear Market						
1937	1	2					
	2	1					
	3	2					
	4	8	rally to Aug. 14, 1937				
	5	1					
	6	2					
1938	7	2					
	8	2					
March 31, 1938 End of 11th Bear Market							

Page 354

DOW JONES 30 RAILROAD AVERAGES

Year	Moves	Weeks
\multicolumn{3}{c}{Reactions in Bull Market}		
1897	1	5
	2	8
1898	3	8
	5	6
	6	8
1899	7	8

End of 1st Bull Market

Year	Moves	Weeks
\multicolumn{3}{c}{Rally in Bear Market}		
1899	1	13
	2	4
1900	3	15

End of 1st Bear Market

2nd Bull Market:

Year	Moves	Weeks
1900	1	5
1901	2	1
1901	3	8
	4	2
	5	3
	6	2
	7	3

End of 2nd Bull Market

2nd Bear Market:

Year	Moves	Weeks
1902	1	4
	2	3
	3	2
	4	2

End of 2nd Bear Market

3rd Bull Market:

Year	Moves	Weeks
1903	1	2
1904	2	7
	3	5
	4	2
1905	5	6
	6	2
	7	3

End of 3rd Bull Market

3rd Bear Market:

Year	Moves	Weeks
1906	1	3
	2	6
	3	9
	5	1
	6	2
	7	5
	8	4

End of 3rd Bear Market

4th Bull Market:

Year	Moves	Weeks
1908	1	4
	2	5
	3	2
	4	8
1909	5	2

End of 4th Bull Market

4th Bear Market:

Year	Moves	Weeks
1909	1	2
	2	4
1910	3	4
	4	2
	5	2
	6	2
	7	1

End of 4th Fourth Bear Market

5th Bull Market:

Year	Moves	Weeks
1910	1	3
	2	7
1911	3	3
	4	3
	5	10
1912	6	10
	7	10

End of 5th Bull Market

5th Bear Market:

Year	Moves	Weeks
1912	1	4
	2	1
	3	3
1913	4	3
	5	2
	6	13
	7	6
	8	2
	9	4
	10	2

5th Bear Market ended Dec. 24, 1914

[W.D. Gann's signature]

[undated, but *circa* 1938 onwards]

Chapter 12

Volume of Sales

AUTHOR:		MEMBER
"Truth of the Stock Tape"	**W. D. GANN**	New Orleans Cotton Exchange
"Wall Street Stock Selector"		Commodity Exchange, Inc N.Y.
"New Stock Trend Detector"	Statistician and Economist	American Economic Ass'n
	82 WALL STREET	Royal Economic Society
	NEW YORK, N.Y.	
	2101 N.W. 18th TERRACE	
	MIAMI. FLA.	

VOLUME OF SALES

After considering the three important factors ... FORMATIONS, TIME and RESISTANCE LEVELS ... the fourth and next very important factor is the VOLUME OF SALES AT TOPS AND BOTTOMS.

The VOLUME OF SALES is the real driving power behind the market and shows whether Supply or Demand is increasing or decreasing. Large buying or selling orders from professional traders, the public or any other source of supply and demand, are bound to be registered on the tape and shown in the volume of sales.

Therefore, a careful study of the VOLUME OF SALES will enable you to determine very closely a change in trend, especially if you apply all of the other rules for judging position according to the Formations, Resistance Levels and Time.

RULES FOR DETERMINING CULMINATIONS BY VOLUME OF SALES

1 - At the end of any prolonged Bull Campaign or rapid advance in an individual stock, there is usually a large increase in the volume of sales, which marks the end of the campaign, at least temporarily. Then, after a sharp decline on heavy volume of sales, when a secondary rally takes place and the volume of sales decreases, it is an indication that the stock has made final top and that the main trend will turn down.

2 - If the stock holds after making a second lower top and gets dull and narrow for some time, working in a sideways movement, and then breaks out on increased volume, it is a sign of a further decline.

3 - After a prolonged decline of several weeks, several months or several years, at the time a stock is reaching bottom, the volume of trading should decrease and the range in fluctuation should narrow down. This is one of the sure signs that liquidation is running its course and that the stock is getting ready to show a change in trend.

4 - After the first sharp advance (when the trend is changing from a Bear Market to a Bull Market) the stock will have a secondary reaction and make bottom, just the same as it had a secondary rally after the first sharp decline. If the volume of sales decreases on the reaction and then the stock moves up, advancing on heavier volume, it will be an indication of an advance to higher levels.

These rules apply to the general market, that is, to the total sales traded in the New York Stock Exchange – daily, weekly or monthly – as well as to individual stocks.

SUMMARY: SALES INCREASE NEAR THE TOP AND DECREASE NEAR THE BOTTOM, except in abnormal markets, like October, and November, 1929 when the market was moving down very fast and culminated on large volume of sales, making a sharp bottom, from which a swift rebound followed. As a rule, after the first sharp rally, there is a secondary decline on decreased volume, as described above under Rule 4.

MONTHLY RECORD OF VOLUME OF SALES
ON NEW YORK STOCK EXCHANGE
1930 – 1935

To understand the importance of Volume, a study of the total number of shares traded in on the New York Stock Exchange is necessary.

1930

JUNE — Sales were 80,000,000 shares, with the market moving lower.

JULY & AUG. — On a small rally the total sales were only 80,000,000 shares for two months.

SEPTEMBER — The market was slightly higher early in the month; then a decline started, which carried prices to new low levels, sales of 50,000,000 shares being recorded.

OCTOBER — The market broke to new low levels. Stocks at this time broke the low levels of November, 1929 and sales increased to 70,000,000 shares.

DECEMBER — The Dow-Jones Industrial Averages declined 46 points under the low levels of November, 1929. Total sales this month were 60,000,000 shares.

1931

JANUARY — A rally started and in January, 1931 the sales were 42,000,000 shares.

FEBRUARY — The market made top of the rally on sales of 64,000,000 shares, which showed that the volume of trading was increasing on the rally and that stocks were meeting resistance. Note that this top was just under the low levels of November, 2929, which showed that stocks met selling when they moved up under the old low levels of the panic.

MARCH — A decline started in March and the sales were 64,000,000 shares, a heavier volume, with prices moving lower.

APRIL — Sales were 54,000,000 shares.

MAY — Sales 47,000,000.

JUNE — There was a sharp decline on a volume of sales totalling 59,000,000, which carried the Averages down to now low levels, reaching 120, the old top of 1919 and the last low of May 1925. A quick rally followed to the end of June and early July, the Averages reaching 157½, but failing to cross the high level made in May, 1931.

JULY The sales were smaller, only 33,000,000, and the market narrowed down.

AUGUST The sales were 24,000,000, still a narrow, dull market, not making much progress on the upside.

SEPTEMBER Activity started and sales reached 51,000,000. On this increased volume the Averages declined 45 points during the month of September. This showed great weakness and indicated a further decline.

OCTOBER A sharp decline occurred which carried the Averages down to 85 on sales of 48,000,000 shares.

NOVEMBER A rally followed, culminating on November 9th. The averages reached 119½, back to the old top of 1919, to the last low of 1925, and to the bottom of a previous rally. Failing to penetrate these old bottoms and cross the previous top, the market showed weakness and indicated that the trend was still down. Sales in November were 37,000,000, the volume decreasing on the rally.

DECEMBER The Averages declined to a new low for the move, making 72 on sales of 50,000,000 shares, the largest since September, 1931. This indicated that big liquidation was still going on.

1932

JANUARY The Averages reached a low of 70 on sales of 44,000,000 shares for the month.

FEBRUARY Rallied to 89¾ on sales of 31,000,000 shares.

MARCH The Averages made about the same high on sales of 33,000,000 shares. Then the market went dead on the rally, stocks narrowing down.

APRIL The Dow-Jones 30 Industrial Averages broke 70, the low of January; and declined to 55 on sales of 30,000,000 shares.

MAY The Averages broke 53, the old low levels of the panic of 1907 and 1914, which indicated lower prices; then decline to 45 on sales of 23,000,000 shares.

JUNE The range between extreme high and extreme low averaged 10 points and the averages reached a new low on sales of 23,000,000 shares.

JULY On July 8, 1932, the extreme low was reached, with the Averages down to 40½. The volume was very small and the Averages and individual stocks moved in a very narrow trading range, indicating the last stages of a bear market. Late in the month the Averages crossed the high of June, which indicated that the trend was turning up. Sales were 23,000,000 shares. The range was about 13 points on Averages. At the low in July the Averages were down 345 points from 1929 high. The volume of sales for the three months – May, June and July – aggregated only 69,000,000 shares, the smallest since 1923, in contrast to over 100,000,000 shares per month at the top in September, 1929 and 141,000,000 in the month of October, 1929. This indicted that after such a drastic decline, liquidation had run its course and the trend was changing. The market really had been sold to a standstill. Traders and investors sold out everything because they feared things were going to get worse. It was the same old story: A bull market begins in gloom and ends in glory. All of the indications were plain: The small volume of sales and narrow range of fluctuations indicated that the end had been reached and that a change in trend was certain.

During the latter part of July, 1932, the advance started.

AUGUST There was a sharp rally in August on sales of 83,000,000 shares, more than for the entire three months past. This was on short covering and wise investment buying.

SEPTEMBER Top of the rally was reached on sales of 67,000,000 shares, with the Averages up 40 points from the low of July 8. After this advance to September on a large volume, distribution took place and the trend turned down. (Note that the total volume from July 8 to the top in September was 168 million shares.) The Averages failed to go higher in the third month. At no time from April, 1930 to July, 1932 had the Averages or most of the individual stocks rallied over two months. Therefore, to show a change in trend to a prolonged bull market, they would have to advance three full months or more.

OCTOBER After September stocks worked slowly down on a smaller volume of sales. In October the sales were 29,000,000.

NOVEMBER Sales were 23,000,000.

DECEMBER Sales 23,000,000.

1933

JANUARY Sales were 19,000,000 shares.

FEBRUARY The whole country was in a state of panic. Banks were failing right and left. People were panic stricken and selling stocks and bonds regardless of price. There were business failures, and when President Roosevelt was inaugurated on March 1, he immediately acted and closed all the banks in the United States. This marked the end of the secondary decline and started a constructive movement.

The Dow-Jones Industrial Averages declined to 50 in February, which was 9 points higher than the low of July, 1932. Sales were only 19,000,000 shares, the smallest volume of any time in over 10 years and the smallest volume for any month since the top in September, 1929, a sure sign of bottom.

MARCH A rally started on increased sales. The volume was 20,000,000 shares.

APRIL The United States went off the gold standard. This started a rapid advance in stocks and commodities. Sales on the New York Stock Exchange were 53,000,000 shares this month.

MAY The advance continued and the volume of trading reach 104,000,000 shares.

JUNE The volume increased to 125,000,000.

JULY The sales were 120,000,000 sales.

From March low to July high, 1933, the total number of shares traded in on the New York Stock Exchange was 422,000,000 shares and the Averages at the top in July were up 60 point from the low of February, 1933. Very few people keep records and study enough to understand what the enormous volume of 422,000,000 shares meant. This was the greatest volume of sales of any bull campaign in the history of the New York Stock Exchange. It was greater than the last advance in 1929. (From the last low in May, 1929 to September, 1929, the Averages advanced 96 points and the total sales on the New York Stock Exchange were 350,000,000 shares.) It was one of the wildest buying waves in history. Commodities advanced by leaps and bounds. People bought stocks regardless of price. Just think about it: Sales of 350,000,000 in three months – May, June, and July, 1933 – equal to the volume from May, 1929 to September, 1929. The signs were plain that volume was telling the story of a wave of inflation. Commodities and stocks had advanced so rapidly and everybody had bought on such thin margin that a wide-open break occurred in four days from July 18th to 21st, carrying the Dow-Jones Averages down 25 points to 85. Cotton and Wheat broke badly at the same time on heavy liquidation. At this time Dr. E.A. Crawford failed. He was involved in commodities, said to be the largest amount carried ever known.

AUG. & SEPT. After the sharp decline in July, a rally followed in August and September, which carried the Averages to within two points of the July high, making a double top. The volume of sales on this second rally was smaller. In August the sales were 42,000,000 and in September 43,000,000 shares. In these two months the volume was only two-thirds of the total volume for July, 1933.

OCTOBER The Dow-Jones 30 Industrial Averages declined to 82½, the last low before the start of a long advance. Sales decreased to 39,000,000 and the market became very dull and narrow. A slow rally started from the October lows.

NOVEMBER Sales were 33,000,000 shares.

DECEMBER Sales 35,000,000.

1934

JANUARY The sales this month were 54,000,000.

FEBRUARY Sales 57,000,000 shares, with the top in February only slightly above the high for January. The Averages failed to get over one point above the high of July, 1933, making a double top. Sales of 111,000,000 shares in two months and the third time at the same level was a signal of top. Individual stocks especially showed plainly by the large volume and the slow progress they were making in February that they were getting ready to start down. The trend turned down in the latter part of February.

MARCH Sales reached 30,000,000 shares.

APRIL There was a slight rally on 29,000,000 shares.

MAY	Prices were lower on 25,000,000 sales.
JUNE	There was a small rally and the volume decreased to 16,000,000 shares for the month.
JULY	On July 26, 1934, stocks made bottom on sales of nearly 3,000,000 shares for the day, with the Dow-Jones Averages down to 85, slightly above the low level of October, 1933.
	For the month of July, 1934 total sales were only 21,000,000 shares. Individual stocks moved in a narrow trading range, which showed that bottom was being made and the foundation laid for another bull campaign. The fact that an extreme high was reached in July, 1933 was an indication that you should watch for a change in trend in July, 1934, according to my rules to watch for a change in trend one year, two years, or three years from any important top and bottom.
AUGUST	The market rallied 11 points on averages on sales of 16,000,000 shares.
SEPTEMBER	The market reacted within one point of the July low. Sales were down to 12,000,000 shares, a sure sign of bottom, being the smallest sales per month in many years.
OCTOBER	The market rallied in October on a slightly increased volume of sales, 15,000,000 shares.
NOVEMBER	The sales increased to 21,000,000 shares.
DECEMBER	Prices were higher on sales of 23,000,000 shares for the month.

1935

JANUARY	There was increased activity on sales of 19,000,000 shares.
FEBRUARY	The market reached the top for the rally. Sales only 14,000,000 shares, which was a sign that there was not enough buying power to carry prices thru.
MARCH	There was a big decline, which was the last before the market advanced to new highs. Sales were 16,000,000 shares.
APRIL	Increased activity shown and stocks started advancing. Volume of sales was 22,000,000 shares, which showed that the bull market was under way.
MAY	The Dow-Jones 30 Industrial Averages crossed the high levels of 1933 and the top of February, 1934, on sales of 30,000,000 shares. Individual stocks showed increased sales and many of them moved up to new high levels.
JUNE	The Averages crossed 120, which was above the last high of November 9, 1931, a sure indication of higher prices. The sales for June were 22,000,000 shares.
JULY	New highs were reached for individual stocks and the Averages. Sales for the month were 29,000,000 shares.

AUGUST	More new highs for individual stocks and new highs for the Industrial Averages. Sales reached 43,000,000 shares, the highest since January and February, 1934.
SEPTEMBER	The advance continued and sales were 35,000,000 shares.
OCTOBER	The Dow-Jones 30 Industrial averages advanced to 142. The total sales for the month were 46,000,000 shares. During the week ending October 26, sales on the New York Stock Exchange were 14,000,000 shares, the largest for any week since September, 1934, which was an indication that you should begin to watch for top in stocks that had had big advances.
NOVEMBER	During the week ended November 2 the sales were 11,000,000 shares and during the week ended November 9 ... a 5-day week ... the sales were 12,000,000 shares. On November 8, the sales were 3,350,000, the largest for any day since the bottom of July 26, 1934

JULY, 1934 TO NOVEMBER, 1935

The total sales from the low of July 26, 1934 to the high of November 8, 1935 were 383,000,000 shares. The total number of points which the Dow-Jones Industrial averages advanced from July, 1934 to November 8, 1935 was 61 points. Note that the total advance from the low of March, 1933 to the top in July, 1933 was 60 points. Therefore, with the averages in November, 1935 up 61 points, as much as in the 1933 campaign, it was time to watch for at least a temporary change in trend.

Note that the volume of sales during this 15-months' campaign from July, 1934 to November, 1935 was about 39,000,000 shares less than the 5 months' campaign from March, 1933 to July, 1933. This shows that since the Securities Administration has been operating, it has reduced trading considerably.

DECEMBER	Volume of sales 57,462,000 shares and a 10-point reaction occurred, a normal reaction in a Bull Market.

LARGEST VOLUME OF SALES BEFORE FINAL TOP

By going over the records you will find that the largest volume of sales often comes before final top is reached; that when the actual high is made, the volume of sales is smaller than in previous months, weeks, or days. This is due to the fact that the public often loads up heavily, buying all they can carry, when the market gets very active; then as the market nears top, their demand having been supplied, they buy less. Example:

1936

JANUARY	Sales 67,500,000, the largest since the low was reached in July, 1934.
FEBRUARY	Sales 60,884,000.
MARCH	Sales 51,000,000.
APRIL	High was reached on April 6, for a reaction. A sharp decline followed. Low April 30, with the Dow-Jones 30 Industrial averages down 21 points. Sales for the month, 39,610,000. The volume on this reaction was smaller than for many months past. You will see that the largest volume came in January before the reaction in April, the public having loaded up on the January rise.

1937

JANUARY   Sales 58,671,000, the largest since January, 1936 ... a signal to watch for a change in trend in the near future.

FEBRUARY   Sales 50,248,000.

MARCH   Dow-Jones averages reached final high at 195½ on March 8. Sales for the month were 50,346,000 and the averages broke back 15 points before the end of the month. This again proves that the public loaded up on stocks in January, as the volume was less in February and when top was reached in March, the public was unable to buy in large volume.

JULY, 1934 TO MARCH, 1937

From July 26, 1934 to October 31, 1936, the total volume was 866,988,000 shares and the market had advanced 94 points on the Dow-Jones averages. This was an average of 88,860 shares per point. From October 31, 1936 to March 8, 1937, when final high was reached, the total volume was 258,392,000 shares and the market had advanced 17 points. This was an average of 151,197 shares per point, showing that the market was meeting with almost twice as many shares per point as it did up to October 31, 1936. This increased volume on a smaller gain was an indication that the market was nearing top. The total sales in the entire Bull Campaign from July 26, 1934 to March 8, 1937 was 1,125,380,000 shares or about one-third of the total shares listed on the New York Stock Exchange.

1937

After the high in March, 1937, the volume decreased on the decline.

MAY   Sales 18,562,000.

JUNE   Sales 16,547,000. Low was reached on June 17 with the averages down 32 points. This decreasing volume indicated that a secondary rally was due.

JULY   Sales 20,721,000.

AUGUST   High secondary rally. Dow-Jones averages reached 190½, up 27½ points. Sales 17,212,000. This will prove that on the secondary rally to within 5 points of the old top the volume was not more than one-third the sales at the first top in March, 1937 ... a sure indication of decreasing demand and a signal to sell the market short.

SEPTEMBER Sharp decline followed. Sales 33,854,000 shares, almost double the volume in August.

OCTOBER   Panicky decline. Sales 51,250,000.

NOVEMBER   Further decline to lower levels, but the volume decreased. Sales, 21,250,000.

1938

JANUARY   There was a rally to January; then decline was resumed. Sales for the month, 24,151,000. This was light volume on the rally, showing that there was not enough buying to turn the trend up.

FEBRUARY   Sales 14,522,000.

MARCH   Sales 23,995,000. This was light volume, considering the fact that the averages declined over 25 points. Final low reached March 21.

MARCH 1937 TO MARCH, 1938

From March 10, 1937 to March 31, 1938 the averages declined 98 points. The total volume of sales was 346,192,000 or an average of 35,325 shares per point, showing a much smaller volume on the decline that when the market advanced in the previous Bull Campaign and more proof of the thin markets due to Securities Exchange regulations.

1938

APRIL   Sales 17,119,000. This was on a 20-point rally in the averages.

MAY   Sales 14,000,000, very small volume on a secondary reaction. The market became very dull and narrow at the bottom when the averages declined to around 106½. This was the same kind of a signal on a secondary reaction that the market was making bottom for an advance as the signal which came in August, 1937, on the secondary rally when the market was making top and getting ready for a big decline.

JUNE   Sales increased to 24,668,000.

JULY   A further great increase to 38,880,000.

AUGUST   Sales 20,788,000. The market made top in July and August; then reacted.

SEPTEMBER   Sales 23,876,000. Low of reaction. The fact that the volume increased on this reaction in September indicated that there was good buying.

OCTOBER   Heavy buying and a great increase in volume this month. Sales were 41,558,000.

NOVEMBER   Sales 27,922,000. November 10, final high; Dow-Jones 30 Industrial averages reached 158¾. The market made a very small gain over the high in October, when there was such large volume. During the first 10 days of November the total volume was 11,800,000, indicating that stocks were meeting some heavy selling and that distribution was taking place.

MARCH, 1938 TO NOVEMBER, 1938

From March 31 to November 10, 1938 the total advance was 61¼ points. Total volume of sales 192,685,000 or 32,080 shares per point, a little less than the same number of shares per point on the decline during 1937 and early 1938.

DECEMBER   Sales 27,492,000, just slightly lower than the sales in November, 1938.

1939

JANUARY   Sales 25,182,000, just a little more than the total sales in Jan. 1938.

V-10

FEBRUARY   The market narrowed down and the volume was very small, 13,873,000.

MARCH   Sales 24,560,000. A sharp decline followed after March 10.

APRIL   Sales 20,246,000. April 11, low.

NOVEMBER, 1938 TO APRIL, 1939

From November 10, 1938 to April 11, 1939 the Dow-Jones 30 Industrial averages declined 38-5/8 points. Total sales 115,232,000 shares. Average volume per point decline was 30,324 shares, slightly less than on the advance to November 10, 1938, but the advance was a greater number of points.

MAY   A rally followed this month but the volume was small. Sales 12,935,000

JUNE   Top of rally was reached on June 9 and a decline of 20 points followed, market reaching low June 30. Sales for the month, 11,963,000. This was a secondary reaction on small volume ... an indication to buy stocks.

JULY   A rally followed on increased volume. Sales in July, 18,067,000.

APRIL TO JULY, 1939

From April 11, 1939 to July 31, 1939 the averages advanced 25¾ points. Total sales were 55,211,000 shares. Average sales per point, 21,234 shares, indicating a thin market, the market being able to advance on a much smaller number of shares than on its decline from November 10, 1938 to April 11, 1939.

If you continue to study the Volume of Sales on the New York Stock Exchange and watch the position of the Dow-Jones Industrial Averages on Formations and at Resistance Levels, you will be able to determine culminations with greater accuracy.

A STUDY OF WEEKLY VOLUME

CHRYSLER MOTORS 1928-35

A study of each individual stock, noting its decrease or increase in Volume and the points at which it narrows down into a slow trading range with small volume and then the other extreme when it advances on large volume and makes a rapid advance, will enable you to determine when tops and bottoms are being made. For example: CHRYSLER MOTORS

1928

On January 21, 1928 Chrysler made low at 54½, June 2, high 88½. Then followed a decline to June 23, making low at 63-5/8, down 25 points in three weeks, on a volume of sale of 1,012,000 shares.

Then followed the final grand-rush lasting 15 weeks. During this time the stock never broke the low of a previous week at any time from the bottom at 63⅝ to 140½, where it reached high on October 6, up 87 points in 15 weeks, on total sales of 9,741,800 shares. During the last two weeks of this rapid advance the sales were 2,768,000.

The total number of shares of Chrysler listed on the New York Stock Exchange is 4,484,000. Thus, you see that on this last great advance the total capitalization changed hands more than twice, and in the last two weeks more than half of the total outstanding stock was traded in. This large volume indicated that during the second advance the stock was making top. During the week ended October 6, the total sales were 1,741,500. This was the largest volume of sales for one week in the history of Chrysler Motors, nearly half of the total stock outstanding.

The following week the price of the stock was lower. It never rallied again to this top until it declined to 5. If you were making a study of the volume of sales, you would see the handwriting plain on the wall and know that this was a final top, especially after it gave all the other indications of a change in trend to the downside.

1929 TO 1932

After Chrysler reached high in October, 1928 there was a panicky decline to the week of November 16, 1929, when the ending of the first section of the bear market was recorded on Averages. The sales during the period were 22,533,000 shares, or over 5½ times the total stock outstanding.

On the rally from the week of November 16, 1929 to April, 1930, when the stock sold at 43, the total number of sales was 3,916,000 on a rally of 17 points. This volume of sales almost equalled the entire outstanding stock.

From April, 1930 high to the low of 5, which was reached in the week ended June 4, 1932, the total number of sales was 14,814,422.

The grand total of sales from the high at 140½ in the week ended October 6, 1928 to the low of 5 in June 1932 was 41,263,622 shares. Thus, the capital stock exchange hands nearly 10 times in this campaign.

1929 – 1935

COMPARISON: DECLINE FROM 88 TO 5 AND ADVANCE FROM 5 TO 88

It is important to review the total number of shares traded in from the time Chrysler sold at 88 in the week ended May 11, 1929 to the low in the week ended June 4, 1932, when it declined to 5. This review is important because we want to make a comparison with the total sales from the low of 5, reached in the week ended June 4, 1932, to the time when Chrysler sold at 88¾ again in October, 1935.

In the week ended May 11, 1929, Chrysler declined below 88 and then failed to get above this level again until it declined to a low of 5 in June, 1932. The total number of sales was 25,154,622 on this decline.

From the extreme low of 5 in the week ended June 4, 1932 to October, 1935, when the stock advanced to 88¾ again, we find that the total volume of sales was 30,628,200 or 5½ million shares more than the total number of shares traded in on the decline from May, 1929 to June, 1932, covering the same range in price.

We know that under normal conditions the volume is always grater when a stock is advancing than when it is declining, because there are more wash sales, pool operations and manipulation. The fact that Chrysler made this advance on only five million shares more than was required to go down the same number of points showed that the operations of the Securities Exchange Commission had reduced the volume of trading in advancing market, especially when we consider that from the week ended June 4, 1932 to March, 1933 low there was a period of accumulation, the stock advancing from 5 to 22 and then declining to 7¾ again in March, 1933, on a volume of 5,105,000 shares. Therefore, deducting this from the total sales for the period from June, 1932 to October, 1935, it would bring the volume of trading down to 25 million shares on this advance, or near the same number of shares traded in on the decline of an equal number of points, from 88 to 5.

1933 – 1935

From the low of 7¾ in the week ended March 4, 1933 to the high at 60⅜ in the week ended February 24, 1934, Chrysler advanced 52⅝ points. Total sales, 15,219,800 shares, over three times the total amount of stock outstanding. Study this first section of the bull campaign and the distribution that took place – then apply the same rules to any other stock in order to determine a change in trend.

RANGE OF DISTRIBUTION:

In the week ended January 6, 1934, Chrysler reached a high of 59½, then reacted to 50, and rallied in the week of February 3 to 59⅜, then reached top at 60⅜ in the week ended February 24, 1934. After three weeks it had failed to gain one point over the high in the week of February 3 and the first high of 59½ in January, which showed that there was real distribution taking place and the stock was meeting with heavy selling. The distribution took place between 50 and 60⅜, or in a range of 10⅜ points. In this range of distribution, there was a total number of 2,779,300 shares traded in, or over half of the total shares outstanding, which indicated that after an advance of 52 points, the stock was making top for at least a sharp decline.

SIDEWAYS DISTRIBUTION:

It is interesting to study a sideways distribution. After a stock turns the minor trend down; then rallies and cannot reach the old highs again, distribution often takes place on the side, which we call a sideways movement. People buy the stock on the reaction because they think it is cheap and don't know that it is getting ready to turn the main trend down. For example:

From the week ended March 3, 1934 to the week ended April 28, 1934, the price range for Chrysler was 49¼ to 56. Total number of shares traded in 1,225,800. Adding this to the distribution at the top, the total volume was 4,002,100, or practically the entire capital stock traded in this 10-point range of distribution. After an advance of over 50 points, when the entire capital stock turned over in a range of 10 points, it certainly was a sign of a change in trend.

It is also interesting to consider that after the advance of 52⅝ points in 51 weeks, the stock was nearing the Time period of one year. One of my rules is to always watch for a change in trend at the end of a year.

A decline followed in Chrysler after this sideways distribution.

BEAR CAMPAIGN – FEBRUARY TO AUGUST, 1934:

From the high at 60⅜ in the week ended February 24, 1934 to the low at 29¼ in the week ended August 11, 1934, the range was 31⅛ points. The total volume of sales was 3,033,900, nearly three-fourths of the capital stock changing hands on this decline. Compared with the large volume on the advance, this volume on the decline, which was a secondary reaction, showed that the pressure of sales was decreasing and that the stock was reaching bottom, at least for a rally. Study this bottom and the volume of sales per week, Also note that the low of 29¼ was practically one-half of 60⅜, the high point.

BULL CAMPAIGN – AUGUST, 1934 TO NOVEMBER, 1935:

From the low of 29¼ in the week ended August 11, 1934 to the high of 42½ reached in February, 1935, the sales were 2,195,500 a smaller volume on the rally. Then the trend turned down again and the stock reached a low of 31 in the week ended March 16, 1935, making a higher bottom than that of August, 1934. The price was down 11½ points from 42½ in three weeks on a small volume of 286,600 shares, which indicated that it was the last decline and that the stock was getting ready to change trend to the upside, especially as it did not go lower in the fourth week of the decline.

LONG UPSWING AFTER SECONDARY BOTTOM:

From the low of 31 in the week of March 16, 1935 to the high of October 25, 2935, when the stock sold at 88¾, making a total range of 57¾ points, the number of shares traded in was 5,091,000 shares, about 3/4 million over the total capital stock outstanding. From the low of 29¼ in August, 1934 to the high of 88¾ in October, 1935, the total range was 59½ points and the total sales 7,287,500, the total number of outstanding shares changing hands nearly twice.

The most important last long swing to consider was from the low of 7¾ in March 1933 to 88¾ in October, 1935, an advance of 81 points on total sales of 25,523,200 shares, which showed that the stock traded in equalled nearly six times the amount of stock outstanding.

When the stock was near the low in March, 1935, the sales per week were around 75,000 shares to as low as 46,000 shares per week until April 27, when the volume was 235,000 shares in the week. After that they were running higher right along. Then, beginning the week of August 31, sales were as high as 229,000 shares a week, 233,000, 254,000, 149,000, 223,000, 209,000, 260,000 in the week of October 19, and during the week ended October 26, when Chrysler reached 88¾, the sales were 256,000. Thus, you see how the volume of sales was increasing rapidly when this stock made a sharp advance to 88¾ from the low of the last reaction around 69.

In determining the extreme high and low points, you will find it will help you to study the Volume of Sales on each individual stock, especially the active leaders, and follow the rules.

Regulations against specialists, pool operators, and against member of the New York Stock Exchange trading for their own accounts have cut down the volume of sales probably as much as 50%. When the Government makes business bad in Wall Street, it hurts business throughout the nation.

The day will come when these reforms and regulations will cease because they are doing harm and helping no one. After these restrictions are taken off, then the market will show a larger volume of sales per point and there will be a more normal market.

When once again we have a free market and everybody is permitted to trade who can put up the money, there will be better business and general prosperity. Let us all pray that the day of reform and regulations will soon cease as it is best for all concerned that they should.

[unsigned]
_____

August 12, 1939

Chapter 13

W.D. Gann Mathematical Formula for Market Predictions -

The Master Mathematical Price, Time and Trend Calculator

W.D. GANN MATHEMATICAL FORMULA FOR MARKET PREDICTIONS

THE MASTER MATHEMATICAL PRICE TIME AND TREND CALCULATOR

This chart is made on transparent plastic so that you can place it over a daily, weekly or monthly high or low chart and see at a glance the position on the time and price based on the geometrical angles. It is designed to give QUICK ACCURATE EASY CALCULATIONS: SAVE TIME AND PREVENT ERRORS.

This square of 12 is always important in working out time periods because there are 12 months in a year. The square of 144 is the GREAT SQUARE and works better then any other square both for TIME AND PRICE because it contains all of the squares from 1 to 144. This chart is divided up into sections of 9 both for time and price because 9 is the highest digit. Nine spaces on the daily chart equals 9 days, 9 weeks or 9 months in time periods and 9 equals 9¢ on grains, 9 points on stocks or 90 points on cotton on the daily high and low chart.

One column in the square of 144 contains 144. This would equal $144 on grain, 144 points on stocks or a using scale of 10 points to 1/8 inch it will equal 1440 points on cotton.

MASTER 144 SQUARE CONTAINS 324 square inches and each square inch contains 64 units which gives 20,736. This is 20,736 weeks or months and the proportionate parts of this are used for the measurement of time and price because this is the great cycle.

THE GREAT CYCLE OF THE SQUARE OF 144
The time period of this square is 20,736 days, weeks or months. One-half is 10,368 days. One-fourth is 5,184 days. One-eighth is 2,592. One-sixteenth is 1,296 days. One-thirty-second is 648 days. One-sixty-fourth is 324 calendar or market days. 1/128 is 162 days and 1/256 is 81 days or the square of 9.

WEEKLY TIME PERIODS
THE GREAT CYCLE in weeks is 2962 and 2 days and 1/2 of this period is 1481 weeks and 1 day. One-fourth is 740 weeks. One-eight is 370 weeks and 2 days. One-sixteenth is 185 weeks, 1 day. One-thirty-second is 92 weeks, 4 days and 1/64 is 41 [46?] weeks, 2 days.

MONTHLY TIME PERIODS
THE GREAT CYCLE in months is 681 months and 23 days. One-half of this is 28 years, 9 months and 23 days. One-fourth is 14 years, 5 months and 8 days. One-eighth is 7 years, 2-1/2 months. One-sixteenth is 43 months and days. The weekly and monthly time periods from any major high and low and be checked to determine the future trend [N.B. transcribed as written].

THE MASTER NUMBERS

The Master Numbers are 3, 5, 7, 9 and 12. The No. 9 and its multiple is the most important because 9 digits added together equal 45. The next number of greatest importance is 7, the number mentioned more times in the Bible than any other number. There are 7 days in the week and 7 calendar days as well as 5 market days, and their multiples should be carried on your Daily, Weekly and Monthly Charts. The square of 7 is 49, which is a very important time period. The 2nd square of 7 is 98 and the third square of 7 is 147 and the fourth square of 7 is 196 and 196 is also the square of 14. The next number in importance is No. 5 which is the balancing number between 1 and 9. The square of 5 is 25 and the second square of 5 is 50 which is just 1 over the square of 7 making 49 to 50 very important for a change in trend. Three squares of 5 is 75 and 5 [4?] squares of 5 is 100 and 100 is the square of 10, which is also important for changes.

The No. 3 is mentioned the Bible next to the No. 7 and 3 is important because 3 x 3 equals 9, the square of 3, and it is the first old [odd?] number that forms a square greater than itself. Three must be used in every way possible. 3 x 7 equals 21, 3 x 5 equals 15, 3 x 9 equals 27 and 3 x 10 [12] equals 36, very important because it is the square of 6. The No. 12 is also spoken of in the Bible many times and is of great importance. Jesus selected 12 disciples. There are 12 months in the year, and 12 signs of the Zodiac. The important 12's in the square of 144 are 12, 24, 36, 48, 60, 72, 84, 96, 108, 120, 132 and 144. These are all important for both time and price in days, weeks and months.

Referring to the No. 9, 7 x 9 is 63 and is of great importance because the square of 8 is 64, therefore around 63 to 64 is very important to watch the [for a?] change in trend. 7 x 12 is 84 and this is of very great importance and the number next to this is 90, which is 10 x 9 and 90 is 1/4 of the circle, which is very important for time and price changes. Next in importance is 9 x 12 which is 108 or 3/4 of 144.

The importance of the circle of 360 deg. must not be overlooked in connection with the square of 144 because the proportionate parts of the circle agree with the parts of 144. 2-1/2 times 144 equals 360 and 1-1/4 times 144 equals 180, 1/2 of the circle, and 90 is 5/8 of 144. 9 is 1/16 of 144, 18 is 1/8, 27 is 3/8, 36 is 1/4, 45 is 5/16 and always very important for time and price changes and for resistance levels. 48 is 1/3 of 144, and 54 is 3/8 and 63 is 7/16, 72 is 1/2 of 144, 81 the square of 9, is 9/16 of 144 and 90 is 5/8, 99 is 11/16, 108 is 3/4, 117 is 13/16 and 126 is 7/8 and 135 is 15/16 of 144. These are the most important in the square of 12 and should be watched closely when time periods in days, weeks or months reach these points on the Master Calculator. Remember that you should always watch the Daily Chart for the first indication of the change in trend and at the same time look at the position on the Weekly Chart or 7 day time periods which is next in importance. The Monthly Chart is of the greatest importance for changes in the main trend.

THE IMPORTANCE OF 3 AND 5

The movement in PRICE and TIME whether on a Daily, Weekly or Monthly chart has three important points, the PRICE, the TIME AND VOLUME of sales, the PITCH or TREND which is the geometrical angle which shows whether time is influencing and driving prices up or down on a slow angle or an acute fast moving angle. There are also four factors that influence prices, PRICE, TIME AND VOLUME AND VELOCITY. Time is the most important factor because when time is up volume increases and the velocity or speed of the market increases and the PITCH or TREND on the angles moves up faster or down faster.

There are three other important points to consider on a Daily, Weekly or Monthly High and Low Chart. These are the LOW PRICE, the HIGHEST PRICE and the RANGE or 1/2 between the high and the low.

FIVE FACTORS FOR TIME AND PRICE

These are high, low, halfway point, opening and closing prices. The trend is indicated by the closing price, especially when the market is very active. If price closes above the half-way point or near the high, the trend is up. If it closes below the half-way point or near the low, the selling is greater than the buying and the trend is down, at least temporarily. In connection with the Master Time and Trend Calculator apply all of the rules with the Master Time Factor and geometric angles.

STRONGEST POINTS FOR TIME AND PRICE RESISTANCE

In using the Master Square of 144, the strongest points are 1/4, 1/3, 2/3, 3/8, 1/2, 5/8, 3/4, 7/8 and the complete square of 144.

The points where the most angles cross are strongest for resistance in PRICE and TIME.

TRIANGLE POINTS

The triangle points or where the green angles cross are the most important. These are 72, 144, 36, 48, 96, 108 and, of course, 72, and the end of the square of 144 at the top and the bottom.

SQUARES IN THE SQUARE OF 144

These squares where the angles cross are of great importance for time and price resistance. These are 36, 45, 54, 63, 72, 90, 108, and at the top end of the square of 144 at the top and the bottom. When the price is at a point equal to 36 and the time periods in days, weeks or months is at 36, TIME and PRICE is SQUARE and it is important to watch for change in trend. With the square of 144 you can get any square from 1 to 144. Suppose you want to get the square of 72; you move across to 72 for time and if the price is at 72 moving up on the chart, PRICE and TIME have balanced, or squared out, and are at the 45 degree angle and at the half-way point on the Master Price, Time and Trend Calculator.

THE W.D. GANN MASTER STOCK MARKET COURSE

WHERE TO WATCH FOR CHANGES IN TREND

Most changes in trend occur when the TIME PERIODS are at one-half of the square of 144 and at the end of a square or at the 1/3, 2/3, 1/4, and 3/4 points in the square of 144; you must always watch the square in time of the HIGHEST PRICE and the MINOR HIGHS and LOWS, also the square in TIME of the LOWEST PRICE and the SECOND OR THIRD higher bottom, and also the time required to square the Range and where the square works out in the Master Square of 144.

EXAMPLE: The lowest price that wheat ever sold was 28¢ per bushel. In March, 1852, therefore, every 28 months would square the lowest price. The highest price that wheat ever sold for was in May 11, 1917 when the May option sold at 325, therefore, it would require 325 months to square the highest price. The lowest price that the May option ever sold was 44¢, therefore, it would require 44 months in time to square the low price. The range between 44 and 325 is 281¢ which would require 281 months, 281 weeks or 281 days to square the range. You would look on the Master Chart and see that 2 squares of 144 equal 288, therefore, you would watch for a change in trend between 281 and 288 or near the end of the second square of 144. 7 x 44, the extreme low, equals 308, therefore, 6-1/2 times 44 would equal 286, which is within two points of the end of the square of 144 or the end of the second square making 286 an important time period to watch for a change in trend. In squaring the range [high?] of 325, the highest price for May wheat would be 2 squares of 144 and 17 [37?] over, therefore, when the time reached 36 days, weeks or months in the Master Square of 144 you can see that resistance would be met because moving up the time period of 136 you see that the 45 deg. angle moving down from 72, which is the INNER SQUARE and the line drawn across from 36 on the price scale crosses at 36. In this way you can see that the Master Chart would indicate a resistance in time and price corresponding with the square of the highest price, the lowest price, and the Range. All other time periods from a high price, low price, or the range of any commodity or of the stock averages or individual stocks should be worked out in this same way.

You will succeed in using the Master Mathematical Price, Time and Trend Calculator by going over the charts and laying the calculator over them and working out past history. In this way you will learn just how it works and prove to yourself the great value of the Master Calculator.

HOURLY TIME PERIODS

When Markets are very active and making a wide range in price, it is important to keep an hourly High and Low Chart, just the same as you keep the Daily High and Low Chart and the Hourly Chart will give the first change in trend.

There are 24 hours in a day, therefore 6 days are required to pass through 144 and a total of 864 days to pass through the square of 144.

-4-

At the present time, all exchanges are open 5 days a week with the exception of holidays and most of them are open 5 hours each day, therefore, it will require 28 days and 4 hours to pass through 144 at the rate of 5 hours per day and 5 days per week. [Trading time for grains is 225 minutes or 3.75 hours per day or 38 days and 1-1/2 hours to pass through 144 at the rate of 3.75 hours per day and 5 days per week.]

GREAT YEARLY TIME CYCLE

To pass through the square of 144, which equals 20,736, it requires 56 years, 9 months and 23 days, which is a very important time cycle. Next in importance is 1/2 of this time period which is 28 years, 5 months and 8 days and 1/4 which is 14 years, 2 months and 19 days. The 14 year cycle is always very important because it is 2 seven year periods. 14 years equals 168 months and 169 months is the square of 13 making it very important for a change in trend and this is also an important time resistance point.

1/8 of the Great Cycle is 7 years, 1 month and 10 days and is quite important. 1/16 is 42 months and 20 days, 1/32 is 21 months and 10 days. This is an important time period because it is close to 22-1/2 months which is 1/16 of the circle of 360 degrees.

NINE SPACES AND NINE TIME PERIODS

The chart being divided up into 9 sections gives all the squares of 9 for price resistance of [or] time resistance which, as referred to above is 9¢ on the Daily Chart for grains and the same for Weekly and Monthly Charts; that is, 1¢ to each 1/8 inch. For different commodities, different scales are used. (See Special Instructions for the different commodities.)

The Chart being divided up into 9 sections gives a 16 the squares of 9 for price resistance or time resistance which, as referred to above, is 90 points of the Daily Chart, 135 on the Weekly Chart, and 270 on the Monthly and 2880 on the 20 point scale and 9 spaces equal 180 points.

The angles in red are all drawn on the squares of 9. The Inner Square of 450 [45°?] is drawn from 72 because 72 is 1/2 of 144. These angles come out at 72, 144 and 72.

The straight lines are in green and are 1/3 the square of 144 in price or time.

GREEN ANGLES

The green angles are the angles of 2x 1 which [move] up two spaces or 2 points in one period of the time. The other angle below the 450 [45°?] angle is the angle of 1 x 2 which requires 2 time periods to move up 1 space or 1¢ per bushel on grains for each time period of 1 day, week or 1 month. These angles move down from the top at the rate of 2 points or 2 spaces per time period or at the rate of 1/2 space, 1/2 point, or 1/2¢ per time period. The distance that the green angles and the red angles are apart determines how far prices can advance or decline.

When the market enters the INNER SQUARE it is important for a change in trend and time angles and Position in the square tell at the time it entered whether the price is going up or down. Also when price breaks below a 45° [angle] on the INNER SQUARE it shows weakness in proportion to the time from high or low price.

- 5 -

WHEN TO START A NEW SQUARE

When the time period of the Daily, Weekly or Monthly Charts has moved 144 you begin a new square. But to get the position you simply move the Master Square over to 144 and place it over the chart to get the position in the next square.

STRONGEST AND WEAKEST POINTS

Where the greatest number of angles cross or bisect each other in the square of 144 are the points of greatest resistance, such as where the 25 and 2 x 1 angles cross each other.

Study and practice on past action of the market and you will soon learn how to determine the trend very quickly by using the Master Chart.

HOW TO USE THE MASTER SQUARE OF 144

Follow all rules on angles as given in the Master Forecasting course.

Place this chart at the bottom or 0 on the Daily, Weekly or Monthly Chart or place the bottom of the chart on the low price or SQUARE of the HIGH PRICE, The LOW PRICE, and the square of the RANGE and show where time end price balances.

When you figure the halfway point of the extreme high or the halfway point of the range, place either the top or the bottom of the chart on the halfway point and it will give the correct POSITION and TREND. However, if you will place the CENTER, or 72, on the halfway point in PRICE you will then get the correct position in time and can see how the price is working out with time in the MASTER SQUARE of 144 and the INNER SQUARE which starts from 72, the gravity center of [or?] 1/2 point of the square.

CALENDAR DAYS AND MARKET DAYS

For any kind of a chart, we move over one space for each unit of time. Therefore it would require 144 market days or 144 calendar days to complete the square of 144. When prices pass out of one square into another, a change of trend usually takes place and the periods and geometrical angles on this MASTER CHART tell you which way the trend is going to change.

LEAP YEARS:

In calculating time periods to get the exact number of days and weeks the LEAP YEAR must be figured out and one extra day added. From 1864 the Leap Years were as follows 1868,1872, 1876, 1880, 1884, 1888, 1892, 1896, 1904, 1908, 1912, 1916, 1920, 1924, 1928, 1932, 1936, 1940, 1944, 1948 and 1952.

THE W.D. GANN MASTER STOCK MARKET COURSE

POSITION WITH MASTER SQUARE

To get the position with the MASTER SQUARE of 144, lay it over the Daily, Weekly or Monthly and start from extreme low, extreme high, 0 or 1/2 point of the range or 1/2 of the high selling price. You can also place the top of the chart at the high selling price. In this way you can get the correct time and positions or angles at a glance.

Place MASTER CALCULATOR on January to get the twelve year periods, each month same way.

You should have all time periods from important highs and lows calculated in days, weeks and months in order that you can look them up quickly on the MASTER CHART.

With all time periods brought up to date in this way, you can get the position on the MASTER CHART and the indicated trend without looking at a daily, weekly or monthly chart. You should have the time periods in months from every important top and bottom.

With the MASTER SQUARE of 144, your work will be cut down but you must learn to practice and bring up all time periods and study the MASTER SQUARE and learn how to use it to get tops and bottoms accurately. Work and practice will bring PRECISION and PROFITS. I have done my part. It is now up to you to work hard and if you do, your success is assured.

HOW TO PLACE THE MASTER CHART
SQUARE OF 144 ON CHARTS

To get correct positions on any of your charts, daily, weekly or monthly, you must place the MASTER CHART OVER THEM correctly. The top of the MASTER CHART has Price and Time Chart by W.D. Gann on it. Always place this on the bottom of your chart unless it is where you move up to a higher price when you place it at 72 or bottom marked "Bottom" 0.

Place the MASTER CHART at 0 on any of your other charts or at a low point on the same date of any high or low point. Place the MASTER CHART at 72 which is 1/2 of 144 or on any one-half point of the price range or 1/2 of the high selling price.

Always place the MASTER CALCULATOR on all previous high and lows to get changes in trends and price resistance. Never overlook the extreme high and low price. Also most important 1/2 of high to low and 1/2 of the highest price any commodity or stock ever sold.

THE W.D. GANN MASTER STOCK MARKET COURSE

TIME PERIODS AND PRICE RESISTANCE

The circle of 360° is most important for time cycles and price resistance. First, we divide the circle by 2 and get 180 which is one-half and is most important for time or price in days, weeks or months. Next we divide the circle by 3 and get the triangle points of 120, 240 and 360. Third, we divide the circle by 4 which gives 90, 180, 270, and 360 which are the squares and most important.

Divide the circle by 8 which give 8 periods of 45 degree angles which are 45, 90, 135, 180, 225, 270, 315, and 360. Next in importance is to divide the circle by 16 which gives the angles of 22-1/2 degrees. We divide the circle by 32 and get the angles and time periods of 11-1/4 degrees and their multiples. Divide the circle by 64 which gives 5-5/8 degrees and their multiples.

The table below shows each division of 5-5/8 and we run down to 16 in the column which equals 90 or 1/4 of the circle and 16 is 1/4 of 64. This arrangement reading across gives each of the multiples and the figures between the heavy lines are among the ones which are the most important.

Table of 64th of the Circle

1.	5-5/8	17.	95-5/8	33.	185-5/8	49.	275-5/8
2.	11-1/4	18.	101-1/4	34.	101-1/4 [191-1/4]	50.	281-1/4
3.	16-5/8 [16-7/8]	19.	106-7/8	35.	196-7/8	51.	286-7/8
4.	22-1/2	20.	112-1/2	36.	202-1/2	52.	292-1/2
5.	28-1/8	21.	118-1/8	37.	208-1/8	53.	298-1/8
6.	33-3/4	22.	123-3/4	38.	213-3/4	54.	303-3/4
7.	39-3/8	23.	129-3/8	39.	219-3/8	55.	309-3/8
8.	45	24.	135	40.	225	56.	315
9.	50-5/8	25.	140-5/8	41.	230-5/8	57.	320-5/8
10.	56-1/4	26.	146-1/4	42.	236-1/4	58.	326-1/4
11.	61-7/8	27.	151-7/8	43.	241-7/8	59.	331-7/8
12.	67-1/2	28.	157-1/2	44.	247-1/2	60.	337-1/2
13.	73-1/8	29.	163-1/8	45.	253-1/8	61.	343-1/8
14.	78-3/4	30.	168-3/4	46.	258-3/4	62.	348-3/4
15.	84-5/8 [84-3/8]	31.	174-3/8	47.	264-3/8	63.	354-3/8
16.	90	32.	180	48.	270	64.	360

The squares from 1 to 10 are important to watch for time and price resistance as they are important degrees in the circle. These are: 1 - 4 - 9 - 16 - 25 - 36 - 49 - 64 - 81 - 100 - 121 - 144 - 169 - 196 - 225 - 256 - 289 - 324 and 361, which is the square of 19.

Divide the circle by 6 and we get two resistance and time periods which are not contained in the other table. These are 60 and 300.

It is also very important to divide the circle by 12 because there are 12 months in the year and this works out accurately for time periods. The following are the degrees not shown in the above table: 30 - 150 - 210 - 330.

- 8 -

Divide the circle by 24 which gives 15 degree periods in longitude and approximately 15 days in time. Because there are 24 hours in a day and the earth makes 1 revolution on its axis in 24 hours these periods are quite important. The following are not contained in the other table: 15 - 75 - 105 - 165 - 195 - 285 - 345.

Under the table of the 64th Circle reading across from left to right the 2nd column is always 90 degrees from the first. Example: The first is 5-5/8 and 17 in the next column is 95-5/8 or a gain of 90. Opposite 33 is 185-5/8 which is 90 from 95-5/8, opposite 49 is 275-5/8 or 90 from 185-5/8.

The column 1 under [row] 8 between the heavy lines is 45 and the next one is 135, 225, and 315 each four 45 [90] degrees apart.

At the bottom of column 1 opposite 16 is 90 and reading across is 180, 270, and 360. These figures are all 45 degrees from the figures in column [row] 8 which are the most important for time and price resistance.

To realize the value and importance of these degrees in the circle you take the price of highs and lows and the time periods, especially in weeks and months and check them over and you will see how well they work out to these important degrees.

Remember you must always figure how many points or cents the prices [are] up from the extreme low or minor lows and how many cents it is down from the extreme highs or minor highs. Also, how many cents it is above or below the main halfway point or the minor halfway points or gravity centers. You will find that the important halfway points form very close to these natural degrees in the circle.

Example: May Soybeans extreme high 436-3/4, extreme low 67, gives the halfway point at 251-7/8. Look in the table and you find the 45th 64th at 253-1/8. This halfway point is very close. Next 1/2 of 436-3/4 is 218-3/8 and the 39th 64th is 219-3/8, very close to this natural resistance degree. The extreme low of Cash beans 44 and the halfway point between 44 and 436-3/4 is 240-3/8. 240 is 2/3 of a circle or a triangle point and 241-7/8 is the 43rd 64th of the circle. 44 the extreme low, was only 1 from 45, the important resistance level. 67, the lowest price May futures ever sold, is within 1/2 point of 67-1/2 which is 12/64 or 3/4 between 0 and 90 and 67-1/2 is halfway between 45 and 90 which was the cause of May beans making lows 5 years between 67-69 which indicated the big advance that followed as there were triple bottoms between 67-69 in three different years.

Next consider the time periods December 28, 1932, was low on May Beans and Dec. 28, 1947, was 15 years or 180 months which is 1/2 of a circle also 1/2 of the 360 degrees making this a very important time cycle. May beans reached extreme high on Jan. 15, 1948, just 18 days beyond the even 15 year cycle. Check all other time periods and time cycles in the same way and you will find how well they work out in the circle of 360 degrees.

W. D. Gann

September 29, 1953

CHAPTER 14

MASTER CALCULATOR FOR WEEKLY TIME PERIODS TO DETERMINE THE TREND OF STOCKS AND COMMODITIES

THE W.D. GANN MASTER STOCK MARKET COURSE

MASTER CALCULATOR FOR WEEKLY PERIODS
TO DETERMINE THE TREND OF STOCKS AND COMMODITIES

by W.D. GANN

This Master Calculator shows Weekly Time Periods of 7 days each or a total of 52 weeks in one year. This represents 364 calendar days, therefore at the end of each year there is a gain of one day and at the end of 7 years, a gain of 7 days, the time period coming out one week before the date of the important high and low prices. You must also add one day for each leap year. Suppose you want to get the time period for 15 years, you multiply 365 by 15, add the number of leap years and then divide the total days by 7 to get the weekly periods of 7 days each in order to use the Calculator. (See Tables for Price and Time Periods).

The total square of 52 is 2704, which we can use to measure weeks, days, months, years or hours. In using days, it would, of course, require 2704 days to pass thru the square of 52. This would give 386 weeks and 2 days or approximately 7 years and 5 months, very close to the important cycle of 7½ years, which is 90 months.

If we used hours to balance or square 2704, we get 112-2/3 days by dividing 2704 by 24, the total number of hours in a day during which time the earth makes one complete revolution on its axis.

The Square of 52, which is composed of 7-day periods, is one of the most important for measuring Price and Time. The number 7 is referred to in the Bible more times than any other number, except the number 3. Both of these numbers are very important to use in connection with price and time changes.

You start Time periods from the actual dates of important high and important low prices and not from the first day of each month or the first day of each year.

The Calculator is 104 weeks wide, which equals 2 years. The time periods run across the bottom of the Calculator, from left to right to 104, which completes 2 years, and to 208, which completes 4 years. At the top of the Calculator, running across to the left, the time periods run to 312, which ends 6 years, and to 416, which ends 8 years, and to 520, which completes a 10-year cycle.

DIVISIONS OF TIME PERIODS

The year is divided by 1/8, which equals 6½ weeks
                                       1/4,   "   "   13   "
                                         1/3,   "   "   17   "
                                         3/8,   "   "   19½   "
                                         1/2,   "   "   26   "   a most important time and resistance level
                                         5/8,   "   "   32½   "
                                         2/3,   "   "   35   "
                                       3/4,   "   "   39   "   very important for a change in trend
                                       7/8,   "   "   45½   "
                       1 year, which is 52 weeks.

MC-2

The angles run from each of the time periods for Price and Time in order to balance the Square and show resistance levels where price and time periods indicate a change in trend.

THIRD AND FOURTH DIMENSIONS OF TIME AND PRICE

We know of three dimensions – height, width and length – but there is a fourth dimensions or element in market movements. We prove the fourth dimension with the Master Calculator or Square of 52 in Time Periods of 7 days each for 7 weeks or more, and the same price relation. 7 x 52 equals 364 or 7 years.

THE CIRCLE, TRIANGLE AND SQUARE

The circle of 360° and the nine digits are the basis of all mathematical calculations. The Square and the Triangle form within the circle, but there is an inner circle and an inner square, as well as an outer square and an outer circle, which prove the fourth dimension in working out market movements.

PRICE

The most important points to consider are:

1. Lowest price.
2. Highest price.
3. The 1/2 point, mean or average between the extreme high and the extreme low. We get the fourth dimension, as shown on the Master Calculator, by drawing 45° angles from the 1/2 point or gravity center, which is the most important for price resistance.
4. Volume of Sales. This is the power which drives the market up or down but remember that TIME is the most essential element and when Time is completed, the volume of sales starts to move the market up or down.

TIME

Time is divided into sections or cycles by which we determine the change in trend.

1. Daily high and low prices
2. Weekly high and low prices
3. Monthly high and low prices
4. Yearly high and low prices

The Weekly and the Yearly Time Periods are most important for trend indications and for changes in trend.

The day is divided into hours, minutes and seconds. The four divisions of the day are: Sunrise, Noon, Sunset and Midnight. Of these the most important are: Noon, when the Sun is straight overhead or on a 90° angle, and Midnight, the opposite point or 180° from Noon and 90° from Sunset.

Because we are using 7-day Time Periods with the Calculator, 1/2 of 7 days or 3½ days is important to watch for a change in trend. Always watch the 3rd and 4th day from any important high or low level for a minor change in trend, which later may become a major change.

7-DAY PERIODS: The time periods of 7 calendar days from any important high or low level is of great importance. 14 days is the most important and 21 days or three weeks is next in importance. Reactions will often run 2 weeks, and sometimes 3 weeks and then resume the main trend. Rallies in a Bear Market often run 14 days, and sometimes 21 days and then resume the downward or main trend.

MULTIPLES OF 7 DAYS: The square of 7 or 49 days is very important for change in trend. You can start to watch for this change after the 42nd day but the first indication of a change may not occur until the 45th or 46th day, which is 1/8 of the year or 365 days. 1/16 of the year is 23 days. Therefore, both the 46-day and 23-day periods are important to watch for change in trend.

Next in importance is 63 to 65 days because 7 x 9 is 63 and the square of 8 is 64. 81 days or the square of 9 is also of great importance. 90 to 91 days is 1/4 of the year or 7 x 13. This is of very great importance to watch for change in trend. Of course, of next importance is around 182 days or 1/2 of the year.

YEARS

Later we will refer to the four seasons or the divisions of the year, which are Spring, Summer, Fall and Winter and important to watch for change in trend. However, the divisions of Time are from the date of the actual important high and low prices.

The important yearly cycles are 1, 2, 3, 5, 7, 9, 10, 12, 14, 15, 18, 20, 21, 22½, 24, 25, 27, 28, 30, 40, 45, 49, 56, 60, 84, and 90 which is the Great Cycle. We divide the cycles into 1/2, which is the most important, and also into the periods of 1/8, 1/3 and 2/3, and watch these proportionate parts of the cycles for a change in trend. For example:

The Great Cycle of 90 years equals 1080 months;
        1/2 is 45 years or 540 months
        1/4 is 22½ years or 270 months
        1/8 is 11¼ years or 135 months
        1/16 is 5-5/8 years or 67½ months

The 30 year cycle or any other cycle is divided up in the same way.

MULTIPLES OF 7 YEARS: The multiples of 7 years or 84 months are all important to watch for change in trend. These are 7 years, 14, 21, 28, 35, 42, and 49, which is most important because it is the square of 7. Next 56 and 63 are very important, 63 because it is 7 x 9. 81, the square of 9, is very important.

Prices can also be used in sevens. Example: 98, 2 x 49. 126, 2 x 63. 162, 2 x 81, etc.

YEARLY TIME PERIODS - TRIANGLES AND SQUARES: When 1/3 of a year from any important low comes out at the same time that 1/4 or 1/2 of a year from another important top or bottom comes out, it is of great importance for change in trend. 1/2 of a yearly time period is always the most important, just the same as 1/2 of the highest selling price and 1/2 of the range of the price is important for resistance levels. By practice, study and comparison and by placing the Calculator over the Weekly high and low Chart, you will see how all these prices and Time Periods work out.

MC-4

TIME, PRICE, VOLUME, VELOCITY, PITCH OR TREND

When a Time Cycle is completed, Volume increases and the market begins to move up faster or move down faster.

The pitch or trend is determined mostly by the 45° angle, which is the most important, but other angles can be used to determine the trend. The pitch or trend is the 4th dimension and shows whether the market is slow or fast by the angles, whether very acute or above the 45° angle or flat and slow, below the 45° angle, which causes a slower creeping market that may later regain important angles and increase the pitch of the angle and start moving up faster.

All of this is shown on the Master Calculator or Square of 52.

3 WAYS TO SQUARE OR BALANCE TIME AND PRICE

(1) Balance the lowest price with time measured in weeks and balance the highest price with time.
(2) Balance the range, which is the total between the extreme high and extreme low.
(3) Get the 4th dimension by balancing Price and Time in weekly time periods as shown on the Master Square of 52.

PRICE SCALE

The price scale runs up and down to 104, 208, 312, 416, and 520, which balances out with the Time Periods. For GRAINS, this scale is for [four?] cents per bushel. For STOCKS, it is $1.00 per share. The Price Periods are divided up into 1/8 and 1/3, the same as the Time Periods.

Scale for COTTON, COFFEE, COCOA and EGGS – each 1/8 cent equals 10 points. Therefore, 52 would indicate 520 in price and 104 would indicate 1040 for Cotton or any other commodity trading in 100 points to 1¢.

EGGS – Weekly high and low chart – Eggs trade at a minimum of 5 points. We use 10 points to 1/8 inch on the daily high and low chart. Experience has proven that a scale of 25 points to 1/8 inch, which represents one week in Time, works best. Therefore, 52 spaces on the Calculator would indicate 1300 or 13¢ for Eggs; 104 would represent 2600; 156 would represent 3900; 208 would represent 5200 or 52¢ per dozen for Eggs, etc. One year Time Period would give a range of 13¢, 1/2 of this would be 6½ cents, 1/4 would be 325 and 1/8 would be 162. Therefore, if you want to get resistance levels for prices above 26¢, you would add 6½, which would give 32½, etc.

All of these are shown on the Table enclosed for prices which run up to the equivalent of 40 years calculated. All you have to do is run across the period marked "1/2" and get the exact date during each year. When the Time is at 1/2 or 182 days from an important high or low, and in the same way from the Table, you get the price resistance levels based on the Square of 52.

HOW TO USE THE MASTER CALCULATOR

One column on the Calculator can be used for one month or one year, but the Calculator is designed to be used on the Weekly high and low Chart for determining the important changes in trend.

HOW TO USE CALCULATOR ON WEEKLY CHART

Place the bottom or "0" of the Calculator on "0" below any price or place it on the low price, then you will see where the angles cross and the resistance levels are indicated.

Place the Calculator marked "Top" at the high price on the exact date the important price is made, then you can see the important angles for resistance from the top down.

THE INNER SQUARE OR 1/2 POINT

Place the Calculator on 1/2 of the highest selling price or 1/2 of the range. Place the Calculator where it is marked 1/2 or 26 weeks over the chart on the same line that low or high is made. Placing the Calculator on 26 over the 1/2 point will show the resistance and whether the price is in a strong or weak position.

THE INNER SQUARE OF 45° ANGLES

The Inner Square of 45° Angles starts from 26, which is 1/2 of 52, and moved up or down. It crosses at 26, which is 1/2 of 52. The 45° angle moving up from "0" crosses at 52 and 104, and the 45° angle moving down from a top or high-level crosses at 52 and terminates at "0". All of these important 45° angles from any important high or low cross on 1/4, 1/2, 3/4, etc., as you can see, and balance out Time and Price.

MOST IMPORTANT TIME PERIODS

The most important Time Periods are the anniversary date of 1, 2, 3 years or more from the dates of the important highs and important lows. Second in importance is 1/2 of the Yearly Time Period; third in importance is the 3/4 or 39 weeks in each year; fourth, the 1/3 point or 17 weeks and the 2/3 point or 35 weeks are also very important Time Periods for change in trend.

When you are working out Weekly Time Periods, you must also consider the importance of the 3-year cycle, the 5-year cycle, 7-year cycle, 10-year cycle, 15 years, which is 1/2 of the 30-year cycle, and 20 years, which is 1/3 of the 60-year cycle, and 30 years, which is a complete cycle of 360 months. The longer the time period from an important top or bottom, the greater the variation, because each year of the time period gains at least one day, and in leap year's gains and additional day before the end of the complete cycle.

The Table for Time and Price Periods shows the exact time in 52 weeks to a year or 364 calendar days. By figuring the leap years and the time gained at the rate of one day per year, you know how much time to subtract and can make the adjustment for the full period.

THE W.D. GANN MASTER STOCK MARKET COURSE

MC-6

SEASONAL TIME PERIODS

In figuring Seasonal Time Periods, we do not start to calculate Time from January 1st but calculate the Time Periods from the date when the Spring Season starts on March 21. These periods are marked on the table in 1/8, 1/3, etc. they are as follows:

May 5	ends	1/8 or	6½	weeks from March 21
Jun. 21	ends	1/4 or	13	"
Jul. 23	ends	1/3 or	17	"
Aug. 5	ends	3/8 or	19½	"
Sep. 22	ends	1/2 or	26	"
Nov. 8	ends	5/8 or	32½	"
Nov. 22	ends	2/3 or	35	"
Dec. 21	ends	3/4 or	39	"
Feb. 4	ends	7/8 or	45½	"
Mar. 20	ends	1 year or	52	"

MIDSEASON TIME PERIODS

These are May 5, August 5, November 8, February 4. Important changes in trend occur around these midseason dates, but all of the above Time Periods should be watched for important changes in trend.

The Table for Time Periods and important high and low prices is shown with the figures at the top running from 1 to 38. The important Time Periods are shown with exact dates, and if you want to look up something in the 7th year, you move over to the column marked "7" and moved down to the 1/2 point. You will find that 7½ years is 390 weeks, etc. and any price on this same line would be an important resistance level.

By studying, practicing and experimenting with the Master Calculator, you will learn how valuable these Time and Price Periods in multiples of 7 are.

[signature]
W. D. GANN

January 10, 1955

Chapter 15a

Master Charts

W. D. GANN

78 WALL STREET
NEW YORK

Scientific Advice
and Analytical Reports
on Stocks and Commodities
Author of "Truth of the Stock Tape"
and "The Tunnel Thru the Air"

Member
American Economic Ass'n
Royal Economic Society
Cable Address
"Ganwade New York"

MASTER CHARTS

The Master Charts are permanent and represent natural angles and permanent resistance points for either price, time or volume. These points do not change and you should study them carefully on each different Master Chart and learn how to apply them.

MASTER "12" CHART

The MASTER CHART is the Square of "12" or 12 x 12, making the first square end at 144. The Second Square of "12" ends at 288, the Third Square of "12" at 432; and the Fourth Square at 576, which will cover most anything that you want, but you can make up as many more squares as you need.

This chart may be used and applied to anything -- TIME, SPACE, PRICE OR VOLUME, the number of points up or down; days, weeks, months and years.

On Square No. 1, which runs from 1 to 144, I have drawn the finer angles to show the grand-center or strongest resistance point in each minor square. The minor centers, which are the strongest for minor tops and bottoms are 14, 17, 20, 23, 50, 53, 56, 59, 86, 89, 92, 95, 122, 125, 128, 131.

The major center is where the strongest resistance is met. These numbers are 66, 67, 78 and 79. Stocks going up or coming down to these prices will meet with stubborn resistance. The next strong angle is the 45°, and the numbers of greatest resistance on it are 14, 27, 40, 53, 66, 79, 92, 105, 118, 151, and 144. The other diagonal 45° angle from 12 is equally strong. The numbers are 12, 23, 34, 45, 56, 67, 78, 89, 100, 111, 122, and 133.

The numbers which are cut by the 45° angles through the center of each of the one 1/4 squares are next in strength. These numbers are 7, 20, 33, 46, 59, 72, 61, 50, 39, 28, 17, and 6, and on the other side of the Square, after you pass the half-way point, these numbers are 73, 96, 99, 112, 125, 138, 139, 128, 117, 106, 95 and 84.

The numbers at the tops and bottoms of the squares are important prices for important tops and bottoms to be made because they are opposition numbers and are equal to the half-way point. These numbers for Square No. 1 are 1, 13, 25, 37, 49, 61, 73, 85, 97, 109, 121, 133. The top numbers are 12, 24, 36, 48, 60, 72, 84, 96, 108, 120, 132, and 144. These are very important to measure time in days, weeks, months and years.

The opposition angle, which runs through the center of the Square, from east to west, equally dividing it, is one of the very strong angles because it equals one-half. Any stock moving up or down and reaching these prices will meet with any resistance and make tops or bottoms. These numbers are 6, 7, 18, 19, 30, 31, 42, 43, 54, 55, 66, 67, 78, 79, 90, 91, 102, 103, 114, 115, 126, 127, 138, 139.

Remember, when anything has moved three sections over from the beginning, it reaches the square of its own place, which is the first strong resistance. When it has moved six sections over it reaches the opposition, or what equals the half-way point of its own place and meets still stronger resistance. Moving over nine places or sections from its own place, it reaches the 3/4 point, another square. The 8th and 9th sections are the strongest and hardest points to pass because this is the "death" zone. The next and still stronger is the 12th section or column which ends at 144. Anything getting into this section meets the strongest resistance but once it moves out of the square and gets as much as 3 points into Square #2, that is, making 147, will indicate much higher. But after reaching this, it should not drop back to 141 or 3 points into Square #1.

When a stock gets into the Second Square of "12", it has faster moves, and when the time or number of months from any bottom or top moves into the Second Square, it is an indication of faster moves, both up and down.

Apply the same rule to the 3rd, 4th, 5th and 6th Squares. In the 3rd and 4th squares of the Master "12", you will find that most of the big bull and bear campaigns culminate, when measured by months, which determines the division, according to time. All of the other rules given you to apply to Space movements, angles and time, can be used with the Master "12" tables.

SQUARE OF NINE

You have already had the MASTER SQUARE OF TWELVE explained, which represents days, weeks, months and years, and the measurements of TIME in the Square of Twelve or the square of the Circle; also used to measure price movements and resistance levels.

The SQUARE OF NINE is very important because nine digits are used in reassuring everything. We cannot go beyond nine without starting to repeat and using the 0. If we divide 360° by 9, we get 40, which measures 40°, 40 months, 40 days, 40 weeks, or 40 months, and shows why bottoms and tops often come out on these angles measured by one-ninth of the circle. This is why the children of Israel were 40 years in the wilderness.

If we divide our 20-year period, or 240 months, by 9, we get 26-2/3 months, making an important angle of 26-2/3°, months, days, or weeks. Nine times 9 equals 81, which completes the First Square of Nine. Note the angles and how they run from the main center. The Second Square of Nine is completed at 162. Note how this is in opposition to the main center. The Third Square of Nine is completed at 243, which would equal 243 months or three months over our 20-year period and accounts for the time which often elapses before the change in the Cycle, sometimes running over 3 months or more. The Fourth Square of Nine ends at 324. Note the angles of 45° cross at 325, indicating a change in cycles here. To complete the 360° requires Four Squares of Nine and 36 over. Note that 361 equals a Square of 19 times 19, thus proving the great value of the Square of Nine in working out the important angles and proving up discrepancies.

Beginning with "1" at the center, note how 7, 21, 43, 73, 111, 157, 211, 273, and 343 all fall on a 45° angle. Going the other way, note that 3, 13, 31, 57, 91, 133, 183, 241, and 307 fall on an angle of 45°. Remember there are always four ways that you can travel from the center following an angle of 45°, or an angle of 180° or an angle of 90°, which all equal about the same when measured on a flat surface. Note that 8, 23, 46, 77, 116, 163, 218, 281 and 352 are all on an angle from the main center; also note that 4, 15, 34, 61, 96, 139, 190, 249, and 316 are on an angle from the main center, all of these being great resistance points and measuring out important time factors and angles.

Study the SQUARE OF NINE very carefully in connection with the MASTER TWELVE and 360° CIRCLE CHART.

SIX SQUARES OF NINE

You will receive six Permanent Charts, each containing 81 numbers. The First Square of Nine runs from 1 to 81. Everything must have a bottom, top, and four sides to be a square or cube. The first Square running up to 81 is the bottom, base, floor or beginning point. Squares #2, 3, 4, and 5 are the four sides, which are equal in containing 81 numbers. The Sixth Square of Nine is the top and means that it is times times as referred to in the Bible, or a thing reproducing itself by being multiplied by itself. Nine times nine equals 81 and six times 81 equals 486. We can also use nine times 81, which would equal 729.

The number 5 is the most important number of the digits because it is the balance or main center. There are four numbers on each side of it. Note how it is shown as the balancing or center number in the Square of Nine.

We square the Circle by beginning at 1 in the center and going around until we reached 360. Note that the Square of Nine comes out at 361. The reason for this is: it is 19 times 19, and the 1 to begin with, and 1 over 360 represents the beginning and ending points. 361 is a transition point and begins the next Circle. Should we leave the first space blank or make it "0", then we would come out at 360. Everything in mathematics must prove. You can begin at the center and work out, or begin at the outer rim and work into the center. Begin at the left and work right to the center or to the outer rim or square.

Note the Square of Nine or the Square of the Circle, where we begin with 1 and run up the side of the column to 19, then continue to go cross until we have made 19 columns, again, the square of 19 by 19. Note how this proves up the circle. One-half of the circle is 180°. Note that in the grand-center, where all angles from the four corners and from the East, West, North and South reach gravity center, number 181 appears, showing that at this point we are crossing the Equator or Gravity center and are starting on the other half of the circle.

We have astronomical and mathematical proof of the whys and wherefores and the cause of the workings of geometrical angles. When you have made progress, proved yourself worthy, I will give you the Master Number and also the Master Word.

THE HEXAGON CHART

Since everything moves in a circle and nothing moves in straight lines, this chart is to show you how the angles influence stocks at very low levels and very high levels and why stocks move faster the higher they get, because they have moved out to where the distance between the angles of 45° are so far apart that there is nothing to stop them and their moves are naturally rapid up and down.

We begin with a circle of "1" in the center and while this only contains 1, yet the circle is 360° just the same. We then place a circle of circles around this circle and 6 circles complete the second circle, making a gain of 6 over the first one, ending the second circle at 7, making 7 on this angle a very important month, year, and week as well as day, the seventh day being sacred and a day of rest. The third circle is completed at 19. The fourth circle around is completed at 37, a gain of 18 over the previous circle. The fifth circle is completed at 61, a gain of 24 over the previous circle. The sixth circle is completed at 91, a gain of 30 over the previous circle, and the seventh circle at 127, a gain of 36 over the last circle. Note that from the first the gain is 6 each time we go around. In other words, when we have travelled six times around we have gained 36. Note that this completes the first Hexagon and as this equals 127 months, shows why some campaigns will run 10 years and seven months, or until they reach a Square of the Hexagon, or the important last angle of 45°.

The eighth circle around is completed at 169, a gain of 42 over the first. This is a very important angle and an important time factor for more reasons than one. It is 14 years and one month, or double our cycle of seven years. Important tops and bottoms culminate at this angle as you will see by going over your charts.

The ninth circle is completed at 217, a gain of 48 over the previous circle. The tenth circle is completed at 271, a gain of 54. Note that 271 is the 9th circle from the first, or is the third 90° angle or 270°, three-fourths of a Circle, a very strong point. All this is confirmed by the Master Twelve Chart, by the four seasons and by the Square of Nine Chart, and also confirmed by the Hexagon Chart, showing that mathematical proof is always exact no matter how many ways or from what directions you figure it.

The eleventh circle is completed at 331, a gain of 60 over the last circle. The 12th circle is completed at 397, which completes the Hexagon, making a gain in 11 circles of 66 from the beginning. 66 months, or five years and six months, marks the culmination of a major campaign in stocks. Note how often they culminate on the 60th month, then have a reaction, and make a second top or bottom in the 66th month. Note the number 66 on the Master Twelve Chart. Note it on the Square of Nine and see that 66 occurs on an angle of 180° on the Hexagon Chart, all of which confirms the strong angle at this point.

We have an angle of 66°, one of 67½, and one of 68, confirming this point to be doubly strong for tops and bottoms or space movements up or down.

Note the number 360 on the Hexagon Chart. It completes a circle of 360°. From our beginning point this occurs at an angle of 150° on the Hexagon Chart going around, but measuring from the center, it would equal an angle of 90° or 180°, making this a strong point, hard and difficult to pass, and the ending of one campaign and the beginning of another.

Again with the center of the Hexagon Chart at "1" notice that 7, 9 [19?], 37, 61, 91, 127, 169, 217, 271, 331, and 397 are all on this direct angle and are important points in time measurement. Beginning with "1" and following the other angle, note that 2, 9, 22, 41, 66, 97, 134, 177, 226, 281, and 342 are all on the same angle of 90°, or an angle of 60° and 240° as measured by the Hexagon Chart.

Go over this chart and the important angles each way and you will see why resistance is met either on days, weeks, months, or years, and why stocks stop and make tops and bottoms at these strong important points, according to time and price.

When any stock has passed out above 120° or especially above 127° or 127 points and gone out of the Square of the first Hexagon, its fluctuations will be more rapid, and it will move faster up and down. Notice near the center that in travelling from 6 to 7 it strikes the angle of 180° or 90°, but when the stock gets out to 162, it can travel up to 169 before striking another strong angle. That is why fast moves occur up and down as stocks get higher and as they move from a center in time.

Remember that everything seeks the center of gravity and important tops and bottoms are formed according to centers and measurements of time from a center, base or beginning point, either top or bottom. The angles formed going straight up and across, may form just the same going across as the stock travels over for days, weeks, months or years. Thus, a stock going up to 22½ would strike an angle of 22½°. If it moves over 22½ days, 22½ weeks, or 22½ months, it would also strike an angle of 22½°, and the higher it is when these angles are struck and the angle it hits going up, the greater the resistance to be met. Reverse the rule going down.

Market movements are made just the same as any other thing, which is constructed. It is just the same as constructing a building. First, the foundation has to be laid and then the four sides have to be completed and last, but not least of all, the top has to be put on. The cube or hexagon proves exactly the law, which works because of time and space in the market. When a building is put up it is built according to a square or hexagon. It has four walls or four sides, a bottom and a top; therefore, it is a cube.

In working out the 20-year Cycle in the stock market, the first 60°, or 5 years, from the beginning forms the bottom of the cube. The second 60°, running to 120, completes the first angle or the first side and runs out the 10-year Cycle. The third 60°, or the second side, ends 15 years or 180°. It is very important because we have the building half completed and must meet the strong resistance at this point. The fourth 60°, or the end of 20 years or 240 months, completes the third side. We are now two-thirds around the building, a very strong point which culminates and completes our 20-year cycle. The fifth 60°, or 300° point, days, weeks, or months, completes 25 years, a repetition of the first 5 years, but it completes the fourth side of our building and is a very important angle. The sixth 60° or 360°, completing the circle and ending 30 years as measured by our Time Factor, which runs 1° per month on an angle of 45°, completes the top. This is a complete cube and we begin over again.

Study this in connection with the Hexagon Chart. It will help you.

[W.D. Gann's signature]

[undated, but likely *circa* early 1931. See note at end of lesson.]

W. D. GANN

91 WALL STREET
NEW YORK

Scientific Advice
And Analytical Reports
On Stocks and Commodities
Author of "Truth of the Stock Tape"
And "The Tunnel Thru the Air"

Member
American Economic Ass'n
Royal Economic Society
Cable Address
"Ganwade New York"

MASTER CHARTS (Continued)

THE MASTER CHART OF 360°

This chart begins at "0" and runs around the circle to "360". We first divide by two and get 180°; then divide 180 by 2 and we get 90°; then divide 90 by 2 and the get 45°; then divide 45 by 2 and we get 22½°; then divide 22½ by 2 and we get 11¼°; then divide 11¼ by 2 and we get 5-5/8° – all of which form the important angles around the circle.

I have only shown all the important angles from 3-3/4 to 360°. All the angles drawn in red, because they are the important square angles.

After dividing the circle by 2, the next important number to divide by is 3. Dividing by 3, we get 120°, 240° and 360°, making the important triangle points. We then divide 120 by 2 and get the angles of 60°, 150°, 210°, 300° and 330°. We divide 60 by 2 and get the angles of 30° and their proportionate parts around. Then divide 30 by 2 and get the angles of 15° and their proportionate angles around the circle. Then divide 15 by 2 and we get the angles at 7½° around the circle.

24 hours in a day divided into the circle equals 15° for each hour. There are 48 divisions of the circle of 7½°, which are important in measuring day, weekly and monthly time periods.

Study the Major Chart of 360° carefully and you will see why cycles repeat. When anything has travelled up 180°, it starts to go down to the opposite point and each angle up to 180° is the opposite on the other side of the circle. That is why tops and bottoms come out at each one of these degrees. For instance, top coming out at 90° or 90 months at one time will occur 90° or 90 months apart, and there will be similar tops causing rapid fluctuations and fast moves up and down because this angle is so acute that stocks can not remain long before starting in the opposite direction.

Note the culminations that occur every 14 and 15 years, 180 months, or when an 180° angle or an angle straight up and down is reached. How rapid the moves are when they near this angle and how fast they move up and down and how quickly reverse. It is the same with the 45°, the 135°, the 225° and the 315° angle. Note how this proves the important campaigns, when tops and bottoms workout in regularity and equal number of months apart. Note the 22½°, and then follow the next important angle, the 30° angle, then the 45°, then note the 60° and 67½° are close together, but both very strong angles. Note also 112½° and 120°, both strong angles and close together, indicating important tops and bottoms. Also note 150° and 157½°, strong angles close together, indicating important tops and bottoms, and so on all the way around.

#2 M.C.

When the circle is divided by 2 and 3 and redivided, we get the following important angles and measurements of time, space and volume around the circle of 360°:-

5-5/8, 7-1/2, 11-1/4, 15, 16-7/8, 22-1/2, 27-7/8, 30, 33-3/4, 37-1/2, 39-3/8, 45, 50-5/8, 56-1/4, 60, 61-7/8, 67-1/2, 73-1/8, 75, 78-3/4, 82-1/2, 84-3/8, 90, 95-5/8, 101-1/4, 105, 106-7/8, 112-1/2, 118-1/8, 120, 123-3/4, 129-3/8, 135, 140-5/8, 146-1/4, 150, 152-7/8, 157-1/2, 163-1/8, 168-3/4, 174-3/8, 180, 185-5/8, 191-1/4, 196-7/8, 202-1/2, 208-1/8, 210, 213-3/4, 219-3/8, 225, 230-5/8, 236-1/4, 240, 241-7/8, 247-1/2, 253-1/8, 258-3/4, 264-3/8, 270, 275-5/8, 281-1/4, 286-7/8, 292-1/2, 298-1/8, 300, 303-3/4, 309-3/8, 315, 320-5/8, 326-1/4, 330, 331-7/8, 337-1/2, 343-1/8, 348-3/4, 354-3/8, 360, which completes the circle.

These points are all made by a division of angles and are measurements of one-half, one-third, one-fourth, one-eight, one-sixteenth, one-thirty-second and one-sixty-fourth.

Compare these points with your Master Twelve Chart, your Square of Nine Chart, your Hexagon Chart and your Major Chart of 360°. You will see how they all confirm the important angles and time factors.

The number "7" being so important in determining the culmination in weeks, days, months and years, we must divide the circle by 7 to get the important points, or the one-seventh points in the circle, which are vital and important angles.

The first one-seventh of 360 equals 51-3/7, the second equals 102-6/7, the third equals 154-2/7, the fourth equals 205-5/7, the fifth equals 257-1/7, the sixth equals 308-4/7, and the seventh completes the circle, equalling 360°, days, weeks, months or years. If you divide each of these points by 2, you'll also get other important and valuable angles which will confirm and correspond to the other angles in the other charts.

One-seventh of a year or one-seventh of the circle shows why so many fast market movements culminate in the 49th day or the 52nd day and why the 7th week is so very important in culminations and also the 7th month as well as the 7th year.

1½ times 51-3/7 equals 77-1/8 and shows why the angles are so very strong around that point, and why the 77th day, 77th week and 77th month are so important for culminations.

MASTER 360° CIRCLE CHART SQUARED

The Master 360 Circle Chart when squared is 90 x 90, and contains 8,100 cells, zones or spaces. Therefore, the Square of 360 will contain 32,400 spaces. This shows why a stock fluctuates up and down so many times over the same territory, because it is working out the number of cells or vibrations of each space in a square. For example:

       1/8 of 90 equals 1,012-1/2.
       1/4 of 90 equals 2,025
       1/2 of 90 equals 4,050
       3/4 of 90 equals 6,075
       1/3 of 90 equals 2,700
       2/3 of 90 equals 5,400

#3 M.C.

The Square of 360, or 360 times 360 equals 32,400.

        1/4 of 360 equals 8,100
        1/3 of 360 equals 10,860
        1/2 of 360 equals 16,200
        2/3 of 360 equals 21,600
        3/4 of 360 equals 24,300
        7/8 of 360 equals 28,350

These points are very important to use for volume of sales as well as time and price measurements.

Suppose you want to know the number of days required to fill or work out the Square of 90. There are 365 days in a year. 20 years will give you 7,300 days, and in counting the leap years will run a little over this. Therefore, about 22 years, 2 months and 10 days are required to work out each vibration in the Square of 90.

THE SPIRAL CHART

The Spiral Chart represents the correct position, time and space of anything that begins at zero and begins to move round and round. It shows just exactly how the numbers increase as the spiral moves round and round and why stocks move faster as they grow older, or swing so much more rapidly as the price reaches higher levels. At center, beginning point or zero, it requires 45° to represent 1 point. When the stock travelled seven times around from the center, it then required seven points to strike a 45° angle. When it has travelled around the spiral twelve times, it will then require a space of 10 points before striking a 45° angle. It would also mean that the stock could move in one direction ten months without striking anything to cause any very great reaction. On this chart, we have only shown the 45, 60, 90, 120, 135, 180, 225, 240, 270, 300, 315 and 360 degree angles. This shows the division of the circle by 2, 4 and 8, and also shows the one-third point and the two-thirds point; being the vital and most important angles, we placed them so you can see how space or time makes rapid fluctuations.

NEW YORK STOCK EXCHANGE PERMANENT CHART

This Chart is a Square of 20, or 20 up and 20 over, making a total of 400, which can be used to measure days, weeks, months or years, and to determine when tops and bottoms will be made against strong angles, as indicated on this Permanent Chart.

For example: the New York Stock Exchange was incorporated May 17th, 1792. Therefore, we began at "0" on May 17, 1792. 1793 ends on a 1, when the Stock Exchange was 1 year old. 1812 will come out on 20;

        1832 on 40   1892 on 100
        1852 on 60   1912 on 120
        1872 on 80   1932 on 140

Note that 139, or 1931, strikes the 45° angle, running from 20 down, and that this is in the 7th zone, or the 7th space over, which indicates that 1931 is the ending of a bear campaign, and

#4 M.C.

the starting of a bull market. But we must watch out for a break around May and June, 1931, when this angle is hit at the end of the 139th year.

You will notice that the numbers which divide the square into equal parts, run across 10, 30, 50, 70, 90, 110, etc., and that the year 1802 comes out on 10, the year 1822 on 30, the year 1842 on 50, the year 1862 on 70. Note that the year 1861, when the Civil War broke out, was on the number 69, which is a 45° angle. Then note that 1882 ended in May on a 90° angle, and at the 1/2 point, 180° angle, running horizontally across.

Again in 1902, it was at 110; the 1/2 point, and in 1903 and 1904, hit the 45° angle.

Note that the years 1920 and 1921 hit the 45° angle on No. 129 and 1922, the first year of the bull market, was at 130 at the 1/2 point.

Note that 1929 was on the 137th number, or 137th month, and hit an angle of 45°, and that the year 1930 was at the 1/2 point on the 4th square, a strong Resistance Point, which indicated a sharp, severe decline.

Again, 138 is at the 1/2 point on the Master 12 Chart.

1933 will be on 141, in the 8th zone, and at the center or 1/2 point of the 2nd quarter of the Square of 20.

The years 1934 and 1935, ending in May, will be on 142 and 143, and 1935 will come out on the 45° angle at the grand center in the 8th zone and at the 1/2 point of the 2nd square, going to 1/2 of the total square, which will indicate a decline and bottom for an advance to run up in 1936, with 1937 striking at 145, which is 1/4th of the column on the way up in the square.

If you will study the weeks, months, as well as the years, and apply them to these important points and angles, you will see how they have determined the important tops and bottoms in the past campaigns.

UNITED STATES STEEL NAME CHART

The name, United States Steel, contains 17 letters. Therefore, to make up a Permanent Square for United States Steel, according to its name, will require 17 x 17, or a Square of 289. Therefore, 17, which is really 2-1/2 times the lowest price at which Steel ever sold is an important point.

The prices 34, 51, 68, 85, 102, 119, 136, 153, 170, 187, 204, 221, 238, 255, 272 are all important because they strike important vibrations on the name and angles of U.S. Steel.

The basic number or low point, for example, 9, the lowest digit on US Steel, and it's vibrations according to its name, all cause slight variations at times from other stocks, because each stock works according to its own base, beginning point, numbers and name.

US Steel works good to the natural angles and Master Chart, because its digit is 9 and comes out on exact 9 vibrations all the way through, finishing at 261, which was 28 nines from its beginning point, or lowest level.

THE W.D. GANN MASTER STOCK MARKET COURSE

#5 M.C.

A study of all these various tables will help you to understand Resistance Levels.

UNITED STATES PERMANENT MASTER CHART

We use the square of 7 for the United States, because the name of America contains 7 letters, and this square is 49, a very important and fatal number.

We begin the United States Chart on October 12, 1492. Make up these Squares of 7 and put on the years. You will note how this indicates the panic years in the United States and the years of prosperity.

You can also make up a Square of 21 x 21, which is the number of letters in the name of United States of America. These angles and important points will all come out about the same as when we use America, because three times 7 is 21. However, you will get some stronger angles and more important points if you make up the Square of 21 x 21, which will run out to 441, with the 1/2 point at 220-1/2.

The more you study these Permanent Chart, the more you will appreciate their great value, and will see that numbers do determine everything in the future, and that geometrical angles and mathematical points measure every Resistance Level, time, price, space or volume.

[unsigned]
_____

[undated, but likely *circa* early 1931]

[N.B. Note the different letterhead addresses between the first and second parts of this lesson. This helps date these lessons at around early 1931, as other (dated) Gann lessons indicate a change of address around this time.]

SQUARE 12

	1	2	3	4	5	6	7	8	9	10	11	12
12	12	24	36	48	60	72	84	96	108	120	132	144
11	11	23	35	47	59	71	83	95	107	119	131	143
10	10	22	34	46	58	70	82	94	106	118	130	142
9	9	21	33	45	57	69	81	93	105	117	129	141
8	8	20	32	44	56	68	80	92	104	116	128	140
7	7	19	31	43	55	67	79	91	103	115	127	139
6	6	18	30	42	54	66	78	90	102	114	126	138
5	5	17	29	41	53	65	77	89	101	113	125	137
4	4	16	28	40	52	64	76	88	100	112	124	136
3	3	15	27	39	51	63	75	87	99	111	123	135
2	2	14	26	38	50	62	74	86	98	110	122	134
1	1	13	25	37	49	61	73	85	97	109	121	133

[Master 360° Square of 12 Chart for Eggs]

THE W.D. GANN MASTER STOCK MARKET COURSE

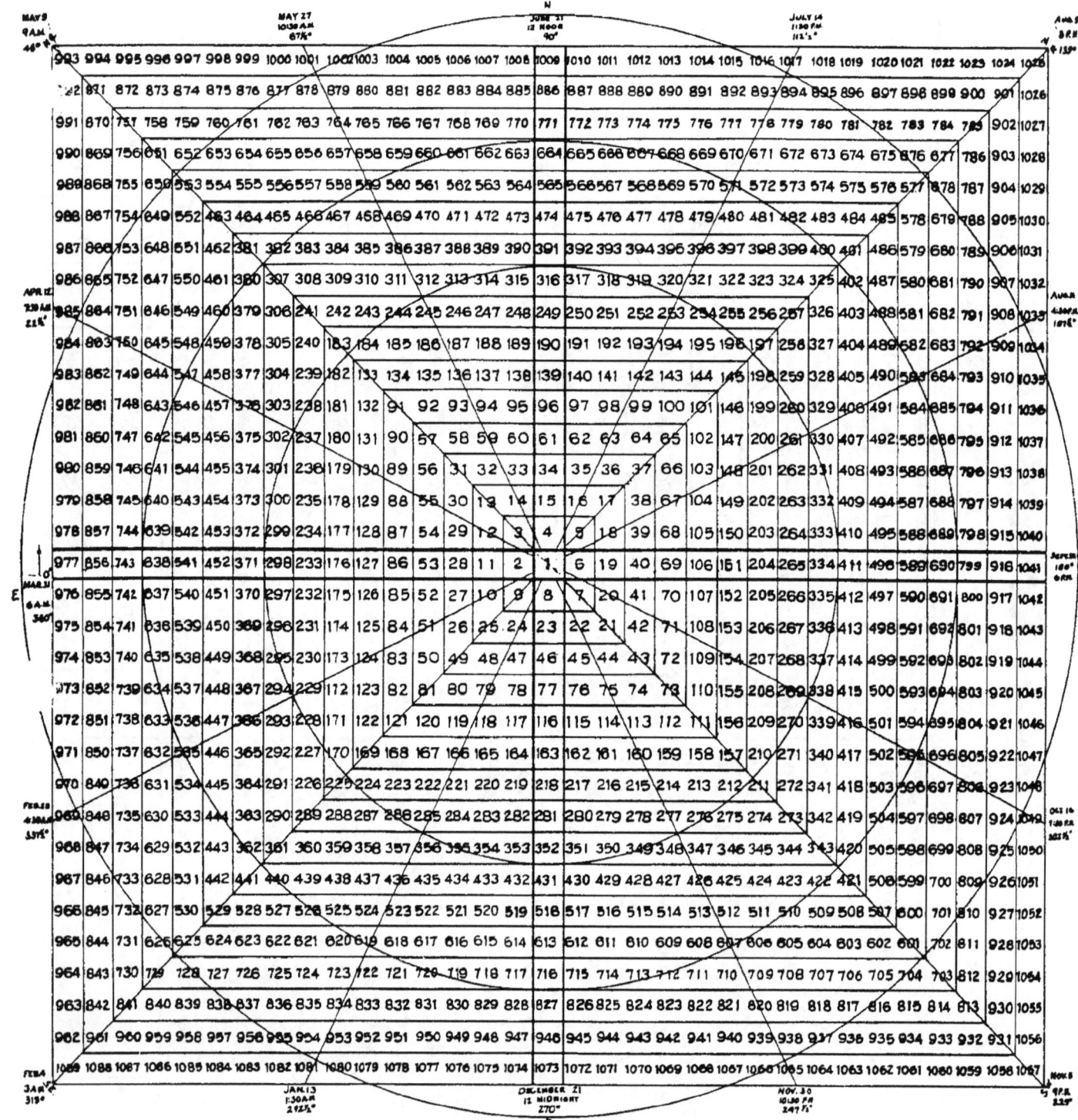

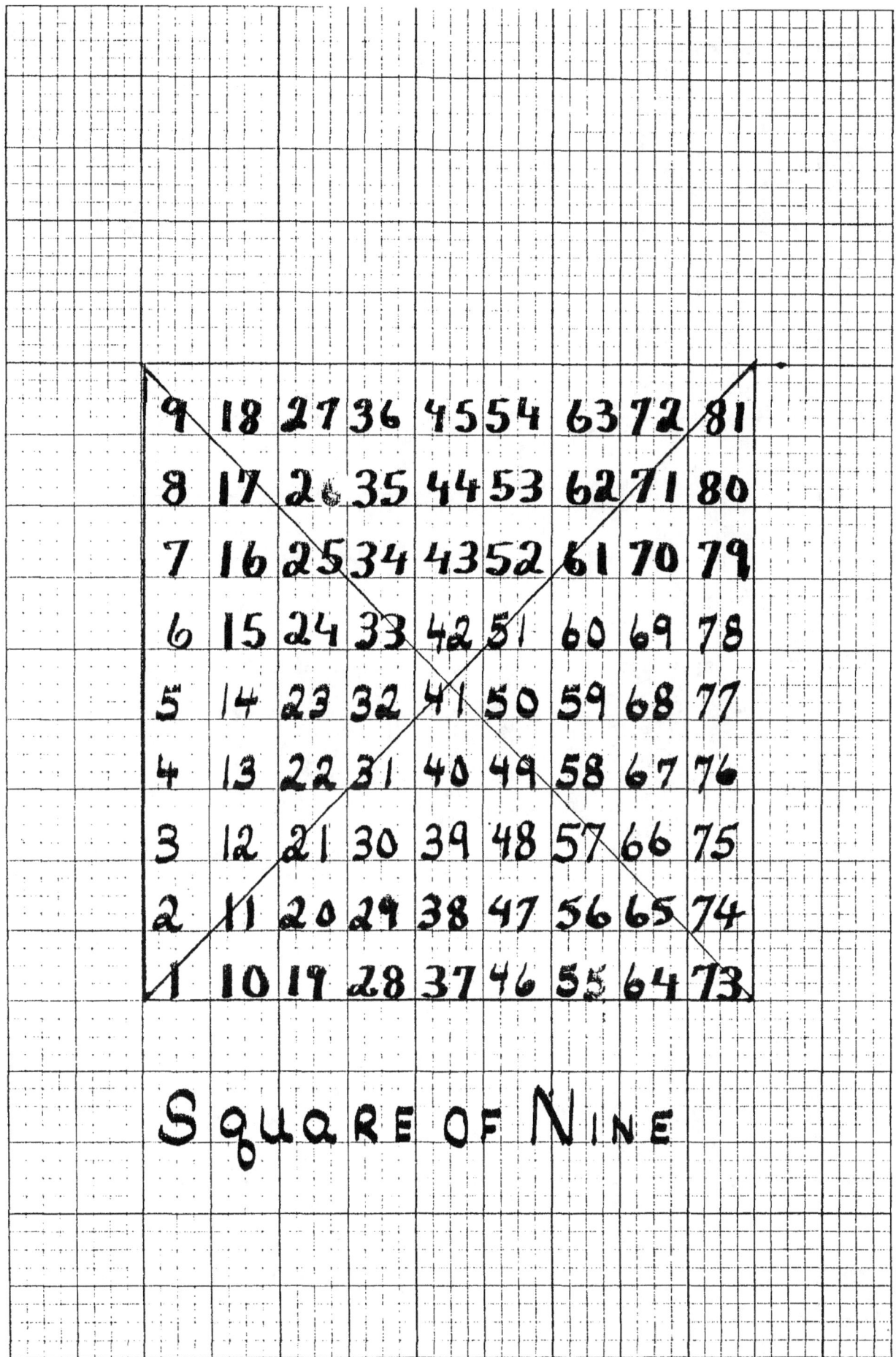

Six Squares of Nine

SQUARE OF THE CIRCLE

	1	2	3	4	5	6	7	8	9	10	11	12	13	14	15	16	17	18	19
19	19	38	57	76	95	114	133	152	171	190	209	228	247	266	285	304	323	342	361
18	18	37	56	75	94	113	132	151	170	189	208	227	246	265	284	303	322	341	360
17	17	36	55	74	93	112	131	150	169	188	207	226	245	264	283	302	321	340	359
16	16	35	54	73	92	111	130	149	168	187	206	225	244	263	282	301	320	339	358
15	15	34	53	72	91	110	129	148	167	186	205	224	243	262	281	300	319	338	357
14	14	33	52	71	90	109	128	147	166	185	204	223	242	261	280	299	318	337	356
13	13	32	51	70	89	108	127	146	165	184	203	222	241	260	279	298	317	336	355
12	12	31	50	69	88	107	126	145	164	183	202	221	240	259	278	297	316	335	354
11	11	30	49	68	87	106	125	144	163	182	201	220	239	258	277	296	315	334	353
10	10	29	48	67	86	105	124	143	162	181	200	219	238	257	276	295	314	333	352
9	9	28	47	66	85	104	123	142	161	180	199	218	237	256	275	294	313	332	351
8	8	27	46	65	84	103	122	141	160	179	198	217	236	255	274	293	312	331	350
7	7	26	45	64	83	102	121	140	159	178	197	216	235	254	273	292	311	330	349
6	6	25	44	63	82	101	120	139	158	177	196	215	234	253	272	291	310	329	348
5	5	24	43	62	81	100	119	138	157	176	195	214	233	252	271	290	309	328	347
4	4	23	42	61	80	99	118	137	156	175	194	213	232	251	270	289	308	327	346
3	3	22	41	60	79	98	117	136	155	174	193	212	231	250	269	288	307	326	345
2	2	21	40	59	78	97	116	135	154	173	192	211	230	249	268	287	306	325	344
1	1	20	39	58	77	96	115	134	153	172	191	210	229	248	267	286	305	324	343

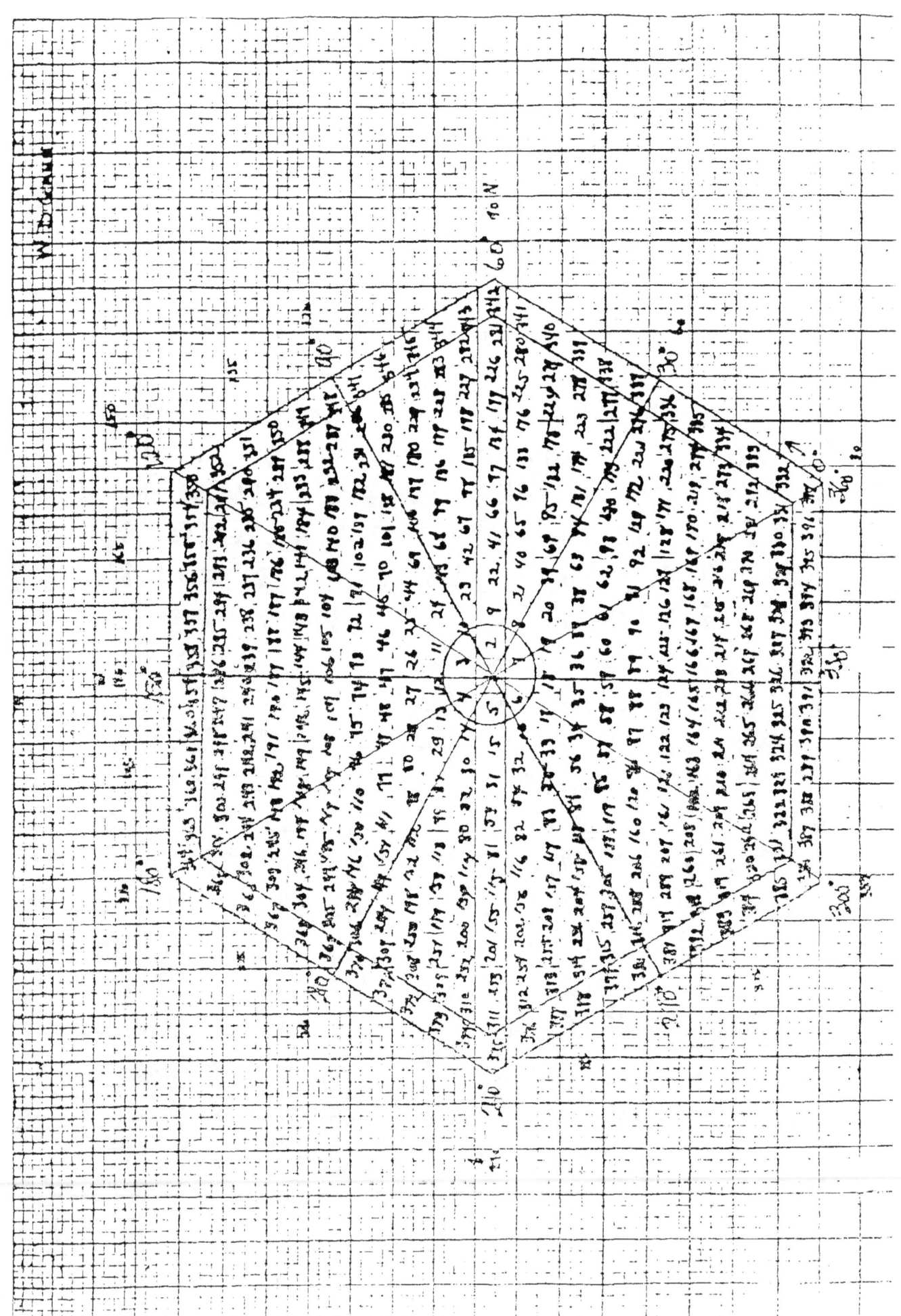

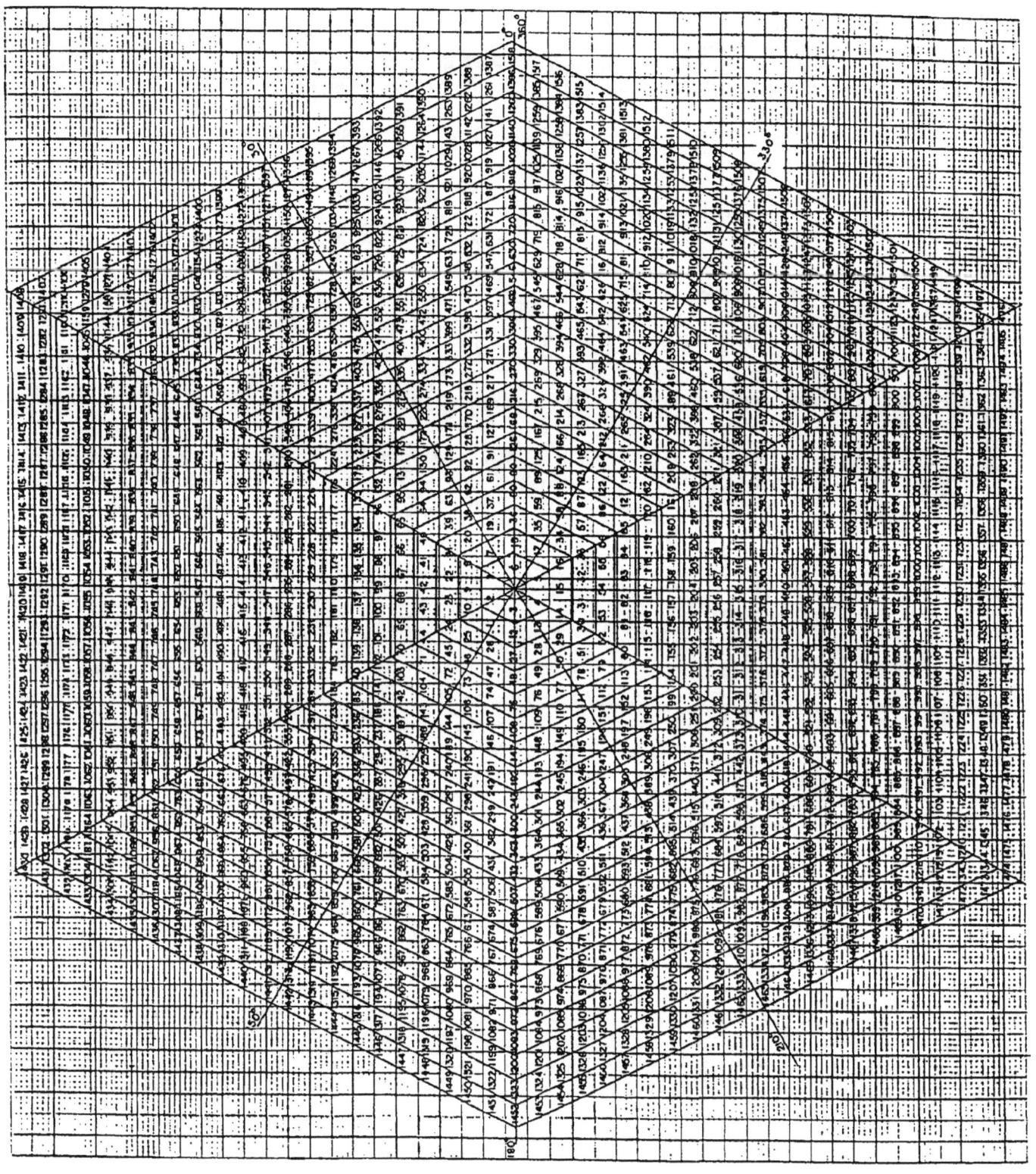

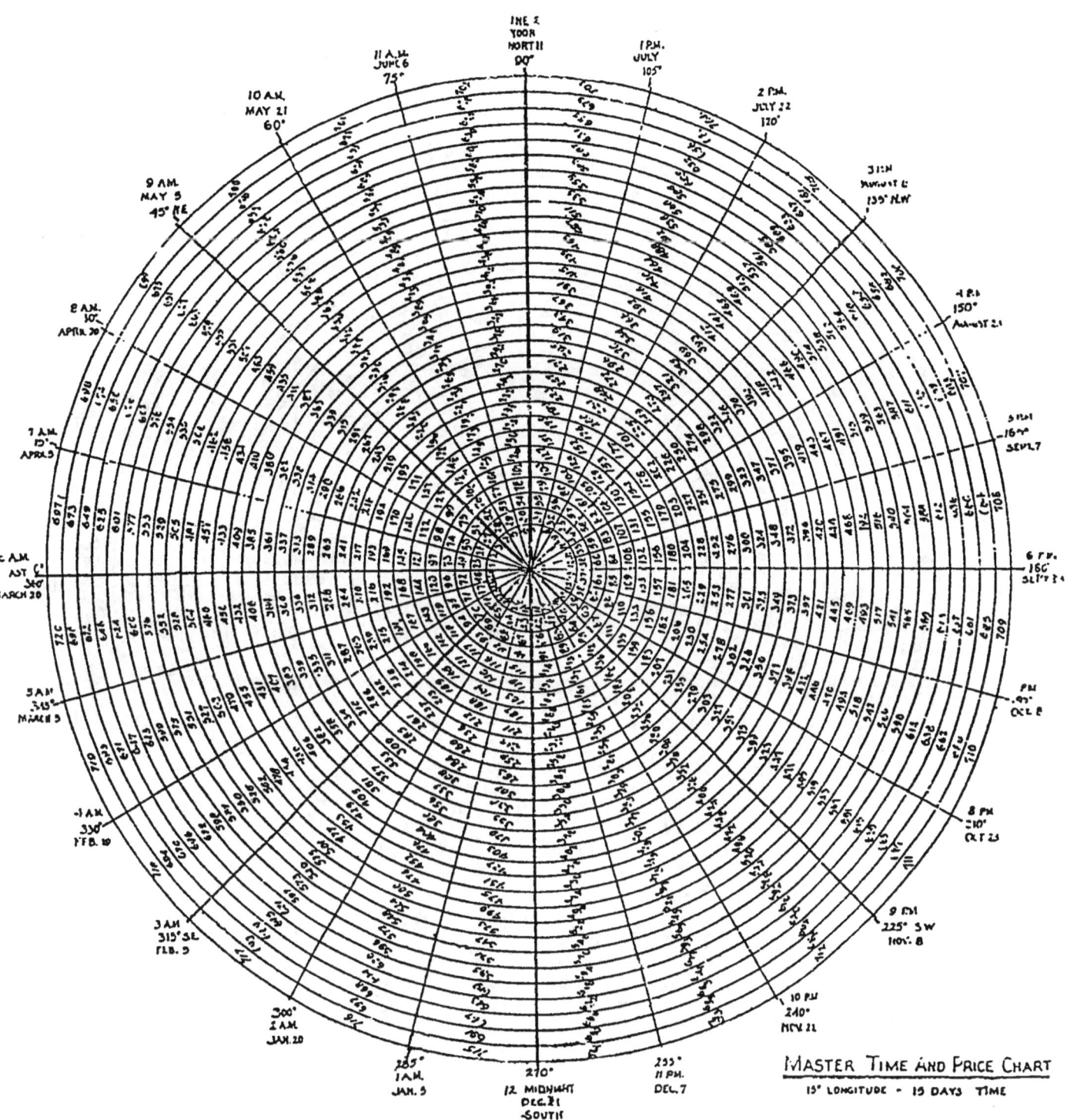

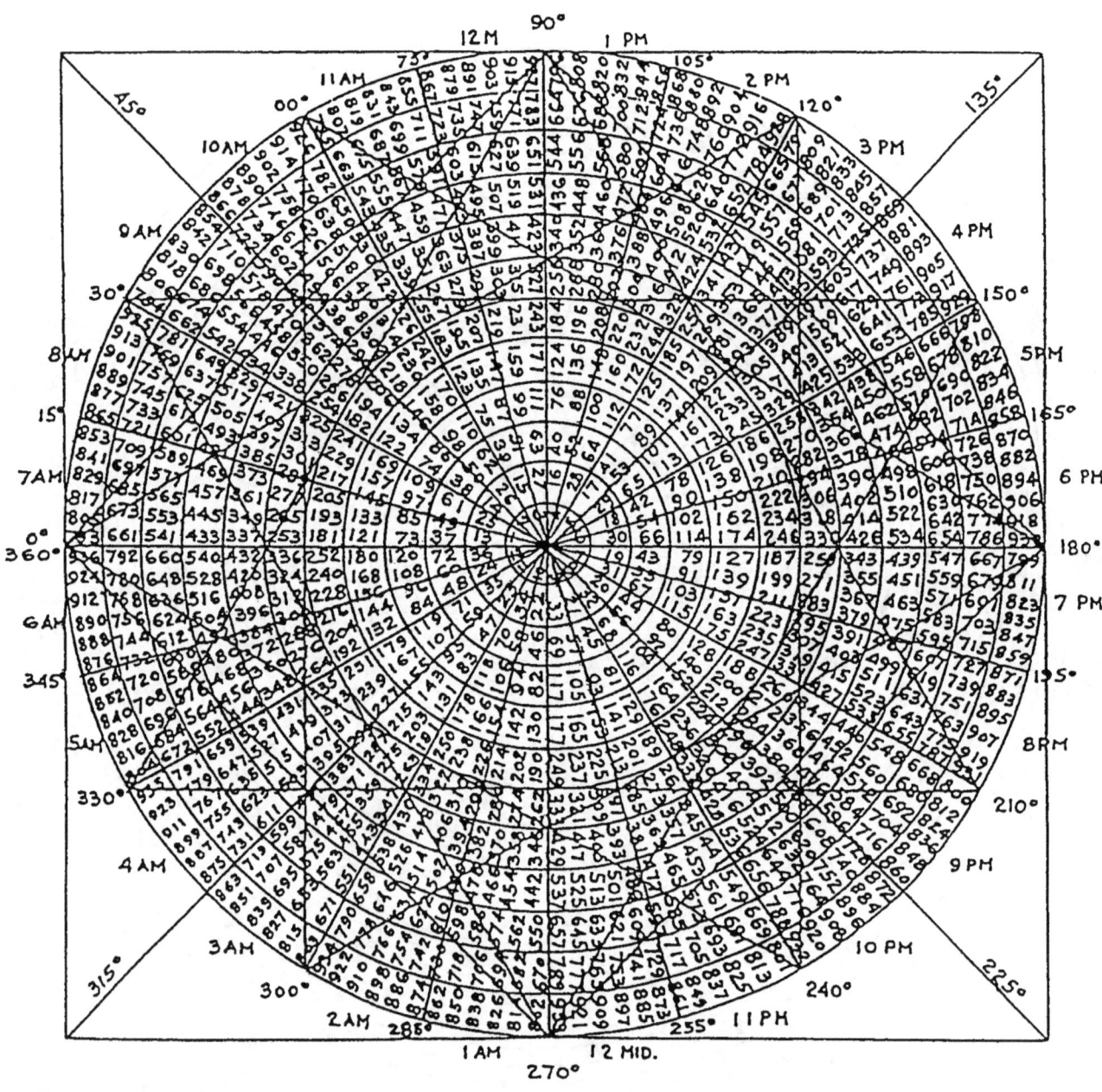

THE W.D. GANN MASTER STOCK MARKET COURSE

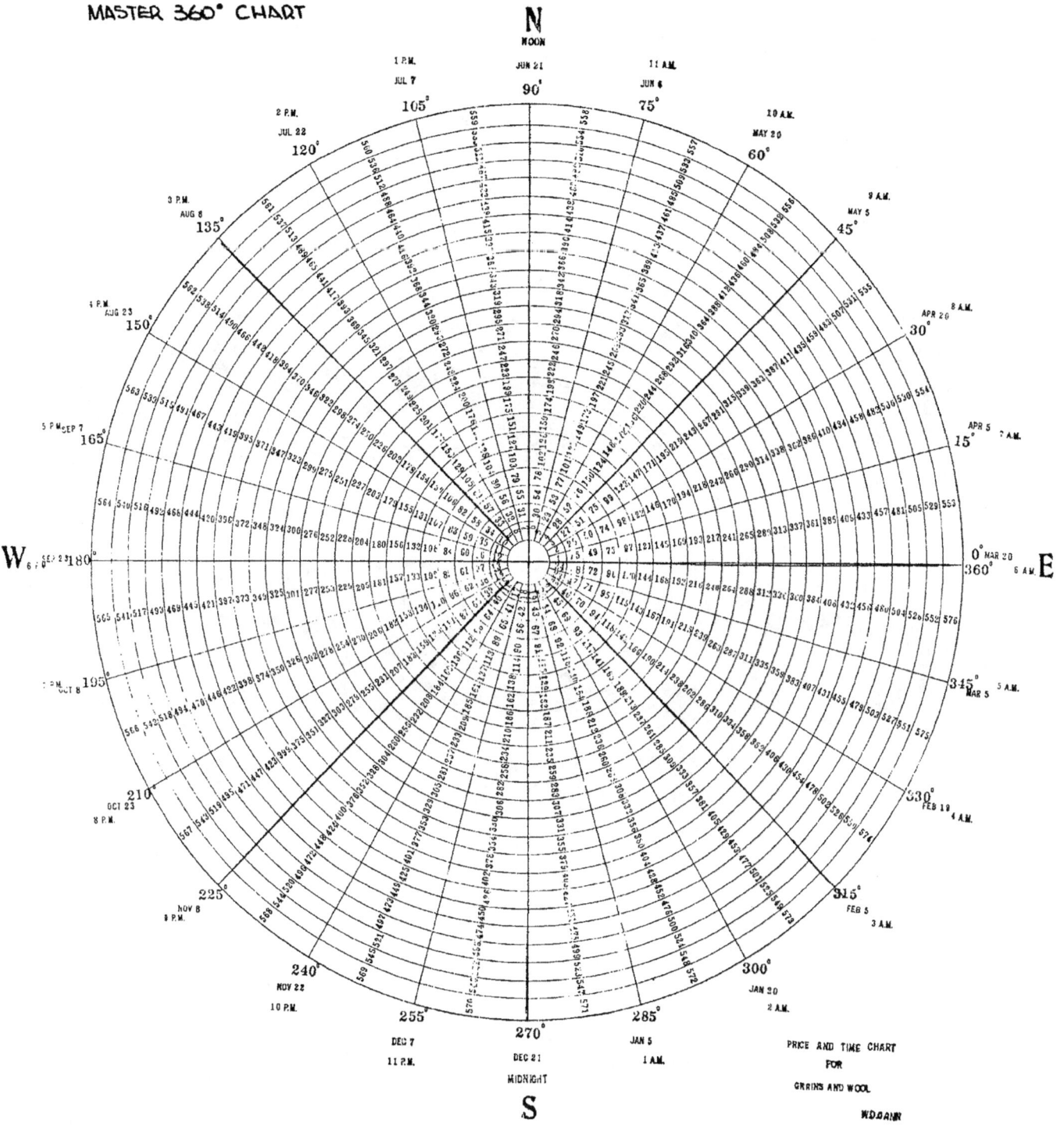

MASTER 360° CHART

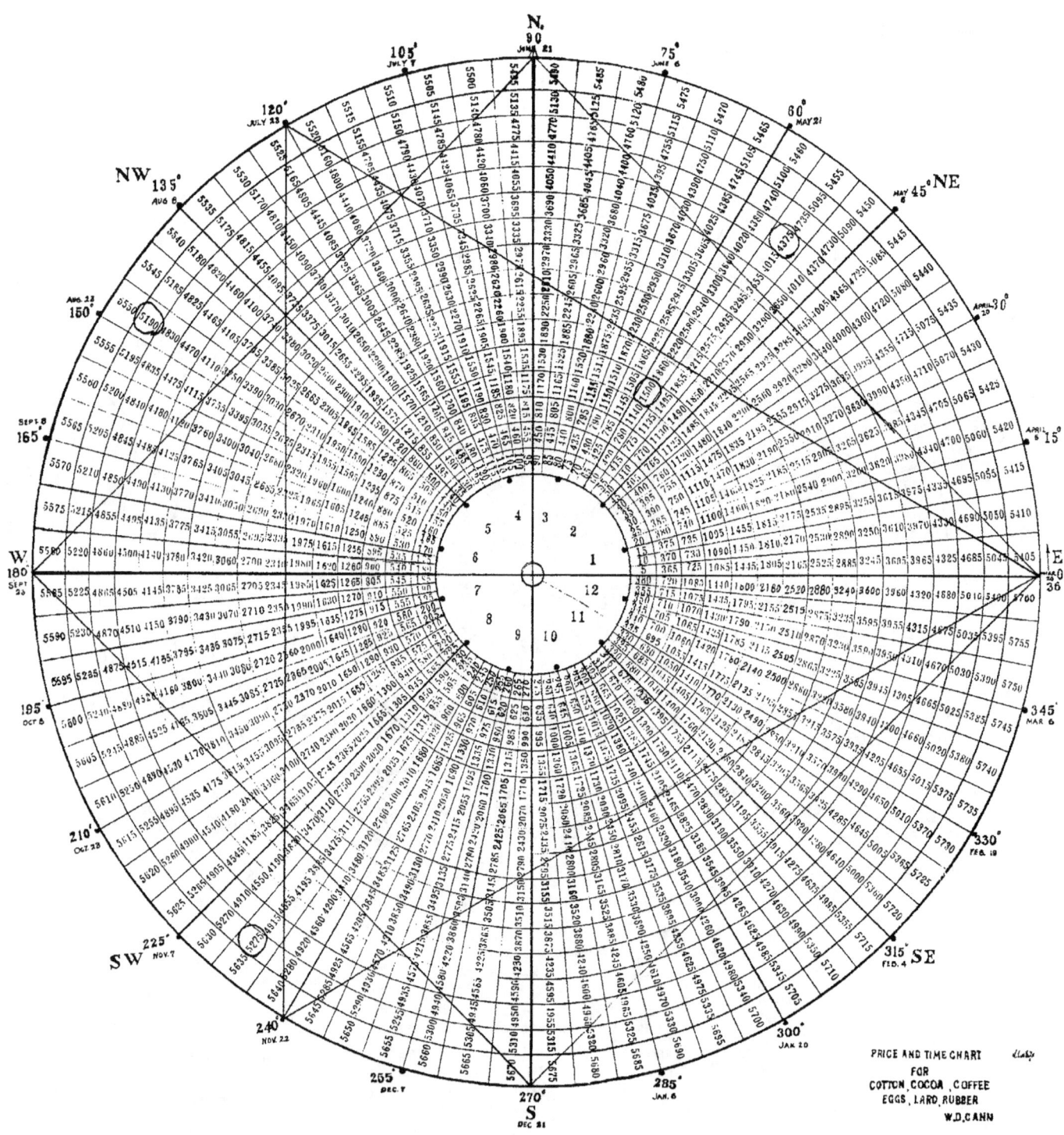

NYSE PERMANENT CHART

	1	2	3	4	5	6	7	8	9	10	11	12	13	14	15	16	17	18	19	20
	1812	1832	1852	1872	1892	1912	1932	1952	1972	1992	2012	2032	2052	2072	2092	2112	2132	2152	2172	2192
20	20	40	60	80	100	120	140	160	180	200	220	240	260	280	300	320	340	360	380	400
19	19	39	59	79	99	119	139	159	179	199	219	239	259	279	299	319	339	359	379	399
18	18	38	58	78	98	118	138	158	178	198	218	238	258	278	298	318	338	358	378	398
17	17	37	57	77	97	117	137	157	177	197	217	237	257	277	297	317	337	357	377	397
16	16	36	56	76	96	116	136	156	176	196	216	236	256	276	296	316	336	356	376	396
15	15	35	55	75	95	115	135	155	175	195	215	235	255	275	295	315	335	355	375	395
14	14	34	54	74	94	114	134	154	174	194	214	234	254	274	294	314	334	354	374	394
13	13	33	53	73	93	113	133	153	173	193	213	233	253	273	293	313	333	353	373	393
12	12	32	52	72	92	112	132	152	172	192	212	232	252	272	292	312	332	352	372	392
11	11	31	51	71	91	111	131	151	171	191	211	231	251	271	291	311	331	351	371	391
	1802	1822	1842	1862	1882	1902	1922	1942	1962	1982	2022	2042	2044	2082	2122	2122	2142	2162	2182	2202
10	10	30	50	70	90	110	130	150	170	190	210	230	250	270	290	310	330	350	370	390
9	9	29	49	69	89	109	129	149	169	189	209	229	249	269	289	309	329	349	369	389
8	8	28	48	68	88	108	128	148	168	188	208	228	248	268	288	308	328	348	368	388
7	7	27	47	67	87	107	127	147	167	187	207	227	247	267	287	307	327	347	367	387
6	6	26	46	66	86	106	126	146	166	186	206	226	246	266	286	306	326	346	366	386
5	5	25	45	65	85	105	125	145	165	185	205	225	245	265	285	305	325	345	365	385
4	4	24	44	64	84	104	124	144	164	184	204	224	244	264	284	304	324	344	364	384
3	3	23	43	63	83	103	123	143	163	183	203	223	243	263	283	303	323	343	363	383
2	2	22	42	62	82	102	122	142	162	182	202	222	242	262	282	302	322	342	362	382
1	1	21	41	61	81	101	121	141	161	181	201	221	241	261	281	301	321	341	361	381

MAY 17 1792

W.D. GANN

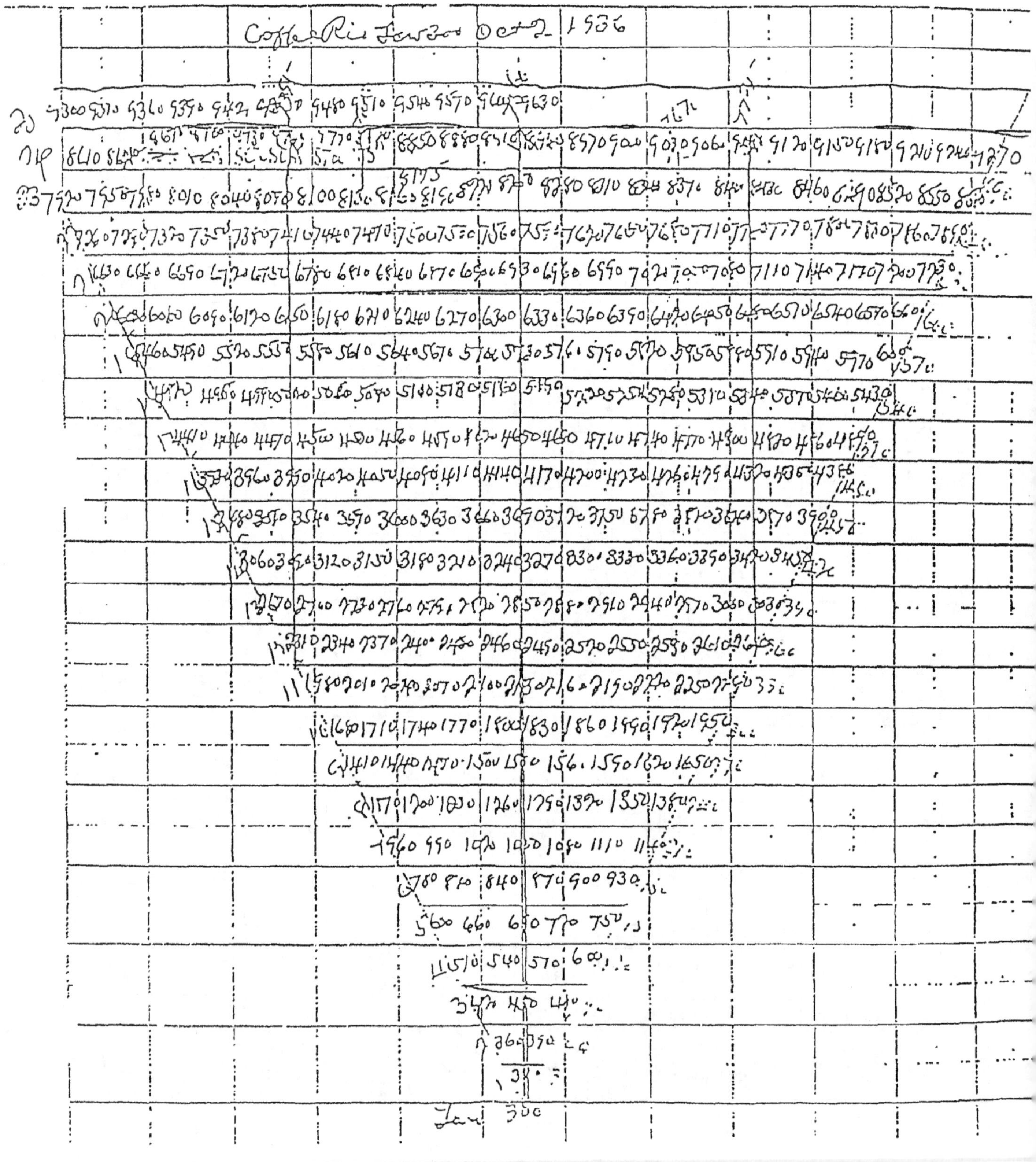
Coffee Rio ... Oct 2 1936
Jan 300

THE W.D. GANN MASTER STOCK MARKET COURSE

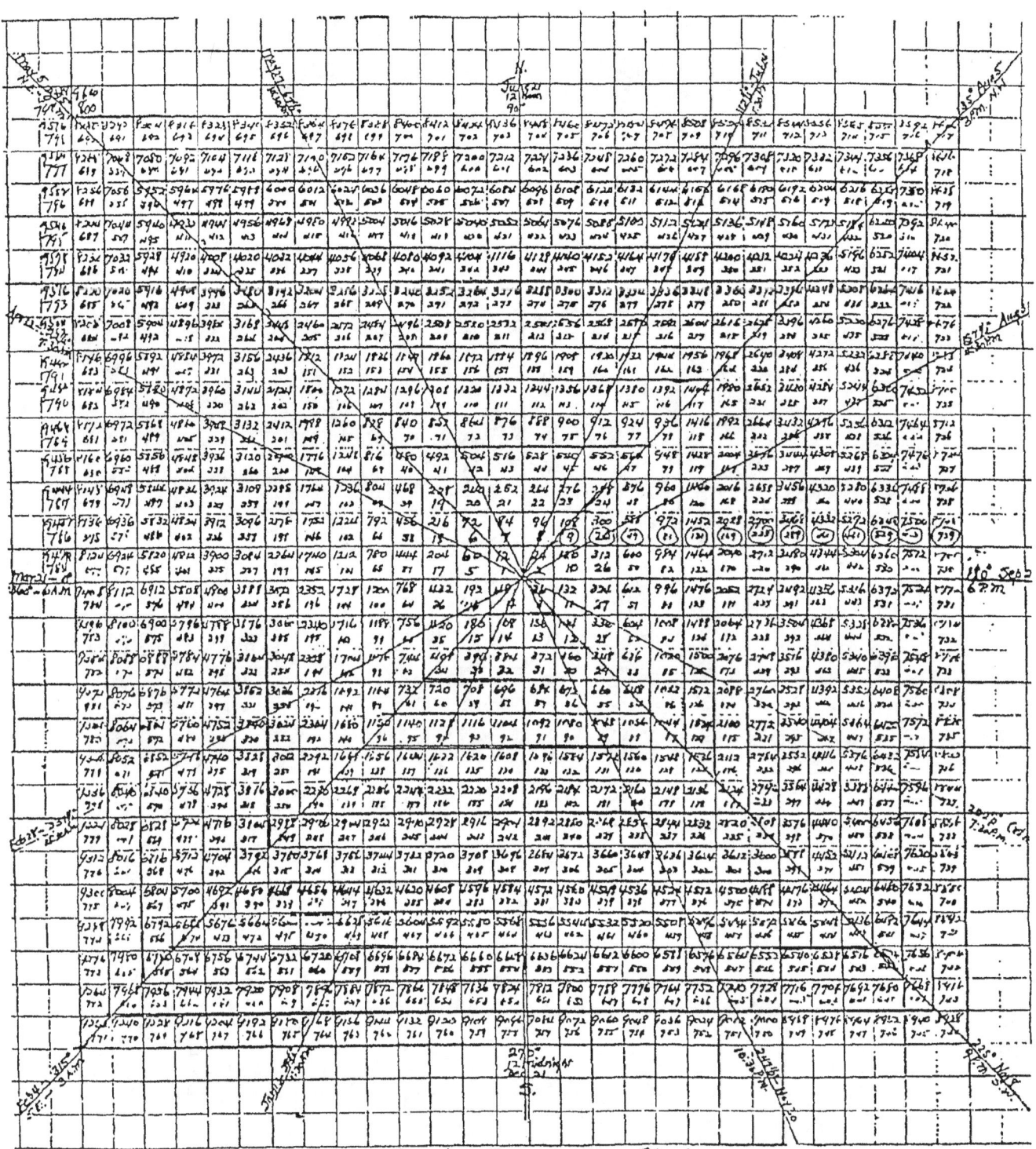

Master Price & Time Chart for Cotton, Coffee, Cocoa, Wool, and Grain

Even Squares for Cotton & Eggs
Time and Price

Dec-28-1920
Dec-28 1948 = 336 Months
April 28, 1949 - 4 "
7×49 = 343 "

July 28, 1948 = 343 "
7×49 = 343 "

Dec 28, 1920 – High 60¢
May 2, 1949 = 1481 weeks

Square of 38 = 1444
" " 39 = 1521
" " √ = 1521

From □ 38 to 39
1/4 = 19 1/4 Weeks
1/2 = 38 1/2 "
1481 + 38 1/2 = 1482 1/2
May 13, 1949 = 1482 1/2

1440 = 4 × 360

May 30, 1949 = 45 weeks
in new 360 cycle.

[Hand-drawn square grid diagram labeled with directional markers: NE 45°, North 90°, SE 315°, East 0°/360°, South 270°, West 180°, SW 225°, NW 135°, with fractional divisions 1/8, 3/16, 1/4, 5/16, 3/8, 7/16, 1/2, 9/16, 5/8, 11/16, 3/4, 13/16, 7/8, 15/16 around perimeter. Grid filled with numerical values.]

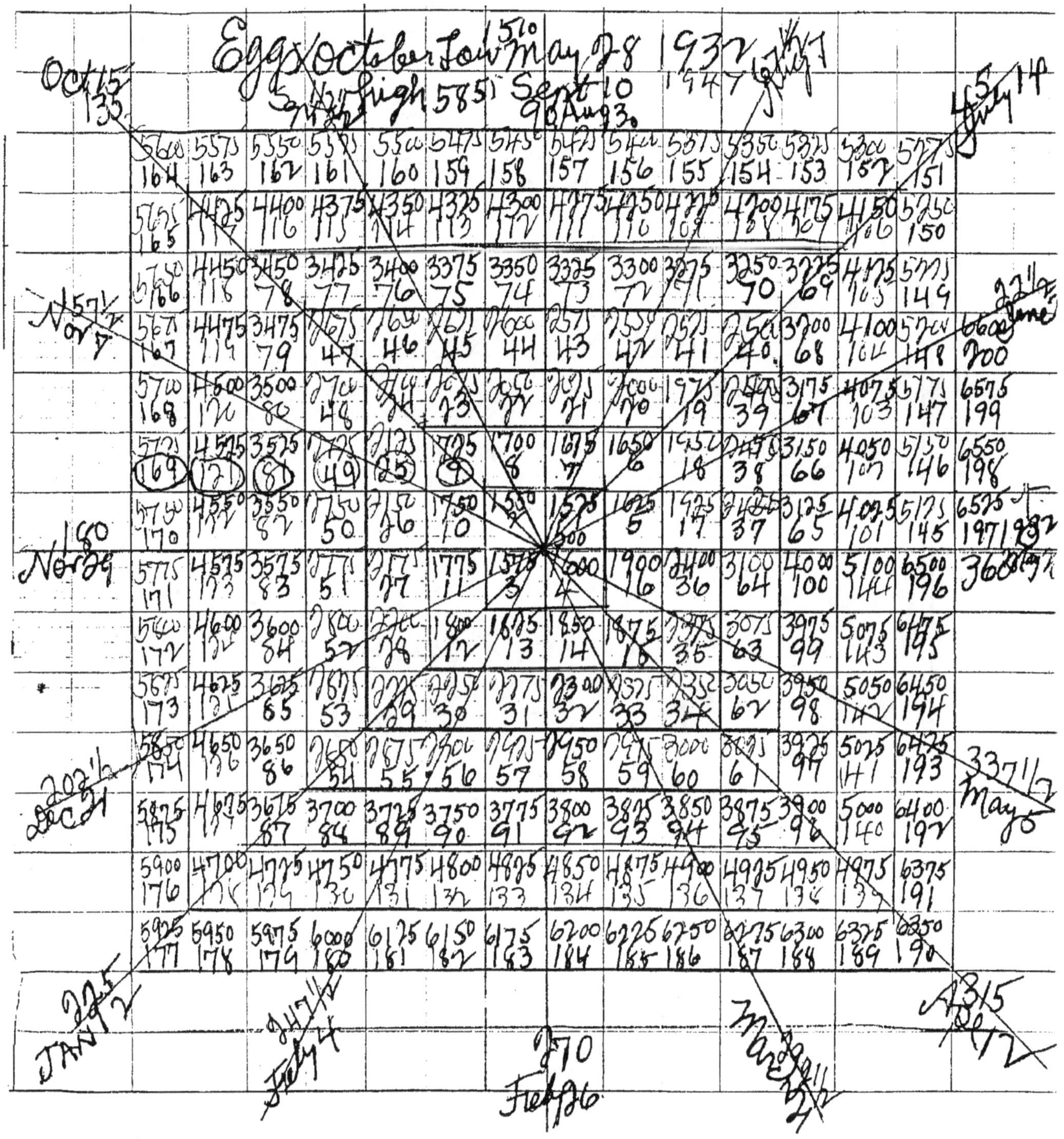

Chapter 15B

The Hexagon Chart

SCIENTIFIC ADVICE	**W. D. GANN**	MEMBER
AND ANALYTICAL REPORTS	78 WALL STREET	AMERICAN ECONOMIC ASS'N
ON STOCKS AND COMMODITIES	NEW YORK	ROYAL ECONOMIC SOCIETY
AUTHOR OF "TRUTH OF THE STOCK TAPE"		CABLE ADDRESS
AND "THE TUNNEL THRU THE AIR"		"GANWADE NEW YORK"

THE HEXAGON CHART

Since everything moves in a circle and nothing moves in straight lines, this chart is to show you how the angles influence stocks at very low levels and very high levels and why stocks move faster the higher they get, because they have moved out to where the distance between the angles of 45° are so far apart that there is nothing to stop them and their moves are naturally rapid up and down.

We begin with a circle of "1" in the center and while this only contains 1, yet the circle is 360° just the same. We then place a circle of circles around this circle and 6 circles complete the second circle, making a gain of 6 over the first one, ending the second circle at 7, making 7 on this angle a very important month, year, and week as well as days, the seventh day being sacred and a day of rest. The third circle is completed at 19. The fourth circle around is completed at 37, a gain of 18 over the previous circle. The fifth circle is completed at 61, a gain of 24 over the previous circle. The sixth circle is completed at 91, a gain of 30 over the previous circle, and the seventh circle at 127, a gain of 36 over the last circle. Note that from the first the gain is 6 each time we go around. In other words, when we have travelled six times around we have gained 36. Note that this completes the first Hexagon and as this equals 127 months, shows why some campaigns will run 10 years and seven months, or until they reach a square of the Hexagon, or the important last angle of 45°.

The eighth circle around is completed at 169, a gain of 42 over the first. This is a very important angle and an important time factor for more reasons than one. It is 14 years and one month, or double our Cycle of 7 years. Important tops and bottoms culminate at this angle as you will see by going over your charts.

The ninth circle is completed at 217, a gain of 48 over the previous circle. The tenth circle is completed at 271, a gain of 54. Note that 271 is the 9th circle from the first, or is the third 90° angle or 270°, three-fourths of a circle, a strong point. All this is confirmed by the Master Twelve Chart, by the four seasons and by the Square of Nine Chart, and also confirmed by the Hexagon Chart, showing that mathematical proof is always exact no matter how many ways or from what directions you figure it.

The eleventh circle is completed at 331, a gain of 60 over the last circle. The twelfth circle is completed at 397, which completes the Hexagon, making a gain in

11 circles of 66 from the beginning. 66 months, or five years and six months, marks the culmination of a major campaigns in stocks. Note how often they culminate on the 60th month, then have a reaction, and make a second top or bottom in the 66th month. Note the number 66 on the Master Twelve Chart. Note it on the Square of Nine and note that 66 occurs on an angle of 180° on the Hexagon Chart, all of which confirms the strong angle at this point.

We have an angle of 66°, one of 67½, and one of 68, confirming this point to be doubly strong for tops and bottoms or space movements up or down.

Note the number 360 on the Hexagon Chart. It completes a circle of 360°. From our beginning point this occurs at an angle of 150° on the Hexagon Chart going around, but measuring from the center, it would equal an angle of 90° or 180°, making this a strong point, hard and difficult to pass, and the ending of one campaign and the beginning of another.

Again with the center of the Hexagon Chart at "1" notice that 7, 19, 37, 61, 91, 127, 169, 217, 271, 331, and 397 are all on this direct angle and are important points in time measurement. Beginning with "1" and following the other angle, note that 2, 9, 22, 41, 66, 97, 134, 177, 226, 281, and 342 are all on the same angle of 90°, or an angle of 60° and 240° as measured by the Hexagon Chart.

Go over this chart and the important angles each way and you will see why resistance is met either on days, weeks, months, or years, and why stocks stop and make tops and bottoms at these strong important points, according to time.

When any stock has passed out above 120° or especially above 127° or 127 points and gone out of the square of the first Hexagon, its fluctuations will be more rapid, and it will move faster up and down. Notice near the center that in travelling from 6 to 7 you strike the angle of 180° or 90°, but when the stock gets out to 162, it can travel up to 169 before striking another strong angle. That is why fast moves occur up and down as stocks get higher and as they move from a center of time.

Remember that everything seeks the center of gravity and important tops and bottoms are formed according to centers and measurements of time from a center, base or beginning point, either top or bottom. The angles formed going straight up and across, may form just the same going across as the stock travels over for days, weeks, months or years. Thus, a stock going up to 22½ would strike an angle of 22½°. If it moves over 22½ days it would strike the angle or 22½ weeks or 22½ months, it would also strike an angle of 22½°, and the higher it is when these angles are struck and the angle it hits going up, the greater the resistance to be met. Reverse the rule going down.

Market movements are made just the same as any other thing, which is constructed. It is just the same as constructing a building. First, the foundation has to be laid and then the four walls have to be completed and last, but not least of all, the top has to be put on. The cube or hexagon proves exactly the law which works because of time and space in the market. When a building is put up it is built according to a square or hexagon. It has four walls or four sides, a bottom and a top; therefore, it is a cube.

In working out the 20-year Cycle in the stock market, the first 60°, or 5 years, from the beginning forms the bottom of the cube. The second 60°, running to 120, completes the first angle or the first side and runs out the 10-year Cycle. The third 60°, or the second side, ends 15 years or 180°. It is very important because we have the building half completed and must meet the strong resistance at this point. The fourth 60°, or the end of 20 years or 240 months, completes the third side. We are now two-thirds around the building, a very strong point which culminates and completes our 20-year Cycle. The fifth 60°, or 300° point, days, weeks, or months, completes 25 years, a repetition of the first 5 years, but it completes the fourth side of our building and is a very important angle. The sixth 60° or 360°, completing the circle and ending 30 years as measured by our Time Factor, which runs 1° per month on an angle of 45°, completes the top. This is a complete cube and we begin over again.

Study this in connection with the Hexagon Chart. It will help you.

[W.D. Gann's signature]
_____

January, 1931.

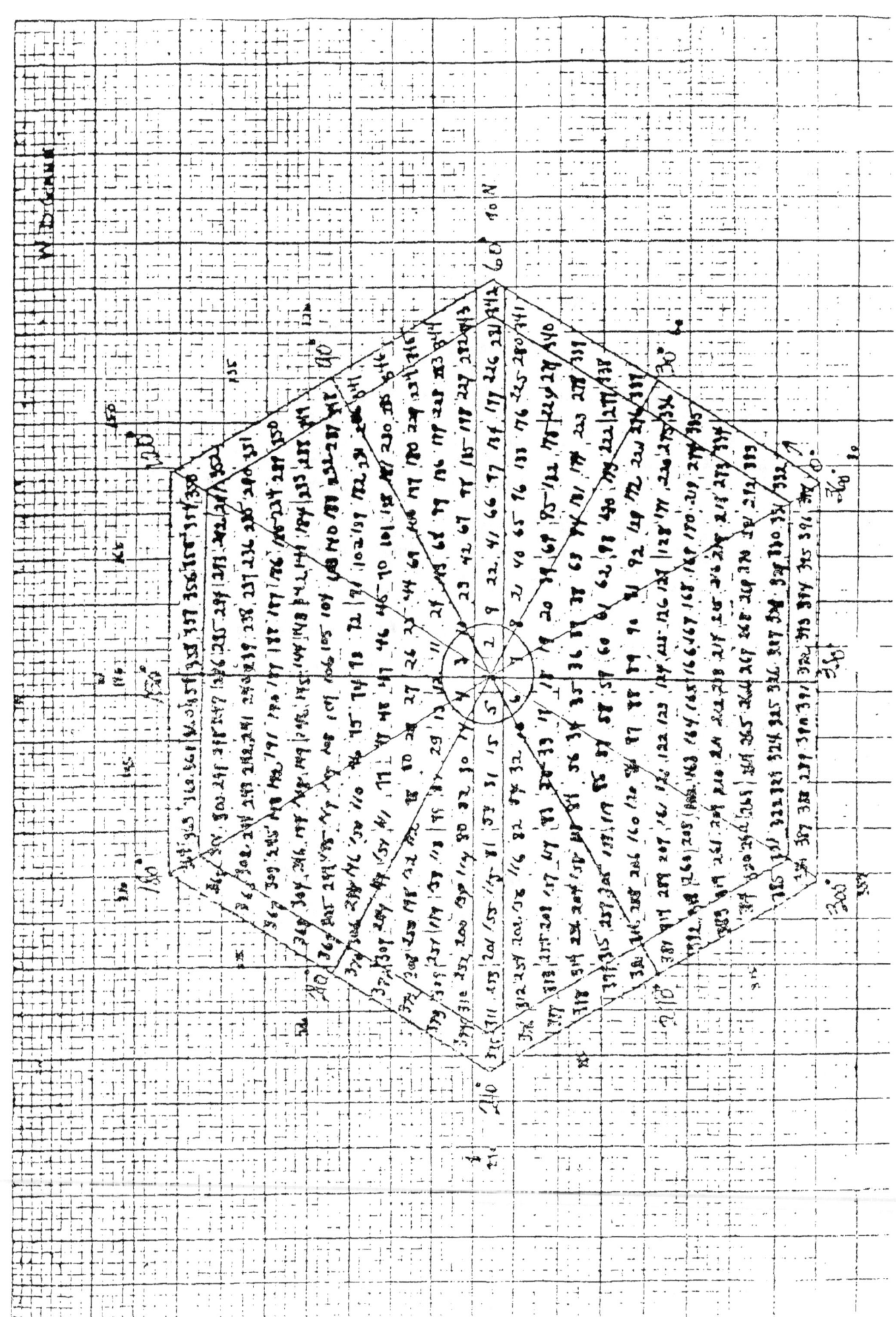

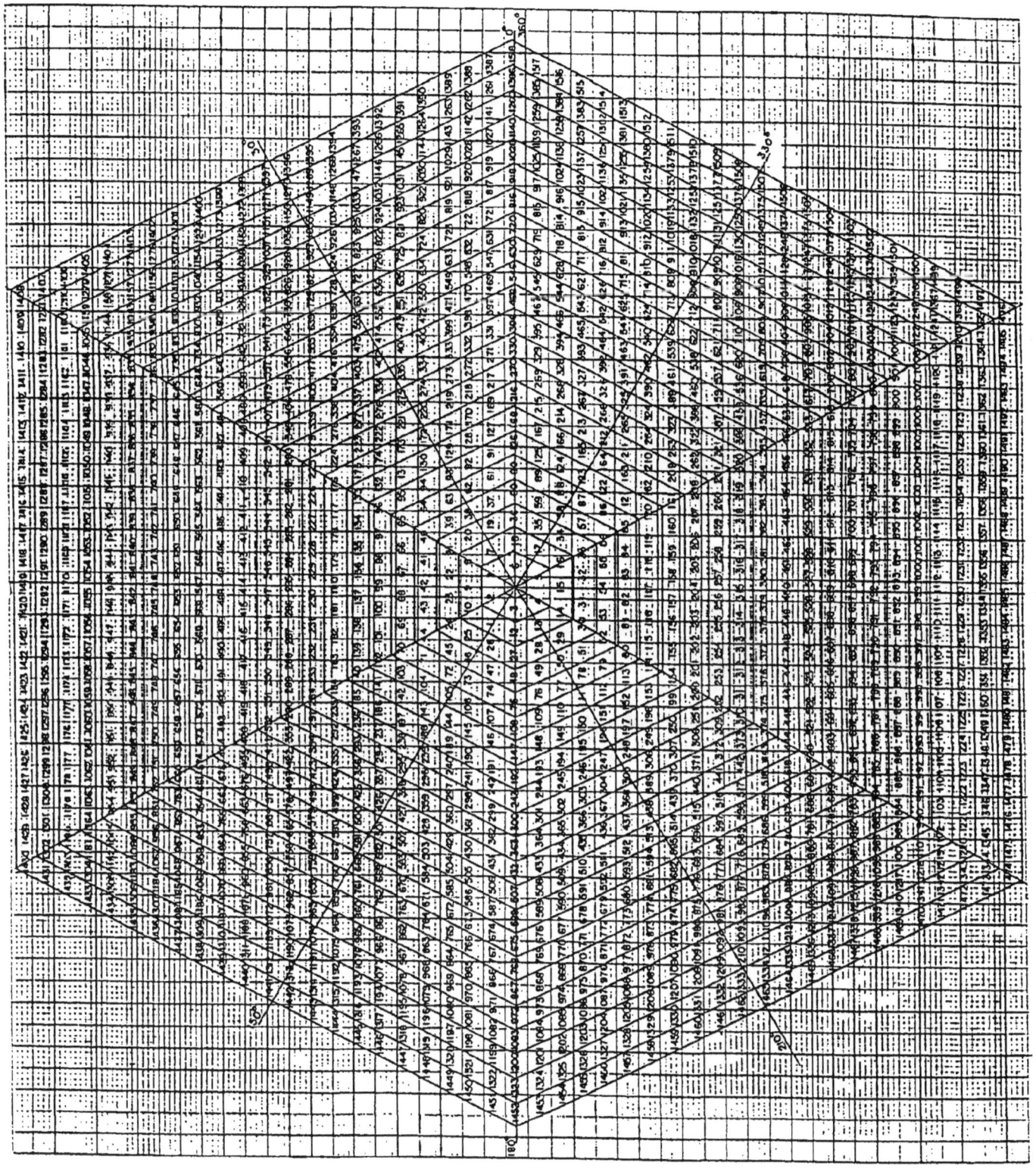

CHAPTER 16

AUBURN MOTORS

W. D. GANN

91 WALL STREET
NEW YORK

SCIENTIFIC ADVICE
AND ANALYTICAL REPORTS
ON STOCKS AND COMMODITIES
AUTHOR OF "TRUTH OF THE STOCK TAPE"
AND "THE TUNNEL THRU THE AIR"

MEMBER
AMERICAN ECONOMIC ASS'N
ROYAL ECONOMIC SOCIETY
CABLE ADDRESS
"GANWADE NEW YORK"

AUBURN MOTORS

The chart enclosed on Auburn Motors has all of the natural important angles placed on it which shows the natural resistance angles obtained by dividing up the circle of 360°. We have used only the 45° angles from tops and bottoms, the 90° angle and the horizontal angle, which is equal to an angle of 90°. Every stock squares itself according to price and time and when it breaks out of the square one way or the other, continues to move in the same direction until it reaches another important 45° angle or resistance point according to the time or price. We use the angles of 11-1/4, 22-1/2, 33-3/4, 45, 56-1/4, 60, 67-1/2, 78-3/4, 90° and so forth. Then draw the 45° angle diagonally where the time crosses the 45° angle from either the important top or bottom.

The crossing of two right angles is very important for a change in trend as we will show on the example of Auburn Motors.

Auburn Motors made the extreme high on April 1, 1930 and 263-3/4; then made a second high on April 10th and the third final high on April 16, 1930, when the price reached 262-3/4. We draw the 45° angle from the top of April 1st, and another 45° angle from the last top made on April 16th; then number the days across and draw the 45° angles bisecting the 45° angles from the top.

Example: April 15th the 45° angle from April 1st and the 45° angle from 11-1/4 days over crossed at the exact point were Auburn made the low price at this time. In other words, on April 15th Auburn made bottom on two 45° angles; then rallied to April 16th, broke the 45° angle and the trend turned down.

Note 23° or days over where we reach the angle of 22-1/2°, and that Auburn made low on the 22nd day, rallied only one day, then broke the day angle or time angle of 33-3/4; next broke the more important 45° angle, showing that it was getting weaker all the time. It made bottom at 180 on the 27th day from the top. 180 is always an important resistance point, because it is one-half of the circle of 360°. Auburn rallied to 201. The next important resistance level is 202-1/2, or 22-1/2° added to 180. Auburn at this top was just under the 45° angle. Next it broke the 45° angle from the day angle of 56-1/4.

May 20th, declined to 150, another important natural angle because it is 5/12 of the circle. This bottom was reached on the 40th market day. Auburn, then rallied to 172 on the 45th market day, which is very important for a change in trend and top. Next it broke the 45° angle drawn from the bottom at 150; continued on down; broke the 45° time angle from 78-3/4, then broke the 45° angle from the 90 timing angle. 90 is twice as strong as 45 and very important for a change in trend.

June 23rd, this is an important date for a seasonal change in trend. Auburn declined to 91, holding one point above the 90° price angle or resistance, which is always important for tops or bottoms. It was on the 67th day and 67-1/2 is a strong angle.

Page #2 A.M.

July 17th, Auburn rallied to 141 on the 86th day and failed to reach the 45° angle from 101-1/4 days. Next it broke the 45° angle from 112-1/2 days; then broke the 45° angle drawn from the low of 91, which indicated that it was in a weak position and going lower. Note that 91 was the lowest parallel angle or lowest 45° angle from the 45° angles drawn from the tops of April 1st and April 16th. This parallel was 53 points wide from April 1st top and 59 wide from April 16th top. The bottom occurred on the 120th day time angle and 120 is important because it is 1/3 of a circle.

August 12th, Auburn declined to 102, which is just above the natural resistance angle of 101-1/4, and this bottom occurred on the 108th day and just above the 45° angle from the 135th day time angle.

September 8th, Auburn rallied to 135 and hit the 45° angle from April 1st top. It was on the 135° natural resistance angle, which is 3/8 of a circle and very strong. A stock is always a short sale, the first time it rallies to the 45° angle from its top, protected with a stop-loss order 3 points above the angle, and at this point it was a safe short sale because the price was 135, which equals the crossing of two right angles. Auburn next broke under the 45° angle from the bottom at 102 and the 45° angle from the 135th day. It continued to break angles and to work into weaker squares until the final bottom was reached.

November 5, 1930, Auburn declined to 60-3/8. 60 is always important because it is 1/6 of a circle. It made this bottom on the 177th market day from April 1st top. Note on the 180th market day Auburn made a higher top and turned the trend up for the first time. The bottom was reached on the 190th day angle or on the 45° angle drawn diagonally from 190 days down from the top.

November 17th, for the first time since April 1930, Auburn crossed the 45° angle from the top of April 1st, when the price reached 77, where the trend turned up, and put Auburn in a very strong position because it crossed the 45 degree angle at such a low level.

Note the top of November 20th was made at 82-1/2, just under the 45° angle from the top of April 16th. Then a decline followed and a bottom was reached at 72-1/2 on November 28, 1930.

November 29th, Auburn crossed the 45° angle from the April 16th top for the first time, indicating that it was in a stronger position and that the main trend had turned up, because it had crossed the extreme outside parallel angle. This low was made around 78-3/4, the natural angle, and Auburn never sold lower after crossing this outside 45° angle until it advance to 295-1/2 on April 14, 1931.

After Auburn regained or got above the 45° angle from the top of April 16, 1930, it started regaining 45° angles and making higher parallels to the left of the 45° angle from 60-3/8 just the reverse of its movement on the way down from 263-3/4 to 60-3/8.

December 18, 1930, Auburn advanced to 119-3/4. This was nearly twice the price of 60-3/8, and the natural angle or 1/3 of a circle, is at 120. This top occurred on the 36th market day.

December 23rd, Auburn declined to 91-1/2 and made a second bottom at 92 on December 27, holding above the 90° resistance point. Note that 90 was the half-way point from 60-3/8 to 119-3/4, which showed that Auburn was in a strong position. The last low of 92 was reached on the 43rd market day, and the price was above the 45° angle from 33-3/4 days.

THE W.D. GANN MASTER STOCK MARKET COURSE

Page #3 A.M.

1931, January 5th, Auburn rallied to 116 on the 225th market day from the top of April 1930. 225 is always strong because it is 5/8 of a circle. Auburn then declined and broke the 45° angle drawn from the bottom of 60-3/8.

January 14th and 17th, declined to 101-1/4, which is the natural resistance angle. Note the cross angle of 101-1/4, and that the price was bottom on the 60th market day, which our rule tells you is very important for a change in trend, because it is 1/6 of a circle. The trend turned up and Auburn continued to get into a stronger position on angles.

January 22, 1931, Auburn crossed the 45° angle, marked in green, from the 60th market day and on January 26th, crossed or regained the 45° angle drawn from the bottom at 60-3/8. The price was 128 on the 67-1/2 market day angle. When a stock regains the 45° angle from the bottom it is in a very strong position. Auburn never got back to the 45° angle from 60-3/8 until it made top on April 14, 1931, at 295-1/2. On the advance after crossing the 45° angle of 60-3/8, it continued to show strength because it worked into higher parallel angles to the left of the 45° angle from the bottom.

February 9, 1931, Auburn crossed the 45° angle drawn from the top at 119-3/4 made in December 18, 1930. This was another indication of a very strong position.

February 26th, Auburn made a top at 217 on the 92nd market day from the bottom or just two days over the 90th day, which is always important for change in trend. Note the natural resistance level at 213-3/4. Auburn then dropped back under this angle and broke back under the 120 day time angle marked in green, which put it into a weaker position and indicated a decline. You can see that Auburn on the way up worked to the 45th, 90th, and other important days on time just the same as it did on the way down.

March 7th, Auburn declined to 175, just 5 points under 180, which is half of the circle, and it reached the 45° angle, which was 1/2 of the distance between the 45° angle drawn from the top of 119-3/4 and the 45° angle drawn from the first top made on November 20, 1930, at 82-1/2. Auburn made this top on the 100th market day, and on the 101st day crossed the 120 green angle, which is time angle. Then made two days tops on the 45 degree angle from 217 top. Then crossed the 45° angle from the top at 217 and never dropped back under it and continued to make higher parallels to the left of the 45° angle from 60-3/8.

April 14th, Auburn reached extreme high of 295-1/2. This was a date for a seasonal change because the last high occurred on April 16th, 1930, from which the big decline followed. Note that the same width of the parallel from the lowest 45° angle drawn from the 101-1/4 and 103-1/2 bottoms made January 14th and 19th, 1931, which was 59 wide. April 14th, the 180th day angle, crossed at 290. This was the crossing of two right angles - one the parallel angle of the same width of the fluctuations from 263-3/4 to 91, and the other from the extreme of 101-1/4 to 295-1/2. The same day that Auburn advanced above the crossing of these parallel angles of 290 it declined and closed at 287, below these angles indicating a weaker position. Auburn only closed 1 day above the width of the same parallel on which it declined. Then it started breaking parallel angles and getting into a weaker position right along.

Page #4 A.M.

It is important to note that 292-1/2 is an important resistance level, because it is 270, which is 3/4 of a circle, plus 22-1/2, and Auburn failed to go over three points above this angle. Another thing to consider is that from 60-3/8 to 295-1/2 Auburn was up 235-1/8 points, which was nearly 2/3 of a circle and another reason for strong resistance. You should look up your resistance card and see the other important points around this level. For example, Auburn's extreme high was 514 and the low on the last move 60-3/8. This would make the half-way point 287-1/8. Auburn's extreme low of history was 31-3/4. This would make the half-way point 272-1/2. Then when Auburn broke back under the first half-way point of 287-1/8 it indicated weakness; next breaking the half-way point of the life fluctuation at 272-7/8, indicating greater weakness. The next important point was 257 or 1/2 of 514, the highest price at which Auburn ever sold. Therefore, when Auburn broke under 257 it was in a very weak position and indicated a further sharp decline.

April 20th, Auburn declined to 180, getting support on the natural angle or 1/2 of the circle. This was on the 315 market day from April 1930, and on the 136th market day from the low of 60-3/8 and on the 166th calendar day. 165 is important because it is 1/2 between the angle of 150 and 180. Auburn made bottom on the 45th market day from the low of 101-1/4 made on January 14, 1931. It rested on the lowest parallel angle of 45°.

From 60-3/8 to 295-1/2 gives the half-way point at 177-3/4 and Auburn holding above this half-way point, showed it was in a strong position and ready to rally. At the time 178-1/2 was on the 45° angle from 103-1/2, the low of January 19, 1931, and being the last and lowest 45° angle it was the strongest support point, from which a rally must take place and the stock was a purchase with stop 3 points under.

April 24th, Auburn rallied to 219 and hit the 45° angle from the bottom of 175 made on March 7th; then broke back under 213-3/4, the price angle, and broke 146-1/4 the day angle.

April 30, 1931, Auburn declined to 187, resting on the 45° angle from the low of 103-1/2. A sharp rally followed and on May 1st Auburn advance to 227-1/2, just under the 45° green angle from 157-1/2 days. This was a cross-angle and also a 45° angle from the top of 119-3/4. The price of 225 was on a strong resistance, or 225°, which is 5/8 of a circle, and Auburn failed to go 3 points above it. A big break followed in the afternoon of the same day and Auburn declined to 184, which was 3 points under the lowest 45° angle from 103-1/2, the bottom of January 19, 1931, and was just above the 45° green angle from the 135th market day and on the 146th market day from November 5, 1930, and on the 179th calendar day from the bottom, which was a strong indication for bottom or a change in trend. Auburn quickly regained the 45° angle from the lowest parallel; then crossed the 45° angle drawn from 60-3/8.

May 5th, Auburn advanced to 225-1/2, where it struck the same resistance of 225 of the natural resistance angles. It hit a 45° angle from the low point of 183 and the 45° angle from the top made on May 1st, and was just under the 45° angle from the 157-1/2 day, a strong resistance point.

May 6th, Auburn declined to 203 on the 45° green angle from the 146-1/4 day and being just above the natural resistance and angle of 202-1/2, it received strong support, rallied and crossed the angle of 45° from 60-3/8 which put it again in a very strong position.

Page #5 A.M.

May 9, 1931, Auburn advanced to 252. This was just under the 45° angle from 219, the low of March 30th, and on the 22nd day from the top of April 14, 1931. You will note that 257 is 1/2 of the highest price at which Auburn ever sold - 514. May 9th was 330 market days from April 1, 1930, which is important, and 103 market days from 60-3/8 and 185 calendar days from 60-3/8. On May 9th Auburn dropped back under the 45° angle from the 168-3/4 day, declined to 237 were rested on the angle of 45° from the top at 119-3/4 may January 18, 1931.

At this writing, May 9, 1931, Auburn is in a strong position on Angles, but is a short sale on rallies with a stop at 260, which is 3 points above the half-way point, or 1/2 of 514. The stock is in a strong position on angles and you have to watch the 45° angle from the top at 295-1/2 and the angle marked in green from 180. As long as Auburn can hold above the 45° angle from 60-3/8 it is still in a position to rally, but when it breaks the 45° angle from 60-3/8 and the lowest 45° angle from 101-1/4 and 101-1/2, the bottoms of January 14th and 19th, 1931, it will then indicate a big decline.

If Auburn can cross 260, the next resistance point will be around 273 and the next around 287, and should it get through the old top of 295-1/2 or cross 300, it will then indicate very much higher prices. You should always watch the 1/4 and 1/2 points from the last important bottom. In Auburn's present position, the point to watch would be between 180 and 252. Also, 237-3/4, which is 1/2 from 295-1/2 to 180. Auburn closed just around this point on May 9th, which is near 240 and an important resistance level, which is 2/3 of the circle. Should Auburn break 234 now or over 3 points under this half-way point it will indicate lower.

May 9, 1931.   [unsigned]

Chapter 17

Time Periods - Seasonal and Yearly

TIME PERIODS, SEASONAL AND YEARLY

The year is not divided according to calendar months to get time periods; it is divided by the 4 seasons of the year, the half-seasons, 1/3 and 2/3 of the year. The year, or any time period of 12 months, can be divided by 16 which gives approximately 23 days which accounts for market moves in stocks which often last 3 weeks to 1 month.

When the trend is advancing in a Bull Market, reactions will last from 3 to 4 weeks and then the main trend will be resumed. In a declining or Bear Market, rallies or advances will last 3 to 4 weeks, and then the downward trend will continue.

NATURAL SEASONAL TIME PERIODS

These seasonal time periods can be started at the beginning of any given season, but my experience has proved that they work out best by starting with the Spring Season, March 21, in a year. These periods run as follows:

March 21 to May 5	=	1/8 of a year or 1/2 of a season
May 6 to June 20	=	1/4 of a year or a season
June 21 to July 23	=	1/3 of a year or a season
July 24 to August 8	=	3/8 of a year or season
August 9 to September 23	=	1/2 of a year
September 24 to November 8	=	5/8 of a year
November 8 to November 22	=	2/3 of a year
November 23 to February 4	=	7/8 of a year
February 5 to March 20	=	1 seasonal year

By checking the dates when extreme highs and extreme lows have occurred, as well as the minor tops and bottoms, you can see how often these prices come out around the dates for seasonal changes.

(Refer to Time Tables showing Time Periods on the Dow Jones 30 Industrial Averages Highs and Lows from 1889 to 1951: W. D. Gann)

To get the correct time period from any high or low, you first add 1/8 of a year or 6½ weeks to the high or low date. Next, add 13 weeks or 1/4 of a year until the anniversary date is reached as you will see on the Table of Time Periods. This time table shows all of the important highs and lows and the date when the prices have been recorded. By looking down the column marked "6½ weeks" or 1/8 of a year, you get all of the periods which are 1/8 of a year from any high or low date.

By going over the record of prices in the past, you will find that the largest percentages of high or low prices have occurred 45 to 50 days before the date of a previous high or low, or 45 to 50 days after the date of a high or low. Therefore, the periods under 1/8 or 6½ weeks, and the periods under 7/8 or 45½ weeks, are very important to watch for a change in trend.

2.

Suppose you wish to look up the time periods from the year 1951, for the month of January you will note from the table that during the past 62 years highs and lows have occurred 8 [82?] times during the month of January, and the periods are as follows:

1/8 - 7 times		5/8 -	10 times
1/4 - 4 times		2/3 -	9 times
1/2 - 10 times		-	9 times
3/8 - 8 times		7/8 -	6 times
1/2 - 11 times Anniversary yearly		-	8 times, making total of 82

All of the other totals are shown in the table.

February 13, 1951, first high 257. May 4, high 264½ and third high, September 14, 1951.

By referring to the anniversary dates you will find that 10 have occurred in the month of September and there was a total of 73 periods of 1/8 to 7/8 of a year, making a total in September of 83. Eleven of these periods occurred on 1/4 of a year, and 11 [8?] on 1/2 of a year, which would be the month of September, based on the seasonal periods, making September very important for a change in trend and the important dates for changes – based on past highs – were September 4, 30, 12, 3, 10, 8, 13, 14. In view of the fact that September 13, 1939 was the last high before the averages declined to April 28, 1942, low 92.69, makes September 13 very important for tops. Figuring 1/4 of a year from June 14, 1948 to June 14, 1949 and June 12, 1950, would make September 12 to 14 the important date to expect extreme high for a change in trend.

Suppose that after the high was made on September 14, 1951, you wish to determine when the next important bottom will occur, you look under December and find 11 periods on 1/4 of a year, and 11 periods on 5/8 of a year. From September 14, 1951, 1/4 of a year will be December 14, 1951. From May 4, 1951, high 5/8 of a year comes out December 20, making December the most important month for a sharp, severe decline, and the next low period after September.

December is also important for low levels because December 24, 1914, low after the stock exchange was closed, and this being in a war period (and we are now in a war period) makes December important for big decline. Also, 1941, December 7 was the starting of the war with Japan. Therefore, all indications point to a sharp decline in December, 1951.

Refer to the table showing extreme lows for each month and you will find that December shows 30 during the past 62 years, and the greatest number of blows have occurred during the month of December.

DOW JONES 30 INDUSTRIAL AVERAGES, HIGH AND LOWS, 1889 TO 1951
(Refer to Times Tables)

The total number of highs and lows for each month during the various years means either an extreme high or a minor high, and an extreme low or minor low.

	Extreme Highs	Extreme Lows		Extreme Highs	Extreme Lows
January	23	18	July	10	16
February	17	18	August	12	18
March	16	17	September	18	18
April	14	15	October	14	16
May	15	22	November	15	17
June	11	24	December	4	30

The table below shows the number of times in each month, when the time is 6½ weeks, 13 weeks, etc., from a previous high or low level, and gives the total number of times the highs and lows have occurred during each month for the total period.

Weeks	Jan	Feb	Mar	Apr	May	Jun	Jul	Aug	Sep	Oct	Nov	Dec
6½	7	9	8	7	7	8	10	10	7	8	4	10
13	4	10	8	8	11	9	7	8	11	11	3	11
17	10	4	14	6	7	11	8	8	9	8	11	3
19½	8	4	9	7	12	7	10	8	9	10	9	8
26	11	3	10	4	12	6	8	11	8	8	8	9
32½	10	6	9	8	4	11	9	8	7	8	7	11
35	9	9	11	3	10	4	12	6	8	11	8	7
39	9	8	9	11	4	9	4	12	6	8	11	8
45½	6	7	9	10	9	8	8	4	9	8	11	8
52	8	8	7	8	8	8	14	3	10	4	12	7
Total	83[82?]	68	94	72	84	81	90	78	83[84?]	84	84	82

RANGE OF PRICES: The price-range in which the averages or an individual stock is moving is very important to consider, as well as the extreme high or low prices have been reached.

1951, May 4, high 264½, you would watch for a top around April 28 because the last extreme low of April 28, 1944, and the high in 1946 was on May 29. If you look under the column for May, under the time periods, you will find that 32 periods occur between May 1 and 10, giving a strong indication that top could occur before May 10. There were 14 periods between May 1 and May 5.

4.

If we use 1/16 of a year, or approximately 23 days, and subtract 23 days from May 29, the high in 1946, we get May 6 as an important time period. From the high of May 4, 1951, Industrial Averages declined 23½ points to June 29. By adding 1/4 of a year to May 4 we get August 4, and the averages moved into new high levels at that time, indicating September as the next important month to watch for a change in trend and final top. If you add 26 weeks, or 1/2 of a year, to May 4, high, it gives November 4 which is near a Seasonal Time Period and the averages started declining again on November 5.

If you will put in the time studying and practicing with these tables and time periods, you will soon learn their value, and by applying all the rules and resistance levels, you will be able to determine a change in trend quite accurately.

[unsigned]

[undated, but likely *circa* August/September, 1951]

Chapter 18

Time and Price Resistance Levels

TIME AND PRICE RESISTANCE LEVELS
by
W.D. GANN

WEEKLY HIGH AND LOW CHART

The Weekly Chart is one of the most reliable trend indicators that we use. The Weekly Tables for Price and Time Resistance are very valuable and enable you to determine ahead of time the prices at which highs and lows will be made and the time or date when these extreme high or low prices will be reached.

These Weekly Tables cover periods of 7 days or 1 calendar week. However you do not start to number time periods from January 1 or the 1st day of any month. You begin to count the time periods from the exact dates of any extreme high or low price. You also use the dates of the minor high and low prices both to begin to count time periods from and to get price resistance and determine a change in trend.

NATURAL SEASONAL TIME PERIODS

These periods do not start with the calendar year but start with the Spring Season March 20. The year is divided up into 8 equal parts and also divided into 1/3's which give two more time periods. These Time Periods are as follows:

       Mar 20 to May   5 is 1/8 of a year or 46 days
                June 21 is 1/4 of a year or 91 days
                July 23 is 1/3 of a year or 121 days
                Aug   5 is 3/8 of a year or 136 days
                Sept 22 is 1/2 of a year or 182 days
                Nov   8 is 5/8 of a year or 227 days
                Nov 22 is 2/3 of a year or 242 days
                Dec 21 is 3/4 of a year or 273 days
                Feb   4 is 7/8 of a year or 319 days
                Mar 20 is 1 year or 365 calendar days

All of these periods are important to watch for changes in trend. The most important are ½ and the end of the season; next important ¼ and ¾, and ⅓ and ⅔.

MID SEASON POINTS

These are May 5, August 5, November 8 and February 4. By checking over past records of prices, you will see how often highs & lows have occurred during these periods.

TABLES FOR TIME PERIODS AND PRICE RESISTANCE

The Tables for Time Periods and Price Resistance are made up to cover 40 years in the future. You can also use them for 40 years in the past.

These Tables measure Price and Time Resistance from 6½ to 2080. Each period of one year or 52 weeks is shown at the bottom of the Table and the division of the yearly time periods are shown both for the Seasonal and Natural Time Periods and for the proportionate parts of a year starting from the date of any high or low price.

Below we give the Tables showing the Price and Time Periods.

1/8	of year	46	days	6½	weeks	Price	6½
1/4	of year	91	days	13	weeks	Price	13
1/3	of year	121	days	17	weeks	Price	17
3/8	of year	136	days	19½	weeks	Price	19½
1/2	of year	182	days	26	weeks	Price	26
5/8	of year	227	days	32½	weeks	Price	32½
2/3	of year	242	days	35	weeks	Price	35
3/4	of year	273	days	39	weeks	Price	39
7/8	of year	319	days	45½	weeks	Price	45½
1	year	365	days	52	weeks	Price	52

From the above table you can see that the year is divided into 10 divisions of Time and starting with 6½ to 52, the price is also divided into 10 divisions. These Tables continue the same for 40 years or more, making equal divisions of Time and Price.

PRICE RESISTANCE

The Price Resistance is calculated in the same way at Time Periods from highs and lows. Always calculate how much the price is up from the low levels or how much it is down from the high levels. In this way you are able to determine all of the important Price Resistance Levels.

Example:

Suppose the low price is 50 and the current price is 102. This is up 52 from the low and equals 52 weeks or 1 year in time, making this price important to watch for change in trend because it is a Time and Price Balance.

Suppose the high price has been 182 and at the time you look it up, the stock or grain is selling at 130. This is at 1/2 or 2½ years in time and the price is down 52 from the high which equals 1 year in time. This is also a Price and Time Balance and is important to watch for change in trend.

Suppose the price makes high or low on 1/4 and the next high or low is on 1/4 of 1/2. This would be important for change in trend.

From the low, suppose the time is on 1/4 and 3/4 and from the high the time is on 1/3 or 2/3, this is important for changes in trend, especially if the price is at 1/2 or 3/4 resistance. (for more proof see example of actual market moves in the past.)

TP-3

INDICATIONS FOR CHANGE IN TREND

1. TIME AND PRICE BALANCE -- Suppose you wish to look up the time period for 5 years, you look at the bottom of column 5 where you find 260, which is 260 weeks. Suppose the price is at 260. This is a Time and Price Balance and is very important for a change in trend.

   Suppose at the end of 262 weeks the price is at 234, which is 1/2 and equals 4½ years in Time. This is next in importance for change in trend.

2. ANNIVERSARY -- DATES Always consider the anniversary date from extreme highs and lows as important for a change in trend.

3. DIVISIONS OF TIME -- Next consider 1/4, 1/3, 1/2, 2/3, and 3/4 of the time periods important for a change in trend.

4. PRICE RESISTANCE LEVELS -- These same Resistance Levels in Price are also important to watch for change in trend, especially when the Time Period comes out at one of these important divisions of price.

5. WEEKLY BOTTOMS AND TOPS -- When you are studying the Weekly Chart, always look to see if a weekly bottom has been broken or a weekly high level has been crossed, which would be important for a change in trend. The greater the time period from any high or low level, the more important it is when prices cross these levels.

6. DOUBLE AND TRIPLE TOPS AND BOTTOMS -- When these occur on important Time Periods and at important Price Resistance Levels, they are very important to watch for change in trend and to expect a move to start that will last for a considerable length of time.

7. SWING BOTTOMS AND TOPS -- The breaking of a swing bottom or the crossing of a swing top is very important for a change in trend.

   SWING CHART -- You can make up a Swing Chart by moving the price up to the top of each week; then the first time the low of the previous week is broken, you move the swing line down to the low of that week. When that week's bottom has been broken, continue to move the line down as long as the price makes lower tops and lower bottoms. The first week that the price makes a higher bottom and a higher top, you move the line on the Swing Chart up to the top of that week and continue to move it up each week until there is a reversal.

WHEN MOST IMPORTANT CHANGES IN TREND OCCUR

These are:

1. Anniversary dates of previous high and lows.
2. Next is 1/2 of each yearly period or 182 days from any high or low.
3. Next in importance is 1/4 and 3/4 or 13 weeks and 39 weeks.

TP-4

4. Next is 1/3 and 2/3 or 17 weeks and 35 weeks.

5. Next is 3/8 and 7/8 of a year or 19½ and 35½ weeks.

You can prove to yourself how well these rules work by going back and checking the Time Periods from highs and lows for several years and checking the price at which the stock or commodity was selling and see how it compares on the Tables for Price and Time Resistance. This will give you the value of these Time Tables and Price Resistance Levels.

W.D. GANN

January 26, 1955

Chapter 19a

How to Make Profits Trading in Puts and Calls

HOW TO MAKE PROFITS TRADING IN PUTS AND CALLS
By
W. D. Gann

To make a success trading in stocks every man should learn everything he can about the stock market and the ways to operate in the market in order to make the greatest success. He should learn to take the smallest risk possible and then try to make the greatest profits possible. The more a man studies and learns, the greater success he will have. We quote Proverbs 1:5 - "The wise man will hear and will increasing learn." Again, Proverbs 2:11 - "Discretion shall preserve thee; understanding shall keep thee." Proverbs 3:9 - "Give instructions to a wise man and he will become wiser. Teach a just man and he will increase in learning." The "Book of the Lambs" says that the fear of the market is the beginning of knowledge.

Many people do not realize that without preparation and knowledge the stock market is dangerous and that it is easier to make losses than it is to make profits. However, the risks in stock speculation or investment are no greater than in any other line of business if you understand and apply the proper rules to speculation, and the profits compared to risks are greater than in any other business.

WHAT ARE PUTS AND CALLS ON STOCKS

PUTS and CALLS are insurance which provide protection for your profits and permit you to trade in stocks with limited risk. A CALL is a contract between you and the seller whereby he agrees to sell you a stock at a fixed price and deliver it in 30 days. You have the option of calling for delivery at any time during the 30 days. Your loss is limited to the prices you pay for the premium, which is the same as buying insurance with a CALL.

For Example:

Suppose a man has a house for sale and agrees to sell it to you for $5,000 and deliver it at that price 60 days later. You pay him $100 for the privilege of buying the house or rejecting it. If at the end of 30 or 60 days you are able to sell the house for $500 profit or for $1000 profit, then you exercise your option to buy the house for $5,000 and sell it to the man so you can make a profit. But if the option expires and you are unable to sell the house for more than the price, them you loose the $100 and do not have to buy the house.

The same applies in buying CALLS on a stock. For example: If you buy a CALL when Chrysler is selling around 105, good for 30 days at 110, you pay $142.50 which includes the Federal taxes. Suppose before the 30 days are up, Chrysler advances to 115, which would give you a profit of $500, you can sell Chrysler any time it reaches 115 and demand delivery of the stock at 110. But if Chrysler sells at 115 within 10 days after you bought the option and you believe that the trend is up and Chrysler is going higher, then you hold and do not exercise your option or sell the stock. Just before the end of the 30 days, if Chrysler is selling at 120, you could sell 100 shares of Chrysler at 120 and then call for delivery on your CALL at 110 making a profit of $1000, less your commission and the amount paid for the CALL. On the other hand, after you have bought the CALL at 110, if at no time it advances above 110 and at the end of 30 days Chrysler is selling below 110, you, of course, make no profit and are only out the amount of money that you paid for the CALL.

A PUT is an option or an agreement with a man from whom you buy the PUT that you can deliver to him the stock at a fixed price any time within 30 days after you buy the PUT. A PUT costs you $137.50 per 100 shares. We will take this example: When Chrysler is selling at 105, say, you believe it is going down and buy a PUT for 30 days at 100, for which you pay $137.50. This means that when Chrysler declines below 100, it puts you in a position of being short 100 shares at that price because the man from whom you bought must take from you 100 shares of Chrysler at 100 any time that you deliver it to him within the 30 day period. We will assume that Chrysler goes below 100 and declines to 95. You can buy 100 shares when it goes to 95 and then hold it to the end of the 30 days. In the meantime if Chrysler advances to 105, giving you 10 points profit, you could sell it out. Then at the end of the time the option expired if Chrysler was still selling above 100, you would have made the profit on the stock that you bought against the PUT and would simply let the option expire and only be out the price you paid for it. But, on the other hand if you do not trade, against the PUT and the stock declines and, we will say, at the end of 30 days is selling around 90, you then buy 100 shares of Chrysler and your broker delivers 100 shares to the man that you bought the PUT from giving you the profit of $1000 less the money you paid for the option and your commission.

PUTS and CALLS are, perfectly safe because every PUT and CALL, sold by a reliable PUT and CALL broker is endorsed by a member of the New York Stock Exchange who is thoroughly reliable and will deliver you the stock that he agrees to deliver on which he sold an option or will receive from you any stock that he agrees to buy on an option.

Again, to make it plainer, when you by a CALL on a stock you are long of the market if it goes above the price at which you bought it, just the same as if you had the stock bought, except that your risk is limited. Again, when you buy a PUT on a stock, it means that you are short at the price at which you bought the PUT, but you do not have to put up any margin or have to stand any loss except the price you paid for the PUT. Then as it declines below the price at which you bought the PUT, you are making money just the same as if you made a SHORT SALE.

SPREAD OR STRADDLE

When you buy a PUT and a CALL on the same Stock it is called a SPREAD. For example: Suppose Chrysler is selling at 100 and you are in doubt whether it will go up or down but you want to take advantage of a move when it gets under way. Therefore we will say that you buy a PUT at 96 and a CALL at 104. Let us assume that the market starts to react and declines to 95, then hesitates and looks like making bottom. Then you buy 100 shares of Chrysler, knowing that if it continues to decline you cannot lose anything because you have a PUT at 96. Let us assume that you are right and the market starts to advance. It continues to advance and before the end of the 30 days Chrysler advances to 110 and there are 6 points' profit in the CALL that you bought at 104. You also still have the stock that you bought against the PUT at 96. Now, you can sell out 200 shares of stock and call for the 100 shares at 104, which gives you a profit and the CALL and your PUT expires because it is of no value.

Often SPREADS can be bought very close to the market when you are buying a PUT and a CALL from the same man. On some stocks you can often buy SPREADS at the market by paying an additional premium. As a rule it would not pay to buy a SPREAD except on very active stocks which have a very wide fluctuation during the 30 days giving you a chance to operate against both the PUT and the CALL during the month. At least when you buy a SPREAD if the stock moves 10 or 15 points or more in either direction, you are sure to make some money. However, it is not always advisable to spend as much as it costs to buy SPREADS unless the market looks like it is going to be very active and you are trading in high-priced stocks.

PUT and CALL brokers, give those definitions: A PUT is a negotiable contract by which the taker may put to the maker a certain lot of securities at a specified price on/or before a fixed date. A CALL is the opposite. A SPREAD is one PUT and one CALL. PREMIUM is the money paid for a PUT, CALL or SPREAD. MAKER is he who writes or sells PUTS, CALLS and SPREADS. ENDORSER is a N.Y. Stock Exchange firm which guarantees a, PUT, CALL or SPREAD contract by endorsing it like a check. The insurance feature provided by these privileges is considered valuable.

HOW PUTS AND CALLS ARE SOLD

PUTS and CALLS are sold by traders and large operators who make it a business trading in and out of the market and selling PUTS or CALLS on the stocks that they have bought or sold, but PUTS and CALLS are always endorsed by members of the New York Stock Exchange. As a rule, a CALL costs you $142.50 and the price that it is away from the market, depends upon the activity of the stock and the condition of the market. A PUT is the reverse, so many points below the price at which the market is selling that day, depending upon the price of the stock and the activity of the market. However, often traders who make it a business of selling PUTS and CALLS, sell them at the market price for an additional premium. For example, Douglas Aircraft might be selling at 56 and by paying a premium $300 to the seller you could buy a CALL or a PUT on Doug for 30 days at 56, therefore when it moved 3 points up or down from the price at which you bought the CALL or the PUT, you would have made the money back or the price of the stock would show you a profit for the money you paid out; then when it went more than 3 points in your favor, you would have a net profit above the price you paid for the privilege, either PUT or CALL, that you bought at the market.

As a rule, I favor buying PUTS and CALLS with risk limited to the price of $142.50 per 100 shares for a CALL or $137.50 per 100 shares for a PUT, and buying PUTS or CALLS a number of points away from the price at which the stock is selling.

WHY PUTS AND CALLS ARE SOLD

The question might be asked: If there is a chance to make large profits on a small risk in buying PUTS and CALLS, why do traders and wealthy speculators sell them?

Often a trader who is out of the market is willing to buy stocks if they decline 4 or 5 points, therefore he will sell you a PUT on a stock 3 or 5 Points away and you pay him the premium of $137.50; then if the stock declines to the level at which he is willing to buy and even though it goes lower, you deliver it to him, he is satisfied to buy it at that level. On the other hand often these big traders have accumulated a large line of stock and already have profits in them, so they are willing to sell all or part of their line should the market advance 5 or 10 points more, therefore they are willing to sell you CALLS on the stocks they hold or part of what they hold 5 or 10 points above the market, as the case may be, and are perfectly willing to deliver you the stock and permit you to have the profit above that price for the premium that you pay. Another reason they sell them is that they know they can always protect themselves. If the market is very strong and you are going to make profits on the CALL they sold to you or you are going to call the stock, they can buy more. On the other hand, suppose they sell you PUTS, the market starts declining fast and looks like going lower, where you will have a profit on the PUT you bought, they can sell short, put up the margin and carry the stock until you deliver it to them against the PUT. It is a perfectly legitimate business just the same as insurance business and is fair to both buyer and seller.

LENGTH OF TIME PUTS AND CALLS ARE SOLD

As a rule, you can buy PUTS and CALLS good 7 days, two weeks, and 30 days, and sometimes you can buy them good 60 or 90 days but most traders who make it a business of selling PUTS and CALLS do not write them for more than 30 days. However, you can always ask your broker or the PUT and CALL broker to make an inquiry and get you a quote on what you can buy PUTS and CALLS for good 30, 60 or 90 days; then if the price looks right, you can buy them.

My advice is that you will make more money buying PUTS and CALLS good 30 days than you will buying them good 7 days or two weeks because the shorter periods of time, except when markets are extremely active, do not give you an opportunity for a wide enough range to make profits. However, when you buy PUTS or CALLS good 7 days or 14 days you pay less premium than for those good 30 days. The premium, as a rule, for 7 days is $62.50; two weeks is $87.50.

HOW TO BUY PUTS AND CALLS

If you live outside You York City, you can give an order to your local broker and he will buy PUTS and CALLS for your account that are endorsed by a New York stock Exchange firm and place them to your credit with your broker in New York City or the correspondent of the house you trade with in your capital city. Then when you want to make a trade against your PUTS or CALLS, or want, to buy or sell and call the stock or put it and take profits, the broker will take care of the transaction for you. Always deal with brokers who are members of the New York Stock Exchange when you buy or sell stocks,

The unit for PUTS and CALLS is 100 shares, but at times you may be able to buy odd-lots or 50-share lots of PUTS and CALLS, but when you buy PUTS or CALLS be sure that they are endorsed by a New York Stock Exchange firm. There are often bucketshops that will Sell you PUTS and CALLS on 10 shares, 25 shares or anything else, but there is no Stock Exchange firm behind them, and you have no assurance of getting your profit if you make them.

PUT AND CALL BROKERS

There are many brokers in PUTS and CALLS in New York City who buy and sell PUTS and CALLS for a commission and have the PUTS and CALLS endorsed by a New York Stock Exchange house and deliver them to you or to your broker. Any honest broker can stand investigation and for your own protection you should ascertain whether the PUT and CALL broker whom you buy PUTS and CALLS from is reliable and will have the PUTS and CALLS guaranteed by a firm that is a member of the Now York Stock Exchange.

ADVANTAGE OF BUYING PUTS AND CALLS DIRECT

Should you want to send orders direct to buy PUTS and CALLS, you can send your check or money order direct to a PUT and CALL broker in Now York and he will buy PUTS and CALLS for your account on your order and mail them direct to you or deliver them to your bank or your broker, as you request.

The advantage in sending your order direct to a PUT and CALL broker instead of over a broker's private wire is that you often get quicker service by using the Postal Telegraph or Western Union because all orders over brokers' private wires to buy and sell stocks have precedence over all messages pertaining to off-the-floor business. This would naturally delay the transmission of your order to buy a PUT or CALL and if the market is very active, it might result in a point or more against you, whereas if your order went direct to the PUT and CALL broker by Western Union or Postal Telegraph, you would get a quicker execution. For example: Suppose you decided to buy a PUT on Chrysler and you thought that Chrysler was about top and wanted to get it in, in a hurry – if you sent your order to a PUT and CALL broker, your telegram would read as follows:

"BUY A PUT 100 CHRYSLER CLOSEST OBTAINABLE 30 DAYS"

On receipt of this order the PUT and CALL broker would immediately buy a PUT on Chrysler to the best advantage and would wire you the price at which he bought it.

You, of course, would have your money on deposit with the PUT and CALL broker before you sent the order because he will not fill orders until the money is in hand. However, you could wire him $137.50 with the above message. On the other hand, if you wanted to buy a CALL on Chrysler, then your order would read as follows:

"BUY A CALL 100 CHRYSLER CLOSEST OBTAINABLE 30 DAYS"

and with this massage to buy a CALL, if you did not have the money on deposit with the broker, you would wire $142,50 to pay for the CALL.

If you were not in a hurry, you could send a telegram to the PUT and CALL broker and ask him to quote you PUTS and CALLS on Chrysler, General Motors, U.S. Steel or any other stocks, good 30 days. He would then wire the price at which he could buy, this price being subject to change any hour or any minute. After receiving the telegram from him, if you thought the price was close enough to the market that you could make money in 30 days, you could then wire your order to buy.

THE ADVANTAGES OF PUTS AND CALLS TO THE BUYER

The great advantage to the man who buys PUTS and CALLS is that his risk is always limited. Another advantage is that he saves payment of interest. For instance, if you buy a CALL and the stock moves up in your favor, for 30 days you do not have to pay any interest until you have called the stock and it has been delivered into your account.

Since the Securities Exchange Commission has raised margin requirements to where it requires 55% margin to buy stocks, it makes it a great advantage to buy PUTS and CALLS. For example: If you wanted to buy 100 shares of stock selling at $100 per share, you would have to put up $5,500 margin and would expect it to go up more than 5 points if you bought it, therefore instead of putting up $5,500 to buy the stock and carry it and also pay interest, you buy a CALL, we will say, 5 points away for 30 days, which costs you $142.50. Then if the stock advances during the 30-day period to where you have a profit of $1,000, you have made nearly 100% on your money. On the other hand, if you put up $5,500 and the stock advances so you have a profit of $1,000, your net return on your capital would be less than 20%, while at the same time if you bought 100 shares of stock, on margin, it might decline 10 or 20 points and your loss would be 10 or 20 points according to whether you held it or used a stop loss order and limited your risk.

HOW TO USE PUTS AND CALLS IN PLACE OF
STOP LOSS ORDERS

Another advantage in buying PUTS and CALLS is to protect the stock that you already have bought or to protect the stock that you are already short of. When markets are very wild and active and unexpected events take place that cause stocks to open up or down several points, as has happened many times in the past and will happen again in the future, you want to be protected against losses. You can always use a stop loss order, but if the stock should open off 3, 4, or 5 points under your stop loss order, then your stock will be sold at the market. On the other hand, if you had 100 shares of Chrysler bought at 100 and it declined and closed some night at 97 and you had a stop loss order at 95 and something unexpected happened overnight and the next morning the stock opened at 90, your stock would be sold on stop at 90 at the market and you would lose 5 points more than you expected to lose by placing a stop loss order. If instead of placing a stop loss order when Chrysler was selling around 100, you bought a PUT at 95, then when the stock opened off at 90 and continued to 80, your stock would be protected at 95 or you could deliver it at 95 on the PUT and would not lose anything by the overnight drop, the PUT having protected you against the unexpected.

Reverse the position. Suppose you are short of Chrysler at 100 and have a stop loss order on it at 105. If the unexpected happened and Chrysler opened at 110, then your stop loss order would be executed 5 points higher than you expected and you would lose $500 or 5 points more than you had figured on. On the other hand if you had a CALL bought on Chrysler to protect your short sale and Chrysler opened 5 points above your stop loss order at 110 some morning, then the CALL would protect you because you would have a contract to buy the stock at a price on the CALL and you could call it and deliver it against your short sale.

Thus, you see that you can use PUTS or CALLS for insurance or for protection when you are long or short of the market just the same as you use them to limit your risk in getting in and out of the market, limiting your loss to the amount you pay for a PUT or a CALL, when you want to take advantage of a stock that you think may have a fast move one way or the other.

WHEN TO BUY PUTS AND CALLS

The time to buy to buy PUTS and CALLS is when stocks are very active or just before activity starts. You can determine when to buy PUTS and CALLS and on what stocks to buy PUTS or CALLS by reading, studying and applying the rules in my books, "Truth of the Stock Tape", "Wall Street Stock Selector", and "New Stock Trend Detector".

I will give you a few rules that will help you to determine the time to buy PUTS or CALLS:

RULE 1 - Buy CALLS around double bottoms or triple bottoms, or buy the stock around double or triple bottoms and buy PUTS, which will protect you should the stock break the old bottom. By this I mean, if a stock has held at a low level, then advances; then reacts to that same low level months later and makes a bottom, this would be a double bottom. Then if it advances and reacts the third time to around the same level, this would be a triple bottom.

Reverse this rule at tops. Buy PUTS around double or triple tops, or sell the stock short, and buy CALLS for protection in case the stock should cross the old tops.

It is always well even when stocks are moving very fast and are active to wait several weeks or several months if a stock holds around a bottom or top before you buy CALLS or PUTS, giving the stock time to complete accumulation or distribution because this has to take place before there is a reverse move of a large number of points. You can easily see this by a study of past action of stocks on charts.

RULE 2 - Buy CALLS when old levels are crossed. If a stock stays for several weeks, several months, or even several years in a narrow trading range around top levels, as referred to in my books, then it breaks over the previous tops, it certainly will indicate activity. That is the time to buy a CALL as I will prove in examples later.

Reverse this rule when a stocks holds for a long time around low levels, then breaks the first support point. Buy PUTS or sell the stock short and buy CALLS for protection.

RULE 3 - If a stock advances to a top that it has made many months previous or many years previous and fails to go through, then has a reaction; then rallies and makes a lower top, that is, a third top and fails to go through, this would be the place to sell the stock short and buy a CALL for protection in case the stock went higher. It would also be the place to buy a PUT for 30 days, because if this top is a final top and the stock is starting on a long decline, you would make money on the PUT and could also be short of the stock at the same time by putting up margin.

Reverse this rule after a prolonged decline. If a stock makes a second or third higher bottom several weeks or months apart, then shows activity on the upside, it is the time to buy CALLS or buy the stock and buy PUTS for protection.

RULE 4 - When a stock holds for several months around the same level and fails to break the first support point, buy a PUT and buy the stock when it begins to show activity, or buy a CALL as soon as activity starts on the upside.

Reverse this rule when a stock holds for several months around top levels and fails to cross the first top. Buy a PUT when activity starts on the downside or buy a CALL and go short.

RULE 5 - After a stock advances through an old top where it has held for several weeks or several months, and advances several points above this top, then reacts to the old top, buy PUTS and buy the stock, or buy CALLS.

Reverse this rule in a bear market. When a stock breaks through an old bottom and goes several points below it, then rallies back to the old bottom, buy CALLS and sell short against them, or buy PUTS.

RULE 6 - In a Bull market when trend is up wait for a reaction of 5, 10 or 12 points, then buy CALLS, or buy the stock and buy PUTS to protect the purchase.

In a BEAR MARKET, wait for rallies of 5, 7, 10 or 12 points, then buy PUTS, or sell short and buy CALLS to protect the trade.

RULE 7 - Buy a CALL when a stock reacts 40 to 50% of the last advance or buy the stock and buy PUTS to protect it.

Reverse this rule in BEAR MARKET: Buy PUTS when a stock rallies 40 to 50% of last move or buy CALLS when it rallies to protect short sales. For example: Suppose a stock advances from 100 to 120. A decline to 110 would be one-half or 50% of the advance. If all indications point to a BEAR MARKET with the main trend DOWN, then you would buy PUTS when the stock rallied 40 to 50%. Example: U.S. Steel, March 6 to 11, 1937, made a top at 126½. After an advance of over 50 points, a big reaction could be expected and it was time to buy PUT. March 22, U.S. Steel declined to 112½, down 14 points from the top. A 50% rally would be 7 points or to 119½, where you would buy PUTS. Steel advanced to 123½, on March 31, better than 50%, giving a good opportunity to buy PUTS for 30 days, which made good as Steel declined 24 points in 30 days.

WHEN TO BUY MORE PUTS AND CALLS ON THE SAME STOCK

Suppose a stock breaks out on the upside, moves up fast and shows uptrend. You have bought CALLS and have profits in them the first month. The trend still shows up and when it crosses previous tops or Resistance Levels, then you buy CALLS the next month and can protect the profits that you have on the first CALLS by buying PUTS under the market and still carry your original stock. Many traders do this when a move of 50 or 60 points takes place in two or three months. They continue to buy CALLS every month and continue to carry their stock and then often buy PUTS to protect their profits instead of placing stop loss orders, thus making a large amount of profit on a very small risk.

HOW TO TRADE AGAINST PUTS AND CALLS

Suppose you buy a CALL on General Motors at 50. At the time you buy the CALL General Motors is selling at 47. You have bought a CALL at 50, good 30 days. When General Motors advances to 50, holds for several days and doesn't look like going through, you could then sell short 50 shares of General Motors; then no matter which way General Motors went, up or down, you would make money. If it advanced to 55, you would still have a profit of 5 points on your CALL, and on the stock that you sold short at 50, you would have a loss of 5 points, but this would be made up because you could call 100 shares. After you sold short at 50, if you were right and General Motors declined to 45 or to 40, then when your CALL expired it would be of no value but the stock that you sold short would be down 5 points or more and you could close your short trade with a profit.

Example of trading against a PUT: Suppose Douglas Aircraft is selling around 50 and you buy a PUT on 100 shares, good 30 days, at 46. Douglas declines to 46 or to 45 and holds for several days and looks like making bottom and not going any lower, but you are not certain which way it will go for the remainder of the time for which your PUT is good, so you buy 50 shares of Douglas at 46 against your PUT, then if it goes up 5 points you are making profit on the stock you bought and you cannot lose because you have a PUT. Then, if it should decline 5 points, you could have a profit of 5 points on your PUT and could deliver 100 shares against what you bought and have no loss except the cost of the commission and the premium paid for your PUT.

Many shrewd traders who buy PUTS and CALLS make money trading against them and at the end of the time the PUT or CALL expires there is no profit in it but they have made a profit because they traded on the fluctuations of the market. Often you can sell against a PUT or buy against a CALL several times during the month and scalp anywhere from 2 to 5 points or more and possibly make 10 points' profit and be protected all the time and yet at the end of the PUT there would be no profit in it.

Some traders handle PUTS and CALLS in this way: Suppose they have bought a CALL on a stock at 100 and it advances to 110; then they buy a CALL for 30 days longer at a higher level, and when the first CALL expires on which they have profit, they CALL the stock in and do not sell it out; then buy a PUT to protect their profit and continue to buy CALLS and buy PUTS, pyramiding all the way up, not selling out their stock until they think the time has come for a change in the main trend.

This way of trading is reversed on the downside of the market. Buying a PUT and getting short, buying more PUTS on the way down; staying short; then buying a CALL to protect the short stock, following the main trend for several months or as long as it indicates that it is down.

KINDS OF STOCKS TO BUY PUTS AND CALLS ON

Stocks always move faster at higher levels than they do at low levels, therefore, as a general rule, you can make the most money by buying PUTS and CALLS on stocks selling between $75 and $150 par share, but there are times when you a buy CALLS on stocks selling between $5 and $10 and make a large percentage on the risk.

The next range of price is between $20 and $36. In this range you can often buy PUTS and CALLS at the market or within one or two points of the price at which the stock is selling. After stocks cross $36 to $40 per share they move much faster, and from there up to $60 to $75 per share you will make more money than you will buying options on stocks in the lower class.

In the same way, by buying CALLS or PUTS on stocks selling at 100 or higher you will make more money as they will decline faster until they get down to around 50 to 40; then in most cases they will decline slower. Therefore your chances of making profits are less in buying PUTS or CALLS on lower-priced stocks. I will give examples later and you can see by watching and studying charts when there are often opportunities for very large profits when a low-priced stock gets out of the zone of accumulation. In the same way, when a stock is in a congested area at high levels and remains in a narrow trading range for a long time, then breaks out, you can then make money buying PUTS just as big decline is ready to start.

EXAMPLES OF TRADING WITH PUTS AND CALLS

CHRYSLER MOTORS
1932 - July 30, note Chrysler on the Weekly Chart had remained in a narrow trading range for 8 weeks after it had made bottom at 5. When it crossed 8 it was over the top of

the previous weeks and indicated higher. At that time you could probably have bought a CALL on Chrysler around 10. It advanced to 16 in 30 days and was up to 21¾ in 6 weeks, giving a possible profit of 10 to 12 points. This trade would have been made by watching the chart and seeing a long period of congestion in a narrow trading range and then not anticipating anything but waiting until the stock showed itself by advancing above the tops of the previous weeks; then you would buy the CALL.

1933 - April 25, again Chrysler crossed 8 weeks' tops. You could probably have bought a CALL at this time around 15, good for 30 days. It advanced to 21½ and the trend did not turn down, the stock continuing up until it reached 39½, showing a possible profit of around 20 [24] points. After the stock advanced to where you had a profit of 10 points or more, you could have bought a PUT which would have protected the profits, or followed it up with a stop-loss order after you had called the stock which you bought lower.

1934 - February 3 to March 1, Chrysler made tops around 60, showing that it was meeting great resistance. Around March 1st you could probably have bought a PUT at 55. The stock started a downward move and declined to 49 in 30 days; then rallied to 56 and you could probably have bought a CALL around 55 before the rally took place, which would have protected your short sales; then you could have stayed short. The stock declined on May 19 to 36½; then rallied to 44 and continued on down to 29¼ on August 7, giving another possibility, for a profit of 20 to 25 points on PUTS and a limited risk of not more than $280 if you bought a PUT and then bought a CALL, after it went down, to protect your profits.

1935 - March 12, Chrysler reached a low of 31; It had made bottom at 29¼ in August, 1934, and made a double bottom at 29-3/8 in September, 1934. This decline to 31 was a third bottom at a higher level and would have been a place at which to buy the stock with a stop under 29¼ or to buy CALLS because this was a double and triple bottom. Around that time you could probably have bought a CALL around 34 or 35 because the stock had been narrow for a long time. In 4 weeks it had advanced to 37 and the trend continued up until May 25, when it reached 49½, giving an opportunity for a profit of at least 10 points net. Then the stock reacted to 41½, which was an old top and a place to again buy a CALL or to buy a PUT and trade against it.

In July and August, 1935, Chrysler crossed 60, the old top of 1934, and held for four weeks without breaking back under 57, which according to the rules in my books, was a place to buy with stop at 57. Having crossed the top of 1934, it indicated higher. After holding for 4 weeks in a narrow trading range, around September 10, you could probably have bought a CALL at 65. In 30 days it was up to 74½, with the main trend UP. You could have bought another CALL and also bought a PUT and held your stock after calling it at the time the first option expired.

In November, 1935, Chrysler advanced to 90 and at no time had it reacted 5 points after it crossed 60. This was another opportunity for make 25 to 30 points' net profit on an original risk of $142.50 and you might have bought more CALLS on the way up after you had profits and started handling a pyramid and made much larger profits.

Always watch a stock if it makes a top or a bottom and holds for several months without making the first support level; then when it begins to show activity by breaking to new lows or advancing to new highs, it is the time to buy a PUT or a CALL. (Refer to Rule 4).

1936 - February 3, Chrysler declined about 10 points, making low at 91½, than advanced on April 13 to 103-7/8; then again declined on April 30 to 91-5/8 and held in this range until June 5, when it was again down to 91-5/8. From February to early June, nearly 5 months, it held in a narrow range without breaking the low level of 91½, and making bottom for so many months around this level indicated that it was due for a big move one way or the other. In the early part of June you could probably have bought a CALL on Chrysler around 97, good 30 days, but if you waited until it crossed several weeks' tops at 98, you would have bought a CALL in the early part of July, good 30 days, which you could probably have bought around 100 to 101. In 30 days it was up to 116, when you would have a profit of 12 to 16 points. It went right on up to 124-7/8 on July 27, advancing 32 points from the low of June 5 without ever reacting 5 points. If you had bought stock when it was near the low or bought a CALL, you could have called the stock; then bought a PUT to protect it and kept it right on through, or you could have PUT a stop loss order on it and carried it through. In the second month you could have bought another CALL. This move certainly gave you an opportunity to make 25 points or more on a CALL.

After a sharp advance of 32 points in less than two months, you could naturally expect a reaction. After these fast moves, as a general rule, the reaction runs one-half or 50%. (See Rule 7.) When Chrysler was around 124, you could probably have bought a PUT at 119 to 117. On August 21 Chrysler declined to 108-5/8, down 16 points, giving you a chance to make profit of 6 to 7 points, anyway, on a PUT. Then it held for 5 weeks between 108-5/8 and 117; then started up. When it started up you could have again bought a CALL. It advanced 18 points in 30 days, advancing to 130½, affording another excellent opportunity for profits on CALLS.

On November 12, 1936, Chrysler made the high of its move at 138¾. This was an important point because the top made on October 6, 1928 was 140½. You would sell out long stock around these levels and go short with a stop above 140½. This was also the level at which to buy PUTS or CALLS. You could buy CALLS and then go short or buy PUTS expecting that it would not go to a new high. You could probably have bought a PUT at 130 or higher. In 30 days Chrysler was down to 121; then continued down to 110¾, which price it reached on January 4, 1937, down 28 points. You certainly would have an opportunity on this decline to make 15 or 20 points on PUTS, or after you bought the first PUT and it declined, you could have bought a CALL for protection and carried the stock on down.

1937 - around January 4 would be a time to buy a CALL or a PUT because the stock was down near the low levels of 108-5/8 made on August 21, 1936. You could have bought a PUT at this level and then bought the stock, figuring that it would not break the old low levels before a good rally, or when it reached 110¾ or anywhere around that level, you could have bought a CALL, probably at 117, good 30 days. Before the 30 days was up Chrysler was up to 124, and on February 11 advanced to 135¼ giving a possible profit of 15 points. This would be another place to buy a CALL and go short figuring the stock would not cross the old top at 138¾, or after you saw it hold and not go through, you could buy a PUT. Chrysler first declined to 124; then rallied to 134-7/8 on March 3. This was the third top around the same level, 135¼ being a lower top than 138¾, and 134-7/8 being slightly lower than the other top. This was an excellent time to go short of the stock with a stop above old tops and also a good time to buy PUTS because the old tops were so close. It declined in 30 days to 120; then you could have bought another PUT good 30 days. By May 13 the stock declined to 106½, down 29 points from the top, giving an opportunity for a profit of 20 points or more on PUTS. Then Chrysler rallied on May 24 to 115, a rally of 8½ points, which was a fair-sized rally in a weak market. On May 24, when Chrysler was selling around 114-5/8 PUTS were offered at 110, good for 30 days at a cost of $137.50.

U.S. STEEL

We will give you some examples as to where PUTS and CALLS could have been bought on U.S. STEEL to advantage:

1932 - May 7 to June 28, high and low on U.S. Steel during this period was 31½ and 21¼. When Steel declined to around 22 you could buy CALLS because the low of 1927 was at 21-7/8. You could probably have bought a CALL at that time at 25 or lower, or you could have bought a PUT and bought the stock against it. Another way to trade would have been to wait until U.S. Steel crossed the top of 32, which was above 7 or 8 weeks' tops, then bought CALLS. In 30 days it advanced to 44 and by September 6 advanced to 52½, giving a possible profit of 25 to 30 points on CALLS.

1933 - July 18, U.S. Steel advanced to 67½ and by July 21 declined to 49, down 18½ points in three days. A PUT good 7 days or two weeks at that time would have made good. However, when it was around the high levels, if you had bought a PUT good 30 days, you could have made profits because the stock declined again to 49 on August 16 and never rallied above 58 until it declined to 34¾ on October 21, 1933.

1935 - January 8, U.S. Steel made high at 40. March 18, declined to 27½. This would have been a place to buy PUTS or CALLS because it was a double bottom against a low made September 17, 1934, when Steel sold at 29¼. You could have bought the stock and bought PUTS as protection, or you could have bought CALLS, or you could have waited until after U.S. Steel crossed 40, the high of January, and then bought CALLS. After it crossed 40, it never sold at 40 again until it advanced to 72 on April 9, 1936. Thus, you can see that if you had bought stock and bought PUTS or bought CALLS and once had profits in them, you could have moved up the stop loss order, or bought a PUT to protect the profits and carried it for big profits.

1936 - April - You could probably have bought PUTS on U.S. Steel good 30 days around 66. Within 30 days it declined to 54¼, giving an opportunity to make a profit of 10 to 12 points in 30 days.

October 3 to January 9, 1937, U.S. Steel held in a range from 72 to 80, or four months in an 8-point range. When Steel narrows down for several months like that, it is getting ready for a big move one way or the other.

On November 23 when it declined to 72, it was at the old top of April 9, 1936, a buying point, or a place to buy PUTS and buy the stock, or to buy CALLS, but a better time and the surest place to buy CALLS was when it crossed 80 on January 7, 1937. You could probably have bought CALLS at that time at 85 good for 30 days. The last low was made at 79 on January 12 and in 30 days or February 11, U.S. Steel sold at 109½, giving a possible profit of 24 points. With the trend still up you could probably have bought PUTS at 5 points down to protect your profit and hold your stock. You could also have bought CALLS good 30 days.

1937 - March 11, U.S. Steel advanced to 126½, up 57½ points in 60 days. Thus, after the long period of dullness in an 8-point range, you had an opportunity in 60 days to make profits of over 50 points by buying CALLS. Then, after this rapid advance you could have bought a PUT. On March 22, U.S. Steel declined to 112½, off 14½ points. On March 31 it rallied, making a top at 123½, lower than the first top. This would have been the time to buy CALLS and go short because it was near the old top, or to buy PUTS. You could probably have bought PUTS at this time around 117. Thirty days later U.S. Steel was down to 99. Then, if you were short on PUTS, you could have bought a CALL to protect your profits or placed a stop loss order to protect profits. On May 18, U.S. Steel declined to 91-5/8, down 32 points in 48 days. This shows you that when activity follows a long period of dullness there are big opportunities for making large profits on small risks trading in PUTS and CALLS.

RULES FOR BUYING PUTS AND CALLS ON LOW-PRICED STOCKS

Many low-priced stocks remain in a narrow trading range for many years and do not offer any opportunity for making profits buying PUTS and CALLS. Therefore, if you bought too often without waiting for definite indications on low priced stocks, you would just lose the money you paid out for PUTS and CALLS.

You must have a rule to determine when to buy PUTS and CALLS on low priced stocks because at times there are really big opportunities for making profits if you study and watch stocks when they start to move from low levels. You either have to wait until a stock holds in a narrow trading range for several years and then crosses the old top levels and shows activity; that is when you can buy CALLS. For example:

JOHNS MANVILLE

1929 - February, Johns Manville advanced to a high of 242. There is no use talking about how much money could have been made buying PUTS even 20, 30 or 50 points away on high priced stocks in 1929 or buying PUTS to protect stocks that people were long of. The opportunities were certainly there. But I want be conservative and point out how profits can be made trading in PUTS and CALLS in normal markets.

1932 - During April, May, June and July Johns Manville made a low each month at 10 and the high during that period was 16. It started up around the middle of July 1932, after the general market had made bottom. Of course, after it stayed several months around 10, you could have bought a PUT, probably one point down, and could have bought the stock, but the safest and best time was in August when it crossed 16; then you could probably have bought a CALL at 19 or 20. It was then above a four-months' range and showed that it was going to move up. In 30 days it advanced to 29 and in the early part of September sold at 33. There was certainly an opportunity to make 10 to 12 points' profit buying CALLS on a low priced stock after it gave a signal to advance.

1933 - March, Johns Manville declined to 13, 3 points above the old low level of 1932 and a place to buy with a stop under 10 a or a place to buy PUTS and buy the stock; also a place to buy CALLS.

In May the stock crossed 33, the high of September 1932, which indicated activity and higher prices. You could nave bought a CALL after it crossed 33, which would have made you at least 15 points' profit in 30 days. In July Johns Manville sold at 60.

1935 - In July Johns Manville crossed a series of tops at 57. This was the time to buy CALLS. In August 1935, it crossed 67, the top of February 1934, another time to buy CALLS because it indicated a definite trend up. It never reacted over 10 points until it sold at 129 in February 1936. You could have bought CALLS right along all the way up or bought PUTS to protect your profits on CALLS and made large profits.

BOEING AIRCRAFT

September 1934, to July 1935, this stock had a range between 11¼ and 6¼, or a range of 5 points. From March 1935 to June 1935, it moved in a range of 2 points between 6¼ and 8¼. In July 1935, it advanced to 9, crossing the tops of the previous three months. This was a place to buy CALLS. However, if you had waited until it crossed 12 in August and bought CALLS when it was above all these high levels, you could have made big profits because it never sold below 12 until it advanced to 26½ in January 1936. Notice how much faster the stock moved up after it reached high levels. I have told you that when a stock gets above 36 to 40, they move much faster. In March 1937, Boeing advanced to 49½, up 13 points in 13 days.

DOUGLAS AIRCRAFT

1935 - March, low 17½. October and November, high 35. December, low 34. Then it crossed the old high levels and advanced to 59 in the same month, making a range of 25 points, the first month after it got above 36. Of course, there was big money in buying CALLS good for 30 days.

1936 - January, Douglas made a low of 50½ and the same month advanced to 75½, making a 25 point range in 30 days, again proving how much faster stocks move after they get above 50 and the greater opportunities for profits as they move into higher levels. November 1936, Douglas high 77. December high 77¾.

1937 - January, high 77. Three months with tops around the same level. This would have been a time to buy CALLS and go short because the high level of the stock was 82, made in October 1936. It was also a time to buy PUTS because they could probably have been bought 5 points down or you could have waited until the stock broke 68, the low of December 1936, and then bought PUTS good 30 days. The stock declined fast and after you had profits on PUTS, you could have bought a CALL and carried it on down.

In May 1937, Douglas declined to 47½, down 30 points from the January high, affording excellent opportunities for pyramiding on the way down and selling the stock short or for staying short after you once had a profit in a PUT and a chance to protect it with a CALL. The percentage of profits compared to the risk would have been enormous.

The above examples show you the advantages and opportunities of using PUTS and CALLS at critical times and when stocks are active. No one can expect to make a great success in any line of business unless they study it constantly and learn more and more about it. There is no business in the world that will return greater profit on the risk and the capital than speculation, using PUTS and CALLS, provided you keep up monthly and weekly high and low charts on quite a few stocks and study them. Follow the rules laid down in my books, "Truth of the Stock Tape", "Wall Street Stock Selector", and "New Stock Trend Detector", and you will learn how to trade successfully in PUTS and CALLS.

The more you study the market and the more you study PUTS and CALLS and learn how to operate, the more advantages you will see in using them.

W.D. GANN

May 26, 1937

Chapter 19B

How to Sell Puts and Calls

HOW TO SELL PUTS AND CALLS

Many people know how to buy PUTS and CALLS but very few know how to sell them or know that they can sell them and get the premium money for the option.

When you sell a PUT or a CALL on stocks, you are simply taking the opposite position to the one when you buy a PUT or a CALL and there are more advantages on the selling side, especially at certain periods of the market.

Suppose you wish to buy U.S. Steel. Naturally, you want to get in the market and buy at the lowest level possible, but you cannot be sure of the exact bottom. For example: We will assume that U.S. Steel is selling at 66, and you feel that you would be willing to buy it if it declines to around 62. You have your account open with your broker and your money on deposit to cover the margin requirements to buy U.S. Steel. You give your broker an order to sell a PUT on 100 U.S. Steel good 30 days -- which is always below the market, varying from 2 to 3 points to as much as 10 to 15 points. We will assume that the broker sells the PUT on U.S. Steel at 62, good 30 days, and receives $112.50, which is credited to your account. This is the premium that you receive from the buyer. Then, we will assume that U.S. Steel does not decline to 62 before the 30-day PUT expires. Therefore, you will have the $112.50 which you received for the PUT.

Then, if you are still willing and want to buy U.S. Steel, you could sell another PUT at 100 shares, good for 30 days, at whatever number of points below the market the broker could get it. In this case, we will assume that Steel is selling around 63 and the broker sells the PUT for you at 59, again receiving $112.50 credited to your account. Then suppose U.S. Steel declines to 58 and closes at the end of 30 days at 58. The man who bought from you the PUT on 100 U.S. Steel at 59 will PUT it to you or deliver it to your broker for 59 and you will have bought Steel at 59 and will have $250.00 to your credit, the money you received on the PUTS sold.

Then, we will assume that you are willing to take 4 or 5 points profit on U.S. Steel, you give your broker an order to sell a CALL on U.S. Steel good 30 days. We will assume he sells it at 64 and again you receive $112.50 premium. If at the end of the 30 days U.S. Steel has not reached 64, you still have the stock and have $375.00 to your credit, which you have received for selling PUTS and CALLS.

We will assume that at the end of the 30 days U.S. Steel is selling at 63. You instruct your broker to sell a CALL on U.S. Steel good 30 days, and he sells it at 67 and receives $112.50 for your account. At the end of the 30 days, or when the CALL expires, U.S. Steel is selling at 69 and the man to whom you sold the CALL demands delivery; then your broker delivers 100 U.S. Steel for 67. You have sold at 67 the Steel that you bought at 59 and have made 8 points profit or $800.00, less commission and interest, and you have received $450.00 premium money for the PUTS and CALLS you sold, which is just that much extra profit because you did not take as much risk as you would if you had just bought U.S. Steel or sold it without selling the PUTS or CALLS.

SELLING CALLS TO GET SHORT OF THE MARKET

Suppose you think the market is about high enough to sell short but you are not sure just when and where the top will be reached. U.S. Steel is selling around 75 when you make up your mind to sell it short. Then you give your broker an order to sell a CALL on 100 U.S. Steel good 30 days. He sells the CALL at 80, which means that if U.S. Steel is selling above 80 at the end of 30 days, the man you sold the option to will CALL it or buy it from you at 80 and you will be short at 80 with a credit of $112.50 which you received for the CALL.

You might be able to sell CALLS twice, three times, five times or more and take in the premium money before the stock is called. Suppose, after you have been called for Steel at 80 which puts you short at 80 - you decide to sell a PUT. You get it at 75, which gives you 5 points profit, and you again receive $112.50 for the PUT good 30 days. We will assume that at the end of 30 days Steel is selling at 74 and the man you sold the PUT to, delivers 100 shares of Steel to the broker for your account. This means that you have bought 100 shares at 75 and covered your short position, making a profit of 5 points or $500.00 less commission and taxes; and at the same time you have made $225.00 extra by selling the PUTS and CALLS and have taken no additional risk.

HOW TO PROTECT YOURSELF IN SELLING PUTS OR CALLS

Whether you want to enter the market or not, you can sell PUTS or CALLS and can protect yourself by buying or selling the stock before the PUT or CALL expires. For example:

Suppose you have sold a CALL on U.S. Steel at 80 and you are not long or have not bought U S Steel. When it advances to 78 or 79 you decide that you do not want to sell it short as the market looks very strong. In order to protect yourself you buy 100 shares of U.S. Steel at 79. Then, we will assume that at the end of 30 days it closes at 87; the man you sold the CALL to demands delivery of the stock and you deliver or sell it to him at 80. You have one point profit, because you bought it at 79, and you have $112.50 premium money that you received for the CALL.

Suppose you sell a PUT on U.S. Steel at 72, good 30 days. Then the market turns weak and is declining fast. When it reaches 74, you decide that it acts as if it is going very much lower, and in order to protect yourself you sell 100 shares of U.S. Steel short at 74. Then, we will assume that the stock declines and closes at 69, and that man you sold the PUT to at 72, delivers you the stock and 72, which PUT you out of the market and still gives you a profit of 2 points and the premium money of $112.50.

When you are long of the market or have stocks bought, it is nearly always to your advantage to sell CALLS good 30 days until your stock is called, because if you are wrong and the market goes against you, will be taking in the premium money you receive for the CALLS, which will help to cover the loss on the stock.

When you are short of a stock, in most cases it will pay you to sell a PUT good for 30 days and take in the money, because if the market declines – as it often does –

and fails to reach the PUT price, you will still have the money you received for the PUT and will still be short of the stock and can sell a PUT for next 30 days and take in another $112.50.

I know many traders, when they are long of the market or have stocks bought, who sell CALLS every 30 days and sometimes carry the stock for six or twelve months before the man who buys the CALLS has an opportunity to CALL the stock. During all that time they are making more than one point a month profit by selling a CALL every 30 days.

BUYING A PUT AND SELLING A CALL AT THE SAME TIME

We will suppose that you buy U.S. Steel at 60 and want to be protected and limit your loss. Then you buy a PUT, good 30 days, at 57, which is 3 points under your purchase price; and at the same time you sell a CALL at 65. This leaves only a small expense or the difference between the Price you pay for the CALL and the price at which you buy the PUT. Should the unexpected happen and some unfavorable news cause U.S. Steel to decline and close at 50 at the end of 30 days, you will be out at 57 because you can deliver on your PUT at 57. This is what we call selling a PUT or a CALL on one side of the market to make the money to pay for protection on the other side.

ARRANGING TO SELL PUTS AND CALLS

You can arrange to sell PUTS and CALLS by getting in touch with your broker. Any brokerage firm that is a member of the New York Stock Exchange can endorse PUTS and CALLS. Many firms, however, do not handle this business, but your broker can recommend a firm that will be glad to endorse the PUTS and CALLS you wish to write. If your broker cannot help you out in this matter, you can get in touch with any member of the PUT and CALL Dealers Association.

In order to sell a PUT or a CALL, it is generally necessary that you deposit at least 30% of the value of the stock, or in case of a CALL, you can deposit the stock itself, so that the broker will always be protected in case the stock is called for or is PUT to you.

PUTS and CALLS are sold not only for 30 days but also for 60 days, 90 days and in some cases for longer periods of time, particularly in dull and inactive markets. Also, instead of selling at a regular rate, such as $125.00 or $112.50, often they are sold for $250, $300, $400, or $500 AT THE MARKET; in other words, instead of getting points up or down, you receive an additional sum of cash which is equivalent to the points.

Your broker or a member of the PUT and CALL Dealers Association can furnish you with prices and quotations and the details for handling such transactions.

If you will read "How to Make Profits Trading in PUTS and CALLS" and supplement the information given, by the use of charts on a few active stocks, you should be able to protect yourself and also operate a profit in both buying and selling PUTS and CALLS.

W. D. GANN

February 1941

Recommended Readings

- 45 Years in Wall Street by W. D. Gann

- Truth of the Stock Tape by William D. Gann

- How to Make Profits In Commodities by W. D. Gann

- Options Made Easy: How to Make Profits Trading in Puts and Calls By W. D. Gann

- The Essence of Success by Earl Nightingale

Avalaible at snowballpublishing.com